Internet and the Law

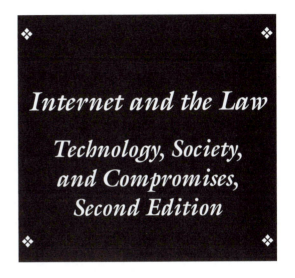

Internet and the Law

Technology, Society, and Compromises, Second Edition

Aaron Schwabach

Santa Barbara, California
Denver, Colorado
Oxford, England

Copyright 2014 by ABC-CLIO, LLC

Library of Congress Cataloging-in-Publication Data

Schwabach, Aaron.
    Internet and the law : technology, society, and compromises / Aaron Schwabach. — Second edition.
        pages cm
    Includes index.
    ISBN 978-1-61069-349-3 (hardback) —
    ISBN 978-1-61069-350-9 (ebook)   1. Internet—Law and legislation—United States—Encyclopedias.
2. Internet—Encyclopedias. I. Title.
    KF390.5.C6S358   2014
    343.7309'944—dc23   2013031062

ISBN: 978-1-61069-349-3
EISBN: 978-1-61069-350-9

18 17 16 15 14   1 2 3 4 5

This book is also available on the World Wide Web as an eBook.
Visit www.abc-clio.com for details.

ABC-CLIO, LLC
130 Cremona Drive, P.O. Box 1911
Santa Barbara, California 93116-1911

This book is printed on acid-free paper ∞
Manufactured in the United States of America

For Daniel, Jessica, Veronica, and Qienyuan

❖ CONTENTS ❖

Internet and the Law

DOING BUSINESS: CONTRACTS AND COMMERCE

Advertising
Adware and Spyware
Business Methods Patent
Clickwrap Agreement
.com
Contracts
Data Mining
Doubleclick
E-Commerce
Federal Trade Commission
French Yahoo! Case
Gambling
Internet Service Providers
Metatags
QR Code
Social Networking Service
Spam
Taxation
Trade Secret
Uniform Computer Information Transactions Act
Voluntary Collective License
Yahoo!

INTERNATIONAL PROBLEMS AND INTERNATIONAL LAW

Activism and Advocacy Groups
America Invents Act
Berne Convention
Censorship
Choice of Law
Digital Divide
International Copyright Protection
International Federation of Reproduction Rights
　　Organizations
International Patent Protection
International Trademark Protection
Internet Corporation for Assigned Names and Numbers
Jurisdiction
Madrid Agreement and Madrid Protocol
Paris Convention
Patent Cooperation Treaty
Recognition and Enforcement of Judgments
Trademark Law Treaty
TRIPS
TRIPS (Copyright)
TRIPS (Industrial Designs and Integrated Circuit
　　Layouts)
TRIPS (Patent)
TRIPS (Trademark)
TRIPS (Trade Secrets)
Universal Copyright Convention
WIPO

WIPO Copyright Treaty
WIPO Performance and Phonograms Treaty

THE INTERNET IN POPULAR CULTURE

Cyber
Cyberpunk
Cyberspace
Data Haven
Phreaking
Worm

INTERNET PESTS AND OTHER NUISANCES

Adware and Spyware
Cookies
Federal Trade Commission
Firewall
Hacking
Malware
Phishing
QR Code
Spam
Trojan
Virus
Worm

KEEPING SECRETS: PRIVACY AND CONFIDENTIALITY OF INFORMATION

Activism and Advocacy Groups
Adware and Spyware
Anonymity
Certificate
Children's Online Privacy Protection Act
Cookies
Defamation
Encryption
Enforcement
Federal Trade Commission
Identity Theft
Internet Service Providers
Privacy
Social Networking Service

LEGISLATING CHANGE: FEDERAL STATUTES AND PROPOSED LEGISLATION

Activism and Advocacy Groups
Audio Home Recording Act
Child Online Protection Act
Child Pornography
Children's Internet Protection Act
Children's Online Privacy Protection Act
Communications Decency Act
Consumer Broadband and Digital Television Promotion Act
Cybersquatting

LITIGATING CHANGE: LANDMARK LAWSUITS

OPEN SOURCE AND OPEN ACCESS

OTHER FORMS OF INTELLECTUAL PROPERTY: BEYOND TRADITIONAL COPYRIGHT, PATENT, AND TRADEMARK

PATENT

TRADEMARK

WHOSE INTERNET?—STRUGGLES FOR INFLUENCE

The roots of the Internet and the current revolution in individual access to information go back for many decades, even centuries, but the Internet as a widespread social phenomenon is just concluding its second decade. Few people had personal computers before the 1980s; few had access to the Internet, or any of its precursors, before the 1990s. The universal acceptance of the Internet happened nearly instantaneously, not only in the United States, but also around the world. Today the Internet is no longer a novelty but a part of daily life in most developed countries, and in many developing ones. Checking email and text messages is as ordinary, and undeserving of comment, as checking phone messages; ordering products from a Web page is as unremarkable as ordering products from a catalog was not long ago. As is true of many technologies that form part of the substrate of our way of life, relatively few people understand how the Internet actually works, but far more are willing to use it without understanding or questioning the technology involved.

A great many books have been written about the hardware infrastructure, the communications protocols, the software, and the people that make the Internet possible. This is not one of those books. Instead, it addresses a different problem: How does society's system of normative expectations—law, in other words—cope with this sudden change in the ground rules? Systems developed over centuries find themselves threatened by sudden change: the U.S. legal system spent two centuries working out a method of coping with the problem of access to pornography by juveniles; almost overnight, the Internet has rendered that system irrelevant. The legal systems of the world spent four and a half centuries—a period twice as long as the history of the United States as an independent nation—working out a system of copyright protection, carefully balancing the interests of creators, publishers, and consumers of copyrighted works. Now anyone can publish a work, or create a million copies of someone else's work, in seconds. Existing copyright law has found itself unable to cope with the threat posed by the Internet, especially by the battle over file-sharing that dominates much of the discussion of Internet law and has created an unprecedented level of animosity between consumers and some sectors of the content industry. Unauthorized copying of intellectual property is nothing new, but on the whole the history of copyright law over the past four and a half centuries would probably appear, to anyone other than a copyright lawyer, to be a tale of unmitigated dullness.

Until now. New battles are fought daily in the three-sided conflict between content owners, consumers, and equipment manufacturers—the latter group sharing interests with both consumers and content owners; there are also signs that the copyright interests of content creators, especially in the music industry, are diverging from those of the content owners. The legal battles in this conflict are fought in Congress and other national legislatures, in the courts, and in international organizations such as the World Intellectual Property Organization and the World Trade Organization. At the same time, there is an ongoing arms race, as content owners create ever more sophisticated means of copy protection and users find ever more sophisticated means of copying.

Many other areas of law are nearly as unsettled. The Internet poses grave threats to privacy, for example. Phone calls and letters are not recorded unless someone takes the trouble to record them, but everything that happens online is, or at least can be, recorded as a matter of course. At the same time, however, the Internet offers the potential for unprecedented privacy, through the use of sophisticated encryption. The balance struck long ago between the individual's desire for privacy and the legitimate crime-detection and national security interests of the government must somehow be adapted to take into account both universal recording of messages and the availability of encryption software.

No book could possibly cover everything that is going on in the world of Internet law; this book attempts, instead, to provide an overview of certain issues in which the degree of social change has been particularly great. The Internet is a tool for transmitting information; the Web and other information exchange services supported on the Internet are composed of information. As a result, the areas of law most affected have been those areas of law that deal with information. All areas of intellectual property law have been deeply affected by the Internet, as intellectual property rights are rights in information. Laws relating to freedom of expression are just as deeply affected; the global soapbox that once belonged only to the owners of large media companies now belongs to everyone. Laws relating to jurisdiction, choice of law, and recognition of foreign judgments are also affected; the global nature of the Internet greatly increases the number of ways in which legal systems may come into conflict with each other. The Congressional struggle to control Internet pornography has highlighted one aspect of this problem: the inability of Congress to control access by U.S. citizens to content originating in other countries. Even if such a thing were possible, it might not be permissible or desirable. The French Yahoo! case has highlighted another aspect: the problem of determining the extent to which Internet users are responsible for complying not only with the laws of their own country, but the laws of other countries in which their message may be received—which is to say, all of the countries of the world.

Just as one book cannot address everything that happens on the Internet, one book cannot address the reaction of all of the world's legal systems to the Internet. This book focuses on one particular legal system—that of the United States. International law—the law governing interactions between nations rather than the law of specific foreign countries—is also addressed in detail where relevant, especially with regard to copyright and other intellectual property rights. Foreign law is addressed in passing, when relevant to a particular case or question. And perhaps fortunately, both intellectual property rights and freedom of expression are governed in the United States mostly (although not entirely) by federal law. Even in areas where state law would ordinarily control, Congress has often preempted state law where the Internet is involved; thus, most of the time this book can focus on a single body of federal law rather than, as is the case in some other areas of law, a bewildering collection of the laws of 50 different states.

In this front section of the book you will find, in addition to the Contents and this Preface, a historical overview of the development of Internet law focusing on relatively recent developments, and a chronology covering a longer timeframe in somewhat less detail. You will also find information on how to use this volume, and on how to understand the various U.S. and international legal materials that are presented and discussed. Finally, before the entries begin, there is a table of abbreviations used in the text. These abbreviations are also explained in the articles in which they appear.

The entries are organized alphabetically. Each entry includes, in addition to the text, a list of legal sources, a list of cross-references, and a list of books, articles, and other sources either referred to in the text or suggested for further information on the topic. The entries are followed by additional general information. Law and Internet each have their own languages, and one of the purposes of this book is to demystify those languages; thus, the first item to follow the topic entries is a glossary of legal and Internet terms used in the book. Another purpose of this book is to serve as a springboard for further discussion and research; the glossary is followed by a documents supplement containing excerpts from some major treaties, statutes, cases, and other legal materials. There is also a selected bibliography, with annotations, a topic finder to assist in locating the material in this book, a table of authorities listing all of the primary sources of law (treaties, statutes, cases, regulations, and the like) discussed in the book, and an index.

This book would not have been possible without the assistance of a large number of people. I'd particularly like to thank my research assistants, Travis Davis and Lorena Garza; Professors Brenda Simon, Richard Winchester, and Claire Wright, for advice and feedback; and my family. I hope that you enjoy reading this book as much as I did writing it, and that it will serve as a starting point for further research on and discussion of Internet and information technology law.

Although our national legal system is flexible and capable of making quick changes, it has often been baffled, at least temporarily, by the social and legal consequences of the rapid adoption of new technology. In the 1960s, for example, as computer programming began to take off, the U.S. Patent and Trademark Office (USPTO) dug in its collective heels and refused to issue any patents for computer programs. At that time computers themselves were new; the USPTO felt overwhelmed by the number of computer hardware patent applications it had received and the difficulty of understanding them, and apparently decided that enough was enough. During the administration of Lyndon Johnson, a presidential commission on software patents was persuaded to the USPTO's point of view; the commission report in turn influenced the Supreme Court's 1972 decision in a case called *Gottschalk v. Benson*. The Supreme Court's opinion in this case was widely understood (including, probably, by the justices themselves) as stating that computer software could not be patented. The USPTO, no doubt with a sigh of relief, suspended all pending applications for patents on computer software. The opinion in *Gottschalk*, which can most charitably be described as ill-advised or perhaps misunderstood, influenced legal developments in other countries; presumably these countries assumed that the United States, as the leader in computer technology at the time, knew what it was doing when it made computer programs unpatentable. Thus, the countries of Europe formed the European Patent Treaty, which to this day excludes computer programs from its definition of patentable material.

Thus one questionable decision, initially made by non-elected bureaucrats at the USPTO, has perpetuated itself throughout the world for decades, and has distorted the development of software law. The Supreme Court eventually realized its error; in 1981 it backtracked a bit, and the USPTO reluctantly began to accept software patent applications. It was not until 1994 that the USPTO actually issued rules for software patent applications, after an opinion of the Federal Circuit (the federal appellate court that deals with patent cases) pointed out that it was just plain wrong to say that software was unpatentable. More recently the waters have been muddied still further by the Federal Circuit's decision in *In re Bilski* and the Supreme Court's decision, on appeal, in *Bilski v. Kappos*; although not dealing specifically with software, these opinions raise continuing questions as to the patentability of software in the abstract. The adaptation of a legal system to new technology takes time; more than 40 years after *Gottschalk*, the question it sought to address is not fully resolved.

Because computer programs were, or were believed to be, unpatentable, some other form of intellectual property right had to be pressed into service to protect them. This turned out to be copyright; computer programs, patented or not, are protected by copyright law. The fit between copyright and computer programs is not perfect, however, and has required some legislative tinkering. Unlike other forms of copyrightable content—books, plays, songs, movies—computer programs are not valued for their content, but for their function. The number of people who read code for the pure pleasure of doing so is rather small. Programs are not "works" in the sense that the term had previously been used in copyright law; they are tools that happen to be made of information rather than of steel or wood. At times, when something new has come along that hasn't quite fit, Congress has carved out new forms of intellectual property protection; for example, the mask work used to create computer chips is given protection that is somewhat like patent but a bit more like copyright. Given a clear directive from the presidential commission or the Supreme Court, Congress might have done something similar for computer programs, which are more numerous and more economically and socially significant than semiconductor chip mask works.

No such category was created, however, and the entire history of intellectual property rights in computer programs has been altered as a result. Whether that alteration is good or bad depends on one's perspective; the point is not so much that computer programs should or should not have been the subject of patent, copyright, or some third form of protection, but that things fell out the way they did more or less by accident. The justices of the Supreme Court in 1972 did not understand computers or computer programs; hardly anyone understood these things in 1972. Of those who understood, not one in a thousand anticipated the growth of something like the Internet beyond a select group of technical users, or that there might be sixth graders in Boise, Brussels, Belgrade, Bangalore, Brasília, and Beijing writing code for class assignments. The law was made without any real awareness of what its consequences might be, for good or for ill; but ever since, the computer programming world has had to work within the confines formed by that initial decision and subsequent attempts to modify it. In contrast, and perhaps as a result, the history of law and the Internet has been one of reaction.

Government created the Internet, but for the most part has managed to avoid regulating it until after a problem has appeared. Although the Internet has no undisputed starting point, most histories trace its ancestry to the linking of four computers to form ARPANET in 1969. ARPANET, a project funded and conducted under the auspices of the United States Department of Defense, grew rapidly in terms of percentages, but by 1981 it was still tiny: a network of 200 host systems.

ARPANET was a network for programmers, scientists, and other specialists using mainframes and sometimes mini-computers. In the mid-1970s, however, a new social phenomenon began: home computing. Computers that by today's standards would be insanely overpriced toys nonetheless fulfilled most of the needs that their owners had for them: word processing, accounting, data storage and sorting, and games. And, with the addition of a device called a modem, they could communicate with other computers. At the time, few foresaw that this would be the single most popular use for home computing.

Purchasers of primitive early computers could use their 300 baud (no, not 300K; 300 baud—300 bits per second, more or less) modems to communicate with other users, one at a time, over a telephone line. For the most part, though, there wasn't much reason to do so. More useful were the bulletin board systems (BBSs) that began to spring up around the country. A BBS allowed multiple users to communicate with each other, and to view information stored on the BBS server, at the same time. BBS users quickly began to use the services to do all of the things that human beings use other media of communication to do: socializing, expounding political theories, conducting business, dating, enjoying, or providing entertainment. Proprietary networks—at first just glorified bulletin boards—came into being: CompuServe, Prodigy, America Online. Throughout the 1980s the various networks became increasingly interconnected; by 1990, when ARPANET officially ceased to exist, its demise was unnoticeable to most users. But the nascent Internet remained technically challenging: Because of the slow speed of the connections and the limited capacity of many computers, most communication was text-only. And a certain amount of technical proficiency was still required.

All of this changed between 1992 and 1994. In 1992, the World Wide Web, created by researchers at the European Center for Nuclear Research in Switzerland, became accessible to the world. And in 1994 the easy-to-use Netscape Web browser became available. Suddenly everyone with access to a computer could view any content on the Web—and, perhaps even more importantly, could create content and place it on the Web for others to view. The Web grew exponentially, in the literal sense of the word: for a while, the number of Web servers increased by an order of magnitude each year.

The legal system was taken by surprise. While the Internet was used by a relatively small number of people, government had been content to ignore it. Suddenly everyone was using it, and some of those users were very unhappy with the ways in which others were using it. Among the first to demand that Congress do something were opponents of pornography, who were concerned both with the amount of pornographic content available on the Web and the fact that the content was available to minors. In 1996, Congress undertook its first, and unsuccessful, attempt to regulate Web content—the first step in a struggle that is not yet finished.

The battle over pornography was to pale in comparison to the battle over copyright. The MP3 file format had been created and developed more or less in chronological parallel with the World Wide Web; the music content industry seemed not to have fully woken up to the danger it faced until 1997, however, with the launch of MP3.com. The content industry then joined the ranks of those demanding that the government Do Something, in this case to protect copyrighted content. This led to the sweeping reforms of copyright law in the Digital Millennium Copyright Act of 1998. While the DMCA greatly tilted the legal balance of interests in favor of content owners, apparently the Congressional thumb on the scale was insufficient to overcome the advantage given to users by technology. While the content industry succeeded in crushing MP3 and later Napster and Grokster, file-sharing continues, and the content industry continues to lobby for additional protection.

As the World Wide Web enters its third decade, the law of the Internet is still in flux; the legal system is still adapting to the widespread social change resulting from technological change. Nor can we predict the way the technology will develop in the future; we have little more idea of the ultimate effects of today's lawmaking on future social and technological development than the Supreme Court had in 1972 when it decided *Gottschalk*. But while this might suggest that the wise course would be to do nothing and await further developments, there are too many people making loud and contradicting demands for immediate action; Congress and the courts will have to choose as wisely as possible and hope for the best.

868: Chinese translation of the Diamond Sutra, the world's oldest surviving block-printed work (the first mass-produced work of literature) is published. The Sutra, now in the collection of the British Library, bears what is arguably a precursor to today's open-source licenses: "Reverently made for universal free distribution by Wang Jie on behalf of his two parents on the 13th day of the 4th moon of the 9th year of Xiantong."

1041: Chinese inventor Bi Sheng creates what is probably the world's first printing machine to use movable type.

1234: Yi Gyu-bo publishes the New Code of Etiquette in Korea; today it is the world's oldest surviving work printed with movable type.

c. 1430–1450: Printing presses are built by Johann Gutenberg and Laurens Coster in Europe.

1455–1468: Johann Gutenberg loses control of his printing business after becoming involved in several lawsuits.

1499: Johannes Trithemius publishes *Steganographia*, in which he sets forth the principles of steganography, or concealed content, later to become important in digital rights management technology. *Steganographia* is an *incunabulum*—a term including all books printed using either block printing or movable type in Europe before 1500. Incunabula are, not surprisingly, rare. Because there was rarely a commercial justification for reprinting them, their content was inaccessible to most of the world's population until the advent of the World Wide Web; today *Steganographia*, like Wang Jie's Diamond Sutra, is available to anyone with Web access. Paradoxically, it is the more recent out-of-print works that are most inaccessible, because although difficult to find in hard copy they are still protected by copyright.

1557: The English government grants a monopoly on book publishing within England to the Stationer's Company. This is England's first serious attempt to cope with the problem of copying printed works that arose soon after the invention of the printing press, and foreshadows modern copyright law.

1661–1663: The Eliot Indian Bible, a translation of the Bible into Algonquin, is published in Cambridge, Massachusetts, becoming the first book printed in the English North American colonies.

1695: After 138 years, the Stationer's Company's monopoly on book printing comes to an end.

1695–1710: Multiple printing companies vie for market share in England; all works are deemed fair game, regardless of who first published them.

1710: The British (Scotland and England having been unified by the Act of Union in 1707) Parliament enacts the Statute of Anne, the first modern copyright law. The Statute sets a copyright term of 14 years for new works, renewable once.

1774: Britain's House of Lords decides *Donaldson v. Beckett*, establishing that copyright terms are of finite duration, even for works published by the Stationer's Company before the Statute of Anne.

1789: U.S. Constitution comes into effect. Article I, Section 8, Clause 8 (the Patent and Copyright Clause) declares that Congress shall have the power "to promote the Progress of Science and useful Arts, by securing for limited Times to Authors and Inventors the exclusive

Right to their respective Writings and Discoveries."

1790: First U.S. Copyright Act provides for the same term of copyright protection as that provided by the Statute of Anne: 14 years, renewable once.

1791: Bill of Rights (Amendments 1 through 10 to the U.S. Constitution) adopted. The first of the 10 amendments declares in part that "Congress shall make no law. . . abridging the freedom of speech, or of the press; or the right of the people peaceably to assemble[.]"

1844: The world's first long-distance electronic communications system, a telegraph line between Washington and Boston, becomes operational.

1847: French composer Ernest Bourget wins a lawsuit against Ambassadeurs, a Paris café that played his music for the entertainment of patrons—without his permission.

1851: World's first successful undersea cable connects British and French telegraph networks.

1858: Transatlantic telegraph cable connects United States and Britain for three weeks before ceasing to function.

1866: Two transatlantic cables are laid, connected Britain to Canada and the United States. Within the next few years, over 100,000 miles of undersea cable are laid, in addition to hundreds of thousands of miles of surface lines, connecting much of the world to the telegraph network.

1876: Telephone patented.

1877: Phonograph invented.

1878: World's first commercial telephone exchange opens in New Haven, Connecticut.

Association Littéraire et Artistique Internationale (International Artistic and Literary Association) founded by Victor Hugo and others to seek an international copyright protection system.

1886: Berne Convention adopted.

1887: Motion pictures invented.

1909: U.S. Copyright Act of 1909 fails to conform to Berne Convention standards, but prohibits "unauthorized mechanical reproduction of musical compositions." The Act doubles the copyright term, providing for a 28-year term, renewable once.

1955: Universal Copyright Convention comes into force for the United States.

1969: ARPANET launched; links four computers.

1971: ARPANET now links two dozen computers.

1972: First email program created.

U.S. Supreme Court decides *Gottschalk v. Benson*, holding that a mathematical algorithm used in a computer program is not patentable. U.S. Patent and Trademark Office (USPTO) suspends all pending computer program patent applications.

1976: Copyright Act of 1976 radically revises U.S. copyright law. The Act preempts state laws, making copyright entirely a federal matter, and provides for a copyright term of the lifetime of the author plus 50 years for individually, non-pseudonymously and non-anonymously authored works, and a term of 75 years from publication or 100 years from creation for most other works. (These terms are later extended by the Sonny Bono Copyright Term Extension Act to lifetime plus 70, 95, and 120 years, respectively.) Nonetheless, U.S. copyright law still fails to conform to Berne Convention norms.

1981: U.S. Supreme Court holds that some computer programs are patentable; USPTO begins to accept applications for software patents.

1983: ARPANET switches to TCP/IP protocol.

1984: William Gibson publishes *Neuromancer*, creating a mystique for a network that does not yet exist.

Congress enacts the Computer Fraud and Abuse Act, an antihacking law.

Supreme Court decides *Sony Corporation of America v. Universal City Studios*, holding that the fact that a VCR can be used for copyright infringement does not make the device unlawful, nor does it make Sony liable for infringement by purchasers of VCRs; the VCR is capable of substantial noninfringing uses and is thus a "staple article of commerce."

1986: NSFNet launched; links five supercomputers.

1988: Internet worm attack infects 10% of Internet host systems.

Congress enacts Berne Convention Implementation Act, bringing U.S. copyright law into conformity with Berne Convention and enabling the United States to join the Convention.

1990: Tim Berners-Lee creates the world's first Web page on a NeXT workstation.

NSFNet replaces ARPANET.

1991: Berners-Lee's first Web page becomes available online, as do many other Web pages, including the first in the United States (at the Stanford Linear Accelerator Center).

Phil Zimmerman releases Pretty Good Privacy (PGP), a powerful encryption program. When PGP becomes available over the Internet, Zimmerman is investigated for violation of U.S. arms export control regulations.

1992: Internet Underground Music Archive offers downloads of copyrighted music to technically savvy (and very patient) users.

Congress enacts Audio Home Recording Act.

1993: National Center for Supercomputing Applications at the University of Illinois releases the Mosaic Web browser.

1994: Netscape Navigator released.

Yahoo! founded.

Agreement on Trade-Related Aspects of Intellectual Property Rights (TRIPS) adopted as part of the Marrakesh Agreement Establishing the World Trade Organization; creates a comprehensive legal regime governing all internationally acknowledged forms of intellectual property.

U.S. Court of Appeals for the Federal Circuit holds that a wide range of computer programs are patentable; USPTO publishes guidelines for software patent applications.

Federal district court in Massachusetts dismisses warez-trading case against David LaMacchia.

1995: MP3 file format patented.

Microsoft Internet Explorer released.

1996: Congress enacts Communications Decency Act and Child Pornography Prevention Act.

John Perry Barlow writes the Declaration of the Independence of Cyberspace.

1997: MP3.com founded.

Congress enacts the No Electronic Theft Act to control warez trading.

Censorship provisions of Communications Decency Act declared unconstitutional by Supreme Court.

1998: Netscape programmers launch Mozilla.org, open-sourcing Netscape's source code.

The Internet Corporation for Assigned Names and Numbers (ICANN) is formed by agreement between the Internet Assigned Numbers Authority and the U.S. Department of Commerce.

The Recording Industry Association of America (RIAA) launches the Secure Digital Music Initiative.

Diamond Multimedia begins marketing the first commercially available portable MP3 player, and is sued by the RIAA.

Congress enacts the Digital Millennium Copyright Act, the Sonny Bono Copyright Term Extension Act, the Child Online Protection Act, and the Children's Online Privacy Protection Act.

1999: Jon Lech Johansen, a 15-year-old Norwegian citizen, makes a program called DeCSS available over the Internet. CSS is the copy protection program used to prevent unauthorized copying on nearly all commercially produced DVDs; CSS-encrypted DVDs cannot be played on Linux systems. DeCSS can be used to play CSS-encrypted DVDs on Linux systems. It can also be used to make unauthorized copies of CSS-encrypted DVDs. Johansen is prosecuted in Norway; persons who distribute DeCSS in the United States are sued by motion picture content companies.

Napster file-sharing service begins operating; Napster is immediately sued by RIAA and others for contributory and vicarious copyright infringement.

Congress enacts Anticybersquatting Consumer Protection Act.

The Ninth Circuit Court of Appeals holds that Diamond Multimedia may lawfully make and distribute its portable MP3 player, and that doing so does not make Diamond liable for copyright infringement.

2000: KaZaA begins operating. MP3.com is purchased by Vivendi; Bertelsmann Music Group invests in Napster.

MP3.com offers MyMP3.com, a service allowing users to download and play music if they can demonstrate a legal right to do so. It is sued by Universal Music Group and others, and subsequently ordered to pay $250 million in damages.

The Children's Internet Protection Act becomes law.

A federal district court holds that the Digital Millennium Copyright Act can constitutionally prohibit the distribution of DeCSS, and that in fact it does so.

2001: Napster is ordered to block sharing of copyrighted files.

Dmitri Sklyarov, a Russian programmer, is arrested while attending a conference in Las Vegas. Sklyarov had written a program enabling users to break the copy protection used by Adobe's Acrobat E-Book Reader. Five months later, the government drops its case against Sklyarov personally, but not against his employer, Elcom.

In response to the September 11 terrorist attacks, Congress enacts the USA PATRIOT Act, which among other things gives the government enhanced powers of surveillance over electronic communications.

The Second Circuit agrees that there is no constitutional bar to the Digital Millennium Copyright Act's ban on the distribution of programs such as DeCSS.

2002: End of Napster, at least in its original form.

WIPO Copyright and Performance and Phonograms treaties come into force.

The Supreme Court's decision in *Eldred v. Ashcroft* upholds the constitutionality of the Sonny Bono Copyright Term Extension Act.

A federal district court in California decides *United States v. Elcom* (Elcom is the employer of Dmitri Sklyarov). The court holds, like the courts in the DeCSS case, that there is no constitutional bar to the Digital Millennium Copyright Act's ban on the distribution of software for the circumvention of copy protection measures.

Aimster, a file-sharing network, is found liable for copyright infringement.

2003: Apple launches iTunes, sells 25 million songs in first year.

Verizon Internet Services refuses to release the name of an individual Verizon subscriber to the RIAA; the RIAA sues, and a federal district court orders Verizon to disclose the information. The Court of Appeals for the D.C. Circuit reverses, holding that Verizon does not have to disclose the subscriber's name.

Hershey's Foods and Mrs. Field's Cookies agree to a settlement with the Federal Trade Commission for collecting information from children in violation of the Children's Online Privacy Protection Act.

RIAA sues individual users for file-sharing; among the first defendants to reach a settlement with the RIAA is Brianna LaHara, a 12-year-old honor student who lives with her mother in public housing in New York City.

Supreme Court upholds constitutionality of Children's Internet Protection Act.

Federal district court in California holds that Grokster and other supernode-based, decentralized peer-to-peer file-sharing networks are not liable for contributory or vicarious copyright infringement.

In Norway, Jon Lech Johansen is acquitted of charges arising from the distribution of DeCSS; the acquittal is upheld on appeal.

2004: Mozilla Foundation releases Firefox, the first browser in many years to seriously challenge Internet Explorer.

RIAA files more suits against individual users.

Ninth Circuit Court of Appeals affirms district court's decisions that Grokster and others are not liable for contributory or vicarious copyright infringement.

In Norway, the government's Economic Crimes Unit drops its case against Jon Lech Johansen.

Supreme Court holds that censorship provisions of Child Online Protection Act may be unconstitutional, and remands for trial on further factual issues.

The social networking site Facebook is founded.

2005: The Second Circuit Court of Appeals decides *1–800 Contacts v. WhenU.com*, holding that a pop-up ad appearing in conjunction with another's Web page is not a "use" sufficient to constitute trademark infringement under the Lanham Act.

YouTube is founded.

2006: Google acquires YouTube.

The Ninth Circuit Court of Appeals decided *Perfect 10 v. Google*, holds that a Google image search result displaying thumbnail images of the plaintiff's copyrighted photos does not constitute copyright infringement.

The social networking and microblogging site Twitter is founded.

2007: Jammie Thomas-Rasset is sued by six major record labels for illegally downloading two dozen songs. The case eventually goes through numerous additional proceedings, with various damage awards ranging from $54,000 to $1.92 million.

2008: The Third Circuit Court of Appeals holds that the Child Online Protection Act (COPA) facially violates the First Amendment and permanently enjoins its enforcement.

YouTube user Stephanie Lenz posts a video of her children dancing to a Prince song. Universal Music, the copyright holder, requests that YouTube remove the video pursuant to the DMCA notice and takedown procedure. Ms. Lenz sues Universal; the federal district court in California holds that the copyright owner must make a good faith consideration of fair use before making a DMCA takedown request.

2009: AACS, which licenses the digital rights management security for Blu-ray disks, releases its "AACS Final Adopter Agreement."

ICANN announces its "Affirmation of Commitments," committing to remain a private not-for-profit corporation not controlled by any one entity.

2010: The Federal Communications Commission (FCC) adopts its "Preserving the Open Internet" rules on net neutrality.

A trial court in Milan, Italy, convicts three Google executives in connection with the posting of an offensive video on YouTube. The video was posted in Italy by Italian citizens; none of the defendants was an Italian citizen or in Italy at the time of the posting.

2011: The Stop Online Piracy Act (SOPA) and Preventing Real Online Threats to Economic Creativity and Theft of Intellectual Property Act (PROTECT IP or PIPA) are introduced in the House of Representatives and Senate, respectively.

2012: Information rights advocates, consumer groups, and Internet entities including Google and Wikipedia protest SOPA and PIPA, both of which are eventually abandoned by Congress.

The Second Circuit Court of Appeals holds, in *Viacom v. YouTube*, that a content provider, in this case YouTube, is not liable for copyright infringement under the DMCA unless they have "actual knowledge" of the alleged infringement occurring on their Web site.

Megaupload, a file-sharing service, is shut down. Founder Kim Dotcom is charged with offenses including conspiracy to commit copyright infringement.

Social networking site Facebook reaches 1 billion users.

Gangnam Style reaches 1 billion YouTube views.

2013: In New Zealand, Kim Dotcom launches next generation of Megaupload while awaiting a hearing to determine whether he will be extradited to the United States.

All professions are a conspiracy against the laity.
—George Bernard Shaw

Two mysterious professional cabals—lawyers and information technology professionals—have conspired to shroud Internet and law in jargon incomprehensible to anyone outside the two professions. This encyclopedia attempts to demystify Internet law; this section takes on the "law" side of Internet law, explaining how the various pieces of the U.S. and international legal systems fit together, as well as how to locate and use the various sources of law.

Overview of the U.S. Legal System

The United States has a federal system of government, meaning that its territorial subdivisions, the states, are not mere administrative divisions, but have a certain degree of sovereignty in their own right. They can, and often do, enact laws that are in conflict with each other. This makes the legal system of the United States extraordinarily complex; it is in fact more than 50 different legal systems (the systems of the states, the District of Columbia, the self-governing territories, and to a certain extent the Native American tribes), all of them subordinate in some, but not all, areas to the federal system.

Fortunately for our purposes, most of the law that governs the Internet in the United States is federal law. The Constitution gives the federal government authority over patents and copyrights, and over interstate and foreign commerce. The First Amendment sets a baseline level of free speech protection below which the states may not go, although they may provide a higher level of protection if they wish. The Copyright Act of 1976, by its terms, specifically preempts state law. The Internet Corporation for Assigned Names and Numbers, though independent, was created by the U.S. Department of Commerce. The National Security Agency, which oversees some encryption technology, is a federal agency.

Even in the areas where state law governs, as in the case of most commercial law, the laws are often uniform: the states have agreed to each adopt the same body of contracts law in order to simplify business transactions. This makes things simpler than they would be if, for example, we were attempting to study the law of marriage and divorce in all 50 states—an area of law in which there is a considerable difference from one state to the next.

The government of the United States, and for that matter of each of the individual states, has three branches: the legislative, the executive, and the judicial. The legislative branch—Congress—enacts statutes subject to the limits imposed by the Constitution. The executive branch carries out these laws; this may involve the making of regulations, if authorized by the statute. The president may also issue proclamations and executive orders that have the substantive effect of statutes, and the executive branch and the Senate have special duties with regard to international law. The judiciary branch can review statutes to determine whether they conflict with or exceed the authority granted by the Constitution, and can review administrative regulations to determine whether they conflict with or exceed the authority granted by the authorizing statute. More often, however, the courts, especially at the trial level, are not involved in such grandiose issues of policy; they are simply resolving disputes or determining how existing law should be applied.

The legislative branch: In addition to Congress itself, the legislative branch includes a handful of Congressional agencies; these report to Congress itself rather than to the executive branch. An agency with particular relevance to the Internet is the Library of Congress; founded in 1800 with the books of Thomas Jefferson, the Library now has over 150 million items. It also includes the United States Copyright Office.

The executive branch: The executive branch of the federal government includes the President and his (or perhaps, someday, her) Executive Office, and various Cabinet-level departments, other departments, and independent executive agencies. Several of these are particularly important to Internet law. The Department of Justice, which includes the Federal Bureau of Investigation, has a wide range of investigative and enforcement duties under various statutes. The Department of Commerce includes the USPTO, and also created and maintains a link to the Internet Corporation for Assigned Names and Numbers. The Department of Defense not only created ARPANET, which in turn gave rise to the Internet, but also includes the National Security Agency, which oversees encryption. The Department of Homeland Security exercises some security-related powers under the USA PATRIOT Act. The Department includes the Secret Service, which shares with the FBI the responsibility for the enforcement of the Computer Fraud and Abuse Act. In addition to these departments, two independent agencies play a large role in Internet law: the Federal Communications Commission, which regulates communication networks, and the Federal Trade Commission, which protects consumers from identity theft, phishing, scams, spam, and a host of other Internet hazards.

The judicial branch: The federal and state court systems in the United States have a three-tiered structure. In the lowest tier are the trial courts; in the federal court system most of these courts are called "district" courts and are assigned responsibility for federal (but not state) cases arising within a particular district, which may be all or part of a state or territory. A few trial courts have specialized jurisdiction defined by subject matter instead of by territory, and have names reflecting their specialty, such as the Court of International Trade.

Almost all federal lawsuits are initially brought in one of these federal trial courts. After the court reaches a decision on a particular matter, the losing party (with one exception) is generally entitled to appeal the decision. The decision from which the losing party appeals need not be a final decision on the merits of the case, although appeals at earlier stages are subject to certain limits; an appeal from some decision prior to that final decision is called an interlocutory appeal. An exception applies to criminal cases: the prosecution cannot appeal a final decision acquitting a defendant.

Decisions that are appealed go before an appellate court; cases may also come before these courts by various other procedural mechanisms. The appellate court will ordinarily review only questions of law, not findings of fact; that is, it will take the facts as found by the trial court and determine whether the trial court correctly applied the law in reaching its result.

Most of the appellate courts, like most of the trial courts, have jurisdiction defined by territory rather than by subject matter. Thus, for example, the Ninth Circuit Court of Appeals has jurisdiction over appeals from federal district courts in the states and territories bordering the Pacific, as well as Arizona, Idaho, Montana, and Nevada.

Reported decisions of appellate courts become part of the body of common law. They are binding precedent in future cases involving the same questions of law; trial courts within the appellate court's jurisdiction must follow the rules set down in the appellate court's decisions. The nonprevailing party on appeal is not entitled to further appellate review; however, he or she may nonetheless seek such review from a high court. In the federal and nearly every state court system (with the exceptions of New York and Maryland) these high courts are called "supreme courts," or some slight variation thereof. (In New York and Maryland the highest courts are called the Court of Appeals; New York complicates matters further by calling its trial courts Supreme Courts, to the great confusion of persons from other states.) Each state high court is the ultimate arbiter (decider) of questions of state law; the U.S. Supreme Court is the ultimate arbiter of questions of U.S. constitutional law.

While nonprevailing parties (except the state in a criminal case) may obtain review before a court of appeals, few decisions of those courts are reviewed at the high court level. The decision to review the case belongs to the court, not to the litigants. High courts are swamped with far more appeals, petitions for certiorari, and other requests for review than they can possibly accommodate; the court of appeals is thus the last stop for most litigants.

International and Foreign Law

International law, or more specifically public international law, is the body of law that governs interactions among nations. The study of the law of foreign countries is not international law but comparative law. The international nature of the Internet makes both international law and comparative law important; however, only international law has force within the U.S. legal system.

International law is either conventional (law made by treaties and other international agreements) or customary (normative expectations based on state practice undertaken out of a sense of legal obligation). In the United States, treaties are ratified by the president upon receipt of the advice and consent of the Senate (but not the House of Representatives). The treaties then become, at least in theory, part of U.S. federal law under Article VI, clause 2 of the Constitution. U.S. law makes a distinction, however, between treaties that are self-executing (and thus require no additional action by Congress in order to take effect in domestic law) and treaties that are not self-executing. Whether self-executing or not, all ratified treaties create obligations on the part of the United States with regard to other nations; however, only a self-executing treaty creates obligations enforceable by individuals in U.S. courts.

Treaties supersede any inconsistent prior federal legislation, but may in turn be superseded by subsequent federal legislation. Because Article VI, clause 2 provides that treaties "shall be the supreme Law of the Land; and the judges in every State shall be bound thereby, any Thing in the Constitution or Laws of any State to the Contrary notwithstanding[,]" treaties supersede inconsistent state law even if the state law is later in time than the treaty.

Customary international law has a hazier status; the nature and even the existence of rules of customary international law is often disputed, and even when a rule is undisputed, pinning an exact date to something that arises from state practice rather than from a document is often an impossible task. The Supreme Court's 1900 decision in *The Paquete Habana*, 175 U.S. 677, is often cited for the principle that customary international law is "part of our law, and must be ascertained and administered by the courts of justice of appropriate jurisdiction, as often as questions of right depending upon it are duly presented for their determination." However, the situation the Court addressed in *The Paquete Habana* was an unusual one, "where there is no treaty, and no controlling executive or legislative act or judicial decision." It is quite a bit less clear what the outcome would be where a rule of customary international law conflicts with a federal statute.

While all sovereign nations share a body of international law, the domestic legal system of each country has its own unique characteristics. Roughly speaking, the legal systems of the world can be divided into four broad groups—Hindu law, Islamic law, common law, and civil law—with a few countries not fitting neatly into any of the groups and many more countries exhibiting characteristics of more than one group. Because the common law system is found in nearly all of the countries of the English-speaking world, there is a tendency on the part of English speakers to think of it as typical. However, it is actually quite atypical; it differs from the other systems most markedly in the importance assigned to judicial opinions. In most of the United States, England, most other English-speaking countries, and a few other countries law is made not only by legislatures but also by judges; this body of judge-made law is known as common law. The legal systems of these countries are often identified as common-law systems (or systems within the common-law tradition) in contrast to the world's other legal traditions, particularly the civil law tradition. The majority of the world's countries, on the other hand, follow legal traditions in some way derived from the Roman law; the legal systems of these countries are often spoken of collectively as belonging to the civil law tradition. (In the United States, civil law systems are found in Louisiana and Puerto Rico, although these have inevitably been influenced by the common-law tradition of the remainder of the country.)

How to Find the Law

Finding federal legislative and administrative materials is fairly straightforward; finding federal cases is a bit more complex. International law materials are easy to find if the United States is a party, but somewhat more difficult if not. These materials—statutes, regulations, cases, and treaties—contain text that has legal effect, and are called primary sources; other materials, such as treatises (not to be confused with treaties) and articles in professional journals contain someone else's opinion about the law, and are called secondary sources.

This is an encyclopedia (a secondary source) of Internet law, and all of the primary sources referred to in this volume are available online. Many of the secondary sources are, too: most of the articles, and a few of the books. Unlike most of the primary sources, however, they are protected by copyright, and some of them may not be available for free.

Statutes enacted by Congress and by state legislatures are collected in compilations, organized by subject matter, for ease of use. Federal statutes are compiled in the United States Code (U.S.C.). The U.S.C. is available online from a variety of sources; lawyers and law students generally use the annotated versions provided by Westlaw or Lexis, but these are proprietary services and charge a fee. One of the many excellent services offering the United States Code online for free is the Legal Information Institute at Cornell University: http://assembler.law.cornell.edu/uscode/; an official Web site is http://www.gpoaccess.gov/uscode/. Bound versions of the U.S.C. are also available from all law libraries and many other libraries. Commercial publishers issue annotated versions of the compiled federal statutes under the titles United States Code Annotated and United States Code Service, abbreviated "U.S.C.A." and "U.S.C.S.," respectively; the annotations include references to cases interpreting each statute and to secondary sources discussing it, if any.

Federal administrative materials are published in the Federal Register, a daily publication. Regulations are initially published in the Federal Register as proposed regulations; after one or more comment periods, they may be published again as interim or final regulations. Final regulations then appear in the Code of Federal Regulations (CFR), available online at http://www.gpoaccess.gov/cfr/index.html. Other administrative publications of Internet law interest include the Federal Communications Commission Record and the Federal Trade Commission Decisions.

Cases are reported, if at all, in case reporters. These reporters include the opinion of the judge deciding the case, as well as information about the case. Important reporters of federal cases include the United States Reports, the Supreme Court Reporter, and the United States Reports (Lawyer's Edition), each of which contains decisions of the U.S. Supreme Court; the Federal Reporter, which includes decisions of the federal Courts of Appeals; and the Federal Supplement, which includes decisions of the federal district courts. Recent editions of the United States Reports are available in PDF format from the Supreme Court's Web site at http://www.supremecourt.gov/.

The easiest way to find a case online is simply to type the case name and cite into the Google search bar. Be careful, however; many cases have given rise to more than one published opinion, so check the cite information and date to be sure you have found the right opinion. Lexis and Westlaw also offer comprehensive case databases for all U.S. and many foreign jurisdictions, for a fee. The Legal Information Institute offers federal and New York cases at http://www.law.cornell.edu/federal/, and most courts' Web sites offer their own cases.

As with cases, the easiest way to find treaties is by using a search engine such as Google. Most of the intellectual property treaties discussed in this volume are available from the World Intellectual Property Organization Web site at http://www.wipo.int/treaties/en/; TRIPS is available from the World Trade Organization Web site at http://www.wto.org/english/tratop_e/trips_e/t_agm0_e.htm.

The professional and academic journal articles cited in this volume are available through Lexis, Westlaw, and Hein-Online, for a fee. Some may also be available for free on the Web sites of the journals or authors; a search for the title will reveal this. Other secondary sources often must be located in hard copy. Only a few of the books cited are available for free online; where available, I have indicated this by providing a Web address. Most will have to be located in hard copy, though, at libraries or booksellers, or purchased as e-books.

Further Reading on Legal Research

- Robert C. Berring et al., *Finding the Law: An Abridged Edition of How to Find the Law* (St. Paul, Minnesota: West, 12th ed. 2005)
- Stephen Elias & Susan Levinkind, *Legal Research: How to Find and Understand the Law* (Berkeley, California: Nolo Press, 16th ed. 2012)
- Kent C. Olson & Morris L. Cohen, *Legal Research in a Nutshell* (St. Paul, Minnesota: West, 10th ed. 2010)

How to Read the Law

Understanding what a statute, regulation, case, or treaty means is not always straightforward. Lawyers spend three or more years as graduate students learning to understand the law, and often emerge realizing how little they actually do understand. If you are not a lawyer, and perhaps even if you are, you should never rely on your interpretation of the law when anything significant is at stake. The same goes for this book: it's intended as a general guide and a starting point for further legal research. It is a good source for a research paper, but do not set up an Internet company, enter into a contract, or sue somebody based on what you read here. Consult a lawyer instead: the law may have changed, or the information in the book may be insufficiently detailed.

There are two problems in understanding the law: understanding the language of the law, and understanding how all the pieces fit together. The first problem is baffling enough for nonlawyers; the second often baffles lawyers and even judges.

In the previous section you read about the sources of law. Statutes are often so verbose that they are difficult to understand, but their place in the scheme of things is fairly simple: later statutes control over earlier statutes, and compiled codes such as the U.S.C. make things simple by deleting the parts that have been superseded and adding the new words. When you look at a compiled statute, you are looking at the law as it stood on the date the compiled statute was last revised. (If you are looking at the statute online, be careful not to mistake the date the Web page was revised for the date the statute was revised.) The statute will also be controlling over a prior case. Compiled regulations are similarly straightforward: the Code of Federal Regulations is published anew each year, and each volume contains the regulations in force as of the publication date.

Note that all of this only applies to authority from a single jurisdiction. A federal statute does not ordinarily control over a prior California statute or case on a question of California law; a California statute never controls over a New York statute or case on a question of New York law.

With cases, however, the situation is complex. Cases are added to reporters more or less chronologically, but each case refers to other cases. Sometimes a case cites other cases approvingly; sometimes it reverses or overturns the decisions in other cases. There's no easy way to find out whether a particular case is still good law—that is, whether it still accurately states a rule of law—using case reporters alone; a citator service must also be used. A citator service employs attorneys to read all of the decisions from a particular jurisdiction, look at the cases cited in each opinion, and come up with a code describing the treatment given to each case.

Two national citator services are available: KeyCite, from Westlaw, and Shepard's Citations, available on Lexis and in hard copy. Understanding the information presented by these services requires specialized training. Although it is relatively easy to spot cases that have been overturned or reversed (marked with a red flag in KeyCite and a stop sign in the online version of Shepard's), even this information can easily be misinterpreted; it would be best to ask a law librarian or lawyer for help interpreting any information provided by citator services.

A large number of books have been written to help laypersons, law students, and lawyers navigate these complexities; many are cited in the "Sources and Further Reading" notes after each entry in this book. The books from Nolo Press are written for nonlawyers; the "Nutshells" and "Understanding" series are written primarily for law students. All three, though, are frequently relied upon by lawyers as well. Books aimed at practicing attorneys and law professors tend to be somewhat inaccessible—Shaw's conspiracy against the laity. A few are included here, though, selected for relative ease of use as well as for comprehensiveness and content.

How to Read the Cites Used in This Volume

The cites in this volume are based on the Harvard Bluebook (*A Uniform System of Citation*, 19th ed.). This is the format most often used by lawyers; it has been modified a bit here for easier understanding, mostly by eliminating some of the more arcane abbreviations and by including publisher information for all, not just some, books. The samples below cover the most frequently cited types of material:

Statute

- **Children's Internet Protection Act, 47 U.S.C. § 254(h)**

"Children's Internet Protection Act" is the popular name of the statute. "U.S.C." indicates that the statute is federal, compiled in the United States Code. The U.S.C. is divided into 50 titles, each assigned a particular subject matter; Title 47 deals with telecommunications. The symbol "§" means "section"; each title of the U.S.C. is further divided into sections. "254(h)" indicates that the statute is codified at section 254, subsection h of Title 47. (A true Bluebook cite would also include the date of publication of the U.S.C. bound volume, which is omitted here because it is confusing and not particularly useful: people mistake it for the date of enactment of the statute.)

Case

- ***Yahoo!, Inc. v. La Ligue Contre le Racisme et L'Antisemitisme*, 169 F. Supp. 2d 1181 (N.D. Cal. 2001), reversed, 379 F.3d 1120 (9th Cir. 2004)**

Case cites, like cases themselves, are the hardest to make sense of. If all you want to do is find the two opinions referred to by this cite, just type the cite into Google or take it to any law librarian. But the cite tells a story, too: This case was brought by Yahoo!, and perhaps others (only the first named plaintiff is listed in the case name) against *La Ligue Contre le Racisme et L'Antisemitisme* (LICRA) and, again, perhaps others. The case was brought in federal trial court in the Northern District (N.D.) of California (Cal.): F.Supp. reports only decisions of federal trial courts, and all federal district courts are trial courts. It was decided in 2001, although it may have been brought earlier. The party who lost in the Northern District of California appealed the decision to the Ninth Circuit Court of Appeals (9th Cir.); three years later, in 2004, the Ninth Circuit reversed the district court's decision. The first (district court) decision can be found in volume 169 of the Federal Supplement, Second Series, beginning on page 1181 (169 F.Supp.2d 1181); the Ninth Circuit's decision can be found in volume 379 of the Federal Reporter, Third Series, beginning on page 1120 (379 F.3d 1120).

Treaty

- **WIPO Copyright Treaty, December 20, 1996, 36 I.L.M. 65 (1997)**

The WIPO Copyright Treaty was signed, or opened for signature, or adopted, or something of the sort on December 20, 1996 (abbreviated to Dec. in cites used in the legal profession, although not in this book); note that this is *not* the date on which the treaty entered into force. A copy of the treaty can be found in volume 36 of *International Legal Materials*, a publication of the American Society of International Law, beginning on page 65 (36 I.L.M. 65). Volume 36 was published in 1997.

Book

- **Richard Stim,** *Patent, Copyright& Trademark: An Intellectual Property Desk Reference* **(Berkeley: Nolo Press, 12th ed. 2012)**

The format used here for books differs from some other formats chiefly in the way the author's name is presented: first name, last name. The cite tells the name of the author, the title of the book, the city in which the book was published, the name of the publisher, and the year of publication. This cite also tells us that the edition cited is the 12th edition of the work. A true Bluebook cite would omit the city and publisher for this particular work.

- **Article (1): "Polynesians Get Free Wireless Web," BBC News (June 26, 2003), available at http://news.bbc.co.uk/1/hi/technology/3020158.stm (visited January 28, 2013)**

This article is dated, but has no named author. If there was a named author, the name would appear before the title, as in the preceding book cite. This article appeared on the Web site ConsumerAffairs.com; because this is an online source, the Web address and date last visited are also given.

- **Article (2): Eric Goldman, "A Road to No Warez: The No Electronic Theft Act and Criminal Copyright Infringement," 82** *Oregon Law Review* **369 (2003)**

Scholarly legal journals are consecutively paginated throughout the volume year. If the first issue in a volume year ends on page 200, the second issue will begin on page 201, not on page 1. Thus, each volume year can be treated as a single volume, like a book; there is no need to cite the month or season in which the issue was printed. The cite format follows the general rules of that used for case reporters and other primary sources: Eric Goldman's article on warez trading appears in volume 82 of the *Oregon Law Review*, beginning on page 369, and was published in 2003. (A true Bluebook cite would abbreviate the name of the journal, somewhat obscurely, as *Or. L. Rev.*)

How to Find Out More about Computer Terms

Law is not the only profession to conspire against the laity; the jargon of information technology professionals is, if anything, even more incomprehensible. Terms used in this volume are defined in the Glossary; for any terms not defined, however, or others that you may encounter in your research, a good source for definitions is PC Magazine's *Encyclopedia* at http://www.pcmag.com/encyclopedia_index/.

A final note: Any attempt to map the changing landscapes of the Internet and the law in print will necessarily yield imperfect results. But this encyclopedia contains links to hundreds of online resources, as well as other print resources; use them!

❖ TABLE OF ABBREVIATIONS ❖

The abbreviations listed here appear in this volume. Most are also explained in the text, so there is no need to commit this list to memory. The use of the notes referring to legal sources is explained in the section "How to Read the Cites Used in This Volume," above. Abbreviations that form company names are mostly omitted, where the company is known primarily by its abbreviation. Some abbreviations have become words, such as DVD (once "digital video disk," now the hokey-sounding "digital versatile disk"); they are not always explained in the text, but are included here for the curious.

AACS: Advanced Access Content System
ACLU: American Civil Liberties Union
ACTA: Anti-Counterfeiting Trade Agreement
ADP: Alliance for Digital Progress
AECA: Arms Export Control Act
AHRA: Audio Home Recording Act
AIA: America Invents Act
ALAI: Association Littéraire et Artistique Internationale (International Artistic and Literary Association)
AOL: America Online
ARPANET: Advanced Research Projects Administration Network
Art.: Article
ASCAP: American Society of Composers, Authors and Publishers

BBS: Bulletin Board System
BIRPI: Bureaux Internationaux Réunis pour la Protection de la Propriété Intellectuelle (United International Bureau for the Protection of Intellectual Property)

CAN-SPAM Act: Controlling the Assault of Non-Solicited Pornography and Marketing Act
CD: Compact disk
CDA: Communications Decency Act
CDR: Campaign for Digital Rights
CD-ROM: Compact disk—read only memory
CERN: L'Organisation Européenne pour la Recherche Nucléaire (European Organization for Nuclear Research; originally Conseil Européene pour la Recherche Nucléaire)
CFAA: Computer Fraud and Abuse Act
CFR: Code of Federal Regulations
CIPA: Children's Internet Protection Act
Cir.: Circuit Court of Appeals
cl.: Clause
COICA: Combating Online Infringement and Counterfeits Act
COPA: Child Online Protection Act
COPPA: Children's Online Privacy Protection Act
CSS: Content Scramble System

D.: Federal District Court
DAT: Digital audio tape
DDoS: Distributed denial of service [attack]
DMCA: Digital Millennium Copyright Act
DOJ: Department of Justice
DOS: (1) Disk operating system; (2) Denial of service
DRM: Digital rights management
DSL: Digital Subscriber Line
DSP: Digital Speech Project
DVD: Digital versatile disk (originally digital video disk)

EEA: Economic Espionage Act
EFF: Electronic Frontier Foundation
EU: European Union
EULA: End-user license agreement

F.: Federal Reporter
F.2d: Federal Reporter, Second Series
F.3d: Federal Reporter, Third Series
FBI: Federal Bureau of Investigation
Fed.: Federal
F.Supp.: Federal Supplement
F.Supp.2d: Federal Supplement, Second Series
FCC: Federal Communications Commission
F.C.C.R.: Federal Communications Commission Record
FSF: Free Software Foundation
FTC: Federal Trade Commission
FTP: File Transfer Protocol

GNU: Gnu's Not Unix (a recursive acronym)
GPL: General Public License
GUI: Graphical user interface

H.: House
H.R.: House of Representatives
HTML: Hypertext Markup Language
HTTP: Hypertext Transfer Protocol

IANA: Internet Assigned Numbers Authority
ICANN: Internet Corporation for Assigned Names & Numbers
IFRRO: International Federation of Reproduction Rights Organizations
I.L.M.: International Legal Materials
INDUCE Act: Inducing Infringement of Copyrights Act (originally Inducement Devolves into Unlawful Child Exploitation Act)
IP: (1) Internet protocol; (2) Internet provider; (3) intellectual property
IRC: Internet Relay Chat
ISP: Internet Service Provider
I-SPY: Internet Spyware Prevention Act

ITAR: International Traffic in Arms Regulation
LICRA: Ligue Contre le Racisme et L'Antisémitisme (League Against Racism and Antisemitism)
L.N.T.S.: League of Nations Treaty Series

MIT: Massachusetts Institute of Technology
MP3: MPEG-1/2 Audio Layer 3
MPAA: Motion Picture Association of America
MPEG: Moving Pictures Experts Group

n.: Note
NCCUSL: National Conference of Commissioners on Uniform State Laws
NCIPA: Neighborhood Children's Internet Protection Act
NCSA: National Center for Supercomputing Applications
n.d.: No date
NET Act: No Electronic Theft Act
NSA: National Security Agency
NSFNet: National Science Foundation Network
NTIA: National Telecommunications and Information Administration

O.J.: Official Journal of the European Community
OSI: Open Society Institute
OSP: Online service provider

P2P: Peer-to-peer
PAA: Protect America Act
PC: Personal computer
PCT: Patent Cooperation Treaty
PDEA: Public Domain Enhancement Act
PDF: [Adobe] Portable Document Format
PGP: Pretty Good Privacy encryption software
PIRATE Act: Protecting Intellectual Rights against Theft and Expropriation Act
PKC: Public-key cryptography
PROTECT Act: Prosecuting Remedies and Tools against the Exploitation of Children Today Act
PROTECT IP Act or PIPA: Preventing Real Online Threats to Economic Creativity and Theft of Intellectual Property Act

RAM: Random access memory
Rep.: Report(s)
RIAA: Recording Industry Association of America
Rptr.: Reporter
RRO: Reproduction rights organization
RSA: Rivest-Shamir-Adleman encryption method

S.: Senate
S. Ct.: Supreme Court Reporter
SAFE Act: Security and Freedom through Encryption Act
SAFE ID Act: Secure Authentication Feature and Enhanced Identification Defense Act

SCA: Stored Communications Act
Sess.: Session
SF: Speculative fiction; also, less accurately, science fiction
SOPA: Stop Online Piracy Act
SPY ACT: Securely Protect Yourself against Cyber Trespass Act
SPY BLOCK Act: Software Principles Yielding Better Levels of Consumer Knowledge Act
SSL: Secure Socket Layer

TCP/IP: Transmission Control Protocol/Internet Protocol
TDRA: Trademark Dilution Revision Act
TLT: Trademark Law Treaty

U.C.C.: (1) Uniform Commercial Code, (2) Universal Copyright Convention
UCITA: Uniform Computer Information Transactions Act
UETA: Uniform Electronic Transactions Act
UFMJRA: Uniform Foreign Money-Judgments Recognition Act
UIGEA: Unlawful Internet Gambling Enforcement Act
UK: United Kingdom
UN: United Nations
U.N.T.S.: United Nations Treaty Series
URL: Uniform Resource Locator
U.S.: (1) United States; (2) when used in case cites, United States Reports
USA PATRIOT Act: Uniting and Strengthening America by Providing Appropriate Tools Required to Intercept and Obstruct Terrorism Act
U.S.C.: United States Code
USCCAN: United States Code Congressional and Administrative News
USPTO: United States Patent and Trademark Office (also abbreviated PTO)
U.S. SAFE WEB Act: Undertaking Spam, Spyware, and Fraud Enforcement With Enforcers beyond Borders Act
U.S.T.: United States Treaties and Other International Agreements

VARA: Visual Artists' Rights Act
VCR: Videocassette recorder
VHDPA: Vessel Hull Design Protection Act
VHS: Video Home System (originally Vertical Helical Scan)

WIPO: World Intellectual Property Association
WL: Westlaw
WTO: World Trade Organization
WWW: World Wide Web

❖ AACS ❖

See Advanced Access Content System

❖ ABANDONWARE ❖

Abandonware is software that is no longer being sold or supported by its author, copyright owner, or licensed distributor. Software that is still being sold, but no longer supported, is sometimes also referred to as abandonware. Software becomes abandonware for various reasons. A software publisher may abandon a program because of declining sales, or because it was written for a hardware platform or operating system that is no longer being sold, such as the Apple II, Atari 800, or Commodore Amiga. Or, the publisher may cease to exist as a corporate entity, for example, through bankruptcy or merger.

Because personal computers have not been around for long enough for the copyright on any programs written for them to expire, all abandonware that was once copyrighted is still copyrighted. Software that has been abandoned because its original publisher no longer exists is not automatically in the public domain, although in a few cases many rights may have been released under an open-source license. Some distributors and sharers of abandonware argue that the ethical objections to sharing copyrighted material do not apply to abandonware; the copyright owner is no longer selling the program, and thus is not being deprived of further sales (Goldman 2003, 405). While there is some logic to this position, it is legally incorrect. When a corporate publisher ceases to exist through bankruptcy or merger with another publisher, its property, including its copyrights, is assigned to some new person. Copyrights held by an individual remain the property of that individual until he or she transfers them to someone else or dies; in the latter case they become a part of his or her estate.

Some corporate publishers do not undergo any formal dissolution process, however; they simply close their doors, without formally transferring their copyrights to anyone. In such a case it can be difficult to locate anyone with the legal right to authorize the making of copies. As a practical matter, such copyrights—and abandonware copyrights generally—are rarely enforced, although some popular sites, such as *Dan's 20th Century Abandonware*, have disappeared from the Web in recent years. The Internet Archive, an online library, maintains a collection of "vintage software," much of which could be classified as abandonware.

Old spreadsheets, word processing programs, and the like are of interest only to a limited number of enthusiasts. Abandoned games, however, are more popular. There has been a renewed interest in older game copyrights as some games are adapted for use on mobile devices. And the content industry generally takes the view that all unlicensed distribution of abandonware is harmful, because the abandoned programs might become valuable again at some point during the life of their copyright term. Balanced against this copyright interest is the valuable function abandonware sites may play in preserving programs that would otherwise be lost (Costikyan 2000).

Under a repeatedly renewed exception to the anticircumvention provisions of the Digital Millennium Copyright Act, libraries are allowed to make copies for archival purposes even where doing so requires circumventing copy protection measures. This exception does not mean, however, that the archived works have entered the public domain.

See also: Copyright Infringement; File-Sharing; No Electronic Theft Act; Public Domain; Warez

Case

- *Bradburn v. North Central Regional Library District*, 231 P.3d 166 (Wash. 2010)

Regulation

- Exemption to Prohibition on Circumvention of Copyright Protection Systems for Access Control Technologies, 37 C.F.R § 201.40 (2010)

Sources and Further Reading

Abandonware: The Official Ring, available at http://www.abandonwarering.com/ (visited May 30, 2012)

Greg Costikyan, "New Front in the Copyright Wars: Out-of-Print Computer Games," *N.Y. Times* (May 18, 2000), available at http://www.nytimes.com/library/tech/00/05/circuits/articles/18aban.html

Eric Goldman, "A Road to No Warez: The No Electronic Theft Act and Criminal Copyright Infringement," 82 *Oregon Law Review* 369 (2003)

Dennis W. K. Khong, "Orphan Works, Abandonware and the Missing Market for Copyrighted Goods," 15 *International Journal of Law & Information Technology* 54 (2007)

"Software Archive," Internet Archive, available at http://web .archive.org/web/20110501034314/http://www.archive .org/details/software (visited May 30, 2012)

❖ ACTIVISM AND ADVOCACY GROUPS ❖

Advances in and increased use of computers and information technology raise a wide variety of political and legal issues. New activist and industry advocacy groups have sprung up to address these issues, while older groups have added new issues to their traditional concerns. Three areas that have given rise to a great deal of litigation and political activism are freedom of expression, privacy, and copyright. Many activist and advocacy groups address a wide range of issues, while others have a single-issue focus.

Freedom of expression is a concern of the American Civil Liberties Union (ACLU), and the ACLU has been a plaintiff in actions brought to determine the constitutionality of federal legislation attempting to regulate or restrict access to Internet content. The action brought by the ACLU challenging the first such Congressional attempt, the Communications Decency Act (CDA), resulted in a U.S. Supreme Court decision holding the content-restricting portions of the CDA unconstitutional (*Reno v. ACLU*, 521 U.S. 824). After the decision striking down the CDA, Congress enacted the Child Online Protection Act (COPA), a second attempt to regulate Internet content, which was also challenged in court by the ACLU. The Supreme Court also expressed doubts about the constitutionality of COPA, and remanded the case to a lower court for trial on the issue of whether blocking and filtering software could provide a less restrictive alternative (*Ashcroft v. ACLU*, 524 U.S. 656). The ACLU has also, although ultimately unsuccessfully, challenged the Children's Internet Protection Act (*American Library Association*, 539 U.S. 194). In the legislative arena it has opposed the Stop Online Piracy Act (SOPA) and the Preventing Real Online Threats to Economic Creativity and Theft of Intellectual Property Act (PIPA), advocated net neutrality, and supported reforms to the Electronic Communications Privacy Act "to provide protection to communications such as email, private social network posts, and other information stored in 'the cloud.'"

On copyright issues, groups can be loosely classified as either users' rights or content owners' rights groups. The division bears no relation to more general left-right political divisions. The division is complicated further by the ambivalent position of equipment and software manufacturers. Equipment manufacturers are naturally inclined toward the users' rights side of the dispute; enhanced copyright controls make equipment more complicated to manufacture and thus either more expensive or less profitable, and also decrease consumer demand because of compatibility issues and because many users want to use the equipment they purchase to make copies, whether within the fair use exception or outside it. But many equipment manufacturers (e.g.,) are also content owners; there is thus an internal conflict.

Software companies suffer a similar conflict, but while the balance for most equipment makers tilts toward the users' rights side, for software makers it tilts toward content owners' rights. Software that allows duplication of copyrighted material will be easier to sell, but software itself is copyrighted content, and software makers have an interest in its protection.

While the ADP is a single-issue group, the Electronic Frontiers Foundation (EFF) is perhaps the best known of several advocacy groups addressing a wider array of computer and Internet law issues. Like the ADP, the EFF is alarmed by Congressional efforts to mandate copyright control mechanisms. On copyright and other intellectual property issues the EFF is a users' rights group. Intellectual property is not the EFF's only concern, however; its "list of issues" includes, among other topics, anonymity, biometrics, censorship, intellectual property, privacy, public records, spam, and the USA PATRIOT Act. On all of these issues the EFF takes a consistent individual rights stance. According to the EFF's Web site, "From the Internet to the iPod, technologies are transforming our society and empowering us as speakers, citizens, creators, and consumers. When our freedoms in the networked world come under attack, the Electronic Frontier Foundation (EFF) is the first line of defense. . . . EFF fights for freedom primarily in the courts, bringing and defending lawsuits even when that means taking on the U.S. government or large corporations." (About EFF). The EFF's activities in pursuit of these freedoms include providing support for lawsuits, education, and reporting on proposed legislation and administrative regulations. Like many other pro-consumer and information-freedom groups, EFF was active in opposing SOPA and PIPA.

SOPA and PIPA brought back a level of public and online activism in opposition to proposed U.S. Internet-law legislation that had not been seen for several years. Among the many opponents of the proposed measures (which found few supporters outside the content industry) was the Center for Democracy and Technology (CDT). The CDT is often aligned with the EFF, although it is somewhat more moderate. The CDT's four stated overarching goals are "preserving the unique nature of the Internet"; "enhancing freedom of expression"; "protecting privacy"; and "limiting government surveillance." It pursues these goals through education, outreach, and legislative advice and advocacy; unlike the EFF, it does not seek to involve itself in litigation.

The Free Software Foundation (FSF) is perhaps the most prominent of several ideologically motivated groups of software designers. Rather than focusing on legal and political solutions to the problem of corporate and government control of users' online autonomy, the FSF and others like it focus on the technological aspect. The core of the problem—that is, the aspect of computers and the Internet that allows them to lend themselves so readily to an architecture of control—is, in the FSF's opinion, the dominance of proprietary operating systems (Philosophy of the GNU Project 2004). Open-source operating systems such as GNU/Linux, a Linux-based operating system distributed by the FSF-sponsored GNU project, are designed by and in the interest of individual users rather than governments or large corporations. The FSF states that its mission is "to preserve, protect and promote the freedom to use, study, copy, modify, and redistribute computer software, and to defend the rights of Free Software users" (GNU Operating System 2012). Despite its anticorporate rhetoric the FSF enjoys support from a number of corporate sponsors, including Google, Oracle, IBM, Hewlett-Packard, Intel, and Nokia. Many of these may feel threatened either by the dominant makers of operating systems for personal computers—Microsoft and Apple—or by content-industry attempts to tighten copyright controls.

Public Knowledge is another users' rights organization concerned with intellectual property law, especially copyright law. According to the organization's mission statement, Public Knowledge has four broad goals:

(1) Ensuring that U.S. intellectual property law [provides] an incentive to creators and innovators while benefiting the public through the free flow of information and ideas.

(2) Preserving an Internet that is built upon open standards and protocols and "end-to-end" architecture, thereby fostering innovation and user control.

(3) Protecting consumers of digital technology from market practices designed to erode competition, choice and fairness.

(4) Ensuring that international intellectual property policies are adopted through democratic processes and with public interest participation (*Public Knowledge Mission Statement*).

Public Knowledge carries out its work through advocacy and reporting on legislation potentially affecting users' rights. It also carries out special projects, including Empowering Creators in the Digital Age, which attempts to determine a workable balance between the need of content creators (rather than distributors) for content protection and the need of those same content creators to be able to make use of prior copyrighted works; and the Open Access Project, the goal of which is the "free and unrestricted world-wide electronic distribution of peer-reviewed journal literature coupled with free and unrestricted access to that literature by scientists, scholars, teachers, students and others" (Open Access Project).

Similar groups exist outside the United States, including the United Kingdom's Campaign for Digital Rights (CDR). Like the EFF, the CDR is concerned with freedom of expression as well as users' rights to fair use of copyrighted material. European Digital Rights (EDRi) focuses on copyright issues in the European Union. Other users' rights advocacy groups in Europe include:

- Association Electronique Libre (Belgium)
- Associazione per la Liberta' nella Comunicazione Elettronica Interattiva (Italy)

- Bits of Freedom (the Netherlands)
- Chaos Computer Club (Germany)
- Cyber-Rights & Cyber-Liberties (United Kingdom)
- Digital Rights (Denmark)
- Electronic Frontier Finland
- Elektronisk Forpost Norge (Norway)
- Förderverein Informationstechnik und Gesellschaft (Germany)
- Forum InformatikerInnen für Frieden und gesellschaftliche Verantwortung (Germany)
- Foundation for Information Policy Research (United Kingdom)
- Fronteras Electronicas España (Spain)
- Imaginons un Réseau Internet Solidaire (IRIS) (France)
- Internet Society Bulgaria
- Netzwerk Neue Medien (Germany)
- Privacy International (United Kingdom)
- Quintessenz (Austria)
- Swiss Internet User Group
- Verein für Internet-Benutzer Österreichs (Austria)

Other groups include Electronic Frontiers Australia and Electronic Frontier Canada.

Because there are many more users than there are content owners, users' rights groups tend to be more numerous and attract a broader base of support than content owners' rights groups. But because content is often worth money, the content owners' rights groups tend to be much better funded. Two groups that have been particularly prominent both legislatively (proposing and lobbying for legislation to enhance copyright protection) and judicially (bringing lawsuits to enforce content owners' rights) are the Motion Picture Association of America (MPAA) and the Recording Industry Association of America (RIAA).

As the names imply, the MPAA is concerned with movies and the RIAA with music. While the interests of the two groups are similar, they are not identical. The MPAA's members may currently be experiencing some lost profits due to piracy, but as long as a substantial portion of movie profits comes from box office receipts rather than video sales, the threat to their business model will remain less severe. The RIAA members' old business model—distribution of bundled music recordings on CDs or other media through retail outlets—has been effectively undermined by technological change. Its new business model, largely based on the sale of individual songs through outlets such as iTunes and rental through subscription services such as Rhapsody, is somewhat less vulnerable, but not immune, to the effects of piracy.

The MPAA's concern that the spread of broadband and DVD recorders would make video piracy as easy as music piracy has been in part forestalled by the advent of the higher-definition (and thus slower-download) BluRay format, but it is only a matter of time until technology makes the sharing of BluRay video content as easy as the sharing of MP3s. Online subscription services such as NetFlix and the packaging of BluRay content, with multiple extras, as gift items aimed at holiday-season sales have also protected the film industry's revenues. The film industry, however, faces a problem the music industry does not: because the total number of films ever made is far smaller than the total number of songs ever recorded, and the number of new films made each year is far smaller than the number of new songs, the film industry will reach market saturation sooner. Recent slowing of video sales may be due to an increasing number of consumers already having all the films they want rather than to piracy, as well as a reduced demand for ownership of recorded media when content is legally available online at a low cost.

Both the RIAA and the MPAA seek to protect content owners' rights through drafting and supporting proposed legislation to enhance copyright protections, through lawsuits against copyright infringers, and through the pursuit of technological solutions.

Statutes

- Child Online Protection Act, 47 U.S.C. § 231
- Children's Internet Protection Act, 47 U.S.C. § 254(h)
- Communications Decency Act, Pub. L. No. 104-104, § 502, 1996 U.S.S.C.A.N. (110 Stat.) 56, 133 (later codified at 47 U.S.C. § 223)
- Copyright Act of 1976, 17 U.S.C. § 101
- Digital Millennium Copyright Act, Title I, Pub. L. No. 105-304, codified at 17 U.S.C. §§ 1201-05
- Electronic Communications Privacy Act of 1986, Pub. L. No. 99-508, codified at 18 U.S.C. § 2703
- Uniting and Strengthening America by Providing Appropriate Tools Required to Intercept and Obstruct Terrorism Act (USA PATRIOT Act) of 2001, Pub. L. No. 107-56, 115 Stat. 272 (codified as amended in scattered sections of the U.S.C.)

Proposed Legislation

- Anti-Counterfeiting Trade Agreement, Oct. 1, 2011, 50 I.L.M. 243 (2011)
- Combating Online Infringement and Counterfeits Act, S. 3804, 111th Cong. (2d Sess. 2010)
- International Cyberspace and Cybersecurity Coordination Act of 2010, S. 3193, 111th Cong. (2d Sess. 2010)
- Internet Freedom Act, H.R. 96, 112th Cong. (1st Sess. 2011)
- Preventing Real Online Threats to Economic Creativity and Theft of Intellectual Property (PROTECT IP) Act (PIPA) of 2011, S. 968, 112th Cong. (1st Sess. 2011)
- Protect America Act of 2007, S. 1927, 110th Cong. (1st Sess. 2007)
- Stop Online Piracy Act, H.R. 3261, 112th Cong. (1st Sess. 2011)

Cases

Supreme Court

- *Ashcroft v. American Civil Liberties Union*, 524 U.S. 656 (2004)
- *Brown v. Entertainment Merchants Association*, 131 S. Ct. 2729 (2011)
- *Reno v. American Civil Liberties Union*, 521 U.S. 844 (1997)
- *United States v. American Library Association, Inc.*, 539 U.S. 194 (2003)

Federal Appellate Courts

- *American Civil Liberties Union v. United States Department of Justice*, 681 F.3d 61 (2d Cir. 2012)
- *Bernstein v. United States*, 176 F.3d 1132 (9th Cir. 1999); rehearing granted, opinion withdrawn, 192 F.3d 1308 (9th Cir. 1999)
- *Steve Jackson Games v. United States Secret Service*, 36 F.3d 457 (5th Cir. 1994)

Federal Trial Courts

- *American Booksellers Foundation for Free Expression v. Coakley*, No. 10-11165-RWZ, 2010 U.S. Dist. LEXIS 114750 (D. Mass. 2010)
- *Gonzales v. Google, Inc.*, 234 F.R.D. 674 (N.D. Cal. 2006)

State Courts

- *Bradburn v. North Central Regional Library District*, 231 P.3d 166 (Wash. 2010)
- *In re Appeal of Application for Search Warrant*, No. 2010-479 (Vt. Dec. 14, 2012)

See also: Budapest Open Access Initiative; Censorship; Child Online Protection Act; Children's Internet Protection Act; Communications Decency Act; Constitutional law; Content industry; Copyright; Declaration of the Independence of Cyberspace; Digital Millennium Copyright Act; Digital Millennium Copyright Act, Title I; Fan Works; File-Sharing; First Amendment; Net Neutrality; Open Source; Preventing Real Online Threats to Economic Creativity and Theft of Intellectual Property Act; Privacy; Recording Industry Association of America; Stop Online Piracy Act; WikiLeaks

Sources and Further Reading

Christina DesMarais, "10 Terrible Tech Laws That Have You in Their Bull's-Eye," *PCWorld* (June 10, 2012), available at http://www.pcworld.com/article/257247/10_terrible_tech_laws_that_have_you_in_their_bulls_eye.html

Electronic Frontier Foundation, "About EFF, General Information about the Electronic Frontier Foundation," available at http://www.eff.org/about/ (visited June 5, 2012)

Virginia Eubanks, *Digital Dead End: Fighting for Social Justice in the Information Age* (Cambridge, MA: MIT Press, 2011)

Free Software Foundation, https://my.fsf.org/associate/support_freedom? (visited Dec. 29, 2012)

GNU Operating System, http://www.gnu.org/ (last updated Dec. 16, 2012)

Mike Godwin, *Cyber Rights: Defending Free Speech in the Digital Age* (Cambridge, MA: MIT Press, 2003)

IFPI Digital Music Report 2012, http://www.ifpi.org/content/library/DMR2012.pdf (visited Sept. 23, 2012)

"Internet Free Speech," American Civil Liberties Union, http://www.aclu.org/technology-and-liberty/internet-free-speech (visited Dec. 20, 2012)

Tim Jordan, *Cyberpower: The Culture and Politics of Cyberspace and the Internet* (New York: Routledge, 1999)

Lawrence Lessig, *Free Culture: How Big Media Uses Technology and the Law to Lock Down Culture and Control Creativity* (New York: Penguin, 2004)

Young Joon Lim and Sarah E. Sexton, "Internet as a Human Right: A Practical Legal Framework to Address the Unique Nature of the Medium and to Promote Development," 7 *Washington Journal of Law, Technology & Arts* 295 (2012)

"Philosophy of the GNU Project," GNU Operating System, http://www.gnu.org/philosophy/ (last updated Jan. 1, 2012)

Public Knowledge Mission Statement, available at http://www.publicknowledge.org/about/what/mission (visited June 6, 2012)

Dan Sabbagh, "Hollywood in Turmoil as DVD Sales Drop and Downloads Steal the Show," *The Guardian* (May 3, 2011), http://www.guardian.co.uk/business/2011/may/03/film-industry-turmoil-as-dvd-sales-drop

Leslie David Simon et al., *Democracy and the Internet: Allies or Adversaries?* (Washington, D.C.: Woodrow Wilson Center Press, 2002)

Daniel Solove, *Nothing to Hide: The False Tradeoff between Privacy and Security* (New Haven, CT: Yale University Press, 2011)

Cass R. Sunstein, *Republic.com 2.0* (Princeton, NJ: Princeton University Press, 2009)

The Open Access Project, "Promoting the Free and Unrestricted World-Wide Electronic Distribution of Peer-Reviewed Journal Literature," Public Knowledge, available at http://www.publicknowledge.org/about/what/projects/open-access.html (visited June 6, 2012)

Siva Vaidhyanathan, *The Anarchist in the Library: How the Clash Between Freedom and Control Is Hacking the Real World and Crashing the System* (New York: Basic Books, 2004)

Anthony E. Varona, "Toward a Broadband Public Interest Standard," 25 *Administrative Law Review* 1 (2009)

❖ ADVANCED ACCESS CONTENT SYSTEM ❖

Advanced Access Content System (AACS) is the name for the motion picture recording digital rights management technology used to protect video recordings using the Blu-ray and the now-defunct HD DVD formats. AACS allows content owners to authorize limited or unlimited copying. The Managed Copy feature allows consumers to transfer AACS-protected movies to other devices, but at the same time makes it more difficult to make and distribute large numbers of unauthorized copies. AACS thus avoids many of the problems with Content Scramble System (CSS, the encryption used to protect DVD recordings). CSS frustrated, and continues to frustrate, consumers because CSS-protected disks can be played back only on CSS-equipped DVD players—the recordings cannot be transferred to other media or devices. And CSS has proved easy to circumvent through the use of such programs as DeCSS; once a CSS key has been leaked or reverseengineered, there is nothing the content industry can do to recapture it. The relative consumer-unfriendliness of CSS, plus the ease of defeating it, provided an incentive for otherwise law-abiding consumers to make unlawful copies. AACS, on the other hand, is designed so that individual keys can be retired without interfering with the functioning of the system as a whole; any keys that enter the public domain can be retired, enabling the content industry to minimize the damage without causing inconvenience to the consumers (Borland 2004).

In order to defend its copyrights, the content industry has been forced to wage a battle on two fronts. One front is legal: the industry fights to increase the scope of copyright protection and penalties for infringement, and sues infringers. The other front is technological: the industry seeks ways to make copyrighted recordings more difficult to copy. To do this effectively requires the cooperation of equipment manufacturers; a recording that cannot be played back on most people's media players, or that freezes, jitters, or stutters on playback, will be difficult to sell.

Historically, equipment manufacturers have been dubious of copyright protection schemes initiated by the content industry. Incorporating copy protection and digital rights management technology makes equipment more expensive to manufacture and increases compatibility problems; at the same time, consumers would prefer not to have it. It is not in the interests of equipment manufacturers to benefit the content industry at their own and their customers' expense. In order to be workable, AACS will have to take the interests of equipment manufacturers (and their customers) into account. That the proposal seems to do so is evident from the number of manufacturers that have joined the AACS Licensing Authority, including IBM, Intel, Panasonic, Sony, and Toshiba; other members include AOL Time Warner, Disney, and Microsoft (Merritt 2004).

Another problem is compatibility with other digital rights management systems. Content delivery is in danger of becoming fragmented: content recorded with a particular digital rights management technology can be played back only with players (whether hardware or software) equipped with that technology. Few consumers want to keep half a dozen different media players around; most seek a single player that can play all of the recordings they own. AACS seeks to resolve this problem as well; the Licensing Authority is working to ensure compatibility with digital rights management systems developed independently by the various members (Borland 2004).

See also: DeCSS; Digital Rights Management; Piracy

Sources and Further Reading
Advanced Access Content System ("AACS") Adopter Agreement, available at http://www.aacsla.com/license/AACS_Adopter_Agrmt_090605.pdf (last updated June 5, 2009)
John Borland, "Tech, Studio Giants Team on New DVD Locks," C/Net News.com (July 14, 2004), available at http://news.cnet.com/Tech,-studio-giants-team-on-new-DVD-locks/2100-1025_3-5269286.html
Clint DeBoer, "2010: The Year AACS and HDMI Kill Off Component Video," Audioholics Online A/V Magazine, available at http://www.audioholics.com/news/industry-news/aacs-hdmi-kill-component-2010 (last updated February 17, 2010)
Kevin Henry, Jiayuan Sui, & Ge Zhong, "An Overview of the Advanced Access Content System (AACS)," available at http://cacr.uwaterloo.ca/techreports/2007/cacr2007–25.pdf (visited September 22, 2012)
Rick Merritt, "Copyright Scheme Could Fuel Transition to High-Definition Systems," *EE Times* (July 15, 2004), available at http://www.eetimes.com/showArticle.jhtml?articleID=23900919
"Time to Revisit Blu-Ray? AACS," Pacific Disc (2010), available at http://www.pacificdisc.com/Article19.html

❖ ADVERTISING ❖

Advertising is an essential component of the modern Internet. Revenues from advertising support many Web sites; without it, content on the Internet would be less plentiful and less varied. Some Internet advertisers, however, make their messages so intrusive that users and Web site operators feel that the advertisement is interfering with their enjoyment of the Internet; in these cases, legal action and demands for regulation may ensue. This unwelcome advertising may raise First Amendment and privacy issues. Internet advertising, welcome or not, may also raise trademark and jurisdictional issues. Adware placed on a user's computer without the user's knowledge or consent may raise an issue of trespass.

There are various types of Internet advertising; among the most common are banner ads, pop-ups, floating and expanding ads, sponsored search engine results, and email advertisements. Banner ads are ads that show up as part of a Web page; they may be still or animated images, and clicking on them generally links to a Web site from which the advertised goods or services may be purchased. In format and visual effect they resemble advertisements in a printed magazine or newspaper; they can usually be ignored by uninterested viewers, although ads that blink, vibrate, or play audio may arouse consumer wrath. Banner ads may also create resentment if they contain indecent or shocking words or images. Ads containing indecent content are generally confined to pornographic Web sites and other Web sites that a user might reasonably expect to contain such advertisements; Web site owners are unlikely to accept such advertising otherwise. A problem may occur, though, when unscrupulous advertisers

hijack a Web site or an ad-placement system, replacing paid advertisers' content with their own. This hijacking is a crime (theft of services) and the hacking required to do it is also illegal.

Pop-ups and pop-unders are advertisements that open as a separate browser page either above or under the page being viewed at the time. They are almost universally disliked by Web surfers, and are declining as now-ubiquitous pop-up blockers render them less useful. The inclusion of pop-up blockers in most Web browsers has proved a mixed blessing, as it has led to the growth of the far more annoying floating ads, which slide across the page being viewed and block the content the viewer actually wants to see; the "X" for closing the floating ad is sometimes artfully concealed, with a decoy box where the "X" would normally be expected, causing unwary consumers to click on the ad by mistake and be subjected to a further unwelcome barrage of ad content. Sponsored search engine results, in contrast, are less intrusive. Like banner ads, they are confined to a certain portion of the page, and for the most part consist only of text.

Email advertising can be roughly divided into two categories. In the first category are advertisements that the recipient has asked or consented to receive, such as notification of the publication of a new book by a favorite author, or of a clearance sale from a clothing company from which the recipient has purchased clothes in the past. In the second category is unsolicited mass email advertising, or spam.

Ads of all sorts can be targeted to the viewer. Some banner ads are placed on a page in response to the nature of the content being viewed; a news story about a baseball game may contain ads for baseball memorabilia. Sometimes the ads are unintentionally absurd: an article about a public school district's ties to religious groups is accompanied by advertisements for men's neckwear decorated with Christian motifs—"religious ties" of a very different sort. Sometimes the ads are tasteless: an article about the fatal crash of a hot-air balloon is accompanied by ads for balloon rides.

More worrisome to privacy advocates is that ads can be targeted based on individual Web surfing habits. Internet users who visit a news site each day and read all of the stories about sailing may soon find that, whatever they view, they see banner ads for sailboats and sailing supplies.

Another category of advertising includes sites that consist entirely of advertisements; these generally cause few legal problems. Users expect a site called www.toyota.com to contain information about Toyota automobiles, and are neither surprised nor offended to learn that it does. Similarly, they expect a retail Web site such as www.amazon.com to advertise goods for sale; they go there expecting, and indeed hoping, to encounter such advertising. Privacy issues may arise, though, from the site's collection of information about viewers. While few visitors of a shopping Web site will find it invasive when the site recommends other items available for purchase on the same site, many or most visitors would be less delighted to have their shopping history sold to other Web sites or bricks-and-mortar retailers, or made available to government agencies. Shopping and other browsing history is poorly protected; however, sites may generally use information collected from visitors as they wish to target future advertising and develop marketing strategies, subject to the terms of a privacy policy written by the company itself and displayed somewhere on the site.

The use of information obtained from children is much more restricted, however. Under the Children's Online Privacy Protection Act (COPPA), commercial Web sites collecting information from children less than 13 years of age must provide a privacy notice explaining what information is collected, how it is used, and under what circumstances and to whom it may be disclosed. In addition, no personal information—defined as information that may identify or permit communication with the child, such as a first or last name, address, email address, telephone number, or social security number—may be obtained from a child without the verifiable consent of the child's parents. The Web site operator must provide the parents with a reasonable means to review the information; the parents must also have the opportunity to refuse to permit the Web site operator to use or maintain the information.

Considerable attention and concern has been focused on Internet "advertainment" and "advergames" aimed at children, such as Neopets or General Mills' now-defunct Millsberry. Under COPPA, a Web site operator may not condition a child's participation in a game, promotional sweepstakes, contest, or other activity upon the collection of any information not reasonably necessary to enable the child to participate in the activity. Some consumers groups feel that in the case of advergames COPPA does not go far enough; Neopets' "immersive advertising" strategy, in which children are not exposed to banners or pop-ups but are instead exposed to product placement within the game itself, strikes some consumers' groups as insidious and dangerous (Guardian 2002). Nonetheless, the sites can inspire considerable loyalty from gamers; the shutdown of Millsberry in 2010 led to outcry from fans and the appearance of several unlicensed imitation Millsberry sites.

The targeting of pop-up and pop-under ads raises the same issues as the targeting of banner ads. In addition, pop-ups may act as parasites on sites to which they have not paid an advertising fee, appearing on the computers of users visiting those sites. These pop-ups and other forms of advertising may be generated by adware placed on the user's computer. Many inexperienced users consent to install this software, under the belief that they are gaining something else: a security program or a new cursor design, for example. Children are especially vulnerable to adware of this sort.

Many users and Internet Service Providers (ISPs) turn to self-help to avoid unwelcome advertising. Users can block ads by using the Windows "hosts" file or downloading an ad blocker. ISPs weed out enormous quantities of spam each day, preventing it from reaching their subscribers' computers. These self-help activities have in turn met with challenges from advertisers. Spammers, for instance, sued America Online (AOL), claiming that its actions violate their First Amendment right to freedom of expression. The courts have rejected this argument; AOL is a private party, not a state actor, and the First Amendment does not require it to deliver email (*America Online*, 948 F. Supp. 456).

Unwelcome advertising, especially spam, has also brought demands for government regulation. COPPA, discussed earlier, is one result. The CAN-SPAM Act, an unsuccessful 2003 law designed to curb spammers, is another. And laws designed for off-line advertising also apply to Internet advertising: commercial speech may be prohibited if it is untruthful, misleading, or deceptive, or if its subject matter or presentation is illegal. It may also be subject to reasonable time, place, and manner restrictions.

Regulating advertising, on the Internet and in many other media, is the job of the Federal Trade Commission (FTC), and more specifically (although not exclusively) of the Division of Advertising Practices of the FTC's Bureau of Consumer Protection. The FTC may take regulatory or administrative action or litigate against unfair, misleading, or false advertising. The FTC may regulate against, or issue a cease and desist order to prevent, advertising acts or practices that are unfair if two additional conditions are met. First, the act or practice must cause or be "likely to cause substantial injury to consumers. . . not reasonably avoidable by consumers themselves." Second, the injury must not be "outweighed by countervailing benefits to consumers or to competition." In determining whether an act or practice is unfair, the FTC may consider public policy, but may not make public policy the primary basis for its action (15 U.S.C. § 45(n)).

An injury to consumers is substantial if a relatively small harm is inflicted upon a large number of consumers or if a greater harm is inflicted on even a small number of consumers; however, the harm must be more than merely trivial or speculative (Greenspan 1999).

The FTC may also take action against deceptive acts and practices: material misrepresentations, omissions, or practices that are "likely to mislead a consumer acting reasonably under the circumstances" (Greenspan 1999). This reasonable person standard can be adapted to match the target audience: a communication to an audience of children would be judged by whether it was likely to mislead a reasonable child.

The FTC has authority to regulate false advertising only if the advertising is for food, drugs, cosmetics, or medical devices, a category that includes a great deal of spam. Advertising for these products is false if it is materially misleading (Greenspan 1999).

The FTC has brought actions against scammers and spammers; it has imposed penalties on Web site operators for violations of their own privacy policies. It has declined, however, to create a federal "do not spam" registry as authorized by the CAN-SPAM Act of 2003, on the grounds that such a registry would be futile, in contrast to the popular "do not call" registry. It is far easier and cheaper to send spam from outside the United States than it is to move a telemarketing operation outside the United States, although the falling cost of international phone calls is undermining the effectiveness of the "do not call" registry as well. Without some form of global control, the FTC's registry would be useless. The FTC has, however, issued a regulation requiring adult-oriented spam to be identified as such in the message header; misidentified adult-oriented spam persists, however.

A few specialized categories of advertising may also be regulated or prohibited. Advertising by attorneys, doctors, and other professionals may be regulated by professional associations, subject to limits imposed by the First Amendment. The status of tobacco advertising is still unclear. Congress can explicitly prohibit tobacco advertising over the Internet, and the European Union has already imposed such a prohibition. As with spam, however, little can be done about advertising originating beyond a nation's borders. A similar problem applies to advertising for gambling.

Statutes
- Controlling the Assault of Non-Solicited Pornography and Marketing (CAN-SPAM) Act of 2003, 15 U.S.C. §§ 7701–7713
- Unfair Methods of Competition, 15 U.S.C. § 45

European Union Directive
- Directive on the approximation of the laws, regulations, and administrative provisions of the Member States relating to the advertising and sponsorship of tobacco products, 2003 O.J. (L 152) 16

Cases
Federal Appellate Court
- *College Source, Inc. v. Academy One, Inc.*, 653 F.3d 1066 (9th Cir. 2011)
- *Gordon v. Virtumundo, Inc.*, 575 F.3d 1040 (9th Cir. 2009)
- *Network Automation, Inc. v. Advanced Sys. Concepts*, 638 F.3d 1137 (9th Cir. 2011)

Federal Trial Court
- *Aitken v. Communs. Workers of Am.*, 496 F. Supp. 2d 653 (E.D. Va. 2007)
- *Ascentive, LLC v. Opinion Corp.*, No. 10 Civ. 4433(ILG)(SMG), 2011 U.S. Dist. LEXIS 143081 (E.D.N.Y. 2011)
- *CJ Prods. LLC v. Snuggly Plushez LLC*, 809 F. Supp. 2d 127 (E.D.N.Y. 2011)
- *Cyber Promotions v. America Online*, 948 F. Supp. 456 (E.D. Pa. 1996)
- *Facebook, Inc. v. MaxBounty, Inc.*, 274 F.R.D. 279 (N.D. Cal. 2011)
- *Fancaster, Inc. v. Comcast Corp.*, No. 08–2922(DRD), 2011 U.S. Dist. LEXIS 147373 (D.N.J. December 13, 2011)
- *Ferguson v. Friendfinders, Inc.*, 94 Cal. App. 4th 1255 (Cal. App. 1st Dist. 2002)
- *Fraley v. Facebook, Inc.*, No. 11-CV-01726-LHK, 2011 U.S. Dist. LEXIS 145195 (N.D. Cal. December 16, 2011)
- *MySpace, Inc. v. Wallace*, 498 F. Supp. 2d 1293 (C.D. Cal. 2007)

State Court
- *Intel Corp. v. Hamidi*, 30 Cal. 4th 1342, 1353 (Cal. 2003)

See also: Adware and Spyware; Censorship; Children's Online Privacy Protection Act; Cookies; Data Mining; Doubleclick; First Amendment; Gambling; Privacy; Spam

Sources and Further Reading
"Advertising on Mobile Phones: Attack of the Covert Commercials," *The Economist*, July 7, 2012, at 60
"An Ad-Block Shock: France v Google," *The Economist*, January 12, 2013
Erik Anderson, "Protection of Trademarks from Use in Internet Advertising Banner Triggers: Playboy v. Netscape," 40 *Jurimetrics Journal* 469 (2000)
Lori Irish Bauman, "Personal Jurisdiction and Internet Advertising," 14 *Computer Lawyer* 1 (1997)
Terence Craig & Mary Ludloff, *Privacy & Big Data* (Sebastopol, CA: O'Reilly Media, Inc., 2011)
Alan N. Greenspan, *Internet Advertising Laws and Regulations*, Practising Law Institute, 19th Annual Institute on Computer Law, February-March 1999
Daniel L. Hadjinian, "Clicking Away the Competition: The Legal Ramifications of Click Fraud for Companies That Offer Pay per Click Advertising Services," 3 *Shidler Journal of Law, Commerce & Technology* 5 (2006)
Martin Headon, "Pet Hates: The Gaming Site Neopets Is a Welcome Relief, Says Martin Headon," *The Guardian* (October 30, 2002), available at http://www.guardian.co.uk/computergames/story/0,11500,822595,00.html
Orin S. Kerr, "Surveillance Law: Reshaping the Framework: A User's Guide to the Stored Communications Act, and a Legislator's Guide to Amending It," 72 *George Washington Law Review* 1208 (2004)
Jason Krause, "The National Pulse: Google Targeted in Trademark Disputes—Rulings Should Help Define What Is Protected in Internet Advertising," *ABA Journal E-Report*, May 28, 2004
Paul Lansing & Mark D. Halter, "Internet Advertising and Right to Privacy Issues," 80 *University of Detroit Mercy Law Review* 181 (2003)
Taiwo A. Oriola, "Regulating Unsolicited Commercial Electronic Mail in the United States and the European Union: Challenges and Prospects," 7 *Tulane Journal of Technology & Intellectual Property* 113 (2005)
"Policy Online Privacy/Data Sharing Internet Advertising Trade Group Issues Guidelines on Use of Web Bugs," *Cybercrime Law Report*, December 16, 2002
Christopher J. Schulte, "Abracadabra International Ltd. v. Abracadabra Creations Inc.—Internet Advertising Just Federalized the Nation's Service Mark Law," 22 *Hamline Law Review* 563 (1999)

Tyson Smith, "Googling a Trademark: A Comparative Look at Keyword Use in Internet Advertising," 46 *Texas International Law Journal* 231 (2010)

"You Shut Down Millsberry and Ruined My Life, and Many More!!!," Pissed Consumer (May 14, 2011), available at http://general-mills.pissedconsumer.com/you-shut-down-millsberry-and-ruined-my-life-and-many-more-20110514237626.html (27 pages, 265 comments)

❖ ADWARE AND SPYWARE ❖

Adware is software installed on a user's computer that causes advertisements to be displayed, often as pop-ups. These pop-ups generally appear while the user is surfing the Web, but may appear at other times; they are neither authorized by nor related to the Web site that the user is viewing at the time. Adware that collects information about the user and passes that information to some other person is spyware. Adware is generally regarded as an annoyance, while spyware may raise privacy and security issues and is considered by many users to be unethical rather than merely annoying.

Some adware is installed as part of commercially distributed programs and is directly related to that program. An antivirus program, for example, may prompt users when their subscriptions are about to expire. This prompt may appear as a pop-up whenever the user turns on the computer. A program that was installed as part of the antivirus program generates the pop-up, and this program could be considered adware. The level of annoyance it produces in the user is likely to be slight, however.

Users may also accept adware as the price of using popular free file-sharing, browser, and email programs. Some users of these programs may be unaware that, by installing the programs, they have consented to the installation of adware. The information is contained in the clickwrap agreements, but few users actually read the agreements.

The Google toolbar includes a "page rank" feature that lets Google know where toolbar users are surfing; some consider this spyware, although the feature can be disabled with a single click. The Google toolbar also includes a pop-up blocker. (Identifying Spyware 2005) But the adware and spyware that arouses the greatest user rage—second only to spam as an unpopular advertising technique—is that installed on a user's computer by stealth or subterfuge.

Computer and smartphone users may be confronted with pop-up dialog boxes asking them to consent to the installation of a program; sometimes these programs are adware, but many users—especially children—may click "yes" to install the program, rather than "no" or "X" to close the dialog box, and thus install the adware. These programs, at least, give users the opportunity to refuse installation. More worrisome are drive-by downloads: programs that install themselves without presenting the user with the option of refusal, and without the user's knowledge (Levinson 2012; Urbach & Kibel 2004).

Adware and spyware can do more than serve pop-up advertising. It can turn a user's computer into a zombie, allowing it to be used in spamming or denial-of-service attacks. Homepage hijackers change the user's browser home page. Spyware can be used not only for annoying advertisements but also for malicious hacking; it can provide hackers with access to and control over the computer on which it is installed. Keystroke loggers, screen capture programs, and similar programs can track and record all activity on a computer, enabling anyone who looks at the log to discover passwords, account numbers, and other vital security information. The infamous Sony BMG rootkit was placed on the computers of purchasers of music CDs and not only transmitted information back to the company but also opened a vulnerability that malicious hackers could, and ultimately did, exploit (Brown 2010). And all of these activities, sinister or not, take up disk space, memory, and processor resources; adware and spyware slow down the operation of the computer on which they are installed, sometimes seriously degrading performance.

Malicious uses of spyware are obviously illegal; however, adware installed with the consent of the user—even when the user does not understand what he or she is consenting to—may not be. Adware has given rise to a great many civil suits for damages and equitable relief. Many of these suits are brought by aggrieved Web site owners and trademark holders. U-Haul, for example, has sued over the unauthorized use of its trademarks in pop-ups generated by WhenU.com, Inc. WhenU.com has been sued frequently. Wells Fargo and Quicken Loans have sued because WhenU's software causes ads for other mortgage lenders to appear when users visit Wells Fargo or Quicken Loans mortgage loan Web sites. These suits have not been successful; although the ad software uses U-Haul's, Wells Fargo's, and Quicken's trademarks to assign particular ads to users visiting the trademark holder's pages, that alone does not meet the elements of trademark infringement. A similar suit against WhenU by 1–800-Contacts likewise led to victory for WhenU in the Second Circuit Court of Appeals.

Opponents of adware and spyware have also pursued legislative change, without much success. Antispyware bills introduced in Congress have included the Safeguard against Privacy Invasions Act and the Software Principles Yielding Better Levels of Consumer Knowledge (SPY BLOCK) Act, introduced in the House of Representatives and in the Senate, respectively, in 2003. The Safeguard against Privacy Invasions Act, renamed the Securely Protect Yourself against Cyber Trespass Act (SPY ACT), passed the House of Representatives by a vote of 399 in favor to one against on October 5, 2004, and reported to the Senate on the following day. Ultimately, however, these attempts at targeted antispyware legislation were unsuccessful, and at the federal level spyware has been dealt with under other statutes, especially the Computer Fraud and Abuse Act.

As with most areas of law governing the Internet, a single uniform body of national (or even transnational) law is preferable to multiple state laws, with all the possibility they present for inconsistencies, conflict, and forum-shopping. But with the federal government unable or unwilling to enact comprehensive antispyware legislation, many states have enacted antispyware laws of their own, beginning with Utah's Spyware Control Act in March 2004 and California's Consumer Protection against Computer Software Act in September of the same year. Alaska, Arizona, Arkansas, Georgia, Illinois, Indiana, Iowa, Louisiana, Nevada, New Hampshire, Pennsylvania, Rhode Island, Texas, Virginia, Washington, and Puerto Rico also have laws designed to be effective against spyware. Adware distributors have brought suits to enjoin enforcement of state statutes (see, e.g., *WhenU.com, Inc. v. Utah; Overstock. com*, 192 P.3d 858).

For most users the main issue that arises from adware and spyware is not its legality, but how to get rid of it. Laws restricting spyware may offer a long-term solution, but will be ineffective against malicious hackers (whose activities are already illegal) and against parties outside the United States. The best way to fight software is with software; many antiadware and antispyware programs are available. As with spam and viruses, there is an ongoing arms race between adware and antiadware software; complete protection may require the use of more than one program. Popular and effective antiadware and antispyware programs include Ad-Aware, HiJack This, Spybot Search & Destroy, and Spy Sweeper; most antivirus programs now offer antiadware and antispyware options as well. Many of these are available as free downloads for individual users, while others are inexpensive. A firewall program can prevent adware from sending information out of the user's computer; this will not solve the problem, but will at least address the privacy issues. A firewall's log may also be useful in identifying spyware.

Statutes and Proposed Legislation
Federal
- Safeguard against Privacy Invasions Act, H.R. 2929, 108th Cong. (1st Sess. 2003), reported to and passed by House of Representatives as Securely Protect Yourself against Cyber Trespass Act (SPY ACT)
- Software Principles Yielding Better Levels of Consumer Knowledge (SPY BLOCK) Act, S. 2145, 108th Cong. (2d Sess. 2003)
- Internet Spyware Prevention (I-SPY) Act of 2007, H.R.1525, 110th Cong. (1st Sess. 2007—2008)

State
- Alaska: Spyware and Unsolicited Internet Advertising, S.B. 140 (Alaska. 2005), Alaska Stat. §§ 45.45.792, -.794, -.798; § 45.50.471(51)
- Arizona: Computer Spyware, H.B. 2414 (Ariz. 2005), Ariz. Rev. Stat. §§ 44–7301 to 44–7304

- Arkansas: Improper Use of Computer Spyware, H.B. 2904 (Ark. 2004), Ark. Code §§ 4–111–101, -102, -103, -104, -105, § 19-6-301, § 19-6-804
- California: Consumer Protection against Computer Software Act, S.B. 1436 (Cal. 2004), Cal. Bus. & Prof. Code §§ 22947 to 22947.6
- Georgia: Computer Security Act, H.B. 127 (Ga. 2005), Ga. Code §§ 16–9-152 to -157
- Illinois: Spyware Prevent Initiative Act, H.B. 380 (Ill. 2005), 720 ILCS 5/17–52.5
- Indiana: Ind. Code § 24–4.8–1 et seq., § 24–4.8–2 et. seq, § 24–4.8–3 et seq.
- Iowa: Deceptive or Unauthorized Computer Software, H.F. 614 (Iowa. 2005), Iowa Code §§ 715.1 to 715.8
- Louisiana: La. Rev. Stat. §§ 51:2006 to 51:2014
- Nevada: Nev. Rev. Stat. § 205.4737
- New Hampshire: Regulating the Use of Computer Spyware, H.B. 47 (N.H. 2005), N.H. Rev. Stat. §§ 359-H:1 to 359-H:6
- Pennsylvania: 73 P.S. 2330.1 et seq.
- Rhode Island: R.I. Gen. Laws §§ 11–52.2–2 to 2–7
- Texas: Consumer Protection against Computer Spyware Act, S.B. 327 (Tex. 2005), Tex. Bus. & Comm. Code §§ 324.001–102
- Utah: Spyware Control Act, H.B. 323 (Utah 2004), Utah Code §§ 13–40–203, 13–40–204, 13–40–301, 13–40–302, 13–40–402
- Virginia: Computer Crimes Act, H.B. 2215 (Va. 2005), Va. Code § 18.2–152.4
- Washington: Wash. Rev. Code §§ 19.270.101–900
- Puerto Rico: 10 L.P.R.A. §§ 2181–85

Cases
- *1–800 Contacts v. WhenU.com, Inc.*, 309 F. Supp. 2d 467 (S.D.N.Y. 2003); reversed & remanded, 414 F.3d 400 (2d Cir. 2005)
- *Overstock.com, Inc. v. SmartBargains, Inc.*, 192 P.3d 858 (Utah 2008)
- *Rescuecom Corp. v. Google, Inc.*, 562 F.3d 123, 131 (2d Cir. 2009)
- *U-Haul International, Inc. v. WhenU.Com, Inc.*, No. 02- V-1469-A, 2003 WL 21673722 (E.D. Va. 2003)
- *Wells Fargo & Co. v. WhenU.com, Inc.*, 293 F. Supp. 2d 734 (E.D. Mich. 2003)
- *WhenU.com, Inc. v. Utah*, No. 040907578 (Utah September 26, 2004)

See also: Advertising; Computer Fraud and Abuse Act; Cookies; Denial-of-Service Attack; Hacking; Malware; Privacy; Spam; Trademark; Trojan; Zombie

Sources and Further Reading
"2d Cir. to Decide Legality of Injunction against Adware 1–800 *Contacts Inc. v. WhenU.com Inc.*," *Andrews Software Law Bulletin*, April 1, 2004, at 12

Bob Brown, "Sony BMG Rootkit Scandal: 5 Years Later," *Network World* (November 1, 2010), available at http://www.networkworld.com/news/2010/110110-sonybmg-rootkit-fsecure-drm.html

Alfred Cheng, "Does Spybot Finally Have Some Allies?: An Analysis of Current Spyware Legislation," 58 *Southern Methodist University Law Review* 1497 (2005)

Terence Craig & Mary Ludloff, *Privacy & Big Data* (Sebastopol, CA: O'Reilly Media, Inc., 2011)

Kevin P. Cronin & Ronald N. Weikers, *Data Security and Privacy Law: Combating Cyberthreats* § 8:44 (St. Paul, MN: West, 2004)

Jonathan I. Ezor, *Privacy and Data Protection in Business: Laws & Practices* (New Providence, NJ: LexisNexis, 2012)

Federal Trade Commission, "Combating Spyware and Malware," available at http://www.ftc.gov/opa/reporter/idtheft/spymalware.shtml (last updated August 28, 2012)

Chad A. Kirby, "Defining Abusive Software to Protect Computer Users from the Threat of Spyware," 10 *Computer Law Review & Technology Journal* 287 (2006)

Meridith Levinson, "Mobile Malware: Beware Drive-by Downloads on Your Smartphone," CIO (March 22, 2012), available at http://www.cio.com/article/702655/Mobile_Malware_Beware_Drive_by_Downloads_on_Your_Smartphone

Paul M. Schwartz, "Privacy Inalienability and the Regulation of Spyware," 20 *Berkeley Technology Law Journal* 1269 (2005)

Small Business Computing Staff, "Inside Spyware," Small Business Computing.com (July 15, 2005), available at http://smallbusinesscomputing.com/webmaster/article.php/3520466/Inside-Spyware.htm

Small Business Computing Staff, "Inside Spyware: Part Two—Identifying Spyware: Malicious, Annoying or Misunderstood?" Small Business Computing.com (July 18, 2005), available at http://www.smallbusinesscomputing.com/webmaster/article.php/3520791/Inside-Spyware-Part-Two.htm

Daniel Solove & Paul M. Schwartz, *Privacy Law Fundamentals* (Portsmouth, New Hampshire: IAPP Publication 2011)

Stop Badware, available at http://www.stopbadware.org (visited September 23, 2012)

Liying Sun, "Who Can Fix the Spyware Problem?" 22 *Berkeley Technology Law Journal* 555 (2007)

Ronald R. Urbach & Gary A. Kibel, "Adware/Spyware: An Update Regarding Pending Litigation and Legislation," *Journal of Proprietary Rights*, July 2004, at 12

Tom Zeller, Jr., "F.T.C. Files First Lawsuit against Spyware Concerns," *N.Y. Times* (October 13, 2004), available at http://www.nytimes.com/2004/10/13/technology/13spy.html?_r=0

❖ AMERICA INVENTS ACT ❖

The Leahy-Smith America Invents Act of 2011 (AIA) was the most dramatic overhaul of U.S. patent law in nearly 60 years. The most dramatic, though by no means only, change wrought by the AIA was to grant patent protection to the first inventor to publicly disclose or to file a successful patent application, rather than, as was previously the case in the United States, to the first person to invent. (Often—perhaps most of the time—the person protected will end up being the same under either rule.) This provision, as well as most of the rest of the AIA, entered into effect on March 16, 2013. Most applications filed before that date, but continued or still in process after that date, will be governed under the earlier law.

First-inventor-to-file: Prior to the AIA, the United States stood alone in protecting the first person to invent, rather than the first to comply with the formalities of the patent process. (Two other first-to-invent jurisdictions, Canada and the Philippines, had switched to first-to-file in 1989 and 1998, respectively.) An international agreement to which the United States was not a party, the Patent Law Treaty, rather opaquely required the use of a first-to-file, rather than first-to-invent, system (Patent Law Treaty arts. 5, 6). The first-to-invent system had strong support in the United States, however, and rather than switch completely to a first-to-file system, the AIA adopted a hybrid approach, the first-inventor-to-disclose-or-file system. The U.S. Patent and Trademark Office (USPTO) explains, less clearly than it might, that:

> The First Inventor to File (FITF) provisions transition the U.S. to a first-inventor-to-file system from a first-to-invent system. The FITF provision includes a 1-year grace period. Specifically, prior art disclosures made publicly available one year or less before the effective filing date can be overcome by applicant showing (1) the prior art disclosure was by another who obtained the disclosed subject matter from the applicant (a deriver), see 102(b)(1)(A), or (2) the applicant or a deriver publicly disclosed the subject matter before the date of the prior art disclosure, see 102(b)(1)(B) (USPTO 2013).

This grace period distinguishes the U.S. first-inventor-to-file system from a true first-to-file system. To critics of the AIA, this means the United States has lost the advantages of a first-to-invent system without achieving the desired uniformity with the patent laws of other countries. Some critics of earlier attempts to reform the first-to-invent system have also suggested that the Patent & Copyright Clause of the U.S. Constitution mandates a first-to-invent system (Simon 2006; Suominen 2001). The clause provides that Congress shall have the power "to promote the Progress of Science and useful Arts, by securing for limited Times to Authors and Inventors the exclusive Right to their respective Writings and Discoveries" (U.S. Const., art. I, § 8, cl. 8). A true first-to-file system would not protect "inventors," but rather "filers." The AIA's first-inventor-to-file system may avoid this constitutional issue.

Other changes: The AIA also made several other changes. It revised the procedures by which a patent, once granted, may be opposed (AIA § 5, to be codified at 35 U.S.C. § 311–330). It allows an entity other than the inventor—for example, the inventor's employer—to apply for a patent, although in such a case the patent will still be issued to the inventor, in presumed compliance with the Patent & Copyright Clause

(AIA § 8, amending 35 U.S.C. § 122; U.S. Const., art. I, § 8, cl. 8). The AIA also created a new category of "small and micro entities," including many or most independent inventors, eligible for a 50% (small entities) or 75% (micro entities) reduction in patent fees (AIA § 10; 35 U.S.C. §§ 41(h)(1), 123). It eliminated most false marking actions; prior to the AIA, individuals could sue anyone who falsely marked goods as "patented," as often happened after patents expired. Such suits may now be brought only by the U.S. government or an injured competitor of the person making the claim, and the fact that a patent has expired no longer makes the claim "false" within the meaning of the statute (AIA § 16(b), amending 35 U.S.C. § 292). This change was in response to the 2009 decision of the U.S. Court of Appeals in *Forest Group,* which had greatly expanded such actions by treating each item sold as a separate false claim (590 F.3d at 1301).

The AIA made many procedural changes as well, and created a Patent Ombudsman Program to support and assist small businesses and independent inventors (AIA § 28).

Constitution
- U.S. Const., art. I, § 8, cl. 8

Statute
- Leahy-Smith America Invents Act, H.R. 1249, 112th Cong., sec. 3 (1st Sess. 2011)

Case
- *Forest Group, Inc. v. Bon Tool Co.,* 590 F.3d 1295 (Fed. Cir. 2009)

Treaty
- Patent Law Treaty, June 1, 2000, 39 I.L.M. 1047 (2000)

See also: Constitutional Law; Court of Appeals for the Federal Circuit; International Patent Protection; Patent; Prosecution History Estoppel; TRIPS (Patent); WIPO

Sources and Further Reading

Tracie L. Bryant, "The America Invents Act: Slaying Trolls, Limiting Joinder," 25 *Harvard Journal of Law & Technology* 673 (2012)

William Hannah, "Major Change, New Chapter: How Inter Partes Review and Post Grant Review Proceedings Created by the America Invents Act Will Shape Litigation Strategies," 17 *Intellectual Property Law Bulletin* 27 (2012)

Sara Jeruss, Robin Feldman, & Joshua Walker, "The America Invents Act 500: Effects of Patent Monetization Entities on US Litigation," 11 *Duke Law & Technology Review* 357 (2012)

J. Andrew McKinney, Jr., "The Most Significant Practical Effects of the America Invents Act ["AIA"] for Business Owners & Transactional Attorneys," *Maryland Bar Journal,* September/October 2012, at 38

Joseph M. Potenza, "The America Invents Act: One Year Later," *Landslide,* January/February 2013, at 1

Karen E. Simon, Comment, "The Patent Reform Act's First-to-File Standard: Needed Reform or Constitutional Blunder?" 6 *John Marshall Review of Intellectual Property Law* 129 (2006)

Edwin Suominen, "Re-Discovering Article 1, Section 8—The Formula for First-to-Invent," 83 *Journal of the Patent Office Society* 641 (2001)

Toshiko Takenaka, "The Best Patent Practice or Mere Compromise? A Review of the Current Draft of the Substantive Patent Law Treaty and a Proposal for a First-to-Invent Exception for Domestic Applicants," 11 *Texas Intellectual Property Law Journal* 259 (2003)

United States Patent and Trademark Office, Patents Examination (March 14, 2013), available at http://www.uspto.gov/aia_implementation/patents.jsp#heading-10

❖ ANALOG HOLE ❖

See Analog Recording

❖ ANALOG RECORDING ❖

Digital rights management technology, including copy protection and copyright management information, can be relatively effective in protecting a digitally recorded work, such as a movie, from digital copying. In order to be played, however, the digital recording must ordinarily be converted to analog form; most households, for instance, have analog television displays. Media players, such as CD and DVD players, are therefore equipped with analog output ports; these can be connected to an analog display device—or to an analog recorder. The analog recording thus made can then be digitized, effectively washing it clean of any copy protection or copyright management information. This digital copy will be somewhat lower in quality than the original, but can be copied freely by anyone, without requiring special knowledge, software, or equipment. This vulnerability to analog copying is referred to as the "analog hole" (see Woodford 2004, 275).

The analog hole represents a threat to copyright interests in movies and music. In the content industry's dream world, all communications between playback devices and displays would be digital, and encrypted. This "analog sunset" will close the analog hole (DeBoer 2010), and should be complete by 2014 (Foresman 2009). Making a recording of a video playing on a monitor, as the RIAA has risibly suggested teachers do in order to show video clips to their classes (Cheng 2009), will still be possible, although the resulting video may be of poor quality.

Closing the analog hole would also make it possible for equipment manufacturers to ensure that, for example, their playback devices could only be used with their video displays and speakers, although so far there seems to be no trend in this direction. Consumers would no longer be able to choose which device to use to play a recording; recordings could only be played back on players and displays equipped with the appropriate decryption keys.

Because cracking copy protection is still fairly easy, however, the analog hole is probably exploited relatively rarely (Woodford 2004, 276). However, the legal status of analog copying is quite different from that of digital cracking-plus-copying. The anticircumvention provisions of the Digital Millennium Copyright Act (DMCA) specifically prohibit the latter (17 U.S.C. § 1201). The making of an analog copy of a digital work, however, may be protected by the fair use exception to copyright infringement. Copying for purposes of space-shifting—that is, for the consumer to play on another type of player, perhaps at another location, such as in a car—is fair use (*Diamond*, 180 F.3d 1072).

Content industry efforts to seal the analog hole have addressed not only digital playback devices but also analog recording devices. One relatively successful content industry initiative has been the use of Rovi (formerly Macrovision) Corporation's copy-protection technology, which exploits the automatic gain control on most videocassette recorders (VCRs) to prevent the VCRs from making viewable copies of protected videotapes and DVDs (Rovi 2005). The content industry has succeeded in making automatic gain control mandatory on new VCRs sold in or imported to the United States, making those VCRs unable to copy Macrovision-protected videos (17 U.S.C. § 1201(k)).

Statute
- Digital Millennium Copyright Act, 17 U.S.C. § 1201

Cases
- *Recording Industry Association of America v. Diamond Multimedia Systems, Inc.*, 180 F.3d 1072 (9th Cir. 1999)
- *Realnetworks, Inc. v. DVD Copy Control Association*, 641 F. Supp. 2d 913, 941 (N.D. Cal. 2009)

See also: Copyright; Copyright Infringement; DeCSS; Digital Millennium Copyright Act, Title I; Digital Rights Management; Fair Use (Copyright); Macrovision; Steganography

Sources and Further Reading
Jacqui Cheng, "MPAA: Teachers Should Videotape Monitors, Not Rip DVDs," *Ars Technica* (May 7, 2009), available at http://arstechnica.com/tech-policy/2009/05/mpaa-teachers-should-video-record-tv-screens-not-rip-dvds/

Susan P. Crawford, "The Biology of the Broadcast Flag," 25 *Hastings Communications and Entertainment Law Journal* 603 (2003)

Clint DeBoer, "2010: The Year AACS and HDMI Kill Off Component Video," Audioholics Online A/V Magazine, available at http://www.audioholics.com/news/industry-news/aacs-hdmi-kill-component-2010 (February 17, 2010)

Chris Foresman, "DRM Licensing Group Presses on with Plan to Plug Analog Hole," *Ars Technica* (June 11, 2009), available at http://arstechnica.com/gadgets/2009/06/drm-licensing-group-presses-on-with-plan-to-plug-analog-hole/

"Secure DVD Content in Today's Digital Home," Rovi Corp. (2005), available at http://www.rovicorp.com/webdocuments/PDF/acpdvd_brochure.pdf?link_id=productsRecursos

Chad Woodford, "Trusted Computing or Big Brother? Putting the Rights Back in Digital Rights Management," 75 *University of Colorado Law Review* 253 (2004)

❖ ANONYMITY ❖

Many Internet users are concerned to some extent about privacy; they do not want all of the information they send or receive over the Internet to be connected to them by name. Paradoxically, the Internet makes anonymity both easier and more difficult. In one sense, all Internet communication, except perhaps live video, is anonymous: there is no way to verify with absolute certainty the identity of any other user. A user can post product reviews on Amazon, send emails to the *Wall Street Journal*, create a blog, start a Facebook page, and participate in an Internet forum—all under a fictitious name, or several fictitious names. (Technically, these communications are generally pseudonymous rather than anonymous, as some name is usually used and used consistently.)

In another sense, however, anonymity on the Internet is impossible. Every Internet communication is recorded. Some, such as the Amazon review, may be matched with the user's actual name, or with the credit card to which the user's Amazon purchases have been billed. Others may be matched to the IP address of the computer from which the user sent the communication. Companies like Google may track users' Web surfing habits and add the information to their databases; sophisticated data-mining techniques may then be used to match and collate this information. As databases grow and data-mining techniques improve, it may eventually become possible for data miners to see, complete with summaries, a report on everything about a particular user that has ever been transmitted over the Internet—and every Web site that user has ever visited, every link that user has ever clicked, and every piece of information that user has ever uploaded or downloaded, or at least every visit, click, upload, and download that has involved that user's computer.

While some users are comfortable with, or at least resigned to, this lack of privacy, others find the implications alarming; as a result, there is support for laws to protect privacy on the Internet, especially in highly sensitive areas such as medical and financial data. The protection of anonymity, however, gathers less support. While most users would probably prefer not to be identified to every Web site they visit, anonymity has also been abused, especially by spammers. Legislative attempts to limit anonymity, such as a Georgia statute requiring all users to correctly identify themselves when sending email (O.C.G.A. § 16–9-93.1), have been aimed at spammers. Anonymous communication is protected by the First Amendment, however, so long as it is not used for fraud or other unlawful purposes; the Georgia statute was declared unconstitutional by a federal court (*Miller*, 977 F. Supp. 1228).

While spammers are a nuisance, other abusers of anonymity are more sinister. Terrorists and child pornographers can use anonymity to conceal their identities and encryption to conceal their communications. Online file-sharers can avoid prosecution and lawsuits by concealing their identities—although not everyone finds this sinister. As a result, however, there has been pressure to enact laws targeting certain uses of anonymity. This has been linked to the pressure to regulate encryption, first through the failed Clipper Chip initiative and later through controls on the export of encryption technology and statutes such as the Communications Assistance for Law Enforcement Act, which requires telecommunication providers to assist the government in conducting surveillance. Some people are willing to accept this, and the enhanced powers granted by the USA PATRIOT Act to pierce Internet anonymity, in order to combat terrorist threats. They may be alarmed, though, at the prospect of using legal and technological tools designed to control terrorism against 12-year-old file-swappers. Businesses are not happy at the prospect of being forced to reveal their customers' identities, either; telecommunications companies have continued to protect users' anonymity against private, rather than governmental, interests, and the courts have agreed: In a December 2003 file-sharing case, a federal appellate court held that Verizon Internet Services did not have to turn over the name of a subscriber to the Recording Industry Association of America, even though the subscriber had allegedly shared copyrighted music files (*Verizon*, 351 F.3d 1229).

As in many areas of Internet law, technology marches ahead of legislation. Advances in encryption technology make it easier for truly determined users to remain anonymous, while services like Anonymizer.com make anonymity available to the less technically sophisticated.

Statutes
Federal
- Communications Assistance for Law Enforcement Act (CALEA) of 1994, 47 U.S.C. §§ 1001–10 (1994)
- Stored Communications Act, 18 U.S.C. §§ 2701–12 (1986)
- Uniting and Strengthening America by Providing Appropriate Tools Required to Intercept and Obstruct Terrorism Act (USA PATRIOT Act) of 2001, Pub. L. No. 107–56, 115 Stat. 272 (codified as amended in scattered sections of the U.S.C.)

State
- Ga. Code Ann., § 16-9-93.1

Cases
Federal Appellate Court
- *In re Anonymous Online Speakers*, 661 F.3d 1168 (9th Cir. 2011)

- *John Doe, Inc. v. Mukasey*, 549 F.3d 861 (2d Cir. 2008)
- *Recording Industry Association of America, Inc. v. Verizon Internet Services*, 351 F.3d 1229 (D.C. Cir. 2003); cert. den., 543 U.S. 924 (2004)
- *Recording Industry Association of America v. Charter Communications, Inc.*, 393 F.3d 771, 772–773 (8th Cir. 2005)

Federal Trial Court
- *American Civil Liberties Union of Georgia v. Miller*, 977 F. Supp. 1228 (N.D. Ga. 1997)

See also: Cookies; Data Mining; Doubleclick; Encryption; Privacy

Sources and Further Reading
Musetta Durkee, "The Truth Can Catch the Lie: The Flawed Understanding of Online Speech in *In re Anonymous Online Speakers*," 26 *Berkeley Technology Law Journal* 773 (2011)

Patrick P. Garlinger, "Privacy, Free Speech, and the Patriot Act: First and Fourth Amendment Limits on National Security Letters," 84 *New York University Law Review* 1105 (2009)

Orin S. Kerr, "Internet Surveillance Law after the USA Patriot Act: The Big Brother That Isn't," 97 *Northwestern University Law Review* 607 (2003)

Ken D. Kumayama, "A Right to Pseudonymity," 51 *Arizona Law Review* 427 (2009)

Declan McCullagh, "Bill Proposes ISPs, Wi-Fi Keep Logs for Police," CNN (February 20, 2009), available at http://www.cnn.com/2009/TECH/02/20/internet.records.bill/

Joshua Rich, "You Don't Know My Name: *In Re Anonymous Online Speakers and the Right to Remain Cloaked in Cyberspace*," 45 *Loyola of Los Angeles Law Review* 325 (2011)

Daniel Solove, *Nothing to Hide: The False Tradeoff between Privacy and Security* (New Haven, CT: Yale University Press, 2011)

Tal Z. Zarsky, "Thinking Outside the Box: Considering Transparency, Anonymity, and Pseudonymity as Overall Solutions to the Problems of Information Privacy in the Internet Society," 58 *University of Miami Law Review* 991 (2004)

❖ ANONYMOUS ❖

See Activism and Advocacy Groups

❖ ANTICIRCUMVENTION PROVISIONS ❖

See Digital Millennium Copyright Act

❖ ANTICYBERSQUATTING CONSUMER PROTECTION ACT ❖

See Cybersquatting

❖ ANTITRUST ❖

See Microsoft Antitrust Litigation

❖ APP ❖

An app (short for "application") is a computer program, usually designed for use on a mobile device such as a tablet or cell phone. The term was also in use as a business buzz-word in the 1990s, referring to any consumer or commercial application of a technological development, as in the then-popular saying "Napster is the Internet's killer app" (see King 2002). It overlaps to some extent with, but should not be confused with, the .app suffix, a file extension used in a variety of operating systems to indicate application software.

Apps face the same legal issues as other computer pro-grams downloaded to and operating from an Internet-capable device. For example, app developers need to be aware of the extent of and limitations on the safe harbors provided by 17 U.S.C. § 512 and 47 U.S.C. § 230, and to comply with restrictions such as the prohibition on the gathering of individual identifying information from persons under the age of 13, as well as privacy protections generally. The use of copyrighted background music or images requires permis-sion. And the tight control exercised by the owners of some mobile device software platforms, notably Apple, may pose additional problems. The treatment of the problem of por-nographic applications by Apple and Google illustrates the different approaches. Apple takes a prior restraint approach, prohibiting all such apps, although with the usual problems of definition. Apple refers to *Webster's Dictionary* (Walters & Wimberly 2010) and specifically invokes Justice Potter Stewart's famous words from *Jacobellis v. Ohio*: "I know it when I see it" (378 U.S. at 197). Google, in contrast, applies a post hoc approach: there is no prior review of apps offered through Google's Android Market, but offending content may be flagged and removed by users. Some commentators have noticed that this approach may actually result in greater restrictions on content than Apple's prior restraint approach (see, e.g., Walters & Wimberly 2010).

Because Apple and Google are not state actors, their restriction of app content does not raise First Amendment concerns. Contract issues may arise, though, both between app developers and platform owners and between app developers and consumers. In the latter case the clickwrap agreement may be an adhesion contract and portions of it may be of questionable validity; for example, a 2011 survey of the 30 then-most popular paid apps found that 22 of them lacked any privacy policy (Beesley 2012; Mullin 2011).

See also: Censorship; Children's Online Privacy Protection Act; Clickwrap Agreement; Computer Program; Contracts; First Amendment; Mobile Device; Privacy

Statutes
- Children's Online Privacy Protection Act, 15 U.S.C. §§ 6501–6506
- Communications Decency Act, 47 U.S.C. § 230
- Online Copyright Infringement Liability Limitation Act (Digital Millennium Copyright Act, Title II), 17 U.S.C. § 512

Case
- *Jacobellis v. Ohio*, 378 U.S. 184 (1964)

Sources and Further Reading
Caron Beesley, "Five Legal Issues to Consider when Developing and Marketing a Mobile App," Small Business Administration (March 2, 2012), available at http://www.sba.gov/community/blogs/community-blogs/business-law-advisor/five-legal-issues-consider-when-developing-and- (visited April 2, 2013)
"Do-it-Yourself Apps: Make Your Own Angry Birds," *The Economist*, July 21, 2012, at 55
Brad King, "The Day the Napster Died," *Wired* (May 15, 2002), available at http://www.wired.com/gadgets/portablemusic/news/2002/05/52540?currentPage=all (visited April 2, 2013)
Joe Mullin, "Most Apps' Privacy Policies Continue to Be Missing in Action," Paid Content (May 27, 2011), available at http://paidcontent.org/2011/05/27/419-most-apps-privacy-policies-continue-to-be-missing-in-action/ (visited April 2, 2013)
Lawrence G. Walters & Kevin W. Wimberly, "Legal Issues Sur-rounding Mobile Apps: Why Apps Are Different than Web-sites," Walters Law Group (September 28, 2010), available at http://lawrencewalters.com/articles/Mobile_App_Article-Final.pdf (visited April 2, 2013)

❖ AUDIO HOME RECORDING ACT ❖

In the mid-1980s the music content industry, having battled unsuccessfully against analog cassette recorders, found itself facing a far greater threat: home digital recorders, which could make unlimited numbers of copies with no degrada-tion in quality. The industry lobbied successfully for protec-tive legislation; perhaps too successfully, as the Audio Home Recording Act (AHRA) that resulted may have killed off the relatively harmless recording format at which it was aimed and made possible the growth of other formats. Of course, market factors and technological progress might have brought about the same result even in the absence of the AHRA.

The AHRA was originally aimed at the digital audio tape (DAT) recorders then on the market, and may have been instrumental in killing the DAT format; DAT today is nearly extinct, used almost exclusively by music professionals and engineers. But although the AHRA's original target is gone, digital recording in other formats has expanded tremendously.

The AHRA attempts to control recording in two ways: through copy-control technology and through a royalty on recorders and tapes. The copy-control technology required by the AHRA for DAT recorders is a primitive form of electronic rights management: the serial copy management system (SCMS). SCMS-equipped recorders place an inaudible identifying code on copies they make, and will not make copies from originals bearing that code. In other words, second-generation copying is impossible; copies can be made only from the master.

The AHRA provides that "no person shall import, manufacture, or distribute any digital audio recording device or digital audio interface device" that does not incorporate SCMS or an equivalent electronic rights management technology (17 U.S.C. § 1002(a)). This provision, unlike the royalty provisions, is by its terms portable to other recording devices, and may be the reason that stand-alone CD recorders and the like never caught on: the statute defines a "digital audio recording device" as one "designed or marketed for the primary purpose of, and that is capable of, making a digital audio copied recording for private use" (17 U.S.C. § 1001(3)). Computers and mobile devices are capable of making such recordings, but that is not the primary purpose for which these devices are marketed and designed; thus the statute does not cover them, and they have become the music copying devices most frequently used by consumers (see, e.g., *Diamond Multimedia*, 180 F.3d at 1078; *Napster*, 239 F.3d at 1024; *Sony BMG*, 660 F.2d at 499 n. 14).

The royalty provisions of the AHRA may have done more than any other provision to kill the DAT format. The AHRA imposes a royalty—from the consumer's point of view, a tax—on digital audio recording equipment and media (17 U.S.C. §1003). Digital audio recorders are taxed at 2%, with a maximum royalty of eight dollars and a minimum of one dollar; digital recording media are taxed at 3% (17 U.S.C. § 1004). The taxes, or royalties, are collected by the Copyright Office and distributed to existing music industry copyright owners. A "digital audio recording medium," according to the AHRA, "is any material object in a form commonly distributed for use by individuals, that is primarily marketed or most commonly used by consumers for the purpose of making digital audio copied recordings by use of a digital audio recording device" (17 U.S.C. § 1001(4)(A)). This definition would seem to exclude most recordable CDs and DVDs, and the statute further provides that the definition of digital recording media specifically excludes any medium "that is primarily marketed and most commonly used by consumers either for the purpose of making copies of motion pictures or other audiovisual works or for the purpose of making copies of nonmusical literary works, including computer programs or data bases" (17 U.S.C. § 1001(4)(B)(ii)).

The royalty provisions have been criticized both as a presumption of guilt and as a tax on aspiring musicians for the benefit of established ones (Smith 2001). The apparent presumption is that all persons who buy digital audio recorders and media are going to use them to pirate music, although in fact some or most will not; the innocent thus subsidize the guilty. And the tax is imposed on legitimate copiers, as well, including those who are making copies of their own music, to which they own the copyright. Although the statute exempts "professional model product"—recorders that are "designed, manufactured, marketed, and intended for use by recording professionals in the ordinary course of a lawful business" (17 U.S.C. § 1001(10))—that exemption is more likely to protect the established, successful professional than the garage band. Professionals with steady incomes can afford professional equipment; teenagers trying to start a band have to make do with what they can afford with their more limited means, or more often with what is already around the house.

As music copying has moved from the old-fashioned stereo system to the computer, and from there to the Internet, the royalty and SCMS provisions of the AHRA have become increasingly irrelevant. The AHRA has had one lasting effect, though, that in contrast to the remainder of the statute is actually beneficial to the consumer. It provides that "no action may be brought under this title alleging infringement of copyright . . . based on the noncommercial use by a consumer of such a device or medium for making digital musical recordings or analog musical recordings" (17 U.S.C. § 1008). The right of consumers to make such recordings had previously been unclear; the AHRA provides an unequivocal immunity for private, noncommercial recordings, including recordings of broadcast music.

Statutes

- Audio Home Recording Act, 17 U.S.C. §§ 1001–1003, 1008
- Digital Performance Right in Sound Recordings Act, 17 U.S.C. § 106(6)

Cases

- *A&M Records, Inc. v. Napster, Inc.*, 239 F.3d 1004 (9th Cir. 2001)
- *Atlantic Recording Corp. v. XM Satellite Radio, Inc.*, No. 06 Civ. 3733(DAB), 2007 U.S. Dist. LEXIS 4290 (S.D.N.Y. 2007)
- *Recording Industry Association of America v. Diamond Multimedia Systems, Inc.*, 180 F.3d 1072 (9th Cir. 1999)
- *Sony BMG Music Entertainment v. Tenenbaum*, 660 F.3d 487 (1st Cir. 2011)

See also: Content Industry; Copyright; Digital Audio Works; Digital Performance Right in Sound Recordings Act; Digital Rights Management; File-Sharing

Sources and Further Reading

Rachel Gader-Shafran, "Confessions of a Serial Infringer: Can the Audio Home Recording Act of 1992 Protect the Consumer from Copy-Protected CDs?" *Intellectual Property Law Newsletter*, Winter 2003, at 10

Aaron L. Melville, "The Future of the Audio Home Recording Act of 1992: Has It Survived the Millennium Bug?" 7 *Boston University Journal of Science and Technology Law* 372 (2001)

Eric Smith, "The DAT Tax," available at http://www.brouhaha.com/~eric/bad_laws/dat_tax.html (last updated April 21, 2001)

Mitchell Zimmerman, "Audio Home Recording Act Does Not Protect Device Distributor against Copyright Claims Arising from Broadcaster Role," Fenwick & West LLP (2007), available at http://www.fenwick.com/FenwickDocuments/No_AHRA_Immunity.pdf

B

❖ BACKUP COPIES ❖

It is not clear whether consumers of a copyrighted work have the right to make at least one backup or archival copy of the work, so that they will still have access to the work if the original is damaged or destroyed. One view is that such a right was recognized by the decision in *Recording Industry Association of America v. Diamond Multimedia Systems*, which recognized the permissibility of copying for space-shifting purposes. On the other hand, the court in *United States v. Elcom* held that "there is as yet no generally recognized right to make a copy of a protected work, regardless of its format, for personal noncommercial use" (203 F. Supp. 2d at 1135).

If such a general right exists, it would be an exception to the exclusive right to make or authorize copies granted to the copyright holder by 17 U.S.C. § 106(1). Any right to make backup copies is itself limited by other statutes. The anticircumvention provisions of the Digital Millennium Copyright Act (DMCA) effectively outlaw the making of backup copies of copy-protected works, especially DVDs. However, analog backup copies may still be made, although they will be inferior in quality to the original. Attempts by content-industry lobbyists to obtain legislation requiring all analog video recorders to be equipped with devices capable of recognizing, and perhaps refusing to copy, protected digital works might cut off this option in the future, though.

The right to make backup copies of computer programs, however, is more definite. Such copies may be made provided "that such new copy or adaptation is for archival purposes only and that all archival copies are destroyed in the event that continued possession of the computer program should cease to be rightful" (17 U.S.C. § 117(a)(2)). This right, too, has limits; while a consumer may be permitted to make backup copies of programs, the sale of devices capable of making such copies—but more likely to be used for copyright infringement—may be prohibited as contributory infringement (*Atari*, 747 F.2d 1422).

Title I of the DMCA directed the National Telecommunications and Information Administration (NTIA) of the Department of Commerce to undertake a study of Section 117 and the making of backup copies of computer programs. The NTIA reported that the DMCA's protection of technological protective measures from circumvention might interfere with the making of archival copies authorized by section 117. A greater worry was that section 117 was out of date; it bore no relation to current practice. Most system administrators and many home users backed up their systems periodically by making a copy of everything on the system. This took time and storage media space, but required little human effort; the backup could be set to take place automatically at a time when no one needed to use the system. This process involved copying copyrighted material other than computer programs, and was thus not authorized by section 117. However, it would be costly, time-consuming, and inefficient to go through each file on a system and identify it as a program or nonprogram file before backing up the system. It would be even more costly, time-consuming, and inefficient to go through each file on each tape, backup, and delete any program files for which a license might have expired. The report observed that "there is a fundamental mismatch between accepted, prudent practices among most system administrators and other users, on the one hand, and section 117 on the other. As a consequence, few adhere to the law" (NTIA Report 2001). While the NTIA found no harm as a result of this noncompliance, it was concerned about the mismatch between law and reality, and recommended that the law be amended to "create a new archival exemption that provides expressly that backup copies may not be distributed" (NTIA Report 2001). No such legislative action has yet been taken, however, and the mismatch persists.

Statutes
- Copyright Act of 1976, 17 U.S.C. §§ 106, 117
- Digital Millennium Copyright Act, 17 U.S.C. § 1201

Cases
Federal Appellate Courts
- *Apple Inc. v. Psystar Corp.*, 658 F.3d 1150 (9th Cir. 2011)
- *Atari v. JS & A*, 747 F.2d 1422 (Fed. Cir. 1984)
- *Krause v. Titleserv, Inc.*, 402 F.3d 119 (2d Cir. 2005)
- *Recording Industry Association of America v. Diamond Multimedia Systems, Inc.*, 180 F.3d 1072 (9th Cir. 1999)

Federal Trial Courts
- *Realnetworks, Inc. v. DVD Copy Control Association*, No. C 08–458 MHP, 2010 U.S. Dist. LEXIS 1433 (N.D. Cal. 2010)
- *United States v. Elcom, Ltd.*, 203 F. Supp. 2d 1111 (N.D. Cal. 2002)

Report
- United States Copyright Office, DMCA Section 104 Report, A Report of the Register of Copyrights Pursuant to §104 of the Digital Millennium Copyright Act (August 2001)

See also: Analog Recording; Copyright; Copyright Infringement; Digital Millennium Copyright Act, Title I; Digital Rights Management; Fair Use (Copyright); First Sale

---

❖ BERNE CONVENTION ❖

The Berne Convention for the Protection of Literary and Artistic Works, an international copyright treaty, was adopted in 1886. Copyrights, like all intellectual property rights, are territorial in nature; they provide the holder of the right with a monopoly for a limited time and within the territory of the sovereign granting the right. In the days before the Berne Convention, states were under no general obligation to recognize within their own territories copyrights granted by other sovereigns. This meant that a book copyrighted in France or the United Kingdom could be, and often was, reproduced without permission and without payment of royalties in other countries, such as the United States. Writers and publishers of the nineteenth century found the situation unacceptable; colonialism had spread European languages around the world, so that the works of British, French, and Spanish authors found a ready market abroad, but those authors received few or no royalties from those overseas sales. To address this situation European writers under the leadership of Victor Hugo, the author of *The Hunchback of Notre Dame* and *Les Miserables*, founded the Association Littéraire et Artistique Internationale (ALAI) in 1878. A central purpose of the ALAI was the adoption of an international copyright convention; this purpose was achieved eight years later with the adoption of the Berne Convention (*ALAI History*).

Since its initial adoption, the Berne Convention has been modified, adjusted, revised, or otherwise revisited several times: in 1896, 1908, 1914, 1928, 1948, 1967, 1971, and 1979. The Convention is nearly universal: 165 countries are parties. This universality was not achieved overnight, however; several major countries have become parties only recently, notably the United States in 1988, China in 1992, and Russia in 1995. (Neither the Soviet Union nor the government of Taiwan, formerly recognized by the United States and many other countries as the government of China, had been parties to the Convention.) New parties continue to be added: the Convention entered into force for Laos on March 14, 2012.

For over a century after the adoption of the Berne Convention, the United States was not a party, largely because U.S. copyright law diverged significantly from the Berne Convention norm. The growth of the (mostly pre-electronic) global information economy during this time, however, made it increasingly desirable for the United States to secure foreign protection of its copyrights and to protect the copyrights of foreign authors within its territory. To this end, the United States entered into multiple bilateral copyright agreements and two major multilateral agreements, the Buenos Aires Convention in 1911 and the Universal Copyright Convention (U.C.C.) in 1955.

The Buenos Aires Convention governed copyright relations between the United States and most of the countries of Latin America until the early 1960s, at which point most of its members had become parties to the U.C.C., although Colombia only became a party in 1976, Bolivia in 1989, and Uruguay in 1993. Honduras never became a party to the U.C.C., but became a party to the Berne Convention in 1990. The Buenos Aires Convention, although still technically in force, is insignificant today, as all of its parties are now parties to the U.C.C., the Berne Convention, or both. It is chiefly of interest as the source of a historical oddity: it is the reason for the words "all rights reserved" almost invariably, and unnecessarily, included on copyrighted works published in the United States. These words were necessary to claim certain rights under the Buenos Aires Convention, but are unnecessary under either the U.C.C. or the Berne Convention.

The U.C.C. came into existence largely as a result of Congressional failure to reform the Copyright Act of 1909. Inconsistencies between the 1909 Act and the Berne Convention made it impossible for the United States to become a party to the Berne Convention; the U.C.C. was developed as an alternative. Because many of the states with which the United States wished to enter into agreement were already parties to the Berne Convention, the U.C.C. includes a Berne Safeguard Clause (UCC 1971, art. XVII(1)). This clause provides that no country that is a party to the Berne Convention may denounce that convention and choose instead to rely on the U.C.C. in copyright matters relating to other parties to the Berne Convention.

Although 100 states are now parties to the U.C.C., the United States and most other U.C.C. parties are also parties to the Berne Convention, so the U.C.C. is nearly as unimportant in modern practice as the Buenos Aires Convention. The U.C.C. may, however, continue to govern such copyright matters as exist between the United States and the one country—Cambodia—that is a party to the U.C.C. but not to the Berne Convention. (Cambodia and the United States are both members of the World Trade Organization (WTO) as well, which has its own intellectual property treaty.) And like the Buenos Aires Convention before it, the U.C.C. has left its mark on copyright notices: the familiar "©" symbol on copyright notices is sufficient to satisfy U.C.C. registration requirements for works published outside the territory of the contracting state (UCC 1971, art. III(1)).

Even as the Berne Convention achieves universality, it in turn is being either supplemented or supplanted by the World Intellectual Property Organization (WIPO) Copyright Treaty and the Agreement on Trade-Related Aspects of Intellectual Property Rights (TRIPS). Eighty-nine countries are parties to the WIPO Copyright Treaty, a special agreement within the meaning of Article 20 of the Berne Convention; the WIPO Copyright Treaty may be viewed as supplementing the Berne Convention. And all of the 157 members of the WTO are parties to TRIPS, although for some newer developing country members its provisions have not yet fully come into effect. TRIPS may be viewed as an alternative approach, outside the WIPO framework, but this analysis is weakened by the near-universality of both treaties. About a dozen countries, plus Taiwan (as Chinese Taipei), Hong Kong, and Macau, are parties to TRIPS but not to the Berne Convention; about two dozen are parties to Berne but not to TRIPS. Several countries are parties to neither; many of these countries are very small (Nauru, Palau, San Marino), experiencing difficulties (Afghanistan, Somalia), recently emerged (Kosovo, South Sudan), or subject to a combination of these factors.

The leisurely evolution of international copyright law for over a century has been replaced by a sense of urgency. Content owners believe that a truly universal copyright regime is necessary to protect their rights. In the age of the Internet, countries once deemed unimportant because of their small size, linguistic or geographical isolation, or limited publishing industry now have the same potential as sources of copyright violation as much larger countries. These previously ignored countries now have the potential to become havens for copyright infringement, and infringing material posted on servers in those countries can be accessed by users anywhere in the world.

The Berne Convention remains the world's most comprehensive copyright agreement. The central obligation it imposes on its parties is to provide national treatment: each state that is a party to the Convention will accord the same recognition of copyright in works authored by nationals of other parties that it would accord to works by its own nationals. Under the Berne Convention, copyright in any qualifying work is automatic; neither registration nor notice on the face of the document is required. The "©" symbol is not required, nor are the words "copyright" and "all rights reserved."

Despite the alterations made to United States copyright law in order to allow the United States to join the Berne Convention, some differences persist. Article 2, for example, defines "literary and artistic works" covered under the Convention as including

> every production in the literary, scientific and artistic domain, whatever may be the mode or form of its expression, such as books, pamphlets and other writings; lectures, addresses, sermons and other works of the same nature; dramatic or dramatico-musical works; choreographic works and entertainments in dumb show; musical compositions with or without words; cinematographic works to which are assimilated works expressed by a process analogous to cinematography; works of drawing, painting, architecture, sculpture, engraving and lithography; photographic works to which are assimilated works expressed by a process analogous to photography; works of applied art; illustrations, maps, plans, sketches and three-dimensional works relative to geography, topography, architecture or science (Berne Convention, art. 2(1)).

This definition is both less concise and possibly less comprehensive than the U.S. Copyright Act's "original works of authorship fixed in any tangible medium of expression." The Copyright Act also includes a list of copyrightable subject matter that, again, is not co-extensive with the Berne list. Works of authorship under the Copyright Act include:

(1) literary works;
(2) musical works, including any accompanying words;
(3) dramatic works, including any accompanying music;
(4) pantomimes and choreographic works;
(5) pictorial, graphic, and sculptural works;
(6) motion pictures and other audiovisual works;
(7) sound recordings; and
(8) architectural works (17 U.S.C. § 102(a)).

The Copyright Act's definition is open-ended. (Computer programs are specifically made copyrightable by section 117 of the Act.) And unlike the Convention, the Copyright Act requires fixation in a tangible medium. The Berne Convention, however, takes into account that among its parties, which include nearly all of the countries in the world, there may be differences; Article 2(2) provides that "countries of the Union [may] prescribe that works in general or any specified categories of works shall not be protected unless they have been fixed in some material form."

Article 3 of the Convention provides that the Convention protects not only nationals of the countries that are parties, but nationals of other countries that are not parties, if the works of those nationals are published in the territory of a party either prior to or simultaneously with publication outside the Union established by the Berne Convention, consisting of all the countries that are parties. This, during the time before the United States was not a party to the Convention, gave rise to another oddity: simultaneous publication in Canada. There may, of course, be sound business reasons for publishing a book or other work simultaneously in the United States and Canada, rather than simply shipping copies of the book printed in the United States to Canada (or, in the case of Canadian books, vice versa). But in the six decades between 1928, when Canada became a party, and 1988, when the United States did, U.S. publishers who could afford to do so published simultaneously in the territory of a Berne Convention party, typically Canada, in order to secure international rights under the Berne Convention.

The point of greatest continuing divergence between the Berne Convention and U.S. law is in the area of moral rights. The most widely recognized moral rights, in copyright law, are the right not to have one's work mutilated or distorted, the right to be acknowledged as the author of the work, and the right to determine when and in what fashion the work shall be presented to the public. These rights are called, respectively, the rights of integrity, paternity, and disclosure. Some legal systems may also recognize a right to recall the work even after disclosure; this is the right of withdrawal.

U.S. law has historically been unreceptive to moral rights, both because copyright is viewed as a purely economic right and because of the potential for conflict with the First Amendment. In contrast, Article 6*bis* of the Berne Convention provides that "[i]ndependently of the author's economic rights, and even after the transfer of the said rights, the author shall have the right to claim authorship of the work and to object to any distortion, mutilation or other modification of, or other derogatory action in relation to, the said work, which would be prejudicial to his honor or reputation." The United States has enacted a moral rights statute, the Visual Artists' Rights Act (VARA), but its coverage is less broad than the international norm (17 U.S.C. § 106A). Some states have also enacted moral rights statutes, some of them broader than VARA, but these may be preempted by VARA and the Copyright Act.

A major obstacle to U.S. adoption of the Berne Convention was the term of copyright protection. Article 7 of the Convention provides minimum terms for various types of works; for most works by individual authors the minimum term is the lifetime of the author plus 50 years. The Copyright Act of 1976 brought U.S. law into compliance with this standard.

Article 8 gives authors the exclusive right to authorize and make translations. Article 9 gives them the core right of the bundle of rights described by the term "copyright": the exclusive right to make or authorize reproductions of copyrighted work, subject to narrowly defined exceptions. This right is detailed in the following articles, and Article 10 describes one of the exceptions: "utilization . . . compatible with fair practice," or fair use.

The duration of copyright had been perhaps the biggest stumbling block to U.S. adoption of the Berne Convention, but other obstacles had to be removed, including U.S. notice and registration requirements. Article 15 of the Convention provides that the only formality necessary for copyright protection is that the author's name or clearly identifiable pseudonym "appear on the work in the usual manner." If the pseudonym does not clearly identify the author, "the publisher whose name appears on the work shall, in the absence of proof to the contrary, be deemed to represent the author." And party states may, by domestic law, designate a competent authority to represent the rights of unknown authors (Berne Convention art. 15).

Article 16 of the Convention provides for seizure of infringing copies of protected works, while Article 20 permits the parties to "enter into special agreements among themselves" granting rights more extensive than those granted by the Berne Convention; the WIPO Copyright Treaty is one such agreement. In the early 1990s the countries of the European Union agreed to a longer term of copyright protection, and the United States followed suit, albeit without any formal agreement, with the Sonny Bono Copyright Term Extension Act in 1998.

Since 1967, the Berne Convention has been administered by WIPO. It is also linked to TRIPS: members of the WTO are required by TRIPS to accept almost all of the conditions of the Berne Convention even if they are not already Berne Convention parties (TRIPS art. 9). Through TRIPS, the WTO's dispute resolution procedure may also provide a forum for actions to enforce portions of the Berne Convention. The United States found itself defending an action in this forum in 2000, albeit an action based on Berne Convention terms incorporated directly into TRIPS. The European Union claimed that the United States had violated Article 13 of TRIPS, which incorporates the Berne Convention's constraints on exceptions to exclusive rights under national law: "Members shall confine limitations and exceptions to exclusive rights to certain special cases which do not conflict with a normal exploitation of the work and do not unreasonably prejudice the legitimate interests of the rights holder." The WTO's dispute resolution body agreed with the European Union that U.S. law failed to provide adequate protection for copyright holders with regard to performance or display of nondramatic musical works. In other words, despite the continuing trend toward greater copyright protection and the shrinking of the fair use and other exceptions, U.S. law still provided less copyright protection in this area than the international standard.

Treaties

- Agreement on Trade-Related Aspects of Intellectual Property Rights (TRIPS), Marrakesh Agreement Establishing the World Trade Organization, Annex 1C, April 15, 1994, 33 I.L.M. 81 (1994)
- Buenos Aires Convention, August 20, 1910, 38 Stat. 1785, 155 L.N.T.S. 179
- Convention Concerning the Creation of an International Union for the Protection of Literary and Artistic Works (Berne Convention), September 9, 1886, as last revised at Paris, July 24, 1971 (amended 1979), 25 U.S.T. 1341, 828 U.N.T.S. 221
- Universal Copyright Convention, September 6, 1952, 6 U.S.T. 2731, revised at Paris July 24, 1971, 25 U.S.T. 1341

- WIPO Copyright Treaty, December 20, 1996, 36 I.L.M. 65 (1997)
- WIPO Performance and Phonograms Treaty, December 20, 1996, 36 I.L.M. 76 (1997)

European Union Directive
- Directive 2006/116/EC of the European Parliament and of the Council of 12 December 2006 on the Term of Protection of Copyright and Certain Related Rights, 2006 O.J. (L 372) 12–18

WTO Case
- Report of the WTO Panel, United States: Section 110(5) of the U.S. Copyright Act, WT/DS160/R, June 15, 2000

Statutes
- Copyright Act of 1976, 17 U.S.C. §§ 101–1332
- Sonny Bono Copyright Term Extension Act, Pub. L. 105–298, 112 Stat. 2827 (1998) (amending and codified at 17 U.S.C. §§ 101, 108, 110, 201, 301–304, 512)
- Visual Artists Rights Act, 17 U.S.C. § 106A

Case
- *Golan v. Holder*, 609 F.3d 1076 (10th Cir. 2010)

See also: Copyright; Copyright Infringement; Digital Millennium Copyright Act, Title I; International Copyright Protection; Moral Rights; Public Domain; Sonny Bono Copyright Term Extension Act; TRIPS (Copyright); Universal Copyright Convention; WIPO; WIPO Copyright Treaty; WIPO Performance and Phonograms Treaty

Sources and Further Reading
"Who Are We," Association Littéraire et Artistique Internationale, available at http://alaiorg.vincelette.net/index.php?option=com_content&task=view&id=76&Itemid=60 (visited September 24, 2012)

Anthony D'Amato & Doris Estelle Long, eds., *International Intellectual Property Anthology* (Cincinnati, OH: Anderson Publishing, 1996)

Daniel Gervais, "Golan v. Holder: A Look at the Constraints Imposed by the Berne Convention," 64 *Vanderbilt Law Review* 147 (2011)

Paul Goldstein & Bernt Hugenholtz, *International Copyright: Principles, Law, and Practice* (Oxford, UK: Oxford University Press, 3d ed. 2012)

Eddan Katz & Ramesh Subramanian, eds., *The Global Flow of Information: Legal, Social, and Cultural Perspectives* (New York and London: New York University Press, 2011)

Makeen Fouad Makeen, *Copyright in a Global Information Society: The Scope of Copyright Protection under International, US, UK, and French Law* (New York: Aspen, 2001)

Sam Ricketson & Jane Ginsburg, *International Copyright and Neighbouring Rights: The Berne Convention and Beyond* (Oxford, UK: Oxford University Press, 2d ed. 2006)

Susan K. Sell, *Private Power, Public Law: The Globalization of Intellectual Property Rights* (Cambridge, UK: Cambridge University Press, 2003)

Martin Senftleben, *Copyright, Limitations and the Three-Step Test: An Analysis of the Three-Step Test in International and EC Copyright Law* (New York: Aspen, 2004)

❖ BITTORRENT ❖

See File-Sharing and the Courts (Attempts to Control Technology)

❖ BLACKBERRY ❖

See Mobile Device

❖ BLOCKING AND FILTERING SOFTWARE ❖

See Children's Internet Protection Act

❖ BOTNET ❖

See Zombie

❖ BRANDJACKING ❖

See Cybersquatting

❖ BROADBAND ❖

Broadband Internet access is notionally Internet access at a higher speed than the maximum speed available through a dial-up connection, 56,000 bits per second, although in general the term is reserved for access at a speed of 512,000 bits per second or higher. Broadband access is either wired or wireless. Wired broadband is available through dedicated Internet lines, as well as through existing telephone and cable lines. Broadband signals can also be transmitted through power lines; this tends to be more useful with a single building than between buildings, because of the problem of sending a signal between lines at different voltage levels. Wireless broadband is either local, via a router usually connected to wired broadband access, or long-distance, most often through a cell phone network or, more expensively, through a satellite network. Of the other existing technologies, one that shows promise for the future in the United States is the use of "white space" television bandwidth left empty by the transition to digital television in 2009. Local wireless broadband is fairly inexpensive to install and maintain, and is provided as a perk to customers of many businesses; in some cities it is a free public service.

Existing telephone lines can be used to provide Digital Subscriber Line (DSL) broadband access; existing cable television lines can be used for Internet access via a cable modem. From the point of view of most consumers, DSL and cable modem broadband access, the two most popular forms of broadband access, are roughly equivalent. The Federal Communications Commission (FCC), however, treats cable and telephone lines differently; consequently, the two forms of broadband access also receive different regulatory treatment.

The disparate regulatory treatment of cable and DSL broadband services has given rise to controversy; the greater popularity and availability of cable modem services has been blamed on regulatory obstacles placed in the path of DSL operators, and the FCC has been criticized for encouraging the unnecessary development of parallel infrastructure rather than guaranteeing competitive access to that infrastructure (Hundt 2004, 239). The FCC regulatory framework provides for different treatment of three categories of information transmission services: information services, cable services, and telecommunications services. Whether cable broadband should be treated as a "cable service" like cable television, or an "information service"—treated much more liberally—has been the subject of considerable litigation. In 2000 the Court of Appeals for the Ninth Circuit had held, in *AT&T Corp. v. City of Portland*, that cable broadband service is not a "cable service" within the meaning of the Communications Act; this prevented local governments from regulating cable modem services through their franchising authority, greatly liberalizing the market for cable modem services and contributing to the growth of the industry (216 F.3d at 871). In 2002 the FCC ruled that cable modem services were information services, not cable services or telecommunications services (17 F.C.C.R. at 4819). The FCC's ruling resulted in challenges raised by at least seven petitions in federal courts. The challenges raised several objections, not so much to the classification of cable modem services alone, but to the disparate treatment of cable and DSL services. The various petitions urged that cable modem service should have received a dual classification as either an information service and a cable service or as an information service and a telecommunications service, or that DSL service should also have been classified as an information service (*Brand X,* 345 F.3d at 1127). The various petitions were brought together before the Ninth Circuit Court of Appeals in *Brand X Internet Services v. FCC,* in which the Ninth Circuit upheld the FCC's ruling classifying cable modem services as information services, but vacated the portion of the ruling stating that cable modem services were not also telecommunication services (345 F.3d at 1132). In 2005 the Supreme Court finally resolved the matter in *National Cable & Telecommunications Association v. Brand X Internet Services,* upholding the FCC's classification of broadband cable modem service as an "information service" but not a "telecommunications service," despite the different treatment of DSL (broadband over phone lines) service (545 U.S. at 984–1001).

Although the Supreme Court's ruling on the issue should be the last word, technological, economic and social changes are making the FCC's distinction increasingly obsolete. Most households in the United States and throughout the developed world have potential broadband access through at least three networks: cable, phone lines, and wireless phone networks. Satellite access, although less widely used, is universally available. All of these can not only serve as information networks, but can also transmit telephone calls and be used to watch television shows and movies. Creating different rules for different infrastructure made more sense when each was linked to a particular type of content; now that all networks can be used for all forms of content, the distinction seems artificial.

However, the Supreme Court's holding does not establish a final rule on the matter; it is not the function of the Supreme Court to regulate telecommunications. Rather, the Court upheld the rule made by the FCC; nothing in the holding prevents the FCC from making a different rule in light of subsequent changes.

Statute

- Telecommunications Act of 1996, 47 U.S.C. §§ 151 et seq. (1996)

Cases

- *AT&T Corp. v. City of Portland*, 216 F.3d 871 (9th Cir. 2000)
- *Brand X Internet Services v. FCC*, 345 F.3d 1120 (9th Cir. 2003), reversed and remanded sub nom, *National Cable & Telecommunications Association v. Brand X Internet Services*, 545 U.S. 967 (2005)

Agency Decision

- *In re Inquiry Concerning High-Speed Access to the Internet over Cable and Other Facilities*, 17 F.C.C. Rcd. 4798, 2002 WL 407567 (2002)

See also: Broadband; Cable; Federal Communications Commission; Federal Trade Commission; Internet; Net Neutrality

Sources and Further Reading

Christian R. Eriksen, "Cable Broadband: Did the Ninth Circuit Beat the FCC to the Punch in Last Mile Regulation?" 6 *Tulane Journal of Technology and Intellectual Property* 283 (2004)

Reed Hundt, "The Ineluctable Modality of Broadband," 21 *Yale Journal on Regulation* 239 (2004)

Mark A. Lemley & Lawrence Lessig, "The End of End-to-End: Preserving the Architecture of the Internet in the Broadband Era," 48 *UCLA Law Review* 925 (2001)

David P. Manni, "National Cable & Telecommunications Ass'n v. Brand X Internet Services: A War of Words, the Effect of

Classifying Cable Modem Service as an Information Service," 13 *Villanova Sports and Entertainment Law Journal* 353 (2006)

Kim Maxwell, *Residential Broadband: An Insider's Guide to the Battle for the Last Mile* (New York: John Wiley & Sons 1998)

"Municipal Broadband: The Need for Speed," *The Economist*, August 11, 2012, at 26

"Polynesians Get Free Wireless Web," BBC News (June 26, 2003), available at http://news.bbc.co.uk/1/hi/technology/3020158.stm (visited January 28, 2013)

Roderick W. Smith, *Broadband Internet Connections: A User's Guide to DSL and Cable* (Boston, MA: Addison-Wesley Publishing Company, 2002)

James B. Speta, "Handicapping the Race for the Last Mile? A Critique of Open Access Rules for Broadband Platforms," 17 *Yale Journal on Regulation* 39 (2000)

❖ BUDAPEST OPEN ACCESS INITIATIVE ❖

Academic articles, as original works of authorship fixed in a tangible medium of expression, are protected by copyright, yet the copyright in these articles is generally of little or no monetary value. The authors publish the articles for the purpose of sharing the results of their research with other scholars; they receive no payment for the articles. Locating the copyright holder for an academic article is not always easy; in the case of a deceased copyright holder or an institution that no longer exists, it can be nearly impossible. The right holder might be the author, the journal in which the work was published, the university or university press that published it, the university or other institution that employed the author at the time the article was written, the foundation or other donor that provided a grant that made the article possible, or some other person. Even when the copyright holder can be located, permission to reprint may be unavailable; a small academic journal may arbitrarily refuse permission to reprint part of a work or may demand an unrealistic fee.

In theory, the Internet should simplify increased sharing of academic work. Yet often attempts to reprint or otherwise share academic work founder—even when the author wants the work to be shared—because of the complexities of copyright law. A system designed to protect valuable property rights in books, movies, songs, and other commercial works is overkill when applied to works written for free and published to an audience of a few hundred readers.

One attempt to address this problem is the Budapest Open Access Initiative. The Open Society Institute (OSI) created the Budapest Open Access Initiative in 2002. The Initiative grew out of OSI's December 2001 meeting in Budapest, thus its name; OSI is the central administrative entity of the Soros Foundations network. The Initiative's goal is, as the title implies, open access: "free and unrestricted availability" of works that "scholars give to the world without expectation of payment." This goal is to be achieved by two mechanisms: open-access journals and self-archiving.

Open-access journals are journals that do not "invoke copyright to restrict access. . . . Instead they will use copyright and other tools to ensure permanent open access to all the articles they publish. Because price is a barrier to access, these new journals will not charge subscription or access fees" (Budapest Open Access Initiative 2002). This does not mean that the journals will not restrict their content; the journals will apply their own peer review or other standards in deciding what to publish.

Self-archiving is the depositing of articles in open-access electronic archives. The goal of the Initiative is to preserve the author's moral rights of integrity and paternity while taking away the economic right to control reproduction of the material:

> There are many degrees and kinds of wider and easier access to this literature. By 'open access' to this literature, we mean its free availability on the public Internet, permitting any users to read, download, copy, distribute, print, search, or link to the *full texts* of these articles, crawl them for indexing, pass them as data to software, or use them for any other lawful purpose, without financial, legal, or technical barriers other than those inseparable from gaining access to the Internet itself. The only constraint on reproduction and distribution, and the only role for copyright in this domain, should be to give authors control over the integrity of their work and the right to be properly acknowledged and cited (Budapest Open Access Initiative 2002).

While this makes sense in the context of academic articles, where the economic rights are in most cases worth nothing and the main incentive for authors, other than sharing knowledge, is to enhance their reputations, it does not reflect current United States copyright law. Instead of seeking to effect change through legislation, the Initiative seeks a voluntary change on the part of academic journals and authors; they are called upon to opt out of the protection guaranteed them under copyright law, in the interest of making their work and other academic work more widely available.

Initiative
- Budapest Open Access Initiative (February 14, 2002), available at http://www.soros.org/openaccess/read.shtml

See also: Copyright; Open Source

❖ BUENOS AIRES CONVENTION ❖

See Copyright, Berne Convention

❖ BUSINESS METHODS PATENT ❖

A business methods patent is, as the name states, a patent on a method of doing business; it grants a right to the patent holder to exclude others from using a particular method of doing business. Historically courts rejected the idea that business methods were patentable (*Hotel Security Checking*, 160 F. at 469). This changed in 1996 with the decision in *State Street Bank & Trust v. Signature Financial Group*. The *State Street* court held that an invention did not become unpatentable merely because it was a business method (149 F.3d at 1375). The decade after *State Street* saw the granting of many business methods patents, some of which became objects of ridicule and have been held up as examples of the U.S. Patent Office's apparent abandonment of the requirements of novelty and nonobviousness. In 2008, the *State Street* standard was overruled and superseded by *In re Bilski*. While the Federal Circuit in *In re Bilski* did not reject the idea of business methods patents entirely, it set a much narrower standard, the "machine or transformation" test: Under *Bilski*, a business method is patentable only "if: (1) it is tied to a particular machine or apparatus or (2) it transforms a particular article into a different state or thing" (545 F.3d 954). While the U.S. Supreme Court later affirmed the outcome in *Bilski*, it rejected the idea that the "machine or transformation" test was the only possible test to apply:

> Today, the Court once again declines to impose limitations on the Patent Act that are inconsistent with the Act's text. The patent application here can be rejected under our precedents on the unpatentability of abstract ideas. The Court, therefore, need not define further what constitutes a patentable "process," beyond pointing to the definition of that term provided in § 100(b) and looking to the guideposts in *Benson, Flook*, and *Diehr*.
>
> And nothing in today's opinion should be read as endorsing interpretations of § 101 that the Court of Appeals for the Federal Circuit has used in the past. *See, e.g., State Street* [.] It may be that the Court of Appeals thought it needed to make the machine-or-transformation test exclusive precisely because its case law had not adequately identified less extreme means of restricting business method patents, including (but not limited to) application of our opinions in *Benson, Flook*, and *Diehr*. In disapproving an exclusive machine-or-transformation test, we by no means foreclose the Federal Circuit's development of other limiting criteria that further the purposes of the Patent Act and are not inconsistent with its text (*Bilski v. Kappos*, 130 S. Ct. at 3231).

The Supreme Court thus agreed that the "machine or transformation" test does not violate patent laws and can be used; however, it left open the possibility that business methods are patentable (see Dallman 2011).

Among the most famous business methods patents issued during the *State Street* period was Amazon.com's patent on one-click ordering, issued in 1999. During the 1999 Christmas shopping season, Amazon succeeded in obtaining an injunction prohibiting a competitor, Barnes & Noble, from using one-click ordering on its Web site (*Barnesandnoble.com*, 239 F.3d 1343). While Amazon's victory was fleeting, it may have been of enormous strategic importance, enabling Amazon to establish a dominant market position in a crucial year.

The international status of business methods patents remains confused. Recent developments, including *Bilski*, have reduced inconsistencies between U.S. and European laws; however, the European Patent Convention still takes the more extreme stance that "schemes, rules and methods for performing mental acts, playing games or doing business, and programs for computers" are not patentable subject matter (European Patent Convention, art. 52(2)(c)). This is apparently inconsistent with the Agreement on Trade-Related Aspects of Intellectual Property Rights (TRIPS), which provides that "patents shall be available for any inventions, whether products or processes, in all fields of technology," with certain exceptions. (TRIPS art. 27). This has been interpreted as requiring parties to TRIPS—most of the world's countries—to issue business methods patents. It remains to be seen whether and for how long the inconsistency will persist.

Treaties

- Agreement on Trade-Related Aspects of Intellectual Property Rights, Marrakesh Agreement Establishing the World Trade Organization, Annex 1C, April 15, 1994, 33 I.L.M. 81 (1994)
- Convention on the Grant of European Patents, 5 Oct. 1973, 13 I.L.M. 276, text as amended through December 10, 1998, available at http://www.epo.org/law-practice/legal-texts/html/epc/2010/e/ma1.html (visited Sept. 24, 2012) [European Patent Convention]

Cases

- *Amazon.com, Inc. v. Barnesandnoble.com, Inc.*, 239 F.3d 1343 (Fed. Cir. 2001)
- *AT&T Corp. v. Excel Communications, Inc.*, 172 F.3d 1352 (Fed. Cir. 1999)
- *Bilski v. Kappos*, 130 S. Ct. 3218 (U.S. 2010)
- *Hotel Security Checking Co. v. Lorraine Co.*, 160 F. 467 (2d Cir. 1908)
- *In re Bilski*, 545 F.3d 943 (Fed. Cir. 2008)
- *State Street Bank & Trust v. Signature Financial Group, Inc.*, 149 F.3d 1368 (Fed. Cir. 1999)

See also: Computer Program; Patent; TRIPS (Patent)

Sources and Further Reading

Andrew S. Dallmann, "Life after Bilski: Is It Time to Bet on Business Method Patents Again?" Jeffer Mangels Butler & Mitchell Patent Lawyer Blog (September 20, 2011), http://patentlaw.jmbm.com/2011/09/life-after-bilski-is-it-time-t.html

Notice 11/2007 from the European Patent Office dated 1 October 2007 concerning business methods, 2007 O.J. (EPO 592)

Matthew G. Wells, "Internet Business Method Patent Policy," 87 *Virginia Law Review* 729 (2001)

❖ CABLE ❖

Broadband Internet access can be provided to homes and businesses over special lines dedicated to the purpose, or more cheaply over existing telephone or cable television lines, or wirelessly via cell phone or satellite networks. For home users, the cost of a dedicated broadband line other than a telephone or cable connection is almost always too high to be worthwhile. At present, though, telephone and cable television companies compete for the home broadband market. To date the cable television industry has proved more adept at reaching and exploiting this market.

Cable lines, like telephone lines, are owned by a relatively small number of companies. Typically, homes will have access to the lines of only one cable company and one telephone company; the use of these lines for broadband Internet access provides these companies with a potential monopoly, or at least a potential local duopoly, on the provision of broadband access. Telephone companies have been compelled to allow other broadband service providers access to their lines. Local governments have attempted to impose similar requirements on cable broadband providers as a condition of granting a cable franchise. However, in 2000, the Court of Appeals for the Ninth Circuit held, in *AT&T Corporation v. City of Portland*, that the Federal Communications Commission (FCC) acted properly in classifying cable broadband service as not a "cable service" within the meaning of the Communications Act, and thus not subject to regulation by local governments through their franchising authority (*AT&T*, 216 F.3d 871).

The FCC subsequently classified cable broadband services as information services and not cable services or telecommunications services. Three years later, a divided three-judge panel of the same court, in three separate opinions, vacated that part of the FCC's ruling stating that cable modem services were not also telecommunications services; the court felt itself to be bound by its earlier decision (*Brand X,* 345 F.3d at 1132). Two years later, in 2005, the Supreme Court rejected the Ninth Circuit's reasoning in *Brand X,* holding that "the Commission's construction was reasonable" (*National Cable & Telecommunications Association,* 545 U.S. at 1000) and stating:

[T]he Federal Communications Commission concluded that cable companies that sell broadband Internet service do not provide 'telecommunications servic[e]' as the Communications Act defines that term, and hence are exempt from mandatory common-carrier regulation under Title II. We must decide whether that conclusion is a lawful construction of the Communications Act. . . . We hold that it is" (*National Cable & Telecommunications Association*, 545 U.S. at 973–74).

This leaves open the possibility of future rulemaking changes on the part of the FCC.

Statute

- Telecommunications Act of 1996, 47 U.S.C. §§ 151 et seq. (1996)

Cases

- *AT&T Corp. v. City of Portland*, 216 F.3d 871 (9th Cir. 2000)
- *Brand X Internet Services v. FCC*, 345 F.3d 1120 (9th Cir. 2003), reversed and remanded sub nom, *National Cable & Telecommunications Association v. Brand X Internet Services*, 545 U.S. 967 (2005)

See also: Broadband; Federal Communications Commission; Internet; Net Neutrality

Sources and Further Reading

Note, "How Chevron Step One Limits Permissible Agency Interpretations: Brand X and the FCC's Broadband Reclassification," 124 *Harvard Law Review* 1016 (2011)

Mark Robichaux, *Cable Cowboy: John Malone and the Rise of the Modern Cable Business* (New York: John Wiley & Sons, 2002)

Steven Semeraro, "The Antitrust-Telecom Connection," 40 *San Diego Law Review* 555 (2003)

Roderick W. Smith, *Broadband Internet Connections: A User's Guide to DSL and Cable* (Boston, MA: Addison-Wesley Publishing Company, 2002)

Phil Weiser, "Paradigm Changes in Telecommunications Regulation," 71 *University of Colorado Law Review* 819 (2000)

Tim Wu, "Network Neutrality, Broadband Discrimination," 2 *Journal on Telecommunications & High Technology Law* 141 (2003)

❖ CAN-SPAM ACT ❖

See Spam

❖ CELL PHONE ❖

See Mobile Device

❖ CENSORSHIP ❖

Censorship is the act or process of inspecting expressive content, such as books, movies, recorded music, or Web pages, and deleting or restricting access to material deemed offensive by the person or organization doing the inspection. The Internet provides new problems for censorship because of its international nature, the ease with which it provides children as well as adults with access to information, the widespread availability of encryption technology, and the quantity of information exchanged. The law of the United States and of the individual states, in accordance with the First and Fourteenth Amendments to the U.S. Constitution, severely restricts the censorship powers of governments.

State action: The First Amendment protects against censorship by the government and not ordinarily against censorship by private parties; state action, rather than private action, is the target of the Amendment. It is perfectly legal, for instance, for a private Internet Service Provider (ISP) such as America Online to block certain mass-mailed email messages even if it would be impermissible for the government to do so; America Online's action is not state action (*America Online*, 948 F. Supp. 456).

Three distinct tests are used in determining whether acts by private parties can be classified as state action for First Amendment purposes: the exclusive public function test, the state-assisted action test, and the joint participant test. The exclusive public function test looks at whether the private entity has exercised powers that are traditionally the exclusive prerogative of the state. The state-assisted action test looks at whether the private entity has acted with the help of, or in concert with, state officials. The joint participant test looks at whether the state has insinuated itself so far into a position of interdependence with the private entity that the state must be recognized as a joint participant in the challenged activity. If the answer to any one of these three questions is "yes," there is state action (*America Online*, 948 F. Supp. 456).

Strict scrutiny for broad content-based prohibitions: Governments or state actors may impose broad content-based restrictions upon expression only in certain narrowly defined situations; most such restrictions are subject to strict constitutional scrutiny. Governments may impose such restrictions when doing so is necessary to achieve a compelling state interest. This interest must be unrelated to the message being communicated; in other words, a government's interest in preventing a message from being heard is not in itself a sufficient basis for restricting that message. The means chosen to restrict the expression must also be the least restrictive alternative available (*Reno v. ACLU*, 521 U.S. 844).

Less-scrutinized restrictions: Noncontent-based restrictions on the time, place, and manner in which expression is permitted must be narrowly tailored to further an important or significant government interest; such restrictions are generally constitutionally permissible unless they unduly constrict the flow of free speech.

Certain types of content-based restrictions are likely to be constitutionally permissible. Governments may prohibit expression such as shouting "Fire!" in a crowded theater, as well as speech that is intended to create a likelihood of imminent violence. Speech or expression may form an element of certain crimes—conspiracy and solicitation, for example—and thus may be prohibited. Defamation and invasion of privacy may be prohibited or made the basis for civil liability, although the scope of this exception is limited when public figures or public officials are involved. The right to duplicate and distribute the expressions of others may be limited by intellectual property rights, particularly copyright. And obscenity, discussed in more detail under the subheading "Pornography" later and in the section of this encyclopedia titled "Obscenity," may be prohibited (*Miller*, 413 U.S. 15).

Broadcast media are traditionally entitled to a lower level of protection than print media, because of the government's role in allocating broadcast frequencies and the limited number of such frequencies available. Courts have held, however, that the Internet is not a broadcast medium and is thus entitled to the highest level of First Amendment protection (*Reno v. ACLU*, 521 U.S. 844). Commercial speech (speech that proposes a commercial transaction) is afforded protection under the First Amendment, although it may be subject to time, place, and manner restrictions, and may be prohibited if it is untruthful, misleading, or deceptive, or if its subject matter or presentation is illegal.

Special problems for the Internet: The two categories of online speech that have been the subject of the greatest number of private and governmental attempts at censorship are pornography and mass email advertising. Free speech that may undermine copyright protections, such as the publishing of encryption/decryption code, is also an Internet-related problem.

Pornography: The term "pornography" covers a variety of sexually explicit material, some of it protected by the First Amendment and some, including child pornography and obscenity, not protected. Although the First Amendment's protection does not extend to obscenity, the term "obscenity" is difficult to define. After wrestling with the problem for some time, the Supreme Court in *Miller v. California* set down the definition that is generally used in U.S. law. Under the *Miller* test, material is obscene if (1) "the average person, applying contemporary community standards would find that the work taken as a whole appeals to the prurient interest"; (2) "the work depicts or describes, in a patently offensive way, sexual conduct specifically defined by the applicable state law; and" (3) "the work, taken as a whole, lacks serious literary, artistic, political, or scientific value" (413 U.S. 39).

Child pornography involving images of actual children is banned even if it does not meet all three prongs of the Miller test, because it is a record of the actual sexual abuse of children and the government has a compelling interest in preventing such abuse (*Ferber*, 458 U.S. 747).

Material that is not obscenity or child pornography may not be banned outright merely on the basis of indecency or offensiveness; much pornographic material is thus protected. The extent to which access to pornographic material may be restricted or controlled has been the subject of much Congressional activity and subsequent litigation.

Access by minors: It is permissible for governments to control minors' access to some material that is permissible for adults. In the pre-Internet era, the access of minors to sexually explicit material could be controlled at the point of sale, by verifying the age of the purchaser. On the Internet it is impossible to determine the age of any user with certainty; any child who can read can access any portion of the Internet accessible to adults. The U.S. legal system has not yet found an effective way to deal with this problem. Statutes enacted by Congress to restrict the access of minors to some Internet content, such as the Child Online Protection Act and the Communications Decency Act of 1996, have been struck down by the Supreme Court on constitutional grounds. Among other flaws, they impermissibly restricted the access of adults to information (*Reno v. ACLU*, 521 U.S. 844).

Software solutions: In the absence of an effective legal solution to the problem of the accessibility of Internet pornography to minors, market-based solutions have emerged. Many filtering programs are available. While the constitutionality of the use of these programs by schools and public libraries has been heavily litigated and has not yet been resolved with any degree of finality, filtering programs can be and are used on home computers. However, such programs are a less than perfect solution for several reasons. They tend to miss some sites, especially foreign-language sites, containing content that the purchasers of the programs would undoubtedly deem offensive. They also err in the other direction, and screen many sites with innocuous content. Finally, they rely to a great degree on the willingness of the child using the computer to comply with the restrictions. Many children are more technologically adept than their parents and can circumvent the programs if they are determined to do so. Even if they are unable to do so, they have the option of using another computer.

International communication: From a U.S. perspective, the international nature of the Internet presents two distinct censorship problems. One is that content that is illegal under U.S. law or the law of a state or local government within the United States may be legal in a foreign country. There is no

practical way for a local government to restrict its inhabitants' access to the illegal content (see *Reno v. ACLU*, 521 U.S. at 878 n. 45). It would be difficult for the national government to do so, and such restriction would probably require the blocking of all or most content from that foreign country; this in turn presents constitutional problems because it restricts the access of persons in the United States to nonprohibited information. In addition, other countries that have tried such draconian measures have found them to be of only limited effectiveness; clever users easily find ways to circumvent the controls. A second problem is that content that is legal in the United States—the advertising for sale of Nazi memorabilia, for example—might be illegal in another country, such as France. U.S. Web publishers may thus unwittingly violate the laws of other countries, risking civil sanctions and even criminal prosecution (*Yahoo!*, 169 F. Supp. 2d 1181). This possibility was demonstrated in 2012 when Google Brazil president Fabio Jose Silva Coelho was imprisoned for refusing to take down a YouTube video after a Brazilian court ruled that it slandered a political candidate; Mr. Coelho was released only after he agreed to take down the offending video (*Google Brazil* 2012). The video would most likely have been protected political speech under U.S. law, just as Mr. Silva Coelho argued, ultimately unsuccessfully, that it was under Brazilian law. Although in this case the defendant was a Brazilian living and working in Brazil (albeit for a U.S. employer), there is no reason to suspect the Brazilian court's decision would have been different had he been a U.S. citizen, or a citizen of any other country, residing outside Brazil. (The eventual outcome, of course, might have been different, as the court would then have had less leverage to force Google to take down the video.) The actual criminal convictions (even though later overturned on appeal) of three non-Italian-resident Google executives in Italy in 2010, based on the content of a YouTube video posted in Italy by Italian citizens, demonstrates the potential for laws controlling content to cross national borders (Hill 2012).

Encryption: The widespread availability of encryption technology poses additional problems. Users can exchange encrypted files over the Internet; even if the communication is being monitored, those monitoring it will have no means to determine whether the encrypted file contains illegal obscene materials, legal but highly confidential corporate secrets, or a collection of recipes. Although breaking the encryption is usually possible, it is time consuming and thus expensive.

Too much information: Finally, the sheer volume of information exchanged on the Internet makes universal monitoring impossible, and thus censorship is a hit-or-miss affair. To some extent this also is being addressed with software, which can be instructed to search for particular types of content. But any time savings gained through the use of such software is offset by the use of encryption.

The state of Internet censorship today: First Amendment advocates continue to battle with opponents of pornography in a struggle that is ultimately without resolution because it pits competing, widely held and incompatible sets of values against each other. The struggle to protect spam, or unsolicited commercial email, is a lonelier one; unsolicited commercial advertising is almost universally detested, while civil liberties advocacy groups may prefer to devote their resources to the defense of noncommercial speech. In December 2003, the U.S. Congress enacted antispam legislation, authorizing the Federal Trade Commission to create a "do not spam" registry similar to the widely popular antitelemarketing "do not call" registry. The Federal Trade Commission (FTC) has declined to do so, pointing out that while such an action may withstand the constitutional scrutiny given to restrictions on commercial speech, it is also likely to prove futile. Unlike telemarketers, spammers incur no cost savings by sending their messages from within the United States; the sources of spam will simply move outside the country's borders. Only action against the companies whose products and services are advertised by spam, rather than against spammers, is likely to prove effective, and even then only against companies with a presence in the United States.

At this point, serious attempts to censor the Internet are focused on a few areas: governments aggressively pursue and prosecute child pornographers and consumers of child pornography (see 18 U.S.C. §§ 2251–2260); the wider campaign against pornography as a whole, though, must be regarded as lost, or at least abandoned for the time being. In response to consumer outrage, governments are now, as Internet service providers have been doing for some time, taking actions to restrict the activities of spammers (bulk email advertisers). And speech that creates a private right of action, such as defamation, invasion of privacy, the commercial appropriation of one's name or likeness, or infringement of an intellectual property right, may be the subject of lawsuits brought by the individuals affected.

Statutes
- Controlling the Assault of Non-Solicited Pornography and Marketing (CAN-SPAM) Act of 2003, 15 U.S.C. §§ 7701–7713
- Child Online Protection Act, 47 U.S.C. § 231
- Child Pornography Prevention Act of 1996, 18 U.S.C. §§ 2251–2260
- Children's Internet Protection Act, 47 U.S.C. § 254(h)
- Communications Decency Act of 1996, Pub. L. No. 104–104, § 502, 1996 U.S.S.C.A.N. (110 Stat.) 56,133 (later codified at 47 U.S.C. § 223)

Cases
Supreme Court
- *Ashcroft v. American Civil Liberties Union*, 524 U.S. 656 (2004)
- *Brandenburg v. Ohio*, 395 U.S. 444 (1969)
- *Miller v. California*, 413 U.S. 15 (1973)
- *New York v. Ferber*, 458 U.S. 747 (1982)
- *Reno v. American Civil Liberties Union*, 521 U.S. 844 (1997)
- *United States v. American Library Association, Inc.*, 539 U.S. 194 (2003)

Federal Appellate Courts
- *Yahoo!, Inc. v. La Ligue Contre le Racisme et L'Antisemitisme*, 169 F. Supp. 2d 1181 (N.D. Cal. 2001), reversed and remanded, *Yahoo! Inc. v. La Ligue Contre Le Racisme et L'Antisemitisme*, 379 F.3d 1120 (9th Cir. 2004), rehearing, 433 F.3d 1199 (9th Cir. 2006)

Federal Trial Courts
- *America Online v. Cyber Promotions*, 948 F. Supp. 456 (E.D. Pa. 1996)
- *Mainstream Loudoun v. Board of Trustees of the Loudoun County Library*, 2 F. Supp. 2d 783 (E.D. Va. 1998)

See also: Activism and Advocacy Groups; App; Child Online Protection Act; Child Pornography; Children's Internet Protection Act; Communications Decency Act; Data Haven; Declaration of Independence of Cyberspace; DeCSS; Defamation; Encryption; First Amendment; French Yahoo! Case; Indecency; Jurisdiction; Obscenity; Pornography; Spam; .xxx

Sources and Further Reading
Jessica E. Bauml, "It's a Mad, Mad Internet: Globalization and the Challenges Presented by Internet Censorship," 63 *Federal Communications Law Journal* 697 (2011)

Giles Castonguay, "Court Quashes Convictions in Google Video Case," *Wall Street Journal* (December 21, 2012), available at http://online.wsj.com/article/SB100014241278873244616045781930936858727 24.html

"Google Brazil to Take Down Controversial Brazil Video," BBC News (September 28, 2012), available at http://www.bbc.co.uk/news/world-latin-america-19753158

Terry Gillespie, "Virtual Violence? Pornography and Violence against Women on the Internet," in *Women, Violence and Strategies for Action*, edited by Jill Radford et al. (Buckingham, UK: Open University Press, 2000)

Mike Godwin, *Cyber Rights: Defending Free Speech in the Digital Age* (Cambridge, MA: MIT Press, 2003)

Kashmir Hill, "The Downside of Being a Google Executive," *Forbes* (September 27, 2012), available at http://www.forbes.com/sites/kashmirhill/2012/09/27/the-downside-of-being-a-google-executive/

"Internet Freedom: Free to Choose," *The Economist*, October 6, 2012, at 70

Tim Jordan, *Cyberpower: The Culture and Politics of Cyberspace and the Internet* (New York: Routledge, 1999)

Kathryn Kolbert & Zak Mettger, eds., *Justice Talking: Censoring the Web: Leading Advocates Debate Today's Most Controversial Issues* (New York: The New Press, 2002)

Lawrence Lessig, *The Future of Ideas* (New York: Random House, 2001)

Saul Levmore & Martha C. Nussbaum, eds., *The Offensive Internet: Speech, Privacy, and Reputation* (Cambridge, MA: Harvard University Press, 2012)

Jeremy Lipschultz, *Broadcast and Internet Indecency: Defining Free Speech* (New York: Routledge, 2007)

Eli Pariser, *The Filter Bubble: What the Internet Is Hiding from You* (New York: Penguin Press, 2011)

Kevin W. Saunders, *Saving Our Children from the First Amendment* (New York: New York University Press, 2003)

Madeleine Schachter, *Law of Internet Speech* (Durham, NC: Carolina Academic Press, 3d ed. 2008)

Bob Sullivan, "Do-Not-Spam List Won't Work, FTC Says," MSNBC (June 15, 2004) available at http://www.msnbc.msn .com/id/5216554/ns/technology_and_science-security/t/ do-not-spam-list-wont-work-ftc-says/#.UAecOpF2r08

"National Differences: The World Is What You Make It—Every Country Has Its Own Internet," *The Economist*, Special Report: Technology and Geography, October 27, 2012, at 20

Andrew Couts, "U.S. Gov't Seizes 70 More Websites for Copyright Infringement—Not the Digital Kind," Digital Trends (July 12, 2012), available at http://www.digitaltrends .com/web/u-s-govt-seizes-70-more-websites-for-copyright-infringement-not-the-digital-kind/

Frank Mosuch & Susan B. Hillson, "Technical Security Measures," in *Data Security and Privacy Law: Combating Cyberthreats*, edited by Kevin P. Cronin & Ronald N. Weikers (St. Paul, MN: West, 2004)

Robert Westervelt, "Microsoft Revokes Additional Digital Certificates due to Encryption Weakness," SearchSecurity (July 11, 2012), available at http://searchsecurity.techtarget.com/ news/2240159440/Microsoft-revokes-additional-digital-certificates-due-to-encryption-weakness

❖ CERTIFICATE ❖

Digital certificates can be used to establish the identity of persons doing business over the Internet. The certificate is issued by a trusted third party known as a certification authority, and includes the name of the party to whom it is issued along with a serial number, an expiration date, and the party's public encryption key and digital signature. Digital certificates commonly use some form of the X.509 standard; because the standard is informal rather than formally defined and approved, different implementations of the standard may differ. The simplest way for companies to avoid difficulties in verifying certificates is to use a third-party verification authority such as VeriSign, Inc. (Mosuch & Hillson 2004, § 3.13).

Digital certificates can be used for a variety of purposes. They can enable secured communications through a virtual private network by identifying persons eligible to use the network. They can verify the identity of buyers and sellers in a transaction in which the parties never meet face to face. They can be used to determine eligibility to view particular content on a Web site, in order to screen the content from certain persons or to ensure that access is limited to authorized persons; these might be persons who have paid a subscription fee, or who work for a particular company, or who are working on a particular project. The Child Online Protection Act of 1998 envisioned the use of digital certificates verifying a user's age as one means to shield children from online pornography (47 U.S.C. § 231(c)(1)(B)).

Statute

• Child Online Protection Act, 47 U.S.C. § 231(c)(1)(B)

See also: Child Online Protection Act; Encryption

Sources and Further Reading

Richard Adhikari, "Hacker Exploits a Loophole to Score Free App Goodies," MacNewsWorld (July 14, 2012), available at http://www.macnewsworld.com/story/75637.html

❖ CHILD ONLINE PROTECTION ACT ❖

Following the Supreme Court's 1997 decision striking down the Communications Decency Act (CDA), Congress made a second attempt to regulate the availability of indecent material to minors with the 1998 Child Online Protection Act (COPA). COPA attempted to address the specific constitutional concerns raised by the Supreme Court when it struck down the CDA. COPA imposed penalties on anyone who "knowingly and with knowledge of the character of the material, in interstate or foreign commerce by means of the World Wide Web, ma[de] any communication for commercial purposes that [was] available to any minor and that include[d] any material that [was] harmful to minors" (47 U.S.C. § 231(a)(1)). COPA included a three-part test for determining whether the material was harmful to minors. Material was harmful if and only if all three of the following requirements were met:

(a) The "average person, applying contemporary community standards, would find" that the material taken as a whole, with respect to minors, was designed to appeal or pander to the prurient interest;

(b) The material depicted, described, or represented, "in a manner patently offensive with respect to minors, an actual or simulated sexual act or sexual contact, an actual or simulated normal or perverted sexual act, or a lewd exhibition of the genitals or post-pubescent female breast; and"

(c) The material, taken as a whole, lacked "serious literary, artistic, political, or scientific value for minors" (47 U.S.C. § 231(e)(6)).

Unlike the CDA's definition, struck down in *Reno v. American Civil Liberties Union*, COPA's definition closely tracked the definition of obscenity set out by the Supreme Court in the 1973 case of *Miller v. California*. Under the Miller test, determining whether material is obscene requires the trier of fact to determine:

(a) whether "the average person, applying contemporary community standards" would find that the work, taken as a whole, appeals to the prurient interest. . .; (b) whether the work depicts or describes, in a patently offensive way, sexual conduct specifically defined by the applicable state law; and (c) whether the work, taken as a whole, lacks serious literary, artistic, political, or scientific value (413 U.S. at 39).

The first prong of the COPA definition was essentially identical to the first prong of the Miller test, with the exceptions of the addition of the words "with respect to minors" and the qualification that the average person must find that the work is designed to appeal or pander to the prurient interest, rather than merely that it does appeal to the prurient interest.

The second prong still differed in one major respect: While *Miller* refers to applicable state law for its definitions of the types of conduct whose depiction is prohibited, COPA attempted to establish its own definition, and this definition extended beyond the depiction of sexual conduct.

The third prong of the COPA definition, other than the addition of the words "for minors," was identical to the third prong of the Miller test.

Like the CDA, COPA provided safe harbors for Web publishers and Internet service providers (ISPs). Under COPA, ISPs were not liable for material merely passing through their systems. And Web publishers were not liable under COPA if they restricted access by minors through the use of a "credit card, debit account, adult access code, adult personal identification number, . . . a digital certificate that verifies age, . . . or by any other reasonable measures that are feasible under available technology" (47 U.S.C. § 231(c)(1)). Inevitably, some minors would be able to circumvent these measures, but COPA insulated complying Web publishers from liability nonetheless.

COPA was immediately challenged by First Amendment advocates; the American Civil Liberties Union (ACLU) and others brought suit in the federal district court for the Eastern District of Pennsylvania to enjoin (prevent) enforcement of COPA. The district court granted the request for an injunction, reasoning that the ACLU had shown that their attack on the constitutionality of COPA was likely to succeed on the merits; in other words, the District Court ordered that COPA not be enforced pending a decision on its constitutionality.

After the grant of the injunction, the government appealed the case to the U.S. Court of Appeals for the Third Circuit, which decided in June 2000 that the District Court had acted correctly in issuing the preliminary injunction. In its opinion, the Circuit Court focused on the problem of applying "community standards" to the World Wide Web, as it existed at that time. In 2000, the architecture of the Web rendered it impossible for a Web publisher to know where, in the real world, the viewer of the published material was located. In contrast, providers of printed pornographic material, pornographic cable television programs, and sexually explicit telephone messages knew where the materials were being sent; they could choose not to send or transmit them to certain communities if the content would violate the standards of those communities. At the time it was difficult or impossible for Web publishers to restrict access to their published content on the basis of geography; the content was published to the whole world or not at all.

Thus, to apply "community standards" to Web content would have required each Web publisher to tailor the content to the standards of the least broad-minded community. The parties conceded that the "contemporary community standards" prong was inapplicable to communities outside the United States, so that there was no need to consider, as the Circuit Court put it, "the more liberal community standards of Amsterdam or the more restrictive community standards of Tehran." Even within the United States, however, there is a wide range of community standards; enforcement of COPA would have had the effect of allowing America's most puritanical community to determine what was the acceptable Web content for the entire population of the United States. (This anomalous result was also produced by the current law governing obscenity generally, but in an Internet context, when every person connected to the Internet was potentially connected to all communities simultaneously, the problem became even more pronounced.)

As so often happens when courts and lawmakers address the Internet, technological developments may render this reasoning obsolete. It is already commonplace for Web site owners to restrict content based on the country in which the recipient is located. While such geographic filtering is imperfect—some users will not be screened and sophisticated users can fool the screening software or otherwise gain access to the content—it successfully blocks most users in a given country. Restricting by state or city within a country might be somewhat more difficult, but the technical problem is not insurmountable. The more difficult problem would lie in determining the standards of each of these communities, and constantly updating filtering software to take these no doubt everchanging standards into account.

The Third Circuit's decision had the interesting effect of granting a higher degree of First Amendment protection to Web content than is enjoyed by print content. It also raised, by implication, an obvious problem with Congressional attempts to censor the Web: It is as easy to publish content outside the United States as within its borders, and as easy to access foreign content from within the borders of the United States as to access domestic content. There is little Congress can do to regulate what is published outside the United States, and little it can do to regulate the access of persons within the United States to foreign Web sites, short of unconstitutionally heavy-handed intervention.

The Third Circuit's decision was not the last word on COPA. In May 2001, the U.S. Supreme Court granted certiorari (a writ directing a lower court to deliver the record in a case for review by a higher court, and the mechanism by which a majority of cases come to the Supreme Court) to review the Third Circuit's decision (*ACLU v. Reno*, 217 F.3d 162).

In 2002, the Supreme Court, in *Ashcroft v. American Civil Liberties Union*, vacated (nullified) the decisions of the Third Circuit and the Eastern District of Pennsylvania enjoining enforcement of COPA. The Court held that the reference to "contemporary community standards" did not in and of itself render COPA facially unconstitutional. A three-justice plurality, with five justices concurring in the result, stated "community standards need not be defined by reference to a precise geographic area," adding that a

> publisher's burden does not change simply because it decides to distribute its material to every community in the Nation. . . . Nor does it change because the publisher may wish to speak only to those in a 'community where avant garde culture is the norm,' . . . but nonetheless utilizes a medium that transmits its speech from coast to coast. If a publisher wishes for its material to be judged only by the standards of particular communities, then it need only take the simple step of utilizing a medium that enables it to target the release of its material into those communities (*Ashcroft v. ACLU*, 535 U.S. at 583).

In other words, COPA might well have the effect of limiting expression on the Web in accordance with the standard of the most puritanical community, but to do so was not unconstitutional.

The Supreme Court remanded (sent back) the case to the Third Circuit for further proceedings. On remand, the Third Circuit held that the plaintiffs had established a substantial likelihood of prevailing on their claim that COPA was not narrowly tailored to achieve a compelling government interest, and that they had also established a substantial likelihood of prevailing on their claim that COPA was unconstitutionally overbroad.

As a restraint on expression in a unique nonbroadcast medium, COPA is subject to strict scrutiny, the highest level of constitutional scrutiny. In order to withstand strict scrutiny, a law or other government action must

(1) serve a compelling governmental interest;
(2) be narrowly tailored to achieve that interest; and
(3) be the least restrictive means of advancing that interest.

It had been agreed by the parties throughout the litigation that the protection of minors from harmful online content was a compelling state interest. However, the Third Circuit found that the statute was not narrowly tailored both because holding all communities to the standard of one would mean that much material that was acceptable in some or all communities would nonetheless be banned in those communities, and because of the difficulty of ascertaining the meaning of the term "as a whole" in the statute "when everything on the Web is connected to everything else" (*ACLU v. Ashcroft*, 322 F.3d at 252). And blocking and filtering software provided a less restrictive means than COPA to achieve the same result; indeed, such software

might be more effective, because it could block foreign Web sites beyond the reach of COPA. The Third Circuit once again affirmed the issuance of the injunction.

The matter did not end there. The Supreme Court once again granted certiorari to consider the matter. On June 29, 2004, a three-justice plurality, with two justices concurring in the result, issued a decision affirming the preliminary injunction and remanding the case for trial. The Court reasoned that the preliminary injunction should stand because the government had not shown that it would be likely to rebut the ACLU's contention that filtering software, a less restrictive alternative to COPA, can protect children from online pornography without infringing the First Amendment rights of adults. A trial was necessary to determine the present-day effectiveness of filtering technology, five years after the grant of the initial injunction.

The Court also reasoned that COPA's "effectiveness is likely to diminish even further if COPA is upheld, because the providers of the materials that would be covered by the statute simply can move their operations overseas" (*Ashcroft v. ACLU*, 544 U.S. 656). Filtering software can block content originating outside the United States; COPA cannot.

In 2007, the ACLU again challenged the constitutionality of COPA. The district court permanently enjoined the Attorney General from enforcing or prosecuting under COPA "at any time for any conduct" (*ACLU v. Gonzales*, 478 F. Supp. 2d at 821). The court reasoned that COPA did not pass the strict scrutiny requirements of the First and Fifth Amendments. On appeal, the Third Circuit affirmed, agreeing that COPA was unconstitutional under the First Amendment. Although COPA served a compelling interest, it was neither narrowly tailored to achieve that interest, nor was it the least restrictive means. In addition, the Court found that COPA was facially unconstitutional: it was both vague and overbroad. The Third Circuit issued a permanent injunction barring enforcement of COPA. The Attorney General appealed to the Supreme Court; however, the Court denied certiorari, effectively putting an end to COPA. Support for COPA eventually diminished. Perhaps, as well-known Internet commentator Declan McCullagh observed, COPA was too limited: "It applies only to material delivered 'by means of the World Wide Web'—meaning that it doesn't cover peer-to-peer file sharing, videos watched via a third-party iPhone application, or streaming porn viewed through the VideoLAN Client, RealPlayer, or Windows Media Player desktop applications" (McCullagh 2009).

The Internet may ultimately bring the entire issue of "community standards," the linchpin of the Miller definition of obscenity, into question. Even without the Internet, the increasing mobility of the U.S. populace and the fragmentation of society, especially in large cities, make "community standards" difficult to determine. On any street in any town in the United States, one may encounter values both more conservative than those in Tehran and more liberal than those in Amsterdam, to use the Third Circuit's examples. Indeed, any person using a computer in any U.S. household may be virtually present in Tehran or in Amsterdam, or in both at once.

Statute

- Child Online Protection Act, 47 U.S.C. § 231

Cases

- *American Civil Liberties Union v. Gonzales*, 478 F. Supp. 2d 775 (E.D. Pa. 2007)
- *American Civil Liberties Union v. Mukasey*, 534 F.3d 181 (3d Cir. 2008), cert. denied sub nom *Mukasey v. American Civil Liberties Union*, 555 U.S. 1137 (2009)
- *American Civil Liberties Union v. Reno*, 217 F.3d 162 (3d Cir. 2000), reversed sub nom, *Ashcroft v. American Civil Liberties Union*, 535 U.S. 564 (2002), on remand, *American Civil Liberties Union v. Ashcroft*, 322 F.3d 240 (3d Cir. 2003), certiorari granted, *Ashcroft v. American Civil Liberties Union*, 540 U.S. 944 (2003), affirmed & remanded, 542 U.S. 656 (2004)
- *Miller v. California*, 413 U.S. 15 (1973)

See also: Censorship; Children's Internet Protection Act; Communications Decency Act; Constitutional Law; First Amendment; Indecency; Obscenity; Pornography

Sources and Further Reading

Mike Godwin, *Cyber Rights: Defending Free Speech in the Digital Age* (Cambridge, MA: MIT Press, 2003)

Kevin F. King, "Personal Jurisdiction, Internet Commerce, and Privacy: The Pervasive Legal Consequences of Modern Geolocation Technologies," 21 *Albany Law Journal of Science & Technology* 61 (2011)

Lawrence Lessig, *Code and Other Laws of Cyberspace, Version 2.0* (New York: Basic Books, 2006)

Saul Levmore & Martha C. Nussbaum, eds., *The Offensive Internet: Speech, Privacy & Reputation* (Cambridge, MA: Harvard University Press, 2012)

Declan McCullagh, "Supreme Court Deals Deathblow to Antiporn Law," CNET (January 21, 2009), http://news.cnet .com/8301–13578_3–10147171–38.html

Joel R. Reidenberg, "Current Debates in the Conflict of Laws: Choice of Law and Jurisdiction on The Internet: Technology and Internet Jurisdiction," 153 *University of Pennsylvania Law Review* 1951 (2005)

Kevin W. Saunders, *Saving Our Children from the First Amendment* (New York: New York University Press, 2003)

❖ CHILD PORNOGRAPHY ❖

The Supreme Court has long held that child pornography is not protected speech under the First Amendment, at least where actual children are involved (*Ferber*, 458 U.S. 747). In 1996, Congress enacted the Child Pornography Prevention Act, which prohibited the possession or distribution of any image that was, "or appeared to be, of a minor engaging in sexually explicit conduct." This covered not only depictions of actual children, but computer-generated images in which no actual children were involved.

A major component of the underlying rationale for Supreme Court decisions on child pornography, particularly *New York v. Ferber*, had been that child pornography is intrinsically related to the sexual abuse of children. It is a record of sexual abuse; actual children are involved in its production and are harmed thereby; and it creates a market for the material, which in turn fuels the problem of sexual abuse of children. When no actual children are involved, the first two of these components are no longer present; the Child Pornography Prevention Act thus presented the Supreme Court with a new question of law. In *Ashcroft v. Free Speech Coalition*, the Court found that the prohibition was unconstitutionally overbroad because it could prohibit expression that was not intrinsically related to the sexual abuse of actual children and was not obscene under the test set out in *Miller v. California* (535 U.S. 234). The Court rejected other arguments offered by the government regarding the potential for harm from virtual child pornography on the grounds that they were speculative and did not justify curtailing First Amendment protections (*Miller*, 535 U.S. 234).

The Court's decision in *Ashcroft v. Free Speech Coalition* does not mean that all images containing virtual child pornography are necessarily protected by the First Amendment, or even that any are. Such images may be, and probably are, obscene under the Miller test, and may thus be prohibited.

Shortly after the Court struck down the Child Pornography Protection Act in *Ashcroft v. Free Speech Coalition*, a new bill, the Prosecuting Remedies and Tools Against the Exploitation of Children Today (PROTECT) Act of 2003, was signed into law. Included in its various provisions was 18 U.S.C. § 1466A, which made illegal visual depictions of child pornography:

> Any person who, in a circumstance described in subsection (d), knowingly produces, distributes, receives, or possesses with intent to distribute, a visual depiction of any kind, including a drawing, cartoon, sculpture, or painting, that—
>
> (1)
> (A) depicts a minor engaging in sexually explicit conduct; and
> (B) is obscene; or
>
> (2)
> (A) depicts an image that is, or appears to be, of a minor engaging in graphic bestiality, sadistic or masochistic abuse, or sexual intercourse, including genital-genital, oral-genital, anal-genital, or oral-anal, whether between persons of the same or opposite sex; and

(B) lacks serious literary, artistic, political, or scientific value;

or attempts or conspires to do so, shall be subject to the penalties provided in section 2252A(b)(1) [18 USCS § 2252A(b)(1)], including the penalties provided for cases involving a prior conviction. (18 U.S.C. § 1466A(a)).

The U.S. Court of Appeals for the Fourth Circuit upheld the constitutionality of this provision in a 2008 case involving hentai—Japanese-style animated pornography. The defendant was convicted of receiving on his computer a number of hentai images depicting minors engaging in sexually explicit conduct. He challenged Section 1466A, claiming that it was "unconstitutional under the First Amendment, as applied to cartoons, because cartoons do not depict actual minors." (*Whorley*, 550 F.3d at 330). This defense failed, however, because Section 1466A(a)(1) "prohibits visual depictions of minors only when they are *obscene*." Obscenity, whether it involves child pornography or not, is not protected under the First Amendment (*Miller*, 535 U.S. 234). Whorley also challenged the constitutionality of Section 1466A(a)(2), which does not invoke the obscenity exception, although it does partially invoke the *Miller* factors. However, Whorley lacked standing to bring this challenge; in the Fourth Circuit's words, "Because Whorley was not convicted of offenses under those provisions, we decline to address his challenges to them" (*Whorley*, 550 F.3d at 337 n.2).

Legislative proposals to strengthen child pornography laws continue to be made. The Protecting Children from Internet Pornographers Act of 2011 would ease the process of collecting information from Internet service providers whose users are viewing and distributing child pornography. Advocacy groups, including EFF and the ACLU, have objected to the proposed Act on the grounds that it is too invasive of the privacy rights of innocent users. Another recent bill is the Child Protection Act of 2012, which would increase funding for task forces dedicated to stopping child pornography.

Statutes and Proposed Legislation

- Child Pornography Prevention Act of 1996, 18 U.S.C. §§ 2251–2260
- Child Protection Act of 2012, S. 3456, 112th Cong. (2d Sess. 2011–2012)
- Prosecuting Remedies and Tools Against the Exploitation of Children Today (PROTECT) Act of 2003, 18 U.S.C. § 1466A
- Protecting Children from Internet Pornographers Act of 2011, H.R. 1981, 112th Cong. (1st Sess. 2011–2012)

Cases

- *Miller v. California*, 413 U.S. 15 (1973)
- *New York v. Ferber*, 458 U.S. 747 (1982)
- *Osborne v. Ohio*, 495 U.S. 103 (1990)
- *Ashcroft v. Free Speech Coalition*, 535 U.S. 234 (2002)
- *United States v. Whorley*, 550 F.3d 326 (4th Cir. 2008)

Sources and Further Reading

Rosalind E. Bell, "Reconciling the Protect Act with the First Amendment," 87 *New York University Law Review* 1878 (2012)

Grant Gross, "Advocacy Group Takes Aim at Anti-Porn Bill," *PCWorld* (February 27, 2012), available at http://www.pcworld.com/article/250803/advocacy_group_takes_aim_at_antiporn_bill_requiring_isp_data_retention.html

See also: Censorship; Child Online Protection Act; Children's Internet Protection Act; Children's Online Privacy Protection Act; Communications Decency Act; Constitutional Law; Encryption; First Amendment; Obscenity; Pornography

❖ CHILDREN'S INTERNET PROTECTION ACT ❖

The Children's Internet Protection Act (CIPA) of 1998 was a companion act to the Child Online Protection Act (COPA). While COPA attempts to control all access to certain types of material by certain persons, CIPA attempts to control access from certain computers by requiring schools and libraries receiving federally subsidized discounted Internet access to install filtering and blocking software.

The federally funded E-rate or School and Libraries Discount program enables qualifying schools and libraries to obtain access to the Internet at discounts of up to 90%, depending upon economic need. Under the Telecommunications Act, the E-rate is only available to schools and libraries if administrators certify that the school or library

(1) is enforcing a policy of Internet safety for minors that includes monitoring the online activities of minors and the operation of a technology protection measure with respect to any of its computers with Internet access that protects against access through such computers to visual depictions that are
(I) obscene;
(II) child pornography; or
(III) harmful to minors; and
(2) is enforcing the operation of such technology protection measure during any use of such computers by minors (47 U.S.C. § 254(h)(5)(B)).

With respect to adults, the school or library must make an identical certification, except that item III (protection against material harmful to minors) is not required. In addition, a school or library administrator or authorized person "may disable the technology protection measure concerned, during use by an adult, to enable access for bona fide research or other lawful purpose" (47 U.S.C. § 254(h)(5)(D)).

CIPA was signed into law in December 2000 by then president Clinton, who expressed disappointment with the statute. Clinton's misgivings included concerns about the efficacy of filtering software and the conflict with First Amendment rights; he stated that he would have preferred locally developed and implemented alternatives.

CIPA required elementary and secondary schools and public libraries providing Internet access to meet two additional requirements for federal funding and benefits. First, schools and libraries were required to purchase and install "technology protection measures"—filtering programs—to filter or block Internet access to specified "visual depictions." In addition, each institution was required to hold a minimum of one public meeting on Internet safety policies to gather input and feedback from community members.

The specified visual depictions to be blocked were those that were obscene or constituted child pornography; the First Amendment protects neither obscenity nor child pornography, and the requirement of one meeting was at least a nod to the "community standards" element of the Miller test for obscenity. "Harmful to minors" is defined in CIPA as meaning

> any picture, image, graphic image file, or other visual depiction that—
>
> (i) taken as a whole and with respect to minors, appeals to a prurient interest in nudity, sex, or excretion;
> (ii) depicts, describes, or represents, in a patently offensive way with respect to what is suitable for minors, an actual or simulated sexual act or sexual contact, actual or simulated normal or perverted sexual acts, or a lewd exhibition of the genitals; and
> (iii) taken as a whole, lacks serious literary, artistic, political, or scientific value as to minors (47 U.S.C. § 254(h)(7)(G)).

Interestingly, this definition differs somewhat from the definition of "harmful to minors" in CIPA's companion act, COPA (47 U.S.C. § 231(e)(6)).

CIPA also includes a subtitle, Neighborhood Children's Internet Protection, that requires schools and libraries to adopt policies that address areas such as minors' access to inappropriate matter on the Web, their safety when using email, chat rooms, and other direct electronic communications (such as instant messaging), and hacking. The term "inappropriate for minors" is to be determined by a "school board, local educational agency, library, or other authority," rather than by an "agency or instrumentality of the United States Government," nor are these locally adopted policies subject to review by these federal agencies or instrumentalities (47 U.S.C. § 254(l)(2)).

Not surprisingly, CIPA was immediately challenged by First Amendment advocates. Plaintiffs, including the `ACLU and the American Library Association (ALA), filed suit in the federal District Court for the Eastern District of Pennsylvania to enjoin enforcement of CIPA on the grounds that it was an unconstitutional abridgement of First Amendment rights, at least as far as libraries and their adult patrons were concerned. With regard to libraries, the plaintiffs argued that CIPA required the imposition of content-based restrictions on library patrons' access to constitutionally protected speech. Although patrons could request that blocked content be unblocked, placing the burden on the library patron to make the request, which might be embarrassing, was likely to discourage many patrons from doing so. And because existing filtering and blocking programs are imperfect, much speech that Congress intended to permit is blocked, and much speech that Congress intended to restrict gets through. In addition, the plaintiffs claimed, the imposition of controls on freedom of expression as a prerequisite to the receipt of federal funds was an impermissible use of the spending power. The existence of an "unblocking" procedure was an insufficient safeguard, because library patrons might feel embarrassed to request the unblocking of certain sites, with a consequent chilling effect on free speech. The district court agreed (*American Library Association*, 201 F. Supp. 2d 401).

The case was appealed directly to the U.S. Supreme Court, which reversed the district court's decision in June 2003. A four-justice plurality of the Supreme Court, with two justices concurring in the result, stated that CIPA was not unconstitutional either as a violation of First Amendment rights or as an impermissible condition attached to Congressional exercise of the spending power. Writing for the plurality, Chief Justice Rehnquist pointed out that "a library reviews and affirmatively chooses to acquire every book in its collection," and that most libraries choose not to acquire pornographic books. The nature of the Web renders it impossible for a library to engage in a similar selection process with the Web content, but the purpose of a library is not to provide a First Amendment forum for Web content publishers. It is to facilitate learning and cultural enrichment, and this process of facilitation invariably involves the making of choices about what material the library will provide to its patrons (*American Library Association*, 539 U.S. 194).

While CIPA's constitutionality has been upheld, its usefulness has been limited by subsequent technological and social developments. Chief among the technological advances have been the advent of local wireless routing and of netbooks, tablets, smartphones, and other ultraportable Internet-capable devices. Where a library provides wireless access but places filtering software only on its own computers, library patrons may be able to use the library's wireless Internet access while bypassing the filtering software. The social changes are harder to track or predict, but it seems likely that the now-universal availability of digital image and video recording devices, combined with a wide variety of options via which recordings can be made with those devices can be communicated, mean that "peer-to-peer" objectionable content may be replacing the traditional distributor-to-audience model of distribution. The ease with which content can be uploaded to a variety of sites, or sent through a variety of means of messaging, makes it impossible to update Web filters quickly enough to block such content (see Spurlin & Garry 2009). Here again, though, technology may race ahead, with image-recognition technology providing the ability to block objectionable content as quickly as it appears.

Statutes

- Children's Internet Protection Act, 47 U.S.C. § 254(h)
- Neighborhood Children's Internet Protection Act, 47 U.S.C. § 254(l)

Case

- *American Library Association v. United States*, 201 F. Supp. 2d 401 (E.D. Pa. 2002); reversed sub nom, *U.S. v. American Library Association, Inc.*, 539 U.S. 194 (2003)

See also: Censorship; Child Online Protection Act; Communications Decency Act; Constitutional Law; First Amendment; Indecency; Obscenity; Pornography

Sources and Further Reading
Kathryn Kolbert & Zak Mettger, eds., *Justice Talking: Censoring the Web—Leading Advocates Debate Today's Most Controversial Issues* (New York: The New Press, 2002)
Eli Pariser, *The Filter Bubble: What the Internet is Hiding from You* (New York: Penguin Press, 2011)
Kevin W. Saunders, *Saving Our Children from the First Amendment* (New York: New York University Press, 2003)
Madeleine Schachter, *Law of Internet Speech* (Durham, NC: Carolina Academic Press, 3d ed. 2008)
Candice J. Spurlin & Patrick M. Garry, "Does Filtering Stop the Flow of Valuable Information?: A Case Study of the Children's Internet Protection Act (CIPA) in South Dakota," 54 *South Dakota Law Review* 89 (2009)
Heidi Wachs, "Permissive Pornography: The Selective Censorship of the Internet under CIPA," 11 *Cardozo Women's Law Journal* 441 (2005)

❖ CHILDREN'S ONLINE PRIVACY PROTECTION ACT ❖

The Children's Online Privacy Protection Act (COPPA) was enacted in 1998; the FTC initially promulgated implementing regulations that took effect in April 2001 (16 C.F.R. § 312), and has engaged in an ongoing rulemaking process since then (see Borges 2011). COPPA was enacted in response to concerns that information about children's use of the Web, routinely gathered by the Web sites the children visited, could be misused. COPPA sets guidelines for operators of commercial Web sites that target children under the age of 13 and for operators of other Web sites who know that they collect information from children under the age of 13.

COPPA requires such operators to provide notice of what information they collect from children, how they use the information, and their practices regarding disclosure of the information. Operators may not collect, use, or disclose personal information obtained from a child without the verifiable consent of the child's parents. Information that will trigger COPPA, if gathered, includes information that may identify or permit communication with the child, such as a first or last name, address, email address, telephone number, or social security number. The parents must be provided with a reasonable means to review the information and to refuse to permit its further use or maintenance. A child's participation in a game, promotional sweepstakes or contest, or any other activity may not be conditioned upon the collection of any information other than that which is reasonably necessary to enable the child to participate in the activity. Web site operators must establish privacy policies that adopt reasonable procedures to protect the confidentiality, security, and integrity of any personal information collected from children (15 U.S.C. § 6502).

COPPA contains a safe harbor provision for certain organizations, but it must be affirmatively applied for; if not previously applied for and granted, it cannot be raised as a defense (15 U.S.C. § 6503). Only four organizations, so far, have been granted exceptions from COPPA under the safe harbor provision: the Children's Advertising Review Unit of the Better Business Bureau (CARU), the Entertainment Software Ratings Board, TRUSTe, and Privo, Inc. The safe harbor provision, along with the rest of the Rule, continues to be amended and strengthened. A review of the Rule was initiated in 2010 to ensure it was remaining effective with the evolving technological landscape. A series of final amendments will go into effect in 2013, including closing a loophole that currently allows third parties to collect personal information from child-directed apps and Web sites. The amendments will also require safe harbor programs to audit members and report their findings annually to the FTC. Overt opposition to COPPA has been limited, with one rare exception provided by Facebook founder Mark Zuckerberg. Zuckerberg has criticized COPPA as limiting children's educational opportunities, stating "My philosophy is that for education you need to start at a really, really young age," adding "We'd take a lot of precautions to make sure that [the children] are safe" (Lev-Ram 2011). This idea has been greeted with concern from some and cautious approval, mingled with a call for stronger protections, from others (*Facebook and Children* 2012).

The FTC, aided by independent watchdogs such as CARU, has actively pursued COPPA violators, often imposing significant fines. In 2003, Hershey's Foods and Mrs. Field's Cookies agreed to settle COPPA charges brought by the FTC for $85,000 and $100,000, respectively (*FTC* 2003). In 2006, Xanga.com, a then-popular social networking site, was fined $1,000,000 for violating

COPPA. Bonzi Software, Inc. was fined $75,000, while UMG Recordings agreed to pay $400,000 for violating COPPA while operating music fan sites targeting children. Similarly, in 2008, Sony BMG Music Entertainment, which then operated over 1000 fan sites for musicians and labels, agreed to settle charges for a $1,000,000 penalty; Imbee.com, a social networking site targeting "tweens," paid a $130,000 penalty. In 2009, Iconix Brand Group, an apparel brand geared toward children, paid $250,000 in 2009. In 2011, Playdom, an online gaming company owned by Disney Enterprises, agreed to settle COPPA charges for $3,000,000 (Khurana 2011). Also in 2011, a mobile apps developer paid $50,000 in fines, and a social networking site for kids, skidekids.com, paid $100,000. In 2012 Artist Arena, the operator of fan Web sites for celebrities, including Justin Bieber and Rihanna, agreed to settlement charges for $1,000,000 and RockYou, a social game site, paid $250,000.

Statute

- Children's Online Privacy Protection Act, 15 U.S.C. §§ 6501–6506

Regulation

- Children's Online Privacy Protection Rule, 64 Fed. Reg. 59,888 (November 3, 1999) (codified at 16 C.F.R. § 312 (2001))

See also: Advertising; Adware and Spyware; Anonymity; App; Privacy; Social Networking Service

Sources and Further Reading

Tsan Abrahamson, "Coping with COPPA: The Practical Aspects of Children's Privacy," *Practical Lawyer*, January 2002, at 49

Rebecca Borges, "In re The Federal Trade Commission's Proposed Revisions to the Children's Online Privacy Protection Rule, Notice of Proposed Rulemaking, 76 Fed. Reg. 59804 (September 27, 2011)," 20 *CommLaw Conspectus* 293 (2011)

Julie Cromer Young, "From the Mouths of Babes: Protecting Child Authors from Themselves," 112 *West Virginia Law Review* 431 (2010)

"Facebook and Children: Let the Nippers Network," *The Economist*, June 9, 2012, at 18

"FTC Charges That Security Flaws in Rock You Game Exposed 32 Million Email Addresses and Passwords," Federal Trade Commission (March 27, 2012), available at http://ftc.gov/opa/2012/03/rockyou.shtm

"FTC Receives Largest COPPA Civil Penalties to Date in Settlements with Mrs. Fields Cookies and Hershey Foods," Federal Trade Commission (February 27, 2003), available at http://www.ftc.gov/opa/2003/02/hersheyfield.shtm

Melanie L. Hersh, "Is COPPA a Cop-Out? The Child Online Privacy Protection Act as Proof that Parents, Not Government, Should Be Protecting Children's Interests on the Internet," 28 *Fordham Urban Law Journal* 1831 (2001)

"Iconix Brand Group Settles Charges Its Apparel Web Sites Violated Children's Online Privacy Protection Act," Federal Trade Commission (October 20, 2009), available at http://www.ftc.gov/opa/2009/10/iconix.shtm

"Imbee.com Settles FTC Charges Social Networking Site for Kids Violated the Children's Online Privacy Protection Act; Settlement Includes $130,000 Civil Penalty," Federal Trade Commission (January. 30, 2008) available at http://www.ftc.gov/opa/2008/01/imbee.shtm

Kevin Khurana, "COPPA Violations? Cop a Settlement for $3 Million," Proskauer Privacy Law Blog (May 18, 2011), available at http://privacylaw.proskauer.com/2011/05/articles/childrens-online-privacy-prote/coppa-violations-cop-a-settlement-for-3-million/

Frederick Lane, *Cybertraps for the Young* (Chicago: NTI Upstream, 2011)

Michal Lev-Ram, "Zuckerberg: Kids under 13 Should Be Allowed on Facebook," CNNMoney (May 20, 2011) available at http://tech.fortune.cnn.com/2011/05/20/zuckerberg-kids-under-13-should-be-allowed-on-facebook/

Lauren A. Matecki, "COPPA is Ineffective Legislation! Next Steps for Protecting Youth Privacy Rights in the Social Networking Era," 5 *Northwestern Journal of Law and Social Policy* 369 (2010)

"Mobile Apps Developer Settles FTC Charges It Violated Children's Privacy Rule," Federal Trade Commission (August 15, 2011), available at http://www.ftc.gov/opa/2011/08/w3mobileapps.shtm

"Operator of Celebrity Fan Websites to Pay $1 Million to Settle FTC Charges That It Illegally Collected Children's Information without Their Parent's Consent," Federal Trade Commission (October 4, 2012), available at http://www.ftc.gov/opa/2012/10/artistarena.shtm

"Operator of Social Networking Website for Kids Settle Charges Site Collected Kids' Personal Information without Parental Consent," Federal Trade Commission (November 8, 2011), available at http://www.ftc.gov/opa/2011/11/skidekids.shtm

Cheryl B. Preston, "CyberInfants," 39 *Pepperdine Law Review* 225 (2012)

"Sony BMG Music Settles Charges Its Music Fan Websites Violated the Children's Online Privacy Protection Act," Federal Trade Commission (December 11, 2008), http://www.ftc.gov/opa/2008/12/sonymusic.shtm

"Xanga.com to Pay $1 Million for Violating Children's Online Privacy Protection Rule," Federal Trade Commission (September 7, 2006), available at http://www.ftc.gov/opa/2006/09/xanga.shtm

❖ CHOICE OF LAW ❖

A choice-of-law problem arises when the law of more than one jurisdiction may be applicable to a particular situation. Choice-of-law problems arise even in the absence of the Internet. If, for example, a California employee of a California corporation travels to Nevada on business and is injured there by a resident of Arizona, it is not instantly apparent whether California, Nevada, or Arizona tort and workers' compensation laws should apply to a suit for damages brought by the injured employee. The answer might depend on where the suit was brought; courts in California, Arizona, and Nevada, each employing their own choice-of-law-rules, might reach three different results.

While states tend, either through stated policy or through their practice over a period of time, to prefer their own law, the preference is not absolute. A Nevada court might well decide that California workers' compensation law should apply and that, if the California workers' compensation law did not bar the tort suit, that Nevada's own tort law should apply.

The Internet increases the possibility of choice-of-law problems. On the Internet, most transactions and interactions involve multiple jurisdictions. With a single click, and without consulting an attorney or reviewing the law of the various jurisdictions involved, a surfer sitting at home in Vermont may purchase and download music from an Australian company with its principal place of business in the Netherlands. The download might take place via a server located in Virginia; the server might belong to an Internet service provider incorporated in the Cayman Islands but with its principal place of business in Louisiana. The order might be paid for with a credit card issued by a bank in Delaware. Without the knowledge of the purchaser, the music downloads might have been illegally copied in Switzerland from disks purchased in Spain by a Norwegian citizen; the copyright owner might be a Mexican corporation with its principal place of business in Florida, which in turn has authorized a California organization to enforce its rights. If the organization in California sues the Norwegian copier, the Dutch/Australian seller, and the Vermont purchaser, and the purchaser in turn sues the seller, the various disputes might conceivably be governed by Vermont, Australian, Dutch, Virginia, Cayman Islands, Louisiana, Delaware, Swiss, Spanish, or Norwegian, Mexican, Florida, or California law. (Although the latter three are the places where the plaintiff, rather than any of the defendants, is located, choice-of-law clauses in the music licensing agreements might dictate the application of the laws of one of these places against the purchaser of the disks. Such clauses might also dictate the application of the law of some other jurisdiction.)

The question of choice of law is separate from, although related to, the question of jurisdiction. The fact that a court in, say, California has jurisdiction over the case does not necessarily mean that the case will be decided under California law. The California court might apply the laws of Vermont, Australian, the Netherlands, Virginia, the Cayman Islands, Louisiana, Delaware, Switzerland, Spain, Norway, Mexico, or Florida, instead. Which state's or nation's law is to be applied will be determined under the forum state's choice-of-law rules; these vary widely among states. Special problems occurring in the resolution of conflicts-of-laws problems include problems of characterization, *renvoi*, *ordre public*, and *depéçage*, and the difficulty of proving the content and meaning of foreign law (Richman & Reynolds 2002, 165–172).

Characterization: In any choice-of-law problem, the issues of characterization of the subject matter, characterization of the problem as substantive or procedural, and characterization of the applicable law must be addressed. The forum state's law is generally applied to problems of characterization.

Characterization of the subject matter and applicable law can affect the outcome because a state's choice-of-law rules may end up dictating that one state's law is applicable if the problem is characterized as a tort problem, and another's is applicable if the problem is characterized as a contract problem. This result may be indirect; for instance, even though a state's law may apply superficially similar rules to torts and contracts conflicts, it may define the locus of a tort as the place where the injury was suffered and the locus of a contract as the place where performance was to take place. If these two loci are not in the same state, the focus of the litigation may be on whether the case is more properly characterized as one in tort or in contract, with each litigant urging the characterization that results in the application of the law most favorable to that litigant's position.

Characterization of the problem as substantive or procedural may also affect the outcome. When a forum's choice-of-law rule refers to the law of another state, it will apply the substantive law of that state but will still use its own procedural law. Thus, in a case in which the law of another state or country may be applied to some issues, the court must characterize each issue as substantive or procedural (Richman & Reynolds 2002, 160–165).

Renvoi: Occasionally, a court will be directed by statute or prior case law to apply the "whole law" of another jurisdiction, meaning that other state's substantive law and its choice-of-law rules. This is *renvoi*, so called because it may result in a "sending back" to the law of the original state: The second state's choice-of-law rules may refer the case back to the law of the first state, whose own choice-of-law rules originally referred the case to the law of the second state. Applying the second state's choice-of-law rules may also result in a "sending on" to the law of some third state. Even in the absence of a statutory or other directive to apply the whole law of some other state, the question may arise whether a court should consider the other state's conflicts law, either in circumstances where the other state's law would refer back to the forum (remission) or to yet another state (transmission). *Renvoi* is rare in the United States; when it does occur, the original state must either accept or reject the *renvoi* to avoid an endless loop in which each state's law dictates the application of the other state's law rather than its own.

Public policy/Ordre public: A state will not apply another state's law if that law offends its local public policy. However, through the process of *depéçage* ("dismemberment," or applying the laws of different states to different issues in a case) the state's court may apply that part of the law that does not offend the state's public policy, eliminating only the part that offends.

Proof of foreign law: At common law, foreign law (including the law of other U.S. states) had to be pleaded/and proved as fact, and the determination of the foreign law was therefore not ordinarily subject to review on appeal. (Appellate courts ordinarily review only a trial court's conclusions of law, not its findings of fact.) Statutory changes now provide for judicial notice of the law of other states of the United States, although not of the law of foreign countries. A uniform act and a federal rule provide that the court, with the assistance of the parties, is to determine foreign law and that its decision is subject to review. When proof fails or the foreign law cannot be determined, a court may presume that the foreign law is the same as the forum's law (Richman & Reynolds 2002, 173–176).

Cases

Supreme Court
- *Alabama Great Southern Railroad Company v. Carroll*, 97 Ala. 126 (1892)

State Courts
- *In re Schneider's Estate*, 96 N.Y.S. 2d 652 (N.Y. Sup. Ct. 1950)
- *Kilberg v. Northwest Airlines, Inc.*, 172 N.E.2d 34 (N.Y. App. Ct. 1961)
- *University of Chicago v. Dater*, 270 N.W. 175 (Mich. 1936)

Restatement
- American Law Institute, *Restatement of the Law Second: Conflict of Laws* (Philadelphia, Pennsylvania: American Law Institute 1971)

See also: Cloud; Jurisdiction

Sources and Further Reading
Joel R. Reidenberg, "Current Debates in the Conflict of Laws: Choice of Law and Jurisdiction on the Internet: Technology and Internet Jurisdiction," 153 *University of Pennsylvania Law Review* 1951 (2005)

William M. Richman & William L. Reynolds, *Understanding Conflict of Laws* (New York: Matthew Bender, 3d ed. 2002)

David D. Siegel, *Conflicts in a Nutshell* (St. Paul, MN: West, 2d ed. 2005)

Russell J. Weintraub, *Commentary on the Conflict of Laws* (New York: Foundation Press, 6th ed. 2010)

❖ CIPHER AND CIPHERTEXT ❖

See Encryption

❖ CIRCUMVENTION OF TECHNOLOGICAL MEASURES ❖

See DeCSS

❖ CLASS ACTION ❖

A class action lawsuit is one in which a small number of named parties—possibly as few as one—represents the interest of a large class. In order for a class action to be brought under rule 23 of the Federal Rules of Civil Procedure, the class must be "so numerous that joinder of all members is impracticable," there must be "questions of law or fact common to the class," "the claims or defenses of the representative parties" must be "typical of the claims or defenses of the class," and the representative parties must "fairly and adequately protect the interests of the class" (Fed. R. Civ. P. 23(a)). In addition to these four basic elements, certain additional elements are necessary to maintain a class action. There are three ways in which these additional elements may be met: A class action may be maintained if the first four elements are met and

(1) Separate actions by or against the class members would create a risk of inconsistent results or would dispose of or impair the interests of other class members, or

(2) "The party opposing the class has acted or refused to act on grounds generally applicable to the class, thereby making appropriate final injunctive relief or corresponding declaratory relief with respect to the class as a whole," or

(3) There are questions of law or fact common to the members of the class that predominate over any questions affecting only individual members so that a class action is the fairest and most efficient means of adjudication available (Fed. R. Civ. P. 23(b)).

The information technology revolution has brought about no fundamental change in the law of class actions, but class actions have been used as a tool to ensure fairness to consumers. The settlement of a class action brought on behalf of users of Toshiba laptop computers on the grounds that a flaw in the computers could cause incorrect recording of data has been particularly influential (see 91 F. Supp. 2d 942). The settlement, for over $2 billion, led to the immediate filing of class action suits against NEC, Compaq, Hewlett-Packard, and other computer manufacturers. It has also encouraged the use of class actions as a tool for the litigation of mass torts: If the number of plaintiffs in the class is large, lawyers can earn substantial fees even when the amount of damage suffered by each individual plaintiff is very, very small. The legal fees for the lawyers representing the class in the Toshiba case, for example, came to $147.5 million.

For this reason, class actions have been criticized as being more valuable in providing employment for lawyers than in protecting consumer rights. A class action plaintiff, who receives an eight-page notice of class action in the mail, spends 15 minutes filling out the enclosed form, mails it back, and finally receives a check for 3 cents may feel that the reward was not justified by the amount of effort involved.

Against this argument is balanced the argument that some harms may be too small to motivate individual plaintiffs and thus go unchecked in the absence of class action litigation. For example, an ISP with 10 million subscribers might, either through a deliberate intent to mislead the subscribers or through sheer inefficiency, overbill each subscriber by 10 cents per month. It would not be worth any subscriber's time to take the effort to correct the error, and most would probably not even notice. Yet the ISP would receive a substantial benefit: a million dollars a month in unearned revenue. This hardly seems fair, yet the government lacks the resources to pursue all cases of such minor injustice. Rule 23 has the effect of enabling private parties—in this case class action lawyers—to enforce public rights where the government is unable or unwilling to do so.

The Internet may also affect class actions by reducing some of the costs involved: defendants and plaintiff/class lawyers may use Web sites as a means of communicating with class members; in the Toshiba case, for example, Toshiba Corporation used a Web site to communicate with the plaintiffs, presumably reducing printing and mailing costs.

Rule
- Rule 23 of the Federal Rules of Civil Procedure

Cases
- *Lance's Gifts & Collectibles, LLC v. Yahoo!, Inc.*, No. 05–8011, 2005 U.S. App. LEXIS 19378 (8th Cir. 2005)
- *Shaw v. Toshiba America Information Systems, Inc.*, 91 F. Supp. 2d 942 (E.D. Tex. 2000)

See also: Activism and Advocacy Groups; Enforcement

Source and Further Reading
Robert H. Klonoff, *Class Actions and Other Multi-Party Litigations in a Nutshell* (St. Paul, MN: West, 2d ed. 2004)

❖ CLICKWRAP AGREEMENT ❖

When software is downloaded over the Internet or when an Internet user registers for an online service, it is generally necessary for the user to click a box indicating that he or she accepts the terms of a licensing agreement. The first few lines of the licensing agreement generally appear in the scroll window of a dialog box. The agreements are almost never read in their entirety by the users, and are rarely read at all. Nonetheless, they purport to affect the rights of the users of the software or the service. The extent to which they actually do so depends on general principles of contract law and law regarding end-user license agreements in particular.

Clickwrap agreements may be adhesion contracts: contracts prepared by one party in which the other party has no opportunity to negotiate and has no option but to take the contract as written or forgo the transaction. The Uniform Commercial Code, the body of contract law adopted, with slight modifications, by the legislatures of all 50 states, looks upon adhesion contracts without favor. While adhesion contracts are not prohibited by the Code, they are not enforceable if they defeat the reasonable expectations of the adhering party or are oppressive or unconscionable (Stone 2008).

Clickwrap and shrinkwrap agreements have been the subject of intensive lobbying by the software industry, which would like them to be free of the restrictions placed on adhesion contracts. This approach is embodied in the Uniform Computer Information Transactions Act, which like the Uniform Commercial Code is a body of law proposed for adoption by all 50 states, but unlike the Code has been adopted by only two (Maryland and Virginia). Consumer advocates and several state governments have united to oppose the adoption of the Act on the grounds that it would unfairly tilt the balance of bargaining power in favor of software companies (Letter from Attorneys General 1999).

Uniform Act
- Uniform Computer Information Transactions Act (2002), available at http://www.uniformlaws .org/Act.aspx?title=Computer%20Information%20 Transactions%20Act (visited July 21, 2012)
- Uniform Commercial Code (2001), available at http://www.law.cornell.edu/ucc/ucc.table.html (visited July 21, 2012)

See also: App; Choice of Law; Cloud; Contracts; Copyright; Uniform Computer Information Transactions Act

Sources and Further Reading
Letter to NCCUSL from Attorneys General Opposing UCITA (July 23, 1999), available at available at http://www .badsoftware.com/aglet1.htm (visited July 21, 2012)
Lucille M. Ponte, "Getting a Bad Rap? Unconscionability in Clickwrap Dispute Resolution Clauses and a Proposal for Improving the Quality of These Online Consumer 'Products'," 26 *Ohio State Journal on Dispute Resolution* 119 (2011)
Bradford Stone, *Uniform Commercial Code in a Nutshell* (St. Paul, MN: West, 7th ed. 2008)

❖ CLOUD ❖

Cloud computing refers to computing services available over a network rather than on physical infrastructure at the user's location. It may be the software which is offered as a service or the computing platform or the entire infrastructure. The user's data will be stored and processed on infrastructure located elsewhere, and typically owned by someone else. Cloud computing offers advantages; it can lower costs, especially for businesses, because there is no need, or at least less need, to buy, maintain, and upgrade equipment. It also offers greater portability: information stored in the cloud can be accessed from anywhere in the world, without the need to transport stored data.

Cloud computing also presents a number of legal challenges. Because information stored at the direction of the user may infringe intellectual property rights, be defamatory, or be otherwise illegal, the cloud service provider can operate only if protected by a safe harbor. In the United States, safe harbors are provided by 17 U.S.C. § 512 and 47 U.S.C. § 230; § 512 protects providers against liability for copyright infringement, while § 230 protects against most liability for tortious content (see, e.g., *Zeran*, 129 F.3d 327).

Cloud service providers may also face liability for interruptions of service, damage to or destruction of data, and for providing inadequate security. The latter worry has slowed down the growth of cloud computing; many companies are reluctant to entrust their confidential data to a service provider even though, objectively, that service provider's security is much better than the client company could provide for itself.

As with any Internet matter, there are problems of jurisdiction and choice of law. With cloud computing, these are magnified, though, because of the difficulty, for the client, of knowing exactly where its files are stored and where services are being provided. The location in the real world where the infrastructure is located may change frequently to suit the cloud service provider's needs, and in the ordinary course of business there would be no need for the service provider to inform the client of the change, or for the client to keep track of such changes.

Matters of provider liability and, to some extent, of jurisdiction and choice of law can be addressed in the contract between the cloud service provider and the client. As with any relatively new business practice, such contracts may not anticipate all of the problems that can arise; in addition, they may be subject to the same concerns as other clickwrap agreements, especially when one party has greater bargaining power.

Statutes
- Communications Decency Act, 47 U.S.C. § 230
- Online Copyright Infringement Liability Limitation Act (Digital Millennium Copyright Act, Title II), 17 U.S.C. § 512

Case
- *Zeran v. America Online, Inc.*, 129 F.3d 327 (4th Cir. 1997)

See also: Choice of Law; Clickwrap Agreement; Contracts; Digital Millennium Copyright Act, Title II; Hacking; Internet Service Provider; Jurisdiction; Open Source; Privacy

Sources and Further Reading

Amazon Web Services, Amazon Elastic Compute Cloud (EC2) User Guide (2012)

"Business Computing: The Cloud Crowd," *The Economist*, October 6, 2012, at 76

"Data Centres: Not a Cloud in Sight," *The Economist Technology Quarterly*, September 21, 2002

Horacio E. Gutierrez, "Peering through the Cloud: The Future of Intellectual Property and Computing," 20 *Federal Circuit Bar Journal* 589 (2011)

Kris Jamsa, *Cloud Computing* (Burlington, MA: Jones & Bartlett Learning, 2012)

David S. Linthicum, *Cloud Computing and SOA Convergence in Your Enterprise: A Step-by-Step Guide* (Boston: Addison-Wesley Publishing Co., 2009)

Lars Nielsen, *The Little Book of Cloud Computing, 2013 Edition: Including Coverage of Big Data Tools* (Wickford, RI: New Street Communications, 2013)

George Reese, *Cloud Application Architectures: Building Applications and Infrastructure in the Cloud* (Sebastopol, CA: O'Reilly Media, 2009)

John Rhoton, *Cloud Computing Explained: Implementation Handbook for Enterprises* (Tunbridge Wells, UK: Recursive Press, 2009)

John Rhoton & Risto Haukioja, *Cloud Computing Architected: Solution Design Handbook* (Tunbridge Wells, UK: Recursive Press, 2011)

Barrie Sosinsky, *Cloud Computing Bible* (Indianapolis: Wiley Publishing, 2009)

Patrick Van Eecke, "Cloud Computing Legal Issues," DLA Piper Brussels, available at http://www.isaca.org/Groups/Professional-English/cloud-computing/GroupDocuments/DLA_Cloud%20computing%20legal%20issues.pdf (visited March 29, 2013)

Vic (J.R.) Winkler, "Cloud Computing: Legal and Regulatory Issues," *TechNet Magazine* (May 2012), available at http://technet.microsoft.com/en-us/magazine/hh994647.aspx

---

CODES AND CODE-BREAKING

See Encryption

❖ .COM ❖

".com" is the most universally familiar of the top-level domains; it is intended to indicate the address of a commercial enterprise, but many noncommercial organizations and individuals use .com addresses as well. The phrase "dot-com" or "dot.com" is also used to refer to Internet-based businesses as a category, particularly in reference to the stock market bubble of the late 1990s.

The .com domain name was originally created in 1984–85 by Jon Postel and Joyce Reynolds of the Network Working Group, along with five other generic top-level domains: .edu, .gov, .mil, .net, and .org (Postel & Reynolds 1984). The .com domain name is now administered by VeriSign (VeriSign 2004).

As the best-known and most popular top-level domain, .com has been especially plagued by cybersquatting and domain name disputes. These disputes can be resolved under the Uniform Domain Name Dispute Resolution Policy of the Internet Corporation for Assigned Names and Numbers, or in court under the Anticybersquatting Consumer Protection Act of 1999 (15 U.S.C. § 1125(d)). The .com top-level domain is also experiencing resource depletion; all or nearly all of the desirable domain names within it have already been registered.

See also: Cybersquatting; Domain Name Registration; Internet Corporation for Assigned Names and Numbers; .xxx

Sources and Further Reading

"About Verisign," Verisign, available at http://www.verisigninc.com/en_US/company-information/about-verisign/index.xhtml (visited October 2, 2012)

Jon Postel & Joyce Reynolds, "Domain Requirements," Network Working Group Request for Comments: 920 (October 1984), available at http://www.ietf.org/rfc/rfc920.txt

"Verisign's Sale of Authentication Services Business to Symantec Closes," Verisign (August 9, 2010), available at https://investor.verisign.com/releasedetail.cfm?releaseid=497643

❖ COMMUNICATIONS DECENCY ACT ❖

The Communications Decency Act of 1996 (CDA) was the first law passed by Congress attempting to address the availability of pornography and obscene materials to minors over the Internet. The CDA was unsuccessful; its censorship provisions were ultimately struck down by the Supreme Court as unconstitutional (although its safe harbor provision remained), and even had it been enforced would have been ineffective against pornography originating outside the United States.

The CDA attempted to restrict the access of minors to pornography in two ways, each of which raised First Amendment issues. The first restrictive provision imposed a penalty on any person who knowingly transmitted "obscene" or "indecent" material to recipients known to the sender to be under 18 years of age. The second imposed a penalty on any person who used an "interactive computer service" to transmit to specific persons under age 18, or to "display in a manner available to" persons under 18, "any comment, request, suggestion, proposal, image, or other communication that, in context, depict[ed] or describe[d], in terms patently offensive as measured by community standards, sexual or excretory activities or organs" (47 U.S.C. § 223(d); amended in 2003 to read "any comment, request, suggestion, proposal, image, or other communication that, is obscene or child pornography" in an attempt to conform to the Supreme Court's holding discussed next; superfluous comma in original).

The constitutional problem posed by the first prohibition involved the definition of "indecent"; the Supreme Court had long since established that obscene material was not entitled to First Amendment protection. The Court had also, however, distinguished indecent speech from obscenity and stated that indecent speech among adults, even though offensive, was constitutionally protected.

The constitutional problem posed by the second prohibition involved the scope of "patently offensive" content covered by the statute. The test developed by the Supreme Court in 1973 in *Miller v. California* provides that material is obscene if

(a) "the average person, applying contemporary community standards would find that the work taken as a whole appeals to the prurient interest;"

(b) "the work depicts or described, in a patently offensive way, sexual conduct specifically defined by the applicable state law; and"

(c) "the work, taken as a whole, lacks serious literary, artistic, political, or scientific value" (413 U.S. at 39).

The CDA's prohibition incorporated portions of this test: the "community standards" prong and part of the "patently offensive" prong (although it omitted Miller's reference to "applicable state law"). Nothing was said about works that might have "serious literary, artistic, political, or scientific value."

The CDA provided a safe harbor for content providers and Internet service providers who took "good faith, reasonable, effective and appropriate actions under the circumstances to restrict or prevent access by minors . . . including any method which [was] feasible under available technology" (47 U.S.C. § 223(d)(5)).

The CDA was immediately challenged by First Amendment advocates, including the ACLU. In a lengthy (175 pages) opinion, a three-judge panel of the U.S. District Court for the Eastern District of Pennsylvania unanimously found the restrictive provisions of the CDA unconstitutional because it had the effect of banning constitutionally protected, albeit "indecent," adult speech over the Internet. Two of the three judges also found that the CDA was unconstitutionally vague under the Fifth Amendment because it did not enable content providers to reasonably distinguish between permitted and prohibited speech (*ACLU v. Reno*, 929 F. Supp. 824).

On appeal, the U.S. Supreme Court affirmed. Seven justices joined in the majority opinion; two (O'Connor and Rehnquist) wrote separate opinions, concurring in part and dissenting in part. The Court affirmed the District Court's finding that the Internet, as a unique communications medium that had never been subject to government regulation, was entitled to the highest level of constitutional protection.

The Court found that the terms "indecent" and "patently offensive" were unconstitutionally vague under the First Amendment. (The Court did not reach the Fifth Amendment vagueness issue addressed by the District Court because it struck down the provisions on First Amendment grounds.) As a result of this vagueness, the CDA functioned as a content-based blanket restraint and could not be analyzed as a time, place, and manner restriction. The CDA's purpose was to regulate children's access to "indecent" material; its effect, however, was to restrict constitutionally protected adult speech. The goal of regulating children's access to indecent material could have been achieved by a less-restrictive alternative; the burden on adult speech thus was not justified by the goal of the CDA (*Reno v. ACLU*, 521 U.S. 844).

Statute
- Communications Decency Act of 1996, Pub. L. No. 104–104, § 502, 1996 U.S.S.C.A.N. (110 Stat.) 56,133 (later codified at 47 U.S.C. § 223)

Case
- *American Civil Liberties Union v. Reno*, 929 F. Supp. 824 (E.D. Pa. 1996), affirmed sub nom, *Reno v. American Civil Liberties Union*, 521 U.S. 844 (1997)

See also: Censorship; Child Online Protection Act; Children's Internet Protection Act; Constitutional Law; Declaration of the Independence of Cyberspace; First Amendment; Indecency; Obscenity; Pornography

Sources and Further Reading
Robert Cannon, "The Legislative History of Senator Exon's Communications Decency Act: Regulating Barbarians on the Information Superhighway," 49 *Federal Communications Law Journal* 51 (1996)

Kevin W. Saunders, *Saving Our Children from the First Amendment* (New York: New York University Press, 2003)

Madeleine Schachter, *Law of Internet Speech* (Durham, North Carolina: Carolina Academic Press, 3d ed. 2008)

Kristina M. Sesek, "Twitter or Tweeter: Who Should Be Liable for a Right of Publicity Violation under the CDA?" 15 *Marquette Intellectual Property Law Review* 237 (2011)

Cass R. Sunstein, *Republic.Com 2.0* (Princeton, NJ: Princeton University Press 2009)

❖ COMPUTER FRAUD AND ABUSE ACT ❖

See Hacking

❖ COMPUTER MAINTENANCE COMPETITION ASSURANCE ACT ❖

See Digital Millennium Copyright Act, Title III

❖ COMPUTER PROGRAM ❖

The Copyright Act of 1976 (as amended in 1980) defines a computer program as "a set of statements or instructions to be used directly or indirectly in a computer in order to bring about a certain result." The definition of copyrightable computer programs extends to operating systems as well as applications.

While computer programs are copyrightable as literary works, their patentability has been much less clear, and the approach of the U.S. and other governments has varied over time. In 1966, the President's Commission on the Patent System issued a report opposing the grant of patents for computer programs. The President's Commission was influenced by the United States Patent and Trademark Office (USPTO), which had been overwhelmed with computer hardware patents and opposed the idea of software patents. Although in 1969 the Court of Customs and Patent Appeals had held that software for an analog computer was patentable, in 1972, the U.S. Supreme Court, relying heavily on the President's Commission report, held that a mathematical algorithm used in a computer program was not patentable (*Gottschalk*, 409 U.S. 63). This was widely, if incorrectly, understood in the United States and Europe as a statement that computer programs themselves were unpatentable, and the USPTO suspended all pending computer program patent applications. As a result, copyright rather than patent became the main mechanism for protecting intellectual property rights in software. This has had significant consequences: it is much easier to obtain a copyright than to obtain a patent, and once obtained a copyright lasts for far longer than a patent; in information technology industry terms copyright, which can easily endure for over a century, might as well be eternal.

It was not until 1981 that the Supreme Court backtracked from this position; the USPTO began to accept applications for, and issue, software patents (*Diamond*, 450 U.S. 175). But the USPTO remained, if not overtly hostile, at least skeptical toward the idea. Only after a 1994 decision of the Court of Appeals for the Federal Circuit did the USPTO publish guidelines recognizing the patentability of a wide range of computer programs and related inventions (*In re Alappat*, 33 F.3d 1526). In yet another reversal, however, the test used to establish patentability in *Alappat* was abrogated by the Federal Circuit's decision in *In re Bilski* (545 F.3d 943), which established (or, arguably, returned to) the "machine or transformation" test. While *In re Bilski* dealt with business methods patents, its logic is equally applicable to software patents. This was hinted at by the U.S. Supreme Court in its opinion affirming the decision of the Federal Circuit, when it approvingly cited *Diamond v. Diehr*, a case upholding the patentability of a procedure for molding rubber with an incorporated computer program (*Bilski v. Kappos*, 130 S. Ct. at 3227; *Diamond*, 450 U.S. 175).

The U.S. position regarding the patentability of computer programs has influenced the development of patent law elsewhere. Some of the changes in the U.S. position on this issue have been followed and some have not, leading to inconsistencies between U.S. law and the law of other countries. For example, the European Patent Convention provides that computer programs are not patentable subject matter (European Patent Convention, art. 52(2)(c)), although a decision of the European Patent Office (EPO) has held otherwise (*International Business Machines*, 1999), and the EPO continues to wrestle with this problem (*Patentability of Programs for Computers*, 2010). The patentability of computer programs remains a controversial issue in both the United States and the European Union (EU), and elsewhere as well; further changes in this area seem likely. The many changes and reversals in direction, continuing in recent years, indicate an area of law that is still in flux. The recent adoption of a unitary EU patent has added an extra layer of complexity.

Treaty
- Convention on the Grant of European Patents, 5 October 1973, 13 I.L.M. 276, text as amended through December 10, 1998, available at http://www.epo.org/law-practice/legal-texts/html/epc/2010/e/ma1.html (visited January 6, 2013) [European Patent Convention]

Statutes
- Copyright Act of 1976, 17 U.S.C. § 114
- Patent Act, 35 U.S.C. §§ 101 et seq.

Cases
Supreme Court
- *Bilski v. Kappos*, 130 S. Ct. 3218 (2010)
- *Diamond v. Diehr*, 450 U.S. 175 (1981)
- *Ebay Inc. v. MercExchange, L.L.C.*, 547 U.S. 388 (2006)
- *Gottschalk v. Benson*, 409 U.S. 63 (1972)

Federal Appellate Courts
- *Apple Computer, Inc. v. Franklin Computer Corp.*, 714 F.2d 1240 (3d Cir. 1983)
- *AT&T Corp. v. Excel Communications, Inc.*, 172 F.3d 1352 (Fed. Cir. 1999)
- *In re Alappat*, 33 F.3d 1526 (Fed. Cir. 1994)
- *In re Bilski*, 545 F.3d 943 (Fed. Cir. 2008)
- *State Street Bank & Trust v. Signature Financial Group, Inc.*, 149 F.3d 1368 (Fed. Cir. 1999), certiorari denied, 525 U.S. 1093

European Patent Office, Technical Board of Appeal
- Case T 0935/97–3.5.1., *International Business Machines Corp.*, Technical Board of Appeal of the European Patent Office, (February 4, 1999)
- Case G 0003/08, *Patentability of Programs for Computers*, Enlarged Board of Appeal of the European Patent Office pursuant to Article 112(1)(b) EPC (November 12, 2010)

See also: App; Copyright; Copyright Infringement; Digital Millennium Copyright Act, Title III; International Patent Protection; Patent

Sources and Further Reading
Press Release, European Parliament, *Parliament Approves EU Unitary Patent Rules* (December 11, 2012), available at http://www.europarl.europa.eu/news/en/pressroom/content/20121210IPR04506/html/Parliament-approves-EU-unitary-patent-rules
Stephen Fishman, *Copyright Your Software* (Berkeley, CA: Nolo Press, 3d ed. 2001)
Pamela Samuelson et al., "A Manifesto concerning the Legal Protection of Computer Programs," 94 *Columbia Law Review* 2308 (1994)
Pamela Samuelson, "Benson Revisited: The Case against Patent Protection for Algorithms and Other Computer-Related Inventions," 39 *Emory Law Journal* 1025 (1990)

❖ CONSTITUTIONAL LAW ❖

Several areas of the U.S. Constitution touch upon problems arising in computer and Internet law. Two areas that have attracted a great deal of legislative activity and litigation are the Patent and Copyright Clause and the First Amendment. The Patent and Copyright Clause (Art. I, §8, clause 8) provides that Congress shall have the power "to promote the Progress of Science and useful Arts, by securing for limited Times to Authors and Inventors the exclusive Right to their respective Writings and Discoveries"; this clause provides the basis for U.S. copyright and patent law.

The First Amendment provides a guarantee of freedom of expression that is at the heart of the ongoing debate over a variety of unpopular uses of the Internet, ranging from spam to pornography and racist hate Web sites. Other areas of constitutional law may also be affected by technological advances. For example, the scope of the Fourth Amendment's protection against unreasonable searches and seizures is growing increasingly difficult to assess as information technology makes it possible for law enforcement officials to view information kept on home computers or exchanged over the Internet.

See also: America Invents Act; Censorship; Child Online Protection Act; Child Pornography; Children's Internet Protection Act; Communications Decency Act; Copyright; Digital Millennium Copyright Act; Digital Millennium Copyright Act, Title I; First Amendment; Indecency; Obscenity; Patent; Pornography; Privacy; Spam

Source and Further Reading
Jerome A. Barron & C. Thomas Dienes, *Constitutional Law in a Nutshell* (St. Paul, MN: West, 7th ed. 2009)

❖ CONSUMER BROADBAND AND DIGITAL TELEVISION PROMOTION ACT ❖

The Consumer Broadband and Digital Television Promotion Act was a proposed law that would have greatly enhanced the content industry's control over digital recordings purchased by consumers. Senator Fritz Hollings (D-SC) introduced the Act, originally drafted as the Security Systems and Standards Certification Act, in the Senate in 2002. The Act was another salvo in the content industry's ongoing fight against digital piracy in general and online file-sharing in particular. Had it become law, it would have required equipment manufacturers, including computing device manufacturers, to incorporate piracy detection and prevention technology into all playback equipment, including computing devices. The Act would also have outlawed the sale or shipment of any devices not incorporating this security technology, and would have prohibited the removal or alteration of the security technology (Consumer Broadband and Digital Television Promotion Act, §§ 3–6). Violations would have been punishable under the scheme set by Title I of the Digital Millennium Copyright Act (DMCA), including fines of up to $1 million and prison terms of up to 10 years (17 U.S.C. § 1204).

The Act was unpopular not only with consumer advocates, who objected to the further restriction of users' already-restricted ability to make copies within the limits of fair use, but also with equipment manufacturers. The law proposed to impose an expense on manufacturers in order to add a feature to their product; because the feature was one the consumers emphatically did not want, it would have been difficult or impossible for the manufacturers to recoup the added cost by passing it along to the consumers. An emotionally heated debate arose between equipment makers and the content industry; at one point Leslie L. Vadasz, then senior vice president of Intel Corporation, described the entertainment industry as "a pimple on the elephant's rear end," the elephant being the equipment manufacturing industry.

In a victory for equipment manufacturers and consumers, the Recording Industry Association of America (RIAA) agreed to withdraw its support for the bill in exchange for concessions on the part of the computer industry (Unexpected Harmony 2003).

Proposed Act
- Consumer Broadband and Digital Television Promotion Act, S. 2048, 107th Cong., (2d Sess. 2002), available at http://thomas.loc.gov/cgi-bin/query/z?c107:S.2048 (visited July 23, 2012)

Statute
- Digital Millennium Copyright Act, §§ 1201–1204

See also: Content Industry; Copyright; Digital Millennium Copyright Act, Title I; Fair Use (Copyright); Macrovision; Piracy

Sources and Further Reading
Declan McCullagh and Milana Homsi, "Leave DRM Alone: A Survey of Legislative Proposals relating to Digital Rights Management Technology and Their Problems," 2005 *Michigan State Law Review* 317 (2005)
"Unexpected Harmony: The Music and Computer Industries Make Peace, but Differences Remain," *The Economist* (January 23, 2003), available at http://www.economist.com/node/1549398
"We've Won, for Now," www.stoppoliceware.org (visited October 22, 2004)

❖ CONTENT INDUSTRY ❖

The content industry is composed of those businesses deriving their profits from the control of intellectual property rights, especially copyright in books, music, and movies. While it could be said to include the creators of content, the term is usually used to refer to the owners of intellectual property rights in that content, who may be but often are not the content creators. Typically, the content industry purchases or licenses intellectual property rights from the creators, or acquires the rights because the content is created for hire. The content industry then reproduces the content—a music CD, for example—and sells it to the public.

The business model of the content industry, especially the music sector, has been under stress in recent years. The music industry's pre-Internet model involves the bundling of a dozen or more songs in a single package; in order to purchase one song, the consumer must also purchase a dozen or so other songs that he or she may not want.

The Internet makes it possible to exchange and record copies of individual songs. Companies not part of the traditional content industry have made varying uses of this capability. In the early days of the Internet a company called MP3.com placed tens of thousands of copyrighted songs on its servers and made them available to subscribers who could demonstrate, by placing a recorded CD in the disk drive of their computers, that they owned, or at least had access to, a legitimate (licensed) copy of the copyrighted version of the material. Representatives of the content industry immediately sued MP3.com; the federal district court for the Southern District of New York found that MP3.com's use of its CDs exceeded the limits of fair use of copyrighted material (*UMG Recordings*, 92 F. Supp. 2d 349).

The content industry faced its next serious threat in Napster, a service that enabled users to view directories of music files on other users' computers and to download those files (*Napster*, 239 F.3d 1004). After intensive litigation, Napster was shut down. The demise of Napster, however, led immediately and predictably to the rise of numerous imitators. Industry attempts at using the Internet to sell music failed to win consumer approval not only because of the cost of the music (which might have been counterbalanced by the greater availability of music on record company sites and the greater reliability of those sites) but also because of restrictions placed on the content, such as a restriction that the downloaded file could be played only on the computer to which it was downloaded and could not be copied for use in a home audio system or car stereo.

The first successful large-scale attempt to offer copyrighted music content with few restrictions was Apple Computer's iTunes.com; iTunes offered (and continues to offer) individual songs, not bundled as albums, for around a dollar each, and has been popular with the public.

The long-term threat to the music content industry is not file-sharing, but the fact that it is no longer necessary for artists to sell songs to a record company for bundling and distribution to the public. Aside from preexisting contract obligations for some established artists, there is nothing to stop musicians from offering their songs directly to an online retailer such as iTunes. The music content industry may eventually find that the most valuable service it can offer musicians is not distribution but publicity.

Eventually, most sales of music may take place directly from the content creators to the consumers through such intermediaries as iTunes; however, the future of other forms of content such as books and movies is more difficult to predict. Music, after all, is cheap to create; while artistic inspiration is priceless, the actual cost of making a studio recording of a song is within the reach of most aspiring musicians. And music files are relatively small; an MP3 of a three-minute popular song may be stored in only three megabytes or so, while a noncompressed 20-minute digital recording sufficient to satisfy the most demanding audiophile can fit in a few hundred megabytes.

Movies are much larger, but increasing broadband speeds and the spread of broadband access have made them easy to copy and share online as well. But while movie piracy is significant, it has proved less of a threat to the industry than music piracy has to the music industry. There are several reasons for this. First of all, box office receipts, or more precisely rentals to cinemas, have traditionally formed a larger part of the movie industry's revenues than concert receipts have of the music industry's watching a movie at home is not a substitute for a night out. Second, movies are not bundled; they are sold as individual works, and the consumer is not forced to buy unwanted movies in order to buy the desired one. Third, movies recorded on DVD or videotape are relatively cheap; a movie that costs tens of millions of dollars to make typically sells for about the same price as a CD that costs tens of thousands of dollars to make. Fourth, the movie industry was quicker to realize the possibilities of digital recording than was the music industry; movie DVDs typically fill the otherwise unused space on the disk with additional content such as alternate language tracks, scenes that ended up on the cutting-room floor, interviews with the cast, video games, and assorted trivia. Fifth, most digitally recorded movies contain copy protection that it is illegal, if not particularly difficult, to circumvent. And sixth, because online movie piracy became technologically practical for most users only after online music piracy was well established, the movie

industry was able to learn from the music industry's mistakes and avoid some of its most disastrous missteps. Finally, because motion picture studios, unlike record companies, are creators as well as marketers of content, they are in a better position than the record companies to offer content directly to the public via the Internet.

Books are also somewhat less threatened by online piracy. Although an entire book will fit in a very small file, many consumers prefer printed books, and the cost of printing, let alone binding, a downloaded book generally exceeds that of purchasing the generally higher-quality printed version. In the case of e-books, retailers have been more effective than content creators or publishers in addressing piracy. Booksellers Amazon.com and Barnes & Noble have also been successful in marketing high-quality, low-cost e-book readers and then selling copy-protected content that can be directed to those readers; convenience and customer loyalty have provided some protection against piracy. Reference works, however, are more threatened, because few people read them in their entirety. High-cost reference works such as the *Oxford English Dictionary* have addressed this problem with copy protection on their software versions and by offering online subscription versions.

Statute
- Copyright Act of 1976, 17 U.S.C. §§ 101–1332

Cases
Federal Appellate Courts
- *A&M Records, Inc. v. Napster, Inc.,* 239 F.3d 1004 (9th Cir. 2001)

Federal District Courts
- *Metro-Goldwyn-Mayer Studios, Inc. v. Grokster, Ltd.,* 259 F. Supp. 2d 1029 (C.D. Cal. 2003), vacated and remanded, 545 U.S. 913 (2005)
- *UMG Recordings, Inc., v. MP3.com, Inc.,* 92 F. Supp. 2d 349 (S.D.N.Y. 2000)

See also: Audio Home Recording Act; Copyright; Copyright Alert System; Copyright Infringement; DeCSS; Digital Audio Works; Digital Millennium Copyright Act, Title I; Digital Rights Management; E-Books; File-Sharing; File-Sharing and the Courts (Attempts to Control Technology); File-Sharing and the Courts (Litigation against Individual Users); File-Sharing (Other Media); Macrovision; P2P; Piracy; Recording Industry Association of America; Sonny Bono Copyright Term Extension Act; Stop Online Piracy Act

Sources and Further Reading
David Carnoy, "Kindle E-Book Piracy Accelerates," CNET (February 18, 2011) available at http://reviews.cnet .com/8301-18438_7-20033437-82.html

Mark A. Lemley, "Media & Content Industry: Is the Sky Falling on the Content Industries?" 9 *Journal on Telecommunications and High Technology Law* 125 (2011)

Lawrence Lessig, *The Future of Ideas: The Fate of the Commons in a Connected World* (New York: Random House, 2001)

Robert Levine, *Free Ride: How the Internet is Destroying the Culture Business and How the Culture Business Can Fight Back* (New York: Doubleday, 2011)

"The Meaning of iPod," *Economist Technology Quarterly* (June 12, 2004), available at http://www.economist.com/node/2724432

Trevor Merriden, *Irresistible Forces: The Business Legacy of Napster and the Growth of the Underground Internet* (New York: John Wiley & Sons, 2002)

"The Music Business: Universal's Gamble," *The Economist*, July 21, 2012, at 57

❖ CONTENT SCRAMBLE SYSTEM ❖

See DeCSS

❖ CONTRACTS ❖

A contract is an agreement between two or more parties that creates legally binding and enforceable rights and obligations. The advent of computer technology and Internet commerce has probably resulted in an increase in the number of contracts formed across state and national boundaries, with consequent conflict-of-laws issues. The two areas in which the law of contracts has been most heavily impacted, however, are e-commerce—now a new area of contracts law—and end-user license agreements: agreements that purport to limit the intellectual property and other rights of consumers of software.

The contracts laws of the states of the United States are for the most part based upon the Uniform Commercial Code (UCC). The UCC limits the enforceability of end-user license agreements of the "take it or leave it" variety, such as shrinkwrap or clickwrap agreements. Contracts of this sort, which are prepared by one party and in which the other party is in a weaker bargaining position and has no opportunity to negotiate terms, are known as adhesion contracts and are disfavored under the UCC. While not automatically invalid, adhesion contracts will generally not be enforced if their terms are oppressive or unconscionable or if they defeat the reasonable expectations of the weaker (or "adhering") party. Ambiguities are generally strictly construed against the drafter and in favor of the adhering party.

The rise of e-commerce has also required changes in contract law, particularly to deal with the problem of signatures when the parties never exchange any physical documents. A federal statute, the Electronic Signatures in Global and National Commerce Act, addresses this problem by providing that in most cases "a signature, contract, or other record relating to such transaction may not be denied legal effect, validity, or enforceability solely because it is in electronic form" (15 U.S.C. § 7001(a)(1)).

Statute

- Electronic Signatures in Global and National Commerce Act (E-Sign), 15 U.S.C. §§ 7001 et. seq.

Uniform Acts

- Uniform Commercial Code (2001), available at http://www.law.cornell.edu/ucc/ucc.table.html (visited July 23, 2012)
- Uniform Computer Information Transactions Act (2002), available at http://www.uniformlaws .org/Act.aspx?title=Computer%20Information%20 Transactions%20Act (visited July 23, 2012)
- Uniform Electronic Transactions Act (1999), available at http://uniformlaws.org/Act .aspx?title=Electronic%20Transactions%20Act (visited July 23, 2012)

See also: App; Choice of Law; Clickwrap Agreement; Cloud; Contracts; E-Commerce; Jurisdiction; Recognition and Enforcement of Judgments

Sources and Further Reading

Jeffrey Ferriell & Michael Navin, *Understanding Contracts* (New York: Matthew Bender, 2d ed. 2004)

Christina Ramberg, *Internet Marketplaces: The Law of Auctions and Exchanges Online* (Oxford, UK: Oxford University Press, 2002)

Claude D. Rohwer et al., *Contracts in a Nutshell* (St. Paul, MN: West, 7th ed. 2010)

Bradford Stone, *Uniform Commercial Code in a Nutshell* (St. Paul, MN: West, 7th ed. 2008)

Julie Cromer Young, "From the Mouths of Babes: Protecting Child Authors from Themselves," 112 *West Virginia Law Review* 431 (2010)

❖ COOKIES ❖

A cookie is a small file (usually a text file) placed by a Web page on computers visiting that page. Cookies generally contain information about the visiting computer; they may store information such as passwords and preferences or pages previously viewed. Because cookies collect information about Web browsing by individual users and because they may remain on a computer long after a page is visited, they can raise security and privacy concerns.

Cookies may be used in conjunction with adware and spyware to track a user's online and off-line computer use; cookies may track Web pages viewed and documents opened, and the adware or spyware may then transmit that information to some third party. Cookies may also be used by Web sites to track a user's behavior in that particular site: the documents viewed, the number of times the user visits the site, and so forth. This information may have benign or even beneficial uses; it can help a commercial site to direct a viewer to products the viewer may find interesting, and it can eliminate the necessity for retyping usernames, passwords, and addresses.

Users who feel uncomfortable with cookies can set their Web browser to refuse cookies, or to notify them when a cookie is being placed on their computer, or to delete cookies periodically (such as when the browser is closed or when the computer is shut down). The former choice will mean that some Web pages cannot be viewed at all; the latter provides a compromise for privacy-conscious Web surfers. Because cookies are within users' control to accept or reject, U.S. law does not prohibit the use of cookies to collect information about users' Web browsing habits, even when it is done without the users' knowledge (*DoubleClick*, 154 F. Supp. 2d 497). An exception is made when the users are children, however: the Children's Online Privacy Protection Act requires Web sites that collect information from children under the age of 13 to provide notice of what information they collect from children, how they use the information, and what their practices are regarding disclosure of the information. When the Web sites gather information that might identify or permit communication with the child, they must first obtain the verifiable consent of the child's parents (15 U.S.C. § 6502). And U.S. companies wishing their Web sites to comply with EU laws must keep in mind that in most cases EU law prohibits the placing of cookies on users' computers unless the user opts in. (This differs from the approach of U.S. law, which allows cookies to be placed unless the user opts out.)

Case
- *In re DoubleClick, Inc. Privacy Litigation*, 154 F. Supp. 2d 497 (S.D.N.Y. 2001)

Statute
- Children's Online Privacy Protection Act, 15 U.S.C. §§ 6501–6506

European Union Directive
- Directive 2009/136/EC of the European Parliament and of the Council of 25 November 2009, 2009 O.J. (L 337) 11, art. 2(5)

See also: Adware and Spyware; Children's Online Privacy Protection Act; Data Mining; Doubleclick; Privacy

Sources and Further Reading
Robert Bond, "The EU E-Privacy Directive and Consent to Cookies," 68 *Business Lawyer* 215 (2012)
Terence Craig & Mary Ludloff, *Privacy & Big Data* (Sebastopol, CA: O'Reilly Media, Inc. 2011)
Stephanie A. Kuhlmann, "Do Not Track Me Online: The Logistical Struggles over the Right 'To Be Let Alone' Online," 22 *DePaul Journal of Art, Technology & Intellectual Property Law* 229 (2011)
Saira Nayak, "How This Cookie Crumbled: Deciphering the Compliance Obligations around the EU's Cookie Directive," *Antitrust Source* 1 (December 2012)
Daniel Solove and Paul M. Schwartz, *Privacy Law Fundamentals* (Portsmouth, NH: IAPP Publication, 2011)

❖ COPYLEFT ❖

See Open Source

❖ COPYRIGHT ❖

Copyright is the main form of protection of the rights of authors of computer programs and Internet content; as the name implies, it provides the holder, for a limited time, with a monopoly on the right to make copies of the copyrighted work. Under the Copyright Act of 1976, "original works of authorship fixed in any tangible medium of expression" may be copyrighted (17 U.S.C. § 102(a)); there is no copyright in U.S. government works (17 U.S.C. § 105). In other words, in order to be eligible for copyright protection the thing to be protected must be original, it must be a work of authorship, and it must be fixed in a tangible medium. If a work meets these three requirements, the copyright holder will have the exclusive right to reproduce, distribute, and publicly display or perform the work (including, in the case of sound recordings, performance by digital audio transmission), as well as to prepare derivative works based upon the work (17 U.S.C. §§ 103, 106). For works created after January 1, 1978, this exclusive right will endure for 70 years after the death of the author or, in the case of a work with multiple authors, for 70 years after the death of the last surviving author. For works made for hire and works published anonymously or under a pseudonym, the copyright will endure for 95 years from the date of first publication or 120 years from the date of creation, whichever is shorter (17 U.S.C. § 302).

History: The concept of copyright in modern law owes its existence to an early revolution in information technology: the invention of the printing press. Anglo-American law's first sweeping attempt to control the reproduction of books came in the century after the introduction of the printing press to Britain, with the granting of a royal monopoly on book publishing to the Stationer's Company in 1557. This monopoly lasted until 1695. In the next 15 years alternative publishers flourished; the Stationer's Company lobbied for further legal protection, and in 1710 the British Parliament passed its first copyright act, the Statute of Anne (Leaffer 2010).

The Statute of Anne preserved the rights of the Stationer's Company in works already published for an additional 21 years, until 1731. But it effectively undermined the position of the Stationer's Company by viewing copyright as stemming from the act of creation of the work, rather than from the act of publishing; the purpose of the statute was to encourage "learned men to compose and write useful work." For works created after the date of the statute, copyright was to endure for 14 years and was renewable for a second 14-year term if the author was still alive at the end of the first. For the next 64 years, however, the Stationer's Company managed to convince the British courts that its rights in the works it published, at least, were perpetual; it was not until 1774 that the House of Lords established, in the case of *Donaldson v. Beckett*, that the term of copyright is invariably finite (Leaffer 2010).

In the United States, the establishment of a law of copyrights was one of the powers granted to Congress by the Constitution. The Patent and Copyright Clause provides that Congress shall have the power "to promote the Progress of Science and useful Arts, by securing for limited Times to Authors and Inventors the exclusive Right to their respective Writings and Discoveries" (Art. I, § 8, cl. 8). In the following year, 1790, the country's first Copyright Act established a 14-year copyright, renewable once for an additional 14 years, in books, charts, and maps. This copyright was held by the author or those to whom the author might assign it. The Act was readily adapted to cover new forms of material in response to rapid technological change; for example, in 1865 photographs became copyrightable. Nonetheless, over the following century or so the Act, despite two major overhauls, became increasingly unworkable. The U.S. law of copyright was increasingly out of step with that developing in the rest of the world, and trade in information was increasingly becoming international (Leaffer 2010).

The Copyright Act of 1909, the culmination of a work begun four years earlier at the urging of President Theodore Roosevelt, failed to solve these problems. It doubled the term of copyright protection—from two 14-year terms to two 28-year terms—but failed to bring U.S. copyright law into compliance with the international norms set forth in the 1886 Berne Convention. Major areas of difference were that U.S. law continued to require compliance with certain formalities before a copyright could be claimed, and that U.S. law granted a shorter term of copyright than the Berne Convention's minimum of the lifetime of the author plus 50years. A domestic problem was created by the 1909 Act's grant of copyright to only a few narrowly defined categories of unpublished works; as a result, an unwieldy parallel system of state common-law copyright protection was necessary to protect copyrights in most unpublished works (Leaffer 2010).

As with the 1790 Act, the 1909 Act evolved to take into account new forms of recorded information. Motion pictures, for example, were added to the list of copyrightable works in 1912. But the difficulties of the 1909 Act were apparent from its inception, and in 1955 Congress began a two-decades-long revision process, culminating in the passage of the Copyright Act of 1976 (Leaffer 2010).

The 1976 Act was designed to bring U.S. law more into line with international practice. The United States, as the world's largest exporter of intellectual property, had far more to gain than to lose from complying with international norms and joining the Berne Convention; its failure to do so had been costly and inconvenient for the U.S. content industry.

The 1976 Act preempted state law, eliminating the problem of common-law copyright (17 U.S.C. § 301). It eliminated the renewable 28-year term of copyright, replacing it with the Berne Convention minimum of the lifetime of the author plus 50 years, and with a term of 75 years from publication or 100 years from creation, whichever was less, for anonymous or pseudonymous works and works for hire. It established the broad and flexible subject matter categories still in use. It defined the rights granted to copyright holders, and the limitations on those rights, far more clearly than had been done previously. It failed in one notable respect to bring U.S. law into compliance with Berne Convention standards: formalities regarding registration and the affixing of copyright notice were still required. This problem was resolved with the Berne Convention Implementation Act of 1988, however, and the United States finally joined the Berne Convention, more than a century after it first came into existence. Legislative tinkering has continued; revisions include the Sonny Bono Copyright Term Extension Act, which increases the duration of copyright terms to the lifetime of the author plus 70 years, with a term of 95 years from publication or 120 years from creation, whichever is less, for anonymous or pseudonymous works and works for hire (17 U.S.C. §§ 320, 304); the No Electronic Theft Act, which allows the government to prosecute those who give away copies of copyrighted material as well as those who sell it (17 U.S.C. §§ 101, 506 & 507); and the Digital Millennium Copyright Act, which makes many changes to accommodate the increase in electronic exchange of information (17 U.S.C. §§ 512, 1201–1204).

The last of these three reforms was at least partially driven by the need to keep U.S. law in compliance with international agreements, while the first was partially driven by concerns about the value of U.S. intellectual property exports and the duration of copyright protection in the EU. To allow valuable copyrights to fall into the public domain in the United States after a term of life plus 50 years would bring them into the public domain in Europe as well, because even though the EU has adopted a term of life plus 70 years, the Berne Convention allows it to adopt another state's term when that state's copyright law provides a term that is in compliance with the Berne Convention but shorter than its own. These recent changes to U.S. copyright law in response to international concerns demonstrate the increasingly international nature of copyright law. Because information can now be exchanged quite freely across international borders, protection of copyright must be international in nature if it is to succeed at all.

The 1909 and the original 1976 Act remain important, however, as they may affect rights to works created before January 1, 1978. Determining exactly which copyright term applies to a particular work is complex and depends on a variety of factors, including the exact date the work was first created or published, whether copyright notice was affixed, and whether the original copyright was renewed.

Originality: The level of originality required for copyright protection is low, but not nonexistent. For example, an alphabetical listing of names in a telephone directory is not copyrightable. The arrangement and page numbering of cases in a case reporter may be, however. The mere fact that an author has put effort into assembling a collection of information does not confer copyright; originality, rather than the "sweat of the brow," is what is protected (*Feist*, 499 U.S. 340).

The *scènes a fàire* doctrine provides that work that is too dependent on basic, common ways of treating particular subject matter is not copyrightable. For example, a movie about Germany in the 1930s may include images of German soldiers drinking in beer halls, saying "Heil Hitler" and singing the German national anthem. Because these images are a standard part of any depiction of Germany in that era, they cannot be copyrighted (*Hoehling*, 618 F.2d 972). Similarly, any video game about baseball, football, or basketball will necessarily follow a certain sequence of play and a certain point-scoring system; any martial arts video game will include certain moves. These elements are *scènes a fàire* and not copyrightable (*Data East*, 862 F.2d 204).

Works of authorship: Works of authorship include literary, musical, and dramatic works, pantomimes and choreographic works, works traditionally thought of as "art" (pictorial, graphic, and sculptural works), motion pictures and other audiovisual works, and sound recordings. Copyright will not protect ideas, although when an idea can be expressed in only a limited number of ways, the idea and the expression merge and the expression is uncopyrightable. Nor will copyright protect procedures, processes, systems, or methods of operation (17 U.S.C. § 102). Computer operating systems, however, are not "mere methods of operation" within the meaning of the Copyright Act and are thus copyrightable (*Apple Computer*, 714 F.2d 1240). The exact boundary between a copyrightable computer program and a noncopyrightable "method of operation" is not always easy to determine. For example, threshold values used to determine the best time to replace a hard disk drive are not mere methods of operation and are copyrightable, but the menu command hierarchy of a computer program is a method of operation and not copyrightable (*Compaq*, 908 F. Supp. 1409; *Lotus*, 49 F.3d 807).

Fixed in a tangible medium of expression: The most common forms in which computer programs are recorded—magnetic and optical storage—cannot be read without mechanical aid. Information recorded in such a way is nonetheless "fixed in a tangible medium of expression."

International copyright protection: Even before the advent of the Internet copyright required international protection. Copyrights are granted by national governments; in the absence of a treaty obligation to do so, countries can and will disregard copyrights issued by their neighbors. Entire industries depend on international recognition of copyrights; if the copyright to the Harry Potter series were honored only in Britain, or copyrights in Hollywood films were honored only in the United States, the greater part of the value of those pieces of intellectual property would be lost.

The need for an international copyright regime was already evident by 1878, when Victor Hugo and others began lobbying for the adoption of an international convention. As a result, the Berne Convention for the Protection of Literary and Artistic Works was adopted in 1886, and has evolved through numerous revisions to become the cornerstone of the modern international copyright regime. For over a century, however, the United States was unable to join the convention because of differences between U.S. copyright law and the Berne Convention's requirements. As a result, a parallel system of bilateral and multilateral treaties arose to protect U.S. copyright interests abroad and foreign copyright interests in the United States; these treaties, some of which are still in force, are now chiefly of historical interest.

The Internet era, with its greatly expanded exchange of copyrighted information across national borders, has seen the adoption of several new international copyright treaties. In addition to the Berne Convention, important treaties to which the United States is a party include the Agreement on Trade-Related Aspects of Intellectual Property Rights (TRIPS) and the World Intellectual Property Organization (WIPO) treaties. TRIPS is an annex to the World Trade Organization (WTO) treaty; it addresses many types of intellectual property and provides, through the WTO, enforcement and dispute resolution mechanisms that other treaties lack. The two 1996 WIPO treaties, although they did not enter into force until 2002, led to the adoption of Title I of the DMCA of 1998, among the most significant changes to U.S. copyright law in the decades since the United States joined the Berne Convention. Further changes seem likely; in addresses at Columbia Law School and before the U.S. Congress in March 2013, U.S. Register of Copyrights Maria Pallante called for a new copyright act, saying "I think it is time for Congress to think about the next great copyright act, which will need to be more forward thinking and flexible than before. . .. [A]uthors do not have effective protections, good faith businesses do not have clear roadmaps, courts do not have sufficient direction, and consumers and other private citizens are increasingly frustrated."

Constitution
- United States Constitution, Article I, Section 8, Clause 8

Statute
- Copyright Act of 1976, 17 U.S.C. §§ 101–1332

Treaties
- Agreement on Trade-Related Aspects of Intellectual Property Rights, Marrakesh Agreement Establishing

the World Trade Organization, Annex 1C, April 15, 1994, 33 I.L.M. 81 (1994)
- Convention Concerning the Creation of an International Union for the Protection of Literary and Artistic Works (Berne Convention), September 9, 1886, as last revised at Paris, July 24, 1971 (amended 1979), 25 U.S.T. 1341, 828 U.N.T.S. 221
- WIPO Copyright Treaty, December 20, 1996, 36 I.L.M. 65 (1997)
- WIPO Performance and Phonograms Treaty, December 20, 1996, 36 I.L.M. 76 (1997)

European Union Materials
- Directive 2006/116/EC of the European Parliament and of the Council of 12 December 2006 on the Term of Protection of Copyright and Certain Related Rights, 2006 O.J. (L 372) 12–18
- Council Directive 93/98/EEC of 29 October 1993 Harmonizing the Term of Protection of Copyright and Certain Related Rights, 1993 O.J. (L 290)

Cases
England
- *Donaldson v. Beckett*, 2 Bro. P.C. 129, 1 Eng. Rep. 837 Burr. (4th ed.) 2408, 98 Eng. Rep. 257 (H.L. 1774)

Supreme Court
- *Eldred v. Ashcroft*, 537 U.S. 186 (2003)
- *Feist Publications, Inc. v. Rural Telephone Service Co.*, 499 U.S. 340 (1991)
- *Wheaton v. Peters*, 33 U.S. (8 Pet.) 591 (1834)

Federal Appellate Courts
- *Apple Computer v. Franklin Computer*, 714 F.2d 1240 (3d Cir. 1983), abrogated by *In re Bilski*, 545 F.3d 943 (Fed. Cir. 2008)
- *Data East USA v. Epyx*, 862 F.2d 204 (9th Cir. 1988)
- *Hoehling v. Universal City Studios, Inc.*, 618 F.2d 972 (2d Cir. 1980)
- *Lewis Galoob Toys, Inc. v. Nintendo of America, Inc.*, 964 F.2d 965 (9th Cir. 1992)
- *Sega Enterprises Ltd. v. Accolade, Inc.*, 977 F.2d 1510 (9th Cir. 1992)
- *Williams Electronics, Inc. v. Arctic International, Inc.*, 685 F.2d 870 (3d Cir. 1982)

Federal Trial Courts
- *Compaq Computer Corp. v. Procom Technology, Inc.*, 908 F. Supp. 1409 (S.D. Tex. 1995)
- *Oasis Publishing Company, Inc. v. West Publishing Company*, 924 F. Supp. 918 (D. Minn. 1996)

See also: App; Berne Convention; Content Industry; Copyright Alert System; Copyright Infringement; DeCSS; Digital Millennium Copyright Act; Digital Millennium Copyright Act, Title I; Digital Millennium Copyright Act, Title II; Digital Millennium Copyright Act, Title III; Digital Millennium Copyright Act, Title IV; Digital Millennium Copyright Act, Title V; Digital Rights Management; Fair Use (Copyright); Fan Works; File-Sharing; File-Sharing and the Courts (Attempts to Control Technology); File-Sharing and the Courts (Litigation against Individual Users); File-Sharing (Other Media); International Copyright Protection; Moral Rights; Open Source; Piracy; Public Domain; Public Domain Enhancement Act; Sonny Bono Copyright Term Extension Act; Stop Online Piracy Act; TRIPS; Universal Copyright Convention; WIPO; WIPO Copyright Treaty; WIPO Performance and Phonograms Treaty

Sources and Further Reading
"A Fine Balance: How Much Copyright Protection Does the Internet Need?" *Economist Technology Quarterly* (January 25, 2003), available at http://www.economist.com/node/1534271
Craig Anderson, "Betting on a Retrial, Oracle Defers Copyright Damages in Java Code Case," *Los Angeles Daily Journal*, May 17, 2012, at 4
Craig Anderson, "Java Language Can't Be Copyrighted, Judge Rules," *Los Angeles Daily Journal*, June 1, 2012, at 1
Craig Anderson, "Jury Hands Google a Sweeping Win in Java Trial," *Los Angeles Daily Journal*, May 24, 2012, at 1
Tanya Aplin, *Copyright Law in the Digital Society: The Challenges of Multimedia* (Oxford, UK: Hart Publishing, 2005)
Richard Chused, ed., *A Copyright Anthology: The Technology Frontier* (Cincinnati: Anderson Publishing Co., 1998)
"Copyright and the Internet: Letting the Baby Dance," *The Economist*, September 1, 2012, at 60
"Copyrights: A Radical Rethink," *The Economist* (January 25, 2003), available at http://www.economist.com/node/1547223
Anthony D'Amato & Doris Estelle Long, eds., *International Intellectual Property Anthology* (Cincinnati: Anderson Publishing, 1996)
Michael H. Davis & Arthur Raphael Miller, *Intellectual Property: Patents, Trademarks, and Copyright in a Nutshell* (St. Paul, MN: West, 4th ed. 2007)
Jane C. Ginsburg, "No 'Sweat'? Copyright and Other Protection of Works of Information after Feist v. Rural Telephone," 92 *Columbia Law Review* 338 (1992)
Marshall Leaffer, *Understanding Copyright Law* (New Providence, NJ: LexisNexis, 5th ed. 2010)
Emmanuel Legrand, "Time to Think about 'The Next Great Copyright Act' in the US?" Flashlight 2013 (April 19, 2013), available at http://flashlight2013.com/blog/b_25960_time_to_think_about_the_next_great_copyright_act_in_the_us.html (visited May 13, 2013)
Lawrence Lessig, *Free Culture: How Big Media Uses Technology and the Law to Lock Down Culture and Control Creativity* (New York: Penguin, 2004)
Lawrence Lessig, *Remix: Making Art and Commerce Thrive in the Hybrid Economy* (New York: Penguin Books, 2008)
Robert Levine, *Free Ride: How the Internet is Destroying the Culture Business and How the Culture Business Can Fight Back* (New York: Doubleday, 2011)

Jessica Litman, *Digital Copyright: Protecting Intellectual Property on the Internet* (Amherst, NY: Prometheus, 2000)

Robert P. Merges & Jane C. Ginsburg, *Foundations of Intellectual Property* (New Providence, NJ: LexisNexis, 2006)

David Nimmer, "Codifying Copyright Comprehensibly," 51 *UCLA Law Review* 1233 (2004)

William Patry, *How to Fix Copyright* (Oxford, UK: Oxford University Press, 2011)

Aaron Schwabach, *Fan Fiction and Copyright: Outsider Works and Intellectual Property Protection* (Farnham, Surrey, UK: Ashgate Publishing, 2011)

Richard Stim, *Getting Permission: How to License & Clear Copyrighted Materials Online & Off* (Berkeley, CA: Nolo Press, 4th ed. 2010)

Richard Stim, *Patent, Copyright & Trademark: An Intellectual Property Desk Reference* (Berkeley, CA: Nolo Press, 12th ed. 2012)

Adam D. Thierer & Wayne Crews, *Copy Fights: The Future of Intellectual Property in the Information Age* (Washington, D.C.: Cato Institute, 2002)

Siva Vaidhyanathan, *Copyrights and Copywrongs: The Rise of Intellectual Property and How It Threatens Creativity* (New York: New York University Press, 2001)

❖ COPYRIGHT ALERT SYSTEM ❖

The Copyright Alert System is an attempt by a group of content industry organizations and companies and ISPs to address the content industry's ongoing file-sharing problem through a combination of education and penalties imposed on individual users, up to and including denial of Internet access. The actual work of administering the Copyright Alert System is carried out by the Center for Copyright Information (CCI), an organization set up for that purpose. The members of the CCI include the Motion Picture Association of America (MPAA), the RIAA, and other content-industry groups, as well as ISPs AT&T, Cablevision, Time Warner, Verizon, and Comcast. The CCI in turn contracts much of the work of detecting infringing BitTorrent activity to MarkMonitor, a private company.

As the CCI's Web site somewhat condescendingly describes the practice, artists, moviemakers, and other owners of content join public peer-2-peer (P2P) networks to see if the music, movies, and TV shows they have made available are being shared without permission and in violation of U.S. copyright law. If they notice that a file is being shared illegally, they notify the appropriate ISP and that ISP, in turn, passes on that notice to their subscriber as a Copyright Alert (Center for Copyright Information 2013).

If CCI identifies, or receives a report from MarkMonitor identifying, an infringing BitTorrent activity, it will use a "six strike" process: After the first detected infringing (or possibly infringing) use, the CCI will notify the user's ISP, which will then send the user (the ISP's subscriber) an "alert." The first alert is informational and educational only; the ISP and the CCI take no other action. If a second infringing use is detected, the ISP will send a second alert, similar to the first.

If the infringing use continues and the ISP sends a third or fourth alert, the ISP will ask its subscriber to acknowledge receipt of the alert. With the fifth alert, the ISP may take "mitigation measures." According to the CCI, these may include the following:

- A temporary reduction in Internet speed;
- A temporary downgrade in Internet service tier; or
- Redirection to a landing page for a set period of time, until a subscriber contacts the ISP or until the subscriber completes an online copyright education program (Center for Copyright Information 2013).

After the sixth alert, the ISP must (not may) take mitigation measures.

Although the CCI does provide for review of alerts possibly sent in error, the review process is not likely to mollify innocent recipients:

> Initial educational Alerts are not eligible for the Independent Review Process. If infringing activity on your account continues and you reach the mitigation stage (where your ISP is going to take corrective measures), you will be offered the opportunity to ask for a review (Center for Copyright Information 2013).

When the mitigation stage is reached, "Once you choose to have your Alerts reviewed, you will be asked to complete a series of steps, including paying a $35 fee (you may request a hardship waiver)." If the wording of the alert is as high handed as the wording mentioned earlier, many frustrated customers may simply abandon their ISPs long before then.

The Copyright Alert System has been criticized by the Electronic Frontier Foundation and other consumer advocates (see Phillips 2011). It remains to be seen whether and how lawsuits and market forces will affect it.

Statute
- Copyright Act of 1976, 17 U.S.C. §§ 101–1332

See also: Content Industry; Copyright; Copyright Infringement; File-Sharing; File-Sharing and the Courts (Attempts to Control Technology); File-Sharing and the Courts (Litigation against Individual Users); File-Sharing (Other Media); Internet Service Providers; P2P; Piracy

Sources and Further Reading

Center for Copyright Information, "Memorandum of Understanding" (July 6, 2011), available at http://www.copyrightinformation.org/wp-content/uploads/2013/02/Memorandum-of-Understanding.pdf (visited April 24, 2013)

Center for Copyright Information, "The Copyright Alert System" (2013), available at http://www.copyrightinformation.org/the-copyright-alert-system/ (visited April 24, 2013)

Cyrus Farivar, "Here's What an Actual 'Six Strikes' Copyright Alert Looks Like: Ars Asks and Comcast Obliges, Giving Us Copies of Alerts 1, 2, 4, and 5," *Ars Technica* (February 27, 2013), available at http://arstechnica.com/tech-policy/2013/02/heres-what-an-actual-six-strikes-copyright-alert-looks-like/ (visited April 29, 2013)

Kashmir Hill, "Will the New 'Copyright Alert System' Actually Stop People from Downloading Music and Movies Illegally?" *Forbes* (February 25, 2013), available at http://www.forbes.com/sites/kashmirhill/2013/02/25/copyright-alert-system/ (visited April 24, 2013)

Mary LaFrance, "Graduated Response by Industry Compact: Piercing the Black Box," 30 *Cardozo Arts & Entertainment Law Journal* 165 (2012)

Robert Levine, *Free Ride: How the Internet is Destroying the Culture Business and How the Culture Business Can Fight Back* (New York: Doubleday, 2011)

Abigail Phillips, "The Content Industry and ISPs Announce a 'Common Framework for Copyright Alerts': What Does It Mean for Users?" Electronic Frontier Foundation (July 7, 2011), available at https://www.eff.org/deeplinks/2011/07/content-industry-and-isps-announce-common (visited April 24, 2013)

David Zax, "The "Six Strikes" Copyright Alert System Is Toothless," *MIT Technology Review* (February 26, 2013), available at http://www.technologyreview.com/view/511841/the-six-strikes-copyright-alert-system-is-toothless/ (visited April 24, 2013)

❖ COPYRIGHT INFRINGEMENT ❖

A copyright is infringed when someone not authorized by the copyright holder reproduces, distributes, or publicly displays or performs a copyrighted work (including, in the case of sound recordings, performance by digital audio transmission), or prepares a derivative work (17 U.S.C. § 106), unless the use of the copyrighted material falls within one of the permissible exceptions: the right to make backup copies, fair use, the first sale doctrine, and the four safe harbors for Internet service providers (ISPs)(17 U.S.C. §§ 107–122, 512). Infringement may be direct, contributory, or vicarious.

Reproduces, distributes, or publicly displays: The making, distribution, or public display of a single copy may be sufficient to constitute a copyright infringement if the other elements of infringement are also present.

Derivative works: The copyright holder has the exclusive right to make or license derivative works, but a device (or perhaps program) that enhances the operation of a computer program may not be a derivative work (*Lewis Galoob Toys*, 964 F.2d 965).

Backup copies: The purchaser of a recording of copyrighted material, such as a computer program, has the right to make a backup copy of the copyrighted material as a safeguard against the destruction of the original recording. However, Title I of the DMCA has the practical effect, although ostensibly not the purpose, of prohibiting the making of digital backup copies of media recordings containing some form of copy protection.

Privileges of ISPs: Under Title II of the DMCA, ISPs are not liable for copyright infringement for material passing through their servers if their connection to the infringing material falls within one of the four statutory safe harbors established by the Act. There are safe harbors for ISPs for transitory communications, system caching, storage of information on systems or networks at the direction of users, and information location tools (17 U.S.C. § 512). The safe harbors are necessary to enable ISPs to function; policing all content transmitted over, cached on, stored on, or located via a network for possible copyright infringement would be extremely costly, if not impossible. The four statutory safe harbors are not absolute, however, and ISPs may be required to remove or block infringing content if the copyright owner complies with certain notice procedures (see *Viacom*, 676 F.3d 19).

Fair use: The right of the copyright owner to prevent unauthorized copying is limited by the fair use doctrine. The exact parameters of fair use are poorly defined and are the subject of an ongoing multisided conflict between the varied interests of content producers, copyright holders, equipment manufacturers, and consumers. The definition created by Congress in section 107 of the Copyright Act allows considerable latitude for interpretation:

> [T]he fair use of a copyrighted work, including such use by reproduction in copies or phonorecords or by any other means specified by that section, for purposes such as criticism, comment, news reporting, teaching (including multiple copies for classroom use), scholarship, or research, is not an infringement of copyright. In determining whether the use made of a work in any particular case is a fair use the factors to be considered shall include—
>
> (1) the purpose and character of the use, including whether such use is of a commercial nature or is for nonprofit educational purposes;
> (2) the nature of the copyrighted work;
> (3) the amount and substantiality of the portion used in relation to the copyrighted work as a whole; and
> (4) the effect of the use upon the potential market for or value of the copyrighted work (17 U.S.C. § 107).

Among the established fair uses of computer software is the right to disassemble or decompile a computer program to reverse engineer for compatibility. Copying a music recording that one has purchased on to one's own computer for one's own listening is fair use, but copying music so that large numbers of anonymous individuals may access it over the Internet is not (*Napster*, 239 F.3d 1004). This latter type of online file-sharing of copyrighted material is perhaps the most hotly contested area in the ongoing battle between the content industry and consumers.

The traditional fair use doctrine provides that the purchaser or licensee of copyrighted software may make backup copies, as noted earlier, and may make copies necessary for the use of the program or for diagnostic purposes. Many media recordings, however, especially movies, contain copy protection that prevents the making of digital backup copies. While this copy protection can be circumvented relatively easily, doing so violates the provisions of the DMCA forbidding the circumvention of technological copy-protection measures (17 U.S.C. § 1201). One compromise between the interests of consumers and content owners is the marketing of DVD recordings on physical media bundled with a license (such as an UltraViolet license) to download and stream copies of the same content to multiple devices.

First sale doctrine: The first sale doctrine, set out in section 109 of the Copyright Act, limits the copyright holder's control over the copyrighted material to its first sale. Once a copy of a work has been sold or given away, the purchaser or recipient may dispose of that copy as he or she wishes. The first sale doctrine does not create a right to make copies, but only to freely dispose of an authorized copy and to display that copy at the place where it is located. It does not include the right to display the copy at some other place than the place where it is located, whether by broadcasting, posting on the Internet, or some other means.

Distributors and resellers of copyrighted materials, such as bookstores, must be permitted to resell the copies they purchase in order to function; similarly libraries must be able to lend out copies of books, and individuals who purchase books must be permitted to give them away as gifts. The first sale doctrine permits all of these persons to do so without infringing on the copyright.

Exceptions to the doctrine have been carved out for holders of copyrights in audio recordings and computer software, who retain the right to control rentals of the copyrighted material. Curiously, no similar exception exists for motion picture recordings. One possible explanation may be that the exceptions for audio recordings and computer programs are designed more to deter piracy than to generate revenue directly for copyright holders. The average consumer watches most motion pictures only once, while the average consumer may listen to a favorite audio recording hundreds of times, so the incentives for piracy are much higher, while the costs in time and recording media or disk storage space are much lower. However, Title I of the DMCA provides motion-picture copyright holders with additional antipiracy protections through its provisions prohibiting the circumvention of anticopying technological measures.

The exceptions for computer programs and sound recordings are themselves subject to exceptions for lending by nonprofit libraries and educational institutions, and rentals of computer programs "embodied in a machine or product and which cannot be copied during the ordinary operation or use of the machine or product; or embodied in or used in conjunction with a limited purpose computer that is designed for playing video games and may be designed for other purposes" (17 U.S.C. §§ 109(b), 109(e)). Section 117 of the Copyright Act adds a further exception for copies of computer programs made as a necessary part of using the program, for archival purposes, or in the course of maintenance or repair.

First sale becomes more complicated when copies are made outside the United States. European copyright laws, for example, have few or no rights equivalent to the right of first sale in U.S. law. And the U.S. Supreme Court has recently decided that gray-market copyrighted goods—copies legally made outside the United States that are then brought into the United States—may be resold by the original individual purchaser in competition with copies made in the United States (*Kirtsaeng*, 133 S.Ct. 1351).

Contractual limitations on purchasers' rights: The software end-user license agreement (EULA) can affect these rights, but its effect will be limited by applicable state law, including restrictions on adhesion contracts, and may be preempted by federal copyright law (*Vault Corp.*, 847 F.2d 255).

Contributory infringement: Contributory infringement requires a direct infringement by someone other than the contributory infringer. The contributory infringer must have actual or constructive knowledge of the violation; that is, the contributory infringer must either know of it or be in such a position that a reasonable person similarly situated would know that direct infringement was taking place. This knowledge requirement is essential to both contributory and vicarious liabilities, but there is no knowledge requirement for liability for direct infringement. Finally, contributory infringement also requires that the contributory infringer makes a material contribution to the direct infringer's activities (*Fonovisa*, 76 F.3d 259).

The sale of devices or programs enabling the copying of copyrighted material may become contributory infringement if the primary use of such devices or programs is copyright infringement. The operation of file-sharing services may also be contributory infringement. Under Title I of the DMCA, it is illegal to distribute to others software or hardware designed to enable users to overcome technological measures designed to prevent copying. A reasonable person distributing software or hardware that had no other use than to overcome these technological protective measures should know that direct infringement is taking place, and the distribution of the software or hardware is a material contribution to the direct infringement. A person distributing such hardware or software might thus be liable for contributory infringement as well as for violation of Title I's anticircumvention provisions.

Contributory infringement and inducement: The 2005 case of *MGM v. Grokster* presented the U.S. Supreme Court with a situation in which a third party, Grokster, had materially contributed to direct copyright infringement, but failed to meet the traditional definition of contributory infringement because it lacked knowledge of any specific infringement at a time when it could prevent the infringement. Rather than leaving this gap in third-party copyright infringement law to Congress to resolve through legislation, the Court imported the doctrine of induced infringement from patent law, stating "One infringes contributorily by intentionally inducing or encouraging direct infringement" (*MGM v. Grokster*, 545 U.S. at 930). This inducement-based liability may be viewed as an alternative way of establishing contributory liability: inducement plus material contribution instead of knowledge plus material contribution. It may also be viewed as an alternate, third form of third-party liability for copyright infringement. This latter approach is arguably more theoretically appealing, but the distinction makes little practical difference.

Vicarious infringement: Like contributory infringement, vicarious infringement is defined by case law rather than by statute. Also like contributory infringement, vicarious infringement requires actual or constructive knowledge of a direct infringement by some other person. In addition, the vicarious infringer must have the right and ability to control the direct infringer's actions, and a direct financial benefit from the infringing activity (*Fonovisa,* 76 F.3d 259). The right and ability to control the infringer's actions may result from a continuing relationship such as an employment relationship; for example, officers and directors of a corporation may be liable for copyright infringement committed by employees of the corporation. It may also result from a contract in which the vicarious infringer retains the right to restrict the direct infringer's actions—for example, a contract between an online file-sharing service and a user of the service in which the file-sharing service reserves the right to restrict access. The direct financial benefit from the infringing activity need not be actual payment; if the possibility of engaging in direct copyright infringement brings more users to a file-sharing service, there is a direct financial benefit for vicarious infringement purposes.

Statute
- Copyright Act of 1976, 17 U.S.C. §§ 101–1332

Cases
Supreme Court
- *Metro-Goldwyn-Mayer Studios, Inc. v. Grokster, Ltd.,* 545 U.S. 913 (2005)
- *Sony Corp. of America v. Universal City Studios, Inc.,* 464 U.S. 417 (1984)
- *Kirtsaeng v. John Wiley & Sons, Inc.,* 133 S.Ct. 1351 (2013)

Federal Appellate Courts
- *A&M Records, Inc. v. Napster, Inc.,* 239 F.3d 1004 (9th Cir. 2001), on remand, No. 00–16401, 2001 WL 227083 (N.D. Cal. 2001), affirmed, 284 F.3d 1091 (9th Cir. 2002)
- *Apple Computer v. Franklin Computer Corp.,* 714 F.2d 1240 (3d Cir. 1983)
- *Computer Associates International, Inc. v. Altai, Inc.,* 126 F.3d 365 (2d Cir. 1997)
- *Data East USA v. Epyx,* 862 F.2d 204 (9th Cir. 1988)
- *F.B.T. Productions, LLC v. Aftermath Records,* 621 F.3d 958 (9th Cir. 2010)

- *Fonovisa, Inc. v. Cherry Auction, Inc.,* 76 F.3d 259 (9th Cir. 1996)
- *Gershwin Publishing Corp. v. Columbia Artists Management, Inc.,* 443 F.2d 1159, 1162 (2d Cir. 1971)
- *In re Aimster Copyright Litigation (Aimster II),* 334 F.3d 643 (7th Cir. 2003)
- *Lewis Galoob Toys Inc. v. Nintendo of America, Inc.,* 964 F.2d 965 (9th Cir. 1992)
- *Lotus Development Corp. v. Borland International, Inc.,* 140 F.3d 70 (1st Cir. 1998)
- *Recording Industry Association of America v. Diamond Multimedia Systems, Inc.,* 180 F.3d 1072 (9th Cir. 1999)
- *Red Baron-Franklin Park, Inc. v. Taito Corp.,* 883 F.2d 275 (4th Cir. 1989)
- *Vault Corp. v. Quaid Software Limited,* 847 F.2d 255 (5th Cir. 1988)
- *Vernor v. Autodesk, Inc.,* 621 F.3d 1102 (9th Cir. Wash. 2010)
- *Viacom International, Inc. v. YouTube, Inc.,* 676 F.3d 19 (2d Cir. 2012)

Federal Trial Courts
- *Capitol Records, LLC v. ReDigi, Inc.,* No. 12-CIV-0095-RJS (S.D.N.Y. 2013)
- *Intellectual Reserve, Inc. v. Utah Lighthouse Ministry, Inc.,* 75 F. Supp. 2d 1290 (D. Utah 1999)
- *Metro-Goldwyn-Mayer Studios, Inc. v. Grokster, Ltd.,* 259 F. Supp. 2d 1029, 1046 (C.D. Cal. 2003); vacated and remanded, 545 U.S. 913 (U.S. 2005)
- *NEC v. Intel,* 10 U.S.P.Q. 2d 1177 (N.D. Cal. 1989)
- *Obodai v. Demand Media, Inc.,* No. 11 Civ. 2503 (PKC), 2012 U.S. Dist. LEXIS 83109 (S.D.N.Y. 2012)
- *Ouellette v. Viacom International, Inc.,* No. CV 10–133-M-DWM-JCL, 2012 U.S. Dist. LEXIS 68109 (D. Mont. 2012)
- *Religious Technology Center v. Netcom On-Line Communication Services, Inc.,* 907 F. Supp. 1361 (N.D. Cal. 1995)
- *UMG Recordings, Inc. v. MP3.Com, Inc.,* 92 F. Supp. 2d 349 (S.D.N.Y. 2000)
- *UMG Recordings, Inc. v. Sinnott,* 300 F. Supp. 2d 993 (E.D. Cal. 2004)
- *Universal City Studios, Inc., v. Reimerdes,* 111 F. Supp. 2d 294 (S.D.N.Y. 2000), affirmed by *Universal City Studios, Inc. v. Corley,* 273 F.3d 429 (2nd Cir. 2001)

European Union
- Case C-128/11, *UsedSoft GmbH v. Oracle International Corp.,* Judgment of the Court of First Instance (Grand Chamber) (July 3, 2012), available at http://curia.europa.eu/juris/document/document.jsf?text=&docid=124564&doclang=en&mode=req (visited Dec. 14, 2012)

See also: Berne Convention; Clickwrap Agreement; Content Industry; Copyright; Copyright Alert System; DeCSS; Digital Millennium Copyright Act; Digital Millennium Copyright Act, Title I; Digital Millennium Copyright Act, Title II; Digital Millennium Copyright Act, Title III; Digital Rights Management; Encryption; Fan Works; File-Sharing; File-Sharing and the Courts (Attempts to Control Technology); File-Sharing and the Courts (Litigation against Individual Users); File-Sharing (Other Media); International Copyright Protection; P2P; Piracy; Steganography; Stop Online Piracy Act; WIPO Copyright Treaty; WIPO Performance and Phonograms Treaty

Sources and Further Reading

Richard Chused, ed., *A Copyright Anthology: The Technology Frontier* (Cincinnati: Anderson Publishing Co., 1998)

Michael H. Davis & Arthur Raphael Miller, *Intellectual Property: Patents, Trademarks, and Copyright in a Nutshell* (St. Paul, MN: West, 4th ed. 2007)

Amir Hassanabadi, "Viacom v. YouTube—All Eyes Blind: The Limits of the DMCA in a Web 2.0 World," 26 *Berkeley Technology Law Journal* 405 (2011)

Marshall Leaffer, *Understanding Copyright Law* (New Providence, NJ: LexisNexis, 5th ed. 2010)

Robert Levine, *Free Ride: How the Internet Is Destroying the Culture Business and How the Culture Business Can Fight Back* (New York: Doubleday, 2011)

J. Thomas McCarthy et al., *McCarthy's Desk Encyclopedia of Intellectual Property* (Washington, D.C.: Bureau of National Affairs, 3d ed. 2004)

Robert P. Merges & Jane C. Ginsburg, *Foundations of Intellectual Property* (New Providence, NJ: LexisNexis, 2006)

William Patry, *How to Fix Copyright* (Oxford, UK: Oxford University Press, 2011)

Pamela Samuelson, "Three Reactions to MGM v. Grokster," 13 *Michigan Telecommunications and Technology Law Review* 177 (2006)

Richard Stim, *Getting Permission: How to License & Clear Copyrighted Materials Online & Off* (Berkeley, CA: Nolo Press, 4th ed. 2010)

Richard Stim, *Patent, Copyright & Trademark: An Intellectual Property Desk Reference* (Berkeley, CA: Nolo Press, 12th ed. 2012)

❖ COURT OF APPEALS FOR THE FEDERAL CIRCUIT ❖

The U.S. Court of Appeals for the Federal Circuit has jurisdiction to hear appeals from a variety of specialized federal courts and administrative tribunals. From a computer and Internet law perspective, its most important function is that it is the court in which patent appeals are heard and decided.

From 1929 until 1982, customs and patent appeals were heard in the aptly named U.S. Court of Customs and Patent Appeals. The court served this function until 1982, when it was abolished and its functions were taken over by the newly created Court of Appeals for the Federal Circuit. The

Court of Appeals for the Federal Circuit was created in 1982 by a merger of most of the functions of the U.S. Court of Customs and Patent Appeals and the U.S. Court of Claims. The trial jurisdiction of the U.S. Court of Claims was spun off to the newly created and confusingly named U.S. Claims Court, later renamed (without reducing the likelihood of confusion to any significant degree) the U.S. Court of Federal Claims.

Decisions of the Federal Circuit have had a profound effect on computer and Internet law; for example, the court's decision in *In re Alappat* led the USPTO to adopt rules for the patenting of computer programs (33 F.3d 1526) and its later abrogation of that decision in *In re Bilski*. The Supreme Court, of course, has the final say. Though respecting the expertise of the Federal Circuit, it will at times reverse the Federal Circuit's decision even on core questions of patent law (see, e.g., *KSR*, 550 U.S. 398).

Cases

- *In re Alappat*, 33 F.3d 1526 (Fed. Cir. 1994), abrogated by *In re Bilski*, 545 F.3d 943 (Fed. Cir. 2008)
- *KSR International Co. v. Teleflex, Inc.*, 550 U.S. 398 (2007)

See also: America Invents Act; Business Methods Patent; Computer Program; Patent

Source and Further Reading

William M. Atkinson & Joey H. Foxhall, "Stating the Obvious Gets Easier: The Supreme Court's KSR Decision," *IPL Newsletter*, Winter 2008, at 1

❖ CRACKING ❖

See Hacking

❖ CRYPTOGRAPHY ❖

See Encryption

❖ CSS ❖

See DeCSS

❖ CYBER ❖

The prefix "cyber" is derived by back-formation from the term "cybernetics," first used in 1948 by mathematician and computer pioneer Norbert Wiener in the book *Cybernetics: Or the Control and Communication in the Animal and the*

Machine. Popular imagination seized on the term not so much to describe the general concept of guided feedback systems but as a shorthand reference for Wiener's conception of the *machinea rationcinatrix*, the reasoning machine. Wiener derived the word "cybernetics" from the Greek word *kybernetes*, meaning the helmsman or steersman of a boat.

The use of the term "cyber" enjoyed its media heyday in the 1990s, when it became an almost automatic indicator of media hype; since then its use in new words has declined considerably, and such new cyber terms as do appear are often ironic. Google Trends shows a steady overall decline in searches for the term, with the exception of spikes every November as shoppers search for Cyber Monday bargains. Congress often lags behind the irony curve, though, and the term surfaced again in 2012 in the name of the proposed Cybersecurity Act.

Proposed Legislation

* Cybersecurity Act of 2012, S. 2105, 112th Cong. (2d Sess. 2011–12)

Sources and Further Reading

Becky Hogge, *Barefoot into Cyberspace: Adventures in Search of Techno-Utopia* (Saffron Walden, Essex: Barefoot Publishing, 2011)

Norbert Wiener, *Cybernetics: Or the Control and Communication in the Animal and the Machine* (Cambridge, MA: MIT Press, 2d ed. 1965)

❖ CYBERLAW ❖

The varied areas of law having to do with computers and the Internet have at times been lumped together under the heading "cyberlaw." Cyberlaw might include, for example, areas of business entity law, constitutional law, contract law, criminal law, intellectual property law, and tort law. The use of the term and the sense that it describes something new in the law has generated a cyberskeptic reaction from many legal theorists, who take the view that the law applicable to computer hardware and software and especially to the Internet is in no way separate from the law applicable to off-line situations. Most or all of the legal problems posed by the Internet, the argument runs, are different in degree rather than in kind from the problems posed by previous technologies (Gomes 2002).

The use of the term "cyberlaw" is thus to some extent associated with a particular ideological approach to problems of computer and Internet law. In the minds of some it is associated with a libertarian, laissez-faire approach that can perhaps be summed up succinctly in the adage that "information just wants to be free" or somewhat less succinctly in the Declaration of Independence of Cyberspace, which concludes "We will create a civilization of the Mind in Cyberspace. May it be more humane and fair than the world your governments have made before" (Barlow 1996). Much like the idealistic Internet-frontier mentality that produced it, the term "cyberlaw" seems to be on a long slide into obsolescence.

See also: Declaration of Independence of Cyberspace

Sources and Further Reading

John Perry Barlow, *A Declaration of the Independence of Cyberspace* (February 8, 1996), available at https://projects.eff.org/~barlow/Declaration-Final.html

Ross A. Dannenberg et al., eds., *Computer Games and Virtual Worlds: A New Frontier in Intellectual Property Law* (Chicago: American Bar Association Publishing, 2010)

Gerald R. Ferrera et al., *Cyberlaw: Your Rights in Cyberspace* (Mason, OH: South-Western College Publications, 2001)

Lee Gomes, "Hot Field of Cyberlaw Is So Much Hokum, Some Skeptics Argue," *Wall Street Journal*, July 1, 2002, at B-1

Steven A. Hetcher, *Norms in a Wired World* (Cambridge, UK: Cambridge University Press, 2004)

David R. Koepsell, *The Ontology of Cyberspace: Law, Philosophy and the Future of Intellectual Property* (Chicago: Open Court, 2000)

Lawrence Lessig, *Code and Other Laws of Cyberspace, Version 2.0* (New York: Basic Books, 2006)

Joseph H. Sommer, "Against Cyberlaw," 15 *Berkeley Technology Law Journal* 1145 (2000)

Timothy Wu, "When Law & the Internet First Met," 3 *Green Bag 2d* 171 (2000)

❖ CYBERPUNK ❖

Cyberpunk is a genre of popular literature, generally thought of as a subgenre of science fiction (or, more properly, SF), which explores the possible evolution of information technology and human society in the relatively near future. Computer technology in general and data networks in particular form the central component of the scientific extrapolation involved, and provide the "cyber" in cyberpunk. A pervading sense of *weltschmerz*, often overdone, provides the "punk" component. Cyberpunk flourished in the 1980s; although it is still being written, most of its best-known practitioners have moved on.

Although proto-cyberpunk works can be traced as far back as the 1950s and perhaps earlier (a late entry is the stylistically definitive 1982 movie *Bladerunner*), the term "cyberpunk" was probably first used by author Bruce Bethke in his short story of that title, although long before Bethke's story was published the term had been picked up by editor Gardner Dozois (of Isaac Asimov's *Science Fiction Magazine*) and widely used by others. Cyberpunk burst out of the narrow world of SF magazines and into the broader popular imagination with William Gibson's 1984 novel *Neuromancer*.

Neuromancer's astonishing cultural impact probably results as much from its timing as its content; it came out at the beginning of the home computing revolution in the developed world. It provided names for things that the world was just beginning to realize existed, or might soon exist. It provided the cultural context and cachet to what otherwise was no more than office equipment. And it was adopted into the canon by the reigning academic elite of the day, providing a body of referents for scholarly discourse on the culture of information.

Cyberpunk's adoption by the mass media resulted in the 1990s habit of tagging anything vaguely connected with information technology with a "cyber" prefix," and in some memorably bad movies. Postmodernists adored cyberpunk (e.g., Jameson 1991); as a literary genre, however, it was necessarily short lived. Its heavy dependence on artifice, particularly on a created slang, meant that it moved from innovation to cliché almost instantly. Many of the writers most closely associated with cyberpunk in its early days—Gibson, Bruce Sterling, and Neal Stephenson—are still actively exploring, in their work, the "cyber" side of cyberpunk: the conjoined evolution of human society and information technology. But while some remain pessimistic, the highly stylized "punk" component has been largely or entirely abandoned. Interesting post-cyberpunk works by these authors include William Gibson's *Zero History*, Neal Stephenson's *Baroque Cycle* trilogy, and some of the short stories collected in Bruce Sterling's *Ascendancies;* stories in the latter collection range from the distinctly cyberpunk *Deep Eddy* (1993) to the upbeat *Maneki Neko* (1998), which despite the shift in attitude addresses the same underlying concern: the ways in which human society will change to adapt to information technology.

See also: Cyber; Cyberspace; Data Haven; Encryption

Sources and Further Reading
Nonfiction
Thomas M. Disch, *The Dreams Our Stuff Is Made of: How Science Fiction Conquered the World* (New York: Touchstone, 1998)
Carl Freedman, *Critical Theory and Science Fiction* (Middletown, CT: Wesleyan University Press, 2000)
Fredric Jameson, *Postmodernism, or the Cultural Logic of Late Capitalism* (Durham, NC: Duke University Press, 1991)
Brian McHale, *Postmodernist Fiction* (London: Methuen Press, 1987)
Fiction
Bruce Bethke, "Cyberpunk," *Amazing Science Fiction*, Volume 57, Number 4 (1983)
William Gibson, The Trilogy: *Neuromancer* (New York: Ace 1984); *Count Zero* (New York: Arbor House 1986); *Mona Lisa Overdrive* (New York: Bantam 1988)
William Gibson, *Burning Chrome* (New York: Arbor House 1986) [collection of thematically linked short stories]
William Gibson, *Zero History* (New York: G.P. Putnam's Sons 2010)
Neal Stephenson, The Baroque Cycle: *Quicksilver* (New York: HarperCollins 2003); *The Confusion* (New York: HarperCollins 2004); *The System of the World* (New York: HarperCollins 2004); Neal Stephenson, *Snow Crash* (New York: Bantam 1992)
Bruce Sterling, *Ascendancies: The Best of Bruce Sterling* (Burton, Michigan: Subterranean Press 2007)
Bruce Sterling, *Islands in the Net* (New York: Arbor House 1988)
Bruce Sterling, ed., *Mirrorshades: The Cyberpunk Anthology* (New York: Arbor House 1986)

❖ CYBERSPACE ❖

Although the idea had been a staple of speculative fiction for decades, the term "cyberspace" was first used by William Gibson in his 1984 novel *Neuromancer* to describe a data network as perceived by a human mind connected directly to it: "the consensual hallucination that [is] the matrix" (Gibson 1984, 5). The idea of a direct connection between a human brain and a computer had been a staple of SF, and a goal of researchers, for some time. The term captured the popular imagination, however, and for a while it became fashionable to refer to the Internet, the World Wide Web, a local area network, or any data network as "cyberspace." Early users began to think of cyberspace as a physical place; importantly, this place was *terra nullius*, not yet under the control of any government. The attitudes of these earlier "settlers" of cyberspace tended toward the libertarianism expressed in the Declaration of Independence of Cyberspace or more succinctly in the aphorism that "information just wants to be free."

A contrasting view was provided by Lawrence Lessig's revolutionary 1999 book *Code and Other Laws of Cyberspace*, and further developed in his later work. Lessig proposed that the architecture of data networks was an architecture of control; liberty is not the natural condition of information systems, and to keep information free requires constant vigilance. In a similar vein Andrew Blum's 2012 book *Tubes: A Journey to the Center of the Internet* focuses on the physical infrastructure of the Internet contrasting its crude physical reality to it perceived ethereal intangibility. While the term "cyberspace" itself has become passé, the attitudes of its early settlers continue to shape and inform debate about the exchange, use and ownership of information on the Internet today.

See also: Cyber; Cyberpunk; Declaration of the Independence of Cyberspace

Sources and Further Reading
Andrew Blum, *Tubes: A Journey to the Center of the Internet* (New York: Harper Collins, 2012)
William Gibson, *Neuromancer* (New York: Ace, 1984)
Becky Hogge, *Barefoot into Cyberspace: Adventures in Search of Techno-Utopia* (Saffron Walden, Essex: Barefoot Publishing, 2011)
David R. Koepsell, *The Ontology of Cyberspace: Law, Philosophy and the Future of Intellectual Property* (Chicago: Open Court, 2000)
Lawrence Lessig, *Code and Other Laws of Cyberspace, Version 2.0* (New York: Basic Books, 2006)
Brian Loader, *The Governance of Cyberspace: Politics, Technology and Global Restructuring* (Basingstoke, Hampshire, UK: Routledge, 1997)

Scott J. Shackelford, "From Nuclear War to Net War: Analogizing Cyber Attacks in International Law," 27 *Berkeley Journal of International Law* 192 (2009)

Vernor Vinge, *True Names and the Opening of the Cyberspace Frontier*, edited by James Frenkel (New York: Tor, 2001)

Timothy Wu, "Cyberspace Sovereignty? The Internet and the International System," 10 *Harvard Journal of Law & Technology* 647 (1997)

❖ CYBERSQUATTING ❖

Cybersquatting is the act of registering a domain name that includes or resembles a trade or service mark with the intent of later selling or licensing that domain name to the owner of the trademark. Cybersquatting was rampant in the early days of the Internet, leading to the passage of the Anticybersquatting Consumer Protection Act of 1999 (ACPA). Despite its name, the ACPA's primary aim is to protect the interests of trademark owners. It provides that one who, with a bad faith intent to profit, registers, traffics in, or uses a domain name that at the time of registration is (1) identical to or confusingly similar to a *distinctive* mark or (2) identical to or confusingly similar to or dilutive of a *famous* mark is liable in a civil action by the owner of the mark. Remedies may include the transfer of the domain name (15 U.S.C. § 1125(d)).

Bad faith intent to profit: In a typical cybersquatting case, the focus is not so much on whether the domain name is identical or confusingly similar to a mark, or whether that mark is famous or distinctive. The distinction would only be important if what was at issue was dilution of the trademark rather than a more direct form of infringement; in the early days of cybersquatting, at least, the infringement was generally direct. Many registrants will seek to register domain names similar to the trademarks of others unwittingly or without malice, however; for example, a person might register his or her own name for a personal Web site without being aware that the name was used as a trademark by another. To address this problem, the ACPA includes a list of nine factors to consider in assessing bad faith. These include the following:

(I) the trademark or other intellectual property rights of the person, if any, in the domain name;

(II) the extent to which the domain name consists of the legal name of the person or a name that is otherwise commonly used to identify that person;

(III) the person's prior use, if any, of the domain name in connection with the bona fide offering of any goods or services;

(IV) the person's bona fide noncommercial or fair use of the mark in a site accessible under the domain name;

(V) the person's intent to divert consumers from the mark owner's online location to a site accessible under the domain name that could harm the goodwill represented by the mark, either for commercial gain or with the intent to tarnish or disparage the mark, by creating a likelihood of confusion as to the source, sponsorship, affiliation, or endorsement of the site;

(VI) the person's offer to transfer, sell, or otherwise assign the domain name to the mark owner or any third party for financial gain without having used, or having an intent to use, the domain name in the bona fide offering of any goods or services, or the person's prior conduct indicating a pattern of such conduct;

(VII) the person's provision of material and misleading false contact information when applying for the registration of the domain name, the person's intentional failure to maintain accurate contact information, or the person's prior conduct indicating a pattern of such conduct;

(VIII) the person's registration or acquisition of multiple domain names which the person knows are identical or confusingly similar to marks of others that are distinctive at the time of registration of such domain names, or dilutive of famous marks of others that are famous at the time of registration of such domain names, without regard to the goods or services of the parties; and

(IX) the extent to which the mark incorporated in the person's domain name registration is or is not distinctive and famous (15 U.S.C. § 1125(d)).

Finally, a catch-all exception provides that bad faith intent shall not be found in any case in which the court determines that the person reasonably believed that the use of the domain name was a fair use or otherwise lawful.

The ACPA has succeeded in rendering traditional cybersquatting unprofitable. It is effective against non-U.S. parties as well as those within the United States, because when it is not possible to proceed in personam (personally) against the person who registered the domain name, the trademark holder may proceed in rem (against a thing rather than a person) against the domain name itself; if the suit is successful, the domain name registration will be transferred to the trademark holder. In addition, many other countries have taken similar measures against cybersquatting.

The "sucks" problem: Some Web site operators may register domain names that include a trademark but clearly indicate that they are intended to criticize the trademark owner, such as www.aolsucks.net (which redirects to www.aolwatch.com) or www.paypalsucks.com. The operators of these sites do not wish to steal business from America Online (AOL), but probably do wish to harm AOL's and PayPal's reputations. However, the registration of the name is not cybersquatting under the ACPA, both because there is no likelihood of confusion and because criticizing a company, so long as there is no defamation, is protected speech; for a court to enjoin the use of the domain name would be state action in violation of the First Amendment (*Bally*, 29 F. Supp. 2d at 1161). If, however, the site is used for some unprotected form of speech, such as the tarnishing of a famous trademark by posting pornographic images unrelated to the mark, use of the site for that purpose may be enjoined to prevent dilution of the famous trademark (*Lucent Technologies v. Johnson*, 2000 WL 1604055).

Typosquatting: The decline in traditional, direct cybersquatting was accompanied by a rise in a form of indirect cybersquatting known as typosquatting. A typosquatter attempts to cash in on the traffic generated by high-volume Web sites. Inevitably, many people will type domain names incorrectly. People also commonly substitute the ".com" top-level domain name for other top-level domain names, or forget the period after "www." A typosquatter registers domain names that are likely to be entered accidentally by persons seeking to visit a popular Web site.

A technique known as mousetrapping was often used to profit from the visitor's mistake. The mousetrapped visitor was trapped in a blizzard of pop-up and pop-under advertisements, often pornographic; inexperienced Web surfers were often unable to extricate themselves from the mousetrap without shutting off the computer. Technology seems to have provided a more effective solution than law: the widespread use of pop-up blockers has made mousetrapping a thing of the past. However, typosquatting—and username-squatting—has found new life on Facebook (Pesochinsky 2010).

Some typosquatters, like some cybersquatters, have other motives than purely financial ones. Persons who have a dispute with the operator of a particular Web site may typosquat in order to express their side of the dispute. Typosquatting has been used for political purposes, for example, especially during presidential election campaigns and in such highly emotionally charged areas as the debate over reproductive rights. Such typosquatting, to the extent that it is not actually trademark infringement, raises First Amendment concerns not raised by the mousetrapping typosquatters.

Brandjacking: Brandjacking is the appropriation of the online identity of another individual or corporate entity in order to appropriate that individual or entity's brand equity. Brandjacking has been used by environmental activists to create fake Twitter account for ExxonMobil and BP, by political opponents to create fake Facebook pages for President Barack Obama, and by pranksters to create fake blogs for celebrities. Brandjacking itself is not necessarily illegal; however, cybersquatting and other trademark laws will apply to brandjacking done for profit, while defamation laws may apply even to noncommercial use of fake celebrity blogs and the like.

Statute
- Anticybersquatting Consumer Protection Act, 15 U.S.C. § 1125(d)

Cases
Federal Appellate Courts
- *Interstellar Starship Services, Ltd. v. Epix, Inc.*, 304 F.3d 936 (9th Cir. 2002)
- *Shields v. Zuccarini*, 254 F.3d 476 (3d Cir. 2001)
- *Sporty's Farm L.L.C. v. Sportsman's Market, Inc.*, 202 F.3d 489 (2d Cir. 2000)

- *Virtual Works, Inc. v. Volkswagen of America, Inc.*, 238 F.3d 264 (4th Cir. 2001)

Federal Trial Courts
- *Bally Total Fitness Holding Corp. v. Faber*, 29 F. Supp. 2d 1161 (C.D. Cal. 1998)
- *Chanel, Inc. v. Chanel255.org*, No. 12–21762-CIV, 2012 U.S. Dist. LEXIS 73894 (S.D. Fla. 2012)
- *E. & J. Gallo Winery v. Spider Webs Ltd.*, 129 F. Supp. 2d 1033 (S.D. Tex. 2001)
- *International Bancorp, L.L.C. v. Société des Baines de Mer et du Cercle des Etrangers a Monaco*, 192 F. Supp. 2d 467 (E.D. Va. 2002)
- *Lucent Technologies v. Johnson*, No. CV 00–05668, 2000 WL 1604055 (C.D. Cal. 2000)
- *Lucent Technologies, Inc. v. Lucentsucks.com*, 95 F. Supp. 2d 528 (E.D. Va. 2000)
- *Petmed Express, Inc., v. Medpets.com, Inc.*, 336 F. Supp. 2d 1213 (S.D. Fla. 2004)
- *Pinehurst, Inc. v. Wick*, 256 F. Supp. 2d 424 (M.D.N.C. 2003)
- *Victoria's Cyber Secret Ltd. Partnership v. V Secret Catalogue, Inc.*, 161 F. Supp. 2d 1339 (S.D. Fla. 2001)

See also: Domain Name Registration; Fair Use (Trademark); Internet; Internet Corporation for Assigned Names and Numbers; Trademark; Trademark Dilution; Trademark Infringement; World Wide Web

Sources and Further Reading

John Brogan, "Much Ado about Squatting: The Constitutionally Precarious Application of the Anticybersquatting Consumer Protection Act," 88 *Iowa Law Review* 163 (2002)

Zohar Efroni, "A Guidebook to Cybersquatting Litigation: The Practical Approach in a Post-Barcelona.com World," 2003 *University of Illinois Journal of Law, Technology and Policy* 457 (2003)

Dara B. Gilwit, "The Latest Cybersquatting Trend: Typosquatters, Their Changing Tactics, and How to Prevent Public Deception and Trademark Infringement," 11 *Washington University Journal of Law and Policy* 267 (2003)

Arik Hesseldahl, " 'Brandjacking' on the Web," *Bloomberg Business Week*, May 01, 2007

IBLS Editorial Board, "Internet Law—Typosquatting and Trademark Infringement Disputes," Internet Business Law Services Internet and E-Commerce Law News (April 12, 2013), available at http://www.ibls.com/internet_law_news_portal_view.aspx?s=articles&id=5533F6E6–4E09–4919–8840-C9BAB7DE6932 (visited May 13, 2013)

Elizabeth D. Lauzon, "Validity, Construction, and Application of Anticybersquatting Consumer Protection Act, 15 U.S.C.A. § 1125 (D)," 177 *American Law Reports Federal* 1 (2002)

Jacqueline D. Lipton, "Who Owns 'Hillary.com'? Political Speech and the First Amendment in Cyberspace," 49 *Boston College Law Review* 55 (2008)

Zorik Pesochinsky, "Almost Famous: Preventing Username-Squatting on Social Networking Websites,"

28 *Cardozo Arts & Entertainment Law Journal* 223 (2010)

Barbara A. Solomon, "Domain Name Disputes: New Developments and Open Issues," 91 *The Trademark Reporter* 833 (2001)

Rebecca S. Sorgen, "Trademark Confronts Free Speech on the Information Superhighway: 'Cybergripers' Face a Constitutional Collision," 22 *Loyola of Los Angeles Entertainment Law Review* 115 (2001)

Bettina Wendlandt, *Cybersquatting, Metatags und Spam* (München: Beck Juristischer Verlag, 2002) (in German)

❖ CYPHERPUNK ❖

See Data Haven; Encryption

D

❖ DATA HAVEN ❖

The term "data haven" was introduced by author Bruce Sterling in a 1988 novel, *Islands in the Net*. The concept appears even earlier in, among other works, John Brunner's mid-1970s novel *The Shockwave Rider*. A data haven is a "place" both on the Internet and in the physical world where data can be safe, especially from government control. All or nearly all national governments attempt to regulate exchange of information within their jurisdiction. The United States, for example, attempts to control or prohibit the exchange over the Internet of child pornography, defamatory material, obscenity, and unauthorized reproductions of copyrighted material and software that may be used to circumvent copyright protections. Other countries may attempt to control political dissent through controlling the exchange of information that criticizes the government or shows it in a bad light.

There are two aspects to keeping data safe in a data haven: a technical aspect and a legal aspect. The technical side of the problem is addressed with computer security tools, especially encryption, and by maintaining the physical security of the servers on which the information is stored. The legal aspect is addressed by locating the data haven in a country that imposes few or no legal restrictions on the information stored. (All or nearly all countries prohibit the use of data havens for child pornography or the furtherance of terrorism or violent crime, so data havens specializing in content of this sort are presumably outside the law wherever they are located and rely on a combination of encryption and lax enforcement to protect their data.)

Because one of the uses of a data haven is the avoidance of copyright restrictions, the countries suitable for data havens are those that are outside the treaty regime governing international copyright law. The Berne Convention, an international copyright protection agreement, includes as parties most of the countries of the world; some of the few that are not parties to the Berne Convention are parties to other agreements. The few countries remaining are mostly small. Sterling's novel anticipated this; the data havens in the story are located in Grenada and Singapore. Neither of these countries was a party to the Berne Convention at the time; both became parties in 1998. Another novel developing the concept, Neal Stephenson's *Cryptonomicon*, locates its data haven in a fictional country bearing some resemblance to Brunei. Brunei was not a party to the Berne Convention at the time the novel was published (it became a party in 2006) but had been a member of the World Trade Organization (WTO) since 1995, and was thus already bound by the Agreement on Trade-Related Aspects of Intellectual Property Rights (TRIPS). Another favored hypothetical site for data havens, Taiwan, is bound by TRIPS as well: Taiwan became a WTO member in 2002, under the confusing name "Chinese Taipei," or more formally the "Separate Customs Territory of Taiwan, Penghu, Kinmen and Matsu." (Taipei is the capital city of Taiwan.)

Only a few countries are neither WTO members nor Berne parties: Afghanistan, East Timor, Eritrea, Ethiopia, Iran, Iraq, Kiribati, Marshall Islands, Nauru, Palau, San Marino, Somalia, Turkmenistan, and Tuvalu. Many of these countries lack the Internet infrastructure to support a data haven, while others lack the inclination or requisite atmosphere of legal tolerance. One of the world's most famous data havens, HavenCo, was located in the world's most famous imaginary country, Sealand. Sealand is a fortified platform in the North Sea; it was built by the United Kingdom for military purposes during World War II and later abandoned. It was occupied by a former British military officer and pirate radio entrepreneur, Paddy Roy Bates, after he was fined for pirate radio broadcasting from another abandoned fortress within the United Kingdom's territorial sea. Although he never used the platform for broadcasting, Bates proclaimed it to be the independent Principality of Sealand in 1967; he became Prince Roy and his wife became Princess Joan. Prince Roy died in 2012; his son, Prince Regent Michael, now administers the "principality" (Woo 2012). No country has recognized the sovereignty of Sealand (Garfinkel 2000). HavenCo went offline in 2008.

There are obvious similarities between pirate radio and data havens; both attempt to deliver information to the populace of developed countries from outside the territory of those countries, thus avoiding censorship and copyright laws. A place like Sealand is a natural venue for both. Further advances in wireless broadband may also make it possible for data havens to be based on ships in international waters, as European pirate radio broadcasters once were.

In theory, HavenCo prohibited only three uses: child pornography, spamming, and "black hat" hacking. As a practical matter, HavenCo was constrained by the ability of mainland governments to shut off its Internet connections; data stored on servers on a platform in the North Atlantic is useless without a connection to the outside world. As a result, HavenCo reserved the right to drop any Web site or service that might threaten its access to the Net; use of HavenCo to assist terrorist activities, for instance, would not be allowed (Garfinkel 2000).

While in theory the idea of a data haven located outside the jurisdiction of any state may be appealing, in practice it has not succeeded. HavenCo never enjoyed financial success (McCullagh 2003). This might have been because of internal conflicts and difficulty serving customers, but was more likely to have resulted from lack of demand for a data haven not bound by the laws of, and located outside the territory of, existing countries, as well as the fact that Sealand was never truly able to operate independently of Great Britain.

Less ambitious but more successful attempts at creating data havens, or approximations thereof, have been of the virtual sort. The long-running Pirate Bay arguably falls into this category, or did in its earlier form, as do many less-infamous but similar projects. Ultimately such projects have been limited by the laws and physical infrastructure of the countries in which they are located. However, the idea of an extraterritorial data haven may find new life with the rise of an increasingly wireless Internet. Like the pirate radio stations that gave Prince Roy of Sealand his start, data havens might be located on ships remaining outside the territorial waters of any state (Kramer 2010).

Treaties

- Agreement on Trade-Related Aspects of Intellectual Property Rights (TRIPS), Marrakesh Agreement Establishing the World Trade Organization, Annex 1C, Apr. 15, 1994, 33 I.L.M. 81 (1994)
- Convention Concerning the Creation of an International Union for the Protection of Literary and Artistic Works (Berne Convention), September 9, 1886, as last revised at Paris, July 24, 1971 (amended 1979), 25 U.S.T. 1341, 828 U.N.T.S. 221
- Universal Copyright Convention, September 6, 1952, 6 U.S.T. 2731, revised at Paris July 24, 1971, 25 U.S.T. 1341
- WIPO Copyright Treaty, December 20, 1996, 36 I.L.M. 65 (1997)

See also: Anonymity; Berne Convention; Copyright; Cyberpunk; Encryption; File-Sharing; International Copyright Protection; Privacy; TRIPS

Sources and Further Reading
Fiction
John Brunner, *The Shockwave Rider* (New York: Ballantine, 1976)
Neal Stephenson, *Cryptonomicon* (New York: HarperCollins, 1999)
Bruce Sterling, *Islands in the Net* (New York: Arbor House, 1988)

Nonfiction
Warwick Ford & Michael S. Baum, *Secure Electronic Commerce: Building the Infrastructure for Digital Signatures and Encryption* (Upper Saddle River, NJ: Prentice Hall, 2d ed. 2001)
Simson Garfinkel, "Welcome to Sealand. Now Bugger Off," *Wired* (July 2000), available at http://www.wired.com/wired/archive/8.07/haven.html?pg=1&topic=&topic_set=(visited July 26, 2012)
Stephen Graham & Simon Marvin, *Splintering Urbanism: Networked Infrastructures, Technological Mobilities and the Urban Condition* (Basingstoke, Hampshire, UK: Brunner-Routledge, 2001)
James Grimmelman, "Death of a Data Haven: Cypherphunks, WikiLeaks, and the World's Smallest Nation," *Ars Technica* (March 27, 2012), available at http://arstechnica.com/tech-policy/2012/03/sealand-and-havenco/ (visited January 28, 2013)
"HavenCo 'Data Center' Offline?" *Security and the Net* (November 18, 2008), available at http://securityandthe.net/2008/11/18/havenco-data-center-offline/ (visited January 28, 2013)
Jeffrey D. Kramer, "Seafaring Data Havens: Google's Patented Pirate Ship," 2010 *University of Illinois Journal of Law, Technology and Policy* 359 (2010)
Declan McCullagh, "Has 'Haven' for Questionable Sites Sunk?" C/Net News.com (August 4, 2003), available at http://news.com.com/2100–1028_3–5059676.html?tag=fd_top (visited January 28, 2013)
Elaine Woo, " 'Prince' Roy Bates Dies at 91; Adventuring Monarch of Sealand," *LA Times* (October 14, 2012), available at http://articles.latimes.com/2012/oct/14/local/la-me-roy-bates-20121014 (visited January 28, 2013)

❖ DATA MINING ❖

Data mining, also known as knowledge discovery in databases (KDD), is a statistical technique that has been rapidly developing since the pioneering work of Usama Fayyad on General Motors defects in the early 1990s. The term "data mining," however, has come to be increasingly and somewhat inaccurately applied in the popular press to a wide range of techniques for extracting information from databases (Zarsky 2002–2003). Data mining has raised privacy concerns, particularly in three areas: consumer behavior, security, and medical records.

The first step in data mining is the compilation of a database. Everything that is done online is at least potentially recordable, although much of it is not actually recorded in any permanent form. Every credit card or ATM transaction is recorded. Nearly every boarding pass issued in the United States is recorded in an airline computer, and nearly every time a prescription is filled, a record is made. Commuters who use FastPass cards to avoid tollbooths may have their movements recorded, as may Web surfers who have a Global Positioning System (GPS) receiver attached to or built into the device used for access. Telephone companies keep records of all numbers dialed from each telephone, and it is possible to track the movement of mobile devices. Private and government surveillance cameras store images of people passing by a given location.

Just a few years ago the gathering of this information was of little concern, for two reasons: there was too much of it, and it was too scattered. Statistical techniques were not yet sophisticated enough to extract meaningful information from all this data, and even if they had been, computers capable of crunching so much data were not widely available. Even with improved computers and KDD algorithms, the information described in the preceding paragraph was inaccessible because it was stored in many different databases, most of them not available to anyone but the owner: telephone company databases could not easily be combined with airline, credit card, pharmacy, or highway authority databases for data mining.

For the most part this is still true; the privacy advocates' nightmare of a world in which Big Brother is aware of every move that every individual takes has not yet arrived. It has become possible, however. Hardware, software, and statistical techniques all continue to improve. Corporate mergers and information-sharing agreements create combined databases of information on disparate areas of activity. And the government engages in data mining of government and perhaps private databases (*Homeland Security* 2003).

Proponents of data mining argue that most uses are benign. Data mining can detect and avoid adverse drug reactions, surely a noble cause; it helps many and harms none. When it comes to protecting national security, data mining is less intrusive and probably more effective than the much-maligned airport security procedures. Data mining may eventually be useful in preventing violent crimes, as well (Jenkins 2012). And the marketing companies that engage in commercial data mining do not want to use that information for any purpose more sinister than trying to sell goods and services.

Privacy advocates are not convinced, however. While avoiding adverse drug interactions is a good thing, data mining of a patient's medical records may make it possible to draw conclusions about the patient's medical history that might not otherwise be obvious—and this information might become available to persons other than pharmacists, physicians, and the FDA.

Security-based data mining and consumer data mining are greeted by many with alarm. The now-defunct Computer Assisted Passenger Prescreening System program (CAPPS II), for example, would have allowed the Transportation Security Administration (TSA) to use data mining techniques in commercial databases to assign air passengers a score, similar to a credit rating, "to determine whether a passenger is a known terrorist, or has identifiable links to known terrorists" (*Criticism Prompts GAO Review* 2003). The successor program to CAPPS II, the Secure Flight initiative, does not make use of commercial databases.

The comparison with credit-rating agencies may highlight the problem with data mining by the TSA: credit-rating agencies make many errors. As a result, they are sued constantly; they are also forced to compete in the marketplace with other companies. The TSA is not competing with any other terror-threat-rating companies or agencies, and is probably immune from most suits for errors. While the credit-rating business has built-in incentives to improve accuracy and reduce the frequency of errors, the TSA has no similar incentive. In addition, an incorrect identification as a terrorist can do far more harm to an individual than a bad credit rating.

Private data mining can also be used in ways more sinister than merely designing junk-mail lists. Private data could conceivably assign scores purporting to reveal the likelihood that a particular individual would be an unsatisfactory employee, for instance. Inevitably, some individuals would be placed in that category incorrectly—yet the low score would make them effectively unemployable. And while private companies have a greater incentive to enhance accuracy, the use of private database information by private individuals and companies is harder to control than use of that information by the government.

Individuals already have some protection against government use of information in electronic databases under a 1988 statute, the Computer Matching and Privacy and Protection Act. But government data mining may have benefits aside from the sometimes-disputed security benefits: in August 2004 data mining of government purchase card data by the Defense Criminal Investigative Service resulted in the indictment of four people, including a senior Defense Information Systems Agency Contracting Officer, who had allegedly improperly awarded over $11 million in contracts to a business in which the Contracting Officer had a financial interest (*Purchase Card Data Mining* 2004).

Statutes
- Computer Matching and Privacy Protection Act of 1988, 5 U.S.C. § 552a(o)
- Privacy Act of 1974, 5 U.S.C. § 552a

European Union Directive
- Directive 2009/136/EC of the European Parliament and of the Council of 25 November 2009, 2009 O.J. (L 337) 11

See also: Advertising; Adware and Spyware; Anonymity; Cookies; Doubleclick; Privacy; Social Networking Service

Sources and Further Reading

Andrew William Bagley, "Don't Be Evil: The Fourth Amendment in the Age of Google, National Security, and Digital Papers and Effects," 21 *Albany Law Journal of Science & Technology* 153 (2011)

Robert Bond, "The EU E-Privacy Directive and Consent to Cookies," 68 *Business Lawyer* 215 (2012)

Terence Craig & Mary Ludloff, *Privacy & Big Data* (Sebastopol, CA: O'Riley Media, Inc., 2011)

Michelle Delio, "Traveling? Take Big Brother Along," *Wired* (April 4, 2003), available at http://www.wired.com/politics/security/news/2003/04/58344 (visited January 28, 2013)

Christopher Elliott, "The Navigator: The TSA's Secure Flight Initiative May Be Making Your Privacy Less Secure," *The Washington Post* (July 30, 2010), available at http://www.washingtonpost.com/wp-dyn/content/article/2010/07/30/AR2010073003907.html (visited January 28, 2013)

Usama M. Fayyad et al., "From Data Mining to Knowledge Discovery: An Overview," *Advances in Knowledge Discovery and Data Mining* 6 (Cambridge, MA: MIT Press, 1996)

Joseph S. Fulda, "Data Mining and Privacy," 11 *Albany Law Journal of Science and Technology* 105 (2000)

David Hand et al., *Principles of Data Mining* (Cambridge, MA: MIT Press, 2001)

"Investigations: Aviation Criticism Prompts GAO Review of TSA Data Mining Program," Cybercrime Law Report, September 22, 2003, at 6

Holman W. Jenkins, Jr., "Can Data Mining Stop the Killing?" *Wall Street Journal*, (July 24, 2013), available at http://online.wsj.com/article/SB10000872396390443570904577546671693245302.html (visited August 28, 2013)

Shahid Khan, "'Apps.Gov': Assessing Privacy in the Cloud Computing Era," 11 *North Carolina Journal of Law & Technology*, Online Edition 259 (2010)

Legislation—Homeland Security: Senate Funding Bill Requires Review of DHS Data Mining, Cybercrime Law Report, August 11, 2003, at 4

"Microsoft and Privacy: Change of Track," *The Economist*, June 9, 2012, at 70

"National Security—Government Databases: Pentagon Concludes DOD Data Mining Plan Doesn't Threaten Privacy Rights," Cybercrime Law Report, June 2, 2003, at 3

Saira Nayak, "How This Cookie Crumbled: Deciphering the Compliance Obligations around the EU's Cookie Directive," *Antitrust Source* 1 (December 2012)

"Privacy Legislation: Sens. Feingold, Wyden Begin Effort to Stop 'Data Mining' by Department of Defense," Cybercrime Law Report, January 27, 2003, at 3

"Purchase Card Data Mining Leads to Co. Indictment," Government Contractor, August 25, 2004, at 330

"Regulatory Affairs—Pharmaceutical: FDA to Use Data Mining to Monitor Adverse Events," 22 Biotechnology Law Report 481 (2003)

"Secure Flight Re-Engineering Welcomed but Watchlist Problems Remain Unaddressed," American Civil Liberties Union (October 22, 2008), available at http://www.aclu.org/technology-and-liberty/secure-flight-re-engineering-welcomed-watchlist-problems-remain-unaddressed (visited January 28, 2013)

Daniel Solove & Paul M. Schwartz, *Privacy Law Fundamentals* (Portsmouth, NH: IAPP Publication, 2011)

Tim Wilson, "Find Sensitive Data in Cloud before Criminals Do," InformationWeek (July 26, 2012), available at http://www.informationweek.com/security/management/find-sensitive-data-in-cloud-before-crim/240004393 (visited January 28, 2013)

Tal Z. Zarsky, "Desperately Seeking Solutions: Using Implementation-Based Solutions for the Troubles of Information Privacy in the Age of Data Mining and the Internet Society," 56 *Maine Law Review* 13 (2004)

Tal Z. Zarsky, "'Mind Your Own Business!' Making the Case for the Implications of the Data Mining of Personal Information in the Forum of Public Opinion," 5 *Yale Journal of Law & Technology* 4 (2002–2003)

❖ DECLARATION OF INDEPENDENCE OF CYBERSPACE ❖

In early 1996, as the Internet exploded into popular consciousness, the Declaration of the Independence of Cyberspace appeared. It was well timed; mainstream media were fascinated by the Internet, governments everywhere were reacting to its advent more with apprehension than with appreciation of the opportunities, and the general public was beginning to log on. The prevailing sentiment of the more experienced users—the Internet old timers—was that there was such a "place" as cyberspace, and that it should remain forever free of interference from real-world governments. John Perry Barlow, a songwriter for the Grateful Dead and cofounder of the Electronic Frontier Foundation, captured this cyber libertarianism in the Declaration of the Independence of Cyberspace.

The Declaration makes eight basic points:

1. The Internet ("Cyberspace") should not be subject to existing governments, nor is it likely to produce a government of its own; "ethics, enlightened self-interest, and the commonweal" will produce the governance (not government) of cyberspace.
2. Cyberspace grows through the cooperation of its users; it cannot be built by governments, "as though it were a public construction project."
3. Internet users, rather than governments, will resolve the problems that have arisen from some users' online activities.
4. Real-world "legal concepts of property, expression, identity, movement, and context" are inapplicable in cyberspace.
5. In cyberspace, all users are equal.
6. Attempts by national governments to control their citizens' access to cyberspace will ultimately prove unsuccessful.
7. Government should not take the place of parents in regulating children's access to Internet content.
8. Intellectual property law, particularly copyright law, is oppressive; information can and should "be reproduced and distributed infinitely at no cost."

A decade later, some of these points seem prescient, others naïve. The first point is largely a matter of opinion, not fact, and thus cannot be definitively shown to be true or untrue. The second seems to ignore the history of the Internet, which after all had its origins in projects of the U.S. Department of Defense and National Science Foundation. The third seems, thus far, to be an open question: the community of Internet users, rather than governments, has been relatively successful in addressing problems such as viruses and spyware. Governments and users have both played a role in suppressing malicious hacking. And neither governments nor users have been notably successful in suppressing annoyances (such as spam) or some crimes.

The fourth point—that real-world legal concepts are inapplicable in cyberspace—represents a viewpoint that must now be considered extreme. Real-world law governs a wide variety of online activities and problems, among them the sale of goods and services; defamation; fraud and identity theft; and malicious hacking and the creation of worms and viruses. And this situation seems to be widely accepted by the overwhelming majority of users. Only in a few areas, such as file-sharing, is there still widespread opposition to the application of "real-world" law to cyberspace; in most other areas it now seems to be accepted by most users that online activities are subject to the same laws as offline activities.

The fifth point (that all users are equal) states a truth that is, as Thomas Jefferson put it, self-evident. The sixth also is proving less and less true with the passage of time. While national governments have for the most part been unable to prevent their citizens from having access to cyberspace, they have been more successful at controlling the content available to most users within their territory and the ways in which those within their territory use that content (*National Differences* 2012). The seventh and eighth served to draw the lines in two fiercely fought battles: the battle over freedom of expression and the battle over intellectual property rights. In the United States, at least, the first battle seems to be winding down; the government has made few recent efforts in this area, and the public has generally accepted and approved the regulation of, for example, Web sites' gathering of information about consumers under the age of 13. The second—the battle over intellectual property rights—is ongoing, but the "information just wants to be free" approach of the Declaration is no longer taken seriously. Most users now accept that in general content should be paid for, and modern battles center on such things as the creation of derivative works and the extent to which content owners should be allowed to invade individual users' privacy or restrict the use of lawfully purchased content.

The U.S. government, in particular, has made three notable attempts to restrict children's access to Internet content. Two of these—the Communications Decency Act and the Child Online Protection Act—attempted to impose a direct governmental prohibition between children and certain forms of content; both statutes were unfavorably received by the courts. The third, the Children's Internet Protection Act, required computers in certain places—schools and libraries—to use filtering software available from private parties. This hybrid approach has been more favorably received; although it might be said that this shows a rejection of the idea of direct government control over children's access to "cyberspace," there is now near-universal acceptance of the idea that children should be shielded from some Internet content. The constitutional problems with the Communications Decency Act and the Child Online Protection Act came not from their shielding of children but from the difficulty of doing so without simultaneously blocking or otherwise interfering with the Internet access of adults to the same content.

The Declaration is somewhat contradictory, as well. On the one hand it scorns governments, or perhaps parents, who would impose laws restricting children's access: "you entrust your bureaucracies with the parental responsibilities you are too cowardly to confront yourselves." The Declaration acknowledges that there is some bad content out there: "In our world, all the sentiments and expressions of humanity, from the debasing to the angelic, are parts of a seamless whole, the global conversation of bits. We cannot separate the air that chokes from the air upon which wings beat." But, while castigating parents who would entrust the government with parental responsibilities, the Declaration also acknowledges that many or most parents lack the skills to police their own children's Internet access: "You are terrified of your own children, since they are natives in a world where you will always be immigrants."

The battle over intellectual property rights also persists. Trademark, patent, and copyright laws are all battlegrounds. The Internet Corporation for Assigned Names and Numbers, perhaps the closest analogue "cyberspace" has produced to a real-world government institution, has been mired in controversy. "Business method" patents for such inventions as one-click online ordering have been much maligned, but they have been granted nonetheless by the real-world United States Patent and Trademark Office. The U.S. government, via the Anticybersquatting Consumer Protection Act, has also stepped in to protect trademark rights online. And courts in many nations have entertained suits by holders of intellectual property rights to protect those rights against online infringement. Suits over online file-sharing of copyrighted information have gained the most attention. From the viewpoint of the Declaration this file-sharing is not a problem: "In our world, whatever the human mind may create can be reproduced and distributed infinitely at no cost." Information, in other words, just wants to be free, and the Internet has given it the keys to its cage.

A large number, possibly even a majority, of Internet users still share the Declaration's opinion of the content industry: "Your increasingly obsolete information industries would perpetuate themselves by proposing laws, in America and elsewhere, that claim to own speech itself throughout the world. These laws would declare ideas to be another industrial product, no more noble than pig iron. . . . The global conveyance of thought no longer requires your factories to accomplish." Nonetheless, laws to protect the content industry persist, and their spirit has entered "cyberspace" through the use of such technological copy-protection and digital rights management measures as encryption and trusted computing.

While some of its points are now accepted aspects of Internet law, and others continue to be debated, the overall sense of community present in the Declaration seems to have vanished. In 1996, the Internet was a new thing to the majority of its users; a core of technically sophisticated, more experienced users was able to guide debate and discourse. The idea of an Internet "community" made far more sense than it does today, when experienced Internet users number in the hundreds of millions, perhaps billions. Cyberspace has vanished as connecting to the Internet has become a part of daily life for the people of North America, Europe, East Asia, and increasingly the rest of the world as well. In this sense, the Declaration's goal of "a civilization of the Mind in Cyberspace" has been achieved; Internet users have "spread [them]selves across the Planet so that no one can arrest [their] thoughts"—or, rather, the Internet has spread itself across the world, entering into the life of people everywhere; what was revolutionary has become mundane.

Declaration

- John Perry Barlow, *A Declaration of the Independence of Cyberspace* (February 8, 1996), available at https://projects.eff.org/~barlow/Declaration-Final.html (visited January 28, 2013)

See also: Activism and Advocacy Groups; Censorship; Child Online Protection Act; Children's Internet Protection Act; Communications Decency Act; Cyberspace; Cybersquatting; Encryption; Fan Works; File-Sharing; Hacking

Sources and Further Reading

Becky Hogge, *Barefoot into Cyberspace: Adventures in Search of Techno-Utopia* (Saffron Walden, Essex: Barefoot Publishing, 2011)

Brian Loader, *The Governance of Cyberspace: Politics, Technology and Global Restructuring* (Basingstoke, Hampshire, UK: Routledge, 1997)

"National Differences: The World Is What You Make It—Every Country Has Its Own Internet," *The Economist* Special Report: Technology and Geography, October 27, 2012, at 20

Berin Szoka & Adam Marcus, eds., *The Next Digital Decade: Essays on the Future of the Internet* (Washington, D.C.: TechFreedom, 2010)

❖ DECRYPTION ❖

See Encryption

❖ DeCSS ❖

DeCSS is a computer program that can be used to decrypt motion picture files encrypted with Content Scramble System (CSS, often incorrectly called Content Scrambling System), used on commercially manufactured DVDs. CSS uses a 40-bit encryption algorithm that is relatively easy to break. Content owners in the United States were initially prevented from using stronger encryption by U.S. export-control regulations; now that a huge number of DVDs and DVD players incorporating the CSS keys have already been sold, there are market pressures against changing the encryption system used on commercial DVDs.

In order to play back movies encrypted with CSS, DVD players must contain a decryption key. The DVD Copy Control Association (DVDCCA), a motion-picture industry trade association, licenses CSS decryption keys to equipment manufacturers (*Reimerdes*, 111 F. Supp. 2d 308; *Bunner*, 113 Cal.Rptr.2d 341). The manufacturers themselves were always a potential source of leakage, but in fact DeCSS and similar programs have been developed by reverse engineering rather than by any compromise of the equipment-makers' security. As a further defense, CSS uses multiple layers of encryption, in which an authentication key ensures that the CSS decryption module can be used only with the DVD drive to which it was originally connected, as a defense against hardware hacking. Each equipment manufacturer is allotted one of the several hundred available player keys; these can be used to decrypt disc keys on DVDs. The disc keys in turn are used to decrypt the title keys, which are used to decrypt the titles—the actual content on the DVD: movies, trailers, and special features. If one has access to the title keys, however, the intermediate steps can be bypassed. (BluRay disks use different digital rights management technology: the Advanced Access Content System to prevent copying, and the High-bandwidth Digital Content Protection to restrict unauthorized playback. However, the legal issues are the same.)

CSS has been used since the mid-1990s. On October 6, 1999, Jon Lech Johansen, a 15-year-old Norwegian citizen, posted the program to a mailing list. Johansen was arrested and tried for violation of Norwegian law. The publicity surrounding the trial made "DVD Jon" an instant Internet celebrity. He was acquitted in January 2003, but the prosecution appealed the verdict. (In many countries, although not in the United States, the prosecution may appeal a verdict of acquittal.) In December, an appellate court upheld the acquittal (*Sunde v. Johansen* (appeal) 2003). In January 2004, Økokrim, the Economic Crimes Unit of the prosecutor's office, announced that it was dropping the case rather than appealing it to Norway's highest court.

Johansen's reason for using (and perhaps writing) DeCSS fell within the boundaries of what in the United States, in the absence of the Digital Millennium Copyright Act (DMCA), might have been called "fair use": CSS-encrypted discs could not be played on Linux systems; DeCSS could decrypt those disks in order to play the movies they contained on Linux systems. The Norwegian appellate court found this use permissible (*Sunde v. Johansen* (appeal) 2003).

Despite the intense interest of the U.S. content industry in the Johansen case, and despite the fact that as a result of Johansen's actions DeCSS became available in the United States, Johansen himself remained effectively outside the reach of the DMCA and the U.S. justice system. The legal test for DeCSS in the United States came when persons within the borders of the United States became involved in the distribution of the program.

In November 1999, activists Shawn Reimerdes, Roman Kazan, and Eric Corley made DeCSS available on their Web sites. They also encouraged others to do the same as an act of civil disobedience. Eight movie studios immediately filed suit against the three. At trial, the federal district court for the Southern District of New York held that CSS effectively controlled access to copyrighted works and that DeCSS was a means of circumventing that control. Thus distribution of DeCSS was unlawful under the DMCA's prohibition against circumvention of technological measures, contained in 17 U.S.C. § 1201(a)(2)(A).

The court rejected the defendants' contention that their conduct was protected under the reverse engineering, encryption research, or security testing exceptions. It also rejected the defendants' two First Amendment arguments. The defendants had argued that Title I's anticircumvention provisions were either an unconstitutional restraint on free speech or were unconstitutionally overbroad because they restricted the fair use of encrypted works. Although the district court agreed that a computer program "is a means of expressing ideas," and that therefore "the First Amendment must be considered before its dissemination may be prohibited or regulated," it then decided that the DMCA's restriction in this expression was content neutral, because it was aimed at the function of the program rather than at the ideas expressed within the code itself. Applying the intermediate standard of review appropriate to a content-neutral restriction of this sort, the court held that the anticircumvention provisions were constitutional. The interest in freely expressing whatever expressive content was contained within the program was outweighed by the interest in protecting copyrights and reducing video piracy, and the potential harm to those interests from the program's function. The trial court also rejected the overbreadth argument, finding that other, not unlawful alternative methods were already available that would allow such fair uses as the making of backup copies, although the image quality would not be as high as that made by the use of DeCSS (*Reimerdes*, 111 F. Supp. 2d 294).

Corley appealed the decision to the Second Circuit Court of Appeals. The Second Circuit largely agreed with the trial court. DeCSS was "speech" within the meaning of the First Amendment, but the focus of the DMCA's restriction was on the functional rather than expressive aspect of the program. The anticircumvention provisions and the injunction against distribution of DeCSS were thus content-neutral and subject only to intermediate scrutiny. Applying this scrutiny, the court found the injunction (and thus Title I of the DMCA) constitutional. In addition, the Second Circuit pointed out that fair use does not guarantee "copying by the optimum method or in the identical format of the original." Title I, the court noted,

> does not impose even an arguable limitation on the opportunity to make a variety of traditional fair uses of DVD movies, such as commenting on their content, quoting excerpts from their screenplays, and even recording portions of the video images and sounds on film or tape by pointing a camera, a camcorder, or a microphone at a monitor as it displays the DVD movie. The fact that the resulting copy will not be as

perfect or as manipulable as a digital copy obtained by having direct access to the DVD movie in its digital form, provides no basis for a claim of unconstitutional limitation of fair use (*Corley*, 273 F.3d at 459).

On the heels of the case against Reimerdes and Corley came a state law case, *DVD Copy Control Association v. Bunner.* Bunner, like Reimerdes and Corley, had made DeCSS available for download on his Web site. (Another of the named defendants in Bunner was "Emmanuel Goldstein," an Internet alias for Corley. The name is drawn from George Orwell's classic dystopian novel *1984*; Orwell's novel suggests that Goldstein, who never appears, probably does not actually exist.) The DVDCCA brought a case against Bunner under California's trade secrets law, arguing that CSS was a trade secret. After the trial court issued a preliminary injunction against Bunner, the California Court of Appeal for the Sixth District reversed. The California appellate court agreed that computer software could be protected as a trade secret. Unlike the *Reimerdes* court, however, it found that the defendant's distribution of DeCSS was protected by the First Amendment. In an opinion that was later reversed by the California Supreme Court, the appellate court stated that DeCSS was "a written expression of the author's ideas and information about decryption of DVDs without CSS," and therefore "the trial court's preliminary injunction barring Bunner from disclosing DeCSS [could] fairly be characterized as a prohibition of 'pure' speech" (*Bunner*, 4 Cal.Rptr.3d 69 (2003)).

The California Supreme Court, in reversing the appellate court's decision, did not have to address the question before the *Reimerdes* court—the characterization of the DMCA's prohibition on DeCSS and similar programs as content-based or content-neutral. The California courts were applying California trade secrets law, not the DMCA, and the particular issue in *Bunner* was the preliminary injunction issued to prevent Bunner from continuing to distribute DeCSS pending the resolution of the trade secrets dispute. The court observed that it was in the nature of any such injunction that it would burden a particular type of content—that which the defendant sought to disclose. The purpose of such an injunction, however, was not to suppress the expression of a particular idea, but to protect the plaintiff's property interest in its trade secret. The injunction could thus be viewed as content-neutral, and under the level of scrutiny applied to content-neutral regulations it was constitutional (*Bunner*, 4 Cal.Rptr.3d 69).

DeCSS was neither the first nor the only program capable of making unencrypted copies of titles on encrypted DVDs. A few weeks earlier, a more limited program, DVD Speed Ripper, had been released. And the release of the DeCSS source code has made possible the development of hundreds of alternative programs, some of them considerably more powerful and effective than DeCSS itself. DeCSS has become a cause célèbre, and the program has been expressed as a series of haiku, as graphic art, and even as a 1,401-digit prime number. Suppression of DeCSS in these forms would seem to invite reexamination of the question of functionality versus expressive content, but that did not stop the DVDCCA from suing (as a codefendant in Bunner) a New Jersey T-shirt company. The T-shirt company, Copyleft, sold shirts with the DeCSS code printed on them. Because DeCSS itself is still widely available on the Internet, and because typing in the code from a T-shirt would be a slow, laborious, and unnecessary process for anyone wishing to decrypt CSS-encrypted DVDs, it seems far more likely that the T-shirts were purchased and worn as a form of political protest, and sold to enable that protest. The fact that the T-shirt company donated $4.00 to the Electronic Frontier Foundation for each T-shirt sold would seem to support this interpretation, as does the name of the company, drawn from the open-source movement. DeCSS and programs like it continue to present a potential for conflict between the DMCA and the First Amendment, and further litigation seems likely. DeCSS has also inspired a decoy program, the perfectly innocuous but confusingly named DeCSS, which can remove Cascading Style Sheets ("CSS") tags from HTML documents.

In the meantime, restrictions on DeCSS and similar programs continue to affect individual users without affecting commercial-scale video piracy. Large-scale video-pirating operations can mechanically reproduce all of the information on a DVD, encryption included, and place it on a new DVD. This new DVD may then be played in a standard DVD player.

Statute
* Digital Millennium Copyright Act, 17 U.S.C. § 1201

Cases
Federal
* *Universal City Studios, Inc., v. Reimerdes*, 111 F. Supp. 2d 294 (S.D.N.Y. 2000), affirmed by *Universal City Studios, Inc. v. Corley*, 273 F.3d 429 (2d Cir. 2001)

State
* *DVD Copy Control Association, Inc. v. Bunner*, 113 Cal.Rptr.2d 338 (2001), *reversed*, 4 Cal.Rptr.3d 69 (2003)

Norway
* *Sunde (for Norway) v. Johansen*, Oslo First Instance Trial Court, January 7, 2003, No. 02–507 M/94; English translation by Professor Jon Bing available at http://w2.eff.org/IP/Video/Johansen_DeCSS_case/20030109_johansen_decision.html (visited January 10, 2013); on appeal, Borgarting Appellate Court, December 22, 2003, No. LB-2003–00731; English translation by Professor Jon Bing available at http://www.efn.no/DVD-dom-20031222-en.html (visited July 28, 2012)

See also: Activist and Advocacy Groups; Advanced Access Content System; Censorship; Content Industry; Copyright; Copyright Infringement; Digital Millennium Copyright Act, Title I; Digital Rights Management; Encryption; File-Sharing; First Amendment; International Copyright Protection; WIPO Copyright Treaty

Sources and Further Reading
Sara Crasson, "Are DeCSS T-Shirts Dirty Laundry? Wearable, Non-Executable Computer Code as Protected Speech," 15 *Fordham Intellectual Property, Media & Entertainment Law Journal* 169 (2004)

Lawrence Lessig, *Free Culture: How Big Media Uses Technology and the Law to Lock Down Culture and Control Creativity* (New York: Penguin, 2004)

Kerry Segrave, *Piracy in the Motion Picture Industry* (Jefferson, NC: McFarland & Company, 2003)

Wendy Seltzer, "The Imperfect Is the Enemy of the Good: Anticircumvention versus Open User Innovation," 25 *Berkeley Technology Law Journal* 909 (2010)

Richard Spinello, *Cyberethics: Morality and Law in Cyberspace* (Burlington, MA: Jones & Barlett Learning, 4th ed. 2011)

❖ DEFAMATION ❖

The tort of defamation is defined in the United States by state law; the elements of the tort thus vary depending on the jurisdiction. The tort will almost invariably include these elements, however. There must be a false statement that is harmful, either because it causes actual damages or because it falls into a category that is deemed harmful per se, even in the absence of any proof of damages. The statement must be published—that is, it must be communicated to some third party, not merely to the person described in the statement (Restatement § 558). Statements that are privileged are not defamatory; the privileges that may be asserted as a defense also vary from state to state, but the First Amendment imposes a nationwide uniform privilege protecting certain types of statements. Defamation may be either libel (written) or slander (spoken). There are several related torts, including injurious falsehood, false light, publicizing of private facts, and appropriation of another's name or likeness (see Restatement §§ 623–629, 652).

By itself, defamation creates no particular legal issues specific to the Internet. The global nature of the Internet, however, means that a statement made in one jurisdiction may be received everywhere in the world. What is defamatory under the laws of one jurisdiction may be acceptable under the laws of another; questions of jurisdiction, choice of law, and recognition and enforcement of judgments then arise.

Jurisdictional issues arise when a statement made in one jurisdiction defames a person located in another, and may be complicated if the message is received in yet a third jurisdiction. The jurisdiction in which the statement is made, as well as the jurisdiction in which the person making the statement is located, will generally be acknowledged as having jurisdiction over the tort. The location where the harm is felt and the location where the defamatory communication is received may also have jurisdiction; in the United States, a combination of state and federal law is applied to this problem.

Where the defendant does not have systematic and continuous contacts with the forum state (the state seeking jurisdiction) sufficient to establish general jurisdiction over the defendant, U.S. states can obtain jurisdiction only if there is grounds for specific jurisdiction: jurisdiction over the defendant for that particular matter, rather than all matters. Specific jurisdiction requires a two-step analysis. First, the state's long-arm statute (a statute providing jurisdiction over out of state defendants) must be examined to determine whether it supports jurisdiction over the defendant for the particular defamation claim. Second, if the long-arm statute does support jurisdiction, the application of the statute must be examined to determine whether the defendant has "certain minimum contacts with [the forum], such that the maintenance of the suit does not offend 'traditional notions of fair play and substantial justice'" (*International Shoe*, 326 U.S. 310).

In the United States, this rule has been applied to give jurisdiction in Internet defamation cases when the defendant knew or reasonably should have known that the injury caused by the defamatory statement would be suffered in a particular state. It has also been applied to give jurisdiction in the state where the server that stores and transmits the statement is located (*Bochan*, 68 F. Supp. 2d 692). The logic underlying this latter application is somewhat more questionable, as the server or servers could be located almost anywhere and its location is generally neither known to the parties nor significant to the communication.

The concerns that apply to jurisdiction also apply to the choice of applicable substantive law: once a court in, say, Virginia has decided that it has jurisdiction over a case, should it apply its own law to the case? Should it apply the law of the state in which the statement was made, or the law of the state in which the server on which the statement was stored is located, or the state in which the harm caused by the statement was felt? Here, though, there is no uniformity even among the states of the United States; there is a wide variety of choice of law rules.

Courts in other countries may be quicker to take jurisdiction over foreign defendants than U.S courts are. In 2002, an Australian court decision caused considerable controversy: the Australian High Court decided that it could exercise personal jurisdiction in a defamation suit against an American publishing company, Dow Jones. The allegedly defamatory article was available on the Dow Jones Web site, from which it could be, and was, viewed in Australia. Had the situation been reversed, these facts alone would not have permitted a court in the United States to exercise jurisdiction over an Australian defendant. The Australian court, though, found that it did have jurisdiction (*Gutnick*, [2002] H.C.A. 56). The reasoning in *Gutnick* has been much criticized as having a potentially chilling effect on Internet speech: if all countries

were to be as liberal in granting themselves jurisdiction as Australia, everything posted on the Internet would have to first be checked against the laws of nearly 200 countries and hundreds or even thousands of states, provinces, territories, dependencies, and colonies.

The problem posed by *Gutnick* is limited by the problem of enforcement of foreign judgments, however. The U.S. courts are unlikely to enforce a foreign judgment in a situation in which the foreign court did not acquire jurisdiction over the defendant in a way that would also have sufficed for jurisdiction in a U.S. court. Most Americans thus have nothing to fear from a judgment in Australia, and even Dow Jones' exposure to Australian judgments is limited to the extent of its assets in Australia.

In addition to the unenforceability of judgments obtained without what U.S. courts regard as proper jurisdiction, U.S. defendants have an additional protection from foreign defamation suits: the First Amendment. Speech protected by the First Amendment includes some speech that in other countries would be considered defamatory. As a result, U.S. courts have refused to apply those countries' defamation law, or to enforce those countries' defamation judgments. In *Bachchan v. India Abroad Publications*, for example, a state court in New York refused to enforce a British defamation judgment on First Amendment grounds, while in *Matusevitch v. Telnikoff* a federal trial court in the District of Columbia did the same. Another nondefamation case, the French Yahoo! case, also stated that a foreign judgment could not be enforced where the First Amendment would have prevented the judgment from being obtained in the United States (*Yahoo! Inc.*, 169 F. Supp. 2d 1181).

While the First Amendment provides some protection against foreign defamation suits for U.S. Internet publishers, the problem is likely to continue to grow. The countries that have already been involved in litigation of this sort are early adopters of the Internet; Australia and the United Kingdom share a legal history and legal culture with the United States, yet incompatibilities between the systems arise. As the Internet continues to increase communication between people from radically different legal cultures, further cross-border disputes over defamation and other real or perceived insults are inevitable. The problem is exacerbated by the possibility of criminal as well as civil actions for defamation, as happened in Italy in 2006.

In 2006, a group of students in Turin, Italy, posted a video on YouTube, showing themselves bullying an autistic child (Fleischer 2012). The video was offensive and shocking, and, regrettably, very popular. In addition to actions taken against the bullies, Italian prosecutors filed charges for criminal defamation and invasion of privacy against Google marketing executive Arvind Desikan, chief legal officer David Drummond, chief privacy attorney Peter Fleischer, and chief financial officer George Reyes. None of these four was an Italian citizen or residents, or even physically present in Italy at the time. Nonetheless, in 2010 three of the four were convicted; Desikan was acquitted (Hill 2012). Although the convictions were overturned on appeal in 2012 (Castonguay 2012), the fact that they were obtained in the first place illustrates the pitfalls for online media companies.

Cases

Australia

- *Gutnick v. Dow Jones & Co.*, [2002] H.C.A. 56 (Austl.)

Italy

- Tribunale Ordinario di Milano (Ordinary Tribunal of Milan) 12 April 2010, Case No. 1972/2010 (It.), available at http://www.giurcost.org/casi_scelti/Google.pdf (visited January 12, 2013)
- Tribunale Ordinario di Milano (Ordinary Tribunal of Milan) 24 February 2010, Sentenza n. 1972/2010 (It.)

United States Supreme Court

- *International Shoe v. Washington*, 326 U.S. 310 (1945)

Federal Appellate Court

- *Cybersell, Inc. v. Cybersell, Inc.*, 130 F.3d 414 (9th Cir. 1997)

Federal Trial Court

- *Bochan v. La Fontaine*, 68 F. Supp. 2d 692 (E.D. Va. 1999)
- *Matusevitch v. Telnikoff*, 877 F. Supp. 1 (D.D.C. 1995)
- *Yahoo!, Inc. v. La Ligue Contre le Racisme et L'Antisemitisme*, 169 F. Supp. 2d 1181 (N.D. Cal. 2001), reversed by *Yahoo! Inc. v. La Ligue Contre Le Racisme et L'Antisemitisme*, 379 F.3d 1120 (9th Cir. 2004); reversal affirmed on rehearing by *Yahoo! Inc. v. La Ligue Contre Le Racisme*, 433 F.3d 1199 (9th Cir. 2006)

State Courts

- *Bachchan v. India Abroad Publications*, 585 N.Y.S.2d 661 (N.Y. Sup. Ct. 1992)

Restatement

- *Restatement (Second) of Torts* (Washington, D.C.: American Law Institute, 1984 & Supp. 2003)

See also: Censorship; Choice of Law; First Amendment; French Yahoo! Case; Jurisdiction; Recognition and Enforcement of Judgments

Sources and Further Reading

"Accused Movie Pirate Sues for Defamation and Millions in Damages," *TorrentFreak* (July 23, 2012), available at http://torrentfreak.com/accused-movie-pirate-sues-for-defamation-120723/ (visited January 28, 2013)

Giles Castonguay, "Court Quashes Convictions in Google Video Case," *Wall Street Journal* (December 21, 2012), available at http://online.wsj.com/article/SB10001424127887324461604578193093685872724.html (visited January 28, 2013)

Todd Cooper, "Fake Facebook Account Prompts Defamation Lawsuit," Omaha.com (July 9, 2012, 1:00AM), available at http://www.omaha.com/article/20120709/NEWS/707099925/1707 (visited January 28, 2013)

Cherie Dawson, "Creating Borders on the Internet: Free Speech, the United States, and International Jurisdiction," 44 *Virginia Journal of International Law* 637 (2004)

Peter Fleischer, "My Italian Appeal," *Peter Fleischer: Privacy . . . ?* (December 6, 2012), available at http://peterfleischer.blogspot.com/ (visited January 28, 2013)

Nathan W. Garnett, "Dow Jones & Co. v. Gutnick: Will Australia's Long Jurisdictional Reach Chill Internet Speech World-Wide?" 13 *Pacific Rim Law and Policy Journal* 61 (2004)

Noah C. N. Hampson, "The Internet Is Not a Lawless Prairie: Data Protection and Privacy in Italy," 34 *Boston College International & Comparative Law Review* 477 (2011)

Kashmir Hill, "The Downside of Being a Google Executive," *Forbes* (September 27, 2012) available at http://www.forbes.com/sites/kashmirhill/2012/09/27/the-downside-of-being-a-google-executive/ (visited January 28, 2013)

Uta Kohl, "Defamation on the Internet—Nice Decision, Shame about the Reasoning," 52 *International & Comparative Law Quarterly* 1049 (2003)

Ken Kraus & Dan Polatsek, "Enforcement of Foreign Media Judgments in the Aftermath of Gutnick v. Dow Jones & Co.," 21 *Communications Lawyer* 1 (2003)

Bryan P. Werley, *Aussie Rules: Universal Jurisdiction over Internet Defamation*, 18 *Temple International and Comparative Law Journal* 199 (2004)

Gary Chan Kok Yew, *Internet Defamation and Choice of Law in Dow Jones & Company Inc. v. Gutnick*, 2003 *Singapore Journal of Legal Studies* 483 (2003)

Vittorio Zambardino, "Il Garante Privacy sulla sentenza di Milano: 'E' sbagliata, ma ora bisogna fare regole non *censorie*," La Repubblica, April 16, 2010), available at http://www.itespresso.it/il-garante-privacy-difende-in-parte-google-dalla-sentenza-di-milano-44937.html (visited August 28, 2013)

❖ DENIAL-OF-SERVICE ATTACK ❖

A denial-of-service attack is an attack on an information service—for example, a Web site—that seeks to deny other users access to the service. In the simplest form, a denial-of-service attack might be launched on a telephone number by setting another telephone to dial that number repeatedly; anyone else trying to reach the same number will receive a busy signal. If the number against which the denial-of-service attack is launched is a toll-free number, the attack will cost the victim not only the loss of the resource, but the cost of the telephone calls as well.

Internet information resources, such as Web sites, are generally not capable of being overwhelmed by repeated requests for access from a single user. In order to deny service, a large number of requests must be sent from several different locations. Internet denial-of-service attacks launched simultaneously from multiple locations are called distributed denial of service (DDoS) attacks; their goal is to deny access to other users. In contrast to a cracker attack, a denial-of-service attack does not attempt to gain entry. Distributed denial-of-service attacks often use zombies—computers that have been backdoored by worms or Trojans—without the consent or knowledge of their users.

The 1996 National Information Infrastructure Protection Act created a private right of action against persons launching a DDoS attack against "protected computers" if the attack meets certain criteria (18 U.S.C. § 1030(g)). Nearly all computers in the United States are likely to fall within the statute's definition of "protected computers" (Jordan 2000). The victim may bring an action against the attacker if any of the six factors in § 1030(4)(A)(i) is present. Section 1030(a) provides in part that:

> (a) Whoever –
> ***
>> (5) (A) knowingly causes the transmission of a program, information, code, or command, and as a result of such conduct, intentionally causes damage without authorization, to a protected computer;
>> (B) intentionally accesses a protected computer without authorization, and as a result of such conduct, recklessly causes damage; or
>> (C) intentionally accesses a protected computer without authorization, and as a result of such conduct, causes damage and loss.[;]
>
> . . .
> shall be punished as provided in subsection (c) of this section.
>
> . . .
> (c) The punishment for an offense under subsection (a) or (b) of this section is—
> ***
>> (4) (A) except as provided in subparagraphs (E) and (F), a fine under this title, imprisonment for not more than 5 years, or both, in the case of—
>> (i) an offense under subsection (a)(5)(B), which does not occur after a conviction for another offense under this section, if the offense caused (or, in the case of an attempted offense, would, if completed, have caused)—
>>
>>> (I) loss to 1 or more persons during any 1-year period (and, for purposes of an investigation, prosecution, or other proceeding brought by the United States only, loss resulting from a related course of conduct affecting 1 or more other protected computers) aggregating at least $ 5,000 in value;
>>> (II) the modification or impairment, or potential modification or impairment, of the medical examination, diagnosis, treatment, or care of 1 or more individuals;
>>> (III) physical injury to any person;
>>> (IV) a threat to public health or safety;
>>> (V) damage affecting a computer used by or for an entity of the United States Government in furtherance of the administration of justice, national defense, or national security; or
>>> (VI) damage affecting 10 or more protected computers during any 1-year period; or
>> (ii) an attempt to commit an offense punishable under this subparagraph;

Subsection (c) then sets out a schedule of fines and prison sentences for various violations.

At first glance, a denial-of-service attack does not seem to fit readily within the terms of § 1030(a)(5). The denial-of-service attack does not allow the attacker to gain entry to the victim's computer, nor does it cause actual damage to any computer; when the denial-of-service attack is over, the victim's computer will continue to operate as before. There is unauthorized access to the zombie computers used in a DDoS, but the zombies' users do not suffer any appreciable economic harm as a result. However, unauthorized access to the zombies, and the transmission of commands from the zombies, may cause economic harm to the victim. The unauthorized access and transmission of commands satisfy the requirements of either § 1030(a)(5)(A) or § 1030(a)(5)(B) and of § 1030(a)(5)(C); only one of these three is needed. And an attack on a business Web site may well cause more than $5,000 in damage, in the form of lost business and the cost of measures taken to end the DDoS attack, thus satisfying the requirement of § 1030(a)(4). In fact, merely "impairing the availability of [the target] computer to other systems in the network" can constitute damage, although the $5,000 threshold must still be met (*Four Seasons*, 267 F. Supp. at 1323). Attacks on hospital computers, emergency 9-1-1 systems, and government computers may satisfy the requirements of subsections (II) through (IV) of § 1030(c)(4)(A). DDoS attacks may also result in prosecution and lawsuits under state law, particularly under the tort of trespass to chattel. The chattels in this case may be the zombie computers or, on somewhat more tenuous reasoning, the target computer; the trespass consists of the unauthorized access to the zombies or the excessive requests and taking up of bandwidth of the target (*eBay*, 100 F. Supp. at 1070).

The problem with private lawsuits as protection against DDoS attacks, however, is that the victim must first identify the attacker. In *Four Seasons* and *eBay*, the partial denial of service was only one of the harms alleged; an attack in which denial of service is the attacker's only goal would be more difficult to trace. Section 1030 includes a statute of limitations of two years from either the date of the act causing damage or the date of discovery of the damage (18 U.S.C. § 1030(g)). Denial-of-service attacks that result in, for example, the disabling of an air traffic control tower, are likely to result in criminal investigations (Nemerofsky 2000, 11). Once the government has located the attacker, the injured parties may pursue private actions. But, where the denial-of-service attack results in the loss of a few thousand dollars' worth of business to a small company, the attacker is less likely to be apprehended, and the victim will be less likely to have sufficient resources to discover the identity of the attacker on its own.

A final category of denial-of-service attacks includes politically motivated "attacks" launched not with the use of zombies but through large numbers of users, by prearrangement, simultaneously attempting to access a political opponent's Web site at the same time. Such an "attack" might fall outside the scope of Section 1030 and might also be protected by the First Amendment.

Statute
- National Information Infrastructure Protection Act (NII) of 1996, codified at 18 U.S.C. § 1030

Cases
- *eBay v. Bidder's Edge*, 100 F. Supp. 2d 1058 (N.D. Cal. 2000)
- *Four Seasons Hotels and Resorts B.V. v. Consorcio Barr, S.A.*, 267 F. Supp.2d 1268 (S.D. Fla. 2003)

See also: Hacking; Malware; Worm; Zombie

Sources and Further Reading
Tom Brewster, "Super-Charged DDoS Attacks Spike in 2012," *TechWeek europe* (July 23, 2012), available at http://www .techweekeurope.co.uk/news/ddos-attacks-power2012–86926 (visited January 28, 2013)
William H. Jordan, "Going after Internet Hackers: Civil and Criminal Responses to Denial of Service Attacks," Electronic Banking Law and Commerce Report, March, 2000, at 6
Joshua McLaurin, *Making Cyberspace Safe for Democracy: The Challenge Posed by Denial-of-Service Attacks*, 30 *Yale Law & Policy Review* 211 (2011)
Jeff Nemerofsky, "The Crime of 'Interruption of Computer Services to Authorized Users': Have You Ever Heard of It?" 6 *Richmond Journal of Law & Technology* 23 (2000)
Margaret Jane Radin, "Distributed Denial of Service Attacks, Who Pays? Part I," *Cyberspace Lawyer*, December 2001, at 2
Margaret Jane Radin, "Distributed Denial of Service Attacks, Who Pays? Part II," *Cyberspace Lawyer*, January 2002, at 2

❖ DERIVATIVE WORKS ❖

The holder of copyright in a work has the exclusive right to make or authorize derivative works. For copyright purposes, a derivative work is a work that builds upon or incorporates a preexisting work. If a Russian novel is translated into English, the translation is a derivative work. If the English translation is adapted for a stage production, the stage play is yet another derivative work. A movie made of the play is derivative, as are a video game based on the movie and a novelization of the movie. To bring the work full circle, the Russian translation of the novelization (which would probably differ substantially from the original) would also be a derivative

work. Each of the authors of these derivative works acquires a copyright in the derivative work, but no copyright in the underlying work. For example, the translator would have the right to prevent others from copying her translation word for word, but no right to prevent others from making their own English translations from the Russian original. If the Russian work is still in copyright, the copyright holder of the original work would, of course, retain the right to authorize the additional translations. And the original translator's contract with the copyright holder might restrict that right.

If the underlying work is copyrighted and the derivative work infringes upon that copyright, the author of the derivative work acquires no copyright in the infringing portion of the work; derivative works that are substantially similar to the copyrighted works upon which they are based require the permission of the copyright holder. If the underlying work is in the public domain, only those parts of the derivative work that differ from the underlying work may be copyrighted.

The exact level of originality required to make a derivative work copyrightable in its own right is unclear. There must be some difference; otherwise, as soon as any work came into the public domain, the first person to copy it could claim to have created a derivative work and the work would once again be copyrighted (see *L. Batlin & Son*, 536 F.2d at 492). However, few if any works can be said to be wholly original. Works of fiction, for example, are necessarily in dialogue with other works of fiction, and many are simply adaptations of earlier existing works and characters. The 1999 film *10 Things I Hate about You* is a fairly straightforward adaptation of Shakespeare's *The Taming of the Shrew* to a modern setting. But the story did not originate with Shakespeare either; elements of it can be found in the Miller's Tale in Chaucer's *Canterbury Tales*, and in other written works and folk tales current in Shakespeare's time. It shows up as well in works in other languages probably unknown to Shakespeare, including Don Juan Manuel's *Tales of Count Lucanor* and in *The Book of the Knight of the Tower*. This does not mean that either the play or the movie is insufficiently "original" to be copyrighted in its own right; rather, "originality" in a legal sense is not coextensive with the term's meaning in a literary sense.

The courts of the United States have long acknowledged the impossibility, or near-impossibility, of requiring absolute originality. In the words of Justice Story, nearly two centuries ago:

> In truth, in literature, in science and in art, there are, and can be, few, if any, things, which, in an abstract sense, are strictly new and original throughout. Every book in literature, science and art, borrows, and must necessarily borrow, and use much which was well known and used before. . . . The thoughts of every man are, more or less, a combination of what other men have thought and expressed, although they may be modified, exalted, or improved by his own genius or reflection. If no book could be the subject of copy-right which was not new and original in the elements of which it is composed, there

could be no ground for any copy-right in modern times, and we should be obliged to ascend very high, even in antiquity, to find a work entitled to such eminence. Virgil borrowed much from Homer; Bacon drew from earlier as well as contemporary minds; Coke exhausted all the known learning of his profession; and even Shakespeare and Milton, so justly and proudly our boast as the brightest originals would be found to have gathered much from the abundant stores of current knowledge and classical studies in their days (*Emerson*, 8 F. Cas. at 619).

The line beyond which a work is legally derivative lies somewhere between mere reference to an earlier work and wholesale adaptation of that work to a new language, setting or medium; exactly where, though, is difficult to determine. The definition of "derivative work" in the Copyright Act is not especially helpful:

> A "derivative work" is a work based upon one or more preexisting works, such as a translation, musical arrangement, dramatization, fictionalization, motion picture version, sound recording, art reproduction, abridgment, condensation, or any other form in which a work may be recast, transformed, or adapted. A work consisting of editorial revisions, annotations, elaborations, or other modifications which, as a whole, represent an original work of authorship, is a "derivative work" (17 U.S.C. § 101).

The first sentence provides only the information that an adaptation from one medium, form, or language to another is a derivative work, as are shortened versions. Fictional treatments based on historical accounts may be derivative works, even though historical facts and theories are not protected by copyright. However, "[a] fictionalization is a treatment of a factual work in which the elements are recast, transformed, or adapted to produce a work of fiction. A work which is only loosely based on the ideas or facts found in an earlier work, is not considered to be a derivative work" (Compendium II of Copyright Office Practices, Ch. 306.02(b)). In other words, the "fictionalization" element seems more aimed at "stories" than at compilations of historical facts. A fictionalization of the true story of one family's escape from German-occupied Poland during World War II might be derivative; a movie or novel drawing heavily on a World War II encyclopedia would probably not be.

The second sentence also points out that even a work that is itself "an original work of authorship" may be derivative. This extension to works that would otherwise be eligible for copyright protection in their own right under 17 U.S.C. § 102 greatly expands the potential scope of the derivative works right.

The copyright holder's exclusive right to authorize derivative works is subject to limitations imposed by fair use and the First Amendment. This is particularly evident in the case of parodies, which are necessarily derivative of the work they parody. A parody may use as much of the original material as necessary to conjure up the original in the mind of the viewer or listener; otherwise the point of the parody would be lost. The exact extent beyond that to which the parody may incorporate material from the original is unclear (*Campbell*, 510 U.S. at 588). In many cases the copyright holder may be unwilling to grant permission to use the material in a parody at any price; parodies can hurt and are often unwelcome.

As with "derivative work," the exact meaning of "parody" can be difficult to pin down. The fact that a derivative work is, or is intended to be, humorous does not make that work a parody (see *Showcase Atlanta*, 479 F. Supp. 351). And while the *Campbell* court seems to address itself to works that attempt (successfully or otherwise) to poke fun at the original, its holding may be applied to a broader category of "transformative works," many of which might not be considered parodies in a literary sense (see, e.g., Tushnet 2008).

Fan works—often parodies and parody-like works created by fans of the original works—form one large category of derivative works on the Internet. A second category includes programs that piggyback on copyrighted programs, Web pages, and other online works. Many companies sell "helper" programs or programs that work jointly with popular programs, such as Microsoft Office: antivirus programs, citecheckers, document makers, metadata cleaners, printer drivers, and many others. These programs may add icons to the taskbars and pull-down menus of the various Microsoft Office programs, making it possible to use the helper program with a single click. If the combined program (Office with one-click helper function) were a derivative work, software makers would be unable to offer this convenient function without prior licensing permission from Microsoft (many, of course, nonetheless take the precaution of obtaining such permission). Similarly, every program loaded onto a Windows system adds information about itself to the Windows Explorer screen, and often to the desktop and various taskbars and menus as well; the altered screen does not become a derivative work, however.

The test for whether such programs are derivative works, and thus require permission, was set out by the Ninth Circuit in *Lewis Galoob Toys v. Nintendo of America*. The plaintiff, Lewis Galoob Toys, made a device called the Game Genie for use with the Nintendo video game system. The Game Genie was inserted between the Nintendo system and the game cartridge; the program on the game cartridge was loaded into the Game Genie, which in turn loaded it onto the system—but allowed the player to increase the number of lives of the player's character and the speed at which the character moved, and allowed the character to float above obstacles (964 F.2d at 967). The Ninth Circuit, in holding that the altered copy of the video game thus created was not a derivative work, pointed out that the Game Genie itself did not physically incorporate any portion of a work copyrighted by another, and that it did not supplant or diminish demand for Nintendo video games (964 F.2d at 969). In addition, the altering of characteristics of the video game for the game-player's enjoyment and convenience was fair use (964 F.2d at 970–972).

This reasoning has been applied to Internet software cases. In an unreported decision, *RealNetworks, Inc. v. Streambox, Inc.*, the federal district court for the Western District of Washington issued an injunction against the distribution of the Streambox Ferret. The Ferret added a button to RealNetworks' RealPlayer graphical user interface (GUI), allowing users to use Streambox's search engine rather than RealNetworks'. The district court considered *Lewis Galoob Toys* and seemed to suggest that the altered GUI might be a derivative work, but reached no definite conclusion; it issued the injunction on other grounds (*RealNetworks*, 2000 WL 127311, *11–12). In another battleground area—adware and spyware—the federal district court for the Southern District of New York held that the creation of a program that triggers popups whenever a particular Web page is viewed does not create a derivative work, and thus does not violate the Web page owner's copyright (*1–800-Contacts*, 309 F. Supp. 2d 467).

Statute

- Copyright Act of 1976, Exclusive Rights, 17 U.S.C. §§ 101, 106(2)

Cases

Supreme Court

- *Campbell v. Acuff-Rose Music, Inc.*, 510 U.S. 569 (1994)

Federal Appellate Courts

- *Lewis Galoob Toys, Inc. v. Nintendo of America, Inc.*, 964 F.2d 965 (9th Cir. 1992)
- *L. Batlin & Son, Inc. v. Snyder*, 536 F.2d 486 (2d Cir. 1976)
- *Pickett v. Prince*, 207 F.3d 402 (7th Cir. 2000)

Federal District Courts

- *1–800 Contacts, Inc. v. WhenU.com*, 309 F. Supp. 2d 467 (S.D.N.Y. 2003), reversed on other (trademark) grounds, 414 F.3d 400 (2d Cir. 2005)
- *Davidson & Associates, Inc. v. Internet Gateway, Inc.*, 334 F. Supp. 2d 1164 (E.D. Mo. 2004)
- *Emerson v. Davies*, 8 F. Cas. 615 (C.C.D. Mass. 1845) (No. 4,436)
- *M.H. Segan Ltd. Partnership v. Hasbro, Inc.*, 924 F. Supp. 512 (S.D.N.Y. 1996)
- *Metro-Goldwyn-Mayer, Inc. v. Showcase Atlanta Co-op. Productions, Inc.*, 479 F. Supp. 351 (N.D. Ga. 1979)
- *Moore Publishing Inc. v. Big Sky Marketing, Inc.*, 756 F. Supp. 1371 (D. Idaho 1990)
- *Radji v. Khakbaz*, 607 F. Supp. 1296 (D.D.C. 1985)
- *RealNetworks, Inc. v. Streambox, Inc.*, No. 2:99CV02070, 2000 WL 127311 (W.D. Wash. 2000)
- *Warner Bros. Entertainment Inc. v. RDR Books*, 575 F. Supp. 2d 513 (S.D.N.Y. 2008)

See also: Copyright; Copyright Infringement; Fan Works, Fair Use; File-Sharing

Sources and Further Reading

Gregory M. Duhl, "Old Lyrics, Knock-Off Videos, and Copycat Comic Books: The Fourth Fair Use Factor in U.S. Copyright Law," 54 *Syracuse Law Review* 665 (2004)

Jaime E. Muscar, "A Winner Is Who? Fair Use and the Online Distribution of Manga and Video Game Fan Translations," 9 *Vanderbilt Journal of Entertainment and Technology Law* 223 (2006)

Aaron Schwabach, *Fan Fiction and Copyright: Outsider Works and Intellectual Property Protection* (Farnham, Surrey, UK: Ashgate Publ., 2011)

Aaron Schwabach, "The Harry Potter Lexicon and the World of Fandom: Fan Fiction, Outsider Works, and Copyright," 70 *University of Pittsburgh Law Review* 387 (2009)

Shira Siskind, "Crossing the Fair Use Line: The Demise and Revival of the Harry Potter Lexicon and Its Implications for the Fair Use Doctrine in the Real World and on the Internet," 27 *Cardozo Arts & Entertainment Law Journal* 291 (2009)

Rebecca Tushnet, "User-Generated Discontent: Transformation in Practice," 31 *Columbia Journal of Law & the Arts* 497 (2008)

United States Copyright Office, "Compendium II of Copyright Office Practices § 306.02(b)" (1984), *Fictionalizations*

Jo-Na Williams, "The New Symbol of 'Hope' for Fair Use: *Shepard Fairey v. The Associated Press*," *Landslide*, September/October 2009, at 55

❖ DIGITAL AUDIO WORKS ❖

In 1986, digital audio recording technology became commercially available to the general public, sending unease through the music content industry. (An earlier attempt to introduce digital recording in the 1970s had failed.) Digital audio recordings, like all digital recordings, can be copied an unlimited number of times with no degradation in quality. The advent of the Internet and of file-compression formats meant that these recordings could then be distributed in moments to countless individuals around the globe. Recorded music is generally sold at prices that make unlawful copying far more attractive than is the case with books and movies; in addition, the music content industry is largely a middleman business, and is thus particularly vulnerable to piracy. As a result, the music content industry successfully lobbied for additional legislation to protect it, including the Audio Home Recording Act of 1992.

The Audio Home Recording Act (AHRA) imposed royalties—in effect, taxes—on digital audio recorders and media, and required digital audio recorders to incorporate electronic rights management technology. These provisions may have succeeded in killing off the digital audio tape (DAT) technology at which the statute was originally aimed, but they have been rendered irrelevant by technological advance. By the terms of the statute and subsequent court decisions, home computers are not digital audio recorders; they are not "designed or marketed for the primary purpose of" making digital audio recordings, and thus are not covered by the AHRA (17 U.S.C. § 1001(3); *RIAA v. Diamond Multimedia*, 180 F.3d at 1078; *Napster*, 239 F.3d at 1024). The AHRA did, however, provide for immunity from copyright liability for private, noncommercial recording of copyrighted music.

Digital audio recording, by itself, was a threat to the music content industry's revenues. Two newer technologies transformed this to a threat to the industry's existence. These new technologies were file compression, especially the MP3 file format, and the Internet. It is now possible for anyone, anywhere on the globe, to make a digital recording and distribute it worldwide, at no significant cost in time or money. The ongoing battle over this online file-sharing has become the defining struggle of the content industry and of Internet copyright law; it is discussed in detail under the heading "File Sharing" in this encyclopedia.

Statute

- Audio Home Recording Act, 17 U.S.C. §§ 1001– 1003, 1008

Cases

- *Arista Records LLC v. Lime Group LLC*, 784 F. Supp. 2d 398 (S.D.N.Y. 2011)
- *A&M Records, Inc. v. Napster, Inc.*, 239 F.3d 1004 (9th Cir. 2001)
- *Recording Industry Association of America v. Diamond Multimedia Systems, Inc.*, 180 F.3d 1072 (9th Cir. 1999)
- *Sony BMG Music Entertainment v. Tenenbaum*, 660 F.3d 487 (1st Cir. 2011)

See also: Audio Home Recording Act; Content Industry; Copyright; Digital Audio Works; Digital Performance Right in Sound Recordings Act; Digital Rights Management; File-Sharing

Sources and Further Reading

Rachel Gader-Shafran, "Confessions of a Serial Infringer: Can the Audio Home Recording Act of 1992 Protect the Consumer from Copy-Protected CDs?" *Intellectual Property Law Newsletter*, Winter 2003, at 10

Aaron L. Melville, "The Future of the Audio Home Recording Act of 1992: Has It Survived the Millennium Bug?" 7 *Boston University Journal of Science and Technology Law* 372 (2001)

Eric Smith, "The DAT Tax," available at http://www.brouhaha.com/~eric/bad_laws/dat_tax.html (visited January 28, 2013)

❖ DIGITAL DIVIDE ❖

The term "digital divide" refers to a gap between rich and poor individuals, communities, or nations in access to information technologies. The origin of the term is uncertain; it has been variously credited to several people, including former president Bill Clinton, the assistant secretary for Communications and Information in Clinton's Commerce Department, and *Los Angeles Times'* reporters Jonathan Webber and Amy Harmon. It came into widespread popular use around the time of its use by Bill Clinton in 1995. While the divide still exists, its nature has changed over the last two decades; the greatest concern now is not the availability of access but the quality of both access and use.

At the individual and community level, wealthy individuals and wealthier or more privileged communities tend to have better access to information technology. In the early days of the Internet, there was widespread concern that this would result in the poor being left behind and missing out on economic and educational opportunities, even in wealthy countries such as the United States. This fear has proved, if not totally unfounded, exaggerated. In 1998, only 26.2% of U.S. households had Internet access; a mere three years later, by 2001, the percentage had nearly doubled, to 50.5% (Statistical Abstracts 2003, 736). Internet access is now available to all, even in most remote rural communities, at little or no cost; debate over the digital divide in the United States now focuses not merely on access but on the quality of access. Broadband access is still relatively expensive, at around $20–$50 per month, and not available in all areas; as of 2010 68% of U.S. households had broadband access (Economics & Statistics Administration 2011), and residents of large cities with stodgy infrastructure look enviously at the ultra-high-speed broadband—over a hundred times as fast as what most broadband users elsewhere enjoy—available in Chattanooga or Kansas City (*Municipal Broadband* 2012). Free broadband access is available in schools and libraries, although it may be subject to content restrictions and does not provide the convenience of home access. Cheap or free access with fewer restrictions is available in many public places. Many businesses provide free wireless Internet access for patrons, and some American cities now provide free wireless access. Children without computers at home have the opportunity to learn to use them at school: in 2009, 97% of teachers in the United States had one or more computers located in the classroom every day. Internet access was available for 93% of the computers located in the classroom every day and for 96% of the computers that could be brought into the classroom. The ratio of students to computers in the classroom every day was 5.3 to 1 (Department of Education 2010).

But if the digital divide has all but vanished in the United States, it still exists among nations. In Europe and East Asia, the divide has also closed rapidly, with many countries surpassing the United States; South Korea, for example, leads the world in the percentage of homes with broadband Internet access—81% and growing—as well as in average broadband access speeds (Sutter 2010); Thailand's capital, Bangkok, offers a free wireless broadband network that would be the envy of many U.S. cities (Joshi 2012). In parts of the world access is less widely available: only about 16% of residents of Africa have Internet access, and Africa accounts for only 6% of total Internet use (*Internet Use in Africa* 2012). However, this is a dramatic change from as recently as 1998, when only one-tenth of 1% of African households had Internet access (Kenny 2000) and Africa's share of total global Internet use was negligible.

To aid in measuring the digital divide, the International Telecommunications Union has created the Digital Access Index (DAI). The DAI attempts to reduce the imprecision of measures such as Internet connections per household, which are useful when making comparisons within a society but not so useful when comparing between societies that may have radically different patterns of work and recreational Internet use, not to mention different concepts of "household." The DAI is based on eight variables drawn from five areas: availability of infrastructure, affordability of access, educational level, quality of information technology and communications technology services, and Internet usage. The results are not surprising in the aggregate: the nations or territories with the highest DAI are the five Scandinavian countries, plus Hong Kong, the Netherlands, South Korea, Taiwan. Canada and the United States are tied for 10th place, followed by the United Kingdom rounding out the top dozen. The 30 with the lowest DAI are all poor countries, all but three of them (Bhutan, Laos, and Haiti) in sub-Saharan Africa (ITU 2007).

This correlation has led some to dismiss the digital divide as a symptom, rather than a cause, of poverty. A decade ago, Michael Powell, then chairman of the Federal Communications Commission, compared it to a "Mercedes divide" (Lemann 2002). Powell's point seems to be that some people can afford to drive a Mercedes, while others cannot, but this is a product of the wealth of the Mercedes drivers, not a cause of it. Driving a Mercedes does not make the Mercedes driver still wealthier, nor do Mercedes drivers have greater access to the roads and highways than Volkswagen drivers, Hyundai drivers, or drivers of rusted 1994 Ford Escorts.

The analogy could be carried yet further: part of the reason for limited Internet access in Niger or Bhutan is its limited usefulness to countries at that stage of development. A dweller on a roadless island has no use for a Mercedes; in Niger, where only 16.5% of the population is literate, 83.5% would be able to make only limited use of an Internet connection. Even those who are literate and able to connect to the Internet will find few Web pages written in Djerba or Fulani, and perhaps a few more in Hausa, although most potential users will also be fluent in French. But even the 127,500 Internet users in the country cannot make the same use of the Internet as users in Tokyo or Toronto. For example, Niger's commercial and physical infrastructure cannot yet support the lively online commerce, with overnight delivery of goods to the user's front door, which is just one of the appealing features of the Internet.

But in Niger, as elsewhere, connectivity is increasing rapidly. As recently as 1998, Niger had only 1.8 telephones per 1,000 people, and there were only about 100 mobile telephones in the entire country (Turner 2001, 1224). By 2011, there were about 270 mobile telephones per 1,000 people (World Bank 2012), giving most families access to long-distance communication, and a higher ratio of cell phones to population than the United States had in 1998 (Elert 2002). The spread of mobile devices in turn is leading to an increase in literacy (Aker 2010), which leads to greater demand for mobile devices and greater economic progress. Soon enough, the roadless island may find itself needing a Mercedes.

There is a flaw in the Mercedes analogy, though. The Mercedes carries no more passengers or cargo than a correspondingly sized Chevrolet, and at the same speeds. A broadband connection, however, carries far more information; it makes possible a number of uses, including most video uses, that are impractical with a dial-up connection. A more accurate comparison might be not between the Mercedes and the Chevrolet, but between either of those and a wheelbarrow. But as mobile devices supplant computers as the primary means of Internet access, developing countries may find themselves bypassing the PC stage altogether. In Kenya, with 650 telephones per 1,000 people, more than half of the phones in use are Internet-capable (*The Economist* 2012). Uses not yet well developed in the United States, especially using the phone for point-of-sale payments in lieu of cash, check, or credit card, are widespread in Kenya. Just as mobile phone technology enabled developing countries to bypass the development of costly landline systems, mobile Internet device technology may enable them to bypass many of the intermediate steps in the development of Internet access and use.

Whether the ongoing international digital access divide is a cause or effect of poverty, it is shrinking; there are few parts of the world, and hardly any parts of Europe, North America, or East Asia, where Internet access is completely unavailable. The availability and quality of access is constantly improving both through market mechanisms and through ongoing efforts by developing-country governments, international organizations, and aid groups.

As access increases, however, concerns about quality of use and the possibility of a new digital divide have arisen. The Internet can be a tool for increased economic productivity; it can help users get jobs, start companies, and create wealth. But, it can also be a time-waster, and for those without proper training it can actually inhibit productivity. In countries with near-universal Internet access, the children of the relatively well-off are more likely to attend schools that offer such training. The children of the poor are more likely to attend schools that do not, and are likely to waste more time online and spend less time online productively than are economically more advantaged children (Kelly 2012; Warschauer 2012). As a result the time-wasting potential of the Internet becomes one more factor inhibiting upward mobility.

See also: Broadband; Internet

Sources and Further Reading

Jenny Aker, "C U L8ter? Using Mobile Phones as a Literacy Tool in Niger," Center for Global Development (September 13, 2010), available at http://blogs.cgdev.org/globaldevelopment/2010/09/c-u-l8ter-using-mobile-phones-as-a-literacy-tool-in-niger.php (visited January 28, 2013)

Economics & Statistics Administration, "Exploring the Digital Nation—Computer and Internet Use at Home," U.S. Dept. of Commerce (November 8, 2011), available at http://www.esa.doc.gov/Reports/exploring-digital-nation-computer-and-internet-use-home (visited January 28, 2013)

Glenn Elert, ed., "Number of Cell Phones in the US," *The Physics Factbook*™ (2002), available at http://hypertextbook.com/facts/2002/BogusiaGrzywac.shtml (visited January 28, 2013)

"Google in Africa: It's a Hit," *The Economist*, May 12, 2012, at 57

Shane Greenstein & Ryan McDevitt, "Why Broadband Prices Haven't Decreased: Creating the First Broadband Consumer Price Index," *Kellogg Insight* (September 2010), available at http://insight.kellogg.northwestern.edu/index.php/Kellogg/article/why_broadband_prices_havent_decreased/ (visited January 28, 2013)

"Information Technology in Africa: The Next Frontier," *The Economist*, February 16, 2013, at 63

"Innovation in Africa: Upwardly Mobile," *The Economist*, August 25, 2012, at 53

"Internet Users in Africa 2012-Q2," Internet World Stats, available at http://www.internetworldstats.com/stats1.htm (visited January 28, 2013)

"ITU Data & Statistics: Digital Access Index," International Telecommunications Union (ITU), available at http://www.itu.int/ITU-D/ict/dai/ (January 19, 2012)

Rahul Joshi, "Digital Inclusion: Thailand Opens 20,000 Free Wifi Spots in Bangkok," *FutureGov Asia Pacific* (January 18, 2012), available at http://www.futuregov.asia/articles/2012/jan/18/thailand-opens-20000-free-wifi-spots-bangkok/ (visited January 28, 2013)

Drew Kelly, "Wasting Time Is New Divide in Digital Era," *New York Times* (May 29, 2012), available at http://www.nytimes.com/2012/05/30/us/new-digital-divide-seen-in-wasting-time-online.html?_r=3&pagewanted=all& (visited January 28, 2013)

Charles J. Kenny (World Bank), "Expanding Internet Access to the Rural Poor in Africa," International Telecommunications Union, African Internet & Telecom Summit, Banjul, The Gambia, June 5–9, 2000

"Kenya's Mobile Telephones: Vital for the Poor," *The Economist*, November 10, 2012, at 52

"Korea, Internet Usage, Broadband and Telecommunications Report," Internet World Stats, available at http://www.internetworldstats.com/asia/kr.htm (visited January 28, 2013)

Nicholas Lemann, "Letter from Washington: The Chairman: He's the Other Powell, and No One Is Sure What He's Up To," *New Yorker*, October 7, 2002

"Mobile Cellular Subscriptions (per 100 People)," World Bank, available at http://data.worldbank.org/indicator/IT.CEL.SETS.P2 (visited November 13, 2012)

"Municipal Broadband: The Need for Speed," *The Economist*, August 11, 2012, at 26

"Niger, Internet Usage, Broadband and Telecommunications Report," Internet World Stats, available at http://www.internetworldstats.com/af/ne.htm (visited January 28, 2013)

Assif Shameen, "Korea's Broadband Revolution: What Korea Is Doing Will Have Global Impact," *Chief Executive Magazine* (April 1, 2004), available at http://chiefexecutive.net/koreas-broadband-revolution (visited January 28, 2013)

John D. Sutter, "Why Internet Connections Are Fastest in South Korea," CNN Tech (March 31, 2010), available at http://articles.cnn.com/2010–03–31/tech/broadband.south.korea_1_broadband-plan-south-korea-broadband-internet?_s=PM:TECH (visited January 28, 2013)

Berin Szoka & Adam Marcus, eds., *The Next Digital Decade: Essays on the Future of the Internet* (Washington, D.C.: TechFreedom 2010)

Barry Turner, ed., *The Statesman's Yearbook: The Politics, Cultures and Economies of the World* (Houndmills, Basingstoke, UK: Palgrave, 139th ed. 2001)

U.S. Census Bureau, *Statistical Abstract of the United States: 2003* (Washington, D.C.: Government Printing Office, 123d ed. 2003)

U.S. Department of Education, "National Center for Education Statistics Teachers' Use of Educational Technology in U.S. Public Schools: 2009" (May 5, 2010), available at http://nces.ed.gov/pubsearch/pubsinfo.asp?pubid=2010040 (visited January 28, 2013)

Mark Warschauer, "The Digital Divide and Social Inclusion," *Americas Quarterly*, Spring 2012, at 131

"Why Broadband Prices Haven't Decreased," *Kellog Insight* (September 2010), available at http://insight.kellogg.northwestern.edu/index.php/Kellogg/article/why_broadband_prices_havent_decreased/ (visited January 28, 2013)

"The World Is What You Make It: Every Country Has Its Own Internet," *The Economist*, Special Report: Technology and Geography, October 27, 2012, at 20

"World Telecommunications/ICT Development Report 2010" (2010), International Telecommunications Union (ITU), available at http://www.itu.int/ITU-D/ict/publications/wtdr_10/material/WTDR2010_e_v1.pdf (visited January 28, 2013)

❖ DIGITAL MILLENNIUM COPYRIGHT ACT ❖

The Digital Millennium Copyright Act (DMCA), enacted in 1998 and signed into law by then-president Clinton, amended several sections of Title 17 of the United States Code, the portion that contains laws governing copyright. The DMCA as enacted contained five titles, four of which addressed various copyright issues. Title I, the WIPO Copyright and Performances and Phonograms Treaties Implementation Act, was designed to bring U.S. law into conformity with the obligations imposed by two World Intellectual Property Organization (WIPO) treaties. The most controversial aspect of Title I is probably its prohibition of the circumvention of copy-protection measures (17 U.S.C. § 1201–1204). Title II, the Online Copyright Infringement Liability Limitation Act, addressed the problem of potential liability of online service providers for copies made in the routine course of storing and transmitting information, hosting Web sites, and providing search services. Copying of information is necessary to the activities of service providers; Title II insulates these service providers from liability for such routine activities so long as they comply with certain conditions (17 U.S.C. § 512). Title III, the Computer Maintenance Competition Assurance Act, was enacted in response to a federal court decision that had exposed third-party computer maintenance and repair companies to copyright infringement liability for copies of computer programs made by the mere act of starting up a computer in the course of maintenance and repair operations (17 U.S.C. § 117). Title IV addressed several issues: functions of the Copyright Office, ephemeral recordings, copies made for distance education purposes, copies made by nonprofit libraries and archives for preservation or interlibrary loan purposes, webcasting, and the assumption of collective bargaining agreement obligations in the case of transfers of rights in motion pictures (17 U.S.C. §§ 106, 108, 110, 112). Title V created a new form of intellectual property protection for vessel hull designs (17 U.S.C. §§ 1301–1332).

Copyright law, once obscure, has become a battleground on which content owners, equipment manufacturers, and consumers all struggle to preserve what each group perceives as its rights. The DMCA, especially Title I, remains among the most controversial of the several controversial developments in copyright law in recent years. In what is surely a rare honor for a federal copyright statute, it even has an activist group, Anti-DMCA, specifically dedicated to its repeal. Congressional efforts to modify the DMCA in ways more friendly to users than to content owners include the Digital Media Consumers' Rights Act (DMCRA), introduced by users' rights advocate Rick Boucher (D-VA, until 2011).

Statutes
- Copyright Act of 1976 (as amended by DMCA), §§ 101, 104, 104A, 106–10, 112, 117, & 411
- Digital Millennium Copyright Act, 17 U.S.C. §§ 512, 1201–05

See also: Activism and Advocacy Groups; Copyright; Copyright Infringement; Digital Millennium Copyright Act, Title I; Digital Millennium Copyright Act, Title II; Digital Millennium Copyright Act, Title III; Digital Millennium Copyright Act, Title IV; Digital Millennium Copyright Act, Title V; File-Sharing; WIPO Copyright Treaty; WIPO Performance and Phonograms Treaty

Sources and Further Reading
David Nimmer, *Copyright: Sacred Text, Technology, and the DMCA* (The Hague: Kluwer Academic/Plenum Publishers, 2004)
Marcia Wilbur, *DMCA: The Digital Millennium Copyright Act* (San Jose, CA: Writers Club Press, 2001)
Christopher Wolf, *Digital Millennium Copyright Act: Text, History, and Caselaw* (Silver Spring, MD: Pike & Fischer, 2003)

❖ DIGITAL MILLENNIUM COPYRIGHT ACT, TITLE I ❖

Title I of the Digital Millennium Copyright Act (DMCA), the WIPO Copyright and Performances and Phonograms Treaties Implementation Act, was designed to bring U.S. law into conformity with the obligations imposed by two World Intellectual Property Organization (WIPO) treaties. The two treaties referred to in the name of the Act—the WIPO Copyright Treaty and the WIPO Performances and Phonograms Treaty—were adopted in 1996 but did not enter into force until 2002. In order to implement the treaties, Title I created new prohibitions against the circumvention of technological protective measures used to prevent unauthorized copying and against tampering with or removing digital rights management information, made technical amendments to various sections of the copyright code, and required the Copyright Office to perform two joint studies with the National Telecommunications and Information Administration of the Department of Commerce (NTIA). The anticircumvention and rights-management provisions have been the focus of nearly all opposition to Title I and of much of the opposition to the DMCA as a whole.

The anticircumvention provisions: Article 11 of the WIPO Copyright Treaty and Article 18 of the WIPO Performances and Phonograms Treaty both require the United States, as a party to the treaties, to "provide adequate legal protection and effective legal remedies against the circumvention of effective technological measures that are used" to prevent unauthorized reproduction of protected works.

Section 103 of the DMCA adds a new chapter 12 to the copyright code. The first section of this new chapter, section 1201, carries out the mandate of Articles 11 and 18 and is titled "circumvention of copyright protection systems." Ostensibly, it aims to prevent circumvention of technological protective measures that prevent unauthorized *access* to a copyrighted work rather than those that prevent *copying* of the work, thus retaining fair use. In practice, however, access is necessary for copying, and section 1201 is widely perceived as having narrowed the scope of fair use. While it is still possible to make a copy of the analog output of a motion picture or music file, and this copying may be permitted by fair use, this means of copying is less convenient and there will inevitably be some loss of quality.

In addition to the provision that, with a few narrow exceptions, "no person shall circumvent a technological measure that effectively controls access to a work," section 1201 also prohibits the enabling of circumvention by others:

No person shall manufacture, import, offer to the public, provide, or otherwise traffic in any technology, product, service, device, component, or part thereof, that—

(A) is primarily designed or produced for the purpose of circumventing a technological measure that effectively controls access to a work protected under this title;

(B) has only limited commercially significant purpose or use other than to circumvent a technological measure that effectively controls access to a work protected under this title; or

(C) is marketed by that person or another acting in concert with that person with that person's knowledge for use in circumventing a technological measure that effectively controls access to a work protected under this title (17 U.S.C. § 1201(a)(2)).

In other words, it is unlawful under the DMCA to distribute hardware or software that will enable the user to violate the underlying prohibition on circumventing a technological measure that effectively controls access to a work, if the hardware or software is designed for that purpose, if it has little other purpose, or if it is marketed for use in circumvention. Only one of these conditions must be met, not all three. It is only permissible to distribute a device or program capable of circumvention if it is not primarily designed for that purpose, it has another commercially significant purpose or use, and it is not marketed for that purpose.

This might seem to create problems for a wide range of equipment manufacturers. Apple's once famous iMac advertisement ("Rip. Mix. Burn. After all, it's your music") could easily be seen as marketing the iMac for circumvention of technological measures, a use of which the iMac is capable. And consumers, even those who have no intention of violating copyright laws, will generally prefer a computer capable of copying protected works to a computer without that capability. The concerns of equipment manufacturers led to the "no mandate" rule of section 1201(c)(3): equipment manufacturers are not required to design their products to "provide for a response to any particular technological measure." There is an exception to this exception, however: within 18 months of the enactment of the DMCA, all analog videocassette recorders were required to conform to "the automatic gain control copy control technology" distributed by Macrovision (now Rovi) Corporation and used to prevent unauthorized copying of analog videocassettes and some analog signals. The statute prohibits the use of Macrovision's technology to prevent copying of free analog broadcast television and basic and extended basic tier cable broadcasts.

In addition to the "no mandate" provision, there are also two savings clauses in section 1201. Section 1201(c)(1) provides that nothing in section 1201 "shall affect rights, remedies, limitations, or defenses to copyright infringement, including fair use, under this title." And section 1201(c)(2) provides that nothing in section 1201 "shall enlarge or diminish vicarious or contributory liability for copyright infringement[.]" Aside from the "no mandate" provision and these savings clauses, section 1201 also includes an exception for law enforcement, intelligence, and other governmental activities. There are also exceptions, under certain circumstances, for nonprofit library, archive, and educational institutions; reverse engineering to achieve interoperability; encryption research; protection of minors; personal privacy, when the technological measure or the work it protects is capable of collecting or disseminating personally identifying information about the online activities of a natural person; and security testing. There is also an ongoing administrative rule-making proceeding, described in section 1201(a)(1)(B)-(E), to evaluate the impact of the anticircumvention provisions.

Challenges to Section 1201: The anticircumvention provisions have been challenged repeatedly in the courts by activists, as well as by the practice of large numbers of users. These challenges are discussed in detail in the entries on DeCSS and file-sharing elsewhere in this encyclopedia. The DeCSS saga can be regarded as a challenge by technically sophisticated activists seeking to protest Title I, while file-sharing, although it contains a not insignificant element of protest, is primarily of concern to content owners because of its ubiquity rather than its ideological underpinnings.

Not long after the anticircumvention provisions came into effect, copies of a program called DeCSS became available on Web sites in the U.S. DeCSS could be used to decode the encryption used to control access to material recorded on DVDs. The operators of these Web sites were immediately sued by the motion picture industry. The case was heard at trial before the federal district court for the Southern District of New York as *Universal City Studios v. Reimerdes,* and on appeal before the federal Court of Appeals for the Second Circuit as *Universal City Studios v. Corley.* Both the trial court and the appellate court found for the movie-industry plaintiffs, rejecting the defendants' constitutional challenge to section 1201.

The DeCSS case presented § 1201 with two major challenges: the defendants questioned the constitutionality of the anticircumvention provisions, which could have resulted in striking down of § 1201 altogether, and the applicability of § 1201 to software as well as hardware, which could have opened a gigantic loophole, effectively eviscerating the statute. The courts found that, although DeCSS contained expression subject to First Amendment protection, the prohibition against its distribution contained in § 1201 was content-neutral, furthered an important governmental interest (protecting copyrighted works stored on digital media), and was no broader than necessary to further this interest. Nor was there a First Amendment violation in applying the statute to enjoin the defendants from posting links to Web sites from which DeCSS could be downloaded. As to the potential loophole, the things included in the categories of "technology, product, service, device, component, or part thereof" listed in the statute were not limited to hardware, but included software as well. And, although CSS was a relatively weak form of encryption (movie studios had been unable to use stronger encryption because of U.S. export control regulations), it was nonetheless a measure that "effectively controlled access" within the meaning of the statute; a technological measure would be deemed to effectively control access so long as controlling access was its function (*Corley*, 273 F.3d 429). (Note that this interpretation raises a question as to whether the word "effectively" in the statute has any effect.)

The federal courts again considered the application of section 1201 to traditionally copyrighted works on digital media in *United States v. Elcom Ltd*. Elcom made a program capable of circumventing access controls on Adobe e-books. The court found that the application of section 1201 to ban distribution of Elcom's program was, like the ban on distribution of DeCSS, not unconstitutional. The court cited extensively from the opinions of the district and circuit courts in the DeCSS case. (In the federal court system, district courts are bound by the holdings of the Circuit Courts to which their decisions may be appealed, but are not bound by the decisions of other Circuit Courts. The court that decided *Elcom* was a federal district court located in California; appeals from it are heard by the Ninth Circuit. Although the decision of the Second Circuit on a question that had not yet been decided by the Ninth Circuit would carry considerable weight, it was quite possible for the *Elcom* court to have disagreed with the Second Circuit, and for the Ninth Circuit to have affirmed the decision. The Ninth Circuit and the Second Circuit would then have been in disagreement. This sort of conflict between the circuits actually happens quite often; if the situation persists, the Supreme Court may eventually resolve the conflict. The resolution would probably come relatively quickly in a case such as this, if two circuits were to disagree as to the constitutionality of a federal statute.)

In holding that section 1201 as applied to Elcom's program was constitutional, the district court explained that "while it is not unlawful to circumvent for the purpose of engaging in fair use, it is unlawful to traffic in tools that allow fair use circumvention." In other words, fair use of protected materials is still available, but only to those who are technically savvy enough to circumvent the protective measures themselves (203 F. Supp 1111).

The anticircumvention provisions, originally envisioned as a way to prevent piracy of movies recorded on DVDs, have also been applied to technological protective measures in things as diverse as printer cartridges, garage door openers, and an investment firm's virtual private network (VPN). This expansion of the application of the DMCA's anticircumvention provisions may ultimately have more far-reaching effects than the application of those provisions to movies, music, and e-books. No one questions, after all, that movies, music, and books are copyrightable; these are traditional subjects of copyright law, and debate over the anticircumvention provisions has tended to focus on the extent to which the DMCA restricts fair use. But printer cartridges, for example, are not traditional subjects of copyright law. Copyright could give printer manufacturers a powerful tool to ensure that those who buy their printers must use their cartridges and no others, bringing about the demise of the printer cartridge aftermarket.

In *Lexmark International v. Static Control Components*, a maker of printers and printer cartridges sued a manufacturer of components for remanufactured computer cartridges. One of these components was the SMARTEK chip, which could be used to allow remanufactured cartridges to work with Lexmark printers. Lexmark had installed chips containing a toner loading program on some of its cartridges; the printers, meanwhile, contained a printer engine program. Neither the toner loading program nor the printer engine program would function unless the printer and the microchip on the toner cartridge "recognized" each other by successfully executing an authentication sequence. Static Control Components ("SCC") designed the SMARTEK chip to enable cartridges remanufactured by persons other than Lexmark to mimic this authentication sequence, thus fooling the printer into believing that it was working with an authentic Lexmark-remanufactured cartridge. SCC reverse engineered a means of bypassing the authentication sequence, but copied the toner loading program on to the SMARTEK chip. The first of these actions gave rise to Lexmark's anticircumvention claim, while the second gave rise to an infringement claim (*Static Control*, 253 F. Supp. 2d 943).

The federal district court for the Eastern District of Kentucky agreed with Lexmark that Lexmark was likely to prevail upon both its anticircumvention and its copyright infringement claims on the merits, and granted injunctive relief against SCC. On appeal, however, the Sixth Circuit Court of Appeals vacated the decision and remanded the case for further proceedings. The Sixth Circuit found that Lexmark had failed to establish a likelihood of success on the merits, and that the bypassing of the lockout code was not necessarily a copyright violation:

> Generally speaking, 'lock-out' codes fall on the functional-idea rather than the original-expression side of the copyright line. Manufacturers of interoperable devices such as computers and software, game consoles and video games, printers and toner cartridges, or automobiles and replacement parts may employ a security system to bar the use of unauthorized components. To 'unlock' and permit operation of the primary device (i.e., the computer, the game console, the printer, the car), the component must contain either a certain code sequence or be able to respond appropriately to an authentication process. To the extent compatibility requires that a particular code sequence be included in the component device to permit its use, the merger and scènes à faire doctrines generally preclude the code sequence from obtaining copyright protection (*Lexmark*, 387 F.3d at 536).

This was in direct contrast to the trial court's rejection of SCC's argument that Lexmark had improperly used copyright law to provide protection to a thing not otherwise copyrightable—the printer cartridge (*Static Control*, 253

F. Supp. 2d 943). The Sixth Circuit pointed out that there were public policy interests favoring interoperability—the "Progress of Science and Useful Arts"—mentioned in the Constitution's copyright clause (U.S. Constitution, Art. I, §8, cl. 8). Congress took these interests into account in designing the DMCA, apparently with things like printer cartridges in mind: "Congress added the interoperability provision in part to ensure that the DMCA would not diminish the benefit to consumers of interoperable devices 'in the consumer electronics environment.'"

The garage door opener case, *Chamberlain Group v. Skylink Technologies*, had superficially similar facts but led to a different result. Chamberlain is a manufacturer of garage door openers; Skylink is a distributor of garage door opener components. Modern garage door openers, including Chamberlain's, use a rolling code signal for added security. (In the absence of the rolling code method, a burglar could leave recording equipment near the garage door, wait until the door opener was used, and then retrieve the door-opening code from the recording equipment.) Because the rolling codes in the remote control and the garage door opener might become desynchronized if the remote control was pressed several times while out of range of the door opener, Chamberlain's door openers also included a process to allow resynchronization of the door opener and the remote control. Skylink distributed universal remotes that used the resynchronization process to operate the Chamberlain garage door openers, thus compromising the rolling code security feature. Chamberlain claimed that the rolling code component of its copyrighted garage door opener program protected the portion of the software that actually operated the door opener, and thus fell within the protection of section 1201. The federal district court for the Northern District of Illinois disagreed and denied Chamberlain's motion for summary judgment. A motion for summary judgment is a legal mechanism that can be used to resolve a case without trial; it can be granted only if there is no genuine issue of material fact and if, based on those undisputed facts, the moving party is entitled to judgment as a matter of law. The court found that there were genuine issues as to two material facts: whether the garage door opener program was in fact protected by copyright, and whether owners of Chamberlain rolling code garage door openers were authorized to use Skylink's remote control (*Skylink*, 292 F. Supp. 2d 1023). On appeal, the Federal Circuit also pointed out that:

> Chamberlain . . . has failed to show not only the requisite lack of authorization, but also the necessary fifth element of its claim, the critical nexus between access and protection. Chamberlain neither alleged copyright infringement nor explained how the access provided by the Model 39 transmitter facilitates the infringement of any right that the Copyright Act protects. There can therefore be no reasonable relationship between the access that homeowners gain to Chamberlain's copyrighted software when using Skylink's Model 39 transmitter and the protections that the Copyright Act grants to Chamberlain (629 F.3d at 1204).

This critical nexus was necessary to prevent "absurd and disastrous" results, as when a burglar disables "a burglar alarm to gain 'access' to a home containing copyrighted books, music, art, and periodicals" and is then charged with "violat[ing] the DMCA" (*id.* at 1201). The Ninth Circuit, however, has taken a somewhat different view, stating (in a now-vacated opinion in *MDY Industries v. Blizzard Entertainment*) that:

> *Chamberlain* . . . viewed an infringement nexus requirement as necessary to prevent "absurd and disastrous results," such as the existence of DMCA liability for disabling a burglary alarm to gain access to a home containing copyrighted materials. In addition, the Federal Circuit was concerned that, without an infringement nexus requirement, §1201(a) would allow copyright owners to deny all access to the public by putting an effective access control measure in place that the public is not allowed to circumvent. Both concerns appear to be overstated, but even accepting them, arguendo, as legitimate concerns, they do not permit reading the statute as requiring the imposition of an infringement nexus. As §1201(a) creates a distinct right, it does not disturb the balance between public rights and the traditional rights of owners of copyright under the Copyright Act. Moreover, § 1201(a)(1)(B)-(D) allows the Library of Congress to create exceptions to the § 1201(a) anti-circumvention right in the public's interest. If greater protection of the public's ability to access copyrighted works is required, Congress can provide such protection by amending the statute (629 F.3d 949).

In general, the Federal Circuit's opinion in *Chamberlain* probably represents the prevailing view in cases where the "content" is sought not for its own sake, but for some other purpose (in that case, in order to open a garage door). While the Ninth Circuit was critical of *Chamberlain*, the facts in *MDY Industries* were different; the circumvention in question was in fact done to gain access to Blizzard's copyrighted content by advancing players in the game more quickly than they could have advanced otherwise, rather than to accomplish some non-informational task such as the opening of a garage door.

In the virtual private network (VPN) case, *Pearl Investments v. Standard I/O*, defendants improperly gained access to the plaintiff's VPN by unauthorized use of access protocols. The federal district court for the District of Maine held that because a "VPN is the 'electronic equivalent' of a locked door" it is a "technological protection measure." This decision, if widely adopted, would represent a further expansion of the scope of section 1201. The district court seems to be willing to apply section 1201 to any unauthorized access to a VPN or similar encryption-protected system, and perhaps to any password-protected Web site, file, folder or disk, even though no device or program—only a password—is used to gain that access (257 F. Supp. 2d 326).

Digital rights management: Article 12 of the WIPO Copyright Treaty and Article 19 of the WIPO Performances and Phonograms Treaty require the parties to prohibit not only the circumvention of technological measures used to prevent actual copying, but also any other circumvention of an electronic rights management scheme. The parties must "provide adequate and effective legal remedies against any person knowingly" removing or altering "any electronic rights management information," or distributing, importing for distribution, broadcasting or communicating to the public any works from which such information has been removed, if in either case the person does not have the authority to do so and knows or has reason to know that doing so "will induce, enable, facilitate or conceal an infringement of any right covered by" the treaties.

The second section of chapter 12, section 1202, carries out the mandate of Articles 12 and 19 and is titled "integrity of copyright management information." Copyright management information is defined in section 1202(c) as information identifying and about the title, author, and copyright owner and, with the exception of audiovisual works and broadcasts of public performance, the performer of a work; the writer, performer, or director credited in an audiovisual work, with the exception of broadcast public performances; "terms and conditions for use of the work"; and "identifying numbers or symbols referring to such information or links to such information." There is also a catch-all category: copyright management information may also include "such other information as the Register of Copyrights may prescribe by regulation, except that the Register of Copyrights may not require the provision of any information concerning the user of a copyrighted work." The text at the beginning of section 1202(c) also specifically excludes "personally identifying information about a user of a work" from the definition of copyright management information.

Section 1202(a) prohibits the knowing use of false copyright management information "with the intent to induce, enable, facilitate, or conceal infringement." Section 1202(b) provides that

No person shall, without the authority of the copyright owner or the law—

(1) intentionally remove or alter any copyright management information, [or]

(2) distribute or import for distribution copyright management information knowing that the copyright management information has been removed or altered without authority of the copyright owner or the law, or

(3) distribute, import for distribution, or publicly perform works, copies of works, or phonorecords, knowing that copyright management information has been removed or altered without authority of the copyright owner or the law.

Section 1202, like section 1201, includes a general exemption for law enforcement, intelligence, and other governmental activities. It also provides exceptions for broadcast stations and cable systems if there is no intent "to induce, enable, facilitate, or conceal infringement of a right" and, in the case of analog transmissions, "avoiding the activity that constitutes such violation is not technically feasible or would create an undue financial hardship on such person"; or, in the case of digital transmissions, certain conditions relating to digital transmission standards for the placement of copyright management information are present.

The next section of Chapter 12, section 1203, provides civil remedies for violations of the provisions of the preceding two sections; section 1204 provides criminal penalties.

The technical amendments: The three technical amendments in Title I dealt with eligibility for national treatment, restoration of protection to some works that had fallen into the public domain in the United States, and copyright formalities.

The WIPO treaties, along with the Berne Convention, require what is called national treatment. Parties to the treaties must provide protection to works and authors from other member countries no less favorable than that accorded to works authored by their own nationals or published in their own territories. Title I amended sections 101 and 104 of the Copyright Act; section 101 deals with general definitions and section 104 deals with subject matter and national origin. Title I added references to the WTO Agreement (which includes the Trade-related Aspects of Intellectual Property Agreement, better known as TRIPS), the WIPO Copyright Treaty, and the WIPO Performances and Phonograms Treaty and striking out the definition of a "Berne Convention work." It also made changes to the language of several subsections and added a provision regarding simultaneous publication of works initially published in states not parties to the various copyright treaties.

The DMCA also amended section 104A of the Copyright Act, which restores copyright protection to certain works that had fallen into the public domain in the United States under earlier U.S. copyright law, but remained protected by copyright in their country of origin. The amendments changed the wording of section 104A to include those states that were parties to the WIPO treaties. The Berne Convention and TRIPS had already required restoration of copyright to works from parties to those treaties, and in 1995 the Uruguay Round Agreements Act, in furtherance of this obligation, had created section 104A. The DMCA's extension of this protection to parties to the WIPO treaties was necessary in order to reflect the treaty obligations accurately, but had no practical effect, as all of the parties to the WIPO treaties were already parties to the Berne Convention, TRIPS, or both.

The next technical amendment concerned section 411(a) of the Copyright Act, which requires that claims of copyright be registered with the Copyright Office before the copyright owner, can initiate a lawsuit for copyright infringement. Prior to the DMCA, section 411(a) contained an exemption for Berne Convention works. The DMCA broadened the exception to include all foreign works. This was not actually required by the various treaty obligations of the United States; even though the Berne Convention, TRIPS, and the WIPO treaties contain "no formalities" requirements, there are a handful of countries that are not parties to any of these conventions; these countries also receive the benefit of the DMCA's "all foreign works" amendment even though the United States was under no obligation to extend it to them. Note also that this amendment, like the restoration of copyright to some foreign works that have fallen into the public domain but not to some U.S. works identically situated, has the odd effect of giving greater protection to foreign works than to U.S. works.

The joint studies: Title I required the NTIA to prepare two reports. The first, to be completed within one year, was to focus narrowly on the effects of section 1201(g) of the copyright code, added by the DMCA, on encryption research. The second, to be completed within two years, had a somewhat broader mandate; it was to address the effects of statutory, technological, and commercial changes on the right of first sale and the right to make backup and other necessary copies of computer programs.

The first of these two required reports—the report on the effect of section 1201(g) on encryption technology research—was mandated by section 1201(g)(5), which provided that:

> Not later than 1 year after the date of the enactment of [the DMCA], the Register of Copyrights and the Assistant Secretary for Communications and Information of the Department of Commerce shall jointly report to the Congress on the effect this subsection has had on—
>
> (A) encryption research and the development of encryption technology;
> (B) the adequacy and effectiveness of technological measures designed to protect copyrighted works; and
> (C) protection of copyright owners against the unauthorized access to their encrypted copyrighted works.

The report was to "include legislative recommendations, if any." The report was completed before the provisions that would have affected encryption technology research went into effect, and forwarded to Congress in May, 2000. It concluded that "every concern expressed [in response to the Copyright Office's and NTIA's solicitation] was prospective in nature, primarily because the prohibition and its attendant exceptions will not become operative until October 28, 2000." As a result, "we conclude that it is premature to suggest alternative language or legislative recommendations with regard to Section 1201(g) of the DMCA at this time" (United States Copyright Office 2000).

The second report was due a year later, 24 months after the enactment of the DMCA, and requires the same parties to evaluate the effects of Title I and technological and e-commerce advances on the first sale doctrine (17 U.S.C. § 109) and on the exemption allowing owners of copies of computer programs to reproduce and adapt them for use

on a computer (17 U.S.C. § 117). The report was also to evaluate the relationship between the operation of sections 109 and 117 on the one hand and existing and emergent technology on the other. The NTIA issued its report in August 2001 (United States Copyright Office 2001).

The right of first sale allows the owner of a lawful copy of a work to dispose of that copy. The right to dispose includes the right to sell, give away, or otherwise transfer the lawful copy, as well as the right to display it at the place where it is located. It does not include the right to display the copy other than where it is located by broadcasting it, transmitting it over the Internet, or by other means. Section 109 also makes exceptions for sound recordings and computer programs, which may not be rented, leased, or lent by the purchaser without the consent of the copyright owner. Further exceptions to the exceptions for computer programs and sound recordings permit such lending by nonprofit libraries and educational institutions, and exempt rentals of computer programs "embodied in a machine or product and which cannot be copied during the ordinary operation or use of the machine or product; or . . . embodied in or used in conjunction with a limited purpose computer that is designed for playing video games and may be designed for other purposes" (17 U.S.C. § 109). The exemption in section 117 provides that

> it is not an infringement for the owner of a copy of a computer program to make or authorize the making of another copy or adaptation of that computer program provided:
>
> (1) that such a new copy or adaptation is created as an essential step in the utilization of the computer program in conjunction with a machine and that it is used in no other manner, [or]
> (2) that such new copy or adaptation is for archival purposes only and that all archival copies are destroyed in the event that continued possession of the computer program should cease to be rightful.

There is an additional exception added to section 117 by Title III of the DMCA: the exception for copies of computer programs made for purposes of maintenance or repair, discussed later. There is also an exception for performance and display of videogames.

In its report, the NTIA observed that "the inclusion of section 109 in the study has a clear relationship to the digital first sale proposal contained in a bill introduced in 1997 by Congressmen Rick Boucher and Tom Campbell. The reasons for including section 117 in the study are less obvious." The NTIA speculated, though, that section 117 was included because of "a proposed exemption for incidental copies found in the Boucher-Campbell bill, which would have been codified in section 117" (United States Copyright Office 2001).

After soliciting and reviewing comments from the content industry, consumer advocates, and others, the NTIA concluded that the anticircumvention provisions of the DMCA had, as yet, no adverse effect on section 109. The concerns expressed to the NTIA about the use of technological measures, particularly Content Scramble System (CSS), were flawed: the fact that DVDs require a special decoding device in order to be viewed does not make them unique. All sound and motion picture recordings require some special device in order to be played back. There is no statutory guarantee of a secondary market for copyrighted works. In any event, while "tethering" a work to a particular hardware device was possible and permissible under the DMCA, the practice was not widespread except in the case of e-books. If the practice were to become widespread, though, there might be a negative impact on the first sale doctrine. There was at least a potential negative impact on section 117, however; technological protective measures might interfere with section 117's archival exception (United States Copyright Office 2001).

While the effect of the DMCA itself on the two sections was minimal, the effect of e-commerce and technological change was significant. With regard to the first-sale doctrine, the advent of computers and the Internet had vastly increased the potential for the owner of a lawful copy of a work to harm the copyright-holder's interest. The first sale doctrine creates a right of distribution, not a right to copy. But because of the ease with which digital copies can be made and distributed—a click of a mouse can send thousands of copies over the Internet, and posting the work on a Web site can make it accessible to billions—the danger of harm to the copyright holder's interest is greater than with, for example, hard copies of books. Technological protective measures deal with this harm without affecting the right protected by section 109: the right to dispose of the original copy of the work that the consumer has purchased. The NTIA recommended no change to section 109 at present, but suggested that problems requiring legislative correction might eventually arise with regard to use by libraries (United States Copyright Office 2001). Complications have also arisen with consumers' right to resell digital works they have purchased (in effect transferring the license) and to import copies legally made in one country to another (see, e.g., *F.B.T. Products*, 621 F. 3d 958; *Kirtsaeng*, 133 S.Ct. 1351). These are discussed in more detail under the heading "First Sale."

A tangentially related and highly controversial area was the making of buffer copies in the course of playing streaming media. Webcasters of streaming media expressed to the NTIA their concerns that they could be forced to pay double royalties on a single download—once for buffering, and once for actual playback. The NTIA found that the making of such buffer copies is "copying" for copyright purposes, adding that a strong case could be made that the making of buffer copies, necessary for smooth playback, was fair use. But the outcome of the fair use argument was not certain; to protect webcasters, the NTIA recommended "that Congress enact legislation amending the Copyright Act to preclude any liability arising from the assertion of a copyright owner's reproduction right with respect to temporary buffer copies that are incidental to a licensed digital transmission of a public performance of a sound recording and any underlying musical work." It made a similar observation, without an explicit legislative recommendation, regarding "performance" of licensed digital music downloads (United States Copyright Office 2001).

In 2002, an arbitral panel decided that music webcasters—"Internet radio stations"—should pay a 9% surcharge for buffer copies. This was coupled with the panel's decision that Web-only stations should pay royalties twice as high as those paid by broadcast stations retransmitting their programs via the Internet; the concerns the webcasters voiced to the NTIA have thus proved well founded (Copyright Arbitration Royalty Panel 2002). This amount was reduced only slightly in the subsequent order of the Librarian of Congress, which set the surcharge for buffer copies at 8.8% (67 Federal Register 45, 239; 37 C.F.R. 261.3(c)).

Since then the Register of Copyrights has gone on record as opposing copyright liability for buffer copies:

> I have already expressed the view that there should be no liability for the making of buffer copies in the course of streaming a licensed public performance of a musical work. On the other hand, RIAA and the Harry Fox Agency have reached an agreement that buffer copies and server copies made for purposes of or in the course of the streaming of performances are included within the scope of the section 115 compulsory license. But perhaps more important than the decision whether to provide an exemption for such copies or to include them within the section 115 license is the need to clarify the status of such copies one way or another. Any reform of section 115 should definitively resolve that issue (Statement of Marybeth Peters 2005).

And in 2008, the U.S. Court of Appeals for the Second Circuit held that transient buffer copies made in the course of video transmission to a digital video recorder (DVR) were not "fixed" within the meaning of the copyright act and thus did not infringe copyright (*Cartoon Network*, 536 F.3d at 129–30).

Nor, at the time of the NTIA's report, was Section 109 the only area of concern. The NTIA found Section 117, dealing with archival copies, to be even more out of date. The provision permitting the making of an archival copy of a program, provided that "all archival copies are destroyed in the event that continued possession of the computer program should cease to be rightful," did not reflect the realities of computer use. Consumers need to back up digital works in digital form because the digital nature of the works renders them vulnerable. Most system administrators and many individual users address this problem with periodic backups of all of the data on a system, even though section 117 does not permit this. It would be costly, time consuming, and inefficient to go through each file on a system and identify it as a program or nonprogram file before backing up the system. Nor would it be practical to examine the contents of past tape backups and delete any program files for which a license might have expired. As a result, the NTIA stated,

"There is a fundamental mismatch between accepted, prudent practices among most system administrators and other users, on the one hand, and section 117 on the other. As a consequence, few adhere to the law." But, the NTIA saw no need for legislative action on this basis alone: "While there is no question that this mismatch exists, nobody was able to identify any actual harm to consumers as a result of the limited scope of the archival exemption." A problem, however, arose from the interaction of fair use (17 U.S.C. § 107) and first sale: the making of backup copies according to the usual practice is probably a fair use, and a court might conceivably conclude that a copy thus made could be sold or otherwise disposed of by the user under section 109. The NTIA therefore recommended that Congress either "amend section 109 to ensure that fair use copies are not subject to the first sale doctrine or . . . create a new archival exemption that provides expressly that backup copies may not be distributed" (United States Copyright Office 2001).

The NTIA also considered the issue of contract preemption that arises when end-user license agreements (EULAs) purport to give copyright-like protection that overrides user rights under copyright law. Enforcement of these contracts under state law raises the preemption issue, because the Copyright Act by its terms (17 U.S.C. § 301) preempts state attempts to make copyright law. Again the NTIA stopped short of making any legislative recommendation; the situation was evolving rapidly, and it was possible that market forces alone would correct the problem, preventing right holders from using EULAs to impose unreasonable limits on consumers' use of copyrighted material. If not, statutory change might be appropriate at some point in the future (United States Copyright Office 2001).

Statutes

- Copyright Act of 1976 (as amended by DMCA Title I), §§ 101, 104, 104A, 107, 109, 117, & 411
- Digital Millennium Copyright Act, 17 U.S.C. §§ 1201–05

Regulation

- Determination of Reasonable Rates and Terms for the Digital Performance of Sound Recordings and Ephemeral Recordings, Final Rule, 67 Fed. Reg. 45,239 (July 8, 2002) (codified at 37 C.F.R. § 261)

Cases

Supreme Court

- *Kirtsaeng v. John Wiley & Sons, Inc.*, 133 S.Ct. 1351 (2013)

Federal Appellate Courts

- *Cartoon Network LP, LLLP v. CSC Holdings, Inc.*, 536 F.3d 121 (2d Cir. 2008)
- *Chamberlain Group, Inc. v. Skylink Technologies, Inc.*, 381 F.3d 1178 (Fed. Cir. 2004)

- *F.B.T. Productions, LLC v. Aftermath Records*, 621 F.3d 958 (9th Cir. 2010)
- *MDY Industries, LLC, v. Blizzard Entertainment, Inc.*, 629 F.3d 928 (9th Cir. 2010)
- *Universal City Studios, Inc. v. Corley*, 273 F.3d 429 (2d Cir. 2001), affirming *Universal City Studios, Inc., v. Reimerdes*, 111 F. Supp. 2d 294 (S.D.N.Y. 2000)

Federal Trial Courts

- *Adobe Systems, Inc. v. Stargate Software Inc.*, 216 F. Supp. 2d 1051 (N.D. Cal. 2002)
- *Arclightz and Films Pvt. Ltd. v. Video Palace Inc.*, 303 F. Supp. 2d 356 (S.D.N.Y. 2003)
- *Chamberlain Group, Inc. v. Skylink Technologies, Inc.*, 292 F. Supp. 2d 1023 (N.D. Ill. 2003), affirmed, 381 F.3d 1178 (Fed. Cir. 2004); certiorari denied, 544 U.S. 923 (2005)
- *Lexmark International, Inc. v. Static Control Components, Inc.*, 253 F. Supp. 2d 943 (E.D. Ky. 2003); reversed, 387 F.3d 522 (6th Cir. 2004); see also *Static Control Components, Inc. v. Dallas Semiconductor Corp.*, No. 1:02CV1057, 2003 WL 21666582 (M.D.N.C. 2003) (same issue)
- *Microsoft Corporation v. Software Wholesale Club, Inc.*, 129 F. Supp. 2d 995 (S.D. Tex. 2000)
- *Pearl Investments, LLC v. Standard I/O, Inc.*, 257 F. Supp. 2d 326 (D. Me. 2003)
- *RealNetworks, Inc. v. Streambox, Inc.*, No. 2:99CV02070, 2000 WL 127311 (W.D. Wash. 2000)
- *United States v. Elcom Ltd.*, 203 F. Supp. 2d 1111 (N.D. Cal. 2002)
- *Video Pipeline, Inc. v. Buena Vista Home Entertainment, Inc.*, 192 F. Supp. 2d 321 (D.N.J. 2002), affirmed, 342 F.3d 191 (3d Cir. 2003)

Reports

- Copyright Arbitration Royalty Panel, Report to the Librarian of Congress (February 20, 2002), Appendix A, available at http://www.copyright.gov/carp/webcast_regs.html#panel (visited July 29, 2012)
- Register of Copyrights, before the Subcommittee on Intellectual Property, Senate Judiciary Committee, 109th Congress (2005) (Statement of Marybeth Peters)
- United States Copyright Office, DMCA Section 104 Report: A Report of the Register of Copyrights Pursuant to § 104 of the Digital Millennium Copyright Act (August 2001)
- United States Copyright Office, Joint Study of Section 1201(g) of the Digital Millennium Copyright Act (May 2000)

See also: Activist and Advocacy Groups; Berne Convention; Censorship; Contracts; Copyright; Copyright Infringement; DeCSS; Digital Millennium Copyright Act, Title II; Digital Millennium Copyright Act, Title III; Digital Millennium

Copyright Act, Title IV; Digital Rights Management; Encryption; Fair Use; File-Sharing; First Amendment; First Sale; International Copyright Protection; Moral Rights; Open Source; Steganography; TRIPS; WIPO Copyright Treaty; WIPO Performance and Phonograms Treaty

Sources and Further Reading

Tanya Aplin, *Copyright Law in the Digital Society: The Challenges of Multimedia* (Oxford, United Kingdom: Hart Publishing, 2005)

"Come Stream with Me: Is There Money in Digital Radio?" *The Economist*, June 16, 2012, at 74

Laura DeNardis, ed., *Opening Standards: The Global Politics of Interoperability* (Cambridge, MA: MIT Press, 2011)

Alessandra Garbagnati, "The Wrath of the Blizz King: How the Ninth Circuit's Decision in MDY Industries, Inc. v. Blizzard Entertainment May Slay the Game Genie," 34 *Hastings Communications and Entertainment Law Journal* 313 (2012)

Tarleton Gillespie, *Wired Shut: Copyright and the Shape of Digital Culture* (Cambridge, MA: MIT Press, 2007)

David Nimmer, *Copyright: Sacred Text, Technology, and the DMCA* (The Hague: Kluwer Academic/Plenum Publishers, 2004)

Pamela Samuelson, "Intellectual Property and the Digital Economy: Why the Anti-Circumvention Regulations Need to Be Revised," 14 *Berkeley Technology Law Journal* 519 (1999)

Pamela Samuelson, *Towards More Sensible Anti-Circumvention Regulations, Cyberspace Lawyer*, July/August 2000, at 2

Christopher Wolf, *Digital Millennium Copyright Act: Text, History, and Caselaw* (Silver Spring, Maryland: Pike & Fischer, 2003)

Jonathan L. Zittrain, *Technological Complements to Copyright* (New York: Foundation Press, 2005)

❖ DIGITAL MILLENNIUM COPYRIGHT ACT, TITLE II ❖

Title II of the Digital Millennium Copyright Act (DMCA), the Online Copyright Infringement Liability Limitation Act, created limitations on the liability of online service providers for copyright infringement when engaging in certain types of activities. The Act created a new section 512 of Title 17 of the United States Code (the copyright code). Section 512 set up and defined safe harbors for service providers for transitory communications, system caching, storage of information on systems or networks at the direction of users, and information location tools. Special rules were also delineated for nonprofit educational institutions. Service providers whose activities fall within the scope of the safe harbor provisions cannot be held liable for damages for copyright infringement arising from those activities, and the availability of injunctive relief against those service providers is limited. The definition of "service provider" in the statute is broad, and could conceivably include online file-sharing services; however, a file-sharing service that deliberately blinds itself (e.g., through the use of encryption) to copyright infringement using its services may not be able to claim the protection of the safe harbors.

In addition to the safe harbor provisions, § 512 permits a copyright owner to obtain a subpoena from a federal court ordering a service provider to disclose the identity of a subscriber who is allegedly engaging in infringing activities (17 U.S.C. § 512(h)). The limits of this subpoena power were defined by the federal appellate court for the District of Columbia Circuit in its December 2003 decision in the case of *Recording Industry Association of America v. Verizon Internet Services*. The RIAA had obtained a subpoena under § 512(h) to compel Verizon to disclose the name of a subscriber who had allegedly shared copyrighted music files. The D.C. Circuit agreed with Verizon that the subpoena, issued before any lawsuit had been filed, could not compel Verizon to disclose the name of the subscriber. The D.C. Circuit distinguished between conduit Internet service providers, which are not subject to a § 512(h) subpoena, and hosting Internet service providers, which may be. In this case Verizon, acting as a mere conduit, was not subject to the subpoena (351 F.3d 1229). As a result, subsequent RIAA file-sharing suits must be brought as "John Doe" actions; once the litigation has been instituted, subpoenas may be obtained as part of the discovery process. Such subpoenas are harder to obtain than § 512(h) subpoenas and require judicial oversight to prevent abuses.

Under § 512, service providers are not required to monitor their services or access material in violation of law (such as the Electronic Communications Privacy Act) in order to be eligible for the protection of any of the safe harbor provisions. A service provider, for purposes of the transitory communications safe harbor provision, is "an entity offering the transmission, routing, or providing of connections for digital online communications, between or among points specified by a user, of material of the user's choosing, without modification to the content of the material as sent or received" (17 U.S.C. § 512(k)(1)(A)). For the other three safe harbors, a service provider is more broadly defined as "a provider of online services or network access, or the operator of facilities therefor" (17 U.S.C. § 512(k)(1)(B)). To be eligible for protection, a service provider must have "adopted and reasonably implemented . . . a policy that provides for the termination in appropriate circumstances of. . . repeat infringers"; and it must also accommodate and not interfere with "standard technical measures" for copyright protection (17 U.S.C. § 512(i)(1)).

Transitory communications safe harbor: Under section 512(a), a service provider is not liable for damages or, except as provided in section 512(j), for injunctive or other equitable relief for copyright infringement where the provider merely acts as a conduit, transmitting digital information from one point on a network to another at someone else's request. The transitory communications safe harbor is available if five elements are present:

(1) the transmission. . . was initiated by or at the direction of a person other than the service provider;

(2) the transmission, routing, provision of connections, or storage is carried out through an automatic technical process without selection of the material by the service provider;

(3) the service provider does not select the recipients of the material except as an automatic response to the request of another person;

(4) no copy of the material made by the service provider in the course of such intermediate or transient storage is maintained on the system or network in a manner ordinarily accessible to anyone other than anticipated recipients, and no such copy is maintained on the system or network in a manner ordinarily accessible to such anticipated recipients for a longer period than is reasonably necessary . . .; and

(5) the material is transmitted through the system or network without modification of its content (17 U.S.C. § 512(a)).

The exception in section 512(j) limits injunctive relief in such cases to two types of orders: orders requiring the service provider to deny access to the infringing user by terminating that user's account and, where the infringing site is outside the United States, orders requiring the service provider to take "reasonable steps . . . to block access to a specific, identified, online location outside the United States." In granting injunctive relief when one of the section 512 safe harbors protects the service provider from an award of damages, the court shall consider four factors:

(A) whether [injunctive relief] would significantly burden either the provider or the operation of the provider's system or network;

(B) the magnitude of the harm likely to be suffered by the copyright owner in the digital network environment if steps are not taken to prevent or restrain the infringement;

(C) whether implementation of such an injunction would be technically feasible and effective, and would not interfere with access to noninfringing material at other online locations; and

(D) whether other less burdensome and comparably effective means of preventing or restraining access to the infringing material are available (17 U.S.C. § 512(j)(2)).

System caching safe harbor: Under section 512(b), a service provider is not liable for damages or, except as provided in section 512(j), for injunctive or other equitable relief for copyright infringement where the copy is made for system caching purposes, that is "by reason of the intermediate and temporary storage of material" on the service provider's system or network, if

(A) the material is made available online by a person other than the service provider;

(B) the material is transmitted from the person described in subparagraph (A) through the system or network

to a person other than the person described in subparagraph (A) at the direction of that other person; and

(C) the storage is carried out through an automatic technical process for the purpose of making the material available to users of the system or network who, after the material is transmitted as described in subparagraph (B), request access to the material from the person described in subparagraph (A) (17 U.S.C. § 512(b)).

Certain additional conditions must also be met: the content of the retained material must not be modified. The service provider must periodically refresh the material by replacing the cached copy with a new copy made from the original location, in accordance with a generally accepted industry protocol, and must not interfere with technology that returns "hit" information to the person who posted the material. Once the service provider has been notified that copyrighted material posted without authorization has been removed or blocked, or ordered to be removed or blocked, at the original site, it must promptly remove or block access to the cached copy. If the person who posted the material has imposed limitations on access, such as password protection, the service provider must also impose these limitations (17 U.S.C. § 512(b)).

The scope of injunctive relief permitted under section 512(j) for the other three safe harbors (system caching, information storage, and information location tools) differs slightly from that permitted with respect to the transitory communications safe harbor. Injunctive relief is limited to orders "restraining the service provider from providing access to infringing material or activity residing at a particular online site on the provider's system or network," and, as with the transitory communications safe harbor, orders requiring the service provider to deny access to the infringing user by terminating that user's account (17 U.S.C. § 512(j)).

Information storage safe harbor: Under section 512(c), a service provider is not liable for damages or, except as provided in section 512(j), for injunctive or other equitable relief for copyright infringement for infringing material stored at the direction of a user on Web sites (or other information repositories) hosted on their systems. The information storage safe harbor is available if the service provider:

(A)
(i) does not have actual knowledge that the material or an activity using the material on the system or network is infringing; [or]

(ii) in the absence of such actual knowledge, is not aware of facts or circumstances from which infringing activity is apparent; or

(iii) upon obtaining such knowledge or awareness, acts expeditiously to remove, or disable access to, the material; [and]

(B) does not receive a financial benefit directly attributable to the infringing activity, in a case in which the service provider has the right and ability to control such activity; and

(C) upon notification of claimed infringement as described in paragraph (3), responds expeditiously to remove, or disable access to, the material that is claimed to be infringing or to be the subject of infringing activity (17 U.S.C. § 512(c)).

In order to receive the benefit of the information storage safe harbor, the service provider must also have filed with the Copyright Office a designation of an agent to receive notifications of claimed infringement.

Section 512(c) also provides a notice-and-takedown procedure. If infringing material is posted on a Web site, the copyright owner must first submit a notification to the service provider's designated agent. If the notice does not contain all of the information required by section 512(c), it will not be considered in determining whether the service provider had knowledge of the infringement. Courts have construed this requirement strictly. For example, if the owner of copyright in a movie notifies eBay, an online auction marketplace, that unauthorized copies of his movie are being listed on eBay, that act alone does not meet the notice requirement. The notification must be in writing and must contain information specific enough to enable eBay to distinguish between authorized and unauthorized listings.

If the service provider acts promptly, upon receipt of proper notification, to remove or block access to the infringing content, the provider is protected within the safe harbor both from monetary liability to the copyright holder and from liability for any claim arising from its having removed or blocked access to the material. The service provider must also promptly notify the user who initially posted the allegedly infringing material that the material has been taken down; if the user believes that the material was incorrectly or fraudulently identified as infringing, the user may then file a counter-notification. Within 10 to 14 business days following the filing of a proper counter-notification the service provider must restore access to the material, unless the service provider's designated agent first receives notice that the person who submitted the original notification has filed an action seeking a court order against the user. Knowing misrepresentation by anyone involved is subject to penalties (17 U.S.C. § 512(c)).

Information location tools safe harbor: amages or, except as provided in section 512(j), for injunctive or other equitable relief for copyright infringement for referring or linking users to sites containing infringing material through tools such as directories, indexes, references, pointers, or hyperlinks. The information location tools safe harbor is available if the service provider does not have the requisite knowledge that the material or activity is infringing; the "knowledge" standard here is the same as that for the information storage safe harbor. In addition, the service provider must not receive

a financial benefit directly attributable to the infringing activity, in a case in which the service provider has the right and ability to control such activity; this standard is drawn from the standard established by the courts for determining vicarious copyright infringement. And finally, section 512(d) provides the same notice-and-takedown procedure as that provided in section 512(c) for the information storage safe harbor.

Nonprofit educational institutions: Under section 512(e), the actions of a faculty member or graduate student employee performing a teaching or research function may affect the eligibility of a nonprofit educational institution for two of the four safe harbors. With regard to the transitory communications and system caching safe harbors, the faculty member or student is a "person other than the provider" and cannot affect the institution's eligibility. Nor will the knowledge or awareness of the faculty member or student be attributed to the institution with regard to the information storage and information location tools safe harbors, so long as

(A) such faculty member's or graduate student's infringing activities do not involve the provision of online access to instructional materials that are or were required or recommended, within the preceding 3-year period, for a course taught at the institution by such faculty member or graduate student; [and]

(B) the institution has not, within the preceding 3-year period, received more than two notifications described in subsection (c)(3) of claimed infringement by such faculty member or graduate student, and such notifications of claimed infringement were not actionable under subsection (f); and

(C) the institution provides to all users of its system or network informational materials that accurately describe, and promote compliance with, the laws of the United States relating to copyright (17 U.S.C. § 512(e)).

Statute
- Digital Millennium Copyright Act, 17 U.S.C. § 512

Cases
Federal Appellate Courts
- *ALS Scan, Inc. v. RemarQ Communities, Inc.*, 239 F.3d 619 (4th Cir. 2001)
- *In re Aimster Copyright Litigation*, 334 F.3d 643 (7th Cir. 2003)
- *Recording Industry Association of America, Inc. v. Verizon Internet Services, Inc.*, 351 F.3d 1229 (D.C. Cir. 2003)
- *Viacom International, Inc. v. YouTube, Inc.*, 676 F.3d 19 (2d Cir. 2012)

Federal Trial Courts
- *Hendrickson v. Ebay, Inc.*, 165 F. Supp. 2d 1082 (C.D. Cal. 2001)
- *Lenz v. Universal Music Corp.*, 572 F. Supp. 2d 1150 (N.D. Cal. 2008)

See also: Cloud; Copyright Infringement; Digital Millennium Copyright Act, Title I; File-Sharing; Internet Service Providers; P2P; Search Engines; Stop Online Piracy Act

Sources and Further Reading

Scott Cleland, *Search & Destroy: Why You Can't Trust Google Inc.* (St. Louis: Telescope Books, 2011)

Eli Pariser, *The Filter Bubble: What the Internet is Hiding from You* (New York: Penguin Press, 2011)

Siva Vaidhyanathan, *The Googlization of Everything: (And Why We Should Worry)* (Berkeley, CA: University of California Press, 2011)

Christopher Wolf, *Digital Millennium Copyright Act: Text, History, and Caselaw* (Silver Spring, MD: Pike & Fischer, 2003)

Mitchell Zimmerman, *DMCA Safe Harbors De-Coded: 17 U.S.C. Section 512 Re-Organized in More Logical Order*, Fenwick & West LLP (May 7, 2012), available at http://www.fenwick.com/Publications/Pages/DMCA-Safe-Harbors-De-Coded.aspx (visited January 28, 2013)

❖ DIGITAL MILLENNIUM COPYRIGHT ACT, TITLE III ❖

Title III of the Digital Millennium Copyright Act (DMCA), the Computer Maintenance Competition Assurance Act, created an exception to liability for copyright infringement in cases in which a person who activates a computer for purposes of maintenance or repair makes a copy of a computer program by doing so. Title III modifies section 117 of the copyright code to permit the making of such copies if they are:

> made solely by virtue of the activation of a machine that lawfully contains an authorized copy of the computer program, for purposes only of maintenance or repair of that machine, if—
>
> (1) such new copy is used in no other manner and is destroyed immediately after the maintenance or repair is completed; and
> (2) with respect to any computer program or part thereof that is not necessary for that machine to be activated, such program or part thereof is not accessed or used other than to make such new copy by virtue of the activation of the machine (17 U.S.C. § 117(c)).

Title III was a Congressional response to the decision of the Ninth Circuit Court of Appeals in the 1993 case of *MAI Systems v. Peak Computer*, which had effectively given software providers the opportunity to use copyright law to retain a monopoly on maintenance of computers running their software (991 F.2d 511). Congress let stand the Ninth Circuit's underlying reasoning: that making a RAM copy of a computer program is "copying" for copyright purposes. But, it added a provision that made such copying for repair or maintenance purposes permissible, thus removing the potential for use of copyright suits to suppress independent repair and maintenance companies.

Statute

- Copyright Act of 1976 (as amended), 17 U.S.C. § 117

Case

- *MAI Systems Corporation v. Peak Computer, Inc.*, 991 F.2d 511 (9th Cir. 1993)

See also: Copyright Infringement; Digital Millennium Copyright Act, Title I; Fair Use (Copyright)

Source and Further Reading

Christopher Wolf, *Digital Millennium Copyright Act: Text, History, and Caselaw* (Silver Spring, MD: Pike & Fischer, 2003)

❖ DIGITAL MILLENNIUM COPYRIGHT ACT, TITLE IV ❖

Title IV of the Digital Millennium Copyright Act (DMCA) contains miscellaneous provisions relating to the functions of the Copyright Office, the making of ephemeral recordings by broadcasters, distance education, nonprofit libraries and archives, webcasting of sound recordings, and the assumption of collective bargaining agreement obligations in the case of transfers of rights in motion pictures.

Ephemeral recordings: It is often more convenient for music broadcasters to record a set of songs and broadcast the recording than to broadcast the set from the original disks each time. Prior to the enactment of the DMCA, section 112 of the Copyright Act allowed radio broadcasters to make such recordings and retain them for up to six months. The Copyright Act as enacted in 1976 contained no general public performance right in sound recordings. In 1995, however, Congress had enacted the Digital Performance Right in Sound Recordings Act (DPRA), creating such a right in public performances by means of digital transmission, with an exemption for digital broadcasts by terrestrial stations licensed by the Federal Communications Commission (FCC) and a statutory license for certain subscription transmissions; the status of some ephemeral recordings made to facilitate such exempt or licensed transmissions was unclear. The DMCA amended the section 112 exemption to include such recordings and even, in some circumstances, to allow broadcasters to circumvent technological protective measures in order to make the ephemeral recording. In some circumstances, organizations may also make multiple ephemeral copies (17 U.S.C. § 112(a)).

Distance education: Prior to the enactment of the DMCA, section 110(2) of the Copyright Act contained an exception for instructional broadcasting. The Copyright Office had recommended changes to section 110(2) that would have updated the language of this exception without broadening the scope. Rather than adopt this proposal, Congress directed the Copyright Office to make recommendations on whether and to what extent exceptions should also be made for Internet-based distance education or other new distance education technologies. After consultation with the public and the affected parties, the Copyright Office issued its report in May 1999. The report suggested several amendments to sections 110(2) and 112 of the Copyright Act, amounting to a restatement of the Copyright Office's pre-DMCA proposal. The report recommended that "it should be clarified through legislative history that the term 'transmission' in section 110(2) covers transmissions by digital means as well as analog." In other words, "transmission" should cover class materials transmitted over the Internet as well as by older means such as television or radio. In addition, the rights covered by section 110(2) should be expanded to cover digital transmissions as well as performance and display; specifically, the rights of reproduction and distribution should be added to "the extent technologically required." And because Internet access to a work posted as part of a distance learning course could substitute for purchase of the work, the exception should emphasize mediated instruction: the statute might be amended to "specify that the performance or display must be made by or at the direction of an instructor to illustrate a point in, or as an integral part of, the equivalent of a class session in a particular course" (United States Copyright Office 1999).

The report also recommended that the requirement of a physical classroom be eliminated, as the Internet had rendered it obsolete. A requirement could be added, though, that materials posted for a class be restricted, "to the extent technologically feasible, [to] the defined class of eligible recipients." Transient copies "should be retained for no longer than reasonably necessary to complete the transmission," but an ephemeral copy exception similar to that for broadcasters should also be added to section 112. Institutions using distance education technology "should be required to institute policies regarding copyright; to provide informational materials to faculty, students, and relevant staff members that accurately describe and promote compliance with copyright law; and to provide notice to students that materials may be subject to copyright protection." In addition, "technological measures should be in place to control unauthorized uses" (United States Copyright Office 1999).

The Copyright Office was less certain whether the distance learning exception should be made available to for-profit educational institutions, but tentatively concluded that it should not. And if audiovisual works were to be added to the list of materials for which the exception was available, "it should be done in a limited way, with greater restrictions than section 110(2) currently imposes." Congress should also clarify the scope of fair use for distance education purposes. Licensing issues, particularly the problem of "orphan works" whose copyright owners cannot be located, should also be addressed (United States Copyright Office 1999).

Congress adopted some of the report's recommendations in the 2002 amendments to section 110(2), contained in the Technology, Education and Copyright Harmonization Act ("TEACH Act"). The TEACH Act adopted the report's recommendations concerning the addition of an ephemeral copy exception for educational uses to section 112. Because access to course information over the Internet requires that a copy of the information also be made on the students' computers, the possibility of downstream infringements—unauthorized reproduction and distribution of the work by the students—arises. The TEACH Act adds a new subparagraph requiring the transmitting institution to use technological measures to prevent "retention of the work in accessible form by recipients . . . for longer than the class session" and "unauthorized further dissemination of the work" (17 U.S.C. § 110(2)(D)(ii)). As a practical matter, this would seem to preclude the use of anything but encrypted streaming formats—a significant, even severe, limitation. And because the schools are required to use technological protective measures, the circumvention of which is prohibited by the DMCA, the student may be unable to lawfully make even a single copy of the work for future study.

The TEACH Act provides the educational institution with a safe harbor analogous to that provided to online service providers by Title II of the DMCA. If the school does not maintain copies of the work on its server "in a manner ordinarily accessible to anyone other than anticipated recipients," or "for a longer period than is reasonably necessary to facilitate the transmissions," it will not be responsible for infringing copies made by others.

The TEACH Act amendments to sec. 110(2) are not altogether draconian, however. The legislative history of the Act reveals that the intent of Congress was to exclude or curtail the reproduction via the Internet of materials that would ordinarily find a market on the Internet; materials intended for use in the physical classroom would fall within the educational materials exception, unless the performance or display over the Internet was made from an unlawful copy with the knowledge of the institution. The making of digital copies of analog works is permitted when otherwise authorized by section 110(2) if no digital version is available to the institution, or the available digital version is protected by technological measures.

Overall, the TEACH Act limits the work that may be displayed via the Internet to a quantity similar to that typically displayed in a live classroom session. The work must be displayed as part of a class session that in turn is part of a mediated instructional activity—in other words, a course. Only accredited, nonprofit educational institutions, and only transmissions made by, at the direction of or under the supervision of the instructor, are eligible for the educational use exception.

Nonprofit libraries and archives: One of the consequences of advances in information technology is that media used for information storage become obsolete. While a book printed hundreds of years ago may remain perfectly readable today, hardly anyone—not even music archives—retains a music player capable of playing music recorded on wax cylinders. Players for vinyl LPs are rare and will be rarer still once the retro-faddishness of vinyl fades. Players for standard cassette tapes will soon be as rare as eight-track cassette players. Digital media, if anything, race to extinction even more rapidly. Information on 5.25 inch or 3.25 inch floppy disks requires a now-obsolete player—and there is more than one type of 5.25 inch floppy; each type requires its own player. Other media flourished only briefly and finding players for them may prove difficult or, in some cases, impossible: Iomega Zip and Jazz drives and Imation 120 megabyte SuperDisk drives can still be found on eBay, but players for other formats—removable hard disk cartridges of various sizes, flopticals, EPROM and EEPROM cartridges for Atari, Commodore and other computers that are no longer made, and numerous others—have in many cases been orphaned by the demise of their original manufacturers, or by abandonment of a particular product line. As no new players are being made for these media, information stored on them is in danger of being lost forever, as nearly happened when the U.S. National Aeronautics and Space Agency (NASA) was reduced to shopping on eBay for readers for the eight-inch floppy disks it used during the golden age of manned space exploration in the 1960s and 1970s (*Storing Information in DNA* 2013, at 71). If a library has information stored on, for example, 5.25 inch Apple II disks, it may be able to borrow an old 5.25 inch Apple drive, connect it to a newer Apple Macintosh, and transfer the information to the hard drive of the Macintosh. It would not be practical for the library to purchase the 5.25 inch drive, keep it permanently connected to the Macintosh, and train library staff to assist patrons in accessing the information from the original 5.25 inch disks. Not only would such an arrangement be costly and cumbersome, but the disks will deteriorate over time, and repeated use would accelerate the process. Copying the information to another computer's hard drive is cheaper, more secure, and more practical.

Making such a copy, however, raises copyright issues. Even media that are not obsolete (including printed materials) deteriorate. Prior to enactment of the DMCA, section 108 of the Copyright Act permitted nonprofit libraries and archives to make a single facsimile copy of a work for purposes of preservation or interlibrary loan. Section 404 of the DMCA extends this exemption to digital information and takes into account the increasing use of digital technology for preservation of information, allowing for digital storage of analog (including hard-copy) information for preservation or interlibrary loan. Section 108, as amended by the DMCA, now permits nonprofit libraries and archives to make up to three copies of works in their collections. The copies may be digital but may not be made available to the public outside the library premises. When the original format in which a work is stored becomes obsolete, the library or archive may also copy the work into a new format (17 U.S.C. § 108).

Webcasting: The Digital Performance Right in Sound Recordings Act, as mentioned, created a performance right in digital transmissions of sound recordings. The DPRA exempted broadcast transmissions from this performance right and made subscription transmissions subject to a statutory license; on-demand transmissions were made subject to the full exclusive right. Between 1995, when the DPRA

was enacted, and 1998, a new category of digital transmission of sound recordings began to appear: streaming audio transmissions over the Internet, or webcasting. Section 405 of the DMCA amends the DPRA to treat non-interactive webcasting in the same manner as subscription transmissions, bringing it within the scope of the statutory license. A statutory or compulsory license is a license created by statute; it allows, in this instance, subscription transmissions and webcasts of audio recordings to be made without requiring the prior permission of the copyright holder. The transmitter or webcaster must still pay a usage fee, however.

Assumption of contractual obligations upon transfers of rights in motion pictures: Typically, a motion picture is produced subject to a collective bargaining agreement between the producers and the actors, director, writers, and other persons involved in the making of the film. The producer or production company is contractually obligated to make residual payments to these persons. At some point, the production company may transfer its rights in the film to a distributor; at this time it is typically obligated to transfer the duty to make residual payments as well. If the production company does not do so, the various persons entitled to residuals may have no recourse against the distributor, because they lack what is called "privity of contract" with the distributor: there is no contractual relationship between them that may be sued upon. And the production company may have no remaining assets, so that even though the film is wildly successful at the box office the persons involved in making it receive nothing. Section 416 of the DMCA addresses this problem by making transferees (such as the distributor) liable in most cases for residual payments for which the producer or production company would have been liable.

Statutes
- Copyright Act of 1976 (as amended by DMCA Title IV), 17 U.S.C. §§ 106, 108, 110, 112
- Digital Performance Right in Sound Recordings Act, codified at 17 U.S.C. §§ 106, 114–15

Case
- *Bonneville International Corp. v. Peters*, 153 F. Supp. 2d 763 (E.D. Pa. 2001), affirmed, 347 F.3d 485 (3d Cir. 2003)

Report
- United States Copyright Office, Report on Copyright and Digital Distance Education (May 1999)

See also: Copyright; Copyright Infringement; Digital Millennium Copyright Act, Title I; Digital Millennium Copyright Act, Title II; Digital Millennium Copyright Act, Title III; Digital Performance Right in Sound Recordings Act; Fair Use (Copyright)

Sources and Further Reading
Chris Priestman, *Web Radio: Radio Production for Internet Streaming* (Boston: Focal Press, 2001)

"Storing Information in DNA: Test-Tube Data," *The Economist*, January 26, 2013, at 70, 71.

Christopher Wolf, *Digital Millennium Copyright Act: Text, History, and Caselaw* (Silver Spring, MD: Pike & Fischer, 2003)

❖ DIGITAL MILLENNIUM COPYRIGHT ACT, TITLE V ❖

Title V of the DMCA, the Vessel Hull Design Protection Act (VHDPA), creates a new type of intellectual property, with aspects of both copyright and patent, for hull designs for vessels of 200 feet or less in length (17 U.S.C. §§ 1301–1332). The VHDPA has no direct application to computer and Internet law, but like the protection granted to semiconductor manufacturing mask work registrations under the 1984 Semiconductor Chip Protection Act (17 U.S.C. §§ 901–914), it is an indicator of Congressional willingness to create new categories of intellectual property when the traditional categories do not seem to fit. This has both worrisome and encouraging aspects: it has the potential to further shrink the public domain, yet the application of patent and copyright law to information technology has proved cumbersome and unwieldy; eventually Congress may see fit to create categories of intellectual property specifically tailored to information technology.

Statute

- Vessel Hull Design Protection Act, codified at 17 U.S.C. §§ 1301–1332

See also: Semiconductor Manufacturing Mask Work Registrations

❖ DIGITAL PERFORMANCE RIGHT IN SOUND RECORDINGS ACT ❖

The Copyright Act of 1976 granted most copyright owners the exclusive right of public performance of their copyrighted works (17 U.S.C. § 106(4)). Holders of copyrights in sound recordings, however, received no such right. The 1995 Digital Performance Right in Sound Recordings Act (DPRSA) added a right for performance by digital audio transmission (17 U.S.C. § 106(6)). This is not a general performance right; it does not cover performance by analog audio transmission, or by public performance of analog or digital recordings. The DPRSA was aimed not at these types of performances, or at possible future digital radio broadcasts, but at so-called Internet radio stations, or webcasters. Internet music services could maintain a large library of music and transmit it to listeners on demand, possibly diminishing the market for sound recordings. A related problem was that consumers might copy the webcast music; this was addressed by the use of encrypted streaming audio. While such encryption is easy to circumvent, doing so might violate the anticircumvention provisions of 17 U.S.C. § 1201. Titles I and IV of the Digital Millennium Copyright Act (DMCA) assisted webcasters by bringing streaming audio transmissions within the scope of the statutory license covering other music performance copyrights. Under the statutory license, webcasters were still required to pay royalties, but the copyright owners could not deny permission to transmit the work.

The DPRSA distinguishes between streaming audio, which it calls "digital transmission," and making a song available for download, which it calls "digital phonorecord delivery" (17 U.S.C. §§ 114(j), 115(d)). Digital rights management technology can be used to reduce the danger that digitally delivered phonorecords will be pirated. The use of encrypted streaming audio for digital transmission, though necessary to avoid vicarious or contributory copyright infringement liability, created an additional problem: in the course of streaming, buffer copies of the work are created. Although these are temporary, partial copies, webcasters were now required to pay royalties twice on a single transmission: once for the buffer, and once for the copy actually played. The webcasters paid a surcharge for the buffer copies, and independent, non-broadcast webcasters also paid royalties twice as high as those paid by broadcast stations retransmitting their programs via the Internet. The Small Webcasters Settlement Act of 2002 provided modified terms to prevent the cost of royalty payments from crushing small and nonprofit webcasters (17 U.S.C. § 114(f)). Webcasters of the "internet radio" variety are increasingly displaced by interactive play-on-demand streaming services such as Spotify, allowing users to choose the songs to be played. This increases the likelihood of displacing sales of sound recordings, and the music industry is slowly coming to terms with technological change and evolving new business models. Play-on-demand services are not included within the scope of the statutory compulsory license, but, in theory, must obtain a voluntary license for each song played—a nearly insurmountable hurdle for small webcasters (such as locally owned independent radio stations) who are not the copyright holders of the recordings they play (17 U.S.C. § 114(d)(3)). The interactive music streaming Spotify (originally from Sweden) was only able to offer access in the United States after two years spent negotiating licensing fees with major record labels. Such negotiated licensing agreements covering large numbers of songs make it possible for interactive services to operate legally (see, e.g., Innovation Asset Group 2012).

Statutes

- Digital Performance Right in Sound Recordings Act, amending and codified at 17 U.S.C. §§ 106(6), 114–15
- Small Webcasters Settlement Act of 2002, amending and codified at 17 U.S.C. § 114(f)

See also: Content Industry; Copyright; Digital Audio Works; Digital Millennium Copyright Act, Title I; Digital Millennium Copyright Act, Title IV; Digital Rights Management; File-Sharing

Sources and Further Reading

ASCAP and the Radio Music License Committee Announce Settlement in Principle, ASCAP (December 5, 2011), available at http://www.ascap.com/press/2011/1205_ASCAP_RMLC .aspx (visited January 28, 2013)

"Come Stream with Me: Is There Money in Digital Radio?" *The Economist,* June 16, 2012, at 74

Ronald H. Gertz, "*Client Memo Re: Summary of Sections 106, 112 & 114 of the Copyright Act of 1976 as Amended by the Digital Performance Right in Sound Recordings Act of 1995 and the Digital Millennium Copyright Act of 1998,*" in *Music on the Internet: Understanding the New Rights & Solving New Problems* (New York: Practising Law Institute, Anthony V. Lupo & Mark F. Radcliffe eds. 2001)

Blake Holland, "The Winding Stream: Entitlement Theories and Intellectual Property Rights in Emerging Media Technologies," 25 *Berkeley Technology Law Journal* 247 (2010)

Lynne B. Lubash, "How the Digital Performance Right in Sound Recordings Act of 1995 Protects Copyright Owners on the Internet," 14 *Santa Clara Computer and High Technology Law Journal* 497 (1998)

Royalty Settlement Signals Change for Music Industry, Innovation Asset Group (April 11, 2012), available at http://www .innovation-asset.com/intellectual-property-news/index .php/2012/04/11/190569/royalty-settlement-signals-change-for-music-industry/ (visited January 28, 2013)

Ben Sisario, "New Service Offers Music in Quantity, Not by Song," *New York Times* (July 13, 2011), available at http:// www.nytimes.com/2011/07/14/technology/spotify-music-streaming-service-comes-to-us.html/?_r=3&adxnnl=1&pagewa nted=all&adxnnlx=1355905217-fNOqqDdkR4Q47I JIOS790w& (visited January 28, 2013)

Ben Sisario, "Pandora and Spotify Rake in the Money and Then Send It Off in Royalites," *New York Times, Media Decoder* (August 24, 2012), available at http://mediadecoder.blogs .nytimes.com/2012/08/24/pandora-and-spotify-rake-in-the-money-and-then-send-it-off-in-royalties/ (visited January 28, 2013)

Jessica Wang, "A Brave New Step: Why the Music Industry Should Follow the Hulu Model," 41 *Idea: The Intellectual Property Law Review* 511 (2011)

❖ DIGITAL RIGHTS MANAGEMENT ❖

Digital rights management (DRM) is the use of technological measures to protect copyrighted digitally recorded material. A typical DRM package may employ some or all of a variety of techniques, including encryption and steganography. DRM software can use encryption to ensure that only authorized users can view the protected data, to control the number of times the protected data can be viewed or copied, and to keep a record of when and by whom the data has been viewed or copied. DRM technology is incorporated into video players, HDTV receivers, MP3 players, e-book readers, and other commercially available hardware and software media players to control the playback of copyrighted information and to prevent the playing of unauthorized copies. This incorporated DRM technology works in combination with DRM information included in the recorded movie, music disk, or other copyrighted information.

Encryption is used to restrict the playback of copyrighted information. For example, the movies stored on DVDs are encrypted using Content Scrambling System (CSS); similarly, movies stored on Blu Ray discs are encrypted using Advanced Access Content System (AACS). Keys to CSS and AACS are integrated into video players to enable them to play the encrypted media. Even relatively simple encryption such as CSS adds a level of complexity to recording and playback; compatibility issues arise, irritating consumers. Eventually, consumers may attempt to reduce their frustration by reverse-engineering the encryption—in this case, the CSS keys. It was apparently a compatibility issue, rather than an attempt at video piracy, that led to the most notorious instance of this reverse engineering: the creation of DeCSS in order to play CSS-encrypted DVDs on Linux systems. Once decryption information has been leaked to the general public, there is little the content industry can do, other than to push for harsher penalties for digital piracy: the keys cannot be changed for future players and disks without rendering them incompatible with DVD players and disks already sold. AACS is somewhat more flexible, allowing transfer of protected movies to other playback devices and permitting individual keys to be retired if they are deliberately or inadvertently disclosed.

Title I of the Digital Millennium Copyright Act (DMCA) provides penalties for the circumvention of copy-protection encryption such as CSS or AACS (17 U.S.C. §§ 1201, 1203–1204). The combination of encryption, which stops the casual user from copying the movie, and criminal penalties, which deter the more sophisticated user, has managed to control, though not eliminate, piracy of movies within the United States. However, the movie industry has united with other content owners in pushing for more powerful DRM tools.

Steganography, the process by which a message can be concealed within and later extracted from another message, can be used to digitally watermark copyrighted content. Any file may include a digital watermark that can be used to detect and track unauthorized copying; the watermark will not be visible or audible to anyone playing back the file, but can easily be detected with the appropriate software. Removal of the watermark can be prevented by employing robust steganography: the watermark can be made impossible to remove without degrading or destroying the recording in which it is contained.

There are several commercially available DRM software packages. Consumer content such as movies and commercial music downloads is often protected with DRM software, but

DRM has drawbacks both from a security and a marketing perspective. The security is limited by the fact that there will always be technologically adept users who can circumvent any copyright-protection safeguards, and by the fact that in order to be useful, content must be capable of being played; anyone can always record a copy of the playback, although there will be some degradation in quality. The marketing disadvantage is that DRM irritates consumers. AACS, which allows some space-shifting, is more user-friendly and less irritating than DeCSS, but a DRM-free version of the same film is less irritating still. While movie and music files have been evolving toward DRM permitting playback on multiple devices, e-books often remain tied to a particular playback device or technology. Also, prices of digital music, and to a lesser extent films, have fallen while prices of e-books have, for the most part. As a result, the incentive to pirate books has risen in relation to the incentive to pirate movies and music. Copying a novel one has purchased for the Kindle in order to be able to read it on one's Nook as well—space-shifting— would ordinarily fall within the "fair use" exception to copyright infringement. Two things, however, prevent this use: first, the anticircumvention provisions of the DMCA make it illegal to circumvent DRM; and second, the consumer is probably contractually obligated, through some form of shrinkwrap or clickwrap agreement, not to make copies, or not to make more than a certain number of copies.

DRM software may also make some recorded movies and music unplayable on some players. Consumers who purchase a music CD to listen to on the computer in their office may find that the disk cannot be played on the computer. They are not likely to purchase a CD player for their office, or ask their companies to do so; instead they will return the disk to the store and demand a refund. Even if the content owner is willing to supply a computer-playable disk upon request, many or most consumers will not have the patience to make the request. Thus the market forces a balance between the desire of the content owner for copy-protection mechanisms and the desire of consumers for convenience in the form of universally playable recordings. Recent developments in copyright law, particularly the anticircumvention provisions of Title I of the DMCA (17 U.S.C. § 1201), have tilted this balance further in favor of the content industry than would otherwise be possible.

DRM also poses difficulties for equipment manufacturers who must design their equipment to play back content recorded with several different DRM techniques. The goal of the DRM and content industries is to make DRM-free content as difficult as possible to play back. This requires the cooperation of equipment manufacturers, who do not share this interest. Not only is there an added cost to the equipment manufacturers; but there is also an impact on those manufacturers' markets. A device that can play back all types of content is more desirable to consumers than a device that can play back only some content; equipment manufacturers have no incentive to bear the content industry's enforcement costs.

An additional potential cost of DRM for consumers is that upgrading to a new computer, or even a significant hardware upgrade to an existing computer, may make downloaded media files unplayable. This imposes a significant burden even on consumers who do not wish to play the downloaded files on a home or car entertainment system, but plan to keep the downloaded files only on their personal computers. All over the United States and much of the rest of the world, countless vinyl records, cassette and 8-track tapes, Betamax tapes, VHS tapes, and increasingly CDs sit abandoned in cardboard boxes in attics, garages, and landfills. The consumers who purchased these media have now replaced them with newer media. Many feel the cost has been worthwhile because of the superior sound and image quality of newer media and recording formats. At some point, however, they will balk if asked to pay for the same copyrighted material yet again, especially if there is no improvement in quality yet less flexibility in how the material may be used. One marketplace solution to the problem is the marketing of bare licenses, or media paired with licenses, to cloud-stored copies of the content that can be downloaded or streamed to multiple devices, as with the movie industry's UltraViolet format for videorecordings.

A final legal problem with DRM is that it will continue to prevent copying after the copyright has expired. The DRM protection of a particular music recording or movie could be set to expire at a certain date, but in the absence of a legislative requirement that it do so (which does not presently exist), content owners have no incentive to set such a limitation on built-in copyright protection. (In the absence of trusted computing, a date limit would disable the copy protection, as the date could easily be spoofed.) And as Congress has frequently adjusted the length of the copyright term, it would be rational for the content owners to assume that the term will be increased yet again and thus avoid limiting their protection by shutting it off after a certain date. Once the protected work is no longer in copyright, the prohibition on circumventing DRM and protective measures would no longer apply—but means for circumventing those measures would be a century out of date, and possibly difficult to locate or reconstruct.

Statutes
- Copyright Act of 1976, 17 U.S.C. §§ 101–1332
- Digital Millennium Copyright Act, §§ 1201–05

See also: Advanced Access Content System; Clickwrap Agreement; Copyright; Copyright Infringement; DeCSS; Digital Millennium Copyright Act, Title I; Encryption; File-Sharing; Steganography

Sources and Further Reading

Megan E. Gray & Will Thomas DeVries, "The Legal Fallout from Digital Rights Management Technology," *Computer & Internet Lawyer*, April 2003, at 20

Daniel Geer, *CyberInsecurity: The Cost of Monopoly*, Cryptome. org (September 27, 2003), available at http://cryptome.org/ cyberinsecurity.htm (visited January 28, 2013)

Timothy B. Lee, "How 4 Microsoft Engineers Proved that the "Darknet" Would Defeat DRM"," *Ars Technica* (November 30, 2012), available at http://arstechnica.com/

tech-policy/2012/11/how-four-microsoft-engineers-proved-copy-protection-would-fail/ (visited January 28, 2013)

Lawrence Lessig, *Free Culture: How Big Media Uses Technology and the Law to Lock Down Culture and Control Creativity* (New York: Penguin, 2004) (also available as a free download)

Robert Levine, *Free Ride: How the Internet Is Destroying the Culture Business and How the Culture Business Can Fight Back* (New York: Doubleday, 2011)

"Music to Their Ears: With Compact-Disc Sales Plummeting, Record Companies Are Rethinking How to Distribute Music Online," *The Economist Technology Quarterly* (September 21, 2002), available at http://www.economist.com/node/1324731 (visited January 28, 2013)

William Patry, *How to Fix Copyright* (Oxford: Oxford University Press, 2011)

Adam Petravicius & Joseph T. Miotke, *Beyond the NDA: Digital Rights Management Isn't Just for Music*, 16 *Journal of Proprietary Rights* 1 (2004)

Bill Rosenblatt et al., *Digital Rights Management: Business and Technology* (New York: John Wiley & Sons, 2001)

Mark Tamminga, "The Sweeping Ambitions of Digital Rights Management: A Potential Hammerlock on Digital Content Has Plenty of Folks Scared," *Law Practice Management*, October 2003, at 24

Siva Vaidhyanathan, *The Anarchist in the Library: How the Clash between Freedom and Control Is Hacking the Real World and Crashing the System* (New York: Basic Books, 2004)

❖ DMCA ❖

See Digital Millennium Copyright Act

❖ DOCTRINE OF EQUIVALENTS ❖

The doctrine of equivalents is a rule of patent law that provides for a finding of patent infringement even if the product or process complained of by the patent holder does not violate the literal terms of the patent. In order not to be infringing, a product or process must differ substantially, not merely slightly, from that described in the patent. The doctrine of equivalents is flexible; whether the difference between the patent and the alleged infringement is substantial depends on how revolutionary the patent is. The doctrine is applied with a wide scope to patents that break significant new ground, called pioneer patents, but with a narrow scope to relatively minor patents in an already crowded field. This flexibility is not unlimited, however; the doctrine of equivalents is limited by rules with colorful names, such as "file wrapper estoppel" and the "nose of wax" rule.

File wrapper estoppel, now more commonly called prosecution history estoppel, draws its name from the file wrapper—a folder in which the patent's prosecution history is stored in the United States Patent and Trademark Office. It prohibits a patent holder from asserting the doctrine of equivalents with regard to any matters that have been conceded during the application process to be outside the scope of the patent (Katz & Riddle 2004, 668).

The nose of wax rule comes from an 1886 patent case, *White v. Dunbar*:

> Some persons seem to suppose that a claim in a patent is like a nose of wax, which may be turned and twisted in any direction, by merely referring to the specification, so as to make it include something more than, or something different from, what its words express. The context may, undoubtedly, be resorted to, and often is resorted to, for the purpose of better understanding the meaning of the claim; but not for the purpose of changing it, and making it different from what it is (119 U.S. at 51–52).

The doctrine of equivalents cannot be used to twist the nose so far that it is no longer recognizable as a nose, and indeed its limits fall somewhat short of that. Most of all, of course, the doctrine of equivalents is limited by the prior art: it cannot be applied to prevent others from doing something they have already done before the patent was issued, or that is insubstantially different from the prior state of the art in the field.

Statutes
- Patent Act, 35 U.S.C. §§ 101–103

Cases
- *Festo Corp. v. Shoketsu Kinzoku Kogyo Kabushiki Co., Ltd.*, 535 U.S. 722 (2002)
- *White v. Dunbar*, 119 U.S. 47 (1886)

See also: Patent; Prosecution History Estoppel

Sources and Further Reading
Paul N. Katz & Robert R. Riddle, "Designing Around a United States Patent," 45 *South Texas Law Review* 647 (2004)

Debra D. Peterson, "The Hydra of Identity Tolerance: Patent Law Heresies Involving 35 U.S.C. § 102," 85 *Journal of the Patent and Trademark Office Society* 639 (2003)

❖ DOMAIN NAME REGISTRATION ❖

A domain name is a portion of the Uniform Resource Locator (URL), the address that allows a computer to find a particular page, file or document on the Internet. Domain names and nonnumeric URLs translate the strings of numbers actually used by computers into a form that is easier for humans to remember. A URL might look like this:

http://www.icann.org/

Within this URL is the domain name:

icann.org

This domain name has two parts: the top-level domain, ".org," and the domain, "icann." The "www" in the URL is a subdomain; there may be many subdomains within "icann" domain, just as there are many domains within the ".org" top-level domain. The Internet Corporation for Assigned Names and Numbers (ICANN), a nonprofit entity formed in 1998 by an agreement between an existing Internet administrative service and the U.S. Department of Commerce, is in charge of establishing and assigning top-level domains. Administrative responsibility for the ".org" top-level domain, designed for use by nonprofit and non-commercial organizations, has been assigned to the Public Interest Registry. Persons wishing to register a domain name within the ".org" top-level domain may do so by checking for the availability of the name at the Public Interest Registry's Web site at http://www.pir.org/registrars/ or at the Web site of a registrar approved by the Public Interest Registry, and then registering that name with one of the approved registrars. In the United States alone, there are over 200 such registrars; some are companies whose primary business is domain names, while others are diversified Internet service companies such as America Online (Public Interest Registry 2013). An individual or organization that has registered a domain name then has authority over the creation and assignment of subdomains within that domain.

Inevitably, disputes arise. While the number of potential domain names is extremely large, the most desirable domain names are those that spell out easily remembered words and names, especially in English. From 1995 through 1998 a company called Network Solutions, Inc. was responsible for resolving disputes regarding domain names within the popular ".com," ".net," and ".org" top-level domains (Gilwit 2003, 271). With the formation of ICANN in 1998, ICANN became responsible for the resolution of some domain name disputes.

Private and administrative dispute resolution procedures are not always successful, however, and disputes over domain names sometimes end up in court. A particular problem in the early days of the expansion of the Internet was cybersquatting: the act of registering a domain name that includes or resembles a trademark, service mark, or other distinctive or famous mark used by someone other than the registrant, with the intent of later selling or licensing the domain name to the owner of the mark. Cybersquatters registered large numbers of domain names; for example, a cybersquatter might register the name "vw.net" and then attempt to sell the name to Volkswagen, the automobile manufacturer (*Virtual Works*, 238 F.3d 264). Volkswagen's "VW" trademark is both distinctive and famous; "vw.net" would be a natural place for Web surfers to seek information about Volkswagen automobiles, and Volkswagen's image could be harmed if inappropriate content were placed at that site instead.

Existing trademark law, however, had not been designed with cybersquatting in mind. To resolve the problem, in 1999 Congress enacted the Anticybersquatting Consumer Protection Act (ACPA) to protect the interests of trademark owners (15 U.S.C. § 1125(d)). The ACPA has proven largely effective in controlling cybersquatting, even when the registrant is unknown or outside the United States: in addition to providing remedies against known registrants, it provides for proceedings against the domain name itself. Even if the cybersquatter cannot be found or brought into court, the trademark owner can obtain an order transferring the domain name to it (15 U.S.C. § 1125(d)(2)(A)).

Other problems arise when there is a conflict between legitimate claimants to a particular domain name. For example, a 13-year-old girl in England created a Web site discussing the plight of endangered species, particularly the South American jaguar. An adult family friend registered the name "jaguarcenter.com" for her site, and was sued by Ford Motor Company, the owner of the Jaguar automobile trademark (Newman 2001). The site at jaguarcenter.com has since been taken down. (A similarly named site, jaguar-center.com, deals in cars.)

New top-level domains have also been proposed as a solution to the continuing problem of Internet pornography. Providing a safe harbor for adult-content Web sites in a top-level domain such as ".xxx," and requiring pornographic sites to move to that domain, could in theory make it far easier for parents and schools to filter inappropriate content from computers used by minors (ICM Registry 2004). But although the ".xxx" top-level domain was approved by ICANN in 2011, there seems to be no discernible impact yet.

Statute

- Anticybersquatting Consumer Protection Act, 15 U.S.C. § 1125(d)

Cases

- *GoPets Ltd. v. Hise*, 657 F.3d 1024 (9th Cir. 2011)
- *Virtual Works, Inc. v. Volkswagen of America, Inc.*, 238 F.3d 264 (4th Cir. 2001)

See also: Cybersquatting; Internet Corporation for Assigned Names and Numbers; Trademark; Trademark Infringement; World Wide Web; .xxx

Sources and Further Reading

W. David Gardner, *Unlikely Alliance Seeks .xxx Top-Level Domain*, TechWeb.com (April 15, 2004), available at http://www.informationweek.com/news/18901730 (visited January 28, 2013)

Dara B. Gilwit, "The Latest Cybersquatting Trend: Typosquatters, Their Changing Tactics, and How to Prevent Public Deception and Trademark Infringement," 11 *Washington University Journal of Law and Policy* 267 (2003)

ICM Registry Inc., *Application for New sTLD RFP Application .xxx*, ICANN (2004), available at http://www.icann.org/tlds/stld-apps-19mar04/xxx.htm (visited January 28, 2013)

Gregory R. Jones, "What's in a Name? Trademark Infringements in Cyberspace," 68 *The Alabama Lawyer* 70 (2007)

Heather Newman, "Web Sites Charge Up Ford's Ire: Owners Sued over Net Names," *Detroit Free Press* (January 24, 2001), available at http://www.whoisfinder.com/news/200101/ford-sue-domain-owners.html (visited January 28, 2013)

Barbara A. Solomon, "Domain Name Disputes: New Developments and Open Issues," 91 *The Trademark Reporter* 833 (2001)

Alexander G. Tuneski, "Hey, That's My Name! Trademark Usage on the Internet," 31 *Franchise Law Journal* 203 (2012)

❖ DOUBLECLICK ❖

DoubleClick, Inc., was an Internet marketing and advertising company and controversy magnet, acquired by Google in 2007; today it is a division of Google. DoubleClick collects information about Internet users' online activities. It then uses this information to target online advertising to particular users. DoubleClick's collection of information raises privacy concerns; while DoubleClick is not the only company to engage in such activities, it has a particularly high profile both as the market leader and as one of the first such firms to attract the attention of the media and privacy advocates.

The controversial nature of DoubleClick's business, combined with its high profile, has led to a certain amount of regulatory attention and litigation. In 1999, the merger with Abacus prompted an investigation by the Federal Trade Commission (FTC) for possible unfair or deceptive trade practices. After receiving assurances from DoubleClick that the two databases would not, in fact, be merged, and that users' information was not being used in ways inconsistent with Doubleclick's privacy policy, the FTC ended its investigation (Macavinta 1999; Weinberg 2001, 36). An FTC employee stated that "we have no grounds to challenge the merger based on privacy concerns" (Macavinta 1999). Antitrust concerns were raised about DoubleClick's 2007 acquisition by Google, but U.S. and European regulators eventually acquiesced to the acquisition.

Users have sued DoubleClick for privacy violations, both individually and as class actions. These suits were consolidated in the federal district court for the Southern District of New York as *In re DoubleClick, Inc. Privacy Litigation*. The Southern District of New York granted DoubleClick's motion to dismiss the federal claims against it; in the absence of a federal claim, it also declined to exercise jurisdiction over the remaining New York state law claim. The decision was seen as a defeat for privacy advocates, but although it was undeniably a victory for DoubleClick, it has not been followed elsewhere: it has been disagreed with by a federal district court in Florida (*In re America Online*, 168 F. Supp. 2d 1359), and decisions of several district and circuit courts have distinguished *In re DoubleClick* on its facts—that is, they have not followed the decision, on the grounds that some factual, procedural, or legal difference makes *In re DoubleClick* inapplicable.

At more or less the same time attorneys general in 10 states (Arizona, California, Connecticut, Massachusetts, Michigan, New Jersey, New Mexico, New York, Vermont, and Washington) were conducting investigations into DoubleClick's business practices. Ultimately these investigations led to a settlement in which DoubleClick, without admitting wrongdoing, agreed to pay $450,000 to cover some of the costs of the investigation, and also agreed to certain restrictions on data use and retention, along with enhanced disclosure and notification requirements (Weinberg 2001, 63–64). This settlement has been criticized as being a step behind recent advances in data mining technology (Zarsky 2002, 4).

Cases

- *In re America Online Version 5.0 Software Litigation*, 168 F. Supp. 2d 1359 (S.D. Fla. 2001)
- *In re Doubleclick Inc. Privacy Litigation*, 154 F. Supp. 2d 497 (S.D.N.Y. 2001)
- *In re Pharmatrak, Inc. Privacy Litigation*, 220 F. Supp. 2d 4 (D. Mass. 2002); 329 F.3d 9 (1st Cir. 2003); on remand, 292 F. Supp. 2d 263 (D. Mass. 2003)

See also: Advertising; Adware and Spyware; Privacy

Sources and Further Reading

Consumer Privacy: $450,000 Payment to States – DoubleClick Reaches Agreement with States on Visibility of Consumer Tracking Activities, Cybercrime Law Report, September 9, 2002, at 6

Terence Craig & Mary Ludloff, *Privacy & Big Data* (Sebastopol, California: O'Riley Media, Inc. 2011)

Jonathan I. Ezor, *Privacy and Data Protection in Business: Laws & Practices* (New Providence, New Jersey: LexisNexis 2012)

Courtney Macavinta, "DoubleClick, Abacus Merge in $1.7 Billion Deal," *C/Net News.com* (November 24, 1999), available at http://news.com.com/2100-1023-233526.html?legacy=cnet (visited January 28, 2013)

Daniel Solove, *Nothing to Hide: The False Tradeoff between Privacy and Security* (New Haven, Connecticut: Yale University Press 2011)

Daniel Solove & Paul M. Schwartz, *Privacy Law Fundamentals* (Portsmouth, New Hampshire: IAPP Publication 2011)

Amy S. Weinberg, "These Cookies Won't Crumble—Yet: The Corporate Monitoring of Consumer Internet Activity, *In re DoubleClick Inc. Privacy Litigation*, 154 F.Supp.2d 497 (S.D.N.Y. 2001)," 21 *Temple Environmental Law and Technology Journal* 33 (2002)

Tal Zarsky, "Cookie Viewers and the Undermining of Data Mining: A Critical Review of the DoubleClick Settlement," 2001 *Stanford Technology Law Review* 1 (2002)

❖ DROID ❖

See Mobile Device

E

❖

❖ E-BOOKS ❖

E-books are books in electronic form: large text files, sometimes with included images, that can be read on computers, dedicated e-book readers, or mobile devices. Because e-books are original works fixed in a tangible medium of expression, they are subject to copyright protection; because they are digitally recorded works, they can easily be copied and distributed over the Internet. As a result, they raise copyright issues similar to those raised by digital music and motion picture recordings, although the e-book industry is smaller than the digital music and movie industries, making e-book piracy smaller as well.

Many e-books can be freely copied and distributed over the Internet either because they are already in the public domain or because the authors have chosen to place few or no restrictions on their copying and distribution. Project Gutenberg, a nonprofit undertaking, offers more than 40,000 previously published books for download, along with a separate self-publishing site and links to partner sites offering over 100,000 additional books (Project Gutenberg 2012). Manybooks.com offers nearly 30,000 titles, many adapted from Project Gutenberg files, formatted for a variety of e-book readers. Commercial sites, including the Baen Free Library and Amazon's free Kindle books section, also offer many titles not in the public domain.

The creation of archives of public domain e-books has renewed interest in many literary classics. While Project Gutenberg's list of top downloads includes works of perennially popular, and still in print, authors such as Jane Austen and William Shakespeare, it also includes more obscure, and long out of print, works such as Elizabeth Kent's *The House Opposite*, as well as less-known works by well-known authors. There is a certain irony in the fact that ancient books once rare and difficult to find are now freely available to all, while others, more recently published and never put into electronic form, are now far harder to find.

Many authors choose to make their works freely available through other Web sites, often their own. The conditions that authors place on the use of e-books still in copyright vary; resources such as Creative Commons provide a variety of prewritten copyright licenses to suit almost all needs. Frequently an author's greatest interest is in having the work read as widely as possible, and unlimited free copying furthers that goal; however, should the work take off commercially, the author would like to be able to make some money from it. The author may reserve the right to commercial reproduction and use of the work, but not to noncommercial use. Authors permitting noncommercial copying and distribution of their works also frequently claim the moral rights of integrity and paternity. The right to integrity is the right to protect the work from changes that could damage the work's or the author's reputation; the right of paternity, also known as the right of attribution, is the right to be identified as the author of a work and to prevent one's name from being associated with a modified version of the work. These rights are not part of U.S. copyright law, but are recognized in many other countries.

Public domain works such as those distributed by Project Gutenberg, along with works whose authors do not wish to restrict copying, are generally delivered in plaintext format: they are not encrypted, and can be read without a decryption key. E-book authors who wish to forbid unauthorized copying must, if they are to rely on anything beyond the good intentions of consumers, encrypt their works. Such encryption then becomes a "technological protective measure" within the meaning of Title I of the Digital Millennium Copyright Act (DMCA), and circumvention of that measure is illegal (17 U.S.C. §§ 1201, 1204). The works may also be digitally watermarked so that unlawfully made copies can be detected.

Although most of the attention given to the DMCA's anticircumvention provisions has focused on the protection of movies, the protection of e-books also gave the world of activists, hackers, and encryption enthusiasts one of its *causes célèbres*: the July 2001 arrest of Dmitri Sklyarov. Sklyarov had written a program, the Advanced E-Book Processor, which made it possible for users to break the copy protection used by Adobe Systems, Inc. for its Acrobat E-Book Reader. Sklyarov was a Russian citizen and had written the program in Russia for a Russian company, Elcom Ltd.; it does not appear that he violated any Russian law by doing so (Samuelson & Scotchmer 2002). Sklyarov then traveled to the United States to give a presentation on Adobe's security flaws at a conference. Acting on a complaint from Adobe, the U.S. Federal Bureau of Investigation arrested Sklyarov at his hotel in Las Vegas on the day after his presentation (Lemos 2001). The Justice Department prosecuted Sklyarov for violation of the DMCA's anticircumvention provisions;

Sklyarov was detained in the United States for five months, free on bail but forbidden to leave the country, and was released only when the Justice Department decided not to pursue the prosecution further (Pravda 2001; Samuelson & Scotchmer 2002, 1647 n. 332).

The Sklyarov case attracted considerable media attention both within and outside the United States (Vaidhyanathan 2004, ix–x). In Russia it was used in the media to ridicule the commitment of the United States to free speech (Pravda, Aug. 30, 2001). Even after the government dropped its case against Sklyarov personally, it continued to pursue charges against Sklyarov's employer, Elcom. Elcom moved to dismiss the charges against it on the grounds that, among other flaws, § 1201(b) of the DMCA violated the First Amendment "because it constitutes a content-based restriction on speech that is not sufficiently tailored to serve a compelling government interest, because it impermissibly infringes upon the First Amendment rights of third parties to engage in fair use, and because it is too vague in describing what speech it prohibits, thereby impermissibly chilling free expression" (*Elcom*, 203 F. Supp. 2d at 1122). The court rejected all of Elcom's First Amendment claims, as well as a due process claim. Section 1201(b) did not violate the First Amendment, the court explained. Even though computer code was speech subject to First Amendment protection, §1201(b) was sufficiently tailored because it did not burden more speech than necessary to attain its goal of protecting copyrighted works and it was not vague. With regard to the fair use argument, the court stated that "it is not unlawful to circumvent for the purpose of engaging in fair use, [but] it is unlawful to traffic in tools that allow fair use circumvention" (*Elcom*, 203 F. Supp. 2d at 1125). Thus had Sklyarov circumvented the copy protection only for his own use, his actions would have been lawful; but for Elcom to distribute his program to those less skilled was unlawful.

More recently library lending of e-books and e-book readers has also become an issue. Lending copies of e-books requires either making copies of those books or lending the device on which those books are stored. Making copies of protected copyrighted works may require the circumvention of technological protective measures, in violation of 17 U.S.C. §1201; the library's making of copies probably falls outside the fairly narrow exceptions for libraries in § 1201(d). The right of first sale (17 U.S.C. § 109) protects the library's right to own the copy of a book (including, presumably, an e-book) it has purchased. Thus a library could load its entire e-book collection on to an e-book reader and lend out that reader. However, lending out the reader would also constitute a lending of the reader's software, possibly in violation of the end-user license agreement (EULA) (*see* Hirtle 2010). One solution might be to use e-book readers running open-source e-book software such as Calibre, FBReader, or Flipbook.

Statutes
- Copyright Act of 1976, §§ 101–106
- Digital Millennium Copyright Act, 17 U.S.C. §§ 1201–1204

Cases
- *Authors Guild, Inc. v. Hathitrust*, No. 11 CV 6351 (HB), 2012 U.S. Dist. LEXIS 146169 (S.D.N.Y. 2012)
- *Kirtsaeng v. John Wiley & Sons, Inc.*, 133 S.Ct. 1361 (2013)
- *United States v. Elcom Ltd.*, 203 F. Supp. 2d 1111 (N.D. Cal. 2002)

See also: Activism and Advocacy Groups; Content Industry; Copyright; Copyright Infringement; DeCSS; Digital Millennium Copyright Act, Title I; Digital Rights Management; Encryption; Fair Use (Copyright); File-Sharing; First Amendment; First Sale; Moral Rights; Piracy; Project Gutenberg; Public Domain; Steganography

Sources and Further Reading
Damien Cave & Katharine Mieszkowski, "Free Dmitry! A Russian Programmer Charged with Violating the Digital Millennium Copyright Act Languishes in Jail," Salon (August 3, 2001, 12:17 PM), available at http://www.salon.com/2001/08/03/dmitry/ (visited January 28, 2013)

Creative Commons, available at http://creativecommons.org/choose/ (visited August 3, 2012)

William M. Cross, "Restoring the Public Library Ethos: Copyright, E-Licensing, and the Future of Librarianship," 104 *Law Library Journal* 195 (2012)

Rachel Ann Geist, "*A* 'License to Read': The Effect of E-Books on Publishers, Libraries, and the First Sale Doctrine," 52 *Idea: The Intellectual Property Law Review* 63 (2012)

Charles Hamaker, "Ebooks on Fire, Controversies Surrounding Ebooks in Libraries," Information Today, Inc. (December 2011) available at http://www.infotoday.com/searcher/dec11/Hamaker.shtml (visited January 28, 2013)

Peter Hirtle, "May a Library Lend E-Book Readers?" LibraryLaw Blog (June 20, 2010), available at http://blog.librarylaw.com/librarylaw/2010/06/may-a-library-lend-e-book-readers.html (visited January 29, 2013)

Edward Lee, "The Public's Domain: The Evolution of Legal Restraints on the Government's Power to Control Public Access through Secrecy or Intellectual Property," 55 *Hastings Law Journal* 91 (2003)

Robert Lemos, "FBI Nabs Russian Expert at DefCon," ZDNet UK (July 18, 2001), available at http://news.zdnet.co.uk/internet/security/0,39020375,2091458,00.htm (visited January 29, 2013)

Laura Hazard Owen, "Ebook Sales Way up in 2011; Overall Trade Book Sales Roughly Flat," PaidContent: The Economics of Digital Content (July 18, 2012), available at http://paidcontent.org/2012/07/18/ebooks-are-now-the-most-popular-format-for-adult-fiction/ (visited January 29, 2013)

Project Gutenberg, available at http://www.gutenberg.net/ (visited January 29, 2013)

"The Project Gutenberg License, License Explained (Informative)," Project Gutenberg, available at http://www.gutenberg.net/license (visited January 29, 2013)

Rally in Support of Russian Programmer Dmitry Sklyarov, Pravda (August 30, 2001), available at http://english.pravda.ru/society/2001/08/30/13827.html

Ira S. Rubinstein, "Export Controls on Encryption Software," in Coping with U.S. Export Controls (New York: Practising Law Institute, 1995)

Pamela Samuelson & Suzanne Scotchmer, "The Law and Economics of Reverse Engineering," 111 *Yale Law Journal* 1575 (2002)

Siva Vaidhyanathan, *The Anarchist in the Library: How the Clash between Freedom and Control Is Hacking the Real World and Crashing the System* (New York: Basic Books, 2004)

"*US v. ElcomSoft Sklyarov,*" Electronic Frontier Foundation, available at https://www.eff.org/cases/us-v-elcomsoft-sklyarov (visited December 4, 2012)

❖ E-COMMERCE ❖

Shoppers today are familiar with the process of viewing pictures of goods on a Web site, reading reviews of those goods on another Web site, using a service such as Google Shopping to shop for the best price on the item selected, and then sending credit card information to an unknown person who claims to have the product available for sale. This convenience has only been made possible, however, by a uniform and uniformly applied body of commercial law. E-commerce has required changes to Article 9 of the pre-existing Uniform Commercial Code, the body of law that, with minor variations from state to state, governs contracts in all 50 states of the United States. It has also required other changes, including changes to tax laws and to the laws of other countries, in order to transform the Internet into a true global marketplace (Kryczka 2004).

One of the first problems presented by e-commerce was the problem of electronic signatures, which arguably did not meet the "signature" requirement for contracts under the Uniform Commercial Code. In 1998, Congress enacted the Electronic Signatures in Global and National Commerce Act, better known as E-Sign. E-Sign provides that, subject to some exceptions, "a signature, contract, or other record relating to such transaction may not be denied legal effect, validity, or enforceability solely because it is in electronic form" (15 U.S.C. § 7001(a)(1)).

Most contract law, however, is state law; the federal government may legislate with regard to interstate and international commerce, which certainly includes e-commerce, but much of the evolution in commercial law to address e-commerce issues has taken place at the state level. Two uniform acts attempt to address e-commerce issues; these acts have been approved by the National Conference of Commissioners on Uniform State Laws, which then urges state legislatures to adopt them. The first of these, the Uniform Electronic Transactions Act (UETA), has been adopted in 47 states, the District of Columbia, and Puerto Rico. UETA's provisions on electronic signatures are similar to E-Sign's (Ring 2003).

The second of the uniform acts is the Uniform Computer Information Transactions Act (UCITA). In contrast to UETA, UCITA proved controversial; it was opposed by consumer advocates and many state attorneys general (Letter from Attorneys General, 1999), and was adopted in only two states, Maryland and Virginia (Ring 2003). The controversy came down to a disagreement over consumer software license agreements; UCITA's opponents pointed out that UCITA placed all of the power in forming such agreements in the hands of software vendors, and none in the hands of consumers. With UCITA apparently permanently stalled, the American Law Institute took up the question, issuing its Principles of the Law of Software Contracts in 2010. The Principles attempt to address many of the same questions, albeit from a somewhat different perspective; they have not been welcomed by consumer advocates.

Statute
- Electronic Signatures in Global and National Commerce Act (E-Sign), 15 U.S.C. §§ 7001 et. seq.

Uniform Acts
- Uniform Computer Information Transactions Act (2002), available at http://www.uniformlaws.org/shared/docs/computer_information_transactions/ucita_final_02.pdf (visited December 4, 2012)
- Uniform Electronic Transactions Act (1999), available at http://www.uniformlaws.org/shared/docs/electronic%20transactions/ueta_final_99.pdf (visited December 4, 2012)

See also: Clickwrap Agreement; Contracts; Taxation; Uniform Computer Information Transactions Act

Sources and Further Reading
American Law Institute, *Principles of the Law of Software Contracts* (Philadelphia: American Law Institute, 2010)
"Chinese E-Commerce: Pity the Parcel People," *The Economist,* November 17, 2012, at 59
Katarzyna Kryczka, "Ready to Join the EU Information Society? Implementation of E-Commerce Directive 2000/31/EC in the EU Acceding Countries—The Example of Poland," 12 *International Journal of Law and Information Technology* 55 (2004)
Letter to NCCUSL from Attorneys General Opposing UCITA, July 23, 1999, available at http://www.badsoftware.com/aglet1.htm (visited August 3, 2012)
"Personalising Online Prices: How Deep Are Your Pockets?" *The Economist,* June 30, 2012, at 69
Christina Ramberg, *The Law of Auctions and Exchanges Online* (Oxford, UK: Oxford University Press, 2002)
Carlyle C. Ring, Jr., *Understanding Electronic Contracting 2003 The Impact of Regulation, New Laws & New Agreements: Overview of the Legal Landscape of E-Commerce,* Practising Law Institute Patents, Copyrights, Trademarks, and Literary Property Course Handbook Series (New York: Practising Law Institute, 2003)
Kurt M. Saunders, *Practical Internet Law for Business* (Norwood, MA: Artech House, 2001)

ELECTRONIC RIGHTS MANAGEMENT

See Digital Rights Management

❖ ENCRYPTION ❖

Encryption is the process by which easily comprehended information, such as ordinary text, a photograph, or a motion picture, is converted into a form that can only be understood with the aid of a key. The process by which this key is used to convert the encrypted message back into its easily understood form is called decryption. The encrypted message is called a ciphertext; the unencrypted message is called plaintext. The method by which the plaintext message is encrypted is called a cipher; it is often incorrectly referred to as a code. While a "code" also converts information into some other form, this is done for technical reasons rather than to keep the information secret. For example, a code such as the American Standard Code for Information Interchange (ASCII) or Unicode, both used to convert the letters and characters of ordinary text to binary numbers for use in computers, is necessary in order to allow human beings to use binary computers; the usefulness of these codes would be destroyed if the information was kept secret, however. Encryption, in which the existence of the message is not hidden but the content of the message is rendered incomprehensible, is also sometimes confused with steganography, in which the existence of the message is hidden; encryption and steganography may be combined, of course.

Most encryption methods can be classified as either symmetric or asymmetric key algorithms. The former and much older type requires that the sender and receiver share a key, kept secret from the rest of the world; the key is used both to encrypt and decrypt messages. The key can be very simple or very complex, but the system has two weaknesses: only persons who know the key can send and receive encrypted messages, and anyone who has the key can decrypt all messages encoded with it. As the number of persons with whom the key is shared increases, the likelihood that one of them will inadvertently or deliberately allow the key to fall into the hands of an unauthorized person increases as well.

Simple and not-so-simple symmetric-key encryption has been in use for millennia. One of the simplest forms, the substitution cipher (in which each letter of the alphabet is represented by some other letter) was used by the ancient Romans. As both ciphers and the ability of cryptographers to break them grew more complex, mechanical devices were invented to encode and decode them. These devices, especially those developed by British and American mathematicians to break German and Japanese ciphers during World War II, were among the early ancestors of modern computers.

The tremendous advances in cryptography for military and intelligence purposes during World War II led to government involvement in and regulation of cryptography. In 1952, during the Korean War, then-President Harry Truman created the National Security Agency (NSA). At the time the primary function of the NSA was cryptography and its counterpart, cryptanalysis, or the breaking of codes used by others. The NSA worked to maintain a United States lead in these areas, which it did successfully until the emergence of asymmetric or public-key cryptography.

Public-key cryptography (PKC) avoids the weakness of symmetric cryptography by using two keys: a public key, available to all, used to encrypt the message, and a private key, known only to the recipient, used to decrypt it. Once the public key is made available, anyone who wishes can use it to send encrypted messages to the recipient. The public key may be made available to anyone without increasing the likelihood that the private key will fall into the wrong hands, so anyone can encrypt messages while only the authorized recipient can decrypt them (Lessig 1999, 36–38).

The "invention" of PKC is generally credited to the team of Martin Hellman, a professor at Stanford University, and two graduate students, Whitfield Diffie and Ralph Merkle, and to the slightly later work of three Massachusetts Institute of Technology professors: Ron Rivest, Adi Shamir, and Len Adleman (Diffie & Landau 2007). The latter group patented their encryption method, known as RSA (the initial letters of the surnames of the inventors) and it forms the basis for asymmetric encryption methods in wide use today. The NSA and its British counterpart later claimed to have been aware of the possibility of PKC for some time and to have kept it secret for security reasons.

The NSA initially attempted to prevent the public's use of PKC. Under the Arms Export Control Act (AECA) and the International Traffic in Arms Regulation (ITAR), cryptographic devices were classified as "significant military equipment." Exporting public-key encryption outside the United States was, at least in theory, a violation of AECA and ITAR. But privacy pioneers like Phil Zimmerman, the developer of the popular PKC program Pretty Good Privacy (PGP), made public-key encryption methods available over the Internet (including, inevitably, to people outside the United States) and emailed their public keys to persons outside the United States (Rubinstein 1995, 425–427). Providing information on the Internet, however, even for free, may constitute an export; after making PGP available as a free download, Zimmerman was investigated for violation of AECA but never prosecuted.

The NSA is a security agency; perhaps its institutional focus on the potential use of PKC by spies and terrorists blinded it to the commercial possibilities. PKC provides obvious advantages to businesses such as financial institutions and online retailers who need an easy way to protect the privacy of communications with their customers; without it, Internet commerce could not have expanded to the extent it has. Thus business interests, as well as privacy advocates, had a strong interest in PKC. The NSA attempted to address the problem with the Clipper chip. The Clipper chip was intended to be included in all communications devices sold in the United States, and would have added a third component to the public/private key pair—a "spare key" to any encrypted message sent or received with the device. This spare key would be transmitted to a government facility and held in escrow, from which it could be retrieved by court order. This would give the government access, subject to constitutional restraints, to all encrypted communications in the United States (Froomkin 1995, 752–763). Needless to say, neither businesses nor privacy advocates were enthusiastic. Neither trusted either the integrity or the competence of the government; the government might use its escrow powers improperly, or the escrow database might be hacked and the spare keys made available to criminals. And, of course, no one outside the United States would want to send encrypted communications using a device that made the content available to the U.S. government, and no non-U.S. manufacturer would incorporate the Clipper chip into devices for sale outside the United States. Consumers would presumably prefer devices made without the Clipper chip, which would also be cheaper to manufacture; the effect on U.S. manufacturers of communications equipment would be disastrous.

Opposition from nearly all sectors of society led to the demise of the Clipper chip (Pednekar-Magal & Shields 2003). The United States was not the only country to attempt such centralized control of encryption; in France, for instance, a Clipper-like program was instituted in the mid-1990s, but abandoned in 1999. Asymmetric encryption is now an accepted part of Internet commerce, transparent to most users. PKC is incorporated into Web browsers in the form of the Secure Socket Layer (SSL), which encrypts messages between the browser and a Web server. Most users will not be aware that SSL is in use unless the Web page tells them or unless they notice the tiny "lock" icon on their Web browser, or by looking at the URL: encrypted pages generally have an address starting with "https" rather than "http." SSL can also be used to confirm a server's or user's identity through the use of a digital certificate, and can be used to ensure that the content of a message has not been altered in transit (Lessig 1999, 39–40).

Public-key encryption is widely available and difficult to break; it has also become an indispensable part of the Internet economy. In addition, PKC has numerous other legitimate uses: it can be used to verify identity through digital certificates and signature, it can be used to preserve the confidentiality of business and personal communications, and it can be used to protect copyrighted information (such as a movie recorded on a DVD) from unauthorized copying. But PKC can also be used by terrorists, child pornographers, and other criminals. The challenge for lawmakers is to create a set of rules that permits the economically and socially beneficial uses of PKC—encryption of credit card numbers, bank account information, business records, confidential business and personal communications, and the like—while controlling the harmful uses.

The first problem is not easily solved; the same encryption tool that can be used to conceal a legal but confidential business plan can be used to conceal an illegal and dangerous terrorist plot. Encryption can create a virtual private network that can save businesses millions of dollars in infrastructure costs—or provide a hidden marketplace for child pornographers. In this situation the encryption technology is merely a tool, and the appropriate legislative approach is to enhance penalties for crimes committed using that tool. A knife that can be used for slicing melons can also be used to commit a robbery; the legislature has responded not by outlawing knives but by providing that the penalty for a crime committed with a knife is more severe than the penalty for a similar crime committed without one.

There seems to be no downside to allowing the use of encryption to verify the identity of Web servers and Internet users. Copy protection encryption, however, has presented significant legislative difficulties in commercial transactions, aside from privacy concerns. The content industry has lobbied heavily for legislative protection for, and even mandate of, copyright protection encryption technologies. Yet users and equipment makers resent copy protection encryption; equipment must be designed to play encrypted material, sometimes with uneven results. And users may want to record protected material to other media for legitimate space-shifting purposes. The use of encryption thus diminishes utility while simultaneously raising the cost: consumers end up with a more expensive but less useful media player.

Within the United States the problem is addressed by a combined legislative and technological approach. Movies could easily be recorded with nearly unbreakable encryption. But in order to make movies that can be played, the recording industry must share the decryption key with the equipment manufacturing industry; the more complex the encryption, the greater the chance of incompatibility, and the greater the number of keys distributed, the greater the chance that a decryption key will be leaked to the general public.

Instead, movies are recorded with relatively simple encryption, and the Digital Millennium Copyright Act (DMCA) provides penalties for the circumvention of this encryption. The combination of encryption to stop the casual user from copying the movie and criminal penalties to deter the more sophisticated user have managed to control, though not eliminate, piracy of movies within the United States.

The problem for the movie industry is the rest of the world. Foreign earnings represent between two-thirds and three-quarters of the U.S. film industry's total revenues in a typical year; about one-third of this amount comes from home video sales, although amounts may vary greatly from year to year. Only a relatively sophisticated user can break the encryption used to copy protect DVDs and Blu-Ray disks. But once the encryption is broken, the key can be distributed to the world at large; anyone can use a program incorporating the key to make copies of encrypted movies. In the United States, the DMCA provides penalties for doing so (17 U.S.C. §§ 1203–1204); outside the United States, however, the movie industry's remedies are limited to an action for copyright infringement under local law (which will generally conform to international treaties).

An intriguing event, and a measure of the level of public fascination with encryption and cipher breaking, has been the emergence of a subgenre of popular fiction on the topic. These novels tend to be multilayered; on the surface they may be read as straightforward adventure novels. On the next level they provide a series of puzzles, related to the story, which the reader can decipher as the plot moves forward. On subsequently deeper levels they provide clues that the reader can use to decipher a variety of messages that may give additional information about the story, or about the author's future work, or about other things unrelated to the story. These novels range from formulaic stories with simple ciphers aimed at a mass market (Dan Brown's *The Da Vinci Code*) and cipher novels for children (the Artemis Fowl series) to the more complex (and thus more rewarding) work of Umberto Eco and to complex ciphers requiring a degree of mathematical sophistication (Neal Stephenson's *Cryptonomicon*).

Statutes
- Arms Export Control Act, 22 U.S.C. § 2778
- Digital Millennium Copyright Act, 17 U.S.C. § 1201
- Security and Freedom through Encryption (SAFE) Act, H.R. 850, 106th Cong. (1st Sess. 1999)

Regulation
- International Traffic in Arms Regulation (ITAR), 22 C.F.R. §§ 120–30

Case
- *U.S. v. Hsu*, 364 F.3d 192 (4th Cir. 2004)

See also: Copyright; Copyright Infringement; Cyberpunk; Digital Rights Management; File-Sharing; Hacking; Phreaking; Privacy; Steganography

Sources and Further Reading
Nonfiction

Andre Bacard, *The Computer Privacy Handbook: A Practical Guide to E-Mail Encryption, Data Protection, and PGP Privacy Software* (Berkeley, CA: Peachpit Press, 1995)

Whitfield Diffie & Susan Landau, *Privacy on the Line: The Politics of Wiretapping and Encryption* (Cambridge, MA: MIT Press, updated ed. 2007)

Niels Ferguson, Bruce Schneier, & Tadayoshi Kohno, *Cryptography Engineering* (Indianapolis: John Wiley & Sons, 2010)

Warwick Ford & Michael S. Baum, *Secure Electronic Commerce: Building the Infrastructure for Digital Signatures and Encryption* (Upper Saddle River, NJ: Prentice Hall, 2d ed. 2001)

A. Michael Froomkin, "The Metaphor Is the Key: Cryptography, the Clipper Chip, and the Constitution," 143 *University of Pennsylvania Law Review* 709 (1995)

Eric Hughes, "A Cypherpunk's Manifesto" (March 9, 1993), available at http://www.activism.net/cypherpunk/manifesto .html (visited August 7, 2012)

David Kahn, *The Codebreakers: The Story of Secret Writing* (New York: Scribner, 1967)

The Law and Practice of Digital Encryption (Amsterdam: Institute for Information Law, 1998)

Lawrence Lessig, *Code and Other Laws of Cyberspace* (New York: Basic Books, 1999)

Lawrence Lessig, *Code and Other Laws of Cyberspace, Version 2.0* (New York: Basic Books, 2006)

Steven Levy, *Crypto: How the Code Rebels Beat the Government—Saving Privacy in the Digital Age* (New York: Penguin Putnam, 2002)

Wenbo Mao, *Modern Cryptography: Theory and Practice* (Upper Saddle River, NJ: Prentice Hall, 2003)

Alfred J. Menezes et al., *Handbook of Applied Cryptography* (Boca Raton, FL: CRC Press, 1997)

Vandana Pednekar-Magal & Peter Shields, "The State and Telecom Surveillance Policy: The Clipper Chip Initiative," 8 *Communication Law and Policy* 429 (2003)

Phillip E. Reiman, "Cryptography and the First Amendment: The Right to Be Unheard," 14 *John Marshall Journal of Computer & Information Law* 325 (1996)

Ira S. Rubinstein, "Export Controls on Encryption Software," in Coping with U.S. Export Controls (New York: Practising Law Institute, 1995)

Ira S. Rubinstein & Michael Hintze, "Export Controls on Encryption Software," in *Coping with US Export Controls 2000* (New York: Practising Law Institute, Commercial Law and Practice Course Handbook Series 2000), available at http://encryption_policies.tripod.com/us/rubinstein_1200_software.htm (visited January 7, 2013)

Simon Singh, *The Code Book: The Evolution of Secrecy from Mary, Queen of Scots to Quantum Cryptography* (New York: Doubleday, 1999)

Daniel Solove, *Nothing to Hide: The False Tradeoff between Privacy and Security* (New Haven, Connecticut: Yale University Press, 2011)

William Stallings, *Cryptography and Network Security: Principles and Practice* (Upper Saddle River, NJ: Prentice Hall, 5th ed. 2010)

"Uncrackable Beams of Light: Quantum Cryptography—Hailed by Theoreticians as the Ultimate of Uncrackable Codes—Is Finally Going Commercial," *Economist Technology Quarterly* (September 6, 2003), available at http://www.economist.com/node/2020013 (visited February 2, 2013)

Peter Wayner, *Disappearing Cryptography—Information Hiding: Steganography and Watermarking* (Burlington, MA: Morgan Kaufmann, 3d ed. 2010)

Fiction

Dan Brown, *The Da Vinci Code* (New York: Doubleday, 2003)

Eoin Colfer, Artemis Fowl series, beginning with *Artemis Fowl* (New York: Hyperion Books, 2001)

Umberto Eco, *The Name of the Rose* (New York: Harcourt Brace & Company, 1983)

Umberto Eco, *Foucault's Pendulum* (San Diego, CA: Harcourt Brace & Company, 1989)

Ari Juels, *Tetraktys* (Newport Coast, CA: Emerald Bay Books, 2009)

Neal Stephenson, *Cryptonomicon* (New York: HarperCollins, 1999)

❖ ENFORCEMENT ❖

The enforcement of laws and legal rights having to do with computers and the Internet involves a wide variety of public and private mechanisms. Intellectual property rights, such as copyright, patent, and trademark rights, are for the most part protected by private lawsuits brought by the victims of infringement on those rights. The same is true of torts against individuals, such as defamation or invasion of privacy. It is the duty of individuals to detect violations of these legal rights and to pursue the violators. In certain cases, however, defamation or infringement of an intellectual property right can result in criminal prosecution.

Certain crimes are especially likely to be committed using the Internet, or are unique to the Internet. These crimes include distribution of unlawful content, identity theft, malicious hacking, phishing, and spamming. Federal and state governments have authority over some Internet crimes, while others are purely federal crimes. While a number of agencies are involved in preventing and pursuing Internet crimes, two in particular—the Federal Trade Commission and the Department of Justice—carry an especially heavy load.

Crimes related to content fall into five general categories: content that infringes upon an intellectual property right; content that is defamatory or invades privacy; content that is obscene, pornographic, or indecent; content that is illegal, including child pornography and criminal conspiracy; and content that threatens national security.

Content that infringes upon an intellectual property right is largely an area for private enforcement, and content industry groups actively pursue civil lawsuits against file-sharing networks (*Napster*, 239 F.3d 1004) and individual file sharers (*Verizon*, 351 F.3d 1229), while trademark owners pursue online trademark violators. The federal government may become involved when the scope of the infringement meets certain requirements (e.g., No Electronic Theft Act, 17 U.S.C. §§ 506–507), or when there may be a violation of the anticircumvention provisions of the Digital Millennium Copyright Act (DMCA) (*Elcom*, 203 F. Supp. 2d 1111); investigation of a possible crime and the making of arrests are the job of the Federal Bureau of Investigation (FBI), while prosecuting the case against the alleged criminal is a matter for the Department of Justice.

Content that infringes on a personal right of reputation or privacy may give rise to a private right of action (*Zeran*, 129 F.3d 327). Ordinarily such content, even if it results in a civil suit, does not lead to criminal prosecution; however, especially egregious defamation may be a crime under state law. Defamation laws in other countries are significantly different, and courts in the United States will not enforce defamation judgments from other countries if enforcement would conflict with the First Amendment (*Bachchan*, 585 N.Y.S.2d 661).

Content that is obscene, pornographic, or indecent has posed an especially difficult problem for U.S. law. Obscene content, as defined in *Miller v. California*, can be prohibited; however, the distinction between obscenity and mere indecency is not always an easy one to draw (413 U.S. 15). Conduct that is merely indecent may not be prohibited, but measures may be taken to render it inaccessible to minors. The difficulty of crafting measures to protect minors from such content without unconstitutionally interfering with the access of adults has occupied considerable Congressional attention. The substantive provisions of the first attempt to do so, the Communications Decency Act of 1996 (CDA), were subsequently struck down as unconstitutional (*Reno v. American Civil Liberties Union*, 521 U.S. 844). A second attempt, the Child Online Protection Act of 1998 (COPA), failed to pass First Amendment scrutiny in the U.S. Court of Appeals for the Third Circuit, which enjoined its enforcement (*Mukasey*, 534 F.3d 181). The Supreme Court denied certiorari, declining to review the Third Circuit's decision.

The next major attempt was the Children's Internet Protection Act of 1998 (CIPA), which fared better in the courts. Unlike the CDA and COPA, which had attempted to restrict Web content, CIPA left the content alone and focused on restricting access. CIPA required blocking and filtering software to be installed and used on computers in schools and libraries receiving discounted (i.e., federally subsidized) Internet access. CIPA's constitutionality has been upheld by the Supreme Court (*American Library Association*, 539 U.S. 194). Enforcement of CIPA is simple: schools and libraries that do not comply do not receive the discount (47 U.S.C. § 254(h)(5)(F)).

Pornographic content provides complex problems of regulation and enforcement because lawmakers wish to restrict access to such content for some users, but not for others. When Congress does not wish to discriminate between groups of users, the lawmaking task is greatly simplified. Some content is prohibited for all users. Child pornography is illegal (18 U.S.C. §§ 2251–2260). Detecting it and arresting violators is the job of the FBI, whose agents infiltrate child pornography rings online; violators are then prosecuted by the Department of Justice. Other illegal content includes content which is part of a crime—for instance, an email soliciting murder for hire, or a Web site offering gambling or prostitution in a jurisdiction where such an offering is illegal, or messages between criminal coconspirators in which they plot to rob a bank. Criminal content of this sort may involve both state and federal law enforcement authorities.

Some content may also be regulated or prohibited on grounds of national security even if it is not otherwise illegal. The USA PATRIOT Act of 2001 greatly enhanced the authority of federal agencies to conduct surveillance of email and other electronic communications and, perhaps more importantly, to disclose the contents of those communications to other law enforcement, intelligence, defense, and national security agencies (18 U.S.C. § 2517(6)). It is possible that the persons sending or receiving the communications may then be detained.

Other crimes are not related to Internet content but to Internet conduct; crimes of this sort include identity theft, malicious hacking, phishing, and spamming. The motivation for these crimes is usually either malicious—a pure desire to cause mischief—or financial. The Federal Trade Commission (FTC) addresses financial crimes directed at consumers. The FTC does this in two ways: through education, outreach, and data collection projects designed to prevent consumers from being victimized; and through prosecutions of violators. It enforces and makes regulations under the Children's Online Privacy Protection Act (COPPA), which governs the collection of personal information from children over the Internet (15 U.S.C. § 6502). The FTC Division of Advertising Practices enforces laws against unfair, misleading, or false advertising, much of which can be found on the Internet, especially in spam; it also monitors e-commerce. The FTC's antiscam office, the Division of Marketing Practices, shuts down Internet scammers, while its ID Theft project addresses the crime of identity theft, which has become far more common as a result of Internet use. The FTC is also responsible for enforcing the CAN-SPAM Act of 2003, an antispam law (15 U.S.C. § 7705(c)) and enforces antispyware measures.

Crimes of mischief, chiefly malicious hacking, are governed by a variety of state and federal statutes; the chief antihacker statute is the federal Computer Fraud and Abuse Act of 1986, enforced by the Department of Justice (via the FBI) and the Department of Homeland Security (via the Secret Service, formerly part of the Department of the Treasury) (18 U.S.C. § 1030(d)).

Statutes
- Children's Online Privacy Protection Act, 15 U.S.C. § 6501–6506
- Child Pornography Prevention Act of 1996, 18 U.S.C. §§ 2251–2260
- Children's Internet Protection Act of 1998, 47 U.S.C. § 254(h)
- Communications Decency Act of 1996, Pub. L. No. 104–104, § 502, 1996 U.S.S.C.A.N. (110 Stat.) 56,133 (later codified at 47 U.S.C. § 223)
- Computer Fraud and Abuse Act of 1986, 18 U.S.C. § 1030
- Copyright Act of 1976, 17 U.S.C. §§ 101–1332
- Digital Millennium Copyright Act, 17 U.S.C §§ 512, 1201–1204
- Identity Theft and Assumption Deterrence Act, amending and codified at 18 U.S.C. § 1028
- No Electronic Theft Act, amending and codified at 17 U.S.C. §§ 101, 506 & 507 & 18 U.S.C. §§ 2319–2320
- USA PATRIOT Act of 2001, 18 U.S.C. § 2517(6)

Cases
Supreme Court
- *Ashcroft v. American Civil Liberties Union*, 524 U.S. 656 (2004)
- *Miller v. California*, 413 U.S. 15 (1973)
- *Reno v. American Civil Liberties Union*, 521 U.S. 844 (1997)
- *United States v. American Library Association, Inc.*, 539 U.S. 194 (2003)

Federal Appellate Courts
- *A&M Records, Inc. v. Napster, Inc.*, 239 F.3d 1004 (9th Cir. 2001)
- *American Civil Liberties Union v. Mukasey*, 534 F.3d 181 (3d Cir. 2008), certiorari denied sub nom *Mukasey v. American Civil Liberties Union*, 555 U.S. 1137 (2009)
- *Recording Industry Association of America, Inc. v. Verizon Internet Services, Inc.*, 351 F.3d 1229 (D.C. Cir. 2003), certiorari denied, 543 U.S. 924 (2004)
- *Zeran v. America Online, Inc.*, 129 F.3d 327 (4th Cir. 1997)

Federal Trial Court
- *U.S. v. Elcom Ltd.*, 203 F. Supp. 2d 1111 (N.D. Cal. 2002)

State Court
- *Bachchan v. India Abroad Publications*, 585 N.Y.S.2d 661 (N.Y. Sup. Ct. 1992)

See also: Adware and Spyware; Censorship; Child Pornography; Children's Internet Protection Act; Communications Decency Act; Copyright; Defamation; Digital Millennium Copyright Act; Federal Communications Commission; Federal Trade Commission; Hacking; Identity Theft; No Electronic Theft Act; Patent; Phishing; Spam; Trademark

Sources and Further Reading

Joe Anastasi, *The New Forensics: Investigating Corporate Fraud and the Theft of Intellectual Property* (Hoboken, NJ: John Wiley & Sons, 2003)

Stuart Biegel, *Beyond Our Control? Confronting the Limits of Our Legal System in the Age of Cyberspace* (Cambridge, MA: MIT Press, 2001)

"FTC Permanently Halts Unlawful Spyware Operations," Federal Trade Commission (November 21, 2006), available at http://www.ftc.gov/opa/2006/11/seismicodysseus.shtm

"Identity Theft Resources," Federal Trade Commission, available at http://www.ftc.gov/bcp/edu/microsites/idtheft2012/ (last updated October 25, 2012)

Chris Marsden, *Internet Co-Regulation: European Law, Regulatory Governance and Legitimacy in Cyberspace* (Cambridge, MA: MIT Press, 2011)

Bill Nelson et al., *Guide to Computer Forensic and Investigations* (Boston: Course Technology, 3d ed. 2009)

Micah Sifry, *WikiLeaks and the Age of Transparency* (Berkeley, CA: Counterpoint, 2011)

Adam Thierer et al., eds., *Who Rules the Net? Internet Governance and Jurisdiction* (Washington, D.C.: Cato Institute, 2003)

Douglas Thomas & Brian D. Loader, eds., *Cybercrime: Law Enforcement, Security and Surveillance in the Information Age* (London: Routledge, 2000)

❖ FACEBOOK ❖

See Social Media

❖ FAIR USE (COPYRIGHT) ❖

Fair use is a doctrine of trademark and copyright law; fair use is a defense to a claim of copyright or trademark infringement. Copyright fair use is somewhat hazily defined by section 107 of the Copyright Code, which provides that

> the fair use of a copyrighted work. . . for purposes such as criticism, comment, news reporting, teaching (including multiple copies for classroom use), scholarship, or research, is not an infringement of copyright. In determining whether the use made of a work in any particular case is a fair use the factors to be considered shall include—
>
> (1) the purpose and character of the use, including whether such use is of a commercial nature or is for nonprofit educational purposes;
> (2) the nature of the copyrighted work;
> (3) the amount and substantiality of the portion used in relation to the copyrighted work as a whole; and
> (4) the effect of the use upon the potential market for or value of the copyrighted work.
>
> The fact that a work is unpublished shall not itself bar a finding of fair use if such finding is made upon consideration of all the above factors.

Copyright fair use is sometimes confused with the idea of the public domain. The distinction is simple: works in the public domain are not copyrighted. Fair use applies to works that *are* copyrighted, but which nonetheless may be copied without the permission of the copyright holder under certain circumstances. Uses that may be protected as fair use include scholarly and "transformative" uses; parody, but not necessarily satire; noncommercial time-shifting and space-shifting, and possibly some commercial time-shifting and space-shifting as well; copying for classroom use; copying in order to reverse engineer computer software; and the use of thumbnail images of copyrighted works on a Web site. One significant Internet use that has been found not to fall within the fair use exception is file-sharing.

Scholarly and transformative uses: The copying of parts of works by scholars is usually fair use under the four section 107 factors. Scholarly works are written for educational purposes, not commercial purposes; the work copied may itself be a scholarly work, and the copying is a way of including the work in an ongoing process of discussion and critical examination of ideas by the scholarly community; the part used is generally a small portion of the whole; and the scholarly examination is unlikely to have an adverse effect on the market for the work—even if the treatment is negative, the attention drawn to the work is likely to enhance the market for the complete original.

While scholarly works are one form of transformative work, they are not the only form. All parodies are transformative works, for example. In discussing one parody, the Supreme Court observed generally that "the goal of copyright, to promote science and the arts, is generally furthered by the creation of transformative works" (*Campbell*, 510 U.S. at 579). The court went on to observe that transformative works "lie at the heart of the fair use doctrine's guarantee of breathing space within the confines of copyright . . . and the more transformative the new work, the less will be the significance of other factors, like commercialism, that may weigh against a finding of fair use."

Parody and satire: In the United States, parody is a form of criticism protected by the First Amendment. Political parodies, literary parodies, and parodies of works of popular entertainment are a staple of discourse in the United States from childhood onward. The urge to parody seems innate; schoolchildren parody the words to the songs they sing in music class, and require no special training to chuckle over the Movie "Satires" (actually parodies) in *Mad Magazine*.

Parodies are transformative works, and in order to be protected as fair use, a sufficient degree of transformation is necessary. In parodying a song, for example, the parodist may use only as much of the original lyrics as is necessary to conjure up the original in the reader's or listener's mind; without such conjuring up, the parody will not be recognized as such. In the case of *Campbell v. Acuff-Rose Music, Inc.*, discussing one such parody, the Supreme Court observed that:

> When parody takes aim at a particular original work, the parody must be able to "conjure up" at least enough of that

original to make the object of its critical wit recognizable. . . . What makes for this recognition is quotation of the original's most distinctive or memorable features, which the parodist can be sure the audience will know. Once enough has been taken to assure identification, how much more is reasonable will depend, say, on the extent to which the song's overriding purpose and character is to parody the original or, in contrast, the likelihood that the parody may serve as a market substitute for the original. But using some characteristic features cannot be avoided (510 U.S. at 588).

The song parodied in *Campbell* was Roy Orbison's 1964 song "Oh, Pretty Woman." The defendants were Luther Campbell and the notorious early rap group 2 Live Crew. (Campbell performed under the name Luke Skyywalker, which despite its extra "Y" raised issues of trademark infringement and dilution.) The parody was, by 2 Live Crew's standards, fairly mild. Nonetheless, it was offensive, as are many parodies. Parodies may generate more litigation than they should not because the copyright owner of the parodied work has suffered economic harm as a result, but because parodies can sting: they are often cruel, and the owner of the parodied work may become emotionally involved to a degree that leads him or her to pursue a lawsuit that does not make good economic or legal sense.

Satire is distinguished from parody for legal (as opposed to artistic) purposes by its target: the purpose of a parody is to make fun of or otherwise criticize the parodied work, while the purpose of satire is to make fun of or criticize some other target, perhaps using a copyrighted work as an instrument. The court in *Campbell* pointed out that satire, unlike parody, does not require such an instrument: satire "can stand on its own two feet and so requires justification for the very act of borrowing" (510 U.S. at 581).

Time-shifting and space-shifting: Time-shifting and space-shifting are terms applied to the copying of copyrighted works that require a player, such as a television screen or speakers, to make them intelligible to a human viewer or listener. Time-shifting occurs when a viewer records a copyrighted work (e.g., a broadcast or cable television program) for later viewing or listening. Space-shifting occurs when a viewer records a copyrighted work to play in some other location (e.g., copying music from a legally purchased music CD to an iPod or other MP3 player in order to play the music in a car with no CD player). The Supreme Court ruled in the landmark case of *Sony Corporation of America v. Universal City Studios* that time-shifting for noncommercial purposes was fair use. The Ninth Circuit applied this reasoning in *Recording Industry Association of America v. Diamond Multimedia Systems* to hold that noncommercial space-shifting was also fair use.

In the years since *Sony* it has become apparent that not all noncommercial space-shifting and time-shifting is fair use; the four factors of section 107 must be applied to each case. Online file-sharing of copyrighted music, for example, might be categorized as noncommercial space-shifting, but it is not fair use, not least because it drastically affects the market for

the work (*Napster*, 239 F.3d 1004). At the same time, some commercial space-shifting and time-shifting may be fair use: the creation of fair-use transformative works may involve space-shifting and time-shifting, for example.

Classroom use: The 1976 Guidelines for Classroom Copying in Not-for-Profit Educational Institutions, prepared as part of the process of drafting the Copyright Act of 1976, provide a safe harbor for teachers who follow some fairly restrictive guidelines on photocopying materials to hand out in class. A more recent concern is the posting of copyrighted materials on course Web sites. Uses of this sort are addressed by Title IV of the Digital Millennium Copyright Act and by the Technology, Education and Copyright Harmonization Act. As amended by these acts, the copyright code now requires the teacher's employing institution to use technological measures to ensure that the work will not be retained by the students in accessible form after the class session ends, and to prevent "unauthorized further dissemination of the work." Schools complying with these rather severe restrictions will be able to avail themselves of a statutory safe harbor providing immunity for further downstream infringements by the students.

Reverse engineering: The copying or decompiling of a copyrighted computer program in order to reverse engineer the program is fair use. Reverse engineering may be necessary either to design a competing program or to achieve interoperability—that is, to ensure that one program can work with another. Congress and the courts have decided that both of these goals are socially desirable (*Sega*, 203 F.3d at 596; *Sony*, 977 F.2d at 1510).

Web site thumbnails: Thumbnails are tiny pictures used on a Web site, usually to provide links either to larger copies of the images, to descriptions of the thing depicted, or to places where the thing depicted may be purchased. In *Kelly v. Arriba Soft*, photographer Leslie Kelly posted copies of his photographs on his own Web site and, under license, on other Web sites. Arriba Soft operated a search engine that displayed results as thumbnails rather than text, like the "Images" search function on Google. The Ninth Circuit Court of Appeals held that this was a fair use of Kelly's photographs. The use, though commercial, was incidental and "not highly exploitative" (*Kelly*, 336 F.3d at 818). The use was transformative because it "created a different purpose for the images": access to information rather than artistic expression (*Kelly*, 336 F.3d at 819). The artistic, rather than factual, nature of the works weighed slightly against a finding of fair use, while the fact that the thumbnail was of the entire work rather than a part was necessary to the search engine's purpose and weighed neither for nor against fair use (*Kelly*, 336 F.3d at 820–821). The fourth factor, like the first, weighed in favor of a finding of fair use: The thumbnails did not adversely affect the market for Kelly's work; they were unsuitable for use as substitutes for the actual photographs, and if anything acted to increase the market by guiding users to Kelly's Web site. Considering all four factors, the court decided that the use of Kelly's photographs (and, by extension, similar uses of copyrighted materials by search engines generally) was fair use (*Kelly*, 336 F.3d at 822).

The Ninth Circuit confirmed this ruling with *Perfect 10, Inc. v. Google, Inc.* Perfect 10 is a pornography site whose subscribers pay a fee for access to photographs. Google's image search function displayed thumbnails of the photos (*Perfect 10*, 416 F. Supp. 2d at 845). Perfect 10 claimed Google's use was "consumptive" because the thumbnails replaced the need for the original image and because Google linked to the original image in full resolution. The Ninth Circuit disagreed, holding Google's use to be transformative and thus a noninfringing fair use. As in *Kelly,* only the thumbnails (which were transformative) were copies made by Google; the full-resolution images were not copies, but links to the original images on Perfect 10's own servers (*Perfect 10*, 653 F.3d at 982).

The President Ford clause: The final clause of section 107 provides that "the fact that a work is unpublished shall not itself bar a finding of fair use if such finding is made upon consideration of all the above factors." This clause was added to the statute after the *Nation* magazine obtained and published excerpts from the then-unpublished memoirs of former president Gerald Ford. The book's publisher sued the magazine, and the U.S. Supreme Court held that "[u]nder ordinary circumstances, the author's right to control the first public appearance of his undisseminated expression will outweigh a claim of fair use" (*Harper & Row*, 471 U.S. at 555). This was widely interpreted as meaning that no use of unpublished work could be fair use; Congress added the final clause to section 107 in 1992 to correct this impression and perhaps to step back a bit from the holding in *Harper & Row*. In an Internet context, the applicability of the clause is limited: all work that is posted on the Internet is published by virtue of being posted. Cases involving unpublished work may still arise, though, if someone obtains a copy of an unpublished work and posts it.

Statutes
- Copyright Act of 1976, 17 U.S.C. § 107
- Digital Millennium Copyright Act, Title IV, 17 U.S.C. §§ 106, 108, 110, 112
- Technology, Education and Copyright Harmonization Act amendments, 17 U.S.C. §§ 110(2), 112

Guidelines
- Guidelines for Classroom Copying in Not-for-Profit Educational Institutions, H.R. Rep. No. 94–1476 (1976)

Cases
Supreme Court
- *Campbell v. Acuff-Rose Music, Inc.*, 510 U.S. 569 (1994)
- *Harper & Row Publishers, Inc. v. Nation Enterprises*, 471 U.S. 539 (1985)
- *Sony Corp. of America v. Universal City Studios, Inc.*, 464 U.S. 417 (1984)

Federal Appellate Courts
- *A&M Records, Inc. v. Napster, Inc.*, 239 F.3d 1004 (9th Cir. 2001)
- *Kelly v. Arriba Soft Corp.*, 336 F.3d 811 (9th Cir. 2003)
- *Perfect 10, Inc. v. Google, Inc.*, 653 F.3d 976 (9th Cir. 2011)
- *Recording Industry Association of America v. Diamond Multimedia Systems, Inc.*, 180 F.3d 1072 (9th Cir. 1999)
- *Sega Enterprises, Ltd. v. Accolade, Inc.*, 977 F.2d 1510 (9th Cir. 1992)
- *Sony Computer Entertainment, Inc. v. Connectix Corp.*, 203 F.3d 596 (9th Cir. 2000)

Federal Trial Courts
- *Lenz v. Universal Music Corp.*, 572 F. Supp. 2d 1150 (N.D. Cal. 2008)
- *Perfect 10 v. Google, Inc.*, 416 F. Supp. 2d 828 (C.D. Cal. 2006)
- *Realnetworks, Inc. v. DVD Copy Control Association*, 641 F. Supp. 2d 913, 941 (N.D. Cal. 2009)

See also: Copyright; Copyright Infringement; DeCSS; Digital Millennium Copyright Act; Digital Millennium Copyright Act, Title I; Digital Millennium Copyright Act, Title IV; Fair Use (Trademark); Fan Works; File-Sharing; Public Domain

Sources and Further Reading

Marshall Leaffer, *Understanding Copyright Law* (New Providence, NJ: LexisNexis, 5th ed. 2010)

William Patry, *How to Fix Copyright* (Oxford: Oxford University Press, 2011)

Aaron Schwabach, *Fan Fiction and Copyright: Outsider Works and Intellectual Property Protection* (Farnham, Surrey, UK: Ashgate Publishing, 2011)

Aaron Schwabach, "Reclaiming Copyright from the Outside In: What the Downfall Hitler Meme Means for Transformative Works, Fair Use, and Parody," 8 *Buffalo Intellectual Property Journal* 1 (2013)

Richard Stim, *Patent, Copyright & Trademark: An Intellectual Property Desk Reference* (Berkeley, CA: Nolo Press, 12th ed. 2012)

Rebecca Tushnet, "Scary Monsters: Hybrids, Mashups, and Other Illegitimate Children," 86 *Notre Dame Law Review* 2133 (2011)

❖ FAIR USE (TRADEMARK) ❖

Trademark fair use is a defense to a claim of trademark infringement just as copyright fair use is a defense to a claim of copyright infringement. As with copyright fair use, trademark fair use does not mean that the trademark in question has fallen into the public domain; it means simply that a particular use is permissible. There are two categories of trademark fair use: classic fair use and nominative fair use.

Classic fair use: Classic fair use occurs when a trademark is also a descriptive term and is used by a person other than the trademark holder in its descriptive sense. For example, a company might obtain a trademark in the name "California's Best Web Hosting." For another company to use the name "California's Best Web Hosting" for its business would then be infringement. But a company with another name—XYZ Web Services Corporation, say—could still claim to offer "the best Web hosting in California"; XYZ would be using the terms in their descriptive sense. XYZ might even be able to claim to offer "California's best Web hosting." A majority of U.S. courts would find the latter use permissible only so long as there was no likelihood that consumers would be confused—that is, no likelihood that consumers would think that XYZ was offering the services of or was in some way associated with California's Best Web Hosting. This majority approach has the effect of making classic fair use a subset of the "no likelihood of confusion" defense to trademark infringement. A minority of courts, however, see the two defenses as separate, and are willing to find that an otherwise infringing use is fair use even if a likelihood of confusion exists (see *Cosmetically Sealed Industries*, 125 F.3d 28).

Nominative fair use: Use of a mark to identify the mark holder's product or service, rather than the secondary user's, is nominative fair use. The idea has been present, if not always accepted, in U.S. law for over a century (see *Saxlehner*, 216 U.S. 375). The U.S. Courts of Appeals for the Third and Ninth Circuits have explored this idea in some depth, reaching rather different conclusions.

Under the Ninth Circuit test, nominative fair use occurs when the person using another's trademark does so not, or not exclusively, to identify his or her own product or service, but to identify the trademark holder's product or service. A software company that describes its software as "Windows 8 compatible" is intending to identify the Windows 8 operating system made by Microsoft. The use is fair: Potential purchasers of the software who use the Windows 8 operating system will want to know whether the software is compatible with their systems; the "Windows 8" trademark is used only to the extent necessary to identify the operating system; and the software company is not suggesting that it is Microsoft, or that Microsoft has endorsed the product.

This analysis follows, more or less, the three-part test for nominative fair use originally developed by the Ninth Circuit Court of Appeals in *New Kids on the Block v. News America Publishing* and later applied to uniquely online uses in *Playboy Enterprises v. Welles*. Playboy Enterprises is a publisher of mildly pornographic print and Internet content. Each year, Playboy selects one of its models as "Playmate of

the Year," a title that may be seen as outrageously offensive, irritatingly condescending, or quaintly archaic, depending on one's point of view, but which apparently has commercial value. The defendant in the case, Terri Welles, had been awarded the title of "Playmate of the Year" in 1981; she operated a Web site containing images of herself and commentary. On the site, she used Playboy's trademarked terms in three ways: she used the term "Playmate of the Year" in banner advertisements and in the headline of the Web page; she used the terms "playboy" and "playmate" in metatags (text which does not appear to the viewer of a site but does appear to search engines); and she used the repeated term "PMOY 1981" as a wallpaper design. The trial court found that Ms. Welles' actions were not infringements; the Ninth Circuit agreed in part. The use of the term "Playmate of the Year" and of the metatags "playboy" and "playmate" was nominative fair use. In order to be nominative fair use, the court explained,

> First, the product or service in question must be one not readily identifiable without use of the trademark; second, only so much of the mark or marks may be used as is reasonably necessary to identify the product or service; and third, the user must do nothing that would, in conjunction with the mark, suggest sponsorship or endorsement by the trademark holder (279 F.3d at 801).

The repeated use of the term "PMOY 1981" on the wallpaper was not a nominative fair use, however. It was not necessary to identify Welles, nor did it appear to do so, as her name or likeness did not appear before or after the term on the wallpaper (279 F.3d at 804–805).

The Ninth Circuit's test has not been adopted by other circuits, and its use has been cast into some doubt by the U.S. Supreme Court's decision in *KP Permanent Make-Up* (543 U.S. at 111; see also Mayberry 2012). The Sixth Circuit has rejected it (*PACCAR*, 319 F.3d at 256), while the Fifth Circuit views nominative fair use as an adjunct to, not a substitute for, traditional fair use analysis (*Pebble Beach*, 155 F.3d at 526). An important alternative approach has evolved in the Third Circuit, which uses a modified version of its traditional fair use test to evaluate nominative fair use as an affirmative defense. The factors considered in the Third Circuit nominative fair use test are:

> (1) the price of the goods and other factors indicative of the care and attention expected of consumers when making a purchase;
> (2) the length of time the defendant has used the mark without evidence of actual confusion;
> (3) the intent of the defendant in adopting the mark; and
> (4) the evidence of actual confusion (*Century 21 Real Estate Corp.*, 425 F.3d at 225–26).

Recently, the Fourth Circuit applied a similar approach, upholding a lower court's application of only three of the Fourth Circuit's nine possible factors:

These "factors are not always weighted equally, and not all factors are relevant in every case." In fact, "there is no need for each factor to support [the plaintiff's] position on the likelihood of confusion issue". . . . Accordingly, there is no hard and fast rule that obligates the district court to discuss each non-mandatory factor (*Rosetta Stone*, 676 F.3d at 154).

The court then added, "This is especially true when the offending use of the plaintiff's trademark is referential or nominative in nature." This was qualified, however, by a statement that "We hasten to add that we are not adopting a position about the viability of the nominative fair-use doctrine as a defense to trademark infringement or whether this doctrine should formally alter our likelihood-of-confusion test in some way. That question has not been presented here and we leave it for another day" (*Rosetta Stone*, 676 F.3d at 155).

Other circuits have taken various approaches; the Ninth Circuit has continued to treat nominative fair use as not infringing (*Toyota Motor Sales*, 610 F.3d at 1175).

Statute
- Lanham Trademark Act, 15 U.S.C. § 1115(b)

Cases
Supreme Court
- *KP Permanent Make-Up, Inc. v. Lasting Impression 1, Inc.*, 543 U.S. 111 (2004)
- *Saxlehner v. Wagner*, 216 U.S. 375 (1910)

Federal Appellate Courts
- *Century 21 Real Estate Corp. v. Lending Tree, Inc.*, 425 F.3d 211 (3d Cir. 2005)
- *Chambers v. Time Warner, Inc.*, 282 F.3d 147 (2d Cir. 2002)
- *Cosmetically Sealed Industries, Inc. v. Chesebrough-Pond's USA Co.*, 125 F.3d 28 (2d Cir. 1997)
- *Interpace Corp. v. Lapp, Inc.*, 721 F.2d 460, 463 (3d Cir. 1983)
- *New Kids on the Block v. News America Publishing, Inc.*, 971 F.2d 302 (9th Cir. 1992)
- *PACCAR Inc. v. TeleScan Technologies, L.L.C.*, 319 F.3d 243 (6th Cir. 2003)
- *Pebble Beach Co. v. Tour 18 I Ltd.*, 155 F.3d 526 (5th Cir. 1998)
- *Playboy Enterprises, Inc. v. Welles*, 279 F.3d 796 (9th Cir. 2002)
- *Rosetta Stone Ltd. v. Google, Inc.*, 676 F.3d 144 (4th Cir. 2012)
- *Scott Paper Co. v. Scott's Liquid Gold, Inc.*, 589 F.2d 1225 (3d Cir. 1978)
- *Toyota Motor Sales, U.S.A., Inc. v. Tabari*, 610 F.3d 1171 (9th Cir. 2010)

Federal Trial Court
- *Health Grades, Inc. v. Robert Wood Johnson University Hospital, Inc.*, 634 F. Supp. 2d 1226 (D. Colo. 2009)

See also: Fair Use (Copyright); Metatags; Trademark; Trademark Dilution; Trademark Infringement

Sources and Further Reading

Tom Abeles, "Trademark's Unfair Nominative Fair Use Defense: Protecting E-Commentary from Censorship by Corporate Monoliths," 33 *Hastings Communications and Entertainment Law Journal* 181 (2011)

G. Peter Albert, Jr. & Rita A. Abbati, "Metatags, Keywords and Links: Recent Developments Addressing Trademark Threats in Cyberspace," 40 *San Diego Law Review* 341 (2003)

Baila H. Celedonia & Kieran Doyle, "Century 21, The New Kid in Town: The Third Circuit Crafts a New Nominative Fair Use Test," 97 *Trademark Reporter* 989 (2007)

Jeffrey P. Dunning, "Whatever Happened to New Kids on the Block? The Nominative Fair Use Defense to Trademark Infringement," 18 *Intellectual Property & Technology Law Journal* 1 (2006)

J. David Mayberry, "Trademark Nominative Fair Use: Toward a Uniform Standard," 102 *Trademark Reporter* 820 (2012)

Douglas G. McCray, "Oh, What a Tangled Web: The Subtle Difference between Metatag Usage as 'Fair Use' and Invisible Infringement," *Michigan Bar Journal* August 2002, at 42

Hope Viner Samborn, "Hiding in Plain Site: The Hunt for Metatags on the Internet Is Changing the Field of Trademark Law," *ABA Journal* September 2000, at 80

Richard Stim, *Patent, Copyright & Trademark: An Intellectual Property Desk Reference* (Berkeley, CA: Nolo Press, 12th ed. 2012)

❖ FAN WORKS ❖

Fan works are works created by fans of particular novels, television shows, movies, and other works of fiction, incorporating elements of the original works. Fans who write their own stories set in Tolkien's Middle-Earth, or who draw their own *Avengers* comics, or who write their own stories about Harry Potter's adventures after Hogwarts are creating fan works. Fan works have been around for as long, or nearly as long, as fiction itself; however, the advent of the Internet has brought greater attention to fan works and their possible intellectual property consequences.

Fan works may include original text, photographic images, artwork, video, and music. They may also include material copied from the original works or from other sources. Fan works are necessarily derivative works in a literary sense, and may be derivative works in a legal sense as well (see 17 U.S.C. § 106). They may also incorporate copyrighted content, including copyrighted characters and story elements. However, they are often parodies or otherwise transformative, and even when they are not, the use of copyrighted elements may be fair use (see 17 U.S.C. § 107).

Cases
- *Salinger v. Colting*, 607 F.3d 68 (2d Cir. N.Y. 2010)

- *Warner Brothers Entertainment, Inc. v. RDR Books*, 575 F. Supp. 2d 513 (S.D.N.Y. 2008)

See also: Copyright; Copyright Infringement; Derivative Works; Fair Use (Copyright); Fair Use (Trademark)

Sources and Further Reading

Anupam Chander & Madhavi Sunder, "Everyone's a Superhero: A Cultural Theory of 'Mary Sue' Fan Fiction as Fair Use," 95 *California Law Review* 597 (2007)

Brian J. Link, "Drawing a Line in Alternate Universes: Exposing the Inadequacies of the Current Four-Factor Fair Use Test through Chanslash," 33 *Thomas Jefferson Law Review* 139 (2010)

Meredith McCardle, "Fandom, Fan Fiction and Fanfare: What's All the Fuss?" 9 *Boston University Journal of Science and Technology Law* 443 (2003)

Aaron Schwabach, *Fan Fiction and Copyright: Outsider Works and Intellectual Property Protection* (Farnham, Surrey, UK: Ashgate Publishing, 2011)

Aaron Schwabach, "The Harry Potter Lexicon and the World of Fandom: Fan Fiction, Outsider Works, and Copyright," 73 *University of Pittsburgh Law Review* 387 (2009)

Rebecca Tushnet, "Legal Fictions: Copyright, Fan Fiction and a New Common Law," 17 *Loyola Los Angeles Entertainment Law Review* 651 (1997)

❖ FEDERAL CIRCUIT ❖

See Court of Appeals for the Federal Circuit

❖ FEDERAL COMMUNICATIONS COMMISSION ❖

Enforcement of federal laws regarding the Internet is divided among many government agencies, with the Federal Communications Commission (FCC) and the Federal Trade Commission (FTC) both playing major roles. In general, the FCC is responsible more for the infrastructure aspect—the Internet itself, and access to it—and the FTC is responsible more for the content transmitted over that infrastructure—the World Wide Web and email. The boundaries of the categories are indistinct, however. For example, the FCC is charged with the administration of the Children's Internet Protection Act (CIPA); while CIPA is an access-control statute, it is aimed more at a particular type of content than at Internet infrastructure.

The FCC, established in 1934, is charged with regulating interstate and international communications by radio, television, wire, satellite, and cable. This includes the Internet's hardware communications infrastructure. In the early years of the Internet, the FCC nurtured the Internet's growth by distinguishing computer and Internet uses of the telephone network from voice and other "basic" uses. The use of the telephone network for transmission of computer and Internet data was classified as "enhanced service," later renamed "information services," and was left unregulated. This lack of regulation made the rapid growth of the Internet possible. The FCC's determination that "enhanced service providers"—dial-up Internet service providers (ISPs)—were exempt from access charges paid by inter-exchange telephone service carriers kept the cost of dial-up access low, increasing the number of households with access to the Internet and thus also helping to drive the medium's growth. Another little-noted FCC decision, without which the Internet might still be in its infancy, was the requirement that telephone carriers allow users to connect their own terminal equipment to the network, rather than equipment leased from the carrier (Oxman 1999). Without this FCC action, modem technology would probably have developed very slowly, from lack of competition.

In the first decade of the 20th century the FCC found itself positioned as a guardian of net neutrality. In 2007, in response to subscriber complaints, the FCC ordered Comcast, an ISP, to cease interfering with its subscribers' use of peer-to-peer (P2P) software. In a blow to consumer advocates, the U.S. Court of Appeals for the D.C. Circuit struck down the FCC's order, holding that the FCC lacked authority to regulate Comcast's internal network management practices (*Comcast*, 600 F.3d 642).

Although the FCC was essential to the Internet's early growth, its later actions have been criticized for what many perceive as an uneven approach to the regulation of broadband Internet access services. Digital subscriber line (DSL) broadband access and cable-modem broadband access are regulated differently; critics feel that the difference in regulation is responsible for the lackluster performance of DSL in the marketplace. This in turn has limited consumer choice in broadband providers, which has kept competition low and prices high. As a result, the percentage of U.S. households with broadband access is lower than the percentages in some less wealthy countries that have come to the Internet more recently (International Telecommunications Union 2010), although this may reflect consumer unwillingness, rather than inability, to pay a higher price. The FCC's National Broadband Plan attempts to remedy this problem by extending broadband to all areas of the United States and "by transforming the $9 billion Universal Service Fund from supporting legacy telephone service to supporting broadband communications service" (Genachowski 2010).

Statute

- Communications Act of 1934, as amended by Telecommunications Act of 1996, 47 U.S.C. §§ 151 et seq.

Cases

- *AT&T Corp. v. City of Portland*, 216 F.3d 871 (9th Cir. 2000)
- *Brand X Internet Services v. FCC*, 345 F.3d 1120 (9th Cir. 2003); reversed and remanded sub nom

National Cable & Telecommunications Association v. Brand X Internet Services, 545 U.S. 967 (2005)
- *Comcast Corp. v. FCC*, 600 F.3d 642 (D.C. Cir. 2010)

See also: Broadband; Cable; Children's Internet Protection Act; Digital Divide; Federal Trade Commission; Internet; Net Neutrality

Sources and Further Reading

Robert W. Crandall et al. "The Empirical Case against Asymmetric Regulation of Broadband Internet Access," 17 *Berkeley Technology Law Journal* 953 (2002)

Julius Genachowski, FCC Chairman, "The Third Way: A Narrowly Tailored Broadband Framework," Federal Communications Commission (May 6, 2010), available at http://www.broadband.gov/the-third-way-narrowly-tailored-broadband-framework-chairman-julius-genachowski.html (visited February 3, 2013)

Jason Oxman, "The FCC and the Unregulation of the Internet," FCC/OPP Working Paper 31, July 1999

Alexander Reicher, "Redefining Net Neutrality after Comcast v. FCC," 26 *Berkeley Technology Law Journal* 733 (2011)

Emily R. Roxberg, "FCC Authority Post-Comcast: Finding a Happy Medium in the Net Neutrality Debate," 37 *Journal of Corporation Law* 223 (2011)

Assif Shameen, "Korea's Broadband Revolution: What Korea Is Doing Will Have Global Impact," *Chief Executive Magazine* (April 1, 2004), available at http://chiefexecutive.net/koreas-broadband-revolution (visited January 18, 2013)

"World Telecommunications/ICT Development Report 2010," International Telecommunications Union (ITU) (2010), available at http://www.itu.int/ITU-D/ict/publications/wtdr_10/material/WTDR2010_e_v1.pdf (visited January 28, 2013)

❖ FEDERAL TRADE COMMISSION ❖

The Federal Trade Commission (FTC) is one of the U.S. government agencies most heavily involved in regulation of the Internet. The FTC was originally founded in 1914 to enforce federal antitrust laws; in 1938 its scope was expanded to include enforcement of laws against unfair and deceptive trade practices (FTC 2011). Subsequently, the FTC has also been empowered by Congress to enforce laws against and make regulations to control a wide variety of trade practices. The FTC's Bureau of Competition carries out the FTC's original mandate—its antitrust and anti-monopoly duties (FTC 2008). The various divisions of the Bureau of Consumer Protection carry out a wide variety of enforcement and regulatory functions with particular significance to the Internet. The Division of Advertising Practices enforces laws against unfair, misleading or false advertising, problems with which the Internet is severely afflicted. The FTC focuses on advertising for products or services claiming to offer health benefits or weight loss; advertising making performance claims for computers, Internet services, and

similar products and services; tobacco and alcohol advertising; claims about product performance; and advertising aimed at children (FTC 2008). The FTC is also charged with enforcement of the Children's Online Privacy Protection Act (COPPA), and with making regulations to carry out COPPA (15 U.S.C. § 6502). Other Bureau of Consumer Protection divisions include the Consumer and Business Education Program, the Division of Enforcement, the Division of Financial Practices, the Division of Marketing Practices, the Division of Planning and Information, and the International Division of Consumer Protection. The Consumer and Business Education Program provides information about consumer protection statutes and regulations, and maintains a Web site at www.consumer.gov. The site attempts to provide a one-stop shop for consumer protection information.

The Division of Enforcement monitors business compliance with consumer protection laws, regulations, and court orders; conducts investigations; and institutes lawsuits when violations are found. A significant part of its workload involves the monitoring of e-commerce (FTC 2008). The Division of Financial Practices is not specifically Internet-related, although the Internet can be a medium through which predatory and fraudulent lending take place. The Division of Marketing Practices pursues and shuts down scammers, including Internet scammers (FTC 2008).

The Division of Planning and Information is, like the Consumer and Business Education Program, involved in consumer education and outreach. It operates a toll-free number, 1–877-FTC-HELP, to receive consumer complaints and provide information, and maintains a database of these complaints. It also operates the Identity Theft Data Clearinghouse, which counsels consumers on how to protect themselves from identity theft and how to respond if they become victims. The Office of International Affairs works with over a hundred foreign competition and consumer protection authorities and participates, along with similar agencies from 41 other countries, in the International Consumer Protection and Enforcement Network (FTC 2012).

The FTC maintains the popular Do Not Call registry, an anti-telemarketing measure, and has been at the forefront of anti-spam measures as well. While an anti-spam registry along the lines of the Do Not Call registry would be unworkable (because most spammers already operate both outside the law and outside the United States), the FTC also takes action against spammers.

Statutes and Proposed Legislation
- Children's Online Privacy Protection Act, 15 U.S.C. §§ 6501–6506
- Federal Trade Commission Act, 15 U.S.C. § 45
- Undertaking Spam, Spyware, and Fraud Enforcement with Enforcers beyond Borders ("SAFE WEB") Act of 2006, Pub. L. No. 109–455, codified at 15 U.S.C. §§ 41 et. seq.

See also: Advertising; Adware and Spyware; Children's Online Privacy Protection Act; Federal Communications Commission; Identity Theft; Phishing; Spam

Sources and Further Reading

"A Brief Overview of the Federal Trade Commission's Investigative and Law Enforcement Authority," Federal Trade Commission, available at http://www.ftc.gov/ogc/brfovrvw.shtm#N_1_ (visited February 3, 2013)

"Federal Trade Commission: A History," Federal Trade Commission, available at http://www.ftc.gov/opa/history/timeline.shtm (visited February 3, 2013)

Paul M. Schwartz, "Property, Privacy, and Personal Data," 117 *Harvard Law Review* 2055 (2004)

"Welcome to the Office of International Affairs," Federal Trade Commission, available at http://www.ftc.gov/oia/index.shtml (visited February 3, 2013)

❖ FILE-SHARING ❖

File-sharing is the sharing of files on one device with other devices to which the first device is linked through some sort of network. Most file-sharing is routine and perfectly legal; however, one type of file-sharing that has created a great deal of controversy is the sharing of copyrighted information over the Internet. The term "file-sharing" is often used in intellectual property law to refer not to all file-sharing but to this particular type of file-sharing. A typical file-sharing network of this type consists of many users who do not know each other making music files on their computers available for others to download, while also downloading music files from the computers of other users. Any type of information may be shared, but the exchange of compressed music files in the MP3 file format is the type of file-sharing that has aroused the most vehement industry response, with the sharing of copyrighted movies in a variety of formats running a close second.

The legal problem created by this type of file-sharing is copyright infringement. Copyright is a private right; detection of and action against copyright infringement must be taken by the copyright holders or their agents, rather than by the state.

Liability for copyright infringement may be incurred in three ways: by direct infringement, by contributory infringement, or by vicarious infringement. The latter two categories are also referred to as third-party infringement.

Direct infringement requires the violation of a reserved use (typically unauthorized copying) of a work in which copyright is owned by another. Direct infringement is evaluated in accordance with a strict liability standard; in contrast to third-party infringement, there is no notice or knowledge requirement. An individual user who downloads copyrighted material through a file-sharing network is a direct infringer (see *Sony BMG Music Entertainment*, 660 F.3d 487). The persons creating and operating the network, however, generally are not. If copyright owners pursue legal action against these persons for the direct infringements by individual users, they must do so on a theory of third-party (contributory or vicarious) copyright infringement.

Contributory infringement requires a direct infringement by someone else, actual or constructive knowledge of the violation, and a material contribution to the direct infringer's activities. Defining "material contribution" is a particular problem area, with various circuits setting varying standards. The Ninth Circuit Court of Appeals has set what may be the lowest standard: In *Fonovisa, Inc. v. Cherry Auction, Inc.*, the Ninth Circuit held that merely providing facilities used in the infringement is a material contribution (76 F.3d 259). At the other end of the spectrum, the Second Circuit Court of Appeals has set what is probably the highest standard: In *Gershwin Publishing Corporation v. Columbia Artists Management, Inc.*, the Second Circuit held that substantial participation in the activity is required (443 F.2d 1159). Contributory infringement may also be found where one person intentionally induces or encourages a direct infringement by another. This can be done by distributing a device or computer program with the object of promoting its use to infringe copyright (*Grokster*, 545 U.S. at 930, 937).

Vicarious infringement requires a direct infringement by someone else, the right and ability to control the infringer's actions, and a direct financial benefit from the infringing activity. The right and ability to control the infringer's actions may result from the continuing relationship between the parties or from the retention of a contractual ability to restrict the infringer's actions. The direct financial benefit from the infringing activity need not be actual payment; if the infringement brings in customers, it generates a financial benefit (*Fonovisa*, 76 F.3d 259).

Two lines of vicarious infringement cases establish the extremes between which the problem of file-sharing falls: the landlord-tenant cases and the dance hall cases. The landlord-tenant cases have held that a landlord who receives fixed rents from tenants regardless of the tenants' activities is not vicariously liable for the tenants' infringement. The dance hall cases, on the other hand, have held that a dance hall owner's relationship with persons hired to provide music to paying customers is analogous to an employer-employee relationship; the dance hall owner is vicariously liable for the musicians' infringement. File-sharing occupies the middle ground between these two lines of cases.

Fonovisa was a vicarious and contributory infringement case involving off-line rather than online pirating of copyrighted music. The defendant, Cherry Auction, was the host of a swap meet. Vendors, including music vendors, paid a daily rental fee to Cherry Auction. Cherry Auction supplied utilities, parking, advertising, plumbing, and customers; the customers paid a fee to Cherry Auction upon entrance to the premises. Cherry Auction knew that many of the vendors sold counterfeit music, infringing upon copyrights owned by the plaintiff, Fonovisa.

The Ninth Circuit held that Cherry Auction was liable for vicarious infringement because there was control and financial benefit. There was control because Cherry Auction could control admission and advertising and had contractually reserved the right to restrict market access and vendor behavior. And there was a financial benefit to Cherry Auction in the form of rental fees from vendors, admissions fees from customers, parking revenues, food sales, and other customer services. In addition, the availability of copyright-infringing materials probably enhanced the appeal of the swap meet to customers (*Fonovisa*, 76 F.3d 259).

Cherry Auction was also liable for contributory infringement because there was knowledge and material contribution. Cherry Auction had actual knowledge of the infringing activity, and made a material contribution by providing the site and facilities for the sale of the unlawfully copied material. The court explained that express encouragement or protection of the identity of the infringers was not required (*Fonovisa*, 76 F.3d 259).

In addition to *Fonovisa,* another prequel to the file-sharing cases is *Sony Corp. of America v. Universal City Studios, Inc.* In 1984, when videocassette recorders (VCRs) were new, producers of television shows sought to have VCRs banned because they could be used to record copyrighted television shows. To this end Universal Studios, a content owner, brought suit against Sony, a manufacturer of VCRs. The Sony Betamax VCRs at issue in the case recorded one-hour tapes. The market for video rentals had not yet emerged and home video camcorders were unknown. The expectation was that the recording function of the VCRs would be used mainly to record television programs.

The U.S. Supreme Court held that Sony was not contributorily liable for infringements committed with the VCRs it manufactured. There was no ongoing relationship between Sony and the end users; the relationship was limited to the sale itself, warranties notwithstanding. In addition, the VCRs were capable of "substantial noninfringing uses" and thus qualified as a "staple article of commerce." (This "staple article of commerce" doctrine apples only to contributory infringement, not to vicarious infringement.) The substantial noninfringing uses included time-shifting (recording programs to watch later), copying noncopyrighted works, and making authorized copies of copyrighted materials (*Sony*, 464 U.S. 417).

Liability for copyright infringement (direct, contributory, or vicarious) is always limited by the fair use doctrine; the noninfringing uses of which the Sony Betamax VCRs were capable included fair uses of copyrighted material such as time-shifting. Four factors are applied to determine the fuzzy parameters of fair use: the nature of the use, especially whether it is personal or commercial; the nature of the protected work; the extent to which the work is copied; and the potential economic effect on the market (*Sony*, 464 U.S. 417; 17 U.S.C § 107).

The advent of the Internet led to disparate results among circuits regarding the liability of an online service provider for content made available on its servers. Congress addressed the disparity with the Digital Millennium Copyright Act (DMCA). Provisions of the DMCA relevant to file-sharing include the safe harbor provisions and the anticircumvention provisions (17 U.S.C. §§ 512, 1201).

Safe harbor provisions The DMCA provides four types of safe harbor, two of which are relevant to file-sharing: the Transitory Digital Network Communications Safe Harbor and the Information Location Tools Safe Harbor. The Transitory Digital Network Communications Safe Harbor provides that a service provider is not liable simply because it transiently stores or transmits, routes, or provides connections for infringing material through a system or network it controls or operates, if:

1. Someone other than the service provider initiates transmission of the material;
2. The transmission, routing, provision of connections, or storage is carried out through an automatic technical process without selection of the material by the service provider;
3. The service provider does not select the recipients of the material except as an automatic response to the request of another person;
4. No copy of the material is maintained on the system or network in a manner ordinarily accessible to anyone other than anticipated recipients, or for longer than reasonably necessary; and
5. The material is transmitted through the system or network without modification of its content (17 U.S.C. § 512(a)).

The Information Location Tools Safe Harbor provides that a service provider is not liable simply because it refers or links users to an online location containing infringing content by using information location tools, including a directory, index, reference, pointer, or hypertext link, if it:

1. Does not actually know that the content is infringing, OR is not aware of facts or circumstances from which the infringing content is apparent, OR upon obtaining such knowledge or awareness, acts expeditiously to remove or disable access to the infringing content, AND
2. Does not receive a financial benefit directly attributable to the infringing activity, in a case in which the service provider has the right and ability to control such activity, AND
3. Upon notification of claimed infringement acts expeditiously to remove or disable access to the infringing content (17 U.S.C. § 512(d)).

Notification must include identification of the reference or link that is to be removed or disabled and information reasonably sufficient to permit the service provider to locate that reference or link.

The safe harbor provisions protect a service provider even if the provider actually knows of the infringement, unless the service provider receives notice of the infringement from the copyright holder or the copyright holder's agent.

Anticircumvention provisions: The anticircumvention provisions of the Digital Millennium Copyright Act work independently of other copyright law protections. No direct or indirect copyright infringement is necessary for liability under the anticircumvention provisions, which prohibit:

1. Tampering with or attempting to circumvent a technological measure that effectively controls access to a copyrighted work;
2. Trafficking in any technology, product, service, device, component or part that is primarily designed or produced for the purpose of circumventing a [protected] technological protection measure (17 U.S.C. § 1201).

The DMCA's use of the word "effectively" calls the entire section into question, however: some forms of "technological protection measures" can be circumvented with a black marker, or by holding down the "Shift" key. Most or even all measures can be circumvented, within days or weeks of their appearance in the marketplace, by software that can be downloaded and used by even the most minimally technically savvy Internet user, often for free. It may be that such measures cannot be said to be "effective"; they create barriers to copying, but they are generally circumvented fairly easily by anyone with the patience and motivation to do so. But courts have held that a technological measure effectively controls access if its function is to control access, even if it can be circumvented. This "intent to control access" test seems perhaps broader than the Congressional intent seen in the plain language of the statute, but Congress has not yet seen fit either to correct this interpretation or incorporate it into the text of the statute.

Statutes
- Audio Home Recording Act of 1992, Pub. L. 102–563, § 1, October 28, 1992, 106 Stat. 4237, amending 17 U.S.C. §§ 1001–1010, 801, 804, 912, and 19 U.S.C.A. § 1337
- Copyright Act of 1976, 17 U.S.C. §§ 101–1332
- Digital Millennium Copyright Act, 17 U.S.C. §§ 512, 1201

Cases
Supreme Court
- *Metro-Goldwyn-Mayer Studios, Inc. v. Grokster, Ltd.*, 259 F. Supp. 2d 1029 (C.D. Cal. 2003); affirmed, 380 F.3d 1154 (9th Cir. 2004); vacated & remanded, 549 U.S. 913 (2005)
- *Sony Corp. of America v. Universal City Studios, Inc.*, 464 U.S. 417 (1984)

Federal Appellate Courts
- *A&M Records, Inc. v. Napster, Inc.*, 239 F.3d 1004 (9th Cir. 2001)
- *Atari, Inc. v. JS & A Group, Inc.*, 747 F.2d 1422 (Fed. Cir. 1984), overruled by *Nobelpharma AB v. Implant Innovations, Inc.*, 141 F.3d 1059 (Fed. Cir. 1998)
- *Bridgeport Music, Inc. v. Justin Combs Publishing*, 507 F.3d 470 (6th Cir. 2007)
- *Capitol Records, Inc. v. Thomas-Rasset*, 692 F.3d 899 (8th Cir. 2011), certiorari denied, 133 S.Ct. 1584
- *Flava Works, Inc. v. Gunter*, 689 F.3d 754 (7th Cir. 2012)
- *Fonovisa, Inc. v. Cherry Auction, Inc.*, 76 F.3d 259 (9th Cir. 1996)
- *Gershwin Publishing Corp. v. Columbia Artists Management, Inc.*, 443 F.2d 1159 (2d Cir. 1971)
- *In re Aimster Copyright Litigation (Aimster II)*, 252 F. Supp. 2d 634 (N.D. Ill. 2002), affirmed in part, 334 F.3d 643 (7th Cir. 2003), certiorari denied sub nom *Deep v. Recording Industry Association of America, Inc.*, 540 U.S. 1107 (2004)
- *Recording Industry Association of America v. Diamond Multimedia Systems, Inc.*, 180 F.3d 1072 (9th Cir. 1999)
- *Recording Industry Association of America, Inc. v. Verizon Internet Services*, 240 F. Supp. 2d 24 (D.D.C. 2003); reversed, 351 F.3d 1229 (D.C. Cir. 2003); certiorari denied, 543 U.S. 924 (2004)
- *Sony BMG Music Entertainment v. Tenenbaum*, 660 F.3d 487 (1st Cir. 2011)
- *Viacom International, Inc. v. YouTube, Inc.*, 676 F.3d 19 (2d Cir. 2012)

Federal Trial Courts
- *Arista Records LLC v. Lime Group LLC*, 784 F. Supp. 2d 398 (S.D.N.Y. 2011)
- *Capitol Records, Inc. v. Does*, No. 07–485 WJ/LFG, 2007 U.S. Dist. LEXIS 97930 (D.N.M. 2007)
- *Elektra Entertainment Group, Inc. v. Barker*, 551 F. Supp. 2d 234 (S.D.N.Y. 2008)
- *Interscope Records v. Does*, 494 F. Supp. 2d 388 (E.D. Va. 2007)
- *Jalbert v. Grautski*, 554 F. Supp. 2d 57 (D. Mass. 2008)
- *London-Sire Records, Inc. v. Doe 1*, 542 F. Supp. 2d 153 (D. Mass. 2008)
- *MGM Studios Inc. v. Grokster, Ltd.*, 243 F. Supp. 2d 1073 (C.D. Cal. 2003)
- *Sony Music Entertainment Inc, v. Does 1–40*, 326 F. Supp. 2d 556 (S.D.N.Y. 2004)
- *Religious Technology Center v. Netcom On-Line Communication Services, Inc.*, 907 F. Supp. 1361 (N.D. Cal. 1995)
- *UMG Recordings, Inc., v. MP3.com, Inc.*, 92 F. Supp. 2d 349 (S.D.N.Y. 2000)

- *UMG Recordings, Inc. v. Sinnott*, 300 F. Supp. 2d 993 (E.D. Cal. 2004)
- *Wolk v. Kodak Imaging Network, Inc.*, 840 F. Supp. 2d 724 (S.D.N.Y. 2011)

See also: Abandonware; Content Industry; Copyright; Copyright Alert System; Copyright Infringement; Digital Audio Works; Digital Millennium Copyright Act, Title I; Digital Millennium Copyright Act, Title II; Encryption; Fair Use (Copyright); File-Sharing and the Courts (Attempts to Control Technology); File-Sharing and the Courts (Litigation against Individual Users); File-Sharing (Other Media); Internet Service Providers; MP3; No Electronic Theft Act; P2P; Piracy; Voluntary Collective License; Warez

Sources and Further Reading

Oliver Abou, *Telechargez vos DIVX et MP3 avec KaZaA et eDonkey* (Paris: Micro Application 2003) (in French)

Michael Albert & Lisa Vertinsky, "From Sony to Napster—and Back? Copyright Law Implications of Decentralized File-Sharing Technology," *Boston Bar Journal*, January/February 2004, at 10

John Alderman & Evan I. Schwartz, *Sonic Boom* (Boulder, CO: Perseus, 2002)

J. Cam Barker, "Grossly Excessive Penalties in the Battle against Illegal File-Sharing: The Troubling Effects of Aggregating Minimum Statutory Damages for Copyright Infringement," 83 *Texas Law Review* 525 (2004)

Michel Barreau, *KaZaA, iMesh, eDonkey et tous les autres* (Paris: CampusPress, 2003) (in French)

David P. Branfman, "What Do Copyrights, Trolls, Sex, & Lawyers Have in Common?" *North County Lawyer*, February 2012, at 19

Fritz Effenberger, *Clever tauschen mit KaZaA und Co.* (Poing: Franzis, 2003) (in German)

"Face Value: The Quiet Iconoclast—With KaZaA, Niklas Zennstrom Undermined the Music Industry," *The Economist*, July 1, 2004, at 54, available at http://www.economist.com/node/2876993 (visited February 3, 2013)

Sheila M. Heidmiller, "RIAA's Latest Attack on P2P File-Sharing," *Intellectual Property Law Newsletter*, Summer 2003, at 10

"I Want My P2P: Record Labels Are Trying to Do Deals with File-Sharing Networks," *The Economist*, November 18, 2004, at 65, available at http://www.economist.com/node/3407417 (visited February 3, 2013)

Jeff Jarvis, *Public Parts: How Sharing in the Digital Age Improves the Way We Work and Love* (New York: Simon & Schuster, 2011)

Jupiter Research Corporation, *File Sharing and the DMCA* [e-book], (MarketResearch.com 2001)

Robert Levine, *Free Ride: How the Internet Is Destroying the Culture Business and How the Culture Business Can Fight Back* (New York: Doubleday, 2011)

Joseph Menn, *All the Rave: The Rise and Fall of Shawn Fanning's Napster* (New York: Crown Business, 2003)

Trevor Merriden, *Irresistible Forces: The Business Legacy of Napster and the Growth of the Underground Internet* (New York: John Wiley & Sons, 2002)

Tom Moon, "Radiohead's 'In Rainbows' Sets Its Own Terms," NPR Music (October 10, 2007), available at http://www.npr.org/templates/story/story.php?storyId=15152703 (visited February 3, 2013)

Lucille M. Ponte, "Coming Attractions: Opportunities and Challenges in Thwarting Global Movie Piracy," 45 *American Business Law Journal* 331 (2008)

"RIAA v. The People: Five Years Later," Electronic Frontier Foundation (September 30, 2008), available at https://www.eff.org/wp/riaa-v-people-five-years-later (visited February 3, 2013)

Pamela Samuelson, "Three Reactions to MGM v. Grokster," 13 *Michigan Telecommunications and Technology Law Review* 177 (2006)

Seagrumn Smith, "From Napster to KaZaA: The Battle over Peer-to-Peer Filesharing Goes International," 2003 *Duke Law & Technology Review* 8 (2003)

Gary Younge, "US Music Industry Sues 261 for Online Song Copying," *The Guardian* (September 10, 2003), available at http://www.richardhartley.com/2003/09/us-music-industry-sues-261-for-online-song-copying/ (visited February 3, 2013)

❖ FILE-SHARING AND THE COURTS (ATTEMPTS TO CONTROL TECHNOLOGY) ❖

The content industry, particularly the music industry, responded to file-sharing technology in much the same way it had previously responded to other copying technologies, from copy machines to tape recorders: by trying to sue it out of existence. The battle of the music industry in particular against online file-sharing was to become the defining intellectual property struggle of the late 20th and early 21st centuries, with battles fought in courts, legislatures, and international organizations across the world. In the United States, a line of cases against file-sharing networks and technologies culminated in a victory, albeit perhaps a Pyrrhic one, for the content industry with the U.S. Supreme Court's decision in *MGM Studios v. Grokster*, 549 U.S. 913 (2005). A major step along the road to that victory was the content industry's earlier victory in *A&M Records, Inc. v. Napster, Inc.*, 239 F.3d 1004 (9th Cir. 2001).

Two other important cases in the run-up to *Napster* and *Grokster* were *Recording Industry Association of America v. Diamond Multimedia Systems, Inc.* and *UMG Recordings, Inc., v. MP3.com, Inc.* The defendant in the first of these, Diamond Multimedia, manufactured the Rio, the first commercially available MP3 player. MP3 files, previously playable by most users only on a computer, could now be transferred to the Rio and played anywhere. The Ninth Circuit Court of Appeals determined that this space-shifting was analogous to the time-shifting in the *Sony* Betamax videorecorder case (*Sony Corp.*, 464 U.S. 417, in which the videorecorder could be used to record television programs for watching at a later time) and was fair use. The Rio could be used to play music already owned, and was thus capable of a substantial noninfringing use (*Diamond Multimedia*, 180 F.3d 1072).

The defendant in the second case, MP3.com, purchased CDs containing tens of thousands of copyrighted songs and placed these songs, as MP3 files, on its servers. It then made the songs on its servers available to subscribers who could demonstrate, by placing a recorded CD in the disk drive of their computers that they owned, or at least had access to, a legitimate (licensed) copy of the copyrighted version of the material. The federal district court for the southern district of New York found that MP3.com's use of its CDs exceeded the limits of fair use of copyrighted material (*MP3.com*, 92 F. Supp. 2d 349).

Napster: On the heels of these two cases came *A&M Records v. Napster.* Napster was a hugely popular file-sharing service. Unlike MP3.com, which stored MP3 files on its own servers, Napster stored no MP3 files; thus Napster, again unlike MP3.com, was not a direct infringer. Instead, Napster's MusicShare software enabled peer-to-peer file-sharing. Files were traded directly between users without passing through Napster's computers. Napster did, however, maintain a central list of available songs; users wishing to download songs would locate them via Napster's list. This list, more than any other single factor, made it possible for A&M Records and others to sue Napster for contributory and vicarious infringement, and win. At least one court has since noted that the newness of the technology at the time of the decision may have led to its being misunderstood by the *Napster* court: "the court's very statement may betray a slight misunderstanding about the way the technology worked" (*London-Sire Records*, 542 F. Supp. 2d at 167).

The suit for contributory infringement required that there be an underlying direct infringement, and that Napster materially contribute to and have actual or constructive knowledge of that direct infringement. The underlying direct infringement required for liability for contributory infringement was committed by Napster's users, many, if not most, of whom were direct infringers unprotected by the fair use exception. Distribution of copies of copyrighted material to anonymous requesters, the Ninth Circuit held, is not a private, personal use. Transfer to unknown, anonymous persons is not mere time-shifting or space-shifting. Typically, the entire work was copied, and distribution adversely affected the market for the songs; users received for free something they would ordinarily have to buy (*Napster, Inc.*, 239 F.3d 1004).

The material contribution was simple enough to establish, using the Ninth Circuit's "but for" test: but for Napster's provision of the list and the file-sharing software, the direct infringement would not have taken place, or would at least have been far more difficult. The "actual or constructive" knowledge element was a bit more difficult to establish. The Ninth Circuit in Napster interpreted *Sony* to mean that knowledge cannot be imputed where a product is capable of a substantial noninfringing use; evidence of *actual* knowledge of *specific* acts of infringement was required. This higher standard (actual rather than constructive knowledge) was met, though: an email from Napster co-founder Sean Parker referred to the fact that Napster users were "exchanging pirated music," and Napster used screen shots showing

copyrighted material to promote its service. The court stated that "the record supports the district court's finding that Napster has *actual* knowledge that *specific* infringing material is available using its system, that it could block access to the system by suppliers of the infringing material, and that it failed to remove the material" (*Napster, Inc.*, 239 F.3d at 1022).

The suit for vicarious infringement also required an underlying direct infringement. In addition, in order to be found vicariously liable, Napster must have had the right and ability to control the direct infringers' actions and must have received a direct financial benefit from the infringing activity. Napster met all of these requirements. There was direct infringement by Napster users. Napster had the right and ability to control the actions of these direct infringers because it reserved the right to block access to the Napster Web site at its discretion. And Napster received a direct financial benefit in the form of an increased customer base on which its future income depended (*Napster, Inc.*, 239 F.3d 1004).

File-sharing after Napster: At the heart of Napster's legal vulnerability was the list of available songs. This list, maintained on Napster's servers, involved Napster in the ongoing file-sharing activity. It gave Napster a financial benefit, by bringing customers to the site. It gave Napster control over the process. And it materially contributed to the process. Post-Napster file-sharing services have sought to avoid this vulnerability by decentralization. Two approaches to decentralization are supernode-based services and Virtual Private Network (VPN) based services.

Supernode: A "supernode" is an individual user's computer that maintains a list of files available for sharing over a file-sharing network. Supernode-based services are based on the FastTrack program from Bluemoon Interactive that allows these services to avoid the necessity of maintaining a centralized directory of available files. (The supernodes are not, except perhaps by coincidence, the same computers on which the files are available.) Napster successors StreamCast Networks, KaZaA, and Grokster were supernode-based systems.

Virtual private network: A VPN piggybacks on an existing network using passwords, tunneling protocols, and encryption to create a virtual network inaccessible by unauthorized users from the larger network. In essence the VPN provides a Web of "secret passages" through the main network.

The lack of centralization made it more difficult for makers of file-sharing software, which is usually distributed for free, to make money. Some, such as KaZaA, made money by advertising generated on (or directed to) the user's computer by the software. Others were not seeking to make a profit, but created file-sharing networks for the sheer pleasure of doing so.

In response, the content industry, led by the Recording Industry Association of America (RIAA), turned to self-help tactics such as spoofing and interdiction. "Spoofing" in an online file-sharing context is distributing fake or damaged copies of popular downloads, wasting users' time and bandwidth. The spoofed files can also contain admonitory messages, as the notorious Madonna files did. Interdiction is the repeated requesting of popular files that are then downloaded very slowly, thus making them inaccessible to others. Although the RIAA denies that interdiction is a denial-of-service (DOS) attack, the underlying principle is the same. Users, in turn, developed software to detect RIAA spoofers and interdictors and bar them from P2P networks. The RIAA also introduced legislation that would allow it to hack file-sharers' computers and delete any MP3s found; needless to say, this provoked widespread public outcry. And, of course, the RIAA continued to sue distributors of file-sharing software. Two important later cases were *In re Aimster Copyright Litigation (Aimster II)*, which dealt a severe blow to VPN-based file-sharing networks, and *MGM Studios v. Grokster*, which dealt an even more severe blow to supernode-based networks.

Aimster: Aimster was a VPN-based file-sharing program that piggybacked on America Online's instant messaging system, AIM (thus the name). Aimster used encryption to prevent anyone other than the users from monitoring or discovering the contents of traded files. The first version of the software, Classic Aimster, identified, by default, all other Aimster users logged on to AIM as "buddies" and therefore members of the VPN. A later version, Club Aimster, charged a monthly fee and included a Web site that listed the 40 most popular downloads and a one-click download option, eliminating the need for manual searching. The Club Aimster Web site also included a tutorial.

At trial, the federal district court for the Northern District of Illinois found Aimster contributorily and vicariously liable. Aimster did not contest the plaintiffs' contention that an underlying direct infringement had occurred (*Aimster II*, 252 F. Supp. 2d 634).

Contributory infringement: The district court found Aimster contributorily liable. Aimster had actual or constructive knowledge of and materially contributed to its users' direct infringement. Various letters from the plaintiffs gave Aimster notice of the direct infringement. Also, the Club Aimster Web site identified and commented on copyrighted material. The court rejected the contention that Aimster could not know what was being traded because of encryption, because Aimster itself had made the encryption available and because specific knowledge of individual transfers was not required; the encryption did not prevent Aimster from having constructive knowledge of the direct infringement (*Aimster II*, 252 F. Supp. 2d 634). Note that this arguably differs from the Ninth Circuit's interpretation of *Sony* as stated in *Napster;* however, the Northern District of Illinois lies in the Seventh Circuit and is not bound by the precedent of the Ninth Circuit.

In addition, Aimster materially contributed to the infringement by providing software and services that enabled users to connect with each other. The Club Aimster Web site also ranked songs and enticed would-be infringers, and Aimster's one-click download service made infringement easier for its users (*Aimster II*, 252 F. Supp. 2d 634).

The district court also reasoned (incorrectly, as it turned out) that the staple article of commerce doctrine applied to the VCRs in *Sony* was inapplicable to Aimster. In the district court's view, Aimster was not an "article of commerce"; it was not a discrete product, but a bundle of services. The mere assertion that Aimster was capable of substantial non-infringing uses, in the absence of supporting evidence that those uses were actually being made of Aimster, was insufficient. And unlike the relationship between Sony and the VCR purchasers, the relationship between Aimster users and Aimster was ongoing. In addition, the Aimster users' activities were not private; each became a global distributor of music (*Aimster II*, 252 F. Supp. 2d 634).

While the federal Court of Appeals for the Seventh Circuit also found Aimster contributorily liable for its users' direct infringements, it rejected the district court's reasoning regarding the "staple article of commerce doctrine" and held that the doctrine was potentially applicable. The Seventh Circuit stated that the doctrine is not categorically inapplicable to services, and that the Supreme Court's concern in Sony was to avoid granting copyright holders an undue degree of control over technology. File-sharing and instant messaging, the Seventh Circuit pointed out, are valuable technologies. And the ongoing relationship between Aimster and its users did not automatically render the doctrine inapplicable; what was at issue was the ability of a service provider or product manufacturer to affect the ability of the end users to infringe. However, although the staple article of commerce doctrine was potentially applicable, Aimster had not met its burden of showing that its service fell within the scope of the doctrine. The mere assertion that Aimster was capable of substantial noninfringing uses, in the absence of supporting evidence that those uses were actually being made of Aimster, was insufficient. If Aimster had met this burden and if the infringing use was also substantial, the Seventh Circuit would then have required a showing that reducing or eliminating the infringing use would be disproportionately costly (*Aimster II*, 334 F.3d 643).

Vicarious infringement: The district court found that Aimster had the right and ability to control the infringers' actions and that Aimster received a direct financial benefit from the directly infringing activity; thus, Aimster was vicariously liable. The appellate court did not address the issue of vicarious liability; it neither affirmed nor reversed the trial court's findings on this issue. It said that it was "less confident" that the plaintiffs would prevail on the merits of the vicarious liability claim than on the merits of the contributory liability claim.

According to the trial court, Aimster met the first of the requirements for vicarious liability because it contractually retained the right to terminate individual users and to take down infringing works. The use of a user name and password to log on to the Club Aimster site was a further measure of control; the fact that communications were encrypted did not mean that Aimster lacked control over the users. In addition, there was a financial benefit because Club Aimster required payment of a monthly fee, Aimster solicited donations for legal fees on its Web site, and the infringing activities attracted customers.

The court also evaluated the applicability of the safe harbor provisions to Aimster. It found that Aimster met the threshold requirement: it was a service provider within the meaning of the DMCA. However, Aimster was ineligible for either the Transitory Digital Network Communications Safe Harbor or the Information Location Tools Safe Harbor because it had not implemented a policy to bar repeat copyright infringers. (Although a policy existed, Aimster stated that it could not implement it because of the encryption.) Although Aimster stated that it would respond to notice of infringement, the court stated that a provider may not willfully create an encryption scheme hiding the information sought and then claim ignorance.

In addition, the Transitory Digital Network Communications Safe Harbor was inapplicable because it applies to materials traveling through a provider's system, and no materials were exchanged through Aimster's system. And the Information Location Tools Safe Harbor is inapplicable to a party who knows of the infringing material or activity or receives a financial benefit therefrom; Aimster was disqualified on both counts (*Aimster II*, 252 F. Supp. 2d 634).

In January 2004, the U.S. Supreme Court rejected Aimster owner John Deep's petition for certiorari, declining to review the Seventh Circuit's decision (*Deep*, 540 U.S. 1107).

Grokster: Grokster was a FastTrack (supernode)-based file-sharing system. Launching the Grokster software on a computer connected to the Internet automatically connected the user to the Grokster P2P network. Some users of Grokster committed direct copyright infringement by using the software to share copyrighted material with large numbers of fellow users unknown to them. In October 2001, Metro-Goldwyn-Mayer (MGM), a content owner, and others brought suit against Grokster for contributory and vicarious infringement. The decisions in Grokster's favor at the trial and circuit court levels were hailed as victories by file-sharers, but victory turned out to be ephemeral; the U.S. Supreme Court vacated the Ninth Circuit's decision, in effect shutting down Grokster and similar networks. Today's Grokster's Web site bears only an intimidating message:

www.grokster.com
The United States Supreme Court unanimously confirmed that using this service to trade copyrighted material is illegal. Copying copyrighted motion picture and music files using unauthorized peer-to-peer services is illegal and is prosecuted by copyright owners. There are legal services for downloading music and movies. This service is not one of them. YOUR IP ADDRESS IS 68.7.243.210 [for example] AND HAS BEEN LOGGED.

Don't think you can't get caught. You are not anonymous. In the meantime, please visit www.respectcopyrights.com and www.musicunited.org to learn more about copyright.

To provide a legal basis for holding Grokster liable as a third-party copyright infringer, the Supreme Court had to make significant changes to the law of contributory infringement as it was then understood.

Contributory infringement: Although there was an underlying direct infringement, the trial court (the federal district court for the Central District of California) found Grokster not liable for contributory infringement because neither the knowledge element nor the material contribution element was met. The trial court (Central District of California) is located within the Ninth Circuit. Like the Ninth Circuit in Napster (and unlike the Northern District of Illinois in Aimster), it applied a high standard to the "knowledge" element: Grokster had to have had "actual knowledge of infringement at a time when [it could] use that knowledge to stop the particular infringement. In other words, Plaintiffs' notices of infringing conduct are irrelevant if they arrive when Defendants do nothing to facilitate, and cannot do anything to stop, the alleged infringement." The fact that Grokster marketed itself as "the next Napster" and knew that its software was being used for copyright infringement did not mean that Grokster knew of any *specific* infringement at a time when it could prevent the infringement.

The "material contribution" element was not met, either, according to the trial court. Grokster originally had control over a root supernode, but no longer had such control by the time of the litigation. At the time of the litigation, searches and downloads were taking place without any information being transferred to or through any computers owned by Grokster. Grokster's contribution to the network was the provision of the software; Grokster was not capable of shutting down the P2P network. This was analogous to the provision of a VCR; the plaintiffs did not introduce "evidence of [Grokster's] active and substantial contribution to the infringement itself." Thus, Grokster was not liable for contributory infringement (*Grokster*, 259 F. Supp. 2d 1029).

The decisions of the district court and Ninth Circuit in *MGM v. Grokster* were good news for file-sharers, but they contained a weakness. All of the elements of third-party liability that were not met came down to a single fact—Grokster's lack of ongoing control over the users of its software. To Grokster's allies, this made Grokster less like Napster and more like Sony, which was not liable for infringements committed with its VCRs. To Grokster's opponents, the better comparison—although they may not have used this specific case—was to *Atari v. JS & A*, a case lost by the distributors of a device for copying Atari game cartridges. JS & A's advertisements seemed to encourage illegal copying; so did Grokster's. To allow Grokster to avoid liability, the content industry claimed, would leave it defenseless. The Ninth Circuit was not unaware of the problem; it was "not blind to the possibility that Defendants may have intentionally structured their businesses to avoid secondary liability for copyright infringement, while benefiting financially from the illicit draw of their wares." But the Ninth Circuit declined to create a new form of third-party liability to cover the situation; the remedy, it said, lay with Congress rather than with the judiciary (*Grokster*, 259 F. Supp. 2d at 1046).

The content industry did not have to wait for Congress to act, however. In 2005, the Supreme Court vacated and remanded, in a plurality opinion, in a way that probably left none of the parties, even the winners, completely satisfied. To create a basis for contributory-infringement liability in the absence of actual knowledge of specific infringements at a time when those infringements could have been prevented, the Court imported the doctrine of induced infringement from patent law, stating "One infringes contributorily by intentionally inducing or encouraging direct infringement" (*MGM v. Grokster*, 545 U.S. at 930). As support for this use of the rule the Court somewhat unconvincingly cited *Gershwin Publishing Corp. v. Columbia Artists Management*. What the *Gershwin* court had actually said, though, was "Similarly, one who, with knowledge of the infringing activity, induces, causes or materially contributes to the infringing conduct of another, may be held liable as a 'contributory' infringer" (*Gershwin Publishing Corp.*, 443 F.2d at 1162). The elements of knowledge and material contribution are present in *Gershwin*. Inducement is an alternative to (or perhaps a synonym for or subset of) one of these elements: material contribution; however, *Gershwin* did not present it as an alternative to the knowledge element, which it would have to be in order for the plaintiffs to prevail in *Grokster*.

However, the Supreme Court is the final authority on such matters. It continued its analysis on the inducement theory it had just introduced, explaining that there was precedent for such borrowing from patent law: in *Sony*, the staple article of commerce doctrine had been so borrowed.

> For the same reasons that Sony took the staple-article doctrine of patent law as a model for its copyright safe-harbor rule, the inducement rule, too, is a sensible one for copyright. We adopt it here, holding that one who distributes a device with the object of promoting its use to infringe copyright, as shown by clear expression or other affirmative steps taken to foster infringement, is liable for the resulting acts of infringement by third parties (*MGM v. Grokster*, 545 U.S. at 936–937).

Once the new rule had been adopted, it was a simple matter to find that Grokster had violated it:

> Grokster's name is apparently derived from Napster, it too initially offered an OpenNap program, its software's function is likewise comparable to Napster's, and it attempted to divert queries for Napster onto its own Web site. Grokster

and StreamCast's efforts to supply services to former Napster users, deprived of a mechanism to copy and distribute what were overwhelmingly infringing files, indicate a principal, if not exclusive, intent on the part of each to bring about infringement (*MGM v. Grokster*, 545 U.S. at 939).

The Court rejected the Ninth Circuit's finding on contributory liability. The Court's wording here is not as clear as it could be; while the view that the Court is presenting the inducement rule as an alternative rule of contributory liability is probably the more widely held, another possible interpretation is that the Court is introducing "inducement" as a third and new form of third-party copyright infringement liability (see Samuelson 2006). This interpretation has the benefit of rendering any inconsistencies with the rule of contributory liability as expressed in *Gershwin* irrelevant: if inducement is a third type of liability, it will necessarily have a different combination of elements than the first two.

The Court went on to explain that the Ninth Circuit had misread *Sony* "as holding that distribution of a commercial product capable of substantial noninfringing uses could not give rise to contributory liability for infringement unless the distributor had actual knowledge of specific instances of infringement and failed to act on that knowledge" (*MGM v. Grokster*, 545 U.S. at 927). This was one more step in the orphaning of *Sony*, which is increasingly coming to look like a relic from an era when the balance between consumer and content owner rights was less heavily weighted in favor of the content owners.

Vicarious infringement: The district court found Grokster not liable for vicarious infringement, either, even though there was an underlying direct infringement and the "direct financial benefit" element was met, because Grokster did not have the right and ability to control the direct infringers' actions. "Direct financial benefit" was defined quite broadly: the district court stated that "because a substantial number of users download the software to acquire copyrighted material, a significant proportion of [Grokster's] advertising revenue depends upon the infringement. [Grokster] thus derive[s] a financial benefit from the infringement" (*Grokster*, 259 F. Supp. 2d at 1044).

Unlike Napster, though, Grokster lacked the right and ability to control its users' access to the file-sharing network. Its software included filters, but the difference between the Napster system architecture (with all searches going through a central server) and the decentralized Grokster architecture meant that there was no obligation on the part of Grokster to police the users' conduct, just as there was no obligation on the part of Sony to police the conduct of those who purchased its VCRs.

The Supreme Court apparently let this stand, declining to address vicarious infringement. "Because we resolve the case based on an inducement theory, there is no need to analyze separately MGM's vicarious liability theory" (*Grokster*, 545 U.S. at 930 n.9).

Knowledge: If inducement liability is treated as a third category of third-party liability, rather than as an alternate way of reaching contributory liability, the question of actual knowledge (as required by the holdings of the Ninth Circuit in *Grokster* and *Napster*) versus constructive knowledge (the lower standard required by the Seventh Circuit in *Aimster II*) remains relevant. Contributory and vicarious liability are not creatures of statute but of case law. The Ninth Circuit's opinion in *Grokster* followed its own reasoning in *Napster* requiring "evidence of actual knowledge of specific acts of infringement." *Aimster's* holding that constructive knowledge is sufficient follows another line of cases, including cases from the Second and Eleventh circuits. However, *UMG Recordings, Inc. v. Sinnott*, a case from a district court within the Ninth Circuit, pointed out that the requirement of actual knowledge of a specific violation is strictly limited to cases involving Grokster-like (decentralized, noncontrolled) online services (*Sinnott*, 300 F. Supp. 2d 993). The defendant in *Sinnott*, like Cherry Auctions (the defendant in *Fonovisa*), was the operator of a real-world flea market at which unauthorized copies of copyrighted music were exchanged. Like Cherry Auctions or Napster, Sinnott had the power to stop the infringing activity at any time after he became aware of it; Grokster, once it had distributed its software, could no longer control the uses of the software.

The *Grokster* and *Aimster II* courts seem to be in agreement on vicarious liability. The results reached in the two cases were different, but the most important factor leading to the different outcomes appears to be not a differing interpretation of the "knowledge" requirement but the existence of Club Aimster. Club Aimster gave Aimster a measure of control that Grokster lacked.

In both cases, financial benefit was defined broadly; *Grokster* requires the broader definition, but it does not appear to be inconsistent with *Aimster* on this element.

Grokster's aftermath: The Supreme Court's decision in *MGM v. Grokster* did not spell the end of file-sharing. It did, however, preempt one possible alternative; while some had speculated that the Court might focus on the fact that Grokster profited from the use of its product for copyright infringement, the inducement rule applies to nonprofit P2P networks as well. Other alternatives remain, though. A file-sharing network that is a staple article of commerce—capable of a substantial noninfringing use—might not be covered. As Justice Breyer pointed out in his separate concurring opinion, about 10% of the files traded over Grokster at the time of the litigation were noninfringing (*Grokster*, 545 U.S. at 933, 947 n. 3, 953–954). This was higher than the percentage of time-shifting uses in *Sony*. Even though times and circumstances have changed since *Sony*, it seems unlikely that the Court would have been willing to decide against Grokster had more than half of the files traded with its software been noninfringing.

There are other lessons as well. File-sharing networks should not advertise themselves as useful tools for copyright infringement. And there is no need for a P2P network to base itself in the United States. While many other countries—Sweden, France, and the United Kingdom—have been as harsh or harsher in their treatment of file-sharing, other have not, and businesses based entirely upon distributing software are extremely mobile. Ultimately, international treaties and the copyright laws of those foreign countries may provide remedies for the content industry, but the process will be delayed.

The internationalization of file-sharing was already well under way by the time of the Supreme Court's decision in *Grokster*. In the wake of *Napster* and *Aimster*, the best-known P2P network was not Grokster but KaZaA (later Kazaa). The KaZaA Media Desktop software was originally distributed by Consumer Empowerment, a company founded by Swedish and Dutch citizens in the Netherlands. After a lawsuit in the Netherlands, Consumer Empowerment applied its decentralization strategy to its corporate structure as well as its software. Sharman Networks, a company incorporated in the Pacific island nation of Vanuatu and headquartered in Australia, became the principal owner, although the original Dutch and Swedish owners retained some influence; the FastTrack software upon which KaZaA Media Desktop (along with many other P2P networks) was based was the intellectual property of the founders and of Bluemoon Interactive, an Estonian company. KaZaA's dispersion made it a difficult target. Sharman Networks was originally a co-defendant in *Grokster* but, as a Vanuatuan company doing business in Australia, was dropped from the suit after the trial stage.

BitTorrent: In the wake of *Grokster*, BitTorrent has emerged as the Internet's most widely used file-sharing protocol. The technical advances (BitTorrent allows the downloading of portions of files from multiple sources, rather than all of a file from a single source) make little legal difference; where the purpose of each partial download is to acquire a copy of the complete original work, the fact that each individual download is partial is not likely to weigh heavily in a fair use analysis. However, BitTorrent has carefully worked around *Grokster* inducement rule by ensuring that there are substantial noninfringing uses.

BitTorrent trackers, however, are another matter. A variety of enterprises and individuals offering tools to enable users to obtain copyrighted content have been sued and shut down by groups representing content owners. The most celebrated ongoing battle is that over the Swedish Web site Pirate Bay, which has survived numerous lawsuits, a police raid, and the conviction and sentencing of at least one of its founders for criminal copyright violations.

A private ISP program, the Copyright Alert System, seeks to detect copyright infringement via BitTorrent and warn users via a "six strikes" system. The Copyright Alert System has been criticized by activist groups, including the Electronic Frontier Foundation, as both over-inclusive (because it may result in the imposition of penalties on innocent users) and under-inclusive (because dedicated infringers can easily take countermeasures to avoid the Copyright Alert System).

Statutes

- Audio Home Recording Act of 1992, Pub. L. 102–563, § 1, October 28, 1992, 106 Stat. 4237, amending 17 U.S.C. §§ 1001–1010, 801, 804, 912, and 19 U.S.C.A. § 1337
- Copyright Act of 1976, 17 U.S.C. §§ 101–1332
- Digital Millennium Copyright Act, 17 U.S.C. §§ 512, 1201

Cases

Supreme Court

- *Metro-Goldwyn-Mayer Studios, Inc. v. Grokster, Ltd.*, 259 F. Supp. 2d 1029 (C.D. Cal. 2003); affirmed, 380 F.3d 1154 (9th Cir. 2004); vacated & remanded, 549 U.S. 913 (2005)
- *Sony Corp. of America v. Universal City Studios, Inc.*, 464 U.S. 417 (1984)

Federal Appellate Courts

- *A&M Records, Inc. v. Napster, Inc.*, 239 F.3d 1004 (9th Cir. 2001)
- *Atari, Inc. v. JS & A Group, Inc.*, 747 F.2d 1422 (Fed. Cir. 1984), overruled by *Nobelpharma AB v. Implant Innovations, Inc.*, 141 F.3d 1059 (Fed. Cir. 1998)
- *Fonovisa, Inc. v. Cherry Auction, Inc.*, 76 F.3d 259 (9th Cir. 1996)
- *Gershwin Publishing Corp. v. Columbia Artists Management, Inc.*, 443 F.2d 1159 (2d Cir. 1971)
- *In re Aimster Copyright Litigation (Aimster II)*, 252 F. Supp. 2d 634 (N.D. Ill. 2002), affirmed in part, 334 F.3d 643 (7th Cir. 2003), certiorari denied sub nom *Deep v. Recording Industry Association of America, Inc.*, 540 U.S. 1107 (2004)
- *Recording Industry Association of America v. Diamond Multimedia Systems, Inc.*, 180 F.3d 1072 (9th Cir. 1999)

Federal Trial Courts

- *MGM Studios Inc. v. Grokster, Ltd.*, 243 F. Supp. 2d 1073 (C.D. Cal. 2003)
- *Religious Technology Center v. Netcom On-Line Communication Services, Inc.*, 907 F. Supp. 1361 (N.D. Cal. 1995)
- *UMG Recordings, Inc., v. MP3.com, Inc.*, 92 F. Supp. 2d 349 (S.D.N.Y. 2000)
- *UMG Recordings, Inc. v. Sinnott*, 300 F. Supp. 2d 993 (E.D. Cal. 2004)

See also: Abandonware; Content Industry; Copyright; Copyright Alert System; Copyright Infringement; Digital Audio Works; Digital Millennium Copyright Act, Title I; Digital Millennium Copyright Act, Title II; Encryption; Fair Use (Copyright); File-Sharing; File-Sharing and the Courts (Litigation against Individual Users); File-Sharing (Other Media); Internet Service Providers; MP3; No Electronic Theft Act; P2P; Piracy; Voluntary Collective License; Warez

Sources and Further Reading
Michael Albert & Lisa Vertinsky, "From Sony to Napster—and Back? Copyright Law Implications of Decentralized File-Sharing Technology," *Boston Bar Journal*, January/February 2004, at 10
"Face Value: The Quiet Iconoclast—With KaZaA, Niklas Zennstrom Undermined the Music Industry," *The Economist*, July 1, 2004, at 54, available at http://www.economist.com/node/2876993 (visited February 3, 2013)
Sheila M. Heidmiller, "RIAA's Latest Attack on P2P File-Sharing," *Intellectual Property Law Newsletter*, Summer 2003, at 10
"I Want My P2P: Record Labels Are Trying to Do Deals with File-Sharing Networks," *The Economist*, November 18, 2004, at 65, available at http://www.economist.com/node/3407417 (visited February 3, 2013)
Robert Levine, *Free Ride: How the Internet Is Destroying the Culture Business and How the Culture Business Can Fight Back* (New York: Doubleday, 2011)
Joseph Menn, *All the Rave: The Rise and Fall of Shawn Fanning's Napster* (New York: Crown Business, 2003)
Trevor Merriden, *Irresistible Forces: The Business Legacy of Napster and the Growth of the Underground Internet* (New York: John Wiley & Sons, 2002)
Pamela Samuelson, "Three Reactions to MGM v. Grokster," 13 *Michigan Telecommunications and Technology Law Review* 177 (2006)
Seagrumn Smith, "From Napster to KaZaA: The Battle over Peer-to-Peer Filesharing Goes International," 2 *Duke Law & Technology Review* 1 (2003)

❖ FILE-SHARING AND THE COURTS (LITIGATION AGAINST INDIVIDUAL USERS) ❖

Lawsuits against file-sharing networks were expensive because the companies behind the networks could fund protracted legal battles. At the same time they were of limited usefulness because the companies could simply move themselves and their operations to other friendlier countries. Frustrated by the slow progress made on this front, the recording industry turned to an alternative strategy, one that may have been effective but also led to near-complete alienation of the consumer base: the industry chose to pursue suits against individual Internet users.

RIAA suits against individual users: In addition to suing file-sharing services, the RIAA filed thousands of suits against individual file-sharers. This was the most controversial tactic in the RIAA's campaign to defend music copyrights. Among the first defendants was 12-year-old Brianna LaHara, who lived with her mother in public housing in New York City. Brianna said that "I thought it was OK to download music because my mom paid a service fee for it." (Her mother had paid a fee to KaZaA) (Younge 2003). Another of the first defendants was 71-year-old Durwood Pickle of Richardson, Texas, whose visiting teenage grandchildren allegedly downloaded music to his computer. Widespread media coverage, including Internet coverage, of the suits was largely unfavorable to the RIAA. Brianna LaHara and Durwood Pickle were portrayed as victims. Extraordinarily large awards of statutory damages helped build a public perception of brutal absurdity. In one 2009 retrial, Jammie Thomas-Rasset, a Native American mother of four, was found liable for $1,920,000 for downloading 24 songs (*Capitol Records*, 799 F. Supp. at 1002), or $80,000 per song. A lifetime's earnings for two dozen songs was almost universally viewed as excessive, and was later reduced to a still-crushing $222,000, or about ten thousand times the market value of the pirated music. The $675,000 in statutory damages awarded against college student Joel Tenenbaum for downloading 30 songs was similarly reduced to $67,500, or $2,250 per song (*Sony BMG*, 660 F.3d at 491).

The excesses of the individual user suits increased public hostility toward the RIAA, making it one of the Internet's favorite punching bags. The RIAA has also met resistance from service providers, who put their users' privacy interests ahead of the RIAA's copyright interests. In December 2003 the federal appellate court for the District of Columbia agreed with Verizon Internet Services that Verizon did not have to turn over the name of a subscriber who had allegedly shared copyrighted music files (*Verizon*, 351 F.3d 1229). The RIAA had previously obtained a subpoena issued pursuant to Title I of the Digital Millennium Copyright Act (DMCA). The D.C. Circuit's decision reversed the decision of the district court for the District of Columbia, which had ordered Verizon to identify the subscriber (*Verizon*, 240 F. Supp. 2d 24). As a result, the RIAA must now bring suit against file-sharing defendants as "John Does" first, and then obtain a subpoena. A subpoena of this sort is harder to obtain than a DMCA subpoena and requires judicial oversight to prevent abuses. The Circuit Court's opinion distinguished between conduit ISPs, which are not subject to a DMCA subpoena, and hosting ISPs, which may be.

File-sharing is speech within the meaning of the First Amendment, and thus any attempt to discover the identity of John Doe defendants must overcome the defendants' First Amendment interest in maintaining their anonymity. Factors to consider in evaluating whether the need for disclosure is sufficient to overcome this interest include:

> (1) a concrete showing of a prima facie claim of actionable harm;
> (2) specificity of the discovery request;
> (3) the absence of alternative means to obtain the subpoenaed information;
> (4) a central need for the subpoenaed information to advance the claim; and
> (5) the party's expectation of privacy (*Sony Music Entertainment*, 326 F. Supp. 2d at 564–565).

Of these, the first two are within the control of the defendant; the third and fourth will generally be met in cases of copyright infringement, as the identity of the defendant is necessary to proceed, and there is generally no other means to obtain it. Assessment of the fifth factor—a defendant's expectation of privacy—depends to some extent on the terms of service in the contract between the subscriber and the ISP (*London-Sire Records*, 542 F. Supp. 2d at 179). Such contracts usually prohibit use of the ISP's service for copyright infringement, reducing the expectation of privacy with regard to copyright-infringing activity.

The intense backlash over the individual-user suits, coupled with the cost and dubious benefit of the strategy, led the RIAA to abandon it in 2008. Since then, it has announced plans to work with ISPs to terminate the Internet service of repeat downloaders; ISPs have responded with a distinct lack of enthusiasm for a strategy that would deprive them of customers.

The music content industry's 20th-century business model—bundling songs in albums—was forced to change to adapt to the Internet. With neither bundling nor recording on a physical medium necessary, it became possible for musicians to sell their works directly to the public over the Internet, without the need of any intermediary, directly or through services such as Apple's iTunes. Without bundling, consumers with a set amount of money to spend are able to buy more of the songs they want while avoiding having to buy songs they do not want. Even when works are bundled, eliminating intermediaries between musicians and consumers may work to the benefit of both, as when albums are made available for download at a "pay what you wish" price.

There are signs, though, that the industry may adapt rather than perish, licensing music for use on YouTube and through streaming music services such as Spotify and Pandora. Consumers have also shown themselves willing to pay fees for upgraded music services versions of file-sharing software in order to avoid advertising. And other segments of the content industry are less threatened by file-sharing than the music industry has been.

Anticircumvention actions: In addition to suits against individual users for direct or third-party copyright infringement, users engaging in file-sharing may violate the anticircumvention measures of 17 U.S.C. section 1201. File-sharing software does not break copy protection. But it may enable trading of copies of copy-protected works on which the copy protection has already been broken. That is, one skillful user may break the copy protection and then share the unprotected copy with less skillful users. That person, if his or her identity is discovered, may be subject to both criminal and civil penalties.

Statutes

- Copyright Act of 1976, 17 U.S.C. §§ 101–1332
- Digital Millennium Copyright Act, 17 U.S.C. §§ 512, 1201

Cases

Federal Appellate Courts

- *Bridgeport Music, Inc. v. Justin Combs Publishing*, 507 F.3d 470 (6th Cir. 2007)

- *Capitol Records, Inc. v. Thomas-Rasset*, 692 F.3d 899 (8th Cir. 2011), certiorari denied, 133 S.Ct. 1584
- *Flava Works, Inc. v. Gunter*, 689 F.3d 754 (7th Cir. 2012)
- *Fonovisa, Inc. v. Cherry Auction, Inc.*, 76 F.3d 259 (9th Cir. 1996)
- *Recording Industry Association of America, Inc. v. Verizon Internet Services*, 240 F. Supp. 2d 24 (D.D.C. 2003); reversed, 351 F.3d 1229 (D.C. Cir. 2003); certiorari denied, 543 U.S. 924 (2004)
- *Sony BMG Music Entertainment v. Tenenbaum*, 660 F.3d 487 (1st Cir. 2011)
- *Viacom International, Inc. v. YouTube, Inc.*, 676 F.3d 19 (2d Cir. 2012)

Federal Trial Courts

- *Arista Records LLC v. Lime Group LLC*, 784 F. Supp. 2d 398 (S.D.N.Y. 2011)
- *Capitol Records, Inc. v. Does*, No. 07–485 WJ/LFG, 2007 U.S. Dist. LEXIS 97930 (D.N.M. 2007)
- *Elektra Entertainment Group, Inc. v. Barker*, 551 F. Supp. 2d 234 (S.D.N.Y. 2008)
- *Interscope Records v. Does*, 494 F. Supp. 2d 388 (E.D. Va. 2007)
- *Jalbert v. Grautski*, 554 F. Supp. 2d 57 (D. Mass. 2008)
- *London-Sire Records, Inc. v. Doe 1*, 542 F. Supp. 2d 153 (D. Mass. 2008)
- *Sony Music Entertainment Inc, v. Does 1–40*, 326 F. Supp. 2d 556 (S.D.N.Y. 2004)

See also: Abandonware; Content Industry; Copyright; Copyright Infringement; Digital Audio Works; Digital Millennium Copyright Act, Title I; Digital Millennium Copyright Act, Title II; Encryption; Fair Use (Copyright); File-Sharing; File-Sharing and the Courts (Attempts to Control Technology); File-Sharing (Other Media); Internet Service Providers; MP3; No Electronic Theft Act; P2P; Piracy; Voluntary Collective License; Warez

Sources and Further Reading

J. Cam Barker, "Grossly Excessive Penalties in the Battle against Illegal File-Sharing: The Troubling Effects of Aggregating Minimum Statutory Damages for Copyright Infringement," 83 *Texas Law Review* 525 (2004)

David P. Branfman, "What Do Copyrights, Trolls, Sex, & Lawyers Have in Common?" *North County Lawyer*, February 2012, at 19

Sheila M. Heidmiller, "RIAA's Latest Attack on P2P File-Sharing," *Intellectual Property Law Newsletter*, Summer 2003, at 10

Tom Moon, "Radiohead's 'In Rainbows' Sets Its Own Terms," NPR Music (October10, 2007), available at http://www.npr .org/templates/story/story.php?storyId=15152703 (visited February 3, 2013)

"RIAA v. The People: Five Years Later," Electronic Frontier Foundation (September 30, 2008), available at https://www .eff.org/wp/riaa-v-people-five-years-later (visited February 3, 2013)

Gary Younge, "US Music Industry Sues 261 for Online Song Copying," *The Guardian* (September 10, 2003), available at http://www.richardhartley.com/2003/09/us-music-industry-sues-261-for-online-song-copying/ (visited February 3, 2013)

❖ FILE-SHARING (OTHER MEDIA) ❖

While movie and e-book publishers lent some support to the music industry's efforts to control file-sharing through litigation, the music industry attracted more attention, much of it unfavorable. The movie and e-book industries' lower profile enabled them to weather the subsequent storm of consumer hostility and emerge in better shape than the music industry.

Books: Books as a medium are less threatened by the Internet than were older forms of music media such as CDs. Even though an entire book will fit in a quite small file, printed books remain popular for their convenience and comfort. Part of the appeal of a book is that the information in it can be accessed without mechanical assistance; it can be carried anywhere, requires no batteries, and can still be read even after being dropped in a puddle or on the floor. Improvements in e-book readers are gradually eroding this advantage, and e-book readers offer an advantage of their own—the ability to carry a large number of volumes easily. Still, e-books are not a substitute for printed books in the same way that MP3s are a substitute for CDs.

A downloaded book can be printed, but the cost of printing usually exceeds the cost of the published version, which will also be bound and will probably be of higher quality. An occasional high-demand item—the latest *Song of Ice and Fire* book, for example—may be pirated by impatient fans before it becomes available in stores, but piracy of this sort seems likely to remain rare. Should e-book reader technology advance to the point that consumers prefer e-books to printed books, however, piracy is likely to accelerate dramatically. E-book files are much smaller than music files, and several orders of magnitude smaller than movies. A single high-definition two-hour movie may occupy as much space as 50,000 books, even uncompressed; downloading every book ever published is actually feasible and will become more so as storage becomes cheaper.

Reference works, such as the one you are currently holding in your hand or reading on your Kindle or iPhone, may be more threatened because they are rarely read in their entirety. Most users read only one recipe or one encyclopedia entry at a time, or look up only one word in a dictionary. High-cost reference works such as the *Oxford English Dictionary* have addressed this problem both legally and economically. A legal approach is the inclusion of copy protection on software versions of the work. The presence of the copy-protection software not only increases the difficulty of copying the work, but perhaps more importantly triggers the anticircumvention provision of the DMCA. An economic, market-based approach is to offer the work online, with frequent enhancements and updates, by subscription.

Movies: Despite widespread downloading of movies, the movie industry has not suffered the disaster previously faced by the music industry. The movie studios are in a more secure position than the recording industry, for several reasons.

First, movies were not traditionally bundled; consumers were not, and are not, forced to buy unwanted movies along with the desired one. Next, recorded movies are relatively cheap when compared to music; a movie may cost ten thousand times as much to make as a song, and have forty times the running time, yet it sells for from five to twenty-five times as much. And while music files generally contain nothing but the music, movie discs often fill the otherwise unused space on the disk with additional content such as alternate language tracks, deleted scenes, cast interviews, and games. And almost all videorecordings contain copy protection, circumvention of which would violate the DMCA and expose those who circumvent it to civil liability and criminal penalties for violation of the anticircumvention provisions in addition to any liability or penalties for the underlying copyright infringement itself.

The role of motion picture studios in the marketplace is also different from that of old-school record companies. Movie studios, unlike record companies, are creators and producers of content, not merely distributors. And, while they have also pursued a limited strategy of suits against individual users and have aroused some public hostility, they have not yet alienated their customer base to the same extent. And finally, a substantial portion of the revenue from a successful movie comes from people viewing the movie in a cinema; while technology is bringing the home-viewing experience closer to the theater experience, it would take some fairly dramatic social shifts to make people stop wanting to go out to the movies.

Statutes

- Copyright Act of 1976, 17 U.S.C. §§ 101–1332
- Digital Millennium Copyright Act, 17 U.S.C. §§ 512, 1201

Cases

- *Sony Corp. of America v. Universal City Studios, Inc.,* 464 U.S. 417 (1984)
- *Viacom International, Inc. v. YouTube, Inc.,* 676 F.3d 19 (2d Cir. 2012)
- *Wolk v. Kodak Imaging Network, Inc.,* 840 F. Supp. 2d 724 (S.D.N.Y. 2011)

See also: Abandonware; Content Industry; Copyright; Copyright Infringement; Digital Audio Works; Digital Millennium Copyright Act, Title I; Digital Millennium Copyright Act, Title II; Encryption; Fair Use (Copyright); File-Sharing; File-Sharing and the Courts (Attempts to Control Technology); File-Sharing and the Courts (Litigation against Individual Users); Internet Service Providers; MP3; No Electronic Theft Act; P2P; Piracy; Voluntary Collective License; Warez

Sources and Further Reading

Joab Jackson, "Google: 129 Million Different Books Have Been Published," *PC World* (August 6, 2010), available at http://www.pcworld.com/article/202803/google_129_million_different_books_have_been_published.html (visited February 3, 2013)

Jeff Jarvis, *Public Parts: How Sharing in the Digital Age Improves the Way We Work and Love* (New York: Simon & Schuster, 2011)

Robert Levine, *Free Ride: How the Internet Is Destroying the Culture Business and How the Culture Business Can Fight Back* (New York: Doubleday, 2011)

Joseph Menn, *All the Rave: The Rise and Fall of Shawn Fanning's Napster* (New York: Crown Business, 2003)

Lucille M. Ponte, "Coming Attractions: Opportunities and Challenges in Thwarting Global Movie Piracy," 45 *American Business Law Journal* 331 (2008)

❖ FILE WRAPPER ESTOPPEL ❖

See Prosecution History Estoppel

❖ FIREWALL ❖

A firewall is a hardware device or software program that can insulate a computer or network from some or all communications with computers on the other side of the firewall. Firewalls are used to prevent the intrusion of hackers, spyware, Trojans, and other dangers, and to prevent any spyware or Trojans that have been installed from reporting back to the outside world. Completely severing all communications links between the computer or network and the outside world is an effective way of insulating it from the outside world, but rarely practical. Instead, firewalls are designed to be partially permeable so that authorized programs can pass information through the firewall while unauthorized programs are blocked (Curtin & Ranum 2000).

A personal firewall protects a single computer; a network firewall protects a network of computers. The personal firewall is usually a software program but may be a hardware device. The network firewall is usually a dedicated hardware device running a firewall program. When the term "firewall" is used generically by information systems professionals, it generally refers to a network firewall. On the smallest scale, most routers for home networks include a hardware firewall; this protects the home network, usually consisting of no more than half a dozen computers. Much larger firewalls exist, of course; some governments have even attempted, with some success, to create firewalls for entire countries (Yu 2002). These national firewalls have been used for censorship as well as security; in Saudi Arabia, for example, a national firewall prevents access to sites not approved by the national government (NeoSmart 2006). The United Arab Emirates (UAE) achieves the same result through the use of a national proxy server; users connect not to the global Internet but to the proxy server, through which all traffic to and from the UAE must run (Turton 2010). While the use of firewalls in this manner has provoked some protests from free-speech advocates, firewalls are viewed mostly as a useful security tool for defending against hackers, spyware, and other Internet pests.

Sources and Further Reading

Matt Curtin & Marcus J. Ranum, "Firewalls FAQ," faqs.org (December 1, 2000), available at http://www.faqs.org/faqs/firewalls-faq/ (visited February 3, 2013)

Stephen Northcutt et al., *Inside Network Perimeter Security: The Definitive Guide to Firewalls, Virtual Private Networks (VPNs), Routers, and Intrusion Detection Systems* (Indianapolis: Sams Publishing, 2d ed. 2005)

Leonard R. Sussman, "The Internet in Flux, in Freedom House, How Free?: The Web & The Press," The Annual Survey of Press Freedom 4 (2001), available at http://epic.org/free_speech/pfs2001.pdf (visited February 3, 2013)

"The Other Great Firewall" NeoSmart Technologies (August 28, 2006), available at http://neosmart.net/blog/2006/the-other-great-firewall/ (visited February 3, 2013)

Stuart Turton, "Dubai's Dubious Internet "Censorship", *PC Pro* (September 6, 2010), available at http://www.pcpro.co.uk/blogs/2010/09/06/dubais-dubious-internet-censorship/ (visited February 3, 2013)

"The World Is What You Make It: Every Country Has Its Own Internet," *The Economist,* Special Report: Technology and Geography, October 27, 2012, at 20

Peter K. Yu, "Introduction to Symposium on Bridging the Digital Divide: Equality in the Information Age," 20 *Cardozo Arts and Entertainment Law* 1 (2002)

❖ FIRST AMENDMENT ❖

First Amendment issues are an inevitable consequence stemming from the nature of the Internet. The Internet is a vehicle for information; it contains the sum of the expression of all of the individuals and groups who publish Web sites or post information on them, who send email or post to newsgroups, or who otherwise provide content that is made available to others. The First Amendment to the Constitution of the United States provides that "Congress shall make no law . . . abridging the freedom of speech, or of the press; or the right of the people peaceably to assemble, and to petition the Government for a redress of grievances." The Fourteenth Amendment extends this prohibition to the governments of the states, as well, as has been explained in numerous Supreme Court decisions. It is also solidly established that "speech" and "press" are not narrow definitions; the First Amendment applies not only to the spoken and written word, but also to expressive conduct. The four protected categories of speech, press, assembly, and petition are generally referred to jointly under the heading "freedom of expression," although there are, or historically have been, subtle differences in the treatment of the four.

The First Amendment regulates the actions of government, and not ordinarily of individuals or private entities.

Private actions may be constructively considered "state action," however, if they meet one of three tests: the exclusive public function test, the state-assisted action test, or the joint participant test. A private entity that has exercised powers that are traditionally the exclusive prerogative of the state meets the exclusive public function test. A private entity that has acted with the help of or in concert with state officials may meet the state-assisted action test. And when the state has insinuated itself so far into a position of interdependence with the private entity that it must be recognized as a joint participant in the challenged activity, the joint participant test is met. Note that only one, and not all three, of these requirements must be met to support a finding of state action subject to the First Amendment (*America Online*, 948 F. Supp. 456).

Even when state action exists, the First Amendment does not, as is sometimes believed, create a universal right for all people to say whatever they want, whenever they want, wherever they want. Some forums are entitled to a higher level of protection than others, as are some forms of expression. The government may ban expression in the schoolroom that it permits on the street corner; it may ban expression on broadcast television that it permits on cable television; it may ban expression on daytime television that it permits on late-night television. The Internet is accorded the highest level of First Amendment protection. Despite some superficial similarities to broadcast media such as radio and television, the government does not have the censorship powers over the Internet that it does over those media. The government does not allocate Web addresses or email accounts as it does radio and television frequency; Internet communication more closely resembles the print media or an exchange of letters among individuals, both of which are also entitled to the highest level of protection.

Even in this highly protected forum, however, some government control is permitted by the First Amendment. Some types of expression, such as obscenity and child pornography, are not protected and may be prohibited by the government (*Miller*, 413 U.S. 15). Other types may be subject to reasonable time, place, and manner restrictions if those restrictions are content-neutral, narrowly tailored to further an important or significant government interest, and do not unduly constrict the flow of free speech. Speech that proposes a commercial transaction may be subject to time, place, and manner restrictions and may be prohibited if it is untruthful, misleading, or deceptive or if its subject matter or presentation is illegal.

The government may issue other broad content-based prohibitions, but in a protected forum such as the Internet, those prohibitions will be subject to strict constitutional scrutiny: they must be necessary to achieve a compelling state interest unrelated to the message being communicated. A government's interest in preventing a message from being heard is not in itself sufficient justification for restricting that message. And the means chosen to restrict the expression must be the least restrictive alternative available.

Speech or expression may constitute an element of certain torts or crimes. Speech in furtherance of a criminal conspiracy, or that solicits the commission of a crime by another, may itself be criminalized. Expression that harms another's reputation and meets certain other requirements may form the basis of a tort action for defamation or invasion of privacy. The copying of someone else's trademark or copyrighted material may give rise to an infringement action. In the latter examples, the aggrieved party, rather than the state, will take action against the defamer or infringer, but the court will enforce a judgment if necessary; thus, there is state action. Computer programs that allow users to break the copy protection on commercial video recordings and other media are prohibited by the Digital Millennium Copyright Act, even though the programs are "expression." Expression such as shouting "Fire!" in a crowded theater or that is likely to lead to imminent violence (but is not otherwise criminal) may also be prohibited, although these seem unlikely to arise in an Internet context, where the communicating parties may be miles apart—perhaps even on different continents.

Expression that is indecent but not obscene is protected by the First Amendment, but may be subject to content-based restrictions. There is probably a compelling state interest, and certainly an important state interest, in preventing the dissemination of indecent, particularly pornographic, material to minors. The problem for Congress has been to design a ban that is the least restrictive means available, or a time, place, and manner restriction that is narrowly tailored, to further this interest. The first Congressional attempt to do so, the Communications Decency Act of 1996, failed to meet these requirements and was declared unconstitutional by the Supreme Court. Congress' second attempt, the Child Online Protection Act of 1998, has been declared unconstitutional by a federal appellate court and has recently been remanded for trial by the Supreme Court.

Spam, as noted, is commercial speech and may be subject to reasonable time, place, and manner restrictions. There is no First Amendment right to have email delivered; an ISP may block mass-mailed messages even if it would be impermissible for the government to do so, because the ISP is not a state actor. The federal government probably also has considerable leeway to restrict spam under the First Amendment; its failure to do so probably stems not from any legislative timidity but from the technical difficulties of enforcing restrictions on spam, and from the fact that a great deal of spam originates outside the United States.

Statutes
- Child Online Protection Act, 47 U.S.C. § 231
- Communications Decency Act of 1996, Pub. L. No. 104–104, § 502, 1996 U.S.S.C.A.N. (110 Stat.) 56,133 (later codified at 47 U.S.C. § 223)

Cases
Supreme Court
- *Ashcroft v. American Civil Liberties Union*, 524 U.S. 656 (2004)
- *Ashcroft v. Free Speech Coalition*, 535 U.S. 234 (2002)
- *Brandenburg v. Ohio*, 395 U.S. 444 (1969)
- *Miller v. California*, 413 U.S. 15 (1973)
- *Reno v. American Civil Liberties Union*, 521 U.S. 844 (1997)
- *United States v. American Library Association, Inc.*, 539 U.S. 194 (2003)

Federal Trial Courts
- *Bradburn v. North Central Regional Library District*, 231 P.3d 166 (Wash. 2010)
- *Cyber Promotions v. America Online*, 948 F. Supp. 456 (E.D. Pa. 1996)
- *Mainstream Loudoun v. Board of Trustees of the Loudoun County Library*, 2 F. Supp. 2d 783 (E.D. Va. 1998)

See also: Activism and Advocacy Groups; App; Censorship; Child Online Protection Act; Child Pornography; Children's Internet Protection Act; Communications Decency Act; Constitutional Law; Data Haven; Declaration of Independence of Cyberspace; French Yahoo! Case; Indecency; Obscenity; Pornography; Spam; WikiLeaks

Sources and Further Reading
Jerome A. Barron & C. Thomas Dienes, *Constitutional Law in a Nutshell* (St. Paul, MN: West, 7th ed. 2009)
Mike Godwin, *Cyber Rights: Defending Free Speech in the Digital Age* (Cambridge, MA: MIT Press, 2003)
Ronald J. Krotoszynski, *The First Amendment in Cross-Cultural Perspective: A Comparative Legal Analysis of the Freedom of Speech* (New York: NYU Press, 2009)
Saul Levmore & Martha C. Nussbaum, eds., *The Offensive Internet: Speech, Privacy & Reputation* (Cambridge, MA: Harvard University Press, 2012)
Jeremy Lipschultz, *Free Expression in the Age of the Internet: Social and Legal Boundaries* (Boulder, CO: Perseus Books, 1999)
Kembrew McLeod, *Freedom of Expression: Resistance and Repression in the Age of Intellectual Property* (Minneapolis, MN: University of Minnesota Press, 2007)
Samuel P. Nelson, *Beyond the First Amendment: The Politics of Free Speech and Pluralism* (Baltimore, MD: The Johns Hopkins University Press, 2005)

❖ FIRST SALE ❖

The first sale doctrine provides an exception to the exclusive right of a copyright owner to make and distribute copies of the copyrighted work. The doctrine provides that "the owner of a particular copy or phonorecord lawfully made under this title, or any person authorized by such owner, is entitled, without the authority of the copyright owner, to sell or otherwise dispose of the possession of that copy or phonorecord" (17 U.S.C. § 109(a)). In other words, once a lawfully made copy of a copyrighted work has been sold, it belongs to the buyer; the buyer can sell it, give it as a gift, throw it away, destroy it, or dispose of it in some other way. There are important rights the buyer does not gain, however: the rights of reproduction, adaptation, and display. The buyer does not gain the right to make copies of the work. The buyer of the printed script of a play does not gain the right to adapt the work or perform the play in public; those rights must be purchased or received separately. And the lawful purchaser of a lawfully recorded videorecording does not gain the right to show (perform) that videorecording in public. In addition, while the lawful buyer of an authorized copy gains the right to display that copy at the place where it is located, the right does not extend to display at some remote location by means such as broadcast or the Internet.

The first sale doctrine is subject to exceptions of its own, and these exceptions have had a dramatic effect on the way computer software is marketed and distributed. Most significantly, the first sale doctrine applies only to sales, not to rentals. Computer software makers can thus retain greater control over the use of their products if they can structure the transaction with the consumer as a rental rather than as a sale.

The first sale rights to dispose of and display the work apply only to purchasers of the work, not to renters:

> The privileges prescribed by subsections (a) and (c) do not, unless authorized by the copyright owner, extend to any person who has acquired possession of the copy or phonorecord from the copyright owner, by rental, lease, loan, or otherwise, without acquiring ownership of it (17 U.S.C. § 109(d)).

Another exception to the first sale doctrine covers "phonorecords"—sound recordings. The purchaser of a phonorecord does not gain the right to rent out that record commercially (17 U.S.C. § 109(b)). Section 109(b) was expanded by the 1990 Computer Software Rental Amendments Act to cover computer programs, but curiously, and despite intense lobbying by the movie industry, it does not cover video recordings.

The rental exception for computer software provides that:

> [U]nless authorized by . . . the owner of copyright in a computer program (including any tape, disk, or other medium embodying such program), [no] person in possession of a particular copy of a computer program . . . may, for the purposes of direct or indirect commercial advantage, dispose of, or authorize the disposal of, the possession of that . . . computer program . . . by rental, lease, or lending, or by any other act or practice in the nature of rental, lease, or lending (17 U.S.C. § 109(b)(1)(A)).

This exception prohibiting the rental of computer software even by the lawful buyer contains three exceptions of its own, for products containing computer programs, for video games, and for nonprofit schools and libraries. Products containing computer programs may be rented if the program itself is not the object of the rental:

> This subsection [109(b)(1)(A)] does not apply to—
> (i) a computer program which is embodied in a machine or product and which cannot be copied during the ordinary operation or use of the machine or product (17 U.S.C. § 109(b)(1)(B)(i))[.]

A car, for example, may contain many software programs: diagnostic programs, onboard navigation programs, noise-reduction programs for the stereo, a CSS decryption program for the DVD players, climate-control programs, antilock braking programs, and so forth. Yet, although these programs may enhance the attractiveness of the rental car to prospective clients, it is not the programs they want to rent, but the car. Nor can the programs be copied during the ordinary operation of the car; few consumers would be able to copy the programs even if they wanted to.

The video games exception provides that

> This subsection [109(b)(1)(A)] does not apply to—
>
> ***
>
> (ii) a computer program embodied in or used in conjunction with a limited purpose computer that is designed for playing video games and may be designed for other purposes (17 U.S.C. § 109(b)(1)(B)(ii)).

The exception applies to arcade games rather than to video games for use on computers or home game systems; in addition to a rental right, the purchaser of the video game receives performance and display rights:

> [I]n the case of an electronic audiovisual game intended for use in coin-operated equipment, the owner of a particular copy of such a game lawfully made under this title, is entitled, without the authority of the copyright owner of the game, to publicly perform or display that game in coin-operated equipment (17 U.S.C. § 109(e))[.]

This statutory provision supersedes an earlier court decision holding that the sale of a video arcade game did not extinguish the seller's performance and display interests (Red Baron, 883 F.2d 275). Once again, there is an exception to the exception:

> [T]his subsection shall not apply to any work of authorship embodied in the audiovisual game if the copyright owner of the electronic audiovisual game is not also the copyright owner of the work of authorship (17 U.S.C. § 109(e)).

In other words, if the video game includes some other copyrighted work—a popular song, for example—purchase of the video game alone does not convey the performance right to the song; that must be conveyed separately.

The third exception to the prohibition on rentals of computer software under the first sale doctrine applies to nonprofit schools and libraries. Nonprofit schools are permitted to transfer lawful copies of computer programs to their own employees and students and to other nonprofit schools:

> The transfer of possession of a lawfully made copy of a computer program by a nonprofit educational institution to another nonprofit educational institution or to faculty, staff, and students does not constitute rental, lease, or lending for direct or indirect commercial purposes under this subsection (17 U.S.C. § 109(b)(1)(A)).

And nonprofit libraries are permitted to lend computer programs to the general public, provided that a copyright warning notice is attached:

> Nothing in this subsection shall apply to the lending of a computer program for nonprofit purposes by a nonprofit library, if each copy of a computer program which is lent by such library has affixed to the packaging containing the program a warning of copyright in accordance with requirements that the Register of Copyrights shall prescribe by regulation (17 U.S.C. § 109(b)(2)(A)).

The nature of computer programs is such that, when a consumer buys a program on disk, he or she will have to make at least one copy in order to run the program. Typically, the consumer will have to make two copies of at least portions of the program: one copy on to the computer's hard drive, and another into RAM (random access memory) when the program is run. The making of these copies is necessarily licensed, explicitly or implicitly, by the sale of the program, rather than permitted by the first sale doctrine.

Attempts to resell downloaded digital recordings of movies and music present some problems for the first sale doctrine, as do e-books. Technically, the copying of any of these to a new user's device falls outside the doctrine, even if the copying process simultaneously deletes the file from the old user's device. However, consumers often tire of, for example, digital music files just as they do of CDs, and wish to resell them. Sites like ReDigi.com have arisen to serve this market.

In principle, the first sale doctrine applies to downloaded digital media, at least in the original downloaded copies (*London-Sire Records, Inc.*, 542 F. Supp. 2d 153). However, "resale" approaches such as ReDigi's—indeed, any approach other than the transfer of the device on which the original downloaded copy is stored—necessitate the making of a new copy and, in the eyes of the content industry, are outside the scope of first sale. ReDigi was sued for copyright infringement by Capitol Records. In March 2013, the federal district court for the Southern District of New York found in favor of Capitol Records, holding that ReDigi's operations resulted in copyright infringement. The court explained that the first sale doctrine was inapplicable in this context because a ReDigi user would have to create a new copy of the digital file on the ReDigi server, making it impossible to sell the original copy. Instead, the new copy would be sold, which would require the making of yet another copy on the buyer's device (*Capitol Records* 2013).

Europe: In most European Union countries, the existence of moral rights has, for the most part, prevented the development of a first sale doctrine as extensive as that in the United States. In 2012, however, the Court of Justice of the European Union ruled that Oracle, a software company, could not prohibit the resale of its software licenses:

> [T]he copyright holder's distribution right is exhausted, in accordance with Article 4(2) of Directive 2009/24, on the occasion of the first sale in the European Union by that rightholder, or with his consent, of any copy, tangible or intangible, of his computer program. It follows that, by virtue of that provision and notwithstanding the existence of contractual terms prohibiting a further transfer, the rightholder in question can no longer oppose the resale of that copy (*UsedSoft GmbH*, ¶77; see contra *Vernor*, 621 F.3d 1102).

International commerce and the sale in the United States of items purchased abroad: In its 2012 October Term, the U.S. Supreme Court heard the case of *Kirtsaeng v. John Wiley & Sons, Inc.* Supap Kirtsaeng, a graduate student in mathematics at the University of California, noticed that textbooks in the United States cost far more than identical versions of the same textbook printed and sold in Thailand. Spotting an opportunity for arbitrage, he asked family members in Thailand to buy textbooks and ship them to him in the United States; he then resold these books on eBay. John Wiley, the publisher of some of the books, considered this a violation of its right to prevent the importation of a copyrighted work without the copyright holder's consent under 17 U.S.C. § 602(a). Kirtsaeng, for his part, asserted the right of first sale under 17 U.S.C. § 109. John Wiley prevailed at trial and on appeal to the U.S. Court of Appeals for the Second Circuit; Kirtsaeng was ordered to pay damages of $600,000.

The books imported by Kirtsaeng were not pirated; they were legally printed in Thailand, bearing the words "Not for sale in the United States" or a similar restriction. Similarly, movie studios authorize the sale of movies on DVD and Blu-ray in other countries at prices far below the prices at which those movies are sold in the United States, relying on region coding to reduce their marketability in the United States. And patented products, especially medicines, are often available for lower prices outside the United States.

Legally manufactured or copied goods, when imported into the United States, become gray-market goods. They are often identical to the same goods produced in the United States, but allow importers to take advantage of price differences between countries; the rule in 602(a) is designed to prevent such arbitrage.

On March 19, 2013, the Supreme Court's opinion resolved the apparent conflict between the two statutes in favor of Supap Kirtsaeng and § 109. The Court explained that:

> To put the matter technically, an "importation" provision, § 602(a)(1), says that
>
> "[i]mportation into the United States, without the authority of the owner of copyright under this title, of copies . . . of a work that have been acquired outside the United States is an infringement of the exclusive right to distribute copies . . . under section 106. . . . "
>
> 17 U.S.C. §602(a)(1) (2006 ed., Supp. V) (emphasis added). Thus §602(a)(1) makes clear that importing a copy without permission violates the owner's exclusive distribution right. But in doing so, §602(a)(1) refers explicitly to the §106(3) exclusive distribution right. As we have just said, §106 is by its terms "[s]ubject to" the various doctrines and principles contained in §§107 through 122, including §109(a)'s "first sale" limitation (568 U.S. ___).

The Court then concluded that Kirtsaeng's interpretation of the two statutes was correct:

> In our view, § 109(a)'s language, its context, and the common-law history of the "first sale" doctrine, taken together, favor a non-geographical interpretation. We also doubt that Congress would have intended to create the practical copyright-related harms with which a geographical interpretation would threaten ordinary scholarly, artistic, commercial, and consumer activities. . . . We consequently conclude that Kirtsaeng's nongeographical reading is the better reading of the Act (568 U.S. ___).

Section 602(a)(2), the Court determined, was applicable only to unlawfully made—that is, pirated—copies. The first sale doctrine permitted Kirstaeng to sell his copies in the United States, so long as they had been lawfully made, regardless of where they were lawfully made.

The application of Section 602(a)(2) to copies lawfully made outside the United States was, in effect, a continuation of a long-abolished statutory provision, the U.S. Manufacturing Clause. The Manufacturing Clause, an outrageously protectionist piece of regulation, had, from 1891 until 1986, prohibited the importation of a substantial number of books printed outside the United States. In the version cited by the Court, "the importation into or public distribution in the United States of copies of a work consisting preponderantly of nondramatic literary material . . . is prohibited unless the portions consisting of such material have been manufactured in the United States or Canada."

The Manufacturing Clause had been one of several factors preventing the United States from joining the Berne Convention; its abolition was an essential step toward allowing the United States to join fully in the global copyright regime. The interpretation sought by Wiley (and previously upheld in other cases by lower courts in decisions abrogated by the Supreme Court's decision in *Kirtsaeng*) would have amounted to a continuation by stealth of the Manufacturing Clause, except where the publishers or their authorized agents were the ones doing the extraterritorial manufacturing and subsequent importing. Although the Court did not discuss the Berne Conventions, it would have been difficult to uphold Wiley's interpretation of 602(a)(2) in a manner consistent with U.S. obligations under the Berne Convention.

The impact of *Kirtsaeng* on e-commerce could be significant, as it does away with geographically segregated pricing, a staple of pre-Internet commerce. Although *Kirtsaeng* involved copies bought in Thailand and sold in the United States, the Court's opinion presents no apparent reason why an enterprising student in Thailand cannot sell books directly from Thailand and then ship copies to individual buyers in the United States. The U.S. publishers' possible defenses against such conduct are either to lower the price in the United States or raise it in Thailand to make the arbitrage less attractive.

Statutes

- Copyright Act of 1976, Limitations on Exclusive Rights: Effect of Transfer of Particular Copy or Phonorecords, 17 U.S.C. § 109
- Copyright Act of 1976, Infringing importation of copies or phonorecords, 17 U.S.C. § 602

Treaty

- Convention Concerning the Creation of an International Union for the Protection of Literary and Artistic Works (Berne Convention), September 9, 1886, as last revised at Paris, July 24, 1971 (amended 1979), 25 U.S.T. 1341, 828 U.N.T.S. 221

Cases

Supreme Court

- *Kirtsaeng v. John Wiley & Sons, Inc.*, 133 S.Ct. 1351 (2013)

Federal Appellate Courts

- *F.B.T. Prods., LLC v. Aftermath Records*, 621 F.3d 958 (9th Cir. 2010)
- *Red Baron-Franklin Park, Inc. v. Taito Corp.*, 883 F.2d 275 (4th Cir. 1989)
- *Vernor v. Autodesk, Inc.*, 621 F.3d 1102 (9th Cir. 2010)

Federal Trial Courts

- *Capitol Records, LLC v. ReDigi, Inc.*, No. 12-CIV-0095-RJS (S.D.N.Y. Order of March 30, 2013)
- *London-Sire Records, Inc. v. Doe 1*, 542 F. Supp. 2d 153 (D. Mass. 2008)

European Union
- Case C-128/11, *UsedSoft GmbH v. Oracle International Corp.*, Judgment of the Court of First Instance (Grand Chamber) (July 3, 2012)

See also: Berne Convention; Copyright; Copyright Infringement; Digital Millennium Copyright Act, Title I; Fair Use (Copyright); File-Sharing; International Copyright Protection; WIPO Copyright Treaty; WIPO Performance and Phonograms Treaty

Sources and Further Reading

G. M. Buechlein, "Burden and Sufficiency of Proof under First Sale Doctrine in Prosecution for Copyright Infringement," 94 *American Law Reports Federal* 101 (1989 & Supp. 2004)

Marshall Leaffer, *Understanding Copyright Law* (New Providence, NJ: LexisNexis, 5th ed. 2010)

Ronald Mann, "Opinion Analysis: Justices Reject Publisher's Claims in Gray-Market Copyright Case," SCOTUSblog: Supreme Court of the United States Blog (March 19, 2013), available at http://www.scotusblog.com/?p=161209 (visited April 15, 2013)

P. Sean Morris, "Knocking on the WTO's Door: International Law and the Principle of First Sale Download in UsedSoft v. Oracle," *ASIL Insights* (January 24, 2013), available at http://www.asil.org/pdfs/insights/insight130124.pdf (visited April 15, 2013)

Richard Stim, *Patent, Copyright & Trademark: An Intellectual Property Desk Reference* (Berkeley, CA: Nolo Press, 12th ed. 2012)

R. "Ray" Wang, "UsedSoft vs Oracle Ruling Opens Up Monopolistic Practices: Used Software Pioneers Gain a Small Victory in a Shrinking On-Premises Software World," *Forbes* (July 4, 2012), available at http://www.forbes.com/sites/raywang/2012/07/04/news-analysis-usedsoft-vs-oracle-ruling-opens-up-monopolistic-practices-by-software-vendors/ (visited April 15, 2013)

Jennifer Waters, "Your Right to Resell Your Own Stuff Is in Peril," *Wall Street Journal Market Watch* (October 12, 2012), available at http://www.marketwatch.com/story/your-right-to-resell-your-own-stuff-is-in-peril-2012-10-04?pagenumber=1 (visited February 3, 2013)

❖ FREEDOM OF EXPRESSION ❖

See Censorship; First Amendment

❖ FREE SPEECH ❖

See Censorship; First Amendment

❖ FRENCH YAHOO! CASE ❖

The term "French Yahoo! case" refers to two related cases, one in France and one in the United States, arising from differences in French and U.S. laws. Yahoo!, Inc. is a U.S. company with its headquarters in Santa Clara, California. Yahoo! offers a wide variety of Internet services, including an online auction service. At the time, Yahoo! auctions could be accessed from anywhere in the world, including France. (Yahoo! has since shut down all of its auction sites except those in Hong Kong, Taiwan, and Japan.) During the 1990s, some Yahoo! users offered Nazi memorabilia for sale on the Yahoo! auctions site; offering such memorabilia for sale is legal in the United States but illegal in France. Yahoo! itself was not a party to the transactions but it made them possible, profited from them, and exhibited pictures of the merchandise offered for sale. This was sufficient to make them legally responsible for certain aspects of the transactions under both French and U.S. laws.

The Yahoo! case in France: In 2000, two civil rights groups, the Ligue Contre le Racisme et L'Antisémitisme (League Against Racism and Antisemitism, generally known by its French acronym LICRA) and the Union Des Étudiants Juifs De France (French Union of Jewish Students) sued Yahoo! in a French court, the Tribunal de Grande Instance de Paris. The plaintiffs claimed, correctly, that some of the goods offered for sale on the Yahoo! auctions site could not be offered for sale in France without violating French law. On May 22, 2000, the French court ordered Yahoo! to block access by French citizens to the offending material and to post a warning to French citizens that searching the Yahoo! site might lead to prohibited material, which could in turn lead to criminal prosecution under French law. Yahoo! was given time until July to demonstrate its compliance with the order. Yahoo! asked the French court to reconsider, explaining that complying with the order was technologically impossible. In the broadest sense this was true; there would be no possible way for Yahoo! to distinguish between a French citizen accessing its auction site from a computer in Manhattan and a U.S. citizen doing the same thing. But the French court was concerned with access from computers in France, and a panel of experts testified to the court that in fact approximately 70% of Internet addresses used by French users or users within France could be identified. An additional 20% of French users could be filtered out by a voluntary identification and registration scheme; in all, 90% compliance was possible—that is, Yahoo! could successfully block access to the prohibited material by 90% of French users (Solum & Chung 2004, 912).

The French court's reaffirmation of its order, and the reasoning accompanying it, sent tremors through the Internet world. The issue was far broader than France's ban on advertising Nazi memorabilia and propaganda; every Web site operator could conceivably be forced to design filters to comply with the laws of nearly 200 sovereign nations, and possibly of administrative subdivisions within those nations as well. Taken to its extreme, the French court's decision could prohibit all Internet speech that violated the law of any country; all Internet users would be held not to the standard of their own country, but to a composite standard forbidding all speech that was forbidden by any nation's law, and was thus far more restrictive than the law of any individual nation.

The Yahoo! case in the United States: Having failed in French court, Yahoo! filed suit against LICRA in a court in the United States, the federal district (trial) court for the Northern District of California. Yahoo! sought a declaratory judgment that the French court's order could not be enforced in the United States because enforcement would violate the First Amendment's guarantee of freedom of speech.

A jurisdictional issue arose: while Yahoo! had a substantial enough business presence in France, including many French users and a French-language site within the .fr (France) top-level domain, LICRA had no comparable presence in the United States. LICRA moved to dismiss the suit on the grounds that the federal court lacked jurisdiction over the organization; the court denied the motion, but its denial would later be reversed by the Ninth Circuit Court of Appeals.

The trial court went on to find that the French ban could not be enforced in U.S. courts. It began with the maxim that "no legal judgment has any effect, of its own force, beyond the limits of the sovereignty from which its authority is derived" (169 F. Supp. 2d at 1192). Foreign judgments, the court pointed out, were enforced in the United States only on a basis of comity, or mutual respect by sovereign states of each other's sovereign acts. In addition, no foreign judgment would be enforced if it "violate[d] American public policy" or was "repugnant to fundamental notions of what is decent and just" in the United States. The French judgment failed this test. The court was careful to point out that the ban on advertising Nazi memorabilia and propaganda was within France's sovereign authority and that it was a perfectly reasonable restriction for France to impose, in light of its historical experience. However, the court was not concerned with the French government's undisputed authority to ban such conduct within France, but with the applicability of that ban to conduct in the United States. Applying the ban to a U.S. party violated the guarantee of freedom of expression in the First Amendment. In reaching this decision, the court followed precedents set in cases involving suits against U.S. parties for defamation allegedly committed in the United Kingdom. Because British laws impose liability for some statements that in the U.S. would be protected by the First Amendment, U.S. courts will not apply the British law in those situations (169 F. Supp. 2d at 1192–1193).

In addition to the jurisdiction and enforcement of judgment issues, the court was presented with a substantive choice of law issue: Should French or U.S. law be applied to the dispute? The court stated that "it must and will decide this case in accordance with the Constitution and laws of the United States" (*Vernor*, 169 F. Supp. 2d at 1187). While this makes sense in a case where the conflict is between the foreign law and a provision of the U.S. Constitution, it would have been less convincing had the French law conflicted only with a U.S. statute, not with the Constitution.

Once the court had established that the First Amendment, not the French statute, was the applicable law, and that a foreign judgment could not be enforced if enforcement would violate the First Amendment, the conclusion was obvious: the French judgment could not be enforced against Yahoo! in the United States (169 F. Supp. 2d at 1194).

LICRA and the Union des Etudiants Juifs de France appealed, however. The appellate court focused not on the constitutional issue but on the narrow jurisdictional issue, and reversed the decision of the trial court. Because Yahoo! had brought the case in the United States without waiting for the French parties to bring an action in a U.S. court to enforce the French judgment, the French parties were the defendants in the action, not the plaintiff. The French parties had not purposely availed themselves of the U.S. forum. As a result, the court could only exercise jurisdiction over the French parties if California's long-arm statute permitted the exercise of jurisdiction and if the exercise of jurisdiction was constitutionally permissible. Even granting the former, jurisdiction could not constitutionally be exercised. LICRA and the Union des Etudiants Juifs de France had no connections to California other than those arising from the dispute. The French parties had done three things that could be considered contacts with the forum state, California: They had sent a cease-and-desist letter to Yahoo! in California; they had used the U.S. Marshals Service to serve process on Yahoo!; and they had asked the French court to require Yahoo! to remove listings of Nazi items from its Web site in California. While the district court had found these three acts sufficient to satisfy the "minimum contacts" standard for the exercise of jurisdiction, the appellate court disagreed (379 F.3d 1124), on the grounds that the acts were not "wrongful conduct targeted at Yahoo!" (379 F.3d at 1125). The appellate court seemed to recognize implicitly that, should the French parties bring suit to enforce the French judgment in a U.S. court, the First Amendment would bar enforcement; but, the court said, Yahoo! would have to wait until the French parties brought suit in the United States before raising the First Amendment claim. As the lower court had done, the appellate court pointed out that the French statute and the French court's decision were completely acceptable exercises of the sovereign authority of the French government within France; there was nothing wrongful about the French parties' pursuit of a remedy in French court under French law (379 F.3d at 1126).

The aftermath of the Yahoo! case: The French Yahoo! case demonstrated the potential for differing applications of law regarding freedom of expression not only between countries with radically different approaches to expression, such as the United States and Saudi Arabia, but between countries with very similar approaches. France and the United States share a history of commitment to a particular concept of civil and political freedoms; the French and American revolutions shaped the concept of freedom of expression as it is generally applied in Europe and North America today. The concept of civil liberties in the two countries is the result not only of shared ideals, but of shared founders, including Thomas Jefferson and the Marquis de Lafayette.

The outcome of the two cases provides no satisfactory solution to the question of jurisdiction over Internet speech (see Pickett 2006); jurisdiction can, at a minimum, be found where the speaker is located, and perhaps where the server storing the speech is located or where the damaging effects of the speech are felt. Internationally there is no uniformity of laws regarding jurisdiction, and further problems are likely to arise in the area of jurisdiction over Internet speech.

Following the cases, Yahoo! and other companies similarly situated engaged in voluntary self-censorship. The list of "Items That Are Prohibited by Yahoo!" in *Yahoo's Auction Guidelines* included:

> Any item that promotes, glorifies, or is directly associated with groups or individuals known principally for hateful or violent positions or acts, such as Nazis or the Ku Klux Klan. Official government-issue stamps and coins are not prohibited under this policy. Expressive media, such as books and films, may be subject to more permissive standards as determined by Yahoo! in its sole discretion (Yahoo! Auctions Guidelines 2013).

Although some free speech advocates criticized Yahoo! for its policy, Yahoo! is not a state actor and its self-censorship raises no First Amendment concerns. If the policy had been arbitrarily or unevenly enforced, however, it could have given rise to lawsuits on other grounds. Other auction sites have adopted similar policies, and the search engine Google has blocked over a hundred Internet sites containing Nazi or hate speech from its French and German versions (Solum & Chung 2004, 910).

Cases

- *Dow Jones & Co., Inc. v. Harrods, Ltd.*, 237 F. Supp. 2d 394 (S.D.N.Y. 2002)
- *League Against Racism and Antisemitism (LICRA), French Union of Jewish Students, v. Yahoo! Inc. (USA), Yahoo France*, Tribunal de Grande Instance de Paris, Interim Court Order, 20 November 2000
- *Yahoo!, Inc. v. La Ligue Contre le Racisme et L'Antisemitisme*, 169 F. Supp. 2d 1181 (N.D. Cal. 2001), reversed, 379 F.3d 1120 (9th Cir. 2004), on rehearing, 433 F.3d 1199 (9th Cir. 2006), certiorari denied, 547 U.S. 1163 (2006)

See also: Censorship; Choice of Law; First Amendment; Jurisdiction; Recognition and Enforcement of Judgments; Yahoo!

Sources and Further Reading

Xavier Amadei, "Standards of Liability for Internet Service Providers: A Comparative Study of France and the United States with a Specific Focus on Copyright, Defamation and Illicit Content," 35 *Cornell International Law Journal* 189 (2001–2002)

Andreas Manolopoulos, "Raising 'Cyber-Borders': The Interaction between Law and Technology," 11 *International Journal of Law and Information Technology* 40 (2003)

Andrew M. Pickett, "Much Yahoo! about Nothing: The Ninth Circuit, Jurisprudential Schizophrenia, and the Road Not Taken in Yahoo! v. La Ligue Contre le Racisme et l'Antisemitisme," 8 *Tulane Journal of Technology & Intellectual Property* 231 (2006)

Peter Singleton, "Personal Jurisdiction in the Ninth Circuit," 59 *Hastings Law Journal* 911 (2008)

Lawrence B. Solum & Minn Chung, "The Layers Principle: Internet Architecture and the Law," 79 *Notre Dame Law Review* 815 (2004)

Yahoo! Auctions Guidelines (2013), http://help.yahoo.com/l/ca/yahoo/auct/agen/agen-09.html (visited August 26, 2013)

❖ FRIENDSTER ❖

See Social Media

G

❖ GAMBLING ❖

Among the most popular and controversial Internet businesses is gambling. Gambling is illegal or restricted in most of the United States, but there is little to stop individual users from sitting at home and gambling. In 2009, the value of the Internet gambling industry was estimated at $25.8 billion, with an annual growth rate of 20% and a predicted value of $35.8 billion by 2012 (Statista 2012). In comparison, in 2011, the value of the legal offline gambling business in the United States was estimated at $35.64 billion (Statista 2012). Over half of the online gamblers were from the United States perhaps because most U.S. states offer their citizens few opportunities for legal offline gambling.

The legality of some types of online gambling in the United States is unclear. In 2011, the U.S. Department of Justice, in what was perceived as a departure from past policy, issued an opinion that the Wire Act (18 U.S.C. § 1084) prohibited online wagering on sports, but not all online gambling within states or across state borders (Memorandum Opinion 2011). This reversal was hailed by gambling law expert I. Nelson Rose as "a big, big present" to the online gambling industry (Jonsson 2011). For the time being, however, the great majority of online gambling sites operate outside the United States, beyond the reach of U.S. law. Considering the problems this situation presents, the Committee on Financial Services of the U.S. House of Representatives has noted that these offshore sites "are not only vulnerable to criminal exploitation by money launderers; they also can easily abuse a customer's credit card information or manipulate the odds of a particular wager to the casino's advantage" (House Report 108–133 2003). In addition, offline gambling is generally considered to represent a trade-off for the jurisdictions that legalize it: the social undesirability of gambling is generally taken as given, and tolerated for the sake of the jobs and tax revenues it provides. Offshore Internet gambling operations provide none of these advantages, nor are they subject to the licensing and regulatory oversight that keeps legalized offline gambling honest.

The Department of Justice's "present" to the gambling industry has led many states to enact or attempt to enact online gambling bills. Delaware was the first state to legalize full-service online casino gambling in June 2012 (Delaware Gaming Competiveness Act of 2012). Illinois followed more cautiously, amending existing law in August 2012 to allow Powerball games to be played online (Ill. S.B. 3497). In New Jersey, a bill authorizing online betting for casino games in Atlantic City was enacted in 2013 (New Jersey Internet Wagering at Atlantic Casinos Act).

Proposed California bills would allow potential operators to apply for a five-year license to run an intrastate online gambling Web site. Licensees would "pay a nonrefundable license fee in the amount of $30,000,000" as well as a non-specified application fee; while this amount would be credited to future monthly fees, the very high start-up cost would impede the entrance of new competitors into the market, protecting existing gambling companies. The bill also allows for the state "to enter into an agreement with other states to provide Internet gambling" (Cal. S.B. 1463; see also S.B. 51, S.B. 678).

Colorado, Hawaii, Iowa, and Mississippi have all attempted to enact bills regulating online gambling, sometimes multiple times, and have thus far failed. Other states, including Maine, Michigan, and Utah, have moved in the opposite direction, strengthening or attempting to strengthen their bans on online gambling following the 2011 Department of Justice opinion. Legislation is also pending in Hawaii and Illinois that would legalize online sales of lottery tickets.

For some gamblers gambling is no more than a form of entertainment; for others it is an addiction. The use of credit cards and the ability to gamble in the privacy of one's home complicate the problem: addicted gamblers can quietly run up debts to the maximum limit on all of their credit cards without anyone, even family members, being aware of what is happening until the bill arrives. Hockey player Jaromir Jagr's Internet gambling loss of $500,000 attracted national attention to the problem, but most online gamblers can be financially ruined by far smaller losses. Age verification is another problem; mere possession of a credit card number is not proof of adulthood, and some gambling sites have accepted bets from minors (House Report 108–133 2003).

Historically, the regulation of gambling has been a matter left to the states; state levels of tolerance of gambling vary widely, so that Nevada, for example, allows most forms of gambling, subject to government regulation and licensing, while its neighbor Utah imposes a strict ban. Occasionally, however, a form of gambling arises that requires the states to seek federal assistance. Thus, in the nineteenth century, states found themselves unable to enforce state laws against mail-order lotteries originating in other states and outside the United States; Congress responded to state concerns with a series of laws culminating in the Federal Anti-Lottery Act, prohibiting the sending of gambling materials through the mails. In 1948, this prohibition was expanded to cover broadcast media, although an exception was later made for the mailing and broadcasting of information relating to state-conducted lotteries. While the Internet is not a broadcast medium, it does involve the transmission of information over wires, and is thus within the scope of another federal anti-gambling statute, the 1961 Wire Act, although the scope of gambling within the Act's prohibition has turned out to be somewhat narrower than originally thought (Memorandum Opinion 2011).

The various states have attempted to enforce their laws against online gambling through lawsuits. Because the online gambling Web site operators are generally beyond the reach of state attorneys general, the targets of these suits have often been credit card companies. Former New York State Attorney General Elliot Spitzer, before his downfall, was especially diligent in pursuing financial institutions that facilitate online gambling. In 2002, Spitzer's activities resulted in two major Internet financial service providers, Citibank and PayPal, prohibiting their services from being used to fund Internet gambling. In a settlement agreement, in which it admitted no wrongdoing, Citibank agreed to stop allowing its cards from being used for Internet gambling; in doing so, it joined American Express, Bank of America, Chase Manhattan, Fleet, and MBNA. In February 2003, Spitzer's office reached similar settlements in which 10 other banks agreed not to allow New York residents to use their cards for online gambling and other credit card issuers have since followed suit on their own initiative. In August 2002, PayPal agreed, also without admitting wrongdoing, not to allow New York residents to use its services for online gambling. Two months later, eBay acquired PayPal and expanded the Internet gambling ban to all PayPal users (Porter 2004, 16).

Actions by state attorneys general are a piecemeal approach to a nationwide problem, however. Like mail lotteries in the nineteenth century, Internet gambling is a nationwide problem that requires a nationwide solution. The United States cannot and should not do anything to regulate gambling operations in other countries aimed at citizens of those countries. When U.S. parties are involved, however, it can take action, as it did in *United States v. Cohen*.

In the late 1990s, the FBI began investigating an offshore gambling operation run by Jay Cohen, a United States citizen. In 1996, Cohen had left the United States and moved to the Caribbean island nation of Antigua and Barbuda, where he opened an online gambling business. The business, World Sports Exchange (WSE), accepted wagers on U.S. sporting events; it had no other business. All of Cohen's partners in WSE were, like Cohen himself, citizens of the United States, and WSE accepted bets by telephone and Internet from the United States (*Cohen*, 260 F.3d at 70). After undercover agents placed bets with WSE from New York, the FBI arrested Cohen and charged him with violation of the Wire Act. Cohen was convicted in the federal district court for the Southern District of New York, and his conviction was upheld on appeal.

An interesting feature of the Wire Act and similar laws is that they criminalize the use of interstate means of communication for acts in violation of *state* law. Conceivably, a state might decide to legalize Internet gambling; had WSE accepted bets from that state, it would have committed no violation of the Wire Act—acts that violate federal law in one state might not violate federal law in another.

Cohen was a U.S. citizen; had he been a foreigner who never set foot in the United States, it would have been difficult or impossible for the government to bring him to trial. While individual prosecution of U.S. persons operating some of the world's two thousand or so sizeable online gambling operations may have some effect, the most likely result is that those persons will be driven out of the business and their places will be taken by non-U.S. persons. If, as it seems, the United States is committed to a policy of controlling and reducing online gambling, the logical point of attack is still the financial mechanisms that make it possible. Actions against banks that issue credit cards have produced results, but the number of banks is large. The number of credit card companies is small, but thus far litigation against them has been less successful. In 2001, a federal district court dismissed several actions against Visa and MasterCard that had been consolidated under the name *In re Mastercard International, Inc. Internet Gambling Litigation*; the decision was subsequently upheld by the U.S. Court of Appeals for the Fifth Circuit (313 F.3d 257).

Several bills have been proposed in Congress to give the federal government a greater ability to control Internet gambling. Bills that would create a federal gambling law tend to be met with distrust from the states; one attempt, the Unlawful Internet Gambling Funding Prohibition Act, would have made no changes in substantive gambling law but would have strengthened the federal government's ability to attack the financial devices that enable illegal Internet gambling from within the United States. The Act was passed by the House but died in the Senate. However, a reformed version of the Act was passed as the Unlawful Internet Gambling Enforcement Act of 2006 as a last-minute attachment to an unrelated bill, the SAFE Port Act of 2006.

Meanwhile, the *Cohen* saga had international law consequences; it gave rise to an international dispute between the United States and Antigua and Barbuda. Antigua and Barbuda hosts other Internet gambling businesses, and felt that the Wire Act, as applied at the time, violated international law regarding trade in services. On November 10, 2004, a World Trade Organization (WTO) dispute resolution panel agreed, potentially making the United States subject to WTO sanctions. In 2007, a WTO arbitration ruled that Antigua could seek sanctions of up to 21 million dollars annually against the United States, far from the $3.4 billion Antigua requested. After unsuccessful negotiations between the two countries, on January 28, 2013, Antigua received final authorization from the WTO to impose the sanctions.

Treaty

- General Agreement on Trade in Services, Marrakesh Agreement Establishing the World Trade Organization, Annex 1B, Apr. 15, 1994, 33 I.L.M. 1168 (1994)

Statutes and Proposed Legislation

- California Authorization and Regulation of Internet Poker and Consumer Protection Act of 2013, S.B. 678 (Reg. Sess. 2013–14)
- California Internet Gambling Consumer Protection and Public-Private Partnership Act of 2012, S.B. 1463 (Reg. Sess. 2011–12)
- California Internet Gambling Consumer Protection and Public-Private Partnership Act of 2013, S.B. 51 (Reg. Sess. 2013–14)
- Delaware Gaming Competiveness Act of 2012, H.B. 333 (Del. 2012), 29 Del. Code §§ 4803, 4805, 4810–4811, 4815, 4819–4820, 4824–4826, 4834–4836, 4 Del. Code 543
- Federal Anti-Lottery Act, 18 U.S.C. §§ 1301–1304
- Hawaii Internet and Lottery Gaming Act, H.B. 2422 (Reg Sess. 2011–12)
- Illinois Amending Lottery and State Finance Act, S.B. 3497 (Ill. 2012), 20 ILCS 1605/7.12, 1605/14.4
- Michigan McCauley-Traxler-Law-Bowman-McNeely Lottery Act, S.B. 1003 (Mich. 2012), Mich. Code § 432.9
- Mississippi Internet Gaming Act of 2012, H.B. 1373 (Reg Sess. 2012)
- New Jersey Internet Wagering at Atlantic Casinos Act (Amending and Supplementing Casino Control Act), A. 2578 (Reg Sess. 2012–13)
- Unlawful Internet Gambling Enforcement Act of 2006, 31 U.S.C. §§ 5361–5367
- Unlawful Internet Gambling Funding Prohibition Act, H.R. 2143, 108th Cong. (1st Sess. 2003)
- Wire Act, 18 U.S.C. § 1084

Committee Report and Attorney General's Opinion

- Report of the Committee on Financial Services on the Unlawful Internet Gambling Funding Prohibition Act, H.R. Rep. No. 108–133 (2003)
- Virgina A. Seitz, Memorandum Opinion for the Assistant Attorney General, Criminal Division: Whether Proposals by Illinois and New York to Use the Internet and Out-of-State Transaction Processors to Sell Lottery Tickets to In-State Adults Violate the Wire Act, Opinions of the Office of Legal Counsel 35 (2011)

Cases

- *In re Mastercard International, Inc. Internet Gambling Litigation*, 313 F.3d 257 (5th Cir. 2002)
- *United States v. Cohen*, 260 F.3d 68 (2d Cir. 2001)
- *Cohen v. United States*, 128 F.App'x 825 (2d Cir. 2005)
- *Dispute Settlement: Dispute DS285, United States—Measures Affecting the Cross-Border Supply of Gambling and Betting Services*, World Trade Organization (December 21, 2007), available at http://www.wto.org/english/tratop_e/dispu_e/cases_e/ds285_e.htm
- Measures Affecting the Cross-Border Supply of Gambling and Better Services (*U.S. v. Antigua & Barbuda*), WT/DS285/ARB, Decision by Arbitrator (World Trade Organization 2007)

See also: E-Commerce; Enforcement

Sources and Further Reading

"2012 Legislation Regarding Internet Gambling or Lotteries," National Conference of State Legislature, available at http://www.ncsl.org/issues-research/econ/2012-online-gambling-legislation.aspx (visited January 9, 2013)

Walter T. Champion, Jr. & I. Nelson Rose, *Gaming Law in a Nutshell* (St. Paul, MN: West, 2012)

Doug Denison, "Delaware to Allow Online Gambling," *USA Today* (June 28, 2012) available at http://usatoday30.usatoday.com/news/nation/story/2012–06–28/delaware-online-gambling/55897914/1 (visited February 3, 2013)

Jack L. Goldsmith, "What Internet Gambling Legislation Teaches about Internet Regulation," 32 *International Lawyer* 1115 (1998)

Jonathan Gottfried, "The Federal Framework for Internet Gambling," 10 *Richmond Journal of Law and Technology* 26 (2004)

"Growth of the World Online Gambling Market from 2003 to 2012 (in Billion U.S. Dollars)," DowJones Statista (2012), available at http://www.statista.com/statistics/168622/market-volume-of-online-gaming-worldwide-since-2003/ (visited February 3, 2013)

Ben J. Hayes & Matthew J. Conigliaro, "The Business of Betting or Wagering: A Unifying View of Federal Gaming Law," 57 *Drake Law Review* 445 (2009)

"House of Cards: Laws Banning Gambling Show the Strength of Sovereignty," *The Economist*, November 20, 2004, at 66, available at http://www.economist.com/node/3411641 (visited February 3, 2013)

"Internet Gambling Scores Its Biggest Win," *Wall Street Journal* (February 26, 2013) available at http://online.wsj.com/article/SB10001424127887323884304578328293465612224.html (visited May 13, 2013)

Patrik Jonsson, "Boom in Internet Gambling Ahead? US Policy Reversal Clears the Way," *Christian Science Monitor* (December 26, 2011), available at http://www.csmonitor.com/USA/2011/1226/Boom-in-Internet-gambling-ahead-US-policy-reversal-clears-the-way (visited February 3, 2013)

Mark D. Lynch, "The Smart Money Is on Prosecutions: Using the Federal Interstate Wire Act to Prosecute Offshore Telephone Gambling Services," 10 *Indiana International and Comparative Law Review* 177 (1999)

Harsh P. Parikh & Heidi McNeil Staudenmaier, "Betting on i-Gambling Could Have Big Returns," *Los Angeles Daily Journal*, May 11, 2012, at 8

Rebecca Porter, "Prosecutors, Plaintiffs Aim to Curb Internet Gambling," *Trial*, August 2004, at 14

Lawrance Kimmel Spiller, "Credit Card Companies Crave More Money and Accumulate More through Illegal Gambling on the Internet—*In re Mastercard International, Inc. Internet Gambling Litigation, 132 F. Supp. 2d 468 (E.D. La. 2002)*," 22 *Temple Environmental Law and Technology Journal* 99 (2003)

State of the States: The AGA Survey of Casino Entertainment 2 (2012), available at http://www.americangaming.org/files/aga/uploads/docs/sos/aga_sos_2012_web.pdf (visited February 3, 2013)

❖ GENERAL AGREEMENT ON TARIFFS AND TRADE ❖

See World Trade Organization

❖ GNU/LINUX ❖

See Open Source

❖ GUTENBERG PROJECT ❖

See Project Gutenberg

❖ HACKING ❖

The term "hacker" is often used to describe a person with sophisticated computer skills and a certain lack of regard for laws and other norms of conduct. The term has its probable origin in student slang at the Massachusetts Institute of Technology. The media and popular fiction have invested the term with a certain outlaw mystique; however, the application of the term "hacking" to illegal activities has aroused resentment among hackers who are careful to keep their activities within the bounds of the law, or to step outside those bounds only to make calculated statements. According to these "white hat" and sometimes "gray hat" hackers, outlaw hackers should properly be referred to as "crackers" or "black hat hackers."

Early computer networks, such as ARPANET and NSFNet, did not support a community of for-profit businesses. Most users were scientists and computer programmers—many, perhaps most, were or aspired to be hackers themselves. Mischievous hacking served a useful purpose; it identified weaknesses and security flaws (Lessig 1999, 194). As a result, legislators and law enforcement ignored it. But as businesses and ordinary people came to rely upon the Internet, the potential for hacking to do harm increased while its usefulness decreased: users whose sites or computers were hacked lacked the technical sophistication to understand which security flaws had been exposed by the hack. The spread of the Internet also gave rise to a generation of "script kiddies"—hackers who in many cases do not actually understand the systems and programs they were hacking, but download and use hacking programs written by others.

The criminalization of hacking coincided with the transformation of the Internet from an experimental network for sophisticated users to a universal information resource. In 1988, hacking was brought to an unprecedented level of public attention by a worm created by Robert Morris, Jr., a graduate student at Cornell University in New York State and the son of National Security Agency data security expert Robert Morris Sr. (Lessig 1999, 282, n. 18). The worm spread across the Internet, shutting down hundreds or perhaps thousands of computers and causing millions of dollars in damage. Morris, in creating the worm, was acting as an old-school hacker: he was pointing out a security flaw in the open-source program Sendmail, which is used to transfer

most of the email on the Internet. Because Sendmail is an open-source program, there is no one person responsible for fixing flaws such as the one discovered by Morris; in a world in which all users were also capable of understanding and rewriting code, the logical way to point out a flaw in Sendmail would be to exploit that flaw in an obvious but harmless way, thus calling it to everyone's attention (Lessig 1999, 195).

Morris used a worm—a self-replicating program—to expose the flaw in Sendmail and another program, Fingerdaemon, as well as in computers' "trusted hosts" and password features (*Morris*, 928 F.2d at 506). He committed two errors of judgment, however: the worm replicated too quickly and most of the new users of the Internet were not technically sophisticated enough to figure out what to do about it. Morris tried to stop the worm after he had released it, but was unable to do so. The worm and its consequences attracted considerable media attention; at the time the Internet was a new and unfamiliar medium, so much so that the appellate opinion in Morris's case referred to it throughout not as "the Internet" or "the internet" but as "INTERNET," in capital letters and without the definite article (*Morris*, 928 F.2d at 504–511). Morris was arrested and charged with violation of what was then a recently enacted statute, the Computer Fraud and Abuse Act (18 U.S.C. § 1030). Section 1030(a)(5)(A) as it then read (it has since been amended) provided for the imposition of penalties on anyone who:

> (5) intentionally accesses a Federal interest computer without authorization, and by means of one or more instances of such conduct alters, damages, or destroys information in any such Federal interest computer, or prevents authorized use of any such computer or information, and thereby (A) causes loss to one or more others of a value aggregating $1,000 or more during any one year period (quoted in *Morris*, 928 F.2d at 506).

Morris was convicted of violating § 1030(a)(5)(A) and "sentenced to three years of probation, 400 hours of community service, a fine of $10,050, and the costs of his supervision" (*Morris*, 928 F.2d at 506).

Morris's worm attack coincided with growing fears on the part of telephone companies that telecommunications networks were vulnerable to attacks by phreakers. The phreaking and hacking communities overlapped to a considerable extent; while phreakers had been more a nuisance than a threat to the phone companies, the possibility of a massive hacker attack shutting down large sections of the telecommunications network motivated federal law enforcement officials to undertake what author Bruce Sterling has called the hacker crackdown. There were several raids by federal agents and New York state police on known and suspected hackers in 1990, including Operation Sundevil in May of that year; "Sundevil" came to be used as a shorthand in the media for all of the anti-hacker activity in 1990 (Sterling 1992, Part 3).

The Computer Fraud and Abuse Act, frequently amended, remains an important weapon in the federal government's anti-hacker arsenal. Other hacker activities may be prohibited by statutes not specifically aimed at hacking but designed instead to control bank fraud (18 U.S.C. § 1344), credit card fraud (18 U.S.C. § 1029), and wire fraud (18 U.S.C. § 1343). Warez trading inspired the No Electronic Theft Act of 1997. And the Digital Millennium Copyright Act prohibits the use of hacker skills to circumvent technological measures used to protect copyrighted works from unauthorized copying.

Many kinds of computer mischief may be lumped by the media under the term "hacking." Sundevil and the other 1990 raids led not only to a polarization of many hackers against the government but to divisions within the hacker community. White-hat hackers have made an attempt to take back the name "hacker" for themselves, encouraging the media to refer to lawbreaking hackers as "crackers" (Lessig 1999, 282, n. 25). In the mainstream media, at least, this attempt has not been successful; it is common to see media reports using the term "hacking" to refer not only to cracking but to a variety of other computer mischief, including phishing, piracy, and online pranks of all sorts.

Hacking has inspired a subculture of literature and movies in which the hackers are almost always seen as outlaw heroes, on the wrong side of the law but (occasionally) with hearts of gold. Most of the now-dated cyberpunk genre falls into this general category; for example, the protagonists of cyberpunk's most celebrated practitioner, William Gibson, tend to be computer users who, despite an astonishing level of technical virtuosity, are down on their luck and suffer from a basic incompatibility with society's notions of law and order. Even in its heyday, however, cyberpunk was not the only genre to romanticize hackers. Hollywood made non-punk heroes of hackers in movies as varied as *Sneakers*, starring Robert Redford and Sidney Poitier as white-hat computer security experts who foil black-hat hacker Ben Kingsley, and the James Bond movie *Goldeneye*, in which Izabelle Scorupco and Alan Cumming play good and evil hackers, respectively; predictably, evil hacker Cumming is part of a plot to rule the world or, failing that, to destroy it, but is foiled by good hacker Scorupco with some help from 007.

As the hacker culture overlapped with and was to some extent an outgrowth of phreaker culture, it in turn contributed to the growth of the cypherpunk movement. Cypherpunk is a largely idealistic commitment to encryption as a means of preserving privacy (Hughes 1993). Cypherpunk, too, has inspired a literary subgenre, whose cryptographer protagonists are not, strictly speaking, hackers, but resemble the hacker protagonists of many cyberpunk works in both their extraordinary technical skills and in their general haplessness when faced with anything other than problems of cryptography.

Among the best-known voices of established hacker culture in the real world is *2600: The Hacker Quarterly*, published by Eric Corley under the name Emmanuel Goldstein. The name "2600" is drawn from the 2600 hertz tone used by early phone phreakers; the "Goldstein" alias is drawn from George Orwell's classic novel of a totalitarian future, *1984*. In the novel, the supposedly dangerous Goldstein never actually appears, although the work attributed to him is quoted extensively; it gradually becomes apparent that Goldstein probably does not actually exist, but is being used by a totalitarian state to justify repression. Corley, both personally and as the editor of *2600*, was involved in the litigation over the DeCSS decryption program (e.g., *Corley*, 273 F.3d 429). The choice of the "Goldstein" alias proved particularly apt in the wake of the terrorist attacks of September 11, 2001; the USA PATRIOT Act and other security legislation imposed harsher sentences for criminal hacking, prompting *2600* to announce that "[t]hose who would use the tragic events of September 11 to create repression will do far more lasting harm to our society than any terrorist ever could" (*Life Imprisonment* 2001).

The rapid growth in Internet use has meant that as each new generation of hackers establishes itself, it almost immediately finds itself overtaken by the next wave. Hacking culture is thus, perhaps appropriately, in constant revolution; hackers of the *2600* school are now outnumbered by /b/ and Anonymous. The latter tend to draw more headlines as well, as in the case of /b/'s hacking and publicizing of 2008 vice presidential candidate Sarah Palin's Yahoo! Mail account.

Statutes

- Bank Fraud Act, 18 U.S.C. § 1344
- Computer Fraud and Abuse Act, 18 U.S.C. § 1030
- Credit Card Fraud Act, 18 U.S.C. § 1029
- Digital Millennium Copyright Act, Pub. L. No. 105–304, codified at 17 U.S.C. §§ 1201–05
- Wire Fraud Act, 18 U.S.C. § 1343
- No Electronic Theft Act, amending and codified at 17 U.S.C. §§ 101, 506 & 507 & 18 U.S.C. §§ 2319–2320

Cases

Federal Appellate Courts

- *United States v. Morris*, 928 F.2d 504 (2d Cir. 1991)
- *Universal City Studios, Inc., v. Reimerdes*, 111 F. Supp. 2d 294 (S.D.N.Y. 2000), affirmed by *Universal City Studios, Inc. v. Corley*, 273 F.3d 429 (2d Cir. 2001)

Federal Trial Court
- *United States v. LaMacchia*, 871 F. Supp. 535 (D. Mass. 1994)

State Court
- *DVD Copy Control Association, Inc. v. Bunner*, 113 Cal. Rptr. 2d 338 (2001), *reversed*, 4 Cal. Rptr. 3d 69 (2003)

See also: Activism and Advocacy Groups; Cloud; Cyberpunk; DeCSS; Encryption; Internet; No Electronic Theft Act; Open Source; Phreaking; Piracy; QR Code; Social Networking Service; Stop Online Piracy Act; Virus; Warez; World Wide Web; Worm

Sources and Further Reading

Nonfiction

Stuart Biegel, *Beyond Our Control? Confronting the Limits of Our Legal System in the Age of Cyberspace* (Cambridge, MA: MIT Press, 2001)

"Businesses and Cyber-Security: A Spook Speaks," *The Economist*, June 30, 2012, at 67

"Hacker Gary McKinnon Will Not Face UK Charges," BBC News (December 14, 2012), available at http://www.bbc.co.uk/news/uk-20730627 (visited February 7, 2013)

Eric Hughes, "A Cypherpunk's Manifesto" (March 9, 1993), available at http://www.activism.net/cypherpunk/manifesto.html (visited August 7, 2012)

Lawrence Lessig, *Code and Other Laws of Cyberspace* (New York: Basic Books, 1999)

Lawrence Lessig, *Code and Other Laws of Cyberspace, Version 2.0* (New York: Basic Books, 2006)

Steven Levy, *Hackers: Heroes of the Computer Revolution* (Sebastopol, CA: O'Reilly Media, Inc., 2010)

"Life Imprisonment for Hackers Could Be Imm*inent*," *2600 News* (September 25, 2001), available at http://www.2600.com/news/view/article/726 (visited February 7, 2013)

Declan McCullagh, "'Aaron's Law' Rewrite Backfires, Reformers Now on Defensive," CNet (April 2, 2013), available at http://news.cnet.com/8301–13578_3–57577520–38/aarons-law-rewrite-backfires-reformers-now-on-defensive/ (visited April 29, 2013)

Kevin D. Mitnick et al., *The Art of Deception: Controlling the Human Element of Security* (Indianapolis: Wiley Publishing, Inc., 2002)

Evgeny Morozov, *The Net Delusion: The Dark Side of Internet Freedom* (New York: PublicAffairs, 2012)

Bruce Sterling, *The Hacker Crackdown* (Electronic edition 1992), available at http://stuff.mit.edu/hacker/hacker.html (visited August 14, 2012)

Siva Vaidhyanathan, *The Anarchist in the Library: How the Clash between Freedom and Control Is Hacking the Real World and Crashing the System* (New York: Basic Books, 2004)

Vernor Vinge, *True Names and the Opening of the Cyberspace Frontier* (New York: Tor, 2001) (fiction and nonfiction)

Fiction

John Brunner, *The Shockwave Rider* (New York: Ballantine, 1976)

William Gibson, *Burning Chrome* (New York: Arbor House, 1986)

William Gibson, *Count Zero* (New York: Arbor House, 1986)

William Gibson, *Idoru* (New York: Putnam Publishing Group, 1996)

William Gibson, *Mona Lisa Overdrive* (New York: Bantam, 1988)

William Gibson, *Neuromancer* (New York: Ace, 1984)

Jeff Moss, ed., *Stealing the Network: How to Own the Box* (Rockland, MA: Syngress, 2003)

Neal Stephenson, *Cryptonomicon* (New York: HarperCollins, 1999)

Bruce Sterling, *Islands in the Net* (New York: Arbor House, 1988)

Bruce Sterling, ed., *Mirrorshades: The Cyberpunk Anthology* (New York: Arbor House, 1986)

❖ ICANN ❖

See Internet Corporation for Assigned Names and Numbers

❖ IDENTITY THEFT ❖

Identity theft is the assumption of another's identity. The most common motive for identity theft is fraud; the criminal assumes the victim's identity in order to use the victim's credit cards, open new credit card accounts, make purchases, take out loans, or otherwise use the victim's identity to obtain money, goods, or services. Identity theft may also be used by terrorists and ordinary criminals hoping to avoid the authorities, by persons wishing to circumvent immigration laws, and by spies for companies and governments. In most cases, the victim is targeted for identity theft for reasons of convenience: the victim may bear a physical resemblance to the thief or may be of the same age and gender, or the thief may choose a particular victim simply because that victim's personal identifying information is available to the thief. Occasionally, identity theft is motivated by a wish to cause harm to a particular victim; the thief may use the victim's identity to make it appear that the victim has committed a crime or other reprehensible act. In addition, identity thieves are criminals who may commit crimes other than the identity theft itself, and their crimes may sometimes be blamed on the victim whose identity was being used at the time the crime was committed.

In order to steal another person's identity, the identity thief needs to assemble several pieces of information. The victim's name, birth date, gender, race, place of birth, father's name, and mother's name can all be obtained from public birth certificate records. The mother's maiden name, if different, can then be obtained from marriage records. If the victim is a homeowner, the victim's home address can be obtained from county property records, as can the price paid for the property, the victim's marital status, how much money has been borrowed against the property, and the names and addresses of the lenders.

This information alone is enough for a diligent identity thief to construct an entirely fictitious identity, which can then be used in fraudulent transactions. Most identity thieves are lazy, though, and prefer to take shortcuts. Identity theft is far easier if the thief has additional information about the victim, such as the victim's social security number, employer and salary information, bank account numbers, and credit card numbers and expiration dates. There are several ways in which thieves may acquire this information. They may steal the victim's wallet, purse, or checkbook; the theft may be temporary, so that the victim never notices that the item is missing. Thieves may steal employee records from a company in which they work, or may raid dumpsters looking for documents with the desired information. They may steal or divert the victim's mail (FTC ID Theft 2012). A thief who can acquire a copy of a victim's tax return will have all of the information he or she needs.

The Internet may serve as a means of identity theft as well. Hackers can obtain salary, credit card, and other information from the records of employers and retailers. Hacking of this sort, however, requires a high level of technical sophistication. Far simpler are phishing scams, in which the thief sends a message to the victim purporting to be from a bank or credit card company. Typically, the message claims that for security reasons it is necessary for the victim to confirm his or her account number and other identifying information, and warns that if this is not done within a certain time, the victim's account will be suspended (FTC Phishing Scam 2006). Phishers make use of spam techniques to send millions or hundreds of millions of copies of the message; if only one person in a million is gullible enough to respond to the message, the scam will still have succeeded.

Identity theft can cause damage that can take years for the victim to correct. Even if the thief is apprehended and the misuse of the victim's identity is halted, bills for purchases and loans initiated by the thief will continue to be reported to credit agencies. Victims may be refused jobs, loans, or rental housing based on the actions of the identity thief, as reported to credit agencies under the victim's name. In extreme cases, victims of identity theft may even be arrested for crimes committed by the thief (FTC ID Theft 2012).

Through its Identity Theft Web site at http://www.ftc .gov/idtheft, the Federal Trade Commission (FTC) collects information on identity theft and offers advice both on preventing identity theft and on repairing the damage if one becomes a victim. A wide variety of federal and state laws also address identity theft. Many of these are preexisting laws regarding fraud, embezzlement, theft, wire fraud, and so forth. Others have been created specifically to deal with the problem of identity theft. Federal statutes in this latter category include the Identity Theft and Assumption Deterrence Act of 1998, the Internet False Identification Prevention Act of 2000, the Fair and Accurate Credit Transactions Act of 2003, the Identity Theft Penalty Enhancement Act of 2004, the SAFE ID Act of 2004, and the Identity Theft and Restitution Act of 2008.

The Identity Theft and Assumption Deterrence Act of 1998 added a new paragraph to 18 U.S.C. § 1028(a), the statute forbidding the use or transfer of unauthorized or false identification documents. The new paragraph makes it unlawful for any person to "knowingly [transfer or use], without lawful authority, a means of identification of another person with the intent to commit, or to aid or abet, any unlawful activity that constitutes a violation of Federal law, or that constitutes a felony under any applicable State or local law" (18 U.S.C. § 1028(a)(7)). This defines the crime that is at the heart of identity theft: the use of false identification, whether in the form of a physical document or an electronic password and account number, to commit some other crime. While the preceding six subsections of § 1028(a) refer to "identification documents," § 1028(a)(7) refers to "means of identification," an apparent acknowledgment that Internet and telephone transactions may rely on means of identification that do not involve physical documents. "Means of identification" is defined in the Act as:

> any name or number that may be used, alone or in conjunction with any other information, to identify a specific individual, including any—
>
> (A) name, social security number, date of birth, official State or government issued driver's license or identification number, alien registration number, government passport number, employer or taxpayer identification number;
> (B) unique biometric data, such as fingerprint, voice print, retina or iris image, or other unique physical representation;
> (C) unique electronic identification number, address, or routing code; or
> (D) telecommunication identifying information or access device . . . (18 U.S.C. § 1028(d)(7)).

These are the type of information that might be obtained from tax returns or employee records, or by phishing.

The Internet False Identification Prevention Act criminalized some types of distribution of counterfeit identification documents and credentials over the Internet that had been left uncovered by loopholes in prior laws; among other things, the Act made it a crime to transfer a false or unauthorized identification document by electronic means (Towle 2004, 268). The Fair and Accurate Credit Transactions Act (FACT) amends the Fair Credit Reporting Act in several ways; among its goals is the protection of consumers from the adverse credit consequences of identity theft and the protection of both consumers and credit card

companies from the theft of identifying information that can be used in identity theft. There is potential for inconsistency or conflict between FACT and state law, and it may be some time before the complexities of the relationship between FACT and state laws are fully worked out (Towle 2004, 270–271).

The Secure Authentication Feature and Enhanced Identification Defense Act of 2003, or SAFE ID Act, was signed by President Bush on April 30, 2004. The SAFE ID Act adds yet another new paragraph to 18 U.S.C. § 1028, and further erases the distinction between "documents" and "means of identification" in the remaining paragraphs of § 1028(a) by adding the words "authentication feature" to the word "document" in sections 1028(a)(1) through 1028(a)(6). This change brings these six paragraphs up to date with § 1028(7), added by the 1998 Federal Identity Theft and Assumption Deterrence Act, and recognizes that physical documents are no longer required for identity theft. The new paragraph added by the SAFE ID Act makes it a crime to "knowingly [traffic] in false or actual authentication features for use in false identification documents, document-making implements, or means of identification" (18 U.S.C. § 1028(a)(8)). The "authentication features" addressed by the Act include "any hologram, watermark, certification, symbol, code, image, sequence of numbers or letters, or other feature that either individually or in combination with another feature is used by the issuing authority on an identification document, document-making implement, or means of identification to determine if the document is counterfeit, altered, or otherwise falsified" (18 U.S.C. § 1028(d)(1)).

The Identity Theft and Penalty Act of 2004 added increased penalties for "aggravated identity theft," meaning the use of the identity of another for the commission of a felony (18 U.S.C. § 1028A). The Identity Theft and Restitution Act of 2008 allowed federal (rather than state) courts to prosecute identity thieves even if the thieves reside in the same state as their victims (18 U.S.C. § 3663(b)). The 2008 Act also provided that a victim may be reimbursed not only for direct losses from the theft, but also for time spent "remediat[ing] the intended or actual harm incurred by the victim from the offense" (18 U.S.C. § 3663(b)).

For consumers, avoiding identity theft remains a concern. While there is no way to avoid a skilled and determined identity thief, there are ways to avoid being an easy target. Consumers should shred tax returns, credit card receipts, paycheck stubs, and similar identifying documents, rather than merely throwing them away. Credit card numbers and other financial information should never be given to unknown persons. Internet phishing is easy to detect: legitimate banks, credit card companies, retailers, Internet service providers, and so forth will never have any reason to email customers asking for their account numbers. The same logic applies to phone phishing and mail phishing: legitimate businesses and financial institutions will never have a reason to call a customer and ask for his or her account number, nor will they have a reason to send a letter requesting it. Any uncertainty as to whether a request is legitimate can be resolved with a telephone call to the credit card company or other business involved; of course, the consumer should call the telephone number provided on the credit card itself or that obtained from the telephone directory, rather than a telephone number provided on the suspected phishing document. And any time a consumer sees charges on a credit card statement that she does not recognize, she should contact the credit card company.

Statutes

- Fair and Accurate Credit Transactions Act, 117 Stat. 1952, amending and codified at 15 U.S.C. §§ 1681 et seq.
- Identity Theft and Assumption Deterrence Act of 1998, amending and codified at 18 U.S.C. § 1028
- Identity Theft Penalty Enhancement Act of 2004, amending and codified at 18 U.S.C. § 1028
- Identity Theft and Restitution Act of 2008, amending and codified at 18 U.S.C. § 3663(b)
- Internet False Identification Prevention Act, amending and codified at 18 U.S.C. § 1028
- Secure Authentication Feature and Enhanced Identification Defense (SAFE ID) Act, amending and codified at 18 U.S.C. § 1028

Cases

- *In re Crawford*, 194 F.3d 954 (9th Cir. 1999), certiorari denied sub nom *Ferm v. U.S. Trustee*, 528 U.S. 1189 (2000)
- *In re Rolando S.*, 197 Cal. App. 4th. 936 (Cal. App. 5th Dist. 2011)
- *Andrews v. TRW, Inc.*, 225 F.3d 1063 (9th Cir. 2000), reversed, 534 U.S. 19 (2001)

See also: Federal Trade Commission; Phishing; Spam

Sources and Further Reading

Federal Trade Commission, "How Not to Get Hooked by a Phishing Scam," FTC Consumer Alert (October 2006), available at http://www.ftc.gov/bcp/edu/pubs/consumer/alerts/alt127.shtm (visited December 17, 2012)

Federal Trade Commission, "ID Theft" (n.d.), available at http://www.consumer.ftc.gov/features/feature-0014-identity-theft (visited December17, 2012)

Federal Trade Commission, "Phishing" (September 2011), available at http://www.onguardonline.gov/phishing (visited December 17, 2012)

"FTC Releases Consumer Fraud Survey: More than One in 10 Americans Fell Victim to Fraud," Federal Trade Commission (August 5, 2004), available at http://www.ftc.gov/opa/2004/08/fraudsurvey.shtm (visited February 7, 2013)

"FTC Releases Survey of Identity Theft in U.S.: 27.3 Million Victims in Past 5 Years, Billions in Losses for Businesses and Consumers," Federal Trade Commission (September 3, 2003), available at http://www.ftc.gov/opa/2003/09/idtheft.shtm (visited February 7, 2013)

Robert Sprague & Corey Ciocchetti, "Preserving Identities: Protecting Personal Identifying Information through Enhanced Privacy Policies and Laws," 19 *Albany Law Journal of Science & Technology* 91 (2009)

Holly K. Towle, "Identity Theft: Myths, Methods and New Law," 30 *Rutgers Computer and Technology Law Journal* 237 (2004)

❖ INDECENCY ❖

In a loosely defined area between expression entitled to the full protection of the First Amendment and obscenity, which is not protected, lies indecency. Indecent expression is expression that does not conform to "accepted standards of morality." It may be "vulgar, offensive and shocking" (*Pacifica*, 438 U.S. 728, 740, 747). It may meet some, but not all, of the elements of the Supreme Court's three-part test for obscenity. That is, it may be material that:

(a) "the 'average person, applying contemporary community standards' would find, taken as a whole, appeals to the prurient interest," or

(b) "depicts or describes, in a patently offensive way, sexual conduct specifically defined by the applicable state law," or

(c) "taken as a whole, lacks serious literary, artistic, political, or scientific value" (*Miller*, 413 U.S. at 39).

It need not meet all three of these, however; content that meets all three criteria is obscene, not merely indecent.

At the federal level, the most significant and pervasive regulation of indecency is that of the Federal Communications Commission (FCC). The FCC does not regulate the Internet, but does regulate broadcast media—at times with absurd results, as when the FCC's response to Janet Jackson's "wardrobe malfunction" at the 2004 Super Bowl invited worldwide mockery of perceived U.S. prudery. Because many providers of mainstream Internet content are also providers of broadcast media, content on these providers' sites may conform to FCC guidelines regarding indecency.

In the Internet context, there has been little or no effort to regulate indecency of the type exemplified by George Carlin's notorious "Filthy Words" (aka "Seven Deadly Words") monologue, the subject of the Supreme Court's decision in *Federal Communications Commission v. Pacifica*. Carlin's monologue is entirely speech, without pictures or other graphic content. It is satirical; it is not designed to appeal to an interest in sex, prurient or otherwise, but to make a point about censorship and, when played on the radio (as it was by the defendant in *Pacifica*) to challenge what the author and the defendant apparently believe to be unnecessarily heavy-handed censorship. It makes its points, however, by deliberate use of shocking and offensive language and examples.

The entire text of the "Seven Deadly Words" monologue is readily available on the Web; it may be found in, among other places, an appendix to the Supreme Court's opinion in *Pacifica*. The widespread availability of this "indecent" content and content like it has aroused no perceptible public or governmental opposition. Rather, concern about indecency has focused on pornography: material that is sexually exciting to some, offensive to others, not obscene or otherwise illegal per se (as child pornography), but generally agreed to be inappropriate for minors. Because the Internet is not a broadcast medium, it is entitled to the highest level of First Amendment protection; the FCC may not regulate Internet content in the way it regulates broadcast television and radio content.

Congress has attempted to restrict the access of minors to pornography, although not necessarily to other forms of indecent content such as Carlin's monologue, both by regulating the supply side (Web sites containing pornographic content) and the user side. To date, neither approach has proven notably effective, as is evident to even a casual Web surfer.

The first Congressional attempt to regulate Internet content was the Communications Decency Act of 1996 (CDA), which, among other things, imposed penalties for the knowing transmission or display of "indecent" material, including depictions or descriptions, "in terms patently offensive as measured by community standards, [of] sexual or excretory activities or organs" to known minors (47 U.S.C. § 223). The Supreme Court held the CDA to be unconstitutional for several reasons, including the difficulty of defining "indecent," the difficulty of verifying the age of the recipient or viewer of the content, and the burden placed on noncommercial sites. These problems rendered it difficult or impossible for content providers to know whether they were violating the CDA, and placed a burden on the operators of some sites, especially noncommercial sites (*Reno v. ACLU*, 521 U.S. 844).

Congress' second attempt was the Child Online Protection Act (COPA) (47 U.S.C. § 231). The federal Third Circuit Court of Appeals has declared COPA unconstitutional (*ACLU v. Reno*, 217 F.3d 162; *ACLU v. Ashcroft*, 322 F.3d 240). The Third Circuit's opinion in *American Civil Liberties Union v. Ashcroft* suggested that user-side control, through blocking and filtering software, might be more effective than supply-side control (322 F.3d 240); the Supreme Court agreed that this was a significant factual question, and therefore remanded the case for trial (524 U.S. 656).

Congress has also enacted legislation (the Children's Internet Protection Act, or CIPA) requiring the use of such software by schools and libraries receiving federally subsidized discounted Internet access (47 U.S.C. § 254(h)); CIPA's constitutionality has been upheld by the Supreme Court (*U.S. v. American Library Association*, 539 U.S. 194). In a purely private context, of course, such as a parent's installation of blocking and filtering software on a child's computer, there is no First Amendment issue, because there is no state action.

The current problems with blocking and filtering software are not legal but technical. Blocking and filtering software may operate by allowing access only to an approved list ("whitelist") of sites, or by prohibiting access to sites on a proscribed list ("blacklist"). It may look for digital certificates of sites that comply with certain standards, or search a site for proscribed keywords. The first approach is effective, but extremely restrictive and suitable only for very young children. Serious online research requires access to a large number of Web sites, many of which will not be whitelisted even though their content is utterly innocuous. The blacklist approach presents the flip side of this problem; for a variety of reasons, many sites containing indecent material will be omitted from the blacklist. The proscribed-keyword approach presents both of these problems: like the whitelist approach, it is over-inclusive; like the blacklist approach, it is under-inclusive. It is over-inclusive because keywords used to identify indecent content may appear on almost any Web site as part of otherwise innocuous content; the proscribed words may appear in academic journals, news stories, encyclopedias, dictionaries, judicial opinions, the text of novels or screenplays, and medical advice Web sites. And it is under-inclusive because Web sites may contain indecent images without containing any of the proscribed words; this is especially true of foreign-language sites.

A hybrid approach that holds promise is the creation of a new top-level domain to which pornographic content, although not other indecent content, could be restricted; children's Web browsers could then be set to block this domain. After many years of debate, in 2011, the Internet Corporation for Assigned Names and Numbers (ICANN) approved the ".xxx" sponsored top-level domain (sTLD). The .xxx sTLD is sponsored by the International Foundation for Online Responsibility (IFFOR), an organization devoted to self-regulation of the pornography industry; according to its own Web site, the IFFOR's goals are to:

- Promote user choice, parental control, and the development and adoption of responsible business practices designed to combat online child abuse images.
- Protect free expression rights as defined in the United Nations' Universal Declaration of Human Rights, Article 19.
- Protect the privacy, security, and consumer rights of consenting adult consumers.
- Foster communication among Internet stakeholders (IFFOR 2013).

The actual operation of the .xxx sTLD registry is carried out by ICM Registry LLC, a company created by entrepreneur Stuart Lawley for that purpose. ICM has applied for additional TLDs for the pornography industry, including porn, although at present the .xxx sTLD is far from oversubscribed.

Nor has the existence of the .xxx domain reduced the presence of pornography in other TLDs. There are two reasons for this: first, the pornography industry grew and matured online before the .xxx domain came into existence; there is no incentive for pornographers to abandon profitable Web sites (even to the minimal extent of replacing the content at those sites with a redirect to a .xxx site) and move the content to the .xxx TLD. Second, there is no disincentive to keeping the content where it is now. The goal of keeping pornographic content quarantined in its own area of the Internet could best be accomplished by the legislative imposition of penalties for online pornographic content, combined with a safe harbor provision exempting content on the .xxx sTLD from those penalties. If crafted as a constitutionally acceptable time, place and manner restriction, rather than an unconstitutional outright ban, this would provide the necessary disincentive to leave pornographic content where it is, with a simultaneous incentive—the safe harbor—to move the content to the .xxx sTLD. At the moment, however, Congress seems to lack the political will to enact such legislation.

Some pornographic content would inevitably remain. Other forms of indecency, such as the transcript of Carlin's monologue, would also continue to be available, but there has been little expression of public concern over such a possibility.

The problem of indecent spam (unsolicited bulk-mailed email advertising) is a more difficult one to address. Most providers of indecent content on the Web have no particular wish to make their content available to minors. Spammers, in contrast, are the outlaws of the Web; they know that no email recipient wants to receive their message, and they know that individuals and Internet service providers (ISPs) employ software designed to screen out their messages. They design their messages to be as difficult to screen out as possible, and have no incentive to assist recipients in blocking indecent content. The problem of blocking indecent spam is thus inseparable from the problem of blocking all spam, a problem that has thus far defied both legislative and technical solution.

Statutes
- Child Online Protection Act, 47 U.S.C. § 231
- Children's Internet Protection Act, 47 U.S.C. § 254(h)
- Communications Decency Act of 1996, Pub. L. No. 104–104, § 502, 1996 U.S.S.C.A.N. (110 Stat.) 56, 133 (later codified at 47 U.S.C. § 223)

Cases
Supreme Court
- *Ashcroft v. American Civil Liberties Union*, 524 U.S. 656 (2004)
- *Ashcroft v. Free Speech Coalition*, 535 U.S. 234 (2002)
- *Federal Communications Commission v. Pacifica Foundation*, 438 U.S. 726 (1978)
- *Federal Communications Commission v. Fox TV Stations, Inc.*, 132 S. Ct. 2307 (2012)
- *Miller v. California*, 413 U.S. 15 (1973)
- *Reno v. American Civil Liberties Union*, 521 U.S. 844 (1997)
- *United States v. American Library Association, Inc.*, 539 U.S. 194 (2003)

Federal Appellate Courts
- *CBS Corp. v. Federal Communications Commission*, 663 F.3d 122 (3d Cir. 2011)

Federal Trial Courts
- *Cyber Promotions v. America Online*, 948 F. Supp. 456 (E.D. Pa. 1996)
- *Mainstream Loudoun v. Board of Trustees of the Loudoun County Library*, 2 F. Supp. 2d 783 (E.D. Va. 1998)

See also: Censorship; Child Online Protection Act; Children's Internet Protection Act; Communications Decency Act; Constitutional Law; First Amendment; Obscenity; Pornography; Spam; .xxx

Sources and Further Reading

Jerome A. Barron & C. Thomas Dienes, *Constitutional Law in a Nutshell* (St. Paul, MN: West, 7th ed. 2009)

Tim Elfrink, ".XXX Sites Are Live Thanks to Stuart Lawley, A South Florida Brit Who Beat the Bush Admin," *Miami New Times* (December 8, 2011), available at http://blogs.miaminewtimes.com/riptide/2011/12/xxx_sites_are_live_thanks_to_s.php (visited February 7, 2013)

International Foundation for Online Responsibility (IFFOR), "Overview" (n.d.), http://www.linkedin.com/company/iffor?trk=tabs_biz_home (visited August 26, 2013)

Madeleine Schachter, *Law of Internet Speech* (Durham, NC: Carolina Academic Press, 3d ed. 2008)

Elizabeth H. Steele, "Examining the FCC's Indecency Regulations in Light of Today's Technology," 63 *Federal Communications Law Journal* 289 (2010)

❖ INDUSTRIAL DESIGNS ❖

See TRIPS (Industrial Designs)

❖ INTEGRATED CIRCUIT LAYOUTS ❖

See Semiconductor Manufacturing Mask Work Registrations; TRIPS (Integrated Circuit Layouts)

❖ INTELLECTUAL PROPERTY ❖

The right of originators of intellectual creations to a monopoly on the use and reproduction of their ideas for a certain period of time has acquired the status of a property right under the laws of the United States and of most other countries. All of these property rights in ideas, rather than in tangible objects, are collectively referred to as intellectual property. Intellectual property includes the well-known areas of copyright, patent, and trademark, as well as less well-known areas such as trade secrets and know-how (McCarthy et al. 2004, 308). National governments may create new forms of intellectual property when a new category of ideas does not seem to fit in to any of the existing categories of intellectual property. Two such new categories created by the U.S. government are discussed elsewhere in this encyclopedia: copyright-like protection for semiconductor manufacturing mask work registrations, used in the making of computer chips, and copyright-like protection for vessel hull designs (17 U.S.C. §§ 1301–1332).

The advent of personal computing and the Internet has raised a wide variety of intellectual property issues, and threatened to undermine the existence of intellectual property in some areas. The first of these areas is copyright: the Internet has transformed the formerly staid world of copyright law into a battleground. File-sharing threatens to undermine copyright protection in certain types of works, especially recorded popular music, and to bring about the demise of the music content industry. The content industry in general, and the music content industry in particular, has responded to this threat with lawsuits and lobbying. Copyright protection has been strengthened and extended by statutes such as the Digital Millennium Copyright Act and the Sonny Bono Copyright Term Extension Act (17 U.S.C. §§ 301–304, 512, 1201–1204). Proposed legislation would strengthen copyright protection still further; for example, the controversial (and defeated) Stop Online Piracy Act (SOPA) and Protect Intellectual Property Act (PIPA) would have allowed the government to bring civil suits to enforce the rights of private property holders, as would the later Online Protection and Enforcement of Digital Trade Act (OPEN).

At the same time, the content industry is pursuing technological anti-copying solutions that could potentially tie copies of copyrighted material to a single playback device, and could continue to prevent copying even after the copyright has expired. Many consumers feel that these measures and legislative initiatives such as the SOPA, PIPA, and OPEN go too far; as a result, activists and advocacy groups have brought lawsuits to block enforcement of certain statutes or to challenge certain interpretations of those statutes, and have engaged in lobbying efforts on behalf of consumers (e.g., *Eldred v. Ashcroft*, 537 U.S. 186). Equipment manufacturers, including computer makers, are caught between the two: on the one hand they are the owners of valuable intellectual property in their own right, but on the other hand their business success depends on pleasing consumers, not on pleasing content owners. Enhanced technological protective measures increase the cost and complexity of playback equipment. Consumers prefer simpler and cheaper equipment, even more so if such equipment can also play back and copy a wider range of material.

While battles over copyright issues capture headlines, the Internet has also led to battles in other areas of intellectual property. In the early days of the Internet, cybersquatters registered domain names incorporating well-known trademarks and then tried to sell those domain names to the trademark owners. Congress responded with the Anticybersquatting Consumer Protection Act, restricting the practice and providing for the transfer of the domain names to the trademark holders when trademark holders were targeted by cybersquatters (15 U.S.C. § 1125(d)). In the mid- and late 1990s, metatag trademark infringement also became an issue: In order to improve their ranking on search engine result pages, Web site operators used trademarked terms as metatags, invisible to the person viewing the page but visible to the search engine. Lawsuits established the limits of trademark protection in such cases and prevented the use of infringing metatags (*Playboy*, 279 F.3d 796); changes in search engine technology have brought about a decline in the use of metatags as a search engine optimization tool, but questionable search engine optimization practices involving the use of trademarks persist.

Business methods patents, such as a patent for a one-click ordering system on a retail Web site, have also proved controversial. The Internet has also been used to disclose trade secrets—a secret, once published on the Internet, is secret no more.

Statutes

- Anticybersquatting Consumer Protection Act, 15 U.S.C. § 1125(d)
- Copyright Act of 1976, 17 U.S.C. §§ 101–1332
- Digital Millennium Copyright Act, Pub. L. No. 105–304, 17 U.S.C. §§ 512, 1201–1205
- Lanham Trademark Act, 15 U.S.C. §§ 1051 et seq.
- Patent Act, 35 U.S.C. §§ 1 et seq.
- Sonny Bono Copyright Term Extension Act, amending and codified at 17 U.S.C. §§ 101, 108, 110, 201, 301–304, 512
- Vessel Hull Design Protection Act, codified at 17 U.S.C. §§ 1301–1332

Proposed Legislation

- Intellectual Property Enforcement Act of 2007, S. 2317, 110th Cong. (1st Sess. 2007)
- Protecting Intellectual Rights against Theft and Expropriation (PIRATE) Act of 2004, S. 2237, 108th Cong. (2d Sess. 2004)
- Stop Online Piracy Act, H.R. 3261, 112th Cong. (1st Sess. 2011)
- Preventing Real Online Threats to Economic Creativity and Theft of Intellectual Property (PROTECT IP) Act of 2011, S. 968, 112th Cong. (1st Sess. 2011)

Cases
- *Eldred v. Ashcroft*, 537 U.S. 186 (2002)
- *Playboy Enterprises, Inc. v. Welles*, 279 F.3d 796 (9th Cir. 2002)

See also: Activism and Advocacy Groups; Business Method Patent; Copyright; Cybersquatting; Digital Millennium Copyright Act; Digital Millennium Copyright Act, Title V; File-Sharing; Metatags; Online Protection and Enforcement of Digital Trade Act; Patent; Protect Intellectual Property Act; Search Engine; Semiconductor Manufacturing Mask Work Registrations; Sonny Bono Copyright Term Extension Act; Stop Online Piracy Act; Trademark; Trade Secret

Sources and Further Reading

Ross A. Dannenberg et al., eds., *Computer Games and Virtual Worlds: A New Frontier in Intellectual Property Law* (Chicago: American Bar Association Publishing, 2010)

Michael H. Davis & Arthur Raphael Miller, *Intellectual Property: Patents, Trademarks, and Copyright in a Nutshell* (St. Paul, MN: West, 4th ed. 2007)

Jane C. Ginsburg, "Copyright in the Digital Environment: Restoring the Balance," 35 *Columbia Journal of Law & the Arts* 1 (2011)

Amy L. Landers, *Understanding Patent Law* (New Providence, NJ: LexisNexis, 2d ed. 2012)

Marshall Leaffer, *Understanding Copyright Law* (New Providence, NJ: LexisNexis, 5th ed. 2010)

Courtney G. Lytle, *Skills & Values: Intellectual Property* (New Providence, NJ: LexisNexis, 2011)

J. Thomas McCarthy et al., *McCarthy's Desk Encyclopedia of Intellectual Property* (Washington, D.C.: Bureau of National Affairs, 3d ed. 2004)

Robert P. Merges & Jane C. Ginsburg, *Foundations of Intellectual Property* (New Providence, NJ: LexisNexis, 2006)

Raymond T. Nimmer, *Licensing of Intellectual Property and Other Information Assets* (Newark, NJ: LexisNexis, 2004)

Aaron Schwabach, *Intellectual Property: A Reference Handbook* (Santa Barbara, CA: ABC-CLIO, 2007)

❖ INTERNATIONAL COPYRIGHT PROTECTION ❖

Copyrights are granted and enforced, if at all, by national governments. No international or global copyright exists. However, most of the countries of the world have entered into one or more treaties by which they undertake to protect, within their national boundaries, the copyrights of foreign authors. The principal multilateral copyright agreements to which the United States is a party are the Buenos Aires Convention, the Universal Copyright Convention (U.C.C.), the Berne Convention, the World Intellectual Property Organization (WIPO) Copyright Treaty and the WIPO Performance and Phonograms Convention, the Brussels Satellite Convention, the Geneva Phonograms Convention, and the Agreement on Trade-Related Aspects of Intellectual Property Rights (TRIPS).

From 1891 through 1955, the United States entered into a series of bilateral copyright agreements and one major multilateral agreement, the 1911 Buenos Aires Convention. (An earlier treaty, the Mexico City Convention of 1902, continued to govern U.S. copyright relations with one country, El Salvador, until 1979; other pan-American copyright conventions included the 1889 Montevideo Convention, the 1906 Rio de Janeiro Convention, the 1911 Caracas Agreement, the 1928 Havana Convention, and the 1946 Washington Convention.) The Buenos Aires Convention, to which the United States and 17 Latin American countries are parties, provides that once a work obtains copyright protection in any member nation, copyright protection will be extended by all of the other member nations without requiring further formalities other than a declaration on the work that intellectual property rights are reserved, typically by the word "all rights reserved." These words probably have no legal significance today, but are included on most published copyrighted works through persistence of prior practice. The Buenos Aires Convention has been, in effect, replaced by the U.C.C. and the Berne Convention, as all states now parties to the Buenos Aires Convention are parties to one or both of the later treaties as well.

The U.C.C. came into existence partly because of the need of the United States for a multilateral copyright agreement at a time when the Copyright Act of 1909 was still in force, making it impossible for the United States to become a party to the Berne Convention. Its principal requirement is that countries accord national treatment to foreign copyrighted works; in other words, that they extend to foreign copyright holders and works published in foreign countries the same copyright protections that they extend to works of their own nationals first published in their own territory. In addition, registration requirements for foreign copyright holders for works published outside the contracting state's territory are satisfied by the use of the symbol "©" upon the work together with the year of first publication and the name of the person claiming copyright.

The U.C.C. came into force for the United States in 1955 and went through a major revision in 1971 to take into account certain concerns of developing countries, many of which had not existed as independent nations in 1955. At the insistence of those countries who were already parties to the Berne Convention, the U.C.C. includes a Berne Safeguard Clause, which provides that no country that is a party to the Berne Convention may denounce that convention and choose instead to rely on the U.C.C. in copyright matters relating to other parties to the Berne Convention. Now that the United States and most other U.C.C. parties are also parties to the Berne Convention, the U.C.C. is of declining importance, although it continues to govern copyright matters between the United States and the one country that is a party to the U.C.C. but not to the Berne Convention:

Cambodia. (Another U.C.C. party, Laos, finally became a party to the Berne Convention on March 14, 2012.)

The Berne Convention, administered by WIPO, is the most important international agreement dealing solely with copyright. Since its creation in 1886, it has been revised six times, most recently in 1971; the United States and most other parties are parties to the 1971 revision as amended in 1979.

Like the U.C.C., the Berne Convention requires national treatment. States parties must grant protection to works first published in the territory of other states parties or created by nationals of those states without formalities. This protection must be granted for a minimum of the lifetime of the author plus 50 years or, for anonymously or pseudonymously authored works, for a minimum of 50 years; for cinematographic works, 50 years from the date the work is released to the public; for photographic works or works of applied art, 25 years. The Berne Convention's subject matter categories include "every production in the literary and artistic domain whatever shall be the mode or form of its expression." Enumerated types of subject matter include:

> books, pamphlets and other writings; lectures, addresses, sermons and other works of the same nature; dramatic or dramatico-musical works; choreographic works and entertainments in dumb show; musical compositions with or without words; cinematographic works to which are assimilated works expressed by a process analogous to cinematography; works of drawing, painting, architecture, sculpture, engraving and lithography; photographic works to which are assimilated works expressed by a process analogous to photography; works of applied art; illustrations, maps, plans, sketches and three-dimensional works relative to geography, topography, architecture or science (Berne Convention art. 2(1)).

Note that this may conceivably be less broad than the definition of subject matter protected by the U.S. Copyright Act of 1976: "original works of authorship fixed in any tangible medium of expression" (17 U.S.C. § 102). It may also be more broad, however, in that it contemplates that some countries, unlike the United States, may wish to protect works that are not fixed in a tangible medium of expression.

The Berne Convention also defines the exclusive rights granted to copyright holders in a way similar to, but not entirely coextensive with, the Copyright Act. The important differences are that the Berne Convention does not address distribution and display rights, and U.S. law does not, for the most part, address what are known as moral rights: the right of the author to "integrity" (the right to protect the work from changes that damage the work's or the author's reputation) and "paternity" (the right to be identified as the author of a work and to prevent one's name from being associated with a modified version of the work; also known as the right of attribution). The United States has accorded limited protection of moral rights to some paintings, sculptures, and similar works under the Visual Artists' Rights Act (17 U.S.C. § 106A), but broader recognition of moral rights has not historically been a part of U.S. law. Recognition of moral rights may present constitutional problems as well; it may not be authorized under the Patent and Copyright Clause and in many situations is likely to conflict with the First Amendment.

The international regime of copyright protection includes two WIPO treaties; the United States became a party to both treaties in 2002. The WIPO Copyright Treaty protects computer programs as literary works and protects original compilations of data. It provides a higher level of protection for these and, with some exceptions, for sound recordings. It includes a clause preventing parties from relying on the Berne Convention's lower level of protection for sound recordings. The second WIPO treaty, the WIPO Performance and Phonograms Treaty, provides for protection of the economic and moral rights of performers of "live aural performances or performances fixed in phonograms" (WIPO Performance and Phonograms Treaty art. 5(1)). Title I of the Digital Millennium Copyright Act of 1998 was designed to, among other things, bring U.S. law into compliance with these two treaties. In most respects it does so, but it does not address the issue of moral rights. U.S. law and practice remains significantly out of step with international norms in the area of moral rights.

The Brussels Satellite Convention, ratified by the United States in 1984, prohibits the hijacking of satellite transmission capability. The Geneva Phonograms Convention, in effect for the United States in 1974, provides international protection for sound recordings. A related convention to which the United States is not a party is the 1961 Rome Convention for the Protection of Performers, Producers of Phonograms and Broadcasting Organizations, which protects performance rights in sound recordings.

The agreement on TRIPS is a comprehensive intellectual property treaty; it addresses not only copyright but also patent, trademark, and other areas of intellectual property. TRIPS is Annex 1C to the Marrakesh Agreement Establishing the WTO; it thus stands outside the WIPO treaty framework, but not aloof from or, for the most part, opposed to it. Most of the world's countries are parties to both the WTO-administered TRIPS and the WIPO-administered Berne Convention.

Under TRIPS, members of the WTO agree to comply with the 1971 revision of the Berne Convention; the Convention's main substantive provisions, with the exception of those dealing with moral rights, are incorporated into TRIPS by reference. The Berne Convention definitions determine the subject matter to be protected, the minimum term of protection, the rights to be conferred, and the permissible limitations to those rights. An appendix allows developing countries to make some exceptions under certain conditions. Developing countries are also given a longer period of time to phase in their TRIPS obligations.

TRIPS mandates national treatment and most-favored nation treatment (TRIPS arts. 3–4). Under the requirement of most-favored nation treatment, parties must accord to all other parties the same level of protection that they accord to any one party; no parties can be singled out for favorable or unfavorable treatment. In addition, TRIPS adds enforcement and dispute resolution procedures, and provides that copyright protection shall extend to expressions and not to ideas, procedures, methods of operation, or mathematical concepts. As provided by the 1971 revision to the Berne Convention, computer programs are protected as literary works; TRIPS adds the clarification that the form in which the program is expressed, whether in source or object code, does not affect the protection (TRIPS art. 10). Databases are eligible for copyright protection if, by reason of the selection or arrangement of their contents, they constitute intellectual creations. The data itself, however, is not necessarily protected. Authors of computer programs and, in certain circumstances, of motion pictures are to be provided with the right to authorize or to prohibit the commercial rental of those works, although in the case of motion pictures ("cinematographic works") member states are exempt from the obligation unless motion picture rentals have led to widespread copying that materially impairs the exclusive right of reproduction. The obligation with regard to computer programs does not apply where the program itself is not the essential object of the rental; for example, a member state would probably not be required to provide the holder of the copyright to an onboard navigation program with the exclusive right to authorize a car-rental company to rent cars incorporating the onboard navigation software; it would certainly not be required to provide the holder of the copyright to an automotive diagnostic program incorporated in these same cars with that right.

States parties to TRIPS are required to provide copyright protection for, at a minimum, the duration set by the Berne Convention. TRIPS also requires member states to provide performers of live audio performances with the right to prevent unauthorized broadcasts and audio, but not audiovisual, recordings of their performances. Producers of sound recordings ("phonograms") are to be given the exclusive reproduction and rental rights to those recordings for a minimum term of 50 years, although many states with other protections for these producers in their domestic law will escape this requirement through a grandfather clause. Broadcasting organizations are to be given the right to prevent unauthorized recording of their broadcasts for a minimum term of 20 years, unless such protection is redundant with protections already granted to the holders of the copyright in the broadcasted material (TRIPS art. 14).

Treaties

- Agreement between the World Intellectual Property Organization and the World Trade Organization, December 22, 1995, 35 I.L.M. 754 (1996)
- Agreement on Trade-Related Aspects of Intellectual Property Rights (TRIPS), Marrakesh Agreement Establishing the World Trade Organization, Annex 1C, April 15, 1994, 33 I.L.M. 81 (1994)
- Buenos Aires Convention, August 20, 1910, 38 Stat. 1785, 155 L.N.T.S. 179
- Convention Concerning the Creation of an International Union for the Protection of Literary and Artistic Works (Berne Convention), September 9, 1886, as last revised at Paris, July 24, 1971 (amended 1979), 25 U.S.T. 1341, 828 U.N.T.S. 221
- Convention Establishing the World Intellectual Property Organization, July 14, 1967, as amended on September 28, 1979 (WIPO Convention), 21 U.S.T. 1749, 828 U.N.T.S. 3
- Convention for the Protection of Producers of Phonograms against Unauthorized Duplication of Their Phonograms, October 29, 1971, 25 U.S.T. 309
- Convention Relating to the Distribution of Programme-Carrying Signals Transmitted by Satellite, May 21, 1974, 13 I.L.M. 1444
- International Convention for the Protection of Performers, Producers of Phonograms and Broadcasting Organizations, October 26, 1961, 496 U.N.T.S. 43
- Universal Copyright Convention, September 6, 1952, 6 U.S.T. 2731, revised at Paris July 24, 1971, 25 U.S.T. 1341
- WIPO Copyright Treaty, December 20, 1996, 36 I.L.M. 65 (1997)
- WIPO Performance and Phonograms Treaty, December 20, 1996, 36 I.L.M. 76 (1997)

Statutes

- Copyright Act of 1976, 17 U.S.C. § 102
- Visual Artists' Rights Act, 17 U.S.C. § 106A

European Union Materials

- Directive 93/98/EEC of 29 October 1993 Harmonizing the Term of Protection of Copyright and Certain Related Rights, 1993 O.J. (L 290) 9
- Directive 2006/116/EC of the European Parliament and of the Council of 12 December 2006 on the Term of Protection of Copyright and Certain Related Rights, 2006 O.J. (L 372) 12–18

See also: Berne Convention; Copyright; Copyright Infringement; Digital Millennium Copyright Act, Title I; TRIPS (Copyright); Universal Copyright Convention; WIPO; WIPO Copyright Treaty; WIPO Performance and Phonograms Treaty

Sources and Further Reading

Michael Boardman, "Digital Copyright Protection and Graduated Response: A Global Perspective," 33 *Loyola of Los Angeles International & Comparative Law Review* 223 (2011)

Daniel C. K. Chow, *A Primer on Foreign Investment Enterprises and Protection of Intellectual Property in China* (The Hague: Kluwer Law International, 2002)

Anthony D'Amato & Doris Estelle Long, eds., *International Intellectual Property Anthology* (Cincinnati: Anderson Publishing, 1996)

Mihaly Ficsor, *The Law of Copyright and the Internet: The 1996 WIPO Treaties, Their Interpretation and Implementation* (Oxford: Oxford University Press, 2002)

Paul Goldstein, *International Copyright: Principles, Law, and Practice* (Oxford: Oxford University Press, 3d ed. 2012)

Jennifer Gong, "Defining and Addressing Virtual Property in International Treaties," 17 *Boston University Journal of Science and Technology Law* 101 (2011)

Alfredo Ilardi & Michael Blakeney, eds., *International Encyclopaedia of Intellectual Property Treaties* (Oxford: Oxford University Press, 2004)

"Imitation v. Inspiration: How Poor Countries Can Avoid the Wrongs of Intellectual-Property Rights," *The Economist*, September 14, 2002, at 13, available at http://www.econo mist.com/node/1325360 (visited February 7, 2013)

Pascal Kamina, *Film Copyright in the European Union* (Cambridge, UK: Cambridge University Press, 2002)

Marshall Leaffer, *Understanding Copyright Law* (New Providence, NJ: LexisNexis, 5th ed. 2010)

Marshall Leaffer, "International Copyright from an American Perspective," 43 *Arkansas Law Review* 373 (1990)

Makeen Fouad Makeen, *Copyright in a Global Information Society: The Scope of Copyright Protection under International, US, UK, and French Law* (New York: Aspen, 2001)

Sam Ricketson, *The Berne Convention for the Protection of Literary and Artistic Works: 1886–1986* (London: Centre for Commercial Law Studies, Queen Mary College, 1987)

Aaron Schwabach, "Intellectual Property Piracy: Perception and Reality in China, the United States, and Elsewhere," 2 *Journal of International Media and Entertainment Law* 65 (2007)

Susan K. Sell, *Private Power, Public Law: The Globalization of Intellectual Property Rights* (Cambridge, United Kingdom: Cambridge University Press, 2003)

Deli Yang, *Intellectual Property and Doing Business in China* (Amsterdam: Pergamon, 2003)

❖ INTERNATIONAL FEDERATION OF REPRODUCTION RIGHTS ORGANIZATIONS ❖

Few individual copyright holders possess the resources to detect and pursue violations of their copyrights in their own country, let alone worldwide; nor is it easy for persons wishing to make copies of copyrighted material to track down the author of each individual work. Reproduction rights organizations (RROs) have arisen to serve this function; the RROs track copyright violators and pursue equitable remedies (getting the violators to stop) and legal remedies (collecting damages). They also act as clearinghouses to authorize reproduction of the copyrighted material (IFRRO Introduction, Operation, and History). The International Federation of Reproduction Rights Organizations (IFRRO, not to be confused with IFFOR) is, as its name states, an umbrella organization that unites and coordinates the activities of over 80 RROs and nearly 60 similar organizations (IFRRO Directory 2012).

IFRRO arose to address the problems posed by photocopying of copyrighted materials for internal use by schools, corporations, and other organizations. The licenses granted by IFRRO members are typically for internal institutional use (IFRRO Introduction, Operation, and History); commercial clearinghouse operations serve the same function with regard to large-scale commercial copying and file-sharing. The Internet has posed new problems for IFRRO. An institution might make copies of a copyrighted work available on a Web site intended for internal use, such as a course Web site, that is nonetheless accessible to the broader community of Internet users. The posted materials would be, in effect, posted to the entire world.

IFRRO coordinates the division of royalties involved in international reproduction of copyrighted works, and sets standards for agreements regarding digital reproduction (s IFRRO 1996). It also coordinates its activities with the WIPO and engages in lobbying in the various states in which it has member organizations.

See also: Copyright; International Copyright Protection

Sources and Further Reading

"What is IFRRO?" International Federation of Reproduction Rights Organizations, available at http://www.ifrro.org/ content/what-ifrro (visited August 16, 2012)

"RRO Members," International Federation of Reproduction Rights Organizations, available at http://www.ifrro.org/rro (visited August 16, 2012)

"Collective Management of Digital Rights," International Federation of Reproduction Rights Organizations (October 15, 1996), available at http://www.ifrro.org/issues_list/641/ (visited February 7, 2013)

❖ INTERNATIONAL PATENT PROTECTION ❖

A patent, like a copyright or trademark, is a territorially limited right. Patents are granted by governments, and are valid only within the territory under that government's control. The holder of a patent on a particular device in Country A can bring an action to stop anyone else in Country A from manufacturing the device, but can do nothing to stop someone in Country B from doing so. If the infringer in Country B tries to export the devices to Country A, the patent holder in country A can request that Country A's customs officials confiscate the infringing devices and not allow them to enter Country A. But if the infringer in Country B wishes only to sell the devices in Country B, or wishes to export them to Countries C, D, E, and F, the patent holder in country A has no recourse.

The solution for the patent holder is to patent the device in every country in which it might be manufactured or sold; however, this might well be over a hundred different countries, each with its own legal system and patent application and approval process, speaking 50 different languages. Patenting an invention in more than a handful of countries would probably pose an insurmountable bureaucratic obstacle to most inventors. To address this problem and the related problem of enforcing patents in other countries, several treaties have been adopted, including the Paris Convention for the Protection of Industrial Property, the Patent Cooperation Treaty, the Patent Law Treaty, and the Agreement on Trade-Related Aspects of Intellectual Property Rights (TRIPS).

The Paris Convention, administered by the World Intellectual Property Organization, requires its 174 member states to provide three forms of protection to patent applicants from other member states. First, member states must provide applicants from other member states with "national treatment"; that is, they must accord to applicants from other member states the same rights and protection that they would accord to their own nationals (Paris Convention, art. 2). Second, the Paris Convention requires that each of its members provide certain minimum levels of protection for all patents (Paris Convention, arts. 4*ter*-5*quater*). And third, the convention guarantees inventors a right of priority: an inventor who has filed a patent application in his or her home country, if that country is a party to the convention, will enjoy a right of priority in all other member states for 12 months from the date of that first filing. Should the inventor file a patent application for the same invention in any of the other member states during that 12-month period, the later application will be treated as if it had been filed on the same date as the original application. The right of priority will enable the inventor to prevail even over another person who has filed a patent application in the second country for the same invention, so long as the second person's filing was later than the inventor's original filing.

While the Paris Convention guarantees a certain degree of uniformity of protection, the Patent Cooperation Treaty (PCT) greatly streamlines the multination patent application process. It provides a process by which an inventor can file a patent application simultaneously in any or all of the 146 countries that are parties to the PCT. It does not create a global patent, however, and the mere filing of simultaneous applications does not mean that all of the countries in which the applications are filed will grant the patent (McCarthy et al. 2004, 437–438).

The Patent Law Treaty addresses a long-standing discrepancy between U.S. patent law and the patent law of other countries: U.S. patent law traditionally protected the first person to invent, while other countries' patent laws protect the first person to file a patent application. Attachment to the first-to-invent system has emotional as well as legal and economic roots in the United States; however, the America Invents Act of 2011 will make the United States a first-to-file country as of March 16, 2013, bringing U.S. law and practice more closely in line with the patent laws and practices of the rest of the world.

Instead of the harmonized system of international patent law sought through measures such as the Patent Law Treaty, an enforceable international system has been reached under TRIPS. All of the 157 members of the World Trade Organization are parties to TRIPS, although for some that have joined recently the patent provisions have not yet come into full effect. TRIPS incorporates the basic protections of the Paris Convention and provides for a uniform patent term of 20 years (TRIPS, arts. 2, 33). A substantive provision of TRIPS with direct application to the Internet is found in Article 27, which has been interpreted as requiring WTO members to grant business method patents (Conley 2003, 8).

Treaties

- Agreement on Trade-Related Aspects of Intellectual Property Rights, Marrakesh Agreement Establishing the World Trade Organization, Annex 1C, April 15, 1994, 33 I.L.M. 81 (1994)
- Budapest Treaty on the International Recognition of the Deposit of Microorganisms for the Purposes of Patent Procedure, April 28, 1977, as amended on September 26, 1980, 32 U.S.T. 1241, 1861 U.N.T.S. 361
- Paris Convention for the Protection of Industrial Property, March 20, 1883, as revised at Brussels on December 14, 1900, at Washington on June 2, 1911, at The Hague on November 6, 1925, at London on June 2, 1934, at Lisbon on October 31, 1958, and at Stockholm on July 14, 1967, and as amended on September 28, 1979, 21 U.S.T. 1583, 828 U.N.T.S. 305
- Patent Cooperation Treaty, Washington on June 19, 1970, as amended on September 28, 1979, and as modified on February 3, 1984, and October 3, 2001, 28 U.S.T. 7645, 9 I.L.M. 978 (1970)
- Patent Law Treaty, June 1, 2000, 39 I.L.M. 1047 (2000)
- Strasbourg Agreement Concerning the International Patent Classification, March 24, 1971, as amended September 1979, 26 U.S.T. 1793

Rule

- World Intellectual Property Organization, Regulations under the Patent Cooperation Treaty (PCT) Rule 19.1(a)(iii), available at http://www.wipo.int/pct/en/texts/rules/r19.htm (visited August 16, 2012)

Statute

- Patent Act, Right of Priority, 35 U.S.C. § 119

See also: America Invents Act; Paris Convention; Patent; Patent Cooperation Treaty; TRIPS (Patent); WIPO

Sources and Further Reading

John M. Conley, "The International Law of Business Method Patents," U.S. Patent and Trademark Office Economic Review (October 2003), available at http://www.frbatlanta.org/filelegacydocs/erq403_conley.pdf

Graeme B. Dinwoodie et al., *International and Comparative Patent Law* (Newark, New Jersey: LexisNexis 2002)

Press Release, European Parliament, "Parliament Approves EU Unitary Patent Rules" (December 11, 2012), available at http://www.europarl.europa.eu/news/en/pressroom/content/20121210IPR04506/html/Parliament-approves-EU-unitary-patent-rules (visited February 7, 2013)

Amy L. Landers, *Understanding Patent Law* (New Providence, NJ: LexisNexis, 2d ed. 2012)

J. Thomas McCarthy et al., *McCarthy's Desk Encyclopedia of Intellectual Property* (Washington, D.C.: Bureau of National Affairs, 3d ed. 2004)

Nuno Pires de Carvalho, *The TRIPS Regime of Patent Rights* (The Hague: Kluwer Law International, 3d ed. 2010)

Toshiko Takenaka, "The Best Patent Practice or Mere Compromise? A Review of the Current Draft of the Substantive Patent Law Treaty and a Proposal for a First-to-Invent Exception for Domestic Applicants," 11 *Texas Intellectual Property Law Journal* 259 (2003)

WIPO, "Basic Facts about the Patent Cooperation Treaty" (April 2002), available at http://www.islandpatent.com/learn/BasicFactsPCT_wipo.pdf (visited February 7, 2013)

WIPO, "Direct Filing of PCT Applications with the International Bureau as PCT Receiving Office" (n.d.), PCT, International Patent System, http://www.wipo.int/pct/en/filing/filing.htm#P20_2204 (visited August 16, 2012)

❖ INTERNATIONAL TRADEMARK PROTECTION ❖

A trademark, service mark, or other protected mark is, like all intellectual property rights, territorially limited. In the absence of international agreements to protect trademarks, each trademark would be protected only in the country or countries in which the holders took appropriate steps to secure trademark protection. The holder would then be able to prevent others in those countries from using the trademark, but would be helpless to prevent the use of the mark in other countries. Complying with the trademark laws of all or most of the world's countries would probably be impossibly burdensome for all but the largest corporate mark holders; however, a system of international agreements simplifies the international trademark registration process and guarantees certain universal norms of protection. These treaties include the Paris Convention for the Protection of Industrial Property, the Madrid Arrangement and Protocol, the Trademark Law Treaty, and the Agreement on Trade-Related Aspects of Intellectual Property Rights (TRIPS).

The Paris Convention, administered by the World Intellectual Property Organization (WIPO), requires its 174 member states to provide two forms of protection to trademark holders from other member states. First, member states must accord "national treatment" to each other's nationals; that is, they must accord to nationals of other member states the same rights and protection that they would accord to their own nationals (Paris Convention, art. 2). Second, the Paris Convention requires that each of its members provide

certain minimum levels of protection (Paris Convention, arts. 6–8).

The Madrid Arrangement (also known as the Madrid Agreement), to which the United States is not a party, and the 1989 Madrid Protocol, to which the United States is a party, make it possible for a mark holder to obtain protection in multiple countries without having to register or otherwise apply for protection in each individual country. The Protocol provides a single filing process for trademark protections in all of the member states; only a single application, in a single language, is required, and only a single fee must be paid. The Trademark Law Treaty, to which the United States is also a party, further harmonizes the administrative requirements for obtaining trademark registration, and reduces the cost of the process (McCarthy et al. 2004, 613). And TRIPS brings trademark law within the World Trade Organization's enforcement and dispute resolution framework.

Treaties

- Agreement on Trade-Related Aspects of Intellectual Property Rights (TRIPS), Marrakesh Agreement Establishing the World Trade Organization, Annex 1C, April 15, 1994, 33 I.L.M. 81 (1994)
- Madrid Agreement for the Repression of False or Deceptive Indications of Source on Goods, April 14, 1891, as revised at Washington on June 2, 1911, at The Hague on November 6, 1925, at London on June 2, 1934, and at Lisbon on October 31, 1958, and Additional Act, Stockholm, July 14, 1967, 828 U.N.T.S. 389
- Madrid Agreement Concerning the International Registration of Marks, April 14, 1891, as revised at Brussels, December 14, 1900; at Washington, June 2, 1911; at The Hague, November 6, 1925; at London, June 2, 1934; at Nice, June 15, 1957; at Stockholm, July 14, 1967; and as amended September 28, 1979, available at http://www.wipo.int/madrid/en/legal_texts/ (PDF download) (visited August 16, 2012)
- Nice Agreement Concerning the International Classification of Goods and Services for the Purposes of the Registration of Marks, June 15, 1957, as revised at Stockholm on July 14, 1967, and at Geneva on May 13, 1977, and amended on September 28, 1979, 23 U.S.T. 1336, 550 U.N.T.S. 45
- Protocol Relating to the Madrid Agreement Concerning the International Registration of Marks, June 27, 1989, available at http://www.wipo.int/madrid/en/legal_texts/ (PDF download) (visited August 16, 2012)
- Singapore Treaty on the Law of Trademarks, March 28, 2006, S. Treaty Doc. No. 110–2
- Trademark Law Treaty, October 27, 1994, available at http://www.wipo.int/treaties/en/ip/tlt/trtdocs_wo027.html (visited August 16, 2012)
- Vienna Agreement Establishing an International Classification of the Figurative Elements of Marks,

June 12, 1973 as amended October 1, 1985, available at http://www.wipo.int/treaties/en/classification/vienna/trtdocs_wo031.html (visited August 16, 2012)

Statute
- Lanham Trademark Act, 15 U.S.C. § 1126

See also: Madrid Agreement and Madrid Protocol; Paris Convention; Trademark; TRIPS (Trademark); WIPO

Sources and Further Reading
Anthony D'Amato & Doris Estelle Long, eds., *International Intellectual Property Anthology* (Cincinnati: Anderson Publishing, 1996)
J. Thomas McCarthy et al., *McCarthy's Desk Encyclopedia of Intellectual Property* (Washington, D.C.: Bureau of National Affairs, 3d ed. 2004)

❖ INTERNET ❖

The Internet is a network connecting numerous computers and local networks so that each connected computer can, in theory, send information to and receive information from every other connected computer. The term "Internet" refers to the physical infrastructure—the computers and transmission lines and facilities—and to the communications protocols that make this worldwide interconnection possible. This infrastructure supports a variety of types of information exchange: cloud computing, email and instant messaging, P2P networks, VPNs, the World Wide Web, and a long list of obsolete information exchange technologies from Gopher to Usenet. The term "Internet" is often used, however, to refer to these information exchange technologies, and especially to the World Wide Web (Wagner 1999).

The Internet's ancestry is usually traced to ARPANET, a computer network established by the Advanced Research Projects Agency (ARPA, thus the name) of the U.S. Department of Defense. ARPANET's humble beginning, in 1969, was as a network of four computers at the University of California at Los Angeles, the Stanford Research Institute, the University of California at Santa Barbara, and the University of Utah (Kristula 2001). ARPANET thrived; two years later, in 1971, it connected two dozen computers at 15 sites, including the Massachusetts Institute of Technology (MIT) and Harvard University. Ten years later, by 1981, ARPANET connected over 200 host systems. The first email program was created in 1972, and in 1978 the first mass emailed commercial message was sent over ARPANET, although the term "spam" was not in use at the time. In 1983, an important technological milestone was achieved, as ARPANET switched to TCP/IP networking protocols; inasmuch as the Internet can be said to have originated at any particular moment, the switch to TCP/IP probably marks that moment. In the same year, ARPANET's military

functions were moved to MILNET, and seven years later, in 1990, ARPANET ceased to exist (Computer History Museum 2006).

The demise of ARPANET did not mean the end of the Internet, nor did it mean that the computers formerly connected to ARPANET ceased to be connected to each other. New networks had grown up; among the most historically important of these were NSFNet, established in the 1980s by the National Science Foundation; USENET, or Unix User Network; and BITNET, a multi-university network originating at the City University of New York, and whose acronym was variously explained as standing for "Because It's Time Network" and "Because It's There Network." These networks and many others were linked to each other, making it possible for any computer connected to any one of the networks to communicate, via a sometimes tortuous route, with any computer connected to any of the others. The Internet spread beyond universities, government, and businesses and into private homes during the 1980s with the growth of proprietary networks such as Compuserve, Prodigy, and America Online. In 1989, a company called The World became the first to offer dial-up Internet access to the public.

In 1989 and 1990, Tim Berners-Lee and Robert Cailliau created a system they called ENQUIRE in order to find documents more quickly on computers at CERN, the European Organization for Nuclear Research in Switzerland. In 1990 and 1991, Berners-Lee expanded ENQUIRE into the storage, search, and retrieval tools essential to the operation of the World Wide Web, and created both the first Web page and the first Web browser. The World Wide Web was made accessible to the world, thus living up to its name, in 1992 (Kristula 2001).

In 1988, Jarkko Oikarinen, a Finnish student, had created the first Internet Relay Chat (IRC) program, and various Web browsers appeared during the early 1990s. The early Internet required a degree of technical sophistication to navigate, however; the dramatic expansion of the Internet became possible after Netscape introduced its browser, Netscape Navigator, in 1994, followed by Microsoft's Internet Explorer in 1995 (Cusumano & Yoffe 2000, 5–12). By October of 1993, the number of World Wide Web servers had increased from Berners-Lee's original one to over 200 (CERN 2008). By June of 1994 that number had increased more than tenfold, to 2,738, and it leaped yet another order of magnitude, to 23,500, by June of 1995, and yet again, to 252,000, by June of 1996. As the number of servers and the number of IP addresses per machine increase, the difficulty of making an accurate count increases as well. Growth seemed to level off a bit by the end of the first decade of the twenty-first century, with 620 million sites (with tens or hundreds of billions of pages) by September 2012 (Netcraft 2012).

The growth of the Internet has raised legal issues at almost every stage. The Internet's potential as a vehicle for the infringement of intellectual property rights, especially copyrights, has led to a number of legislative adjustments to copyright laws in the United States and in other countries. The ease with which the Internet provides access to information has led to attempts to censor Internet content and restrict access. The battle for dominance in the market for Internet browsers led to antitrust litigation against Microsoft. The Internet has been used as a vehicle for scams and frauds. And Internet users and the Internet itself have come under repeated attack from viruses, worms, and hackers since the first major Internet worm attack in 1988. The Internet has become an accepted part of life for a large part of the world's population, but society and the legal system are still digesting its implications.

See also: Censorship; Copyright; File-Sharing; Hacking; Microsoft Antitrust Litigation; Net Neutrality; Spam; Virus; Web Browser; World Wide Web

Sources and Further Reading

Andrew Blum, *Tubes: A Journey to the Center of the Internet* (New York: Harper Collins 2012)

John Brockman, ed., *Is the Internet Changing the Way You Think? The Net's Impact on Our Minds and Future* (New York: HarperCollins, 2011)

Computer History Museum, Exhibits: Internet History (2006), available at http://www.computerhistory.org/internet_history/internet_history_90s.html (visited January 11, 2013)

Michael A. Cusumano & David B. Yoffe, *Competing on Internet Time: Lessons from Netscape and Its Battle with Microsoft* (New York: Touchstone, 2000)

Dave Kristula, "The History of the Internet" (n.d.), available at http://www.davesite.com/webstation/net-history.shtml (visited August 16, 2012)

"September 2012 Web Server Survey," Netcraft (September 10, 2012), available at http://news.netcraft.com/archives/2012/09/10/september-2012-web-server-survey.html (visited February 7, 2013)

Sherry Turkle, *Alone Together: Why We Expect More from Technology and Less from Each Other* (New York: Basic Books, 2012)

Ronald L. Wagner, *Road Runner Guide to Cyberspace* (Herndon, VA: Citapei Communications, 9th ed. 1999)

"Welcome to info.cern.ch: The Website of the World's First-Ever Web Server," CERN (2008), available at http://info.cern.ch/ (visited February 7, 2013)

Robert H. Zakon, "Hobbes' Internet Timeline v10.2," available at http://www.zakon.org/robert/Internet/timeline/ (visited February 7, 2013)

❖ INTERNET CORPORATION FOR ASSIGNED NAMES AND NUMBERS ❖

As the Internet grew in the 1990s from an academic network to a global medium, some form of governance became necessary to ensure that the various sites and servers remained connected and accessible. In particular, some uniform way of allotting Internet addresses and domain names was needed. In the early and mid-1990s, this function was carried out by relatively informal organizations such as the Internet Engineering Task Force. In 1998, at the time that the Internet Corporation for Assigned Names and Numbers (ICANN) was created, the function of assigning addresses and domain names was performed by the Internet Assigned Numbers Authority (IANA), the project of Dr. Jon Postel at the University of Southern California (Palfrey 2004, 419). Since 1995, Network Solutions Inc. had been in charge of registering domain names within the popular ".com," ".net," and ".org" top-level domains (Gilwit 2003, 271).

Dr. Postel died in October 1998. In November 1998, representatives of IANA reached an agreement with the U.S. Department of Commerce under which a new entity, ICANN, took over the functions of IANA, as well as other functions relating to the operation of the Internet. ICANN was incorporated as a nonprofit organization under the laws of California; its guiding documents were its Articles of Incorporation and the Memorandum of Understanding between ICANN and the Department of Commerce (Palfrey 2004, 420–421).

In an industry that has grown as rapidly and as chaotically as the Internet information industry, it is not surprising that there has been controversy, and that ICANN has frequently found itself embroiled in controversy; in fact, it is perhaps more surprising that ICANN has survived. Much of this controversy has centered on the issue of representation. Paragraph II.C.4 of the Memorandum of Understanding, under the heading "Representation," declares that:

> This Agreement promotes the technical management of the DNS in a manner that reflects the global and functional diversity of Internet users and their needs. This Agreement is intended to promote the design, development, and testing of mechanisms to solicit public input, both domestic and international, into a private-sector decision making process. These mechanisms will promote the flexibility needed to adapt to changes in the composition of the Internet user community and their needs (Memorandum of Understanding 1998).

Although ICANN has maintained its commitment to transparency, openness, and public representation, the scale of the Internet has altered so dramatically since its inception that

> [w]hereas one representative used to have a constituency of 100, now he or she has a constituency of hundreds of millions (in the case of North America), or even billions of people (in the case of Asia). Similarly, openness—particularly in the sense of transparency—becomes harder with scale, as not all decisions can be made by a small group of directors and officers in front of the world at large (Palfrey 2004, 425).

ICANN's structure has undergone changes over the years, with the U.S. Department of Commerce gradually privatizing many of the functions of Internet administration while retaining oversight over some crucial operations (Joint Project Agreement 2006) and retaining control of the authoritative root zone file, which allows the resolution of textual URLs to IP addresses. Today ICANN continues, amid controversy, to administer the top-level domain name system. Top-level domains are the parts of a domain name that appear after the last dot in the URL, such as ".com," and ".gov." (generic top-level domains, or gTLDs), ".de," and ".uk." (country-code top-level domains), and others. It authorizes new top-level domains, and authorizes private registrars to assign domain names to within some of those top-level domains (ICANN Welcome 2012; ICANN-Information for Registrars and Registrants 2012). Country-code top-level domains are delegated in accordance with the wishes of the national governments concerned (ICANN 1999); other TLDs can involve commercial concerns, and controversy can arise as a result. In 2012, ICANN unveiled over 1,400 new gTLDs, triggering a land rush among those seeking to run the new gTLD registries, and many complaints of unfairness in the allocation of these registries (*Dot dash* 2012).

The ICANN also performs a dispute resolution function: under its Uniform Domain Name Dispute Resolution Policy it resolves disputes regarding rights to domain names (ICANN Welcome 2012).

Not everyone is happy with a system in which the Internet is administered by an organization with links to the U.S. government, however. Almost from its outset, ICANN has been beset by attempts to either pry it loose from its U.S. government connections or pry the Internet loose from ICANN's control (such as it is). In recent years, one form this has taken is a proposed UN convention to wrest many of ICANN's administrative functions away and assign them to a non-U.S. body such as the International Telecommunications Union (ITU) (*U.S. and UK Refuse to Sign* 2012). During the World Conference on International Telecommunications (WCIT) in December 2012, only 89 of 144 countries signed a proposed treaty that would have granted the ITU more power to control the Internet. In a unanimous vote in December 2012 the U.S. House of Representatives adopted a resolution reaffirming its unwillingness to give the ITU control over the Internet (H. Con. Res. 127).

Congressional Resolution
- H. Con. Res. 127, 112th Cong. (2011–13)

ICANN Governing Documents
- Affirmation of Commitments by the United States Department of Commerce and the Internet Corporation for Assigned Names and Numbers, U.S.-ICANN (September 30, 2009), available at http://www.icann.org/en/news/announcements/announcement-30sep09-en.htm (visited February 7, 2013)
- *Articles of Incorporation of Internet Corporation for Assigned Names and Numbers*, ICANN, available at http://www.icann.org/general/articles.htm (visited February 7, 2013)
- *Bylaws for Internet Corporation for Assigned Names and Numbers, a California Nonprofit Public-Benefit*

Corporation: As amended 13 October 2003, available at http://www.icann.org/general/archive-bylaws/bylaws-13oct03.htm (visited February 7, 2013)
- Joint Project Agreement between the U.S. Department of Commerce and the Internet Corporation for Assigned Names and Numbers, U.S.-ICANN, September 26, 2006, Approved Resolution 06.71, available at http://www.ntia.doc.gov/files/ntia/publications/signedmou290906.pdf (visited February 7, 2013)
- Memorandum of Understanding between the U.S. Department of Commerce and the Internet Corporation for Assigned Names and Numbers, November 1998, available at http://www.icann.org/general/icann-mou-25nov98.htm (visited February 7, 2013)

See also: Cybersquatting; Domain Name Registration; Internet; World Wide Web; .xxx

Sources and Further Reading
Stuart Biegel, *Beyond Our Control? Confronting the Limits of Our Legal System in the Age of Cyberspace* (Cambridge, MA: MIT Press, 2001)

David P. Fidler, "Internet Governance and International Law: The Controversy concerning Revision of the International Telecommunication Regulations," *ASIL Insights* (February 7, 2013), available at http://www.asil.org/pdfs/insights/insight130207.pdf

A. Michael Froomkin, "Almost Free: An Analysis of ICANN's Affirmation of Commitments," 9 *Journal on Telecommunications and High Technology Law* 187 (2011)

A. Michael Froomkin, "Wrong Turn in Cyberspace: Using ICANN to Route around the APA and the Constitution," 50 *Duke Law Journal* 17 (2000)

Dara B. Gilwit, "The Latest Cybersquatting Trend: Typosquatters, Their Changing Tactics, and How to Prevent Public Deception and Trademark Infringement," 11 *Washington University Journal of Law and Policy* 267 (2003)

"ICANN and Top Level Domains: Dot Dash," *The Economist*, June 16, 2012, at 76

"ICANN CEO Talks about the New Affirmation of Commitments," ICANN (September 30, 2009), available at http://www.icann.org/en/news/announcements/announcement-30sep09-en.htm (visited February 7, 2013)

"ICANN's Major Agreements and Related Reports," ICANN (2013), available at http://www.icann.org/en/about/agreements (visited August 26, 2013)

Information for Registrars and Registrants, ICANN (2013), available at http://www.icann.org/en/resources/registrars (visited August 26, 2013)

"Internet Domain Name System Structure and Delegation (ccTLD Administration and Delegation)," ICANN (May 1999), available at http://www.icann.org/icp/icp-1.htm (visited February 7, 2013)

"Internet Domain Names: Combat," *The Economist*, June 2, 2012, at 73

"Internet Governance: System Error," *The Economist*, December 1, 2012, at 67

Christopher T. Marsden, ed., *Regulating the Global Information Society* (New York: Routledge, 2000)

Milton Mueller, *Ruling the Root: Internet Governance and the Taming of Cyberspace* (Cambridge, MA: MIT Press, 2002)

John Palfrey, "The End of the Experiment: How ICANN's Foray into Global Internet Democracy Failed," 17 *Harvard Journal of Law & Technology* 409 (2004)

Patricia Paoletta & Peter McElligott, "Perspectives—U.S. and European Union Stay United in Opposition to ITU Efforts to Change Internet Governance," The European Institute (2012), available at http://www.europeaninstitute.org/EA-December-2012/patricia-paolette-and-peter-mcelligott.html (visited January 10 2013)

Amy Thomas, "UN Telecom Treaty Approved amid U.S. Web-Censorship Concerns," Bloomberg (December 14, 2012), available at http://www.bloomberg.com/news/2012–12–13/u-s-and-u-k-refuse-to-sign-un-agreement-on-telecommunications.html (visited February 7, 2013)

"U.S. and UK Refuse to Sign UN's Communications Treaty," BBC News (December 14, 2012), available at http://www.bbc.co.uk/news/technology-20717774 (visited February 7, 2013)

Jonathan Weinberg, "Governments, Privatization, and "Privatization": ICANN and the GAC," 18 *Michigan Telecommunications & Technology Law Review* 189 (2011)

"Welcome to ICANN," ICANN (2012), available at http://www.icann.org/en/about/welcome (visited December 17, 2012)

"World v. Web: America Does Not Want the United Nations to Run the Internet," *The Economist*, November 20, 2004, at 65

❖ INTERNET SERVICE PROVIDERS ❖

An Internet service provider (ISP) is, in the broadest sense, any company or organization that provides Internet services. The term ISP is generally used more narrowly, however, to refer to companies that provide Internet access and transmission, email, and Web hosting services. Specialized service providers such as search engines are generally discussed separately.

Telecommunications and cable television companies may also function as Internet service providers (ISPs). There are also companies that exist solely or primarily to provide Internet access, such as America Online; these are a subgroup in their own right, sometimes referred to as online service providers or OSPs.

ISPs, in addition to confronting the same legal problems confronted by any business, face two categories of problems unique to the business of providing Internet services. The first of these is the so-called battle for the last mile, often pitting ISPs against each other and against federal regulators in the struggle to gain subscribers and improve infrastructure. The second problem is inherent in the business of providing Internet services; ISPs transmit and store enormous amounts of information, beyond the capacity of any person or organization to scrutinize; inevitably, some of this information violates intellectual property rights, censorship laws, or other laws.

The last mile: ISPs provide Internet access to their subscribers in a variety of ways: home subscribers may connect through dial-up modem connections, cable modem broadband connections, wireless broadband connections, and use of new or existing phone lines as Digital Subscriber Line (DSL) connections. Business subscribers, and a few home subscribers, may opt for costlier direct high-speed, high-bandwidth connections. Legal disputes have arisen over the allocation and required sharing of infrastructure, particularly in the area of broadband access (access at a speed of 512,000 bits per second or higher) through cable and DSL lines. The Federal Communications Commission (FCC) treats cable and telephone lines differently for regulatory purposes, although from the consumer's point of view the two offer similar levels of service. Cable modem services have done better in the marketplace, so far, and the FCC has been blamed for the relative underperformance of the DSL sector (Hundt 2004, 239). The FCC provides different regulatory structures for three different categories of information transmission services: information services, cable services, and telecommunications services. In the context of the Internet and ISPs, however, the categories are so arbitrary as to be nearly meaningless. From the consumer's point of view, either a cable or a telecommunications connection is also an Internet connection; and the function of the Internet is to provide information, communication, and entertainment.

Internet service providers and unlawful content: ISPs deal in information; billions of users continually transmit enormous quantities of information around the globe, and this information passes over the networks and through the servers of the ISPs. Some of this information is illegal; some of it may infringe upon the intellectual property rights of others or may defame others; other information may be inherently illegal because it is part of a criminal act or transaction or because it violates censorship laws. There is no way for the ISPs to police all of the content stored on and passing through their systems; if they were required to do so, they would be unable to operate, and the Internet would collapse. In order to prevent this, laws have been created to protect ISPs from liability and prosecution in cases where they are innocent of any wrongful intent—that is, cases in which information merely passes through or is stored upon the ISPs system without the ISP being aware of the content.

Internet service providers and content that infringes copyright: Title II of the Digital Millennium Copyright Act (DMCA) was enacted in 1998 to shield ISPs from liability for copyright infringement by creating four safe harbors: the transitory communications safe harbor, the system caching safe harbor, the information storage safe harbor, and the information location tools safe harbor. Compliance with the terms of these safe harbors will shield an ISP from awards of damages and from most forms of injunctive relief (17 U.S.C. § 512(j)).

The transitory communications safe harbor shields a service provider from liability where the provider merely acts as a conduit, transmitting digital information from one point on a network to another at someone else's request. Five elements must be present for a service provider to avail itself of the transitory communications safe harbor: the transmission must be "initiated by or at the direction of a person other than the SP"; it must be "carried out through an automatic technical process without selection of the material by the" service provider; the service provider must "not select the recipients of the material except as an automatic response to the request of another person"; the service provider must not maintain a copy of the material "in a manner ordinarily accessible to anyone other than anticipated recipients" or "for a longer period than is reasonably necessary"; and the material must be transmitted "without modification of its content" (17 U.S.C. § 512(a)).

The system caching safe harbor shields a service provider from liability where the provider makes a copy of material for system caching purposes. In order for a service provider to be eligible for the system caching safe harbor, the material must be "made available online by a person other than the service provider"; it must be transmitted from that person to another person at the direction of the second person; and the caching "must be carried out through an automatic technical process for the purpose of making the material available to users of the system or network who . . . request access" (17 U.S.C. § 512(b)). In addition, the ISP must not modify the retained material, must periodically refresh it, and must not interfere with technology that returns hit information to the person who posted the material. Finally, the system caching safe harbor includes a notice and takedown provision: once the service provider has been notified that copyrighted material posted without authorization has been removed or blocked, or ordered to be removed or blocked, at the original site, the service provider must promptly remove or block access to the cached copy. If the person who posted the material has imposed limitations on access, such as password protection, the ISP must also impose these limitations (17 U.S.C. § 512(b)(2)).

The information storage safe harbor shields a service provider from liability where the service provider stores information at the direction of a user. The information storage safe harbor will then protect the ISP if it does not have actual or constructive knowledge that the content is infringing, and upon acquiring such knowledge acts "expeditiously to remove, or disable access to, the material" (17 U.S.C. § 512(c)). However, the information storage safe harbor is not available to a service provider that "does not receive a financial benefit directly attributable to the infringing activity, in a case in which the service provider has the right and ability to control such activity" (17 U.S.C. § 512(c)(1)(B)). This exception, drawn from the rule established by the federal courts for determining vicarious copyright infringement, rules out the use of this safe harbor by online file-sharing services, other than perhaps nonprofit enthusiast services (see *Fonovisa*, 76 F.3d 259).

The information storage safe harbor also includes a notice and takedown provision: in order to receive the benefit of the safe harbor, the ISP must "upon notification of claimed infringement" respond "expeditiously to remove, or disable access to, the material that is claimed to be infringing or to be the subject of infringing activity" (17 U.S.C. § 512(c)(1)(C)). The notice and takedown procedure has potential for abuse; it can be used maliciously to block access to innocent Web sites. The DMCA seeks to reduce the potential for abuses by setting forth detailed requirements for the "notice" portion of the notice and takedown process:

> (3) Elements of notification.—
>
> (A) To be effective under this subsection, a notification of claimed infringement must be a written communication provided to the designated agent of a service provider that includes substantially the following:
> (i) A physical or electronic signature of a person authorized to act on behalf of the owner of an exclusive right that is allegedly infringed.
> (ii) Identification of the copyrighted work claimed to have been infringed, or, if multiple copyrighted works at a single online site are covered by a single notification, a representative list of such works at that site.
> (iii) Identification of the material that is claimed to be infringing or to be the subject of infringing activity and that is to be removed or access to which is to be disabled, and information reasonably sufficient to permit the service provider to locate the material.
> (iv) Information reasonably sufficient to permit the service provider to contact the complaining party, such as an address, telephone number, and, if available, an electronic mail address at which the complaining party may be contacted.
> (v) A statement that the complaining party has a good faith belief that use of the material in the manner complained of is not authorized by the copyright owner, its agent, or the law.
> (vi) A statement that the information in the notification is accurate, and under penalty of perjury, that the complaining party is authorized to act on behalf of the owner of an exclusive right that is allegedly infringed (17 U.S.C. § 512(c)(3)(A)).

The protection of § 512(c)(3)(A) is not perfect, of course; a malicious person could still submit a false notification, complete with false contact information, and escape undetected. To protect innocent Web site operators from such actions, the DMCA also provides penalties for misrepresentation (17 U.S.C. § 512(f); see also *Lenz*, 527 F. Supp. 1150) and a procedure for counter-notification:

> *Contents of counter notification.*—
> To be effective under this subsection, a counter notification must be a written communication provided to the service provider's designated agent that includes substantially the following:
>
> (A) A physical or electronic signature of the subscriber.
> (B) Identification of the material that has been removed or to which access has been disabled and the location at which the material appeared before it was removed or access to it was disabled.
> (C) A statement under penalty of perjury that the subscriber has a good faith belief that the material was removed or

disabled as a result of mistake or misidentification of the material to be removed or disabled.

(D) The subscriber's name, address, and telephone number, and a statement that the subscriber consents to the jurisdiction of Federal District Court for the judicial district in which the address is located, or if the subscriber's address is outside of the United States, for any judicial district in which the service provider may be found, and that the subscriber will accept service of process from the person who provided notification under subsection (c)(1)(C) or an agent of such person (17 U.S.C. § 512(g)(3)).

The notification process is thus simpler for the Web site operator than for the copyright owner, perhaps because only one person—the Web site owner—is likely to file the counter-notification; other persons have nothing to gain by doing so maliciously or as a prank. Once the counter-notification is received, the ISP must restore the removed or blocked material within not less than 10 and not more than 14 business days, unless the copyright owner or other person alleging copyright infringement notifies the ISP that it has "filed an action seeking a court order to restrain the subscriber from engaging in infringing activity relating to the material on the service provider's system or network" (17 U.S.C. § 512(g)(2)(c)). This provision helps to protect the rights of Web site operators; in addition, a notice that fails to comply with the provisions of § 512(c)(3)(A) in any way has no effect on the rights of the ISP. In other words, if a copyright owner informs the ISP that a particular Web site contains infringing content, but fails to include any of the required elements of the notice—a signature, for example— the ISP has no duty to act; it can safely ignore the notice and continue to claim the protection of the safe harbor.

The information location tools safe harbor is designed with search engines, Internet portals, and similar services in mind, rather than the broader category of ISPs generally. Its provisions are substantially similar to those of § 512(c) (the information storage safe harbor).

Internet service providers and trademark law: Trademark law contains no safe harbor for ISPs along the lines of that provided for copyright violations under the DMCA; trademark is a much riskier area for ISPs than copyright is. Congress once attempted to provide a safe harbor for ISPs from liability for any content that they innocently transmitted or stored: 47 U.S.C. § 230(c)(1) provides that "no provider or user of an interactive computer service shall be treated as the publisher or speaker of any information provided by another information content provider." However, § 230(c)(1) seems to provide no protection from liability for trademark infringement; indeed, if it did, its safe harbor would be so broad that the four DMCA safe harbors would have been unnecessary. 47 U.S.C. § 230(e)(2) further provides that "[n]othing in this section shall be construed to limit or expand any law pertaining to intellectual property." A federal district court has held that § 230(e)(2) prevents the use of § 230(c)(1) as a defense to trademark infringement (*Gucci*, 135 F. Supp. 2d 409).

The exposure of ISPs to liability for trademark infringement is potentially vast; any Web site or Internet communication might contain trademark-infringing content. The protection of ISPs from trademark infringement liability must rely on traditional doctrines of trademark law, however, particularly the innocent infringer defense. Ordinarily the ISP should not be held liable until it has had notice of the alleged infringement and an opportunity to act upon it, but the law in this area remains in flux (Walsh 2004).

Internet service providers and tortious speech: A tort, to lawyers, is an injury that entitles the victim to receive some form of legal remedy from a person causing the injury. Tortious speech includes defamation, traditionally divided into libel (written defamation) and slander (spoken defamation), as well as injurious falsehood, false light, publicizing of private facts, and appropriation of another's name or likeness. Just as some of the content posted or transmitted on the Internet inevitably infringes on intellectual property rights, some of it is inevitably defamatory or otherwise tortious. The speech component of these torts must be "published"—communicated to someone other than the speaker and the person spoken about. Many tortious statements are published on the Internet; the question for ISPs then becomes whether they can be held liable as publishers for statements made over their networks or on their servers.

47 U.S.C. § 230(c)(1) protects ISPs from liability as publishers, for the most part; under § 230(c)(1), ISPs are not "treated as the publisher or speaker of any information provided by another information content provider." In the most celebrated harmful-speech case to date, *Zeran v. America Online*, Section 230(c)(1) was applied to shield an ISP from liability. Kenneth Zeran, the plaintiff in the case, had been the victim of a malicious prank committed using the services of America Online (AOL), an ISP. In 1995, a week after the bombing of the Alfred P. Murrah Federal Building in Oklahoma City, an unidentified person posted a message on an AOL bulletin board advertising T-shirts with tasteless slogans relating to the bombing; among the milder examples was "Visit Oklahoma—It's a Blast!" The message instructed interested persons to call "Ken" at Zeran's home telephone number; not surprisingly, Zeran received numerous angry and insulting calls and some death threats. Zeran relied on his telephone number for a business he ran from his home, and could not change it without losing a significant amount of business; instead he called AOL and asked AOL to remove the notice and print a retraction. AOL said that it would remove the notice, although the parties disagreed as to the date on which this was done; AOL refused, as a matter of policy, to print a retraction. Over the next several days, another person or persons, using the name KenZZ03, posted many similar messages; Zeran called AOL repeatedly and was told that the individual account from which the messages were posted would soon be closed. By April 30, five days after the first message, Zeran was receiving an abusive phone call approximately every two minutes; on May

1, an announcer for Oklahoma City radio station KRXO was apparently taken in by the hoax and read the first AOL posting on the air. The announcer urged listeners to call "Ken," and the calls intensified; Zeran requested and received protection from the Seattle police. Two weeks later, by May 14, after an Oklahoma City newspaper published a story exposing the shirt advertisements as a hoax and after KRXO made an on-air apology, the number of calls subsided to 15 per day (*Zeran,* 129 F.3d at 329).

Zeran, not surprisingly, sued AOL for defamation. He lost; under Section 230, the case was not even a close one. The trial court granted AOL judgment on the pleadings; there was no need for a trial, since even if all of the facts were as alleged by Zeran, the law would entitle him to no relief against AOL. The Fourth Circuit Court of Appeals affirmed the trial court's decision. From the point of view of ISPs, the decision is beneficial; the defamation in *Zeran* and its effects were about as bad as they possibly could be, yet the ISP was immune from suit under § 230. From the point of view of individuals, the result is a bit unsettling; what happened to Kenneth Zeran could happen to anyone. Even a person without enemies could become the target of such an attack; the person making the statements might have picked Zeran's name, or some other name, out of a telephone book. Congress has apparently decided, however, that the potential harm to the development of the Internet from forcing ISPs to undertake the probably impossible task of policing Internet content for possible defamation outweighs the potential for harm to individuals through defamation.

Internet service providers and criminal speech: Some Internet content is illegal, either in its own right (such as child pornography) or because it is part of a crime (such as the crime of conspiracy). Different governments ban different speech, yet speech posted on or transmitted through ISPs may be received anywhere in the world. Internet content is thus potentially subject to the law of every jurisdiction on the planet. Within the United States, ISPs are broadly protected under § 230. However, content that is legal in the United States may be illegal elsewhere, even in countries that share many of their legal, political, and cultural values with the United States. In France, for example, advertising Nazi artifacts and memorabilia for sale is illegal; the U.S. ISP Yahoo! has found itself in violation of French law for postings originating in the United States, where they are legal, but accessible in France, where they are not (*Yahoo,* 433 F.3d 1199). Although U.S. courts are likely to continue to refuse to enforce such judgments, U.S. ISPs with assets in other countries may have to modify their behavior to conform to the laws of those countries, or risk the seizure of those assets in satisfaction of judgments.

Internet service providers and privacy: One of the most valuable services an ISP can offer its customers is privacy; most, perhaps all, Internet users would prefer their Internet activities to remain private. Some concerns have been raised over the use of information by ISPs; ISPs could potentially sell user information for marketing purposes and may allow government agencies access to confidential user information. While in these areas the interests of the ISPs may be opposed to those of the users, more frequently the interests of the ISPs and their subscribers are aligned, as when an outside party attempts to compel the ISP to disclose information about a user.

The DMCA provides a subpoena process by which content owners seeking to enforce copyrights may obtain subpoenas to compel ISPs to disclose the identities of subscribers (17 U.S.C. § 512(h)). The subpoenas thus obtained require no judicial oversight; this streamlined subpoena process is aimed at file-sharing, the biggest single threat to music (and, to a lesser extent, movie and e-book) copyright interests. Its use has been significantly restricted by the courts, protecting the interests of both ISPs and users against the interests of the content industry. In 2003, the Recording Industry Association of America (RIAA) had obtained a § 512(h) subpoena requiring Verizon Internet Services to turn over the name of a subscriber who had allegedly shared copyrighted music files, and Verizon refused to comply. The federal appellate court for the District of Columbia held that Verizon did not have to comply with the subpoena; Verizon was a conduit ISP, rather than a hosting ISP; it served only to transmit the shared music files, rather than to store them for access by other users. The D.C. Circuit's holding appears to limit the use of § 512(h) subpoenas to a small number of cases (see also *Viacom,* 676 F.3d 19).

Statutes

- Communications Decency Act (immunity) of 1996, 47 U.S.C. § 230
- Digital Millennium Copyright Act, 17 U.S.C. § 512
- Telecommunications Act of 1996, 47 U.S.C. §§ 151 et seq.

Cases

Supreme Court

- *American Civil Liberties Union v. Reno,* 929 F. Supp.824 (E.D. Pa. 1996); affirmed sub nom *Reno v. American Civil Liberties Union,* 521 U.S. 844 (1997)

Federal Appellate Courts

- *AT&T Corporation v. City of Portland,* 216 F.3d 871 (9th Cir. 2000)
- *Brand X Internet Services v. FCC,* 345 F.3d 1120 (9th Cir. 2003), reversed and remanded sub nom, *National Cable & Telecommunications Association v. Brand X Internet Services,* 545 U.S. 967 (2005)
- *Fonovisa, Inc. v. Cherry Auction, Inc.,* 76 F.3d 259 (9th Cir. 1996)
- *Name.Space, Inc. v. Network Solutions, Inc.,* 202 F.3d 573 (2d Cir. 2000)
- *Playboy Enterprises Inc. v. Netscape Communications Corp.,* 354 F.3d 1020 (9th Cir. 2004)

- *Playboy Enterprises, Inc. v. Welles,* 279 F.3d 796 (9th Cir. 2002)
- *Recording Industry Association of America, Inc. v. Verizon Internet Services,* 351 F.3d 1229 (D.C. Cir. 2003), certiorari denied, 543 U.S. 924 (2004)
- *Universal Communication Systems, Inc. v. Lycos, Inc.,* 478 F.3d 413 (1st Cir. 2007)
- *Time Warner Telecom, Inc. v. FCC,* 507 F.3d 205 (3d Cir. 2007)
- *Viacom International, Inc. v. YouTube, Inc.,* 676 F.3d 19 (2d Cir. 2012)
- *Yahoo! Inc. v. La Ligue Contre Le Racisme et L'Antisemitisme,* 433 F.3d 1199 (9th Cir. 2006), reversed and remanded, *Yahoo! Inc. v. La Ligue Contre Le Racisme et L'Antisemitisme,* 379 F.3d 1120 (9th Cir. 2004), rehearing, 433 F.3d 1199 (9th Cir. 2006), certiorari denied, 547 U.S. 1163 (2006)
- *Zeran v. America Online, Inc.,* 129 F.3d 327 (4th Cir. 1997)

Federal Trial Courts
- *Ford Motor Co. v. Greatdomains.com, Inc.,* No. 00-CV-71544-DT, 2001 WL 1176319 (E.D. Mich. 2001)
- *Gucci America, Inc. v. Hall & Associates,* 135 F. Supp. 2d 409 (S.D.N.Y. 2001)
- *Lenz v. Universal Music Corp.,* 572 F. Supp. 2d 1150 (N.D. Cal. 2008)
- *Perfect 10, Inc. v. Cybernet Ventures, Inc.,* 213 F. Supp. 2d 1146 (C.D. Cal. 2002)

Agency Decision
- *In re Inquiry Concerning High-Speed Access to the Internet over Cable and Other Facilities,* 17 F.C.C. Rcd. 4798, 2002 WL 407567 (2002)

See also: Broadband; Cable; Censorship; Child Pornography; Cloud; Communications Decency Act; Copyright; Copyright Alert System; Copyright Infringement; Data Mining; Digital Millennium Copyright Act, Title II; Federal Communications Commission; File-Sharing; File-Sharing and the Courts (Attempts to Control Technology); File-Sharing and the Courts (Litigation against Individual Users); File-Sharing (Other Media); French Yahoo! Case; Metatags; Net Neutrality; Search Engines; Social Networking Service; Stop Online Piracy Act; Trademark Dilution; Trademark Infringement

Sources and Further Reading

Timothy D. Casey, *ISP Liability Survival Guide: Strategies for Managing Copyright, Spam, Cache, and Privacy Regulations* (New York: John Wiley & Sons, 2000)

Scott Cleland, *Search & Destroy: Why You Can't Trust Google Inc.* (St. Louis, MI: Telescope Books, 2011)

Cherie Dawson, "Creating Borders on the Internet: Free Speech, the United States, and International Jurisdiction," 44 *Virginia Journal of International Law* 637 (2004)

Julieta Andrea Grinffiel, "Don't Shoot the Messenger: Civil Liability for ISPs after Virginia da Cunha v. Yahoo! Argentina & Google Inc.," 17 *Law & Business Review of the Americas* 111 (2011)

Jennifer L. Hanley, "ISP Liability and Safe Harbor Provisions: Implications of Evolving International Law for the Approach Set out in Viacom v. Youtube," 11 *Journal of International Business & Law* 183 (2012)

Reed Hundt, "The Ineluctable Modality of Broadband," 21 *Yale Journal on Regulation* 239 (2004)

Mark A. Lemley & Lawrence Lessig, "The End of End-to-End: Preserving the Architecture of the Internet in the Broadband Era," 48 *UCLA Law Review* 925 (2001)

William Patry, *How to Fix Copyright* (Oxford, United Kingdom: Oxford University Press, 2011)

Alfred C. Yen, "Internet Service Provider Liability for Subscriber Copyright Infringement, Enterprise Liability, and the First Amendment," 88 *Georgetown Law Journal* 1833 (2000)

❖ IPHONE ❖

See Mobile Device

❖ JUNK EMAIL ❖

See Spam

❖ JURISDICTION ❖

Even in the absence of the Internet it is possible for an act in one state or country to have legally significant consequences in another. But the advent of the Internet makes multiple-jurisdiction transactions the norm rather than the exception. In very little time, and with no review of the laws of the various jurisdictions involved, a person located in Canada can order goods from a company in New York via a server located in California; the server might belong to an Internet service provider incorporated in Delaware but with its principal place of business in Virginia. The order might be paid for with a credit card issued by a bank in South Dakota, and result in goods being shipped by a third party located in Illinois to a fourth party located in Singapore. If disputes arise from the transaction, any or all of the states and countries involved might conceivably have jurisdiction over the matter.

When the territorial jurisdiction of state courts of the United States is at issue, the first question that must be addressed is the reach of the state's long-arm statute. A long-arm statute is a state law that permits that state's courts to exercise jurisdiction over parties outside the state. If the long-arm statute, by its own terms, permits jurisdiction over the out-of-state party, the next step is to determine whether the long-arm statute's reach exceeds what is constitutionally permissible.

The territorial jurisdiction of a court may be either general or specific. A person who is subject to the general jurisdiction of a forum (that is, a court or other dispute-resolution body) may be compelled to defend any action in that forum, even if the action is unrelated to the defendant's contacts with the forum state. Nonresidents are only subject to the general jurisdiction of a forum if they have contacts that are sufficiently systematic and continuous that they might reasonably anticipate being required to defend an action in that forum. In other words, people who live in a state are subject to the general jurisdiction of that state's courts, as are other people closely connected to that state.

Problems are more likely to arise with specific jurisdiction. The U.S. Supreme Court established in *International Shoe v. Washington* that specific jurisdiction exists over a nonresident defendant only if that defendant has "certain minimum contacts with [the forum], such that the maintenance of the suit does not offend 'traditional notions of fair play and substantial justice.'" This "minimum contacts" standard requires that a defendant purposefully avail himself or herself of the privilege of conducting activities in the forum. Because the jurisdiction thus created is specific, not general, the suit against the defendant must arise from his or her activities in or related to the forum. Finally, in order to comport with traditional notions of fair play and substantial justice, the exercise of jurisdiction must be reasonable (326 U.S. 310).

Thus, among the states of the United States, there are certain universally agreed upon and constitutionally mandated concepts regarding the territorial jurisdiction of courts. Among the nations of the world, however, there is no such universal agreement. The variability of national standards means that online activity may subject a person to the jurisdiction of the courts of a country in which he or she has never set foot, and with which he or she has not established anything approaching the minimum contacts of *International Shoe*.

The 2002 case of *Gutnick v. Dow Jones & Co.*, in which an Australian court found it had jurisdiction over a U.S. defendant without a business presence in Australia, created alarm among online businesses. Gutnick, an Australian businessman living in Australia, alleged that he had been defamed by an article published in print and online by *Barron's*, a business journal, in New Jersey. Only five copies of the print edition reached Australia; however, the online edition was as accessible from Australia as from anywhere else. The High Court of Australia viewed the act of "publication" as not a single act (as in U.S. law) but two—being published and being received. Because the publication was received in Australia and (allegedly) caused its harm there, the Australian court had jurisdiction over the non-Australian defendant.

Gutnick was greeted with alarm by businesspeople and commentators, who saw the decision as opening the door to potentially limitless lawsuits; anything that might be actionable under the law of some jurisdiction somewhere might, if that jurisdiction adopted a similarly broad view of territorial jurisdiction, result in lawsuits the defendants would be ill-equipped to defend. The *Gutnick* court itself downplayed this possibility:

> [T]he spectre which Dow Jones sought to conjure up in the present appeal, of a publisher forced to consider every article it publishes on the World Wide Web against the defamation laws of every country from Afghanistan to Zimbabwe is seen to be unreal when it is recalled that in all except the most unusual of cases, identifying the person about whom material is to be published will readily identify the defamation law to which that person may resort (*Gutnick*, para. 54).

Subsequent events have proven the court at least partially correct. The decade since, *Gutnick* has not seen the once-feared explosion of litigation. Problems of territorial jurisdiction involving multiple nations have grown more complex, but *Gutnick*-like excesses remain rare. But while the problem may not be as drastic as it could have been, it is not nonexistent either. Dow Jones ultimately paid Gutnick the nontrivial sum of $580,000 (Australian dollars; about $443,500 U.S. at the time) to settle the action (Cooper 2005; *Dow Jones Settles* 2004).

The bizarre prosecution of Joseph Weiler raised some alarm as well. Weiler's problems began when Thomas Weigend, a German professor living in Germany, wrote (in Germany, but in English) an unfavorable review of a book by Dr. Karine Calvo-Goller, a French citizen living in Israel. The review was published on GlobalLawBooks.org, a Web site associated with the *European Journal of International Law* and hosted on a U.S. server, edited by South African-born U.S. professor Joseph Weiler. Although Weiler had taught in France in the past, there was no nexus between France and Weiler's allegedly defamatory publication of Weigend's review, although of course the Web site could be accessed from France. The French court declined jurisdiction and awarded Weiler €8,000 "to compensate the harm caused by her abuse of process" (*Public Prosecutor v. Weiler*). While *Public Prosecutor v. Weiler* provides a welcome sanity check after Gutnick, there are still some worrisome aspects. First, this was a criminal case; it was theoretically possible for Weiler to have ended up facing jail time. And the lengthy proceedings meant that Weiler and his employer were put to significant expense—probably more than the €8,000 awarded—to defend the action, which dragged on for four years, no doubt causing considerable stress and loss of productivity as well.

In contrast, the ongoing effort of the U.S. Department of Justice to obtain the extradition of Megaupload founder Kim Dotcom from New Zealand shows the difficulty a country may have in protecting its interests from online activities originating beyond its borders. Mr. Dotcom, a German citizen residing in New Zealand, was accused by the United States of enabling online piracy worth over $500 million, an act that is a crime in New Zealand as well. For the time being, Mr. Dotcom remains in New Zealand, awaiting an April 2014 extradition hearing while appealing a decision in favor of the U.S. extradition attempt to the New Zealand Supreme Court (*Dotcom Fight* 2013; *Megaupload Case* 2012).

Meanwhile, the possibility of Web postings leading to travelers being arrested while changing planes at another country's airport remains. The imprisonment in 2012 of Google Brazil president Fabio Jose Silva Coelho for refusing to take down a YouTube video after a Brazilian court ruled that it slandered a political candidate did not raise this concern, as Mr. Silva Coelho—a Brazilian living and working in Brazil—was already subject to the Brazilian court's jurisdiction. However, criminal charges filed in Italy in 2006 against other Google executives were more alarming: in response to the popularity of a highly offensive YouTube video of the bullying of an autistic child, Italian prosecutors filed charges for criminal defamation and invasion of privacy against Google marketing executive Arvind Desikan, chief legal officer David Drummond, chief privacy attorney Peter Fleischer, and chief financial officer George Reyes. None of the four defendants were Italian citizens or residents, or even physically present in Italy at the time charges were filed. Jurisdiction could be based only on the nationality of the victim. Nonetheless, the defendants traveled to Italy to defend themselves in court, and in 2010, three of the four were convicted; Desikan was acquitted (Hill 2012). Even when convictions in a foreign country do not lead to immediate imprisonment, they are not purely symbolic, and may have severe consequences. The convict must exercise care when traveling, not only to the country in which the conviction was obtained, but to any other country that might extradite the convict to the convicting country. And the convict's future employment options may be limited; many employment opportunities require convictions to be reported at the application stage, and attorneys must report convictions to their bar associations (and may face disciplinary action as a result).

Fortunately, for the future of the Internet, the convictions were overturned on appeal in 2012 (Castonguay 2012). However, the possibility of Web administrators facing criminal prosecution in other countries as a result of content posted on Web sites they administer remains. The legal systems of Australia, Brazil, and Italy do not create normative expectations wildly different from the U.S. norm; indeed, in the case of Australia, the legal system and resultant expectations are about as similar to those in the United States as might be found anywhere in the world. The legal systems of other countries with far more divergent ideas of what is tortious or criminal may only now be awakening to the possibility of exercising jurisdiction over foreign Web administrators. The disastrously idiotic YouTube video *Innocence of Muslims* led to riots around the world, with dozens of deaths; Google blocked the video in many countries, while in others, national governments blocked YouTube altogether. While the video has not yet led to charges against any Google employees, a court following the same chain of logic, or illogic, as the Italian trial court in the 2010 case might reach a similar result—with a more severe sentence, as deaths have resulted.

Cases

Australia
- *Gutnick v. Dow Jones & Co.*, [2002] H.C.A. 56 (Austl.), available at http://www.austlii.edu.au/cgi-bin/sinodisp/au/cases/cth/HCA/2002/56.html?stem=0&synonyms=0&query=dow%20jones (visited February 8, 2013)

France
- Tribunal de Grand Instance de Paris [TGI], [ordinary court of jurisdiction] Paris, Mar. 3, 2011, Case No. 0718523043 (Fr.) (*Public Prosecutor v. Weiler*), English translation available at http://www.ejiltalk.org/wp-content/uploads/2011/03/Public-Prosecutor-v-Weiler-judgement-March-3–2011–3.pdf (visited December 18, 2012)

Italy
- Tribunale Ordinario di Milano (Ordinary Tribunal of Milan) April 12, 2010, Case No. 1972/2010 (It.), available at http://www.giurcost.org/casi_scelti/Google.pdf (visited January 12, 2013)
- Trib. Ordinario di Milano, February 24, 2010, Sentenza n. 1972/2010 (It.)

Supreme Court
- *International Shoe v. Washington*, 326 U.S. 310 (1945)

Federal Appellate Court
- *Cybersell, Inc. v. Cybersell, Inc.*, 130 F.3d 414 (9th Cir. 1997)

See also: Censorship; Choice of Law; Cloud; Defamation; French Yahoo! Case; Piracy; Recognition and Enforcement of Judgments

Sources and Further Reading

Giles Castonguay, "Court Quashes Convictions in Google Video Case," *Wall Street Journal* (December 21, 2012), available at http://online.wsj.com/article/SB10001424127887324461604578193093685872724.html (visited January 28, 2013)

Kevin M. Clermont, *Civil Procedure: Territorial Jurisdiction and Venue* (New York: Foundation Press, 1999)

Blake Cooper, "The U.S. Libel Law Conundrum and the Necessity of Defensive Corporate Measures in Lessening International Internet Libel Liability," 21 *Connecticut Journal of International Law* 127 (2005)

George B. Delta & Jeffrey H. Matsuura, *Law of Internet* (New York: Aspen Publishers, 2d ed. 2001)

"Dotcom Fight Set to Reach Highest Court," Stuff (March 2, 2013), available at http://www.stuff.co.nz/national/8372108/Dotcom-extradition-fight-set-to-reach-highest-court (visited April 29, 2013)

"Dow Jones Settles Gutnick Action," ABC News (November 12, 2004), available at http://www.abc.net.au/news/2004–11–12/dow-jones-settles-gutnick-action/584404 (visited February 8, 2013)

Peter Fleischer, "My Italian Appeal, Peter Fleischer: Privacy . . . ?" (December 6, 2012), available at http://peterfleischer.blogspot.com/ (visited January 28, 2013)

"Google Brazil to Take Down Controversial Brazil Video," BBC News (September 28, 2012), available at http://www.bbc.co.uk/news/world-latin-america-19753158 (visited February 8, 2013)

John O. Haley, *Fundamentals of Transnational Litigation: The United States, Canada, Japan, and the European Union* (New Providence, New Jersey: LexisNexis 2012)

Noah C.N. Hampson, "The Internet Is Not a Lawless Prairie: Data Protection and Privacy in Italy," 34 *Boston College International & Comparative Law Review* 477 (2011)

Kashmir Hill, "The Downside of Being a Google Executive," *Forbes* (September 27, 2012), available at http://www.forbes.com/sites/kashmirhill/2012/09/27/the-downside-of-being-a-google-executive/ (visited January 28, 2013)

Jeralyn, "Dueling Briefs Filed in Megaupload Case," TalkLeft: The Politics of Crime (May 10, 2013), available at http://www.talkleft.com/story/2013/5/10/52233/2140/foreignaffairs/Dueling-Briefs-Filed-in-Megaupload-Case (visited May 13, 2013)

"Megaupload Case: New Zealand Court Wants FBI Evidence," BBC News (August 16, 2012), available at http://www.bbc.co.uk/news/technology-19280898 (visited February 8, 2013)

Erin F. Norris, "Why the Internet Isn't Special: Restoring Predictability to Personal Jurisdiction," 53 *Arizona Law Review* 1013 (2011)

Tracie E. Wandell, "Geolocation and Jurisdiction: From Purposeful Availment to Avoidance and Targeting on the Internet," 16 *Journal of Technology Law & Policy* 275 (2011)

"The World Is What You Make It—Every Country Has Its Own Internet," *The Economist*, Special Report: Technology and Geography, October 27, 2012, at 20

Vittorio Zambardino, "Il Garante Privacy sulla sentenza di Milano: 'E' sbagliata, ma ora bisogna fare regole *non censorie*," La Repubblica, April 16, 2010, available at http://www.itespresso.it/il-garante-privacy-difende-in-parte-google-dalla-sentenza-di-milano-44937.html (visited August 28, 2013)

Jonathan L. Zittrain, *Jurisdiction* (New York: Foundation Press, 2005)

❖ LAST MILE ❖

See Broadband

❖ LIBRARIES ❖

See Children's Internet Protection Act

❖ LIKELIHOOD OF CONFUSION ❖

See Trademark Infringement

❖ LINKEDIN ❖

See Social Networking Service

❖ LINUX ❖

See Open Source

❖ LIVEJOURNAL ❖

See Social Networking Service

❖ LOOK AND FEEL ❖

Computer programs and Web sites interact with users through a graphical user interface (GUI). The look and feel of a program or a Web site are often distinctive. The "look" consists of the site's or program's graphics, fonts, colors, and so forth. The "feel" describes the way in which buttons, menus, links, dialog boxes, and the like, help the user navigate the site or use the program. A user who is familiar with one program or site may be reluctant to switch to another, even one that is better at performing the same functions, if the new site is unfamiliar. There is thus an incentive

for developers of new software and new sites to copy the look and feel of popular existing programs and sites, whose owners have turned to two areas of intellectual property law to protect what they see as their rights in the look and feel of those programs and sites: copyright and trade dress.

Copyrightability of look and feel: Copyright protects the expression of ideas rather than the underlying ideas themselves; when an idea can be expressed only in a very limited number of ways, those means of expression are not copyrightable. The copyrightability of look and feel has thus depended on whether a program or Web site looks and feels the way it does because there are only a few possible ways for it to look and feel, or whether it looks and feels the way it does because that look and feel is one of many possible expressions and reflects the designer's originality (see Terry 1994, 144). In the early days of personal computing, look and feel litigation was a major battleground, culminating in the dispute between Apple and Microsoft over Windows, which looks and feels a lot like Apple's operating system for the Macintosh.

In 1985, Apple and Microsoft had reached an agreement regarding the development of Windows, but the agreement fell apart after Microsoft granted Hewlett-Packard (HP) a license to use Windows to develop HP's New Wave software desktop. The release of New Wave and Windows 2.03 in 1988 led to more than six years of litigation between Apple and Microsoft, culminating in a decision by the Ninth Circuit Court of Appeals (Cole 1995).

In *Apple v. Microsoft*, the Ninth Circuit affirmed the district court's opinion, in which the district court had used a two-step analysis for finding copyright infringement. The first step of the test (the "extrinsic test") was to compare the disputed works and to determine if, according to an objective standard, they were substantially similar. If they were, the second step (the "intrinsic test") was to apply a subjective standard to only the copyrightable elements of the work, in order to determine whether "the similarity of the works in suit stems solely from unprotectible [*sic*] features" (*Apple Computer*, 799 F. Supp. at 1020). Under this test, for example, two children's software programs might each employ a "Print" button without either infringing upon the other. One button might be shaped like a rabbit, and the other like a flower; each might have the word "Print" across the button. The use of a Print button and the use of the word "Print" to identify it are substantially similar, and meet the requirements of the extrinsic test. However, both are methods of operation and thus not copyrightable; there are few if any other practical ways to make it easy for a user to print from the program. The shapes of the buttons may well be copyrightable, but they are not at all similar; they fail the intrinsic test, and thus there is no infringement.

In the year following the Ninth Circuit's 1994 decision in *Apple*, the First Circuit, in a decision later affirmed by the Supreme Court, declared that the menu command hierarchy of a computer program was not copyrightable. This was seen as another blow to the copyrightability of look and feel (*Lotus Development*, 49 F.3d 807).

Look and feel as trade dress: Even as *Apple* and *Lotus* seemed to herald the decline of look and feel suits for computer software, the World Wide Web was growing and creating new ground for look and feel lawsuits. Popular Web sites, like popular programs, have a particular look and feel, and if that look and feel cannot be protected by copyright, perhaps it may be protected as trade dress. Trade dress is a form of trademark protection that protects the "total image and overall appearance of a product" (*Two Pesos*, 505 U.S. at 764–765, n. 1). The Restatement (Third) of Unfair Competition describes trade dress as the "manner in which the goods or services are presented to prospective purchasers[.]" Once trade dress has acquired significance as an identifier of the source of goods and images offered for sale, it functions as a trademark (Restatement § 16, comment a). The interface of a Web site such as Google or Amazon may well serve the requisite identifying function and thus be protectable as trade dress.

There are problems with the use of trade dress law to protect Web site designs, however. One is that the appearance of a Web site on a user's screen is the result of not only the Web design, but also the interaction of the site with the user's computer or mobile device and browser. Not all users use the same device or browser, and even two users of the same browser, running on the same device, at the same connection speed, may have chosen quite different display settings; as a result, they may see the same Web site differently (Nguyen 2000, 1250–1252). Another is that Web sites constantly change their appearance, although in many cases the changes may not be significant enough to affect the look and feel of the site. For example, the text and images on the news Web site www.cnn.com change several times a day, but the look and feel of the site have remained unchanged for years. Finally, just as methods of operation are not copyrightable, purely functional elements of the presentation of a product or service are not eligible for trade dress protection. "Print this screen" buttons and similar functional Web site elements are no more eligible for trade dress protection than they are for copyright protection. Attorneys advise clients on how to avoid possible trade dress infringement, and scholars speculate as to how the novel trade dress issues raised by Web sites might be resolved, but at present

possible trade dress infringement of Web site designs is an issue more anticipated than litigated (see Nguyen 2000, 1244). However, the look and feel of the video game Tetris have been successfully defended against imitators (Tetris Holding, 2012 U.S. Dist. LEXIS 74463), and a look and feel argument (along with the patent claims) was central to the long-running dispute between Apple and Samsung, which ultimately came to include dozens of lawsuits in at least 10 countries.

Statutes
- Copyright Act of 1976, 17 U.S.C. §§ 101–105
- Lanham Trademark Act, 15 U.S.C. § 1125

Cases
Supreme Court
- *Lotus Development Corp. v. Borland International, Inc.*, 49 F.3d 807 (1st Cir. 1995), affirmed, 516 U.S. 233 (1996)
- *Two Pesos, Inc. v. Taco Cabana, Inc.*, 505 U.S. 763 (1992)

Federal Appellate Court
- *Apple Computer, Inc. v. Microsoft Corp.*, 799 F. Supp. 1006 (N.D. Cal. 1992), affirmed, 35 F.3d 1435 (9th Cir. 1994)

Federal Trial Court
- *Apple Inc. v. Samsung Electronics Co. Ltd.*, No.: 12-CV-00630-LHK (N.D. Cal. Order Granting Motion for Preliminary Injunction June 19, 2012)
- *Tetris Holding, LLC v. Xio Interactive, Inc.*, 2012 U.S. Dist. LEXIS 74463 (D.N.J. May 30, 2012)

Australia
- *Apple Inc. v. Samsung Electronics Ltd. Co.* (No. 2) 2012 FCA 1358 (Austl.), available at http://www.judgments .fedcourt.gov.au/judgments/Judgments/fca/ single/2012/2012fca1358 (visited January 12, 2013)

France
- Tribunal De Grand Instance de Paris [TGI], [ordinary court of jurisdiction] Paris, Case No. 11/10464, December 8, 2011 (Fr.) (*Samsung Electronics Co. Ltd and Samsung Electronics France v. Apple France et al.*), English translation available at http://www.eplawpatentblog.com/2011/ December/2011–12–08_Samsung_Apple_comments .pdf (visited January 12, 2013)

Italy
- Tribunale di Milano (Milan first-instance court) (preliminary proceedings) December 8, 2011, Docket No. 11/58301 (It.) (*Samsung Electronics Italia s.p.a v. Apple Inc.*)

Japan
- Tōkyō Chihō Saibansho [Tokyo District Court] August 31, 2012, Case No. 2011 (Yo) No. 22027 (Japan) (*Japan Samsung Electronics Co., Ltd v. Apple Japan, Inc.*)

Republic of Korea
- Seoul Central District Court Decision, Case No. 2011 Kahap 39552, August 24, 2012 (S. Kor.) (*Samsung Electronics Co., Ltd. v. Apple Korea Ltd.*)

United Kingdom
- *Samsung Electronics Co., Ltd v. Apple Retail UK et al.* [2012] EWHC 1882 (Pat) (U.K.) available at http://www.judiciary.gov.uk/Resources/JCO/Documents/Judgments/samsung-apple.pdf (visited January 12, 2013)

See also: Business Method Patents; Copyright; Copyright Infringement; Menu Command Hierarchy; Trademark; Trademark Infringement

Sources and Further Reading

"Apple v. Samsung: iPhone, uCopy, iSue," *The Economist,* September 1, 2012, at 12

Lisa M. Byerly, "Look and Feel Protection of Web Site User Interfaces: Copyright or Trade Dress?" 14 *Santa Clara Computer and High Technology Law Journal* 221 (1998)

Rodger R. Cole, "Substantial Similarity in the Ninth Circuit: A 'Virtually Identical' 'Look and Feel'?" 11 *Santa Clara Computer and High Technology Law Journal* 417 (1995)

Lauren Fisher Kellner, "Trade Dress Protection for Computer User Interface 'Look and Feel'," 61 *University of Chicago Law Review* 1011 (1994)

George Likourezos, "Trademark Law in the Computer Age: Applying Trademark Principles to the 'Look and Feel' of Software," 77 *Journal of the Patent and Trademark Office Society* 451 (1995)

Josh Lowensohn, "Apple-Samsung Trial: The End Is Nigh," C/Net (August 17, 2012), available at http://news.cnet.com/8301–13579_3–57495807–37/apple-samsung-trial-the-end-is-nigh/ (visited February 8, 2013)

Xuan-Thao N. Nguyen, "Should It Be a Free for All? The Challenge of Extending Trade Dress Protection to the Look and Feel of Web Sites in the Evolving Internet," 49 *American University Law Review* 1233 (2000)

Steven Schortgen, "'Dressing' Up Software Interface Protection: The Application of Two Pesos to 'Look and Feel,'" 80 *Cornell Law Review* 158 (1994)

Nicolas P. Terry, "GUI Wars: The Windows Litigation and the Continuing Decline of 'Look and Feel,'" 47 *Arkansas Law Review* 93 (1994)

❖ MACROVISION ❖

Rovi Corporation, previously known as Macrovision Corporation, is a software company specializing in copy protection and digital rights management software. The term "Macrovision" is often used, however, to refer to a particular Rovi product: a technique to prevent analog copying of video recordings. The Macrovision copy protection is remarkable because it can prevent analog copying of either an analog or a digital recording, thus closing the "analog hole" in most digital rights management systems. It does this by sending a signal that manipulates the automatic gain control and automatic tracking control features built in to most videocassette recorders (VCRs); in Rovi's own words, this causes the "VCRs to make distorted copies, devoid of entertainment value" (Macrovision 2003, 2). VCRs without automatic gain and tracking control are unaffected, however. To address this problem, Congress included a requirement in Section 1201(k) of the Digital Millennium Copyright Act (DMCA) that VCRs made in or imported to the United States after April 26, 2002, must contain automatic gain control, and thus be vulnerable to Macrovision's copy protection:

(k) Certain Analog Devices and Certain Technological Measures –

(1) Certain analog devices –

(A) Effective 18 months after the date of the enactment of this chapter, no person shall manufacture, import, offer to the public, provide or otherwise traffic in any –

(i) VHS format analog video cassette recorder unless such recorder conforms to the automatic gain control copy control technology;

(ii) 8 mm format analog video cassette camcorder unless such camcorder conforms to the automatic gain control technology;

(iii) Beta format analog video cassette recorder, unless such recorder conforms to the automatic gain control copy control technology, except that this requirement shall not apply until there are 1,000 Beta format analog video cassette recorders sold in the United States in any one calendar year after the date of the enactment of this chapter;

(iv) 8mm format analog video cassette recorder that is not an analog video cassette camcorder, unless such recorder conforms to the automatic gain control copy control technology, except that this requirement shall not apply until there are 20,000 such recorders sold in the United States in any one calendar year after the date of the enactment of this chapter; or

(v) analog video cassette recorder that records using an NTSC format video input and that is not otherwise covered under clauses (i) through (iv), unless such device conforms to the automatic gain control copy control technology.

(B) Effective on the date of the enactment of this chapter, no person shall manufacture, import, offer to the public, provide or otherwise traffic in—

(i) any VHS format analog video cassette recorder or any 8mm format analog video cassette recorder if the design of the model of such recorder has been modified after such date of enactment so that a model of recorder that previously conformed to the automatic gain control copy control technology no longer conforms to such technology; or

(ii) any VHS format analog video cassette recorder, or any 8mm format analog video cassette recorder that is not an 8mm analog video cassette camcorder, if the design of the model of such recorder has been modified after such date of enactment so that a model of recorder that previously conformed to the four-line colorstripe copy control technology no longer conforms to such technology. Manufacturers that have not previously manufactured or sold a VHS format analog video cassette recorder, or an 8mm format analog cassette recorder, shall be required to conform to the four-line colorstripe copy control technology in the initial model of any such recorder manufactured after the date of the enactment of this chapter, and thereafter to continue conforming to the four-line colorstripe copy control technology. For purposes of this subparagraph, an analog video cassette recorder "conforms to" the four-line colorstripe copy control technology if it records a signal that, when played back by the playback function of that recorder in the normal viewing mode, exhibits, on a reference display device, a display containing distracting visible lines through portions of the viewable picture.

The statute was aimed primarily at VHS recorders, as the VHS format was the market leader, and at 8-mm analog camcorders for the same reason. But other formats were also included, in case equipment manufacturers might try to circumvent the intent of the statute by reviving the Betamax format or bringing in some other analog format.

Section 1301(k) and Macrovision have been criticized for infringing on fair use. Apologists for the DMCA's anti-circumvention provisions had pointed out that, although individual users were prohibited from making digital copies of protected works, they could still make analog copies for fair use purposes such as space-shifting—recording the work onto a different medium in order to play it on a different device. Because of its simplicity, Macrovision can be circumvented fairly easily through the use of devices to disable the VCR's automatic gain control or to filter out the manipulating information sent by the playback device. Rovi Corporation owns patents not only on its copyright protection software, but also on many means of circumventing it; as a result, such devices usually disappear from the market as soon as Rovi discovers them (see, e.g., *Macrovision Wins Preliminary Injunction* 2004).

With the obsolescence of analog video recording, first Macrovision Corporation and then Rovi have turned their attention to copy protection of digital recordings, creating RipGuard and CopyBlock to increase the difficulty of copying DVDs. However, copy protection technology now forms only a small part of Rovi's business.

Statute
- Digital Millennium Copyright Act, 17 U.S.C. §§ 1201(c)(3), 1201(k)

Case
- *Recording Industry Association of America v. Diamond Multimedia Systems, Inc.*, 180 F.3d 1072 (9th Cir. 1999)

See also: Analog Recording; Copyright; Copyright Infringement; Digital Millennium Copyright Act, Title I; Digital Rights Management; Fair Use

Sources and Further Reading
"Content Protection," Rovi Corp. (2012), available at http://www.rovicorp.com/products/distribution/content-protection.htm (visited February 8, 2013)

"Macrovision Wins Preliminary Injunction against 321 Studios in Patent and Copyright Infringement Lawsuit," Macrovision Press Release (May 20, 2004), available at http://www.realwire.com/releases/macrovision-wins-preliminary-injunction-against-321-studios-in-patent-and-copyright-infringement-law (visited August 19, 2012)

"What Is Macrovision?" DVD Buying Guide (2010), available at http://www.dvdbuyingguide.com/codefreedvd/tip6.html (visited February 8, 2013)Macrovision Corporation, *Preserving an Effective DVD Copy Protection System* (Mar. 3, 2003), available at http://www.macrovision.com/pdfs/Preserving-an-effective-DVD-Copying-System_0303.pdf (visited October 21, 2004; archived copy visited August 25, 2013)

❖ MADRID AGREEMENT AND MADRID PROTOCOL ❖

The Madrid Agreement Concerning the International Registration of Marks (Madrid Agreement), originally adopted in 1891, sets up the Madrid Union, an international system for the registration of trademarks and other marks. The United States, however, is not a party, nor are several other major manufacturers and exporters of trademarked goods, including Japan, Korea, Sweden, and the United Kingdom. All of these countries, including the United States, have since become parties to the Madrid Union under the Protocol Relating to the Madrid Agreement Concerning the International Registration of Marks (Madrid Protocol), originally adopted in 1989. Eighty-eight countries and the European Community are now parties to the Madrid Union via the Madrid Agreement, the Madrid Protocol, or both; the United States became a party in November 2003. The countries of Latin America are conspicuous by their absence. In 2003, the Madrid Protocol adopted Spanish as a third official language, in addition to French and English, in the hope of encouraging Latin American countries to join (Hines 2004). This hope has been in part fulfilled: Colombia became a party in August 2012 and Mexico in February 2013 (Cuba, a party to the Agreement since 1989, has also been a party to the Protocol since 1995). The Madrid Agreement, despite its name, has only French as its official language (Madrid Agreement art. 17).

The one country that is party to the Agreement but not the Protocol (Algeria) and the 32 countries that are parties to the Protocol but not the Agreement, plus the European Union, are nonetheless all parties to the Union (Madrid Protocol art. 1; Madrid Agreement art. 1).

Under the Madrid Protocol, persons who wish to seek protection for a trademark or other mark in any or all of the Madrid Union's member countries may do so with a single application (in English, Spanish, or French) at any office authorized to accept applications for protection in a member state; the U.S. parties, for example, may do so with the U.S. Patent and Trademark Office (Madrid Protocol arts 2–3). States that are parties only to the Agreement, in contrast, must file a registration of the mark in French with the World Intellectual Property Organization (Madrid Agreement art. 2). The Madrid Protocol, unlike the Agreement, also permits international registration as soon as an application is filed in the home country, rather than after the registration is granted in the home country (McCarthy et al. 2004, 360). After a mark has been registered for five years, the Protocol also allows the international protection to remain valid even if the home country registration lapses; after five years, the international registration becomes independent of the home country registration (Madrid Protocol art. 6).

Treaties
- Madrid Agreement Concerning the International Registration of Marks, April 14, 1891, as revised at Brussels, December 14, 1900; at Washington, June 2, 1911; at the Hague, November 6, 1925; at London, June 2, 1934; at Nice, June 15, 1957; at Stockholm, July 14, 1967; and as amended September 28, 1979, available at http://www.wipo.int/madrid/en/legal_texts/ (PDF download) (visited August 20, 2012)
- Protocol Relating to the Madrid Agreement Concerning the International Registration of Marks, June 27, 1989, available at http://www.wipo.int/madrid/en/legal_texts/ (PDF download) (visited August 20, 2012)

See also: International Trademark Protection; Paris
Convention; Trademark; TRIPS; WIPO

Sources and Further Reading
P. Jay Hines, "The Year That Was: Madrid Protocol Milestones
in 2003," Oblon, Spivak, McClelland, Maier & Neustadt,
P.C. (July 2004), available at http://www.oblon.com/
publications/year-was-madrid-protocol-milestones-2003
(visited February 8, 2013)
J. Thomas McCarthy et al., *McCarthy's Desk Encyclopedia of Intellectual Property* (Washington, D.C.: Bureau of National Affairs,
3d ed. 2004)
Peter Wilner, "The Madrid Protocol: A Voluntary Model for the
Internationalization of Trademark Law," 13 *DePaul University
Journal of Art and Entertainment Law* 17 (2003)

❖ MALWARE ❖

Malware is a catchall term, a contraction of "malicious software." Malware includes viruses, worms, Trojans, backdoors, and spyware (and, to many users, adware as well). Viruses and worms can spread from one computer to another by replicating themselves. Trojans do not replicate themselves, but are disguised as legitimate software in order to trick the user into installing them. Viruses usually do little besides replicating themselves, infecting other programs and files to do so; however, they may destroy data on a computer and render the computer unusable. Worms and Trojans can serve as vehicles for a variety of programs, including spam mailers and backdoor programs that allow the computer to be used as a zombie in denial-of-service attacks. More malicious uses are also possible, and worms and Trojans can install or enable the installation of programs that allow "black-hat" (malicious) hackers to access information on another user's computer and to perform any action that the legitimate user of the computer would be able to perform. Users of dial-up Internet connection are also vulnerable to dialer programs, often installed via a drive-by download—one in which the user is not notified that a program is being installed. These dialers may switch the user's dial-up connection number to a 900 number or other number that will result in a hefty charge to the user's account. Adware and spyware can slow the user's computer by increasing the amount of advertising the user receives, and spyware can report information on the user's Web-surfing habits and computer use to persons unknown to the user without the user's consent (Symantec 2004).

Not all malware comes from scammers, spammers, and black-hat hackers. Perhaps the most infamous instance of malware being installed on unsuspecting users' computers was the Sony BMG rootkit episode. In 2005, Sony BMG, a music-content company, published and sold CDs incorporating software that, if the CD were played on a computer running Microsoft Windows, would install a rootkit on the computer; the number of computers potentially infected was in the millions, if not higher. A rootkit allows certain processes to operate undetected. Presumably this was done to allow Sony BMG to surreptitiously detect and block file-sharing of the songs on the CD, but a malicious hacker who was aware of the rootkit could also use it to gain undetected access to the computer, and everything on it, including, for example, valuable personal information, bank account passwords, trade secrets, tax returns, and credit card numbers. The rootkit episode came at the height of the music industry's ultimately self-destructive panic over file-sharing, and shows a peculiarly misplaced sense of values, placing the sanctity of music copyright above, say, the sanctity of millions of innocent users' bank accounts. This was reflected in Sony BMG's surprisingly clumsy initial response to what would become one of the most spectacular content-industry public relations disasters of the decade. When software engineer Mark Russinovich discovered and publicized the existence of the rootkit, Sony BMG executive Thomas Hesse responded "Most people don't even know what a rootkit is, so why should they care about it?" (Brown 2010). The company took a somewhat different line after multiple lawsuits were filed; in the United States alone, these included a class-action suit on behalf of the purchasers of Sony BMG music CDs, suits by states and by the Federal Trade Commission (FTC), a suit by the Electronic Frontier Foundation, and even a public scolding from an official of the Department of Homeland Security (Brown 2010; Krebs 2005). Ultimately, Sony BMG backed down and agreed to install no further rootkits.

Despite the expensive public relations meltdown, Sony BMG got off more lightly than might a malicious hacker installing similar software on another user's computer. Malware that enables one user to gain access to another's computer without that user's knowledge or consent is governed by the Computer Fraud and Abuse Act (CFAA) of 1986 (18 U.S.C. § 1030). Section 1030(a)(5) of the CFAA, as amended, deals with malware; it provides for criminal penalties for any person who:

(A) knowingly causes the transmission of a program, information, code, or command, and as a result of such conduct, intentionally causes damage without authorization, to a protected computer;
(B) intentionally accesses a protected computer without authorization, and as a result of such conduct, recklessly causes damage; or
(C) intentionally accesses a protected computer without authorization, and as a result of such conduct, causes damage and loss.

In plain English, at the risk of some oversimplification and loss of detail, the statute prohibits any person from doing two things with regard to another's computer: no one may knowingly transmit any "program, information, code or command" that intentionally damages another's computer; this covers the sending of harmful viruses, worms, and Trojans. Nor may any person intentionally or knowingly gain unauthorized access or exceed authorized access to another's computer; courts have interpreted this to cover not only the installation of backdoors and other remote access tools, but also the "access" gained by the worms and other programs themselves (*Morris*, 928 F.2d 504).

However, for criminal penalties to attach for unauthorized access or exceeding authorized access, the damage must either be caused recklessly or must be nontrivial; §1030(c)(4) lists the various types of damage that will make the access a crime even if the damage done by the access was caused accidentally or negligently, with penalties increasing with the severity of the damage. Thus, a first "offense under subsection (a)(5)(B) [intentional access recklessly causing damage]" can result in "a fine under this title, imprisonment for not more than 5 years, or both . . . if the offense caused (or, in the case of an attempted offense, would, if completed, have caused)"—

(I)   loss to 1 or more persons during any 1-year period (and, for purposes of an investigation, prosecution, or other proceeding brought by the United States only, loss resulting from a related course of conduct affecting 1 or more other protected computers) aggregating at least $5,000 in value;

(II)   the modification or impairment, or potential modification or impairment, of the medical examination, diagnosis, treatment, or care of 1 or more individuals;

(III)   physical injury to any person;

(IV)   a threat to public health or safety;

(V)   damage affecting a computer used by or for an entity of the United States Government in furtherance of the administration of justice, national defense, or national security; or

(VI)   damage affecting 10 or more protected computers during any 1-year period (18 U.S.C. § 1030(c)(4)(A)).

The term of imprisonment can be increased to 10 years if the offense is committed not under subsection (a)(5)(B) [intentional access recklessly causing damage] but under subsection (a)(5)(A) [knowing transmission intentionally causing damage] (18 U.S.C. § 1030 (c)(4)(B)), and to 20 years for repeat offenses under either of these two sections (18 U.S.C. § 1030 (c)(4)(C), or for a violation of subsection (a)(5)(A) in which "the offender attempts to cause or knowingly or recklessly causes serious bodily injury" (18 U.S.C. § 1030 (c)(4)(E)). "If the offender attempts to cause or knowingly or recklessly causes death from conduct in violation of subsection (a)(5)(A)," imprisonment for life may result (18 U.S.C. § 1030 (c)(4)(F)). For lesser violations, including first offenses under subsection (a)(5)(C), the maximum term of imprisonment is one year (18 U.S.C. § 1030 (c)(4)(G)); repeat offenses under subsection (a)(5)(C) [intentional access causing damage, without reference to whether the damage was intended or recklessly caused, or merely negligently or accidentally caused] may lead to a

sentence of up to 10 years, in addition to the usual fine (18 U.S.C. § 1030 (c)(4)(D)).

Other statutes may also be applicable to malware. Depending on the type of harm caused, malware users may violate federal statutes against bank fraud (18 U.S.C. § 1344), credit card fraud (18 U.S.C. § 1029), and wire fraud (18 U.S.C. § 1343). They may also violate state privacy and burglary statutes.

Statutes

- Controlling the Assault of Non-Solicited Pornography and Marketing Act of 2003, 15 U.S.C. §§ 7701–7713
- Bank Fraud Act, 18 U.S.C. § 1344
- Computer Fraud and Abuse Act, 18 U.S.C. § 1030
- Credit Card Fraud Act, 18 U.S.C. § 1029
- Wire Fraud Act, 18 U.S.C. § 1343
- Unfair Methods of Competition, 15 U.S.C. § 45

Cases

- *United States v. Morris*, 928 F.2d 504 (2d Cir. 1991)
- *Zango, Inc. v. Kaspersky Lab, Inc.*, 568 F.3d 1169 (9th Cir. 2009)

See also: Adware and Spyware; Denial-of-Service Attack; Hacking; Spam; Trojan; Virus; Worm; Zombie

Sources and Further Reading

Bob Brown, "Sony BMG Rootkit Scandal: 5 Years Later," *Network World* (November 1, 2010), available at http://www.networkworld.com/news/2010/110110-sonybmg-rootkit-fsecure-drm.html (visited February 8, 2013)

"Businesses and Cyber-Security: A Spook Speaks," *The Economist*, June 30, 2012, at 67

Brian Krebs, "DHS Official Weighs in on Sony," *Washington Post* (November 11, 2005), available at http://voices.washington-post.com/securityfix/2005/11/dhs_official_weighs_in_on_sony.html (visited February 8, 2013)

Richard G. Kunkel, "Protecting Consumers from Spyware: A Proposed Consumer Digital Trespass Act," 28 *The John Marshall Journal of Computer & Information Law* 185 (2010)

"Security Response Glossary," Symantec U.S. (2012), available at http://securityresponse.symantec.com/avcenter/refa.html (visited August 20, 2012)

❖ MENU COMMAND HIERARCHY ❖

The menu command hierarchy of a computer program consists of the commands by which a user tells the program to do certain things and the order in which those commands are arranged. When more than one program performs the same function, the commands and command hierarchies of those programs may be similar or identical, raising questions of copyright infringement.

Copyright does not protect ideas, but the expression of ideas. When an idea is capable of only one or a small number of means of expression, those means of expression are not copyrightable. In addition, methods of operation are not copyrightable (17 U.S.C. § 102). The copyrightability of menu commands and menu command hierarchies thus depends on whether there are multiple ways of expressing the same idea, whether the idea is original enough to merit copyright protection, and whether the idea is a method of operation. For example, every keyboard driver has some method by which users may type letters and have them appear on the screen. All of these programs use the same commands: the user types the key marked "E," and the letter "E" appears on the screen. The use of the key marked "E" to enter the letter "E" fails the copyrightability test on all three counts. There are no other practical ways of expressing the same idea; for the user to strike some other key or combination of keys in order to enter the letter "E" would be nonsensical. The idea is not original; the reason the key is marked "E" is so that it can be used to enter the letter "E," an idea derived from typewriter keyboards that predate the advent of personal computing by over a century. And the "idea" is a method of operation; it serves to operate the computer rather than to express any idea apart from the task of placing the letter "E" on the screen.

The noncopyrightability of menu commands and command hierarchies may not be so obvious, however. The use of "Control-S" as a command to save a document is intuitive and scarcely original; the use of the F10 key for the same purpose is not intuitive, and might meet the originality requirement for copyrightability. It also meets the "multiple means of expression" test; any of the function keys on the keyboard, or any other key, might be used for the same purpose. It is thus copyrightable unless it is a mere method of operation.

The U.S. Supreme Court addressed this problem in the case of *Lotus Development v. Borland*, and concluded that the hierarchy of commands in Lotus Development's Lotus 1–2–3 spreadsheet program was a noncopyrightable method of operation. The Supreme Court affirmed the decision of the appellate court, which had compared the command hierarchy to the buttons on a VCR:

> Users operate VCRs by pressing a series of buttons that are typically labeled "Record, Play, Reverse, Fast Forward, Pause, Stop/Eject." That the buttons are arranged and labeled does not make them a "literary work," nor does it make them an "expression" of the abstract "method of operating" a VCR via a set of labeled buttons. Instead, the buttons are themselves the "method of operating" the VCR.
>
> When a Lotus 1–2–3 user chooses a command, either by highlighting it on the screen or by typing its first letter, he or she effectively pushes a button. Highlighting the "Print"

command on the screen, or typing the letter "P," is analogous to pressing a VCR button labeled "Play" (*Lotus,* 49 F.3d at 817).

Clicking "Print," like pressing "Play," is not an expressive act; its purpose is not to express the idea "Print" or "Play," but to perform the act of printing a document or playing a video. The set of commands that operate a computer program, as well as the hierarchy in which they are ordered, is also a method of operation and not copyrightable. Although the court's decision has been criticized on the grounds that "user interfaces, including menu commands," may be expressive, original works and thus "should receive at least narrow protection under copyright law," the issue has not been revisited (Stagnone 1997, 948).

Statute
- Copyright Act of 1976, 17 U.S.C. §§ 101–105

Case
- *Lotus Development Corporation v. Borland International, Inc.,* 49 F.3d 807 (1st Cir. 1995), affirmed, 516 U.S. 233 (1996)

See also: Business Method Patents; Copyright; Copyright Infringement; Look and Feel

Source and Further Reading
Lauren A. Stagnone, "Copyright Law—Computer Program Menu Command Hierarchy: An Uncopyrightable Method of Operation? *Lotus Development Corporation v. Borland International, Inc.,* 49 F.3rd 807 (1995), aff'd, 116 S. Ct. 804 (1996)," 30 *Suffolk University Law Review* 939 (1997)

❖ METATAGS ❖

Metatags are text inserted into an HTML document so as to be invisible when the document is viewed as a Web page. The metatag is inserted near the top of the HTML document, just after the title; it typically takes the form <META name = "category" content ="thing(s) in category">. Metatags on a Web page can be viewed from a Web browser by selecting "View/Source." There are several uses for metatags; they can contain copyright information or direct the viewer to a new Web page. Legally, however, the most problematic use of metatags has been to include terms that increase the page's chance of being located by search engines, and its rank when located. This by itself is perfectly acceptable, but trademark issues arise when trademarked terms are used as metatags.

The use of a trademark as a metatag by a person other than the trademark holder or someone licensed by the trademark holder is trademark infringement unless an exception applies. The exception most likely to be applicable is the defense of nominative fair use. The Ninth Circuit Court of Appeals sets out the elements of nominative fair use as applicable to metatags in the case of *Playboy Enterprises, Inc. v. Welles:*

> First, the product or service in question must be one not readily identifiable without use of the trademark; second, only so much of the mark or marks may be used as is reasonably necessary to identify the product or service; and third, the user must do nothing that would, in conjunction with the mark, suggest sponsorship or endorsement by the trademark holder (279 F.3d at 801).

The defendant in *Welles*, a former model for *Playboy* magazine, had used the words "playboy" and "playmate" in metatags. In holding this use to be nominative fair use, the Ninth Circuit explained that the first element was met because "Welles has no practical way of describing herself without using trademarked terms. In the context of metatags, we conclude that she has no practical way of identifying the content of her website without referring to PEI's trademarks" (279 F.3d at 803). The second element was met because "[t]he metatags use only so much of the marks as reasonably necessary" and the third element was met because "nothing is done in conjunction with them to suggest sponsorship or endorsement by the trademark holder" (279 F.3d at 804). While a single use of each term was thus nominative fair use, repeated use of the terms might not be: "We note that our decision might differ if the metatags listed the trademarked term so repeatedly that Welles' site would regularly appear above [Playboy Enterprises'] in searches for one of the trademarked terms" (279 F.3d at 804).

Playboy Enterprises' trademark has been particularly subject to infringement; in cases where the metatag infringement was accompanied by other, more egregious infringement, it has sometimes prevailed (*Playboy Enterprises, Inc. v. AsiaFocus, Int'l*, 1998). And while feuding pornographers may attract little sympathy, mainstream businesses have also been involved in metatag trademark infringement litigation. *Niton Corporation v. Radiation Monitoring Devices, Inc.* involved metatags on the Web pages of Radiation Monitoring Devices, Inc. (RMD) that said "The Home Page of Niton Corporation, makers of the finest lead, radon and multi-element detectors" (27 F. Supp. 2d at 104). The district court issued an injunction prohibiting RMD from using this and similar metatags, holding that Niton had shown that it was likely to succeed on the merits of its trademark infringement claim (27 F. Supp. 2d at 104–105).

Thus the use of trademarks as metatags solely to identify the user's products or services and not to mislead is generally permissible, while the use of the trademarks with the intent to mislead search engines and Web surfers or to harm the trademark holder seems not to be. There is one special case, however: some Web sites may use trademarks as metatags not because they wish to steal business that would otherwise have gone to the trademark owner, but because they wish to criticize the trademark owner. The problem is analogous to the "sucks" problem in cybersquatting, in which critics of, say, PayPal register the domain name www.paypalsucks.com in order to post their criticisms. However, metatags are not covered by the Anticybersquatting Consumer Protection Act (Computer & Internet Lawyer 2000, 44). Such use of metatags is likely to meet the three prongs of the *Playboy Enterprises* test and thus is generally permissible, although the content of the site may give rise to other claims for trademark infringement and defamation.

The ongoing technology race between search engine spammers and search engine companies has long since left metatag spamming behind, although nonspamming metatags are still used to provide useful information; however, the legal principles that apply to metatags apply to other forms of hidden text and use of competitors' trademarks as well.

Statute
- Lanham Trademark Act, 15 U.S.C. § 1115(b)

Cases
Federal Appellate Courts
- *Network Automation, Inc. v. Advanced Systems Concepts, Inc.*, 638 F.3d 1137 (9th Cir. 2011)
- *Playboy Enterprises, Inc. v. Welles*, 279 F.3d 796 (9th Cir. 2002)
- *Rearden LLC v. Rearden Commerce, Inc.*, 683 F.3d 1190 (9th Cir. 2012)
- *Rosetta Stone Ltd. v. Google, Inc.*, 676 F.3d 144 (4th Cir. 2012)

Federal Trial Courts
- *Bihari v. Gross*, 119 F. Supp. 2d 309 (S.D.N.Y. 2000)
- *Lucent Technologies, Inc. v. Lucentsucks.com*, 95 F. Supp. 2d 528 (E.D. Va. 2000)
- *Niton Corp. v. Radiation Monitoring Devices, Inc.*, 27 F. Supp. 2d 102 (D. Mass. 1998)
- *Playboy Enterprises, Inc. v. AsiaFocus, Int'l*, No. 97–734-A, 1998 U.S. Dist. LEXIS 10359 (E.D. Va. 1998)

See also: Cybersquatting; Fair Use (Trademark); Trademark; Trademark Dilution; Trademark Infringement

Sources and Further Reading
G. Peter Albert, Jr. & Rita A. Abbati, "Metatags, Keywords and Links: Recent Developments Addressing Trademark Threats in Cyberspace," 40 *San Diego Law Review* 341 (2003)

Katherine Ivancevich, "Promatek Industries, Inc. v. Equitrac Corporation: Promoting the Metatag Fallacy," 12 *DePaul-LCA Journal of Art and Entertainment Law* 351 (2002)

Douglas G. McCray, "Oh, What a Tangled Web: The Subtle Difference between Metatag Usage as 'Fair Use' and Invisible Infringement," *Michigan Bar Journal*, August 2002, at 42

Alex Michael & Ben Salter, *Marketing through Search Optimization: How to Be Found on the Web* (Burlington, MA: Butterworth-Heinemann, 2d ed. 2007)

"No Lanham Act Claim Where Trademark Was Used in Metatags for Web Site Criticizing Trademark Owner," *Computer & Internet Lawyer*, December 2000, at 44

Hope Viner Samborn, "Hiding in Plain Site: The Hunt for Metatags on the Internet Is Changing the Field of Trademark Law," *ABA Journal* September 2000, at 80

Shari Thurow, *Search Engine Visibility* (Berkeley, CA: New Riders Press, 2d ed. 2007)

"Webmaster Tools: Metatags," Google, available at http://support.google.com/webmasters/bin/answer.py?hl=en&answer=79812 (visited February 8, 2013)

Bettina Wendlandt, *Cybersquatting, Metatags und Spam* (München: Beck Juristischer Verlag, 2002) (in German)

❖ MICROSOFT ANTITRUST LITIGATION ❖

At one time Microsoft Corporation enjoyed a near-complete monopoly in the personal computer operating system and Web browser markets, and its Works and Office packages dominated the markets for word-processing software, spreadsheets, and presentation software. Microsoft was an aggressive business competitor; many smaller businesses, including former market leaders such as Netscape, were unable to thrive in the face of competition from Microsoft. In Microsoft's heyday private companies and government attorneys sought to restrain it using laws designed to prevent single business entities from monopolizing entire industries.

Chief among these laws is the Sherman Antitrust Act, under which "[e]very contract, combination in the form of trust or otherwise, or conspiracy, in restraint of trade or commerce among the several States, or with foreign nations, is declared to be illegal" (15 U.S.C. § 1). Many state laws contain similar restrictions. The FTC had taken an interest in possible monopolistic practices by Microsoft as early as 1991; the FTC closed its investigation in 1993 without bringing any suit, and in the same year the Department of Justice commenced its own investigation. In July 1994, the government and Microsoft entered into a consent decree under which Microsoft agreed not to tie other Microsoft products to the Windows operating system (Software Publishers Association 1998). In 1995, however, the consent decree was rejected by a federal district court as too lenient; this decision was overturned by an appellate court, which transferred the case to a new judge, Penfield Jackson. Judge Jackson approved the consent decree just as the browser wars between Microsoft and Netscape were beginning. Microsoft began giving away Internet Explorer, its Web browser, for free at a time when Netscape was still charging for its browser (Software Publishers Association 1998). In 1996, the Department of Justice began a new investigation, this time into whether Microsoft had violated the terms of the consent decree. The browser wars continued and in 1997, Netscape's share of the browser market fell from 90% to 60%. At the same time, Microsoft attracted

other opponents: Sun Microsystems filed a suit accusing Microsoft of attempting to undermine Sun's Java technology by not using Java with Internet Explorer (*Sun*, 81 F. Supp. 2d 1026). Not long after Sun filed its suit, the Justice Department also filed a suit alleging that Microsoft had violated the 1994 consent decree by forcing PC makers to use Internet Explorer on new PCs as a condition of obtaining a Windows license. Judge Jackson agreed, and the court issued an injunction requiring Microsoft to "cease and desist . . . from the practice of licensing the use of any Microsoft personal computer operating system software (including Windows 95 or any successor version thereof) on the condition, express or implied, that the license [*sic*] also license and preinstall any Microsoft Internet browser software" (980 F. Supp. at 545). Six days later, the Justice Department asked the court to hold Microsoft in contempt after Microsoft allegedly offered computer makers old and defective copies of Windows 95. In January 1998, Microsoft signed an agreement permitting computer makers to install Windows without the Internet Explorer icon (Software Publishers Association 1998).

The Justice Department's suit centered on the bundling of Internet Explorer with Windows in new computers; Microsoft appealed Judge Jackson's decision and sought the removal of the Special Master, Lawrence Lessig, appointed by Jackson. In 1998, the District of Columbia Circuit Court of Appeals reversed Judge Jackson's grant of an injunction against Microsoft (147 F.3d at 956).

The Justice Department and several state governments then brought suit against Microsoft. The various lawsuits against Microsoft in the United States eventually ran out of steam, however; while there were some findings of improper conduct on Microsoft's part, the company was not broken up, and Microsoft retained its near-monopoly in browsers and operating systems. The final blow to the effort to break up Microsoft came on June 30, 2004, with the D.C. Circuit's decision in *Massachusetts v. Microsoft*. Massachusetts, along with several other states, had refused to join in an earlier consent decree, and had continued to pursue an "unbundling" solution, separating Internet Explorer and other programs from the Windows operating system. Microsoft had rejected the solution as technically not feasible; opponents of Microsoft had hoped that Microsoft would be split into two companies, one making operating systems and the other making applications software. This, it was further hoped, would open up both fields—operating systems and applications—to increased competition (Cohen 2004). By rejecting Massachusetts' challenge to the consent decree, the D.C. Circuit seems to have eliminated any possibility that Microsoft will be split into two companies or otherwise forced to unbundle its operating systems and applications (see 373 F.3d 1241–1242).

But as the antitrust suits against Microsoft in the United States slowly wound down, European Union regulators began to consider similar suits. The European Commission lacked the ability to impose the profound structural changes upon a company that a U.S. court might have imposed; there was never a possibility that the EU action might break up Microsoft. The EU Commission could and did enjoin future violations, impose a substantial fine, and require Microsoft to disclose previously confidential information about its products in aid of interoperability and to unbundle Windows Media Player from the Windows operating system (*Microsoft (EU)* 2007).

The European Commission focused on two areas related to the Sun Microsystems complaint but largely overlooked by the U.S. Justice Department's antitrust efforts: the effect of Microsoft's Windows Media Player on the market for streaming media technology, and Microsoft's creation of applications programs that can only achieve full interoperability when used with Microsoft server software. The first of these arises from concerns similar to Sun's, while the second directly follows on Sun's complaint. In March of 2004 the Commission found against Microsoft on both charges; the decision was, for the most part, upheld on appeal in 2007 (*Microsoft (EU)* 2007).

Statute
- Sherman Antitrust Act, 15 U.S.C. § 1

Cases
United States
- *In re Microsoft Corp. Antitrust Litigation*, 127 F. Supp. 2d 702 (D. Md. 2001)
- *New York v. Microsoft Corp.*, No. CIVA 98–1233 CKK, 2006 WL 3949168 (D.D.C. 2006)
- *Novell, Inc. v. Microsoft Corp*, 429 Fed. App'x.254 (4th Cir. 2011)
- *Novell, Inc. v. Microsoft Corp.*, No. 2:04-cv-01045-JFM, 2012 U.S. Dist. LEXIS 98710 (D. Utah 2012)
- *Sun Microsystems, Inc. v. Microsoft Corp.*, 81 F. Supp. 2d 1026 (N.D. Cal. 2000)
- *United States v. Microsoft Corp.*, 980 F. Supp. 537 (D.D.C. 1997), reversed, 147 F.3d 935 (D.C. Cir. 1998)
- *United States v. Microsoft Corp.*, 87 F. Supp. 2d 30 (D.D.C. 2000); affirmed in part, reversed in part, 253 F.3d 34 (D.C. Cir. 2001); certiorari denied sub nom *Microsoft Corp. v. United States*, 534 U.S. 952 (2001); on remand, *U.S. v. Microsoft*, 231 F. Supp. 2d 144; affirmed by *Massachusetts v. Microsoft Corp.*, 373 F.3d 1199 (D.C. Cir. 2004)

European Union
- Case T-201/04, *Microsoft Corp. v Commission of the European Communities*, Judgment of the Court of First Instance (Grand Chamber) (September 17, 2007)

Complaint
- Complaint of State Attorneys General, United States v. Microsoft Corp., 1998 U.S. Dist. Ct. Pleadings

LEXIS 23 (1998) (No. 98–1232 (TPJ)), available at http://www.justice.gov/atr/cases/f1700/1763.htm

See also: Internet; Open Source; Web Browser; World Wide Web

Sources and Further Reading
Chris Butts, "The Microsoft Case 10 Years Later: Antitrust and New Leading "New Economy" Firms," 8 *Northwestern Journal of Technology and Intellectual Property* 275 (2008)

Amanda Cohen, "Surveying the Microsoft Antitrust Universe," 19 *Berkeley Technology Law Journal* 333 (2004)

Barbara Crutchfield George et al., "Increasing Extraterritorial Intrusion of European Union Law into U.S. Business Mergers and Competition Practices: U.S. Multinational Businesses Underestimate the Strength of the European Commission from G.E.—Honeywell to Microsoft," 19 *Connecticut Journal of International Law* 571 (2004)

Robert A. Levy, "Microsoft and the Browser Wars," 31 *Connecticut Law Review* 1321 (1999)

Ramona Mateiu, "In re Microsoft Corporation Antitrust Litigation," 17 *Berkeley Technology Law Journal* 295 (2002)

David McGowan, "Between Logic and Experience: Error Costs and United States v. Microsoft Corp.," 20 *Berkeley Technology Law Journal* 1185 (2005)

Holger Metzger, *Netscape History*, (n.d.), available at http://www.holgermetzger.de/Netscape_History.html (visited August 22, 2012)

Press Release, Netscape, "Mosaic Communications Corporation Changes Name to Netscape Communications Corporation" (November 14, 1994), available at http://www.holgermetzger.de/netscape/NetscapeCommunicationsNewsRelease.htm (visited December 21, 2012)

John Paczkowski, "Novell Antitrust Suit against Microsoft Sputters to a Close," All Things (July 16, 2012), available at http://allthingsd.com/20120716/novell-antitrust-suit-against-microsoft-sputters-to-a-close/ (visited February 8, 2013)

Software Publishers Association, "Timeline of Events Surrounding Microsoft Antitrust Case" (1998), available at http://www.procompetition.org/litigation/timeline.html (visited November 9, 2004; archived copy visited August 25, 2013)

❖ MOBILE DEVICE ❖

A mobile device, in the context of Internet technology and law, is an easily portable device such as a cell phone or tablet that can function as a computer and provide Internet access. In the early days of the World Wide Web and mass Internet use—the early 1990s—most Internet access took place at fixed work stations. Laptops provided some mobility, but truly mobile Internet devices such as the PDAs and primitive smartphones then available were rare. By the middle of the next decade the technology had improved considerably, and phones and tablets began to displace desktop and laptop computers as the main means of access for many users. This de-anchoring of Internet access, along with the integration of Internet links into the everyday world through such mechanisms as the QR code, has changed the way the Internet affects its users. Internet access no longer requires a workstation; it can be carried in one's pocket or worn as a wristwatch. The location of the user is now as flexible as the locations of the content the user accesses, making problems of jurisdiction still more complex; for example, an Internet transaction might take place while the user is passing from one jurisdiction to another.

Another impact of mobile devices has been the reduction of the digital divide. Mobile devices are smaller and cheaper than desktops and laptops; they are often provided for free or at a deep discount by mobile telephone service providers. In some developing countries, an entire generation is leapfrogging the workstation phase altogether and growing up with mobile devices as the primary means of Internet access (see, e.g., Kenya's Mobile Telephones 2012).

See also: App; Digital Divide; Jurisdiction; QR Code; Social Networking Service

Sources and Further Reading

Jenny Aker, "C U L8ter? Using Mobile Phones as a Literacy Tool in Niger," Center for Global Development (September 13, 2010), available at http://blogs.cgdev.org/globaldevelopment/2010/09/c-u-l8ter-using-mobile-phones-as-a-literacy-tool-in-niger.php (visited January 28, 2013)

"Innovation in Africa: Upwardly Mobile," *The Economist*, August 25, 2012, at 53

"Kenya's Mobile Telephones: Vital for the Poor," *The Economist*, November 10, 2012, at 52

"Mobile Cellular Subscriptions (per 100 People)," World Bank, available at http://data.worldbank.org/indicator/IT.CEL.SETS.P2 (visited November 13, 2012)

"Over-the-Top Phone Services: Joyn Them or Join Them," *The Economist*, August 11, 2012, at 60

"Struggling Smart-Phone Makers: Biting Back at Apple," *The Economist*, September 1, 2012, at 62

"Video Games: Japan Fights Back," *The Economist*, November 17, 2012, at 61

❖ MORAL RIGHTS ❖

Traditionally European, but not United States, copyright law protected the so-called moral rights of an author: the right to integrity (the right to protect the work from changes that could damage the work's or the author's reputation); the right of paternity (also known as the right of attribution: the right to be identified as the author of a work and to prevent one's name from being associated with a modified version of the work); and the right of withdrawal (the right to withdraw a work from distribution if it no longer represents the views of the author). Not only are these not economic rights of the author; they may actually harm the economic interests of others if exercised.

U.S. law has historically been unreceptive to moral rights, both because copyright is viewed as an economic right (and moral rights are noneconomic) and because of the potential for conflict with First Amendment freedom of expression. If, as Richard Wilbur wrote, "Edgar Degas purchased once/A fine El Greco, which he kept/Against the wall beside his bed/To hang his pants on while he slept," then Degas might conceivably have violated El Greco's moral rights (Wilbur 1987, 292; the point is moot, however, as El Greco had been dead for more than two centuries when Degas was born). After Armand Vaillancourt painted the slogan "Vive le Quebec libre" on his fountain-sculpture at Justin Herman Plaza in San Francisco, the city government sent workers to remove his words. This action, too, might have violated the artist's moral rights had they been recognized under U.S. law at the time. Both actions, however—expressing one's disregard for a painting by hanging one's pants on it, and erasing a political slogan—are probably protected expression under the First Amendment. The United States has accorded limited protection of moral rights to some paintings, sculptures, and similar works under the Visual Artists' Rights Act (17 U.S.C. § 106A), which has been fairly narrowly construed (see, e.g., *Kelley*, 635 F.3d 290; *Kleinman*, 597 F.3d 323). As noted above, recognition of moral rights may present Constitutional problems as well; it may conflict with the First Amendment and may also not be authorized under the Patent and Copyright Clause. Taken to its extreme, the idea of moral rights, even in paintings, becomes untenable: most people would probably be appalled at the idea that the estate of serial killer John Wayne Gacy might be able to recover damages from people who bought his paintings in order to burn them.

European legal systems have also recognized moral rights in trademarks. At one time U.S. law was willing to recognize the rights of integrity and attribution with regard to trademarks under the Lanham Trademark Act. The U.S. Supreme Court's decision in *Dastar v. Twentieth Century Fox* seems to have severely limited the enforceability of these rights, however (539 U.S. 23).

U.S. law and practice remains significantly out of step with international norms in the area of moral rights; because of the conflict between moral rights and First Amendment freedoms, this situation is likely to persist. Under TRIPS, members of the World Trade Organization agree to comply with the 1971 revision of the Berne Convention; its main substantive provisions, with the exception of Berne Convention Article 6bis (dealing with moral rights), are incorporated into TRIPS by reference. This exception takes into account the concerns of those countries, especially the United States, that are unwilling to impose broad protections of moral rights.

Treaties
- Agreement on Trade-Related Aspects of Intellectual Property Rights, Marrakesh Agreement Establishing the World Trade Organization, Annex 1C, April 15, 1994, 33 I.L.M. 81 (1994)
- Convention Concerning the Creation of an International Union for the Protection of Literary and Artistic Works (Berne Convention), September 9,

1886, as last revised at Paris, July 24, 1971 (amended 1979), 25 U.S.T. 1341, 828 U.N.T.S. 221

Statutes
- Copyright Act of 1976, 17 U.S.C. §§ 101–1332
- Visual Artists Rights Act, 17 U.S.C. § 106A

Cases
Supreme Court
- *Dastar v. Twentieth Century Fox, Inc.*, 539 U.S. 23 (2003)

Federal Appellate Courts
- *Kelley v. Chicago Park District*, 635 F.3d 290 (7th Cir. 2011)
- *Kleinman v. City of San Marcos*, 597 F.3d 323 (5th Cir. 2010)
- *Massachusetts Museum of Contemporary Art Foundation, Inc. v. Buchel*, 593 F.3d 38 (1st Cir. 2010)

See also: Berne Convention; Copyright; International Copyright Protection; Trademark; TRIPS (Copyright)

Sources and Further Reading
Stephen R. Elias, *Patent, Copyright & Trademark: An Intellectual Property Desk Reference* (Berkeley, CA: Nolo Press, 6th ed. 2003)

Justin Hughes, "American Moral Rights and Fixing the Dastar 'Gap,'" 2007 *Utah Law Review* 659 (2007)

Marshall Leaffer, *Understanding Copyright Law* (New York: Matthew Bender, 5th ed. 2010)

J. Thomas McCarthy et al., *McCarthy's Desk Encyclopedia of Intellectual Property* (Washington, D.C.: Bureau of National Affairs, 3d ed. 2004)

"Some of John Wayne Gacy's Artwork Displayed in West Palm Beach," Associated Press (June 5, 2004), available at http://www.fadp.org/news/MGBIUQQU3VD.html (visited February 8, 2013)

Richard Wilbur, "Museum Piece," in *New and Collected Poems* 292 (Fort Washington, PA: Harvest Books, 1987)

MOUSETRAPPING

See Cybersquatting

❖ MP3 ❖

MP3 is both the name of a file format and the name of a company, MP3.com. The file format is actually MPEG-1/2 Audio Layer 3, but is abbreviated as MP3 when used in a Windows file suffix or referred to in a nontechnical sense. "MPEG," in turn, stands for "Moving Picture Experts Group," often incorrectly given as "Motion Picture Experts Group." The Moving Picture Experts Group is an organization that seeks to develop formats for video and multimedia storage and playback.

The MP3 format has proven to be especially well adapted to the compact storage of audio files of about three to five minutes in length that demand polyphony and a range of tones and intensities, but for which some loss during compression can be tolerated. This makes it ideal for compressing popular songs; large numbers of songs can be stored on just about anything capable of digital storage, including a computer's hard drive, a portable MP3 player, a CD, a flash drive, an iPod, or a mobile phone. The quality, compactness, and versatility of the MP3 format make it a consumer's dream: a huge number of songs will fit on a very small device, and once the consumer has purchased an authorized copy of a popular song, he or she may make an MP3 compressed copy and space-shift it to play it on just about any other device he or she owns.

Unfortunately, the same qualities that make the MP3 format a consumer's dream made it the music content industry's worst nightmare. Before the advent of the MP3 format and the Internet, the music content industry had learned to accept, if not like, the fact that home recording for space-shifting purposes was a fair use of copyrighted material. But MP3 files are small enough to be shared across the Internet in seconds; they can be emailed and posted on Web sites, or shared over file-sharing networks. Teenagers who might once have had to save their allowances for a month to buy a single album at the music content industry's retail price, and might want only one song on the album, can now download hundreds of songs in an evening, for free—as long as they can find someone who has a copy of the song and is willing to share it online. While sharing with a friend might still fall within the fuzzy parameters of fair use set by 17 U.S.C. § 107, sharing with large numbers of unknown strangers does not (*Napster*, 239 F.3d 1004).

MP3.com, a company based in San Diego, California, was an early entrant into the Internet music field. MP3.com purchased CDs containing tens of thousands of copyrighted songs and converted them to MP3 format. It then placed these MP3 files on its servers; any subscriber to MP3.com's MyMP3.com service could access the servers and obtain the MP3 files. To protect against copyright infringement, MyMP3.com customers were required to demonstrate that they owned, or at least had access to, an authorized copy of the work they wished to download; this was done by placing an authorized recorded CD in the subscriber's computer. While this seems absurdly cumbersome today even for machines with legacy optical drives, it made a certain amount of sense at the time. MP3.com's other line of business (the one in which it is still engaged, now under the ownership of C/Net) was the direct offering of musical works to the public; these were almost exclusively works of artists without record contracts with the music content industry.

On the day of its initial public offering, MP3.com's share price opened at an astonishing $92 per share (Nerney 1999), in an outstanding example of what Alan Greenspan had earlier called "irrational exuberance." At the height of the dot-com madness, MP3.com's stock was still trading at $44 a share and a total market capitalization of nearly three billion dollars—more than twenty-four hundred times its annual earnings.

The music content industry reacted with alarm to MyMP3.com, and sued for copyright infringement. The federal district court for the Southern District of New York held that MP3.com's copying and posting of its CDs were not protected fair use. The district court's decision may have played a part in the collapse of MP3.com's share price and the bursting of the dot.com bubble, but the share prices were so outrageously inflated in any event that the collapse was inevitable.

The music content industry's victory over MP3.com may have paved the way for other file-sharing networks. File-sharers took the decision as a sign that centralized file-sharing networks on the MP3.com model, rather than all file-sharing networks, were illegal, and began to design around the decision, eventually building P2P networks.

Cases
Federal Appellate Courts
- *A&M Records, Inc. v. Napster, Inc.*, 239 F.3d 1004 (9th Cir. 2001)
- *Recording Industry Association of America v. Diamond Multimedia Systems, Inc.*, 180 F.3d 1072 (9th Cir. 1999)

Federal Trial Court
- *UMG Recordings, Inc., v. MP3.com, Inc.*, 92 F. Supp. 2d 349 (S.D.N.Y. 2000)

See also: Content; Copyright; Copyright Infringement;.com; Fair Use (Copyright); File-Sharing; P2P

Sources and Further Reading
Bruce Haring, *Beyond the Charts: MP3 and the Digital Music Revolution* (Los Angeles: JM Northern Media LLC, 2000)
Chris Nerney, "Early MP3.com Investors May Be Singing Sad Tune," Internetnews.com (July 26, 1999), available at http://www.internetnews.com/bus-news/article.php/168501 (visited February 8, 2013)

N

❖ NAPSTER ❖

See File-Sharing and the Courts (Attempts to Control Technology)

❖ NCIPA ❖

See Children's Internet Protection Act

❖ NET NEUTRALITY ❖

According to proponents of net neutrality (also known as network or Internet neutrality), the Internet functions best (and most fairly) if Internet service providers (ISPs) do not discriminate among users or data, but instead treat all equally. Differential pricing for different users or types of data violates net neutrality, as does giving higher priority to certain users or types of data. In particular, any attempt by ISPs to create tiered pricing or service, especially to discriminate against subscribers of their competitors, violates net neutrality.

Because the marketplace provides more incentives for ISPs to discriminate against their competitors and in favor of their own content and subscribers than it does to provide neutral access, proponents of net neutrality have attempted to convince the U.S. Congress to enact legislation requiring it. These attempts have been unsuccessful; however, the Federal Communications Commission (FCC) has, for the most part, acted as a guardian of net neutrality. Its authority is limited, however. In 2008, the FCC ruled against Comcast, an ISP, in a complaint brought by Comcast subscribers over Comcast's interference with their use of BitTorrent, a peer-to-peer networking application. Comcast then petitioned for review in the U.S. Court of Appeals for the District of Columbia Circuit, which held that the FCC had lacked authority to rule against Comcast, because "the Commission has failed to tie its assertion of ancillary authority over Comcast's Internet service to any 'statutorily mandated responsibility'" (Comcast Corp., 600 F. 3d at 661).

Case

- *Comcast Corp. v. FCC*, 600 F.3d 642 (D.C. Cir. 2010)

See also: Activism and Advocacy Groups; Broadband; Cable; Federal Communications Commission; Internet

Source and Further Reading
"Internet Governance: System Error," *The Economist*, December 1, 2012, at 67

❖ NO ELECTRONIC THEFT ACT ❖

The No Electronic Theft Act (NET Act) was enacted in 1997 to address the specific problem of warez trading and the general problem of intellectual property piracy. The NET Act was a response to an early unsuccessful attempt to prosecute a warez trader, David LaMacchia, a twenty-one year old student at the Massachusetts Institute of Technology (MIT). LaMacchia operated a bulletin board service (BBS), making use of MIT's network to do so. In the early 1990s, LaMacchia's BBS, Cynosure, enabled users to upload and download popular software of the day, such as WordPerfect 6.0, Excel 5.0, and SimCity 2000. Because LaMacchia did not operate Cynosure for financial gain, he could not be charged directly with criminal copyright infringement under the law at the time. In 1994, LaMacchia was arrested and charged with conspiracy to violate the federal wire fraud statute, 18 U.S.C. § 1343 (LaMacchia, 871 F. Supp. at 536). The federal district court for the District of Massachusetts dismissed the charges against LaMacchia. An earlier Supreme Court decision, *Dowling v. United States,* had held that intellectual property, including copyright, could not be taken by fraud; thus LaMacchia could not have conspired to commit a fraud to take the copyright owners' property interests in the software (LaMacchia, 871 F. Supp. at 545). The district court was not particularly pleased with its own result, and called LaMacchia's conduct "at best . . . heedlessly irresponsible, and at worst . . . nihilistic, self-indulgent, and lacking in any fundamental sense of values" (LaMacchia, 871 F. Supp. at 545). Congress, the court suggested, should modify the law: "Criminal as well as civil penalties should probably attach to willful, multiple infringements of copyrighted software even absent a commercial motive on the part of the infringer" (LaMacchia, 871 F. Supp. at 545).

It took three years for Congress, at the urging of content industry lobbyists, to make the modifications suggested by the court. In 1997 Congress enacted the NET Act in order, according to the House of Representatives report on the bill, "to reverse the practical consequences of *United States v. LaMacchia*" (House Report, *3). Eric Goldman, an expert commentator on the NET Act, describes its effects as follows:

> The Act effected six principal changes to criminal copyright law. First, the NET Act expanded the Copyright Act's definition of "financial gain" to include the receipt (or expectation of receipt) of anything of value, including other copyrighted works. Second, in addition to willful infringement for commercial advantage or private financial gain, the Act criminalized the reproduction or distribution, in any 180 day period, of copyrighted works with a total retail value of more than $1,000. Third, the Act said that evidence of reproducing and distributing copyrighted works does not, by itself, establish willfulness. Fourth, the Act changed the punishments for criminal infringement. For infringements of more than $1,000, the punishment includes imprisonment of up to one year and a fine. For infringements of $2,500 or more, the punishment includes imprisonment of up to three years and a fine. For second or subsequent offenses involving commercial advantage or private financial gain, the punishment includes imprisonment of up to six years. Fifth, the Act permits copyright infringement victims to submit victim impact statements. Finally, the Act instructed the United States Sentencing Commission . . . to adjust the United States Sentencing Guidelines . . . for criminal copyright infringement to make the punishments sufficiently stringent to deter the crimes and to reflect the infringed items' retail value and quantity (Goldman 2003, 373–374).

After reviewing the provisions and the legislative history of the Act, Goldman concludes that "Congress specifically targeted warez trading" of the nonprofit enthusiast type engaged in by LaMacchia and others (Goldman 2003, 375).

The first 18 months after the passage of the NET Act brought no prosecutions, leading Congress to convene hearings to inquire as to the lack of activity. Following the hearings, the Justice Department began to pursue prosecutions under the NET Act, and by February 2004 at least 80 warez traders and pirates had been convicted. Many of these, including many enthusiast warez traders with no financial motive, were sent to prison (Goldman 2003, 427). Several of the prosecutions resulted from the 2001 Department of Justice crackdown on the long-running cracker/warez group, DrinkOrDie (see Tresco Slashdot Interview 2002).

Statute
- No Electronic Theft Act, amending and codified at 17 U.S.C. §§ 101, 506 & 507 & 18 U.S.C. §§ 2319–2320

Legislative History
- House Report on the No Electronic Theft Act, H.R. Rep. No. 339 (1997)

Cases
Supreme Court
- *Dowling v. United States*, 473 U.S. 207 (1985)

Federal District Court
- *United States v. LaMacchia*, 871 F. Supp. 535 (D. Mass. 1994)

See also: Abandonware; Copyright; Copyright Infringement; File-Sharing; Hacking; Warez

Sources and Further Reading
Eric Goldman, "A Road to No Warez: The No Electronic Theft Act and Criminal Copyright Infringement," 82 *Oregon Law Review* 369 (2003)

"Former DrinkOrDie Member Chris Tresco Answers," *Slashdot* (October 4, 2002), available at http://interviews.slashdot .org/story/02/10/04/144217/former-drinkordie-member-chris-tresco-answers (visited February 9, 2013)

U.S. Department of Justice, "Six Formerly Associated with Fox Cable Charged with Copyright Infringement for Running Warez Site That Had Pirated Movies, Software" (May 14, 2004), available at http://www.justice.gov/criminal/ cybercrime/press-releases/2004/sarnaCharge.htm (visited February 9, 2013)

❖ OBSCENITY ❖

Expression that is obscene is not protected by the First Amendment. Defining "obscene" in universally comprehensible and applicable terms has presented some difficulty, however. The legal definition currently in use, established by the U.S. Supreme Court in the 1973 case of *Miller v. California*, was arrived at only after much litigation and deliberation and many false starts. The Supreme Court's first attempt to address the problem came in the 1957 case of *Roth v. United States*. The Roth court defined expression as obscene if "to the average person, applying contemporary community standards, the dominant theme of the material, taken as a whole, appeals to prurient interest" and if it is "utterly without redeeming social importance" (354 U.S. 484, 489). This rule contains elements of the rule finally adopted; however, it proved difficult to apply and resulted in many erroneous decisions in lower courts. The Supreme Court revisited the issue in the 1964 case of *Jacobellis v. Ohio*. In *Jacobellis* the Court added a requirement that expression, in order to be obscene, must go "substantially beyond customary limits of candor in description or representation" (378 U.S. at 191). The *Jacobellis* court also struggled with the difficulty of determining "community standards"; at that time it decided that the "community" referred to in the phrase "contemporary community standards" was a national, not local, community (378 U.S. at 192). Nine years later the Supreme Court was to reverse itself on this point in *Miller v. California*, the case that set the standard currently in use.

In 1973, the Court decided *Miller v. California*, a case involving the mass mailing of sexually explicit advertising. Miller is thus relevant not only to the general problem of Internet pornography and obscenity but also to the specific problem of sexually explicit spam. The *Miller* court created a three-part test. In order to determine whether content is obscene it must be determined

(a) whether the "average person, applying contemporary community standards" would find that the work, taken as a whole, appeals to the prurient interest,
(b) whether the work depicts or describes, in a patently offensive way, sexual conduct specifically defined by the applicable state law, and

(c) whether the work, taken as a whole, lacks serious literary, artistic, political, or scientific value (413 U.S. at 39).

This definition, with its "community standards" element, covers a broader range of material than the definitions in *Roth* and *Jacobellis*. It has also proven capable enough of application to endure, with occasional clarifications, for more than 40 years so far.

In making determinations as to obscenity, jurors are to apply the standards of the area from which they come as "community standards." An appeal to the prurient interest, under the California law addressed in *Miller*, was an appeal to "shameful or morbid interests" in sexual conduct, but not something that incites "normal" lust, despite the obvious problems of moral relativity and value judgments implicit in distinguishing between "shameful" and "normal" lusts.

The term "average person" includes only adults, not children. "Serious artistic, political, or scientific value" is determined according to a national, not local, standard. Material that meets some, but not all, of the criteria of the *Miller* test may be indecent, but not obscene. According to the Supreme Court's opinion in *Federal Communications Commission v. Pacifica*, indecent material can be identified by its "nonconformance with accepted standards of morality." The objectionable material in the *Pacifica* case was comedian George Carlin's notorious "Filthy Words" (also known as "Seven Deadly Words") monologue. The monologue appeals to no prurient interest in sex; thus, it does not meet the first element of the Miller test. It is not about sex or intended to titillate; its apparent purpose is to make a point about censorship and about what makes certain speech offensive in some contexts but not in others. However, Carlin makes his points in part by explicit sexual and scatological descriptions apparently intended to shock (and, by extension, offend) at least part of his audience; thus, the monologue may meet the second of the three elements of the Miller test. It probably does not meet the third element of the test: the monologue has at least some literary, artistic, and political value, perhaps even serious value. Because the three elements are not all met, the monologue is not obscene, even though it is vulgar, offensive, and shocking. It can be, and is, indecent, however, and thus subject to some restrictions (*Pacifica*, 438 U.S. 726).

Cases

- *Ashcroft v. Free Speech Coalition*, 535 U.S. 234 (2002)
- *Brockett v. Spokane Arcades Inc.*, 472 U.S. 491 (1985)
- *Federal Communications Commission v. Pacifica Foundation*, 438 U.S. 726 (1978)
- *Hamling v. United States*, 418 U.S. 87 (1974)
- *Jacobellis v. Ohio*, 378 U.S. 184 (1964)
- *Miller v. California*, 413 U.S. 15 (1973)
- *Mishkin v. New York*, 383 U.S. 502 (1966)
- *Paris Adult Theatre v. Slaton*, 413 U.S. 49 (1973)
- *Pinkus v. United States*, 436 U.S. 293 (1978)
- *Pope v. Illinois*, 481 U.S. 497 (1987)
- *Reno v. American Civil Liberties Union*, 521 U.S. 844 (1997)
- *Roth v. United States*, 354 U.S. 476 (1957)

See also: Censorship; Child Online Protection Act; Children's Internet Protection Act; Communications Decency Act; Constitutional Law; First Amendment; Indecency; Pornography; Spam; xxx

Sources and Further Reading

Jerome A. Barron & C. Thomas Dienes, *Constitutional Law in a Nutshell* (St. Paul, MN: West, 7th ed. 2009)

Mike Godwin, *Cyber Rights: Defending Free Speech in the Digital Age* (Cambridge, MA: MIT Press, 2003)

Kevin W. Saunders, *Saving Our Children from the First Amendment* (New York: New York University Press, 2003)

Madeleine Schachter, *Law of Internet Speech* (Durham, NC: Carolina Academic Press, 3d ed. 2008)

❖ ONLINE COPYRIGHT INFRINGEMENT LIABILITY LIMITATION ACT ❖

See Digital Millennium Copyright Act, Title II

❖ OPEN SOURCE ❖

The term "open source" originally referred to software whose source code is freely distributed and may be modified by users. "Open source" is now used for other information resources as well, including the open source encyclopedia Wikipedia (Economist 2004). Because computer software is too new to have fallen into the public domain through the expiration of copyright terms, it can be made open source only by a deliberate act of the author. The author must make the software available under an open-source license, of which the best known is probably the GNU General Public License (GPL). An author's use of an open-source license is sometimes, but inaccurately, referred to as "placing the software in the public domain." Technically, the software is still copyrighted and thus not in the public domain; a better term is "copyleft," developed as an alternative to "copyright" to refer to the use of the GNU GPL.

Other fields have imitated, or are attempting to imitate, the open-source approach. Copyright restrictions are often seen as stifling creativity, which may be a fair exchange when the copyrighted work is valuable but serves to hinder the development of ideas as in the case of articles in academic journals; the academic articles are worth no money but subject to the same level of copyright protection as works worth millions of dollars. The term "open access" is used to refer to a process equivalent to copylefting through which journals and scholars would make their works available with few restrictions other than the acknowledgment of authorship and first publication (Budapest Open Access Initiative 2002). Open-source approaches to areas of intellectual property other than copyright have also been proposed, including open-source pharmaceuticals (Economist 2004).

The best-known open-source software program is the GNU/Linux operating system, but others abound. Two-thirds of the Web's 50 million or so servers run Apache, an open-source HTTP server program (Apache 2012; Economist 2004). The open-source email program Sendmail is even more universal (Economist 2004); however, these programs tend to operate out of the sight of most users and have not attracted the same level of media attention as GNU/Linux.

Document

- Budapest Open Access Initiative (February 14, 2002), available at http://www.soros.org/openaccess/read.shtml

See also: Budapest Open Access Initiative; GNU/Linux; Project Gutenberg; Public Domain

Sources and Further Reading

"The Number One HTTP Server on The Internet," Apache HTTP Server Project (April 2012), http://httpd.apache.org/ (visited January 12, 2013)

"Open Source: Beyond Capitalism?" *The Economist*, June 10, 2004, available at http://www.economist.com/node/2747734 (visited February 8, 2013)

❖ ORPHANED TECHNOLOGY ❖

See Abandonware

P

❖ P2P ❖

P2P, an abbreviation for peer-to-peer, refers to a type of file-sharing network in which files are exchanged directly between users rather than through a central server. The use of P2P networks in the abstract is perfectly legal, and there are many perfectly innocuous P2P networks, such as SETI@home, a distributed computing project that allows users to participate in the search for extraterrestrial intelligence by devoting unused computer resources to analyzing radio telescope data for possible transmissions from the stars. These uses of P2P networks rarely grab headlines, however (although SETI@home surely will if it ever succeeds in its mission). Most attention to P2P networks focuses on the fact that they are often, perhaps primarily, used to trade unauthorized copies of copyrighted material, especially popular songs compressed as MP3 files. The volume of MP3 file-sharing has grown so large that, in the opinion of many in the music content industry, it threatens the industry's continued existence. The content industry has pursued P2P networks and their users with lawsuits for copyright infringement, but these lawsuits may have been counterproductive. The content industry's early victory over Napster led P2P services to design around existing law. The currently popular "supernode" systems avoid the centralization of search functions that made Napster vulnerable to suits for contributory and vicarious infringement. These systems designate certain computers in the network, with their users' consent, as supernodes; search lists are maintained on these machines rather than on a centralized server. The legality of this approach, at least when marketed as a tool for music file-sharing, was undercut by the Supreme Court's decision in *Metro-Goldwyn-Mayer Studios, Inc. v. Grokster, Ltd.*, 545 U.S. 913 (2005). In the post-*Grokster* world BitTorrent has emerged as the most popular P2P file-sharing protocol.

The legality of the P2P networks themselves, however, does not mean that using those networks to share copyrighted material is lawful. The P2P operators do not copy files themselves; if they are to be held liable, it must be as contributory or vicarious infringers, or through some new category of copyright infringement liability to be defined by Congress in future legislation. The users who copy files, however, may be committing direct copyright infringement, and the content industry has filed hundreds of lawsuits against individual users of P2P networks (Bergen 2004, 200).

Cases
Supreme Court
- *Metro-Goldwyn-Mayer Studios, Inc. v. Grokster, Ltd.*, 545 U.S. 913 (2005)

Federal Appellate Court
- *A&M Records, Inc. v. Napster, Inc.*, 239 F.3d 1004 (9th Cir. 2001), on remand, No. 00–16401, 2001 WL 227083 (N.D. Cal. 2001), affirmed, 284 F.3d 1091 (9th Cir. 2002)
- *In re Aimster Copyright Litigation (Aimster II)*, 252 F. Supp. 2d 634 (N.D. Ill. 2002); affirmed in part, 334 F.3d 643 (7th Cir. 2003); certiorari denied sub nom *Deep v. Recording Industry Ass'n of America, Inc.*, 540 U.S. 1107 (2004)
- *Recording Industry Association of America, Inc. v. Verizon Internet Services, Inc.*, 351 F.3d 1229 (D.C. Cir. 2003)

Netherlands Appellate Court
- *Buma & Stemra v. KaZaA*, Amsterdam Court of Appeal (2002), unofficial English translation available at http://w2.eff.org/IP/P2P/BUMA_v_Kazaa/20020328_kazaa_appeal_judgment.html (visited December 19, 2012)

See also: Activism and Advocacy Groups; Copyright; Copyright Alert System; Copyright Infringement; DeCSS; Digital Rights Management; File-Sharing; File-Sharing and the Courts (Attempts to Control Technology); File-Sharing and the Courts (Litigation Against Individual Users); File-Sharing (Other Media); Stop Online Piracy Act; Voluntary Collective License; Warez

Sources and Further Reading
Grace J. Bergen, "Litigation as a Tool against Digital Piracy," 35 *McGeorge Law Review* 181 (2004)
John Buford, Heather Yu, & Eng Keong Lua, *P2P Networking and Applications* (Burlington, MA: Morgan Kaufmann, 2008)
"Face Value: The Quiet Iconoclast—With KaZaA, Niklas Zennstrom Undermined the Music Industry," *The Economist*, July 3, 2004, at 54

Patrick Gray, "Sharman Presses for Evidence," *Wired News* (May 18, 2004), available at http://www.wired.com/news/digiwood/0,1412,63509,00.html (visited February 8, 2013)

Jay Lyman, "Google Pulls P2P Links over Kazaa Copyright Claims," *TechNewsWorld* (September 2, 2003, 3:39 PM), available at http://www.technewsworld.com/story/31481.html (visited February 8, 2013)

Seagrumn Smith, "From Napster to KaZaA: The Battle over Peer-to-Peer Filesharing Goes International," 2003 *Duke Law & Technology Review* 8 (2003)

❖ PALLADIUM ❖

See Digital Rights Management

❖ PARODY ❖

See Fair Use (Copyright)

❖ PARIS CONVENTION ❖

The Paris Convention creates the Paris Union, which governs issues relating to trademarks, patents, and unfair competition in international law among its members. The Paris Union is administered by the World Intellectual Property Organization (WIPO). As of December 2012, 174 countries were parties to the Paris Convention. The United States has been a party since 1887; the most recent party, Brunei, joined in February 2012. The Paris Convention provides three forms of protection to intellectual property right holders from member states. The first of these is national treatment. Article 2 of the convention requires member states to give national treatment to right holders from other member states:

> Nationals of any country of the Union shall, as regards the protection of industrial property, enjoy in all the other countries of the Union the advantages that their respective laws now grant, or may hereafter grant, to nationals; all without prejudice to the rights specially provided for by this Convention. Consequently, they shall have the same protection as the latter, and the same legal remedy against any infringement of their rights, provided that the conditions and formalities imposed upon nationals are complied with (Paris Convention, art. 2(1)).

Article 3 extends this protection to "[n]ationals of countries outside the Union who are domiciled or who have real and effective industrial or commercial establishments in the territory of one of the countries of the Union," as well.

Second, the Paris Convention requires each of its members to guarantee to provide a defined minimum level of protection for various types of intellectual property. Third, it requires its members to provide a right of priority to applicants for trademarks, patents, and utility model and design registrations from other member countries:

> Any person who has duly filed an application for a patent, or for the registration of a utility model, or of an industrial design, or of a trademark, in one of the countries of the Union, or his successor in title, shall enjoy, for the purpose of filing in the other countries, a right of priority during the periods hereinafter fixed (Paris Convention, art. 4(A)(1)).

In other words, once the applicant has applied for a patent, utility model registration, trademark, or design registration in Country A, he or she may apply for the same form of protection in other member countries within a set period of time and that application will be treated as if it had been filed on the same date as the filing in Country A—assuming that Country A is a party to the Paris Convention. For patents and utility models, the right of priority extends for 12 months; at any time within 12 months after filing the initial application in Country A, the inventor may file another application in Country B—even if someone else has filed an application for the same invention in the interim. So long as the second inventor's filing is dated later than the first inventor's original filing in Country A, the first inventor's filing in Country B will be treated as if it had been filed first in Country B as well. For trademarks and industrial design registrations, the right of priority works in the same way, but for a period of 6 months rather than 12 months (Paris Convention, art. 4(C)(1)).

The Paris Convention is incorporated into the World Trade Organization's Agreement on Trade-Related Aspects of Intellectual Property Rights (TRIPS) by Article 2 of TRIPS:

> 1. In respect of Parts II, III and IV of this Agreement, Members shall comply with Articles 1 through 12, and Article 19, of the Paris Convention (1967).
> 2. Nothing in Parts I to IV of this Agreement shall derogate from existing obligations that Members may have to each other under the Paris Convention, the Berne Convention, the Rome Convention and the Treaty on Intellectual Property in Respect of Integrated Circuits.

Thus WTO members, even the handful not already parties to the Paris Convention, are required to abide by the Paris Convention's substantive terms. And in the event that the terms of TRIPS impose less of an obligation on a member state than the Paris Convention would, the member states may not use TRIPS as an excuse to avoid the Paris Convention obligation.

Treaties

- Agreement on Trade-Related Aspects of Intellectual Property Rights, Marrakesh Agreement Establishing the World Trade Organization, Annex 1C, April 15, 1994, 33 I.L.M. 81 (1994)

- Paris Convention for the Protection of Industrial Property, March 20, 1883, as revised at Brussels on December 14, 1900, at Washington on June 2, 1911, at The Hague on November 6, 1925, at London on June 2, 1934, at Lisbon on October 31, 1958, and at Stockholm on July 14, 1967, and as amended on September 28, 1979, 21 U.S.T. 1583, 828 U.N.T.S. 305

See also: International Patent Protection; International Trademark Protection; Patent; Patent Cooperation Treaty; Trademark; TRIPS; WIPO

Sources and Further Reading

Graeme B. Dinwoodie et al., *International and Comparative Patent Law* (Newark, NJ: LexisNexis, 2002)

J. Thomas McCarthy et al., *McCarthy's Desk Encyclopedia of Intellectual Property* (Washington, D.C.: Bureau of National Affairs, 3d ed. 2004)

Nuno Pires de Carvalho, *The TRIPS Regime of Patent Rights* (The Hague: Kluwer Law International, 2d ed. 2005)

Nuno Pires de Carvalho, *The TRIPS Regime of Patent Rights* (The Hague: Kluwer Law International, 3d ed. 2010)

❖ PARIS UNION ❖

See Paris Convention

❖ PATENT ❖

A patent is an intellectual property right that grants the right holder the right to exclude others from making an invention, as well as from selling it, using it, offering to sell it, or importing it into the United States. It does not, as is sometimes believed, grant the holder the right to make, sell, use, offer to sell, or import the invention. Patents are often granted for improvements upon already patented previous technology, and the patent on the underlying invention would prevent the holder of the patent on the improvement from making, and so on, the improved invention (McCarthy et al. 2004, 433–435).

In order to be patentable under U.S. law, an invention must meet these basic requirements: it must be useful (35 U.S.C. § 101); it must be novel (35 U.S.C. § 102); and it must not be obvious (35 U.S.C. § 103). Assessing the latter two requirements requires an examination of the "prior art"—the existing body of inventions and technical knowledge in the area.

An invention that meets these three requirements must go through a lengthy patent application process. Until recently, U.S. patent law protected the first person to invent, rather than the first person to file a patent application. The patent laws of other countries have traditionally protected the first person to file. Under the America Invents Act, the United States became a first-inventor-to-disclose-or-file country in March 2013.

Other countries also take different approaches to the process of granting patents and the substantive rules applied. As a result, gaining international patent protection is considerably more complex than gaining international copyright or even trademark protection. The Patent Cooperation Treaty simplifies the subject somewhat, but both the U.S. and Patent Cooperation Treaty processes are time-consuming, complex, arduous, and expensive, and should not be undertaken without the assistance of someone experienced in the process.

Patent protection in the United States lasts for 20 years from the date on which the patent application was filed, in accordance with the Agreement on TRIPS (35 U.S.C. § 154(a)(2)). The TRIPS term replaces the earlier U.S. term of 17 years from the date on which the patent is granted; as the law adopting the TRIPS standard specifies that no patent application shall remain pending for more than three years, the TRIPS term will in no case be shorter than the original 17-year term (35 U.S.C. § 154(b)(1)(B)). As with other intellectual property rights, it is the duty of the right holder, not of the government, to detect and pursue infringers.

Patent law played an important role in the early development of software by its absence; from the 1960s onward, the United States Patent and Trademark Office (USPTO) opposed the idea of software patents. The report of the 1966 President's Commission on the Patent System adopted this approach, and the 1972 decision of the U.S. Supreme Court in *Gottschalk v. Benson*, holding that a mathematical algorithm used in a computer program was not patentable, was also widely understood as stating that computer programs were unpatentable. Although the Supreme Court appeared to soften its position on software patents in the 1981 case of *Diamond v. Diehr*, it was not until 1994 that the USPTO explicitly accepted the idea of software patents by publishing guidelines regarding the patentability of computer programs. The USPTO's reversal followed the 1994 decision of the Federal Circuit Court of Appeals in *In re Alappat*, specifically recognizing the patentability of certain types of computer programs (33 F.3d 1526). *Alappat* was later abrogated by the Federal Circuit in *In re Bilski* (545 F.3d 943).

In the meantime, however, copyright, rather than patent, had become the main form of protection for computer software, and other countries had followed the U.S. lead in declaring software to be the subject of copyright rather than patent. Patent law has become important in an Internet context not because of the patenting of computer software but because of the advent and proliferation of business method patents. Prior to the decision of the Federal Circuit in the 1998 case of *State Street Bank & Trust*, business methods had been viewed as unpatentable "methods of operation" under U.S. law (149 F.3d 1368). Ten years later, in 2008, *State Street* was abrogated by *In re Bilski*, which set a much narrower "machine or transformation" standard: under *Bilski*, a business method is patentable only "if: (1) it is tied to a particular machine or apparatus, or (2) it transforms a particular article into a different state or thing" (545 F.3d at 954). Article 27 of TRIPS has had the same effect internationally; it has been interpreted as requiring WTO members to grant business method patents (Conley 2003, 8).

Treaties

- Agreement on Trade-Related Aspects of Intellectual Property Rights, Marrakesh Agreement Establishing the World Trade Organization, Annex 1C, April 15, 1994, 33 I.L.M. 81 (1994)
- Paris Convention for the Protection of Industrial Property, March 20, 1883, as revised at Brussels on December 14, 1900, at Washington on June 2, 1911, at The Hague on November 6, 1925, at London on June 2, 1934, at Lisbon on October 31, 1958, and at Stockholm on July 14, 1967, and as amended on September 28, 1979, 21 U.S.T. 1583, 828 U.N.T.S. 305
- Patent Cooperation Treaty, June 19, 1970, as amended on September 28, 1979, and as modified on February 3, 1984, and October 3, 2001, 28 U.S.T. 7645, 9 I.L.M. 978 (1970)

Statute

- Patent Code, 35 U.S.C. §§ 1–376

Cases

Supreme Court

- *Gottschalk v. Benson*, 409 U.S. 63 (1972)
- *Diamond v. Diehr, II*, 450 U.S. 175 (1981)

Federal Appellate Courts

- *Apple Computer, Inc. v. Franklin Computer Corp.*, 714 F.2d 1240 (3d Cir. 1983)
- *In re Alappat*, 33 F.3d 1526 (Fed. Cir. 1994), abrogated by *In re Bilski*, 545 F.3d 943 (Fed. Cir. 2008)
- *In re Bilski*, 545 F.3d 943 (2008)
- *State Street Bank & Trust Co. v. Signature Financial Group*, 149 F.3d 1368 (Fed. Cir. 1998), certiorari denied, 525 U.S. 1093

See also: America Invents Act; Business Methods Patent; Computer Program; International Patent Protection; Paris Convention; Patent Cooperation Treaty; Prosecution History Estoppel; Three-Dimensional Printing; TRIPS (Patent); WIPO

Sources and Further Reading

John M. Conley, "The International Law of Business Method Patents," *U.S. Patent and Trademark Office Economic Review* (October 2003), at 15, available at http://www.frbatlanta.org/filelegacydocs/erq403_conley.pdf (visited February 8, 2013)

Graeme B. Dinwoodie et al., *International and Comparative Patent Law* (Newark, NJ: LexisNexis, 2002)

Amy L. Landers, *Understanding Patent Law* (New Providence, NJ: LexisNexis, 2d ed. 2012)

J. Thomas McCarthy et al., *McCarthy's Desk Encyclopedia of Intellectual Property* (Washington, D.C.: Bureau of National Affairs, 3d ed. 2004)

Robert P. Merges & Jane C. Ginsburg, *Foundations of Intellectual Property* (New Providence, NJ: LexisNexis, 2006)

Aaron Schwabach, *Intellectual Property: A Reference Handbook* (Santa Barbara, CA: ABC-CLIO, 2007)

Toshiko Takenaka, "The Best Patent Practice or Mere Compromise? A Review of the Current Draft of the Substantive Patent Law Treaty and a Proposal for a First-to-Invent Exception for Domestic Applicants," 11 *Texas Intellectual Property Law Journal* 259 (2003)

❖ PATENT COOPERATION TREATY ❖

The Patent Cooperation Treaty (PCT) greatly streamlines the multination patent application process. Prior to the adoption of the PCT, patenting an invention in multiple countries was a daunting task, involving long, expensive, and complex application procedures in multiple languages, cultures, and legal systems. The PCT has simplified the process; through the PCT, an inventor can file a patent application simultaneously in any or all of the countries that are parties. One hundred and twenty-four states are now parties to the PCT, the most recent being Panama, for which the treaty became binding on June 7, 2012.

The PCT does not, as is sometimes believed, create any sort of global patent, nor does it guarantee the success of patent applications in other countries (McCarthy et al. 2004, 437–438). Different countries have different standards for granting patents and different histories of patents already granted and refused, and an invention that is patentable in one country may well be unpatentable in another. The United States Patent and Trademark Office is considered to be lenient, even lax, in granting patents; many patent applications that are denied elsewhere may be granted in the United States.

In order to gain the benefit of the PCT, the inventor must file a patent application with a designated Receiving Office; the national patent offices of PCT member states can function as Receiving Offices. A separate fee must eventually be paid for each country in which a patent is sought and for each language into which the application must be translated; fee is not payable at the time of filing but much later in the process. Only one application is required; once the fee is paid, the Receiving Office will handle much of the complexity of separate national application processes and translations (PCT arts. 10, 12, 15, 22). The initial application, however, must be in Arabic, Chinese, English, French, German, Japanese, Korean, Portuguese, Russian, or Spanish (WIPO, *Direct Filing of PCT Applications* 2012).

The WIPO administers the PCT, and PCT filing fees provide a significant portion of WIPO's budget. The

International Bureau of WIPO is also designated as a Receiving Office under the PCT (PCT Rule 19.1(a)(iii)). The PCT works in conjunction with regional patent agreements, so that an applicant from a PCT member state may apply for and receive a regional patent where some agreement permitting regional patents exists. Regional patent agreements under which patents may be granted under the PCT include the Eurasian Patent Convention, the European Patent Convention, the Harare Protocol of the African Regional Industrial Property Organization, and the agreement forming the Organisation Africaine de la Propriété Intellectuelle (WIPO, *Regional Patents* 2012).

Treaty

- Patent Cooperation Treaty, Washington, D.C., June 19, 1970, as amended on September 28, 1979, and as modified on February 3, 1984, and October 3, 2001, 28 U.S.T. 7645, 9 I.L.M. 978 (1970)

Rule

- World Intellectual Property Organization, Regulations under the Patent Cooperation Treaty (PCT) Rule 19.1(a)(iii), available at http://www.wipo.int/pct/en/texts/rules/r19.htm (visited December 19, 2012)

See also: International Patent Protection; Patent; WIPO

Sources and Further Reading

J. Thomas McCarthy et al., *McCarthy's Desk Encyclopedia of Intellectual Property* (Washington, D.C.: Bureau of National Affairs, 3d ed. 2004)

WIPO, "About the Patent Cooperation Treaty," PCT, International Patent System (2012), available at http://www.wipo.int/pct/en/treaty/about.html (visited February 8, 2013)

WIPO, "Direct Filing of PCT Applications with the International Bureau as PCT Receiving Office," PCT, International Patent System (2012), available at http://www.wipo.int/pct/en/filing/filing.html (visited August 16, 2012)

WIPO, "PCT Contracting States for which a Regional Patent can be Obtained via the PCT," PCT, International Patent System (May 1, 2012), available at http://www.wipo.int/pct/en/texts/reg_des.html (visited February 8, 2013)

❖ PEER-TO-PEER ❖

See P2P

❖ PHISHING ❖

Phishing is an Internet scam technique used to obtain credit card numbers, account numbers, passwords, and other confidential information, often as the first stage of identity theft. The word is derived from "password harvesting fishing," and has no connection to the band Phish. Phishing and related techniques that aim at exploiting the gullibility or good will of other users are known as social engineering.

A phishing attack is typically carried out by email or instant messaging. The attacker sends an email or instant message to the victim; the message purports to be from a bank, a government agency, an ISP, an online payment service, or some similar entity with which the victim might have an account. The text of the message is designed to convince the victim to send the desired information to the phisher in the mistaken belief that he or she is sending it to a company that will use it to the victim's benefit. A sample phishing email is reproduced next:

Subject: Verify Your E-Mail with Citibank
This email was sent by the Citibank server to verify your email address. You must complete this process by clicking on the link below and entering in the small window your Citibank ATM/Debit Card number and PIN that you use on ATM.

This is done for your protection—because some of our members no longer have access to their email addresses and we must verify it.

To verify your email address and access your bank account, click on the link below:
***

Thank you for using Citibank

The top of the email reproduces the blue and white Citibank logo. Clicking on the link takes the user to a site that also uses the Citibank logo and purports to be a Citibank site; the site may even spoof the Citibank URL in the browser's address bar. Choosing "Sign On to a Citi Account" from a list of options gives the user the opportunity to enter his or her Citibank account number and password. A search in the Lookup database at www.whois.com reveals that the site is not, in fact, owned by Citibank. (Given the nature of the site, the name that does appear as registrant, administrative contact and technical contact is most likely either the name of a nonexistent person or the name of some innocent person chosen either at random or maliciously by the site's true operator.) The most likely explanation is that some person is deliberately attempting to trick people into believing that the site is a Citibank site, and then harvesting any account numbers and passwords that are entered.

Phishing can be, and in the case of the preceding email is, combined with spamming. Few people would be taken in by the previous letter; if it is emailed to 100,000,000 Citibank card holders, however, and only one-one hundredth of one percent are taken in, the phisher will still have harvested 10,000 credit card numbers. If an average of only $100 is stolen from each card, the phisher will have made a million dollars with only a couple of hours' effort, or less. (Creating the fake site actually requires little effort, as it can be copied from the real site, changing only the crucial links.)

The easiest way to avoid being taken in by a phishing scam is not to respond to any emails asking for confidential personal or financial information; the real Citibank will have no reason to request anyone's credit card number or login information by email. The crimes involved in phishing, including fraud, wire fraud, and theft, have long been prohibited by state and federal law; phishers face long prison sentences if caught and convicted. Crimes involved in phishing scams include bank fraud (18 U.S.C. § 1344), computer fraud (18 U.S.C. § 1030(a)(4)), credit card fraud (18 U.S.C. § 1029), identity theft (18 U.S.C. § 1028(a)(7)), and wire fraud (18 U.S.C. § 1343). Phishing operations involving spamming also violate the CAN-SPAM Act (18 U.S.C. § 1037), while phishing operations involving viruses, worms, or other malicious code violate 18 U.S.C. § 1028(a)(5).

Phishers are also subject to civil lawsuits. In addition to the obvious suits by the victims for compensation, they may be subject to suits by the companies whose names are used and whose Web sites and logos are copied. The misuse of the name may be trademark dilution by tarnishment, while the copying of the trademark and of material from the company's Web site involves trademark infringement and copyright infringement.

Phishers are actively pursued by the Federal Trade Commission and the Anti-Phishing Working Group formed by companies whose names have been abused, and whose customers have been targeted, by phishing scams. Copies of suspected phishing emails can be sent to these organizations at spam@uce.gov and reportphishing@antiphishing.org, respectively (FTC 2012).

Statutes

- Bank Fraud Act, 18 U.S.C. § 1344
- Controlling the Assault of Non-Solicited Pornography and Marketing (CAN-SPAM) Act, 18 U.S.C. § 1037
- Computer Fraud and Abuse Act, 18 U.S.C. § 1030
- Credit Card Fraud Act, 18 U.S.C. § 1029
- Identity Theft and Assumption Deterrence Act, 18 U.S.C. § 1028
- Wire Fraud Act, 18 U.S.C. § 1343

See also: Enforcement; Federal Trade Commission; Hacking; Identity Theft; Spam

Sources and Further Reading

"Avoid Scams: Phishing," OnGuardOnline.gov (September 2011), available at http://www.onguardonline.gov/phishing (visited February 8, 2013)

"Binational Working Group on Cross-Border Mass Marketing Fraud," Report on Phishing: A Report to the Minister of Public Safety and Emergency Preparedness Canada and the Attorney General of the United States (October 2006), available at http://www.justice.gov/opa/report_on_phishing.pdf (visited February 8, 2013)

❖ PHREAKING ❖

Phreaking bears the same relationship to telecommunications systems that hacking bears to information systems. Like hacking, it is a tech-counterculture phenomenon that originated, insofar as it can be traced to any one origin, at the Massachusetts Institute of Technology (MIT) in the 1960s. The term "phreaking" is derived from "phone freaking"; it is important to the Internet world both because of the effect it has had on hacking and because many early phreakers developed technical skills which they later put to use to build home computing and the Internet.

In the 1960s, early phreakers at MIT used computers to generate the tones used by the then-existing telecommunications network for billing, switching, and dialing calls. Early phreakers at MIT were more interested in exploring the telecommunications system than in stealing telephone services; they were technology enthusiasts. At the time, however, long-distance telephone calls were very expensive, and the phreaking techniques developed by enthusiasts soon spread beyond the MIT campus into the 1960s counterculture (Jammer & Jack the Ripper 1987, 30). Phreaking became widespread in the early 1970s, when Abbie Hoffman's Youth International Party devoted a magazine, *Youth International Party Line*, to teaching and discussing phreaking techniques. Although phreakers did not damage or disrupt the telecommunications network, they made calls that arguably resulted in substantial lost revenues to the phone companies; Hoffman argued that free phone calls harmed no one (Cronin & Weikers 2004, n. 4). As with the music industry's arguments regarding lost sales, the total value of calls made by phreakers was probably far greater than the amount of business lost, as most of those calls would not have been made had the callers been required to pay for them.

Nonetheless, the phone companies felt threatened by phreaking, and prevailed upon the federal government to criminalize it (Cronin & Weikers 2004). Phreakers including the celebrated Captain Crunch were imprisoned for violation of the Wire Fraud Act and other telecommunications statutes (Draper 2007). Eventually, for reasons related to technological advances rather than to phreaking, the telephone companies replaced their voice transmission and signal-transmission hardware, rendering old-school phreaking impossible. At the same time long-distance telephone costs dropped dramatically, decreasing the popular appeal of phreaking.

The phreaking culture had its own slang and its own celebrities, foreshadowing the hacking culture of today. Captain Crunch (John Draper) took his name from a whistle found in a box of Captain Crunch cereal; the whistle, when blown, generated a 2600 hertz tone, necessary for phone phreaking (and the source of the name of *2600: The Hacker Quarterly*). Joe the Whistler (Joe Engressia), who was blind, could whistle the tone. Many phreakers found their way into Silicon Valley and the high-tech industry; Captain Crunch went to work for Apple, and Apple founders Steve Wozniak and Steve Jobs were rumored to have been phreakers (Freiberger & Swaine 1999).

While phreaking still goes on, it is largely confined to enthusiast groups. One exception is cell phone phreaking, or phone cloning, in which phreakers copy the identifying digital footprint of a cell phone in order to connect to the telecommunications network on that phone's account. Prankster phreaking of phone networks, in which the purpose is to lock up phones, also goes on, both through traditional phreaking techniques and through denial-of-service attacks. The growth of phones into portable computing devices has also made cell phone hacking possible; this hacking is sometimes, although incorrectly, referred to as phreaking (Weingarten 2002). And Van Eck phreaking, which has nothing to do with telephones, is a (perhaps largely hypothetical) technique for eavesdropping on computers from a distance, using electromagnetic radiation given off by now-obsolete cathode-ray tube monitors and possibly by printers and other devices (Van Eck 1985).

Statute
- Wire Fraud Act, 18 U.S.C. § 1343

See also: Encryption; Hacking

Sources and Further Reading
Kevin P. Cronin & Ronald N. Weikers, "Electronic Security Risks and the Need for Privacy, § 1.17," *Data Security and Privacy Law: Combating Cyberthreats* (St. Paul, MN: West, 2004)
John Draper, "Phone Phreaking Stories," (2007), available at http://www.webcrunchers.com/stories/ (visited February 8, 2013)
Paul Freiberger & Michael Swaine, *Fire in the Valley* (New York: McGraw-Hill, 2d ed. 1999)
The Jammer & Jack the Ripper, *The Official Phreaker's Manual* (February 14, 1987), available at http://www.phreak.ch/files/phreakmanual.txt (visited February 8, 2013)
Wim Van Eck, "Electromagnetic Radiation from Video Display Units: An Eavesdropping Risk?" 4 *North-Holland Computers & Security* 269 (1985), available at http://cryptome.org/emr.pdf (visited February 8, 2013)
Marc Weingarten, "Phone Phreaks," The Feature (February 25, 2002) available at http://www.thefeaturearchives.com/topic/Archive/Phone_Phreaks.html (visited February 8, 2013)
Youth International Party Line (aka *TAP Magazine*) archive, available at http://flag.blackened.net/daver/misc/yipl/ (visited December 19, 2012)

❖ PIPA ❖

See Preventing Real Online Threats to Economic Creativity and Theft of Intellectual Property Act

❖ PIRACY ❖

To an international or admiralty lawyer, piracy is any of several crimes committed against ships at sea and their occupants, including robbery, theft, kidnapping, and murder. Piracy of this sort was for decades little more than a historical curiosity, romanticized by Hollywood; from the 1990s onward, however, pirate attacks on shipping began to rise, to more than 200 per year. Pirate attacks are now a serious threat to shipping and to the lives of sailors, costing billions of dollars each year. Piracy is a crime against the law of nations; were Congress today to exercise its constitutionally granted power to license privateers, or government-sponsored pirates, by "grant[ing] Letters of Marque and Reprisal, and mak[ing] Rules concerning Captures on Land and Water" (U.S. Constitution, art. I, § 8, cl. 8), the United States would almost certainly be in violation of international law.

The term "piracy" is also applied to the hijacking of aircraft; to intellectual property lawyers, however, and these days to the media, "piracy" refers to something far less violent, if potentially more economically harmful: the infringement of intellectual property rights by large-scale unauthorized copying. These intellectual property "pirates" create and distribute unauthorized copies of things that are copyrighted, trademarked, or patented. In an Internet context most pirated material infringes on copyright, with trademark-infringing materials running a distant second. The term "piracy" can be used to refer to all unauthorized reproduction, but more often it is used to refer specifically to the operation of businesses specializing in the sale of unlawfully reproduced material. Thus, software pirates make and sell copies of copyrighted software; video pirates make and sell DVDs; music pirates make and sell CDs with hundreds of unlawfully copied MP3 files on them; apparel pirates make and sell imitation designer-label clothes, complete with unlawfully reproduced labels; and so forth. These businesses involve the Internet only peripherally, for the most part. Spam (unsolicited mass email advertising) is often used to advertise pirated goods, from unlawfully copied software to fake Rolex watches. These goods may also be sold on online auction sites or other marketplaces. Some pirated materials, especially computer programs, are offered for download over the Internet. But for the most part the unlawfully copied e-books, movies, music, and computer programs available over the Internet are exchanged for free via P2P file-sharing networks or through warez sites.

Directives
- Directive 2009/136/EC of the European Parliament and of the Council of 25 November 2009, 2009 O.J. (L 337) 11, 30

Constitution
- United States Constitution, art. I, § 8, cl. 8

See also: Copyright; Copyright Alert System; Copyright Infringement; DeCSS; Digital Rights Management; File-Sharing; File-Sharing and the Courts (Attempts to Control Technology); File-Sharing and the Courts (Litigation against Individual Users); File-Sharing (Other Media); Internet Service Providers; Look and Feel; No Electronic Theft Act; P2P; Search Engines; Stop Online Piracy Act; Trademark; Trademark Infringement; Warez

Sources and Further Reading

Robert Bond, "The EU E-Privacy Directive and Consent to Cookies," 68 *Business Lawyer* 215 (2012)

"Dutch Court Bans Pirate Party Links to the Pirate Bay," BBC News (May 10, 2012), available at http://www.bbc.co.uk/news/technology-18016819 (visited February 8, 2013)

"The Economic Cost of Piracy," Oceans Beyond Piracy (2012), available at http://oceansbeyondpiracy.org/cost-of-piracy/economic (visited February 8, 2013)

"Google's Copyright Complaints Flag Up Piracy of Microsoft," BBC News (May 25, 2012), available at http://www.bbc.co.uk/news/technology-18204411 (visited February 8, 2013)

Noah C. N. Hampson, "The Internet Is Not a Lawless Prairie: Data Protection and Privacy in Italy," 34 *Boston College International & Comparative Law Review* 477 (2011)

Saira Nayak, "How This Cookie Crumbled: Deciphering the Compliance Obligations around the EU's Cookie Directive," *Antitrust Source* 1 (December 2012)

"Pirated Rihanna Songs Land Frenchman in Court," BBC News (September 14, 2012), available at http://www.bbc.co.uk/news/technology-19597429 (visited February 9, 2013)

Vittorio Zambardino, "Il Garante Privacy sulla sentenza di Milano: 'E' sbagliata, ma ora bisogna fare regole non *censorie*," La Repubblica (April 16, 2010), available at http://www.itespresso.it/il-garante-privacy-difende-in-parte-google-dalla-sentenza-di-milano-44937.html (visited August 28, 2013)

❖ PORNOGRAPHY ❖

One of the most widely observable social effects of the Internet, and among those that has inspired the greatest amount of legislation and litigation, has been the ease with which it makes pornographic content available and the consequent expansion of the pornography industry. The Internet's early growth may have owed more to pornography than is generally acknowledged. Large media companies that had invested heavily in the provision of Internet services ran "hype" stories about Internet pornography, ostensibly decrying it as a menace but perhaps hoping to pique the prurient interest of the public and increase Internet use.

Pornographers have also played a significant role in the development of payment systems on the Web, and have aggressively pursued copyright infringers. At the same time, they have been the target of lawsuits, Congressional legislation, and content-screening software. These Web sites were among the first profitable Internet businesses. Estimates of the number of pornographic Web sites, the number of visits made to those sites, and the total revenues of the industry vary greatly. Both the pornography industry and its dedicated opponents have reasons for exaggerating these figures; *Forbes* magazine, which has taken a skeptical approach to the claims of both sides, estimates that pornography accounts for 4% of Web sites and 13% of Web searches (Ruvolo 2011), while its continued profitability is in doubt, in part because "there is so much free stuff out there on the web, so many amateur exhibitionists willing to produce new material for free"—a telling statement about the social changes brought about by the ubiquity of online pornography (Worstall 2012). At the other end, a 2010 study estimated that 37% of Web sites were pornographic (Optenet 2010).

The pervasiveness of Internet pornography has caused concern for numerous reasons. A broad spectrum of social activists, from religious fundamentalists to radical feminists, see pornography as both a cause and a symptom of social problems. Almost everyone is concerned by the possibility that children may be exposed to pornography. Companies worry that employees waste work hours surfing pornography, and may expose their employers to potential liability in sexual harassment lawsuits brought by other employees who are exposed to unwelcome images. Some who are otherwise tolerant of pornography are disturbed not so much by the increase in the availability of "traditional" pornography as by the increase in overtly violent pornographic content.

One reason that it has been difficult to regulate pornography, or even to estimate its quantity, is the lack of agreement as to what, exactly, it is. Most people probably share the sentiments of Justice Potter Stewart, who, trying to define "hardcore pornography," said "perhaps I could never succeed in intelligibly doing so. But I know it when I see it" (*Jacobellis*, 378 U.S. at 197). Some might define pornography as words or images that are sexually exciting to some while offensive to others, acknowledging that there might be a number of viewers—in some instances even a majority—who would be neither excited nor offended. Others reject this definition, preferring to separate "pornography," which in this definition includes an element of exploitation or degradation of the subject, from "erotica," which does not. Courts and lawmakers have for years attempted to define pornography by reference to particular body parts and particular acts; this tends to create a difficulty in distinguishing between materials produced as pornographic entertainment and materials produced for medical or scientific purposes.

Under current law, "pornography" (however defined) is not in itself illegal. Two categories that overlap with the category of pornographic material, however, are obscenity and child pornography. A great deal of content that is "indecent" but not "obscene" and not child pornography may be permissibly distributed to adults but not to minors; this probably includes most of the material that most people would think of as pornographic.

The First Amendment protects neither material that is obscene nor child pornography. In modern U.S. law "obscenity" is defined according to the test set forth by the Supreme Court in *Miller v. California* in 1973. Child pornography is relatively easy to define when images of actual persons are involved: if the persons in "depictions of explicit sexual conduct" in photographs, film, or video are minors, the material is illegal as child pornography even if not otherwise "obscene" under the Miller test. Computer-generated or hand-drawn images of minors engaged in sexually explicit conduct can also be child pornography, even if the works are created without involving any children. Shortly after the Court struck down the Child Pornography Protection Act in *Ashcroft v. Free Speech Coalition* (535 U.S, 234), Congress enacted a new law, the Prosecuting Remedies and Tools against the Exploitation of Children Today (PROTECT) Act of 2003. Under the PROTECT Act, 18 U.S.C. § 1466A bans visual depictions of child pornography, "including a drawing, cartoon, sculpture, or painting." The constitutionality of the ban was upheld in a 2008 decision of the U.S. Court of Appeals for the Fourth Circuit (*Whorley*, 550 F.3d 326).

If material is not illegal as child pornography or obscenity, its transmission via the Internet presents an additional legal problem. Children use the Internet, and nothing about the architecture of the Internet makes it intrinsically more difficult for children to access pornographic materials than for adults. Most pornographic content cannot, for constitutional reasons, be banned outright. The protection of minors from pornographic Internet content thus requires the imposition of some sort of barrier between the minor's computer and the pornographic content.

There are two ways in which such barriers may be imposed: either by restricting access to the Web site containing the content or by using blocking and filtering software on the minor's computer. Both approaches present problems; a hybrid approach may be the most effective, although as a practical matter no attempt to block pornographic content will be completely effective.

Congress has twice attempted to control minors' access to pornography from the "supply" end. The first of these attempts was the Communications Decency Act of 1996 (CDA)(47 U.S.C. § 223). The CDA attempted to restrict the access of minors to pornography in two ways. The first restriction imposed a penalty for the knowing transmission of "obscene" or "indecent" material to recipients known to the sender to be under 18 years of age. The second imposed a penalty for use of an "interactive computer service" to transmit to specific persons under 18 years of age, or to "display in a manner available to" persons under 18, "any comment, request, suggestion, proposal, image, or other communication that, in context, depict[ed] or describe[d], in terms patently offensive as measured by community standards, sexual or excretory activities or organs" (47 U.S.C. § 223).

The second prohibition was clearly unconstitutional to a court applying the *Miller* test: its prohibition of depictions or descriptions "in terms patently offensive as measured by community standards, sexual or excretory activities or organs" covers a much broader category of materials than the three-part test in *Miller*, as it incorporates only a portion of the *Miller* test.

The unconstitutionality of the first prohibition is less instantly obvious. Among the problems it presented were the difficulty of defining "indecent," the difficulty of verifying the age of the recipient or viewer of the content, and the burden placed on noncommercial sites. The lack of a clear definition of "indecent" (as opposed to "obscene") made it difficult or impossible for content providers to know exactly what material could permissibly be made available to minors. Actually verifying the age of any viewer on the Internet is as a practical matter impossible, although the senders were only required to avoid transmitting prohibited content to persons known to them to be minors. And while commercial sites could easily include age verification as one of the conditions of providing access (indeed, many already did so indirectly, by requiring credit cards for payment), requiring some form of documentary proof of age would impose a burden on noncommercial sites both by discouraging users from visiting the site and by increasing the cost of maintaining the site.

After the CDA was struck down in 1997, Congress tried again in 1998 with the Child Online Protection Act (COPA) (47 U.S.C. § 231). COPA included a definition of obscenity that was similar to, but oddly (in light of Congress' desire to enact a constitutional statute, avoiding the problems of the CDA) not identical to, the Miller test. COPA has been declared unconstitutional by the federal Court of Appeals for the Third Circuit (*ACLU v. Reno*, 217 F.3d 162; *ACLU v. Ashcroft*, 322 F.3d 240). In addressing COPA, the Third Circuit suggested that blocking and filtering software, rather than supply-side control, might ultimately provide a more effective, as well as more constitutionally palatable, means of achieving the goal of protecting minors from exposure to pornography. The Supreme Court agrees that there are factual questions regarding the efficacy of such software; the case was argued before the U.S. Supreme Court in March 2004, and in June 2004 the Supreme Court remanded the case for trial to determine whether user-side control, through blocking and filtering software, might be more effective than supply-side control as a means of shielding minors from Internet pornography (*Ashcroft v. ACLU*, 524 U.S. 656).

The problem with this solution is not primarily a constitutional one, but a technical one. The First Amendment protects freedom of expression against government interference; if a parent installs blocking and filtering software on his or her child's computer, there is no state action and thus no First Amendment issue. The use of blocking and filtering software by government entities such as libraries and schools, however, does present a constitutional issue. The Children's Internet Protection Act (CIPA), enacted as a companion statute to COPA, requires schools and libraries receiving federally subsidized discounted Internet access to install filtering and blocking software (47 U.S.C. § 254(h)). The constitutionality of CIPA has been upheld by the Supreme Court, which reasons that schools and libraries exist to facilitate learning and cultural enrichment rather than to provide a First Amendment forum for Web content publishers. This facilitation process inevitably involves selecting content (*U.S. v. American Library Association, Inc.*, 539 U.S. 194).

CIPA is not a supply-side control like COPA or the CDA. It regulates an intermediary (schools and libraries) but in effect is more of a demand-side than a supply-side control. To date, then, Congress has been more successful in enacting laws intended to restrict access to pornography from the demand side, or at least the user side, than from the supply side.

The technical problems with blocking and filtering software are more difficult to address, however. There are at least three ways in which such software may operate: it may allow access only to an approved list ("whitelist") of sites; it may allow access to all sites other than those on a proscribed list ("blacklist"); or it may prohibit access to sites containing forbidden keywords. The first approach is the most effective, but also the most restrictive; as a practical matter it is suitable only for very young children who are just learning to use the Internet. Serious online research will require access to a very large number of Web sites; new sites are being created every day, and the whitelist cannot be updated quickly enough to keep track of all of them. A similar approach using digital certificates runs into the same problem: most Web site creators do not bother to, or even know how to, create such certificates for their nonpornographic sites. The blacklist approach presents the problem from the opposite direction. New pornographic Web sites are created daily, and blacklists cannot be updated quickly enough to screen them all out.

The proscribed-keyword approach presents both the problem of overbreadth (as with the whitelist approach) and the problem of ineffective blocking (as with the blacklist approach). It is overbroad because keywords used to describe sexual behavior may appear on almost any Web site as part of otherwise innocuous content; the proscribed words may appear in academic journals, news stories, encyclopedias, dictionaries, the text of novels or screenplays, and medical advice Web sites. Even if the program looks for frequency of certain words or certain relationships between words, many nonpornographic sites are likely to be blocked. At the same time, sites that contain pornographic images may contain none of the proscribed words; this is especially true of foreign-language sites. At present there is no way for software to screen the content of the images themselves.

An approach that seems obvious, and that has been advocated for years by some both on the free-speech and on the anti-pornography sides of the issue, is the creation of a "red-light district" on the Web. This was finally achieved, although perhaps too tardily to be effective, with the creation of the ".xxx" sponsored top-level domain (sTLD). The hope was that the .xxx domain could be made a safe haven for pornographic content, although not for obscenity or child pornography. Congress could then constitutionally restrict pornographic content, including pornographic Web advertising, to this top-level domain. Creating software to restrict access to certain top-level domains is easy; in fact, it can be done using the security settings (rather than the

less effective "content advisor" features) of existing Web browsers.

There has been no significant migration from other TLDs to .xxx, nor will there be until both a carrot (the safe haven) and a stick (restriction of pornographic content in other TLDs) are put in place. The next step is for Congress to enact legislation providing an incentive for pornographers to move their content to .xxx and a disincentive for them to remain in the .com and other domains. Few, if any, pornographers want their content to be available to minors, but there are costs associated with moving a Web site. The costs of registering new domain names will be small, and measures have been taken by the .xxx registrar to ensure that, for example, the owners of www.pornography.com have a right of first refusal to the domain name www.pornography.xxx; additional protection is provided by the Anticybersquatting Consumer Protection Act, although problems may arise if different pornography businesses are currently using the same name in different top-level domains. There will also be labor costs, but these problems might be minimized by providing a phaseout period during which penalties would not be applied. Problems of definition will still arise, of course, and borderline cases will probably continue to be litigated for many years. But given sufficient positive and negative incentives, most pornographers may choose to self-define their content as pornographic and voluntarily transfer it to the .xxx domain, which may itself become a marketing tool.

At the moment, however, such legislation seems unlikely. Even if it is enacted, effective and constitutional legislation restricting pornographic content to the .xxx domain will not completely solve the problem. Congress has legislative jurisdiction over actions, things, and persons within the territory of the United States and over some actions of U.S. persons outside the country; it can thus, subject to the Constitution, regulate content on servers in the United States or published by persons within the United States or by U.S. persons even outside the country. The scope of Congressional authority to regulate actions of non-U.S. persons outside the country is unclear and the subject of some debate; as a practical matter, however, there is little or nothing the U.S. government can do about Web content published in a foreign country by a foreign person. Yet such content is as accessible as any other content on the Web.

In addition, any screening software can be and will be circumvented by clever minors. Attempts to restrict the availability of pornography to minors can never achieve absolute success. Just as laws prohibiting the sale of pornographic magazines to minors do not actually prevent all minors from gaining access to at least some of those magazines, screening software will not prevent some minors from gaining access to pornographic Internet content, or for that matter from sharing that content with other minors. The goal, rather, is to prevent pornography from becoming so pervasive that it becomes part of the cultural background noise, and to prevent the unsought exposure to pornography that is all too familiar to many Web surfers and email users; attempts to restrict the access of minors to pornography are an exercise in control rather than in elimination.

A related problem, and a more difficult one to address, is the problem of sexually explicit spam (unsolicited bulk-mailed email advertising). A high percentage of spam contains sexually explicit language; a smaller but not insignificant amount contains pornographic images. Spammers are already outside the rules of the Internet, if not outside the law. Whether they send advertisements for pornographic Web sites or nonpornographic advertisements for low-cost mortgages, they are often operating in violation of agreements with their own Internet service providers. A solution to the problem of pornographic spam must await a solution to the problem of spam generally.

Statutes

- Anticybersquatting Consumer Protection Act, 15 U.S.C. § 1125(d)
- Child Online Protection Act, 47 U.S.C. § 231
- Child Pornography Prevention Act of 1996, 18 U.S.C. §§ 2251–2260
- Communications Decency Act of 1996, Pub. L. No. 104–104, § 502, 1996 U.S.S.C.A.N. (110 Stat.) 56,133 (later codified at 47 U.S.C. § 223)

Cases

Supreme Court

- *American Civil Liberties Union v. Reno*, 217 F 3d 162 (3d Cir. 2000); reversed sub nom *Ashcroft v. American Civil Liberties Union*, 535 U.S. 564 (2002), on remand, *American Civil Liberties Union v. Ashcroft*, 322 F.3d 240 (3d Cir. 2003), certiorari granted, *Ashcroft v. American Civil Liberties Union*, 124 S. Ct. 399 (2003); affirmed & remanded, 525 U.S. 656 (2004)
- *Ashcroft v. Free Speech Coalition*, 535 U.S. 234 (2002)
- *Jacobellis v. Ohio*, 378 U.S. 184 (1964)
- *Miller v. California*, 413 U.S. 15 (1973)
- *New York v. Ferber*, 458 U.S. 747 (1982)
- *Osborne v. Ohio*, 495 U.S. 103 (1990)
- *Reno v. American Civil Liberties Union*, 521 U.S. 844 (1997)
- *United States v. American Library Association, Inc.*, 539 U.S. 194 (2003)

Federal Trial Courts

- *America Online v. Cyber Promotions*, 948 F. Supp. 456 (E.D. Pa. 1996)
- *Mainstream Loudoun v. Board of Trustees of the Loudoun County Library*, 2 F. Supp. 2d 783 (E.D. Va. 1998)
- *United States v. Whorley*, 550 F.3d 326 (4th Cir. 2008)

See also: Censorship; Child Online Protection Act; Children's Internet Protection Act; Communications Decency Act; Constitutional Law; First Amendment; Indecency; Obscenity; Spam; .xxx

Sources and Further Reading

Rosalind E. Bell, "Reconciling the Protect Act with the First Amendment," 87 *New York University Law Review* 1878 (2012)

Andrea Dworkin, *Pornography: Men Possessing Women* (New York: Perigee Books, 1981)

Tim Elfrink, ".XXX Sites Are Live Thanks to Stuart Lawley, A South Florida Brit Who Beat the Bush Admin," *Miami New Times* (December 8, 2011), available at http://blogs.miaminewtimes.com/riptide/2011/12/xxx_sites_are_live_thanks_to_s.php (visited February 7, 2013)

Terry Gillespie, "Virtual Violence? Pornography and Violence against Women on the Internet," in *Women, Violence and Strategies for Action: Feminist Research, Policy, and Practice*, edited by Jill Radford et al. (Buckingham, UK: Open University Press, 2000)

Mike Godwin, *Cyber Rights: Defending Free Speech in the Digital Age* (Cambridge, MA: MIT Press, 2003)

Kathryn Kolbert & Zak Mettger, eds., *Justice Talking: Censoring the Web: Leading Advocates Debate Today's Most Controversial Issues* (New York: The New Press, 2002)

Jeremy Lipschultz, *Free Expression in the Age of the Internet: Social and Legal Boundaries* (Boulder, CO: Perseus Books, 1999)

Jason Mick, "Study: One Third of Internet Is Crammed with Porn," DailyTech (June 17, 2010), available at http://www.dailytech.com/Study+One+Third+of+Internet+is+Crammed+With+Porn/article18760.htm (visited February 17, 2013)

"More Than One Third of Web Pages Are Pornographic," Optenet Press Release (June 16, 2010), available at http://www.optenet.com/en-us/new.asp?id=270 (visited February 17, 2013)

National Research Council, *Technical, Business, and Legal Dimensions of Protecting Children from Pornography on the Internet: Proceedings of a Workshop* (Washington, D.C.: National Academies Press, 2002)

Andy Patrizio, "XXX Domains May Be Hard Sell," *Wired News* (March 6, 2001), available at http://www.wired.com/news/business/0,1367,42217,00.html (visited February 17, 2013)

"Porn 3x More Popular than Searches: Tracking Firm Finds That 18.8% of All U.S. Users Went to 'Adult' Sites, 5.5% Went to Search Engines," CNNMoney (June 4, 2002), available at http://www.freerepublic.com/focus/f-news/1147848/posts (visited February 17, 2013)

Julie Ruvolo, "How Much of the Internet Is Actually for Porn?" *Forbes* (September 7, 2011), available at http://www.forbes.com/sites/julieruvolo/2011/09/07/how-much-of-the-internet-is-actually-for-porn/ (visited February 17, 2013)

Kevin W. Saunders, *Saving Our Children from the First Amendment* (New York: New York University Press, 2006)

Dick Thornburgh & Herbert S. Lin, *Youth, Pornography and the Internet* (Washington, D.C.: National Academies Press, 2002)

Tim Worstall, "The Declining Economics of the Pornography Industry," *Forbes* (June 8, 2012), available at http://www.forbes.com/sites/timworstall/2012/06/08/the-declining-economics-of-the-pornography-industry/ (visited February 17, 2013)

❖ PREVENTING REAL ONLINE THREATS TO ECONOMIC CREATIVITY AND THEFT OF INTELLECTUAL PROPERTY ACT ❖

The awkwardly named Preventing Real Online Threats to Economic Creativity and Theft of Intellectual Property Act, introduced by Senator Patrick Leahy (D-VT) and more often known as the PROTECT IP Act or PIPA, was one of the two proposed U.S. statutes in 2011 that managed to reignite online consumer and information rights activism after a period of complacency. The two statutes, PIPA and the Stop Online Piracy Act (SOPA), would have enabled, and in many cases required, the U.S. government to block access to certain foreign Web sites from within the United States. In its most extreme proposed form, PIPA would have allowed the removal of these rogue domains from the Domain Name System, in effect making them unfindable and unresolvable by Web browsers. After an objection from the U.S. government that the widespread use of such an extreme remedy might wreck the Internet, proponents of PIPA and SOPA stepped back from this position. PIPA did, however, retain the requirement that "an operator of a non-authoritative domain name system server shall take the least burdensome technically feasible and reasonable measures designed to prevent the domain name described in the order from resolving to that domain name's Internet protocol address" (PIPA § 3(d)(2)(A)(i)). Search engines were also required to take measures to block access to rogue sites by taking:

> technically feasible and reasonable measures, as expeditiously as possible, to—
>
> (i) remove or disable access to the Internet site associated with the domain name set forth in the order; or
> (ii) not serve a hypertext link to such Internet site (PIPA § 3(d)(2)(D)).

Advertising for or on the proscripted sites could also be forbidden, as could the making of payments by U.S. financial services. While most opponents of PIPA and SOPA agreed that preventing intellectual property piracy was a desirable goal, they argued that the means chosen were excessive. Internet service providers worried about structural harm to the Internet; advocacy groups worried about censorship. Some, pointing out that once such broad censorship powers had been granted they might eventually be used for other things than preventing intellectual property piracy, raised the specter of a U.S. Internet cut off from the rest of the world, as in more restrictive societies.

By early 2012, U.S. legislators had received more than 14 million contacts from persons expressing opposition to PIPA and SOPA (Weisman 2012). Opposition reached a peak with the "Internet blackout" protest on January 18, 2012. Over 115,000 Web sites blacked out all or part of their content as part of the protest. Internet encyclopedia Wikipedia replaced its home page with a page reading "Imagine a world without free knowledge." Other protesters included such popular sites as BoingBoing, Failblog, Google, Reddit, WordPress, and xkcd.

The protests were successful; several senators who had originally supported PIPA withdrew their support, and Senate Majority Leader Harry Reid (D-NV) postponed a vote on or further discussion of PIPA, in effect killing the bill (Weisman 2012).

Proposed Statute

- Preventing Real Online Threats to Economic Creativity and Theft of Intellectual Property Act, S. 968, 112th Cong. (1st Sess. 2011)

See also: Activism and Advocacy Groups; Stop Online Piracy Act

Sources and Further Reading

Bill D. Herman, *The Fight over Digital Rights: The Politics of Copyright and Technology* (Cambridge, UK: Cambridge University Press, 2013)

Larry Magid, "What Are SOPA and PIPA and Why All the Fuss?" *Forbes* (January 18, 2012), available at http://www.forbes.com/sites/larrymagid/2012/01/18/what-are-sopa-and-pipa-and-why-all-the-fuss/ (visited April 24, 2013)

Jonathan Weisman, "After an Online Firestorm, Congress Shelves Antipiracy Bills," *New York Times* (January 20, 2012), available at http://www.nytimes.com/2012/01/21/technology/senate-postpones-piracy-vote.html?_r=0 (visited April 24, 2013)

Jenna Wortham, "Public Outcry over Antipiracy Bills Began as Grassroots Grumbling," *New York Times* (January 19, 2012), available at http://www.nytimes.com/2012/01/20/technology/public-outcry-over-antipiracy-bills-began-as-grass-roots-grumbling.html?pagewanted=all (visited April 24, 2013)

❖ PRIVACY ❖

The Internet is a two-way information tool; individuals use the Internet to locate information on the Web, to send and receive information by email, and to upload and download information using FTP and file-sharing programs. All of this activity creates information about the user. Web sites collect information about visitors; copies of visited pages, email messages, and uploads and downloads are stored on the user's computer and on servers through which they pass on their journey across the Internet. Together, all of this information may reveal things that the user would prefer to keep private.

Many users prefer to maintain privacy, at least from the world at large, about their income and financial status, health and medical history, personal correspondence, sexual preference, employment history, and history of brushes with the law, if any. Yet information gained from observing the user's Internet use can reveal all of these things. Anyone who files an electronic tax return or uses online banking or bill payment is allowing detailed financial information to travel across the Internet and to be stored on Internet servers. The danger that this information will be accidentally disclosed is fairly low, as such information is always encrypted. More general information can also provide a thorough picture of an individual's financial status, however. A user who purchases a Patek Phillippe watch online has revealed information about his or her level of disposable income; one who purchases first-class tickets to Fiji can be placed in a different marketing category from one who flies coach class to Cleveland. A user who surfs debt-relief sites is announcing his or her indebtedness by doing so; one who uses a real estate site to shop for houses in the $300,000 price range and mortgages in the $250,000 range has given anyone familiar with real estate a fairly accurate idea of his or her annual income.

In the same way, visits to support groups for a particular disease, or searches for information on that disease, are usually a good indicator that the user or someone in the user's family suffers from the disease. Visits to pornographic Web sites can provide information about an individual's sexual orientation, as can purchasing a secondhand copy of the *Spartacus International Gay Guide* on eBay. Few people would have difficulty deducing a great deal of information about a person who buys the following items:

- *Surviving Law School*, by Michael Brogan and David Spencer
- *Irish Wedding Traditions: Using Your Irish Heritage to Create the Perfect Wedding*, by Shannon McMahon-Lichte
- Iron Man Halloween costume, size 8
- Little Mermaid Halloween costume, size 6
- Woman's sweatshirt, size S, reading "Obama 2012"

All of these items can be, and are, purchased over the Internet; the combination allows a casual observer to make fairly accurate guesses as to the user's age, education, marital status and plans, political affiliation, religion, and national origin, as well as the number, age, and gender of the user's children. It is not even necessary that the user actually purchase the items; he or she leaves a trail of information simply by shopping for them. Of course, some or all of the items might be gifts for someone else, but an examination of a larger sample of the user's shopping and purchases would still reveal patterns. Online marketing companies such as Doubleclick.com (now owned by Google) gather together far more pieces of data than the five items listed here. Data mining and advanced statistical techniques can then be used to come up with fairly accurate guesses about the user.

Many users feel uncomfortable at the idea that strangers can find out so much about them. The hypothetical shopper described earlier probably makes no effort to conceal her religion or political beliefs from her friends and acquaintances, but might be disconcerted to find her name on a Web site under the heading "Irish Catholic Democrats." In the same way, most people probably agree in the abstract with the idea that political campaign contributions should not be anonymous, but feel disconcerted when they visit www.fundrace.org and discover a record of the fact that they once donated $200 to the ill-fated presidential campaign of former governor and ambassador Jon Huntsman, Jr. The feeling of unease is increased by the fact that the listings include the donors' home addresses and occupations.

Individual concerns about privacy fall into three general categories: privacy from the government, privacy from other legitimate private parties, and privacy from malicious users. Each of these types of privacy is protected in different ways.

Concerns about privacy from the government can in turn be divided into two categories: concerns about the government's use of information about individuals and concerns about the government's disclosure of that information. The government collects a great deal of information about individuals, and that information is stored electronically. It can conceivably be used to create lists of individuals on the basis of race, national origin, or exposure to a certain disease. Worries about the uses of this information were raised in the aftermath of the September 11 attacks, when the FBI used existing information in government databases to identify and conduct interviews with thousands of Arabs and Muslims in the United States, including U.S. citizens (Sheridan 2004). In the minds of civil libertarians, the FBI's action was not only improper in its own right but also raised the specter of more sinister uses of the information, as in the case of the internment of Japanese-Americans during World War II.

The government may collect, use, and disclose data on individuals so long as the collection and use does not invade a constitutionally protected "zone of privacy." Protection of privacy requires that the government use both legal and technical safeguards to prevent improper use or disclosure of the information. With these safeguards in place, the government may collect and use even quite personal information, such as the names and addresses of all persons who have received certain prescription drugs (*Whalen*, 429 U.S. 589). The government may also collect information in which the individual cannot reasonably expect to be private, such as postings in a chat room (*Charbonneau*, 979 F. Supp. 1177), and may subpoena records of electronic communications on private companies' servers (18 U.S.C. § 2703). And the government may conduct analysis and data mining of its own records, creating abstracts of existing information (*Pippinger*, 129 F.3d 519).

Collection of private information may be overt, as when a product registration screen asks for information about a consumer's hobbies, marital status and income, or covert, as when spyware tracks a user's surfing habits. The overt collection of information usually arouses fairly little concern, as consumers have the option of refusing to provide the information. An exception is made in the case of the collection of information from children, however. Under the Children's Online Privacy Protection Act (COPPA), Web sites that collect information from children under the age of 13 must provide notice of what information they collect from children, how they use the information, and what their practices are regarding disclosure of the information. Personal information, including information that might identify or permit communication with the child, may only be collected, used, or disclosed with the verifiable consent of the child's parents (15 U.S.C. § 6502).

Covert collection of information arouses greater concerns. Adware and spyware are almost universally despised by consumers, and are a current target of legislative efforts. But much covert collection of information is less intrusive. Commercial Web sites track consumer purchases and shopping and then make suggestions as to further purchases. These sites are generally open about the process; consumer anxiety seems to be directed not at the maintenance of such information by retail Web sites but at the possibility that the information will be disclosed to third parties unknown to the consumer, without the consumer's knowledge or consent. Web sites post privacy policies, but reading and interpreting each site's policy would be a time-consuming task.

There are certain restrictions on private parties' collection, use, and disclosure of information about individuals even when those individuals are adults. However, the use of cookies to collect information about users' Web browsing habits is not illegal; concerned users can always block the cookies, at the cost of some browsing functionality (*DoubleClick*, 154 F. Supp. 2d 497). And there is no reasonable expectation of privacy in workplace email or Web surfing; workers who use their office email to complain about the boss may be embarrassed, or worse, when the boss reads the messages (*Smyth*, 914 F. Supp. 97).

The third category of privacy worries, about disclosure of information to malicious users, is related to the first two. Information can be stolen from users' own computers, but users can take steps to prevent that. Once the information has been placed in a private or government database, however, the user can no longer protect it; a malicious hacker might crack the database's protection. Such unauthorized access to private records occurs frequently; sometimes the information is used by identity thieves, and sometimes it is gleefully posted on Web sites. The activities of the crackers and identity thieves are already illegal; privacy concerns focus more on the inadequate protection of many databases, especially government databases. The concern is that, although government agencies are required to use technical safeguards to protect the information (*Whalen*, 429 U.S. 589), those safeguards will not be updated quickly enough to keep pace with the development of cracking techniques.

Statutes

- Children's Online Privacy Protection Act, 15 U.S.C. §§ 6501–6506
- Electronic Communications Privacy Act, 18 U.S.C. § 2703

Cases

Supreme Court
- *Whalen v. Roe*, 429 U.S. 589 (1977)

Federal Appellate Courts
- *Pippinger v. Rubin*, 129 F.3d 519 (10th Cir. 1997)

Federal Trial Courts
- *Bohach v. City of Reno*, 932 F. Supp. 1232 (D. Nev. 1996)
- *In re DoubleClick, Inc. Privacy Litigation*, 154 F. Supp. 2d 497 (S.D.N.Y. 2001)
- *Smyth v. Pillsbury*, 914 F. Supp. 97 (E.D. Pa. 1996)
- *United States v. Charbonneau*, 979 F. Supp. 1177 (S.D. Ohio 1997)

See also: Adware and Spyware; App; Children's Online Privacy Protection Act; Cloud; Cookies; Data Mining; Doubleclick; Hacking; Identity Theft; Social Networking Service

Sources and Further Reading
"A Knight in Digital Armour," *The Economist Technology Quarterly*, September 1, 2012, at 23

Robert Bond, "The EU E-Privacy Directive and Consent to Cookies," 68 *Business Lawyer* 215 (2012)

Michael A. Caloyannides, *Computer Forensics and Privacy* (Norwood, MA: Artech House, 2001)

Fred H. Cate, *Privacy in the Information Age* (Washington, D.C.: Brookings Institution Press, 1997)

Terence Craig & Mary Ludloff, *Privacy & Big Data* (Sebastopol, CA: O'Reilly Media, Inc. 2011)

"Data Privacy: Out of Shape," *The Economist*, July 21, 2012, at 14

Jonathan I. Ezor, *Privacy and Data Protection in Business: Laws & Practices* (New Providence, NJ: LexisNexis, 2012)

"Government Surveillance: Little Peepers Everywhere," *The Economist*, July 21, 2012, at 23

Susan Landau, *Surveillance or Security? The Risks Posed by New Wiretapping Technologies* (Cambridge, MA: MIT Press, 2011)

"Microsoft and Privacy: Change of Track," *The Economist*, June 9, 2012, at 70

Ciaran McEvoy, "Listserv Privacy Unsettled Issue," *Los Angeles Daily Journal*, May 21, 2012, at 1

Terry W. Posey, Jr., "Tony Soprano's Privacy Rights: Internet Cookies, Wiretapping Statutes, and Federal Computer Crimes," 29 *University of Dayton Law Review* 109 (2003)

Paul M. Schwartz, "Property, Privacy, and Personal Data," 117 *Harvard Law Review* 2055 (2004)

Mary Beth Sheridan, "Interviews of Muslims to Broaden: FBI Hopes to Avert a Terrorist Attack," *Washington Post*, July 17, 2004, at A01

Daniel Solove, *Nothing to Hide: The False Tradeoff between Privacy and Security* (New Haven, CT: Yale University Press, 2011)

Daniel Solove & Paul M. Schwartz, *Privacy Law Fundamentals* (Portsmouth, NH: IAPP Publication, 2011)

Hayley Tsukayama, "Google: 'Government Surveillance Is on the Rise'," *Washington Post* (November 13, 2012), available at http://articles.washingtonpost.com/2012–11–13/business/35506267_1_dorothy-chou-google-senior-policy-analyst-requests (visited February 17, 2013)

❖ PROJECT GUTENBERG ❖

The duration of copyright protection is so long that by the time a work finally enters the public domain, it is often not only out of print but unavailable even from resellers. Project Gutenberg makes these works, and others in the public domain, available in electronic form. According to its mission statement, "The mission of Project Gutenberg is simple: To encourage the creation and distribution of eBooks. This mission is, as much as possible, to encourage *all* those who are interested in making eBooks and helping to give them away." In furtherance of this mission, Project Gutenberg makes over 40,000 e-books available for free download, with more constantly being added. For over four decades, the work of Project Gutenberg has been carried out entirely by volunteers. While most of the available works are in English, it also includes works in Chinese, Dutch, Finnish, French, German, Italian, Spanish, and other languages.

Most of the texts available via Project Gutenberg are in the public domain in the United States; a few are copyrighted texts that the copyright holders have licensed Project Gutenberg to distribute. Project Gutenberg in turn attaches restrictions to the copies it distributes, although the enforceability of these restrictions with regard to works already in the public domain is questionable. The main restrictions are on commercial uses, modification, and use of copyrighted materials. Project Gutenberg also attaches a warning that works in the public domain in the United States might still be protected by copyright in other countries. Other Project Gutenberg networks exists; because the extent of the public domain is not identical from one country to the next, works available from one country's Project Gutenberg might still be in copyright in other countries.

Project Gutenberg cannot claim copyright in the public domain works it distributes. It cannot and does not demand royalties from commercial use of those works. It can and does claim a trademark in the name "Project Gutenberg," however, and the licensing agreement includes a royalty schedule for commercial use of the trademark.

The condition that "only unmodified copies of these eBooks may be redistributed without limitation" would be unenforceable as to works in the public domain, but is attached to use of the trademark rather than to use of the work: altered works may not include the Project Gutenberg header or trademark, nor may they otherwise indicate that they are associated with Project Gutenberg.

Copyrighted works distributed via Project Gutenberg are, of course, subject to conditions attached by the copyright holder; these vary from work to work, but generally include restrictions on commercial use and protection of the moral rights of integrity and paternity.

A look at the most downloaded Project Gutenberg works raises some questions about Project Gutenberg's possible effect on the marketplace. Most of the most popular works are or recently have been in print, and are readily available in print form: *Alice's Adventures in Wonderland, The Art of War, Grimm's Fairy Tales, The Notebooks of Leonardo Da Vinci, Pride and Prejudice*, and *Ulysses* are perennial favorites. Even many obscure titles, such as an 1860 book on casting hand shadows, are still readily available. Printed editions of the work, *Hand Shadows to Be Thrown upon the Wall*, by Henry Bursill, can be purchased secondhand in the United States for under a dollar (or as a Kindle e-book for 99¢), and it is currently in print in the United Kingdom, where it sells for £4.00, new. Throughout December 2012 the most popular download was, not surprisingly, Charles Dickens' *A Christmas Carol*, with 11,386 downloads in the week ending December 19 (it was originally published on December 19, 1843). This does not mean that an additional 11,386 copies of the book could have been sold during that week; many downloaders probably chose the book because it was in the public domain and available for free. It does suggest, though, that public domain archives such as Project Gutenberg can be a source of information to commercial publishers as to which books it might be worthwhile to reprint (not that, in the case of Dickens, that information is needed; *A Christmas Carol* has remained continuously in print for 169 years).

See also: Budapest Open Access Initiative; Copyright; Open Source; Public Domain

Sources and Further Reading

Henry Bursill, *Hand Shadows to Be Thrown upon the Wall: A Series of Novel and Amusing Figures Formed by the Hand* (Yorkletts, Whitstable, Kent, UK Pryor Publications 1993 (1860)), reviews and ordering information available from Amazon UK at http://www.amazon.co.uk/exec/obidos/ASIN/0946014248/qid=1097002589/ref=sr_8_xs_ap_i1_xgl/202–0143568–6564612 (visited January 13, 2012)

Charles Dickens, *A Christmas Carol* (London: Chapman & Hall, 1843)

"Free eBooks by Project Gutenberg," Project Gutenberg, available at http://gutenberg.nl/ (visited February 17, 2013)

Michael Hart, "Project Gutenberg Mission Statement," available at http://www.gutenberg.org/wiki/Gutenberg:Project_Gutenberg_Mission_Statement_by_Michael_Hart, Project Gutenberg (visited February 17, 2013)

Edward Lee, "The Public's Domain: The Evolution of Legal Restraints on the Government's Power to Control Public Access through Secrecy or Intellectual Property," 55 *Hastings Law Journal* 91 (2003)

"Project Gutenberg," available at http://www.gutenberg.net/ (visited January 29, 2013)

"The Project Gutenberg License," Project Gutenberg, available at http://www.gutenberg.net/license (visited January 29, 2013)

"Project Gutenberg of Australia: A Treasure-Trove of Literature," PGA, available at http://www.gutenberg.net.au/ (visited February 17, 2013)

❖ PROSECUTION HISTORY ESTOPPEL ❖

Prosecution history estoppel, also called file wrapper estoppel, is a limit on the application of the patent law doctrine of equivalents. The "file wrapper" is the folder in which the United States Patent and Trademark Office (USPTO) keeps the papers filed during the process of a patent application. The doctrine of equivalents allows a patent holder or assignee to sue for patent infringement if the infringing conduct or product is not literally within the scope of the patent, but differs only insubstantially from the description in the patent. Prosecution history estoppel prevents a patent holder from asserting the doctrine of equivalents if the alleged infringement lies in an area that was given up by the patent holder during the prosecution of the patent. In order to obtain a patent, the patent holder may have conceded that certain processes or products were outside the scope of the patent even though they may have been substantially similar to those described in the patent. The patent holder is then *estopped*—prohibited—from attempting to recapture the area that was conceded; he or she may not later sue for infringement for activities within that area, even though those activities would otherwise be covered by the patent under the doctrine of equivalents.

File wrapper estoppel has been applied to many cases involving computer technology patents. Both *Texas Instruments v. U.S. International Trade Commission* and *Wang Labs v. Toshiba Corporation* involved arrangements of computer chips in ways only slightly different from that described in allegedly infringed patents; in both cases prosecution history estoppel was applied to preclude the patent infringement claim. More recently, the Supreme Court has held that the doctrine is flexible: the range of subject matter surrendered by the patent applicant when submitting an amended application must be determined for each particular case, rather than by applying an inflexible complete bar (*Festo*, 535 U.S. at 737–738).

Cases
Supreme Court
- *Festo Corp. v. Shoketsu Kinzoku Kogyo Kabushiki Co., Ltd.*, 535 U.S. 722 (2002)

Federal Circuit
- *Marine Polymer Technologies, Inc. v. HemCon, Inc.*, 672 F.3d 1350 (Fed. Cir. 2012)
- *Texas Instruments Inc. v. U.S. International Trade Commission*, 988 F.2d 1165 (Fed. Cir. 1993)
- *Wang Labs, Inc. v. Toshiba Corporation*, 993 F.2d 858 (Fed. Cir. 1993)

See also: America Invents Act; Doctrine of Equivalents; Patent

Sources and Further Reading
"Impact of *Marine Polymer Tech. v. HemCon Inc.* on Post-Grant and Inter Partes Review," Patent Review Blog (March 16, 2012), available at http://patentreviewblog.wordpress.com/tag/file-wrapper-estoppel/ (visited February 17, 2013)

Stephen B. Maebius & Harold C. Wegner, "The Honeywell Nail in the Festo Coffin: A Narrowing Amendment Does Create a Presumption of Prosecution History Estoppel," 23 *Biotechnology Law Report* 417 (2004)

Steven J. Moore, "America Invents Act: Impact on Patent Processing and Litigation Strategies," *Metropolitan Corporate Counsel* (October 24, 2011, 2:56 PM), available at http://www.metrocorpcounsel.com/articles/16306/america-invents-act-impact-patent-processing-and-litigation-strategies (visited February 17, 2013)

❖ PROTECT IP ACT ❖

See Preventing Real Online Threats to Economic Creativity and Theft of Intellectual Property Act

❖ PSEUDONYMITY ❖

See Anonymity

❖ PUBLIC DOMAIN ❖

In intellectual property law, the public domain consists of those works and inventions unprotected by copyright or patent. Intellectual property rights protected by trademark or trade secret law are also spoken of as "falling into the public domain" if they lose that protection. The exact limits of the public domain are uncertain, and are fiercely contested by the content industry on the one hand and users' and consumers' advocates on the other. The limits are also constantly changing: new works enter the public domain as copyrights and patents expire, and Congressional modification of copyright and patent law can take works out of the public domain and restore intellectual property protection. Works created by the U.S. government are in the public domain, although the U.S. government may acquire ownership of copyrights in works created by others (17 U.S.C. § 105).

The concept of the public domain is inherent in the legislative creation of limited terms of copyright and patent protection. It was implicit in the 1710 Statute of Anne and the 1774 decision of the House of Lords in *Donaldson v. Beckett*. In the United States, it is built into the Constitution: the Patent and Copyright Clause provides that Congress shall have the power "To promote the Progress of Science and useful Arts, by securing for limited Times to Authors and Inventors the exclusive Right to their respective Writings and Discoveries." After the "limited Times" set by Congress have expired, works fall in to the public domain. Works that are unprotected by copyright from the outset, such as U.S. government works, are also in the public domain.

In the nineteenth century, the federal courts fought off attempts by the content industry to invade the public domain using another form of intellectual property protection: trademark. In the 1890 case of *Merriam v. Holloway Publishing Company*, the publishers of an 1847 edition of *Webster's Dictionary*, on which the copyright had expired, brought suit against another publisher that had reproduced and distributed for sale the entire 1847 edition. Among the arguments advanced by Merriam was that even though the copyright had expired, the entire dictionary was still protected by trademark. Speaking for the court, Justice Miller stated that:

> this proceeding is an attempt to establish the doctrine that a party who has had the copyright of a book until it has expired, may continue that monopoly indefinitely, under the pretense that it is protected by a trade-mark, or something of that sort. I do not believe in any such doctrine, nor do my associates. When a man takes out a copyright, for any of his writings or works, he impliedly agrees that, at the expiration of that copyright, such writings or works shall go to the public and become public property. I may be the first to announce that doctrine, but I announce it without any hesitation. If a man is entitled to an extension of his copyright, he may obtain it by the mode pointed out by law. The law provides a method of obtaining such extension. The copyright law gives an author or proprietor a monopoly of the sale of his writings for a definite period, but the grant of a monopoly implies that, after the monopoly has expired, the public shall be entitled ever afterwards to the unrestricted use of the book (*Merriam*, 43 F. at 451).

Six years later, the U.S. Supreme Court addressed the same issue in a patent law context in the landmark case of *Singer Manufacturing Company v. June Manufacturing Company*. As Merriam had with its copyrighted dictionary, Singer asserted a trademark right in its patented sewing machine even after the patent had expired. The Supreme Court disagreed; while Singer could still claim a trademark in the name "Singer" and could require other manufacturers to identify themselves, not Singer, as the manufacturer, it could not use its trademark in the Singer name to prevent others from manufacturing Singer machines on which the patent had expired, and from using the name "Singer" to identify those machines. Writing for the Court, Justice White explained:

> It is self-evident that on the expiration of a patent the monopoly created by it ceases to exist, and the right to make the thing formerly covered by the patent becomes public property. It is upon this condition that the patent is granted. It follows, as a matter of course, that on the termination of the patent there passes to the public the right to make the machine in the form in which it was constructed during the patent. . . . It equally follows from the cessation of the monopoly and the falling of the patented device into the domain of things public that along with the public ownership of the device there must also necessarily pass to the public the generic designation of the thing which has arisen during the monopoly in consequence of the designation having been acquiesced in by the owner, either

tacitly, by accepting the benefits of the monopoly, or expressly by his having so connected the name with the machine as to lend countenance to the resulting dedication. To say otherwise would be to hold that, although the public had acquired the device covered by the patent, yet the owner of the patent or the manufacturer of the patented thing had retained the designated name which was essentially necessary to vest the public with the full enjoyment of that which had become theirs by the disappearance of the monopoly. In other words, that the patentee or manufacturer could take the benefit and advantage of the patent upon the condition that at its termination the monopoly should cease, and yet, when the end was reached, disregard the public dedication and practically perpetuate indefinitely an exclusive right.

> The public having the right, on the expiration of the patent, to make the patented article, and to use its generic name, to restrict this use, either by preventing its being placed upon the articles when manufactured or by using it in advertisements or circulars, would be to admit the right, and at the same time destroy it. It follows, then, that the right to use the name in every form passes to the public with the dedication resulting from the expiration of the patent (*Singer*, 163 U.S. at 185–186).

The *Singer* opinion served both to clearly define the public domain and to introduce the term (as "the domain of things public") to American law. The public domain in *Singer* is more inclusive than the nineteenth-century concept of *domaine publique* in French law and in the Berne Convention, from which the term may have been drawn (Lee 2003, 106–07).

In contrast to copyrights and patents, which are of limited duration, trade secrets and trademarks are of potentially infinite duration. Trade secrets fall into the public domain as soon as they become public; the person who makes them public may be liable for penalties, but the protection cannot be regained once the secrecy is lost. Trademarks may fall into the public domain by coming into common use as a generic term for an item; words like "aspirin" and "shredded wheat" now suggest generic classes of products, rather than particular brand names; owners of trademarks such as Xerox and Frigidaire have battled valiantly—and successfully—to keep their trademarks from being similarly extinguished.

The battle over the limits of the public domain is particularly intense in the area of copyright law. Most recently, the Sonny Bono Copyright Term Extension Act, which extended most copyright terms by 20 years, has inspired a movement to defend the public domain against further encroachment. The Act was challenged, unsuccessfully, in the case of *Eldred v. Ashcroft*. In the aftermath of *Eldred*, opponents of the Act proposed a Public Domain Enhancement Act to require copyright registration and payment of a minimal fee in order to extend the copyright term beyond 50 years, thus allowing a great number of copyrighted works of no significant commercial value—most of them no longer in print—to fall into the public domain.

Constitution
- United States Constitution, Article I, Section 8, Clause 8

Statute
- Copyright Act of 1976, 17 U.S.C. § 105

Proposed Legislation
- Public Domain Enhancement Act, H. R. 2601, 108th Cong. (1st Sess. 2003), available at http://thomas.loc.gov/cgi-bin/query/z?c109:H.R.2408: (visited December 19, 2012)

Cases
England
- *Cheavin v. Walker*, 5 Ch. Div. 850 (1877)
- *Donaldson v. Beckett*, 2 Bro. P.C. 129, 1 Eng. Rep. 837 Burr. (4th ed.) 2408, 98 Eng. Rep. 257 (H.L. 1774)

United States
- *Eldred v. Ashcroft*, 537 U.S. 186 (2002)
- *Merriam v. Holloway Publishing Co.*, 43 F. 450 (C.C.E.D. Mo. 1890)
- *Singer Manufacturing Co. v. June Manufacturing Co.*, 163 U.S. 169 (1896)

See also: Budapest Open Access Initiative; Copyright; Patent; Project Gutenberg; Sonny Bono Copyright Term Extension Act; Trademark

Sources and Further Reading

James Boyle, "The Second Enclosure Movement and the Construction of the Public Domain," 66 *Law & Contemporary Problems* 33 (2003)

James Boyle, ed., *Collected Papers, Duke Conference on the Public Domain* (Durham, NC: Center for the Study of the Public Domain, 2003)

Stephen Fishman, *The Public Domain: How to Find & Use Copyright-Free Writings, Music, Art & More* (Berkeley, CA: Nolo Press, 5th ed. 2010)

Wendy J. Gordon, "A Property Right in Self-Expression: Equality and Individualism in the Natural Law of Intellectual Property," 102 *Yale Law Journal* 1533 (1993)

David Lange, "Recognizing the Public Domain," 44 *Law & Contemporary Problems* 147 (1981)

Marshall Leaffer, *Understanding Copyright Law* (New Providence, NJ: LexisNexis, 5th ed. 2010)

Lawrence Lessig, *Free Culture: How Big Media Uses Technology and the Law to Lock Down Culture and Control Creativity* (New York: Penguin, 2004) (also available as a free download)

Jessica Litman, "The Public Domain," 39 *Emory Law Journal* 965 (1990)

Edward Samuels, "The Public Domain Revisited," 36 *Loyola (Los Angeles) Law Review* 389 (2002)

Pamela Samuelson, "Mapping the Digital Public Domain: Threats and Opportunities," 66 *Law and Contemporary Problems* 147 (2003)

Symposium, "The Public Domain," 66 *Law & Contemporary Problems* (2003)

R. Polk Wagner, "Information Wants to Be Free: Intellectual Property and the Mythologies of Control," 103 *Columbia Law Review* 995 (2003)

❖ QR CODE ❖

A QR code, or Quick Response Code, is a type of two-dimensional bar code, familiar to most consumers as a black and white square formed of smaller black and white squares. A QR code can hold more information than a one-dimensional Universal Product Code (UPC) bar code, and can be scanned with a cell phone or other mobile device to convey this information in user-readable form to the device. This information may take the form of a Uniform Resource Locator, allowing the user to open a Web page on his or her phone by scanning the QR code. This makes QR codes useful in advertising; in effect a QR code becomes a real-world hyperlink.

The QR code was originally developed by Denso Wave, a subsidiary of the Toyota Group, for tracking components during manufacturing. Denso holds Japanese, U.S., and European patents on the QR code, as well as a trademark in the name. However, Denso has chosen not to enforce its patents; QR codes can be freely used by anyone.

Because they contain hyperlinks, QR codes are a possible conduit for malware, phishing, and other malicious uses. A malicious user can print a QR code on an adhesive label and stick it over the genuine QR code on an advertising sign; unsuspecting users may then be directed to a phishing site or a site that allows the malicious user to gain access to the scanning phone's camera, Global Positioning System (GPS) information, microphone, passwords, email, text messages, contacts, and other personal information.

Sources and Further Reading

Matt Liebowitz, "QR Tags Can Be Rigged to Attack Smart Phones," *Scientific American* (September 13, 2011), available at http://www.scientificamerican.com/article.cfm?id=qr-tags-can-be-rigged-to (visited February 17, 2013)

"Square Deal: After Many False Starts, QR Codes Are Finally Taking Off," *The Economist*, June 16, 2012, at 76

What Is a QR Code? Denso ADC (2013), available at http://www.denso-adc.com/learning-center/what-are-qr-codes (visited December 20, 2012)

R

❖ RECOGNITION AND ENFORCEMENT OF JUDGMENTS ❖

The Internet increases the likelihood of international litigation. Material may be posted on a Web site in the United States that is completely legal and permissible under U.S. law, but exposes the publisher to civil liability for defamation under some other country's law. Because the posted material is accessible from that other country, a plaintiff might bring an action in that country's court and obtain a judgment against the U.S. defendant. This could happen without the participation or even the awareness of the defendant. A problem may arise, however, if a court in the United States is asked to recognize or enforce the foreign court's judgment.

"Recognition" and "enforcement" are terms of art. A court *recognizes* the judgment of the courts of another state or nation when it acknowledges that the result reached by the foreign court was correct. It *enforces* a judgment when it takes some action, such as attaching assets or transferring property, as a result of a judgment reached by a court in another jurisdiction. The threshold required for enforcement of foreign judgments is, naturally, higher than that required for recognition. While the Internet presents no fundamentally new problems in recognition and enforcement of foreign judgments, it may increase the number of cases in which courts are called upon to address the issue.

States of the United States are required by Article IV, § 1 of the U.S. Constitution to give full faith and credit to the judgments of the courts of other states, although certain limitations apply, particularly where real property is involved. The Full Faith and Credit Clause and Full Faith and Credit Statute also require the federal courts to recognize judgments of state courts, but interestingly do not require state courts to recognize federal judgments (28 U.S.C. § 1738). However, the Supreme Court has repeatedly stated that the states do have such an obligation, although the source upon which the Court bases this obligation is obscure.

No similar requirement of full faith and credit exists among nations, absent a treaty provision imposing it. This acts as a check on jurisdiction: the nation of Ruritania may decide that its courts have jurisdiction over all parties and all controversies arising anywhere in the world, but the probable result will be that no court outside Ruritania will recognize Ruritania's judgments in the absence of some more concrete basis for jurisdiction.

There is no constitutional or statutory requirement for any court in the United States to recognize any foreign court's judgment. Two canons of construction apply to the recognition and enforcement of foreign judgments: (1) no law has any independent effect outside the territory of the government that creates it, and (2) no sovereign government is bound to recognize or enforce within its territory judgments rendered by the courts of other nations, absent some agreement to the contrary. Foreign country judgments are thus recognized and enforced in the United States, if at all, on a basis of comity or mutual respect by sovereign states of each other's legislative, executive, and judicial acts (Richman & Reynolds 2002, 355–356).

U.S. federal courts will generally recognize and enforce foreign-country judgments on a basis of reciprocity, except where the foreign law is contrary to fundamental U.S. moral, legal, and policy principles (Richman & Reynolds 2002, 356–357). Default judgments seem to be less likely to be enforced. Where the foreign law conflicts with a fundamental constitutional right (such as freedom of expression) the foreign judgment will not be enforced. And U.S. courts may recognize, but need not enforce, penal and tax judgments of foreign countries.

The Uniform Foreign Money-Judgments Recognition Act (UFMJRA) has been adopted by 31 states plus the District of Columbia and the U.S. Virgin Islands. Foreign money judgments (but not for taxes, fines, or penalties, or in family law matters) will be recognized unless one of the UFMJRA's mandatory or discretionary grounds for nonrecognition is present. Nonrecognition is mandatory (that is, a state in which the UFMJRA has been adopted is not permitted to recognize the judgment) where the judgment was rendered:

(1) Under a system that does not provide impartial tribunals or procedures compatible with the requirements of due process of law;

(2) By a court that did not have personal jurisdiction over the defendant; or

(3) By a court that did not have jurisdiction over the subject matter (UFMJRA § 4(a)).

Note that the presence of any one of these three factors will prohibit recognition of the judgment; all three need not be present. Nonrecognition is discretionary (that is, a court in a state in which the UFMJRA has been adopted may choose not to recognize the judgment) where

(1) There was insufficient notice to the defendant;
(2) The judgment was obtained by fraud;
(3) The cause of action or claim for relief on which the judgment is based is repugnant to public policy;
(4) The judgment conflicts with another final and conclusive judgment;
(5) The judgment is contrary to the parties' choice of a forum (as expressed in a contract);
(6) Jurisdiction over the defendant was based only on personal service of process and the forum is an inconvenient one for the defendant (UFMJRA § 4).

Because these factors render nonrecognition discretionary, a court might choose not to recognize a judgment if only one of the six factors was present; conversely, it might conceivably choose to recognize a judgment even if all six were present, so long as none of the three mandatory grounds was present.

Constitution
- United States Constitution, Art. IV, § 1

Statute
- Full Faith and Credit Statute, 28 U.S.C. § 1738

Uniform Act
- National Conference of Commissioners on Uniform State Laws, Uniform Foreign Money-Judgments Recognition Act, August 4, 1962, available at http://www.uniformlaws.org/shared/docs/foreign%20money%20judgments%20recognition/ufmjra%20final%20act.pdf (visited December 20, 2012)

Case
- *Hilton v. Guyot*, 159 U.S. 113 (1895)

See also: Choice of Law; Defamation; French Yahoo! Case; Jurisdiction

Sources and Further Reading
John J. Barcelo III & Kevin M. Clermont, *A Global Law of Jurisdiction and Judgments: Lessons from the Hague* (Dordrecht, Netherlands: Kluwer Law International, 2002)
William M. Richman & William L. Reynolds, *Understanding Conflict of Laws* (New York: Matthew Bender, 3d ed. 2002)
Mark D. Rosen, "Exporting the Constitution," 53 *Emory Law Journal* 171 (2004)

❖ RECORDING INDUSTRY ASSOCIATION OF AMERICA ❖

The Recording Industry Association of America (RIAA) is an industry association representing music content industry companies. The advent of home computing, digitally recorded music, and the Internet threatened the music content industry's business model by making it far easier for consumers to copy and share recordings of popular music; in the past two decades the RIAA has been involved in ceaseless litigation and advocacy to defend the interests of its members on several fronts. It has sued a maker of MP3 players, fearing that MP3 players might enable and encourage piracy of copyrighted music (*Diamond Multimedia*, 180 F.3d 1072). It has sued file-sharing services, usually as a co-plaintiff with music and motion picture content industry companies (e.g., *Napster*, 239 F.3d 1004). It has sued Internet service providers in an attempt to compel them to disclose the names of their subscribers who may be engaging in sharing of copyrighted music files (*Verizon Internet Services*, 351 F.3d 1229). And it has filed thousands of suits against individual users of file-sharing services.

The RIAA has also pushed to protect its members' interests through changes in legislation. It has lobbied for increased copyright protection, particularly against online file-sharing. Its lawsuits and lobbying may have backfired, however, at least to some extent: The RIAA has acquired iconic status, representing to many consumer advocates the excesses of the current regime of copyright law. The RIAA has been sued in turn, for example, by distributors of file-sharing software (*Grokster [Antitrust]*, 269 F. Supp. 2d 1213). The RIAA Web site has become a target for technically skilled pranksters, and the suits against individual file sharers—especially when those file sharers are children—have attracted adverse publicity.

Cases
Federal Appellate Courts
- *A&M Records, Inc. v. Napster, Inc.*, 239 F.3d 1004 (9th Cir. 2001)
- *In re Aimster Copyright Litigation*, 334 F.3d 643 (7th Cir. 2003)
- *Recording Industry Association of America v. Diamond Multimedia Systems, Inc.*, 180 F.3d 1072 (9th Cir. 1999)
- *Recording Industry Association of America, Inc. v. Verizon Internet Services*, 351 F.3d 1229 (D.C. Cir. 2003)

Federal Trial Court
- *Metro-Goldwyn-Mayer Studios Inc. v. Grokster, Ltd. [Antitrust claims]*, 269 F. Supp. 2d 1213 (C.D. Cal. 2003)

See also: Activism and Advocacy Groups; Content Industry; Copyright; File-Sharing; Open Source; P2P; Piracy; Voluntary Collective License

Sources and Further Reading

"What Is Online Piracy?" RIAA, available at http://riaa.com/physicalpiracy.php?content_selector=What-is-Online-Piracy (visited December 20, 2012)

"Why We Do What We Do," RIAA, available at http://riaa.com/physicalpiracy.php?content_selector=piracy-online-why-we-do-what-we-do (visited December 20, 2012)

❖ RIAA ❖

See Recording Industry Association of America

❖ ROOTKIT ❖

See Malware

❖ ROVI CORPORATION ❖

See Macrovision

S

❖ SAFE HARBOR ❖

See Digital Millennium Copyright Act, Title II

❖ SEARCH ENGINE ❖

A search engine is a computer program that locates files stored on one or more computers. The user specifies values, such as words, numbers, or dates, for the files sought; the search engine then examines the files in the location it is designed to search and returns a list of files containing those values. There are a wide variety of search engines for different tasks. The Windows Search function is a search engine that searches a single personal computer. Library online catalogs search a network of library computers, and may connect to search engines at other libraries or search a shared inter-library database. Search engines make P2P networks possible. Search engines for large proprietary professional databases such as Westlaw and Lexis offer sophisticated search functions that require training to use. But the search engines that attract the greatest amount of attention, and are most likely to raise legal issues, are those that search the World Wide Web. Some of these search only a portion of the Web, while others attempt to search the entire Internet, and actually do search a large portion of it. The most popular of these general-purpose search engines is Google, followed by Microsoft's Bing, Yahoo! Search, and Ask; Google, however, has more unique monthly visitors than all of its competitors combined.

Internet search engines may become involved in legal disputes in several ways. They may be vehicles for copyright and trademark infringement. Because they may be used from anywhere in the world, they may violate local censorship laws. And they are subject to abuse by search engine spammers.

Search engines and copyright infringement: Internet search engines are generally considered to be service providers within the meaning of Title II of the Digital Millennium Copyright Act (DMCA), although Title II as a whole seems not to have been designed with search engines in mind: references to "subscribers" and "account holders" have no application to search engines, for example. As service providers, search engines are eligible for the protection of the four statutory safe havens from liability for copyright infringement: the transitory communications safe harbor, the system caching safe harbor, the information storage safe harbor, and the information location tools safe harbor. The fourth of these, the information location tools safe harbor, is the one designed with search engines in mind; however, the nature of most search engines means that some search engine activities may also fall within the other three safe harbors. Most Internet search engines, including the most popular ones, work by crawling the Web and storing information about each crawled Web site in the search engine's database. Searches then take place in the database rather than in the Web as a whole, which makes the searches much faster. Some, such as Google, also make cached versions of Web sites available to the public.

The transitory communications safe harbor shields a service provider from liability where the provider merely acts as a conduit, transmitting digital information from one point on a network to another at someone else's request. Five elements must be present for a service provider to avail itself of the transitory communications safe harbor: the transmission must be "initiated by or at the direction of a person other than the" service provider; it must be "carried out through an automatic technical process without selection of the material by the" service provider; the service provider must "not select the recipients of the material except as an automatic response to the request of another person"; the service provider must not maintain a copy of the material "in a manner ordinarily accessible to anyone other than anticipated recipients" or "for a longer period than is reasonably necessary"; and the material must be transmitted "without modification of its content" (17 U.S.C. § 512(a)).

Many search engine activities are likely to meet these requirements: the search engine can be viewed as a conduit for conveying information about Web sites between Web site operators and users. The users initiate the search, which is carried out by an automatic technical process, although it might be difficult to establish that the process does not involve selection of the material by the service provider. The service provider does not select the recipients of the material; the recipients select themselves. The results of a particular search are accessible only to the person running that search, and are maintained only until the recipient closes the search window or runs another search. However, there are problems with this reasoning; it may well be that the automated process of selecting search results is "selection of material" within the meaning of the statute. The transitory communications safe harbor is not generally applied to search engine activities.

The system caching safe harbor shields a service provider from liability where the provider makes a copy of material for system caching purposes. This system caching is a necessary part of the operation of all search engines that rely on searching their own databases of crawled Web sites, which is to say nearly all Internet search engines. In order for a service provider to be eligible for the system caching safe harbor, three requirements must be met: the material must be "made available online by a person other than the service provider"; it must be transmitted from that person to another person at the direction of the second person; and the caching "must be carried out through an automatic technical process for the purpose of making the material available to users of the system or network who . . . request access" (17 U.S.C. § 512(b)). These conditions appear to be met in the case of Internet search engines, although again the poorness of the fit between the statute and the reality of search engine operation is evident. Information about Web pages is made available online by the Web site operators, not by the search engines. It is "transmitted," or at least communicated in some way, to search engine users at their request. And the caching is done by an automatic process for the purpose of making the information available to search engine users.

Even if these requirements are met and the search engine service meets the threshold requirement of eligibility for the system caching safe harbor, however, additional conditions must be met before the search engine is shielded from liability. The search engine must not modify the retained material, must periodically refresh it, and must not interfere with technology that returns hit information to the person who posted the material. Search engines are likely to meet these conditions, but an additional condition has caused some controversy: once the service provider has been notified that copyrighted material posted without authorization has been removed or blocked, or ordered to be removed or blocked, at the original site, the service provider must promptly remove or block access to the cached copy. If the person who posted the material has imposed limitations on access, such as password protection, the service provider must also impose these limitations (17 U.S.C. § 512(b)(2)). This provision may be necessary to protect the interests of the copyright owner, but it interferes with the use of large cached databases such as Google's cached pages as archives for research into the history of the Web.

The information storage safe harbor is not really applicable to search engines; it shields a service provider from liability where the service provider stores information at the direction of a user. Search store information provided by Web site operators, but on their own initiative rather than at the direction of the operators; this storage is more likely to fall within the system caching safe harbor or the information location tools safe harbor. Search engines may, however, store information provided by Web site operators for use in targeted advertising or paid search results, and conceivably this information could contain infringing content. The information storage safe harbor would then be available to the search engine if it does not have actual or constructive knowledge that the content was infringing, and upon acquiring such knowledge acts "expeditiously to remove, or disable access to, the material" (17 U.S.C. § 512(c)). However, the information storage safe harbor is not available to a service provider that receives "a financial benefit directly attributable to the infringing activity" (17 U.S.C. § 512(c)(1)(B)). The fact that the search engine is paid for the advertising is probably not a benefit attributable to the infringing content in the advertisement. The search engine's advertising revenue will be the same whether the advertisement does or does not include infringing content, although where the advertisement is for something that is inherently infringing, such as (arguably) an online music file-sharing service, the ad revenue would be directly attributable to the infringement, possibly making the search engine ineligible for this safe harbor. The question seems unlikely to arise, however, as this safe harbor is designed to protect services hosting Web pages from liability for infringement posted on those pages; as with the previous two safe harbors, it is a poor fit when applied to search engines.

The information location tools safe harbor is designed with search engines in mind, although search engine operations have evolved and changed since the passage of the DMCA in 1998. The information location tools safe harbor shields a service provider from liability for referring or linking users to sites containing infringing material through tools such as directories, indexes, references, pointers, or hyperlinks. In order to be eligible for the information location tools safe harbor, the search engine or other service provider must not have actual or constructive knowledge that the located content is infringing; the "knowledge" standard here is the same as that for the information storage safe harbor. Again, like the information storage safe harbor, the information location tools safe harbor requires that the search engine must "not receive a financial benefit directly attributable to the infringing activity, in a case in which the service provider has the right and ability to control such activity" (17 U.S.C. § 512(d)(2)). This standard is drawn from the rule established by the federal courts for determining vicarious copyright infringement (see *Fonovisa*, 76 F.3d 259). The information location tools safe harbor includes the same notice-and-takedown procedure as the information storage safe harbor.

This notice-and-takedown procedure has given rise to controversy. The importance of search engines cannot be overestimated; a site that is overlooked by search engines will receive little or no traffic. In order to guarantee themselves the protection of the information location tools safe harbor, search engines will take down any potentially infringing links as soon as they are informed of them. This gives actual and purported copyright holders tremendous power over Web use patterns. No court order is required; the person claiming to own certain content has merely to notify the search engine of the alleged infringement, and the site will be blocked without first giving the Web site operator a chance to argue that there is no infringement. There are several reasons why a use might not be infringing: perhaps because the material is in the public domain or because the use is a fair use, or because the person claiming to be the content owner is not, in fact, the owner and the true owner has authorized the use. The operator may make these arguments after the fact, but search engines are safer ignoring such arguments until they have been resolved by a court; the requirements of the information location tools safe harbor encourage the search engine to err on the side of removing links, even at the cost of harm to the Web traffic (and thus the revenue) of the allegedly infringing Web site.

By removing the links, the search engine cuts off a sizable portion of the Web traffic that would otherwise have reached those sites. It is easy to imagine how such a procedure might be abused, especially by businesses seeking to block traffic to the Web sites of their competitors. To guard against such abuses, the DMCA establishes strict requirements for the notice that must be given to the service provider by the copyright owner:

(3) Elements of notification.—

(A) To be effective under this subsection, a notification of claimed infringement must be a written communication provided to the designated agent of a service provider that includes substantially the following:

    (i) A physical or electronic signature of a person authorized to act on behalf of the owner of an exclusive right that is allegedly infringed.

    (ii) Identification of the copyrighted work claimed to have been infringed, or, if multiple copyrighted works at a single online site are covered by a single notification, a representative list of such works at that site.

    (iii) Identification of the material that is claimed to be infringing or to be the subject of infringing activity and that is to be removed or access to which is to be disabled, and information reasonably sufficient to permit the service provider to locate the material.

    (iv) Information reasonably sufficient to permit the service provider to contact the complaining party, such as an address, telephone number, and, if available, an electronic mail address at which the complaining party may be contacted.

    (v) A statement that the complaining party has a good faith belief that use of the material in the manner complained of is not authorized by the copyright owner, its agent, or the law.

    (vi) A statement that the information in the notification is accurate, and under penalty of perjury, that the complaining party is authorized to act on behalf

of the owner of an exclusive right that is allegedly infringed (17 U.S.C. § 512(c)(3)(A)).

All of the information required could be faked, of course; anyone could send a letter (or, with an electronic signature, an email) claiming to be the owner of copyrighted material on a particular site. Although the person sending the letter must provide contact information, no duty is imposed upon the service provider to use that contact information. A business could thus send a letter complaining of copyrighted content on its rival's site, claiming to be—and giving accurate contact information for—the true owner of the copyrighted material. Even though the copyright owner had actually authorized the use of its material on the site, the search engine might simply block the site without contacting the copyright owner. The business sending the letter would have violated requirements (v) and (vi), but would be unlikely to be caught; the rival's business would suffer harm until the confusion could be straightened out—and it would be the rival who would bear the cost in time and money of straightening out that confusion.

The alleged infringer may contest the allegation of infringement by submitting a counter-notification. Within 10 to 14 business days following the filing of a proper counter-notification the service provider must restore access, unless it first receives notice that the person who submitted the original notification has filed a court action against the user. A great deal of harm can be done to a business in 10 to 14 business days, however, and the counter-notification procedure has been criticized as inadequate (Yen 2000). The search engine is given every incentive to place a higher value on the interests of the copyright holder than on any harm to the business of the alleged infringer: the DMCA insulates the search engine from liability to the Web site owner for blocking the site, so there is no risk to the search engine in doing so (17 U.S.C. § 512(g)(1)). At the same time, the DMCA shields the search engine from all monetary liability and most injunctive relief, other than orders "restraining the service provider from providing access to infringing material or activity residing at a particular online site on the provider's system or network" (17 U.S.C. § 512(j)).

Search engines as copyright infringers: In addition to being sued as contributory or vicarious infringers for linking to allegedly copyright-infringing content, search engines may be sued as direct infringers. A search engine results page typically includes short text excerpts, and sometimes thumbnail images copied from the site on which that result is found. These are likely to increase traffic to the found sites; nonetheless, some content owners have taken exception to the practice. In 2007, the U.S. Court of Appeals for the Ninth Circuit held that the use of such thumbnail images by Google was fair use within the meaning of 17 U.S.C. § 107 (*Perfect 10*, 508 F.3d at 1168) and that in-line linking to the picture on the found site, even when appearing with a frame on the Google results page, was not a display of the original full-resolution picture (*Perfect 10*, 508 F.3d at 1161). Nor was it a copy, as no copying of the image took place on Google's servers; the user's computer was directed to the found site.

Search engines and trademark law: The DMCA provides search engines with a safe harbor from liability for copyright infringement; it provides no similar safe harbor from liability for trademark infringement. Section 230(c)(1) of the Communications Decency Act provides that "no provider or user of an interactive computer service shall be treated as the publisher or speaker of any information provided by another information content provider." At one time, this was thought to provide protection for service providers from liability for some trademark infringement along lines similar to those of the DMCA copyright infringement safe harbors. However, § 230(e)(2) of the same statute provides that "nothing in this section shall be construed to limit or expand any law pertaining to intellectual property." Sections 230(c)(1) and 230(e)(2) survived the Supreme Court's decision in *Reno v. American Civil Liberties Union*, which struck down the Internet censorship portions of the Communications Decency Act as unconstitutional. The federal district court for the Southern District of New York has since explained that the effect of § 230(e)(2) is that § 230(c)(1) conveys no immunity upon service providers from liability for trademark infringement; in other words, there is no safe harbor (*Gucci*, 135 F. Supp. 2d 409).

Search engines may be involved in trademark infringement and dilution in many ways. They may reproduce trademark infringing text or domain names on search result pages; search engines that show images as well as text may reproduce trademark logos exactly, and the trademarks may be used in a way that infringes upon or dilutes the mark holder's interest. And, as with copyright, search engines may provide links to sites with infringing content.

Abuse of search engines: Search engine results are crucial to the success of an online business; the higher a company shows up on a list of search results, the more hits it will receive. As a result, companies use a variety of tricks to increase search engine rank. Some of these tricks are simply sensible Web design, such as prominently displaying the terms most descriptive of the company's business on the Web site's front page, and publicizing the business to encourage other businesses to link to the Web site. Other tricks raise ethical questions: the use of terms, often repeated far more times than necessary simply for identification purposes, in metatags; paid placement; the use of competitors' trademarks as a part of either of these techniques; and link farming. Unethical use of these techniques to trick search engines into ranking a site higher than it ordinarily would is called search engine spamming.

Metatags are text inserted into an HTML document so as to be invisible when the document is viewed as a Web page. To view the metatags, a user can select "View/Source" from the browser menu. Metatags, if any, will appear near the top of the HTML document, just after the title; they typically take the form <META name = "category" content = "thing(s) in category">. While there are legitimate uses for metatags, such as to identify the Web page author and copyright holder, they have acquired notoriety for their abuse in search engine spamming. While metatags are invisible to the viewer, they are visible to search engines; thus, a term could be repeated thousands of times in metatags, potentially raising the page's rank, without changing the visible appearance of the page.

This use of metatags is not in itself illegal; however, a business may go too far if it seeks to gain an advantage over its competitors by using the competitor's name as a meta tag, so that searches for one Web site will detect the other as well. This use of a competitor's name may be unlawful trademark infringement, subject to such exceptions as fair use: for example, it would probably not be infringement for an independent bicycle dealer, Citywide Bicycles, to use the trademarked name "Trek" as a meta tag, if Citywide sells or repairs Trek bicycles; this may fall within the nominative fair use exception to trademark infringement. If, however, Citywide's chief competitor is Urban Cycles, it would be trademark infringement for Citywide to use the name Urban Cycles as a meta tag; the tag is not being used to identify Urban Cycles, but to attempt to divert business from its Web site (see *Playboy v. Welles*, 279 F.3d at 801). Use of metatags may be nominative fair use so long as three conditions are met:

> First, the product or service in question must be one not readily identifiable without use of the trademark; second, only so much of the mark or marks may be used as is reasonably necessary to identify the product or service; and third, the user must do nothing that would, in conjunction with the mark, suggest sponsorship or endorsement by the trademark holder (279 F.3d at 801).

While technological advances have rendered meta tag spamming no longer worth the effort, the same reasoning applies to the use of protected marks in more sophisticated search engine spamming techniques.

Paid placement is one way in which companies may obtain higher search result rankings for their Web sites: the company pays a sum of money to a search engine to move its site up the rankings when a particular search term is entered. The use of trademarks as search terms raises concerns similar to those raised by the use of metatags: if Citywide Bicycles pays to be ranked at or near the top of the list when the term "Trek" is entered, there is probably no problem; the use of the name "Trek" is nominative fair use. Applying the same factors applied to metatags yields the same result: Citywide cannot identify its business (selling and repairing Trek bicycles) without using the trademark; it is using no more of the mark than necessary to identify its service; and it is not using the mark in a way that suggests the sponsorship or endorsement of the bicycle maker, Trek.

However, if Citywide pays to be ranked first when the name of its competitor, Urban Bicycles, is entered as a search term, a problem arises. This use may well constitute trademark infringement, although the question is a new enough one that it has not yet been resolved by the courts (Padawer 2003). While Google does not actively screen for trademarks used as advertising keywords (AdWords), it will act on complaints by the mark owners (Google *AdWords Trademark Policy*). A search engine following such a policy (analogous to the notice and takedown policy set by statute for copyright violations) is unlikely to be liable for misuse of trademark terms by others. In 2004, the Ninth Circuit Court of Appeals reversed a lower court ruling in favor of Playboy Enterprises against Netscape and Excite, which had allowed advertisers of pornographic content to link their advertisements to search results for the trademarked terms "Playboy" and "Playmate" (*Playboy v. Netscape*, 354 F.3d 1020). The liability of the party initiating the possibly infringing use may be, as one author observes, a bit more "difficult to predict because of conflicting opinions among jurisdictions" as to fair use and likelihood of confusion in such cases (Winkler 2012, at 1005). Results in other countries may differ as well: in a 2005 French judgment, Google was found to have infringed trademarks by allowing trademarked terms to be used as advertising keywords. The decision was upheld on appeal in 2006. Google then appealed to France's highest court, the Court of Cassation, which in turn referred the question to the Court of Justice of the European Union. The Court of Justice held that Google, in allowing others to use trademarked terms as AdWords, was not "using" the terms within the meaning of EU copyright law, and was in any event protected from liability by provisions equivalent to the safe harbors for Internet service providers under U.S. law (*Google France v Louis Vuitton*, 2008). Similar suits have been filed against Google by trademark holders in Germany and Italy, but are likely to run into the same barrier.

Link farming: A link farm is "a network of pages on one or more Web sites, heavily cross-linked with each other, with the sole intention of improving the search engine ranking of those pages and sites" (Perkins 2004). Link farming is aimed at Google and related search engines that rank pages by the number and type of links to those pages from other pages, just as meta tag spamming was aimed at other search engines. Link farm spamming is considered unethical (Perkins 2004) but is not illegal; the best cure is probably not legislation but, as with metatags, advances in search engine technology that diminish the usefulness of the tactic.

Internet search engines and censorship: Search engines risk running afoul not only of copyright and trademark laws, but of censorship laws. Search engines, like all Internet resources, are accessible from nearly all of the world, and content that is legal, even accepted as mainstream, in one country may be completely illegal in another. The French Yahoo! case raised awareness of the fact that the actions of an Internet service provider in its home country may expose it to liability in another. In the aftermath of the Yahoo! case, Google has removed listings for Nazi and racist hate sites from the French and German versions of its search engines, www.google.fr and www.google.de. The power of search engines over access to information on the Internet poses the problem of private censorship; while Google blocked sites from its French and German search engines in response to complaints from the French and German governments, it has also blocked search-engine access to sites critical of the Church of Scientology at the request of the Church (McCullagh 2002). Search engines with a political agenda might even decide to remove sites from search results on their own initiative, rather than out of fear of litigation by some aggrieved outside party. (A search for "Google's liberal bias" turns up an apparently inexhaustible vein of semiliterate paranoia.) Self-censorship of this sort poses no First Amendment concerns, as search engine operators are private companies and not state actors. However, some users' rights advocates have begun to demand transparency in the process: search engines, they say, may remove sites from search databases if they wish, but they should publish information about which sites have been removed (McCullagh 2002). Compromise steps include Google's promise to report legal threats (which tend to be accompanied by demands to remove or block search access to certain sites) to the free-speech Web site www.chillingeffects.org.

Statutes

- Communications Decency Act, 47 U.S.C. § 230
- Digital Millennium Copyright Act, 17 U.S.C. § 512

European Union Directives

- First Council Directive 89/104/EEC of 21 December 1988 to approximate the laws of the Member States relating to trade marks, 1989 O.J. (L 40) 1
- Article 9(1) of Council Regulation (EC) No 40/94 of 20 December 1993 on the Community trade mark, 1994 O.J. (L11) 1
- Article 14 of Directive 2000/31/EC of the European Parliament and of the Council of 8 June 2000 on certain legal aspects of information society services, in particular electronic commerce, 2000 O.J. (L 178) 1

Cases

Supreme Court

- *Reno v. American Civil Liberties Union*, 521 U.S. 844 (1997)

Federal Appellate Courts
- *1–800 Contacts, Inc. v. WhenU.com, Inc.*, 414 F.3d 400 (2d Cir. 2005)
- *Fonovisa, Inc. v. Cherry Auction, Inc.*, 76 F.3d 259 (9th Cir. 1996)
- *Kelly v. Arriba Soft Corp.*, 336 F.3d 811 (9th Cir. 2003)
- *Name.Space, Inc. v. Network Solutions, Inc.*, 202 F.3d 573 (2d Cir. 2000)
- *Perfect 10, Inc. v. Amazon.com, Inc.*, 508 F.3d 1146 (9th Cir. 2007)
- *Playboy Enterprises Inc. v. Netscape Communications Corp.*, 354 F.3d 1020 (9th Cir. 2004)
- *Playboy Enterprises, Inc. v. Welles*, 279 F.3d 796 (9th Cir. 2002)
- *Yahoo! Inc. v. La LigueContre Le RacismeetL'Antisemitisme*, 433 F.3d 1199 (9th Cir. 2006), reversed and remanded, *Yahoo! Inc. v. La LigueContre Le Racisme et L'Antisemitisme*, 379 F.3d 1120 (9th Cir. 2004), rehearing, 433 F.3d 1199 (9th Cir. 2006), certiorari denied, 547 U.S. 1163 (2006)

Federal Trial Court
- *Gucci America, Inc. v. Hall & Associates*, 135 F. Supp. 2d 409 (S.D.N.Y. 2001)

European Union
- Case C-236/08, *Google France v. Louis Vuitton*, Judgment of Court (Grand Chamber) (March 23, 2010), available at http://curia.europa.eu/juris/liste.jsf?language=en&num= C-236/08 (visited February 18, 2013)

See also: Censorship; Communications Decency Act; Copyright; Copyright Infringement; Data Mining; Digital Millennium Copyright Act, Title II; File-Sharing; French Yahoo! Case; Metatags; Trademark Dilution; Trademark Infringement

Sources and Further Reading
"An Ad-Block Shock: France v Google," *The Economist* (January 12, 2013), available at http://www.economist.com/news/business/21569414-xavier-niel-playing-rough-internet-giant-france-v-google (visited February 18, 2013)
"AdWords Trademark Policy," Google, available at http://support.google.com/adwordspolicy/bin/answer.py?hl=en&answer=6118 (visited December 20, 2012)
Jesse Drucker, "Google Shifts $10b into Bermuda Subsidiary Tax Bill," *Royal Gazette Online* (December 11, 2012, 8:00 AM), available at http://www.royalgazette.com/article/20121211/BUSINESS/712109923 (visited February 18, 2013)
"Google and Antitrust: Transatlantic Tussles," *The Economist* (December 22, 2012), at 105, available at http://www.economist.com/news/business/21568757-investigations-google-approach-climax-america-and-europe-transatlantic-tussles (visited February 18, 2013)
"Google's Copyright Complaints Flag Up Piracy of Microsoft," BBC News (May 25, 2012), available at http://www.bbc.co.uk/news/technology-18204411 (visited February 8, 2013)

"Google in Africa: It's a Hit," *The Economist* (May 12, 2012), at 57, available at http://www.economist.com/node/21554566 (visited February 18, 2013)
"Google Threatens French Media Ban over Proposed Law," BBC News (October 18, 2012), available at http://www.bbc.co.uk/news/technology-19996351 (visited February 18, 2013)
Jessica Leber, "EmTech: French Minister Says Google Faces Critical Questions over Copyright," *MIT Technology Review* (October 25, 2012), available at http://www.technologyreview.com/view/506296/emtech-french-minister-says-google-faces-critical-questions-over-copyright/ (visited February 18, 2013)
Declan McCullagh, "Google Excluding Controversial Sites," CNET News.com (October 23, 2002), available at http://news.cnet.com/2100–1023–963132.html (visited February 18, 2013)
Heidi S. Padawer, "Google This: Search Engine Results Weave a Web for Trademark Infringement Actions on the Internet," 81 *Washington University Law Quarterly* 1099 (2003)
Alan Perkins, "The Classification of Search Engine Spam," Search Mechanics, available at http://www.ebrandmanagement.com/whitepapers/spam-classification/ (visited October 28, 2004)
"Search Tools Listing: Open Source Search Engines," Search Tools, available at http://www.searchtools.com/tools/tools-opensource.html (visited February 18, 2013)
Craig W. Walker, "Application of the DMCA Safe Harbor Provisions to Search Engines," 9 *Virginia Journal of Law & Technology* 1 (2004)
Katelynn Winkler, "Functionality Failure: How Rosetta Stone v. Google Misapplies the Trademark Functionality Doctrine to AdWords," 44 *Arizona State Law Journal* 995 (2012)
Alfred C. Yen, "Internet Service Provider Liability for Subscriber Copyright Infringement, Enterprise Liability, and the First Amendment," 88 *Georgetown Law Journal* 1833 (2000)

❖ SECURE SOCKET LAYER ❖

See Encryption

❖ SECURITY SYSTEMS STANDARDS AND CERTIFICATION ACT ❖

See Consumer Broadband and Digital Television Promotion Act

❖ SEMICONDUCTOR MANUFACTURING MASK WORK REGISTRATIONS ❖

A semiconductor manufacturing mask work is a design pattern used in the manufacture of computer chips. These chips are manufactured in a three-stage process. The first stage is the manufacture of the blank wafers from which the chips will be etched; the wafers are usually made of silicon, gallium arsenide, or indium phosphide, and are made at a plant solely dedicated to wafer manufacturing; the second stage—the transformation of the blank wafer into a chip –generally takes place elsewhere. The third stage is the assembly and packaging; the etched wafers are cut apart and mounted in a ceramic or metal package, and leads are soldered on (Lee & Elliot 2006).

The second stage of the process, the transformation of blank wafers into computer chips, is the most technically complex. The surface of the wafer is first oxidized by being exposed to oxygen at a high temperature. Much of the rest of the manufacturing process is devoted to selectively removing portions of this oxidized layer. This is done by first applying a coating of photoresist, a light-sensitive compound, over the oxidized layer. Portions of the photoresist are then exposed to light through a mask (Lee & Elliot n.d.). The mask is the informational portion of the manufacturing process; it determines which parts of the photoresist shall be exposed, in the same way, although not by the identical process, that a laser printer, photocopier, or photographic negative determines what part of a print drum or photographic paper shall be exposed. In essence, an image of the mask is being recorded on the photoresist-coated surface of the wafer.

Exposure to light causes a portion of the photoresist to either harden or soften. (Photoresist may be either positive or negative: positive photoresist softens when exposed to light, while negative photoresist hardens.) A photoresist-developing chemical is then used to strip away the soft portion of the photoresist; the hard portion remains. Where the photoresist has been removed, the silicon dioxide layer is exposed. This layer is then etched by exposure to acid or a reactive gas plasma. The channels left by the etching are then "doped"—conducting and semiconducting materials are deposited in them by one or more of several processes. A new layer of silicon is then deposited on the surface of the wafer, and the process begins again for as many layers as necessary. Finally, the wafers are polished and enter the third stage of production (Lee & Elliot n.d.).

The semiconductor manufacturing mask work is crucial to the process; the design of the mask is a long and complex process. Once designed, however, it can be imitated by reverse engineering. Conceivably a mask work could be made the subject of copyright or patent, but instead Congress has chosen to create a new category of intellectual property, giving the mask work copyright-like protection. The Semiconductor Chip Protection Act of 1984 provides for the registration of semiconductor mask work designs with the U.S. Copyright Office (17 U.S.C. § 908; 37 C.F.R. § 211.4). The registrant must then alert the world to the claim of an intellectual property right in the mask work by placing the words "mask work," the symbol "Ⓜ," or the letter "M" in a circle in a visible location on the exterior surface of the finished chip or its receptacle (17 U.S.C. § 909; 37 C.F.R. § 211.6). The registrant will enjoy the exclusive right to reproduce the mask work and to import or distribute a semiconductor chip embodying the mask work, as well as the exclusive right to authorize, induce, or knowingly cause

any other person to do either of these things (17 U.S.C. § 905). This exclusive right will last for 10 years from the date of registration or from "the date on which the mask work is first commercially exploited anywhere in the world, whichever occurs first" (17 U.S.C. § 904). The Act also includes a right of first sale (17 U.S.C. § 906(b)) and an exception to the exclusive rights for reverse engineering (17 U.S.C. § 906(a)). Innocent infringers are also protected (17 U.S.C. § 907).

Semiconductor manufacturing masks are not like other protected works such as MP3s; they are not subject to widespread piracy and infringement. Anyone can copy and use the MP3, but without a chip-manufacturing factory, the mask is useless. Chip factories are relatively rare, and setting up a new factory may require an investment of hundreds of millions of dollars. As a result, infringements of registered mask works are rare. The Semiconductor Chip Protection Act has given rise to relatively little litigation, resulting in only a handful of reported cases, only one of which—*Brooktree v. AMD*—deals with the substantive application of the Act. The others include *Anadigics v. Raytheon* and *Atari v. Nintendo*. The reported opinion in *Anadigics* dealt with procedural issues, however (903 F. Supp. 615), while the court in *Atari* concluded that the Act did not apply (975 F.2d at 842 n. 5).

Brooktree v. Advanced Micro Devices involved the reverse engineering exception. The defendant, Advanced Micro Devices (AMD), claimed to have reverse-engineered the chip, resulting in a different chip that performed the same function. The court agreed that such reverse engineering would be permitted under the Act. However, at trial, a jury had found that AMD's chip design did infringe upon Brooktree's registered mask work; the appellate court held that a reasonable jury could have reached this conclusion, and declined to reverse the trial court's decision. The appellate court pointed out that, as a witness had testified to Congress in hearings on the Act,

> Whenever there is a true case of reverse engineering, the second firm will have prepared a great deal of paper—logic and circuit diagrams, trial layouts, computer simulations of the chip, and the like; it will also have invested thousands of hours of work. All of these can be documented by reference to the firm's ordinary business records. A pirate has no such papers, for the pirate does none of this work. Therefore, whether there has been a true reverse engineering job or just a job of copying can be shown by looking at the defendant's records. The paper trail of a chip tells a discerning observer whether the chip is a copy or embodies the effort of reverse engineering (*Brooktree*, 977 F.2d at 1566).

The trial court had instructed the jury to "place great weight on the existence of the reverse paperwork trail" (977 F.2d at 1567); the jury had apparently done so. The trial court had also instructed the jury that AMD's mask work could be considered original if it incorporated new design elements either superior to or merely alternative to those in

Brooktree's design; apparently the jury found that it did not. The appellate court announced that it would not revisit "these fact-dependent areas"; appellate courts are concerned with questions of law rather than fact, and based upon the facts found by the jury, AMD had in fact infringed upon the rights of Brooktree under the Act.

Anadigics aside, the 12 years since *Brooktree* have been quiet ones for the Semiconductor Chip Protection Act. Given the relatively small number of firms in the chip-making industry, it may be that industry self-regulation has resolved most problems before they reached the litigation stage.

Statute

- Semiconductor Chip Protection Act, 17 U.S.C. §§ 901–914

Cases

Federal Appellate Courts

- *Atari Games Corp. v. Nintendo of America, Inc.*, 975 F.2d 832 (Fed. Cir. 1992)
- *Brooktree Corp. v. Advanced Micro Devices, Inc.*, 977 F.2d 1555 (Fed. Cir. 1992)

Federal Trial Court

- *Anadigics, Inc. v. Raytheon Co.*, 903 F. Supp. 615 (S.D.N.Y. 1995)

Code of Federal Regulations

- Mask Work Protection, 37 C.F.R. § 211

See also: Copyright; Digital Millennium Copyright Act, Title V; Intellectual Property

Sources and Further Reading

Gerard V. Curtin, Jr., "The Basics of ASICs: Protection for Semiconductor Mask Works in Japan and the United States," 15 *Boston College International and Comparative Law Review* 113 (1992)

The Industry Handbook—The Semiconductor Industry, Investopedia.com, available at http://www.investopedia.com/features/industryhandbook/semiconductor.asp (visited December 20, 2012)

M. K. Carol Lee & J. Julian Elliot, "Semiconductor Manufacturing," in *Bay Area Air Quality Management District Permit Handbook* § 7, Chapter 4 (2006), available at, http://hank.baaqmd.gov/pmt/handbook/rev02/PH_00_05_07_04_mem_1.pdf (visited December 20, 2012)

❖ SOCIAL NETWORKING SERVICE ❖

Social media, in an Internet context, refers to a large number of platforms on which users place self-generated content to be viewed by other users, and which they also use to view other users' content, and to interact with those users. The entire Internet is, in a sense, a social network, and many Web sites and services have a social component. E-commerce sites such as Amazon and eBay allow users to create profiles, post reviews, and enter into discussions; even the comments section of a news Web site allows social interaction. Blogging, Twitter, video-sharing sites (for user-generated videos) are all "social media." But the term "social networking service" (often shortened to "social network") is generally reserved for platforms for which the social component is not ancillary to some other purpose, such as commerce or news reporting, but is the primary function; such social networks include Facebook, Google +, LinkedIn, MySpace, and LiveJournal.

Social networking was one of the first uses of the Internet. In the days before the World Wide Web, many bulletin board services (BBS) and Usenet newsgroups existed solely for social networking purposes. The advent of mass use of the Web in the mid-1990s saw the emergence of Web-based social networking platforms such as Geocities, Theglobe, and Tripod, as well as email-based services such as Classmates.com. By the late 1990s, profile-based, searchable services emerged, with Six Degrees in 1997 and LiveJournal in 1999. Other briefly ubiquitous services included Friendster (beginning in 2002) and MySpace in 2003.

One feature of all of these social networking services was their short lifespan; all of those named in the preceding paragraph are now extinct, moribund, or have suffered a marked decline from their peak popularity. Many social networking platforms have turned out to be very sensitive to trends and fads, abandoned in favor of newer platforms, although specialized networks such as LinkedIn, used for resume-sharing and job-finding, have had more staying power. But the growth of Facebook from its launch in 2004 to its emergence as the world's most popular social networking services has eclipsed most other networks; it remains to be seen whether it will prove immune to the faddishness that doomed so many other services.

Social networking services present many of the legal problems of the entire Internet. They enable the sharing of copyrighted and other illegal content, albeit on a smaller scale (and although such use is generally prohibited by the services' Terms of Service). Some of the content that is posted is bullying, abusive, defamatory, or otherwise actionable. A user's history of posts gives information that may lead to that user being denied a job, or even fired. Privacy concerns have led to laws prohibiting employers from demanding access to employees' social networking accounts, and have led to scrutiny of the privacy policies of Facebook and other services. A 2011 class action lawsuit against Facebook for using users' names and images in connection with advertising without permission led to a $20 million settlement (Fraley, No. 11-CV-01726). On August 26, 2013, the settlement was approved by the district court. During the course of the suit the named plaintiff, Angel Fraley, withdrew after Facebook's attorneys succeeded in "digging up embarrassing material about her from her Facebook account" (Hill 2013).

Facebook and other services are also popular with children, despite a federal statute, the Children's Online Privacy Protection Act (COPPA), prohibiting these services from collecting personal information from children without the verifiable consent of the parents. Facebook founder Mark Zuckerberg has criticized COPPA as limiting children's educational opportunities, stating "My philosophy is that for education you need to start at a really, really young age," adding "We'd take a lot of precautions to make sure that [the children] are safe" (Lev-Ram 2011).

Cases

- *Fraley v. Facebook, Inc.,* No. 11-CV-01726-LHK, 2011 U.S. Dist. LEXIS 145195 (N.D. Cal. December 16, 2011)
- Order Granting Motion for Final Approval of Settlement Agreement, No. 3:11-cv-01726-RS (N.D. Cal. August 26, 2013), available at http://www .fraleyfacebooksettlement.com/docs/2013-08-26-Order_Granting_Final_Approval.pdf

Statute

- Children's Online Privacy Protection Act, 15 U.S.C. §§ 6501–6506

Regulation

- Children's Online Privacy Protection Rule, 64 Fed. Reg. 59,888 (November 3, 1999) (codified at 16 C.F.R. § 312 (2001))

See also: Children's Online Privacy Protection Act; Data Mining; Mobile Device; Privacy

Sources and Further Reading

"Facebook and Children: Let the Nippers Network," *The Economist*, June 9, 2012, at 18

"Facebook: Work in Progress," *The Economist*, August 4, 2012, at 60

Kashmir Hill, "Yes, That Legal Notice You Got from Facebook Is Real," *Forbes* (January 26, 2013), available at http://www .forbes.com/sites/kashmirhill/2013/01/26/yes-that-legal-notice-you-got-from-facebook-is-real/ (visited April 24, 2013)

"Imbee.com Settles FTC Charges Social Networking Site for Kids Violated the Children's Online Privacy Protection Act; Settlement Includes $130,000 Civil Penalty," Federal Trade Commission (January 30, 2008), available at http://www.ftc.gov/ opa/2008/01/imbee.shtm (visited April 24, 2013)

Michal Lev-Ram, "Zuckerberg: Kids under 13 Should Be Allowed on Facebook," CNNMoney (May 20, 2011, 11:02 AM), available at http://tech.fortune.cnn.com/2011/05/20/ zuckerberg-kids-under-13-should-be-allowed-on-facebook/ (visited April 4, 2013)

"Operator of Social Networking Website for Kids Settle Charges Site Collected Kids' Personal Information without Parental Consent," Federal Trade Commission (November 8, 2011), available at http://www.ftc.gov/opa/2011/11/skidekids .shtm (visited April 5, 2013)

"Video Games: Japan Fights Back," *The Economist*, November 17, 2012, at 61

❖ SONNY BONO COPYRIGHT TERM EXTENSION ACT ❖

The Sonny Bono Copyright Term Extension Act (CTEA), named for the late singer, songwriter and U.S. Representative Sonny Bono, extends the duration of copyrights in the United States by 20 years. The Copyright Act of 1976 had brought U.S. copyright terms in line with the Berne Convention requirements: the lifetime of the author plus 50 years for most individual works, and 75 years from publication or one hundred years from creation, whichever was less, for anonymous or pseudonymous works and works for hire. The CTEA extended these terms to life plus 70 years and 95 years, respectively (17 U.S.C. §§ 302, 304).

In the early 1990s, the countries of the European Union had agreed among themselves to a longer term of copyright protection than that required by the Berne Convention. The copyright terms specified in the Berne Convention are minimum rather than maximum terms, and Article 20 of the convention specifically permits countries to agree among themselves to a longer term. The EU directive extending copyright terms was applied to foreign works and foreign authors on a basis of reciprocity; that is, in order for a foreign author to receive the benefits of the EU directive, the author's country would have to offer works by EU authors the same term of copyright protection (Council Directive 93/98/EEC). The CTEA was ostensibly enacted, at least in part, to bring U.S. law into conformity with EU law. Although there was no treaty obligating the United States to achieve this conformity, there is a benefit in that American works and authors can now receive the same copyright term in the European Union as EU works and authors do.

Its detractors, however, see another and more immediate purpose, and derisively refer to the CTEA as the Mickey Mouse Protection Act (*Economist* 2002, 67). Among those lobbying for the passage of the CTEA was the Walt Disney Corporation. Copyrights on early Mickey Mouse cartoons would have begun to expire in 2003, and the 75-year term for works for hire would have become a moving terminator, constantly bringing more Disney works (and those of the other entertainment conglomerates that arose after Disney) into the public domain.

This does not mean that the characters themselves would fall into the public domain, allowing anyone who wished to make his or her own Mickey Mouse cartoons; Mickey Mouse is protected by trademark law as well as by copyright law, and trademarks are of potentially infinite duration. But Disney still receives substantial royalties from its early works; the first full-length animated feature, *Snow White and the Seven Dwarfs*, was 75 years old in 2012, yet it remains among the best-selling movies of all time. Thanks to the CTEA, Disney will receive another 20 years of profits from *Snow White*. This provides a considerable windfall for Disney and is strikingly different from the way patents are treated. Pharmaceutical companies would surely be delighted to receive a 20-year extension to the term of existing drug patents, which may be the product of far more expense and effort than even a Disney animated film. Yet, Congress has quite wisely held the line against any such extension of patent terms, reasoning that the shorter patent term encourages greater effort devoted to research and development and thus greater and more rapid technological advance.

In the past four decades, Congress has extended the copyright term 11 times. It is quite possible that in the next decade or two the copyright term will be extended yet again, creating a "limited" copyright term that never actually expires. Some consumer advocates fear that this is what the CTEA and future Congressional action aim to achieve: Sonny Bono's widow, U.S. representative Mary Bono, stated in the House of Representatives that "Sonny wanted the term of copyright protection to last forever." However, she said, because she was "informed by staff that such a change would violate the Constitution," Congress might instead consider a copyright term of "forever less one day" (Statement of Mary Bono 1998, H9952).

The "forever less one day" proposal has been attributed (by Mary Bono and many others) to Jack Valenti, content-industry advocate and, until his retirement in March 2004 at the age of 82, president of the Motion Picture Association of America (MPAA). The constitutional problem to which Ms. Bono referred is the Patent and Copyright clause of the U.S. Constitution, which provides that Congress shall have the power "to promote the Progress of Science and useful Arts, by securing for limited Times to Authors and Inventors the exclusive Right to their respective Writings and Discoveries." A perpetual copyright, even one of forever less one day, would not be for a limited time and would thus be unconstitutional.

The CTEA helps the content industry in the short term by protecting its revenues from already created works. Opponents, however, point out that there is potential for long-term harm to the content industry by inhibiting creativity. Many of Disney's successful animated features have been based on works already in the public domain: *Snow White*, *Sleeping Beauty*, *Cinderella*, *Beauty and the Beast*, *The Little Mermaid*, *Mu-lan*, *Hercules*, and the *Hunchback of Notre Dame*, to name a few. Had the CTEA and the EU copyright directive been in force at the time, the copyright on the fairy-tale collections of the Brothers Grimm would have expired in 1933, 70 years after the death of Jakob Grimm; *Snow White* would just barely have fallen in to the public domain. Had the 1857 edition of *Grimm's Fairy Tales* been a work for hire, the CTEA would have protected it until 1952.

In addition, holders of patents have enjoyed no similar extension of protection; patents have durations roughly similar to that which they had two centuries ago, while the term of copyright has increased from 14 years, renewable once, to 95 years or life plus 70 years.

Although the CTEA passed Congress with little opposition, after its passage it became the subject of a lawsuit seeking to have it declared unconstitutional. The named plaintiff, Eric Eldred, operated Eldritch Press, an online publisher of out-of-copyright materials. The plaintiffs were represented by consumer advocate and Internet law guru Lawrence Lessig.

The arguments of the plaintiffs were rejected, and the CTEA was upheld, both at trial in the federal district court and on appeal to the Circuit Court of Appeals for the District of Columbia. The U.S. Supreme Court granted certiorari to review the questions of whether Congress had the power under the Copyright Clause to retroactively extend the term of existing copyrights, and whether a law that extends the term of existing and future copyrights is categorically immune from challenge under the First Amendment. The plaintiffs did not challenge Congress' authority under the Copyright Clause to apply a longer copyright term to works created after the passage of the statute, but its ability to extend the term for works already in existence—the "Mickey Mouse Protection Act" aspect of the CTEA. The constitutional arguments advanced by Eldred and Professor Lessig were, first, that the "limited time" in the Copyright Clause is the time limit in effect when the copyright is granted, and subsequent Congressional expansion of the term for existing works means, in effect, that the term is not "limited." The second argument was that the preambular language in the Copyright Clause—"To promote the Progress of Science and useful Arts"—was a substantive limitation on the length of the "limited time" for which Congress could grant copyright protection; any grant longer than that necessary to promote the progress of science and the useful arts was unconstitutional. This would prohibit extension of the terms of existing copyrights; as the longer copyright term would not have been in existence at the time of creation of the work, it could not have served as an incentive. The First Amendment argument was that the CTEA unconstitutionally restricted the right to make use of the copyrighted works of others (*Eldred*, 537 U.S. 186).

The Supreme Court, like the lower courts, rejected the plaintiffs' arguments on both questions and held that the CTEA was constitutional. The term "limited" did not mean "fixed" or "inalterable." It meant "not unlimited." A perpetual term was prohibited, but Congress was free to adjust the limits. Historically, Congress had repeatedly included existing works when extending the term of copyrights so that all copyrights would be governed evenhandedly. The Supreme Court had also previously found the extension of existing patents constitutional.

The Court evaluated the CTEA under a "rational basis" test, and found that it was a rational exercise of legislative authority, with purposes including harmonizing U.S. copyright terms with those of the European Union in order to provide U.S. copyright holders with the same copyright term as European copyright holders under EU law. The Court rejected the First Amendment argument as well. The fact that the First Amendment and the Copyright Clause were adopted at about the same time showed that the framers of the Constitution viewed copyright protection as consistent with freedom of expression. In addition, copyright law incorporates First Amendment protections both by prohibiting copyright in an idea and through the fair use exception. The CTEA itself includes two additional exceptions to its 20-year extension of copyright terms, one for reproduction by libraries and other institutions for scholarly purposes, if the work is not already being exploited commercially and further copies are unavailable at a reasonable price, and the other exempting small businesses from payment of royalties on music played from licensed broadcasting facilities. The Court noted that the goal of the First Amendment is to protect the individual's freedom to make his or her own speech rather than to protect the freedom to make someone else's speech (*Eldred*, 537 U.S. 186).

Constitution
- United States Constitution, Article I, Section 8, Clause 8

Statute
- Sonny Bono Copyright Term Extension Act, 17 U.S.C. §§ 302, 304.

Congressional Record
- 144 Cong. Rec. H9946–01, H9952 (Sonny Bono Copyright Term Extension Act, October 7, 1998) (Statement of Representative Mary Bono)

Cases
- *Eldred v. Ashcroft*, 537 U.S. 186 (2002)
- *Harper & Row Publishers, Inc. v. Nation Enterprises*, 471 U.S. 539 (1985)

European Union Materials
- Council Directive 93/98/EEC of 29 October 1993 Harmonizing the Term of Protection of Copyright and Certain Related Rights, 1993 O.J. (L 290) 9

See also: Berne Convention; Constitutional Law; Copyright; International Copyright Protection; Public Domain

Sources and Further Reading
"Face Value: Lawrence Lessig Wants Less Copyright Protection, Including for Disney's Famous Rodent," *The Economist*, October 12, 2002, at 67

Michael Jones, "Eldred v. Ashcroft: The Constitutionality of the Copyright Term Extension Act," 19 *Berkeley Technology Law Journal* 85 (2004)

Cecil C. Kuhne III, "Forcing the Copyright Genie Back into the Bottle: Public Policy Implications of Copyright Extension Legislation," 33 *Southwestern University Law Review* 327 (2004)

William M. Landes & Richard A. Posner, "Indefinitely Renewable Copyright," 70 *University of Chicago Law Review* 471 (2003)

Lawrence Lessig, *Free Culture: How Big Media Uses Technology and the Law to Lock Down Culture and Control Creativity* (New York: Penguin, 2004)

Makeen Fouad Makeen, *Copyright in a Global Information Society: The Scope of Copyright Protection under International, US, UK, and French Law* (New York: Aspen, 2001)

Susan K. Sell, *Private Power, Public Law: The Globalization of Intellectual Property Rights* (Cambridge, UK: Cambridge University Press, 2003)

Symposium, "Panel II: Mickey Mice? Potential Ramifications of Eldred v. Ashcroft," 13 *Fordham Intellectual Property, Media and Entertainment Law Journal* 771 (2003)

❖ SOPA ❖

See Stop Online Piracy Act

❖ SPAM ❖

Few features of the Internet arouse more widespread ire than spam, or unsolicited mass email advertising. Everyone with an email account has received unsolicited advertisements, many of them unsavory. Emails offering generic Viagra, enlargement of various body parts, pornography, fake university degrees, and too-good-to-be-true interest rates have become a form of information pollution. Years of transparently fraudulent emails from purported Nigerian colonels proposing shady business transactions, or from phishers requesting credit card or bank account information, have prompted first outrage, then laughter, and finally resigned annoyance.

So why do the spammers bother? The answer lies in economics. The marginal cost of sending additional copies of a message is low; the cost of transmitting spam is born by Internet Service Providers (ISPs), not by the spammers; and the cost of deleting unwanted messages is borne by the users. By forcing others to bear these external costs, spammers are able to continue operating a business that results in a net loss to the overall economy. Suppose that a spammer spends $15 (including the cost of the spammer's time) writing and sending 10 million copies of an email message advertising the infamous "patch" for sale for $20. ISPs may spot and delete 99% of the messages before they arrive, but 100,000 messages will still be transmitted, and the ISPs will have incurred costs in transmitting and deleting the messages. Ninety-nine percent of the recipients may delete the message unread, but a thousand messages will still be read. Ninety-nine percent of those who read the message may ignore or delete it; if 1% of those who actually read the message order the product, the spammer will receive $200. If the spammer is a legitimate enough businessperson to actually ship some goods in exchange, there will be further costs—perhaps as much as 50% of the total. This leaves the spammer with a profit of $85: the $200 received, minus $100 for the cost of the goods and shipping, minus the original $15 cost of the advertisement.

The other economic actors involved, though, have much higher costs. If it costs one-one thousandth of a cent to transmit a message over the Internet or to delete the message before it reaches its intended recipient, the ISPs involved will have incurred costs of $100. If it takes the average user half a second to identify a message as spam and delete it, and the average user's time is valued at $10 per hour, the 99,000 messages deleted will have cost their recipients a total of $137.50. And if the average time spent by the 990 users who read the message but did not order the product was 10 seconds, an additional $27.50 worth of time has been expended without recompense, assuming those users received no other value (such as entertainment) from the message. The users and their ISPs will thus have spent a total of $265 to support the spammer's $85 profit, representing a net loss to the Internet economy of $180. Expanding this to a larger scale reveals the scope of the problem: in 2002, advertisers spent an estimated $1.3 billion on spam marketing; this spam cost ISPs and corporations—not even taking into account individual users—an additional $11.9 billion (Alongi 2004). In effect, the ISPs and users unwillingly gave a $12 billion subsidy to the spammers.

Similar arguments can be made with regard to other forms of advertising, but abuses are generally limited by the fact that other forms of advertising cost money. Spamming is very nearly free; after the initial set-up costs, unlimited copies of an advertisement can be sent at little or no additional cost. In addition, various tricks can be used to lower costs and increase profits. Many spam messages include a bogus "unsubscribe" option, saying something like "This e-mail has been sent to you because you have expressed an interest in receiving messages about low-interest loans. If you wish to unsubscribe, click here." When a recipient clicks on the "unsubscribe" message, the recipient's email address will be identified to the spammer as a "live" address—one at which there is an actual person receiving and reading email, and one naïve enough to click on the bogus "unsubscribe" link. The email address will then become more valuable, and may be sold to other spammers at a higher rate.

Spammers may also trick users into installing spam-sending programs on their computers, often by clicking an email attachment. Once installed, this program may send out copies of spam messages, and forward additional spam messages, to millions of other users. The user will be unaware that his or her computer has been turned into a spam zombie; the spammer will be able to send far more messages at no additional cost. The zombie computer may also send out additional copies of the spam-sending program, further multiplying the number of spam messages.

The dubious honor of being the first Internet spammers goes to two Arizona lawyers who, in 1994, sent an advertisement for legal services to 8,000 Usenet newsgroups, reaching 20 million users and crashing the spammers' ISP. Not surprisingly, the advertisement itself was also on the dubious side: it offered to assist would-be immigrants to the United States in applying for the Diversity Visa program, better known as the green card lottery. Application for the lottery is actually quite simple, and requires no fee other than a postage stamp (Fogo 2000). Historical purists may put the origin of spam much earlier, though: in 1978 the first mass commercial email was sent over ARPANET, a predecessor to the Internet (Zakon 2011). And spam is as old as information networks; as early as 1864 dentists Arnold and Maurice Gabriel were using the telegraph network to annoy people with their advertising, prompting a strongly worded letter to the *Times* (*Getting the Message* 2007; M.P. 1864).

Spamming is a serious burden for users and ISPs alike. Users spend a great deal of time deleting spam, and may inadvertently delete important personal or business messages in the process. Children may be exposed to sexually explicit advertising. Some users may be taken in by scams. Users may find themselves unable to communicate with each other because one's ISP identifies the other's ISP as a source of spam; this is a particular problem for international email. A user whose email address is spoofed by a spammer may find himself or herself blocked or terminated by his or her ISP. Blind and visually impaired users suffer especially grievously from spam, and may find themselves unable to use email; where a sighted person can scan email headers quite rapidly and delete spam with a fair degree of accuracy, a blind person must wait for screen-reading software to read the headers, one at a time, before identifying each message as spam.

ISPs are burdened by the sheer bulk of spam. Spam has made up the majority of email since shortly after May 2003, when spam first accounted for 50% of email; two studies in May 2004, a year later, put the percentage at 64% and 78% (Greenspan 2004). In 2003, spammers sent an estimated 25.5 billion messages every day. According to a study by Kaspersky Lab, spam peaked at above 90% of all email in 2008, and has since declined, but still makes up about two-thirds of all email (*Read this* 2013).

Unlike spammers, ISPs do incur additional costs in transmitting additional messages; the ISPs have to pass these costs along to users and legitimate advertisers, who are thus also subsidizing the spammers.

A small number of people send most spam. According to the Register of Known Spam Operations (ROKSO) maintained by Spamhaus, an antispam organization, a mere 100 spam operations, consisting of probably no more than 400 individuals, account for 80% of all spam received in North America and Europe (ROKSO 2012). Many spammers have been sued by ISPs; at least one, the Buffalo Spammer, has been sent to prison for identity theft and falsification of business records related to spamming (Roberts 2004). The techniques used by spammers often involve theft of services from ISPs; breaches of contracts with ISPs; illegal hacking, trespass, and theft of services to users whose computers are made into zombies; violation of the federal Controlling the Assault of Non-solicited Pornography and Marketing

(CAN-SPAM) Act of 2003 and an implementing federal regulation regarding adult email; false advertising, false statements, fraud, identity theft, and a variety of other torts and crimes. Spammers often use stolen credit card numbers to set up accounts.

Yet spam persists; the legal system has not, so far, been able to deal with it effectively. Antispam legislation has limited impact because spammers are already operating outside the law, and have no reason to comply with these additional rules. A spammer who uses stolen credit card information and plants spam Trojans on other users' computers is already facing serious legal penalties, and is unlikely to be deterred by more. The CAN-SPAM Act's requirements may convince some of the more reputable mass emailers to comply, but are not likely to have a significant effect on the overall volume of spam without some additional measures.

The other point at which spam may be attacked is the demand side. Many businesses pay money to spammers; the CAN-SPAM Act makes these businesses responsible for violations by spammers. Persons or entities providing goods, products, property, or services to another person or entity that violates the statute may also be liable under two sets of circumstances: (1) if they have a greater than 50% ownership interest in the violator or (2) if they have actual knowledge that the goods, products, property, or services are promoted in a prohibited spam message and they "receive, or expects to receive, an economic benefit from such promotion" (15 U.S.C. § 7705(b)). The CAN-SPAM Act provides for hefty damages of from $20 million to $60 million for violations. Aggravated violations such as address harvesting, automated creation of multiple email accounts, and unauthorized use of a network for spamming purposes trigger the highest penalties.

The CAN-SPAM Act also authorizes the Federal Trade Commission (FTC) to create a "Do Not Spam" registry along the lines of the "Do Not Call" registry established to control telemarketing. The FTC has not done so, because of the difficulties of putting such a registry into operation and its probable futility; only spammers who comply with the other requirements of the CAN-SPAM Act can be reported for violations of the "Do Not Spam" registry.

Even if the CAN-SPAM Act and additional federal legislation creates a workable regime for U.S. spammers and advertisers, the U.S. law can do little or nothing to solve the problem of spam originating outside the United States and advertising goods or services sold by non-U.S. parties. Spam is an international problem, and it will not be controlled until it can be addressed internationally. The email marketer sued by Verizon now says "I've gone overseas . . . I now send most of my mail from other countries. And that's a shame. I pay a fortune to providers to do this, and I'd much rather have it go to American companies. But I have to stay in business, and if I have to go out of the country, then so be it" (Wendland 2002).

Other countries have taken steps to outlaw spam, many of them more far-reaching than the CAN-SPAM Act. CAN-SPAM

has been criticized as an "opt out" rather than "opt in" approach: all users are fair targets for commercial email that otherwise complies with the statute unless and until they specifically request not to receive it. The European Union (EU), on the other hand, has chosen an "opt in" approach: its 2002 Directive on Privacy and Electronic Communications prohibits spam, telemarketing calls, and junk faxes unless consented to by the user or unless consent can be inferred from a preexisting business relationship; even when spam is sent, it must include an opt-out option. The EU Directive also contains identification and valid email address requirements similar to CAN-SPAM's. Many EU members, including Austria, Denmark, Finland, Germany, Greece, and Italy, have enacted domestic opt-in legislation along these lines. At least two, Belgium and Spain, have chosen opt-out legislation similar to CAN-SPAM. Australia has also adopted an opt-in law, while South Korea and Japan have adopted opt-out laws (Alongi 2004, 266–68). An opt-in law has obvious advantages in stopping spam, but in the United States and other countries it may run into problems because of constitutional protections of freedom of expression.

In the United Kingdom, an older law, the 1990 Misuse of Computers Act, may prove useful in deterring spammers. The Act prohibits unauthorized access to computers, potentially including the planting of spam Trojans and the use of zombies. Microsoft has filed suits under the Act against persons it alleges have engaged in illegal account name harvesting. A newer set of regulations, adopted pursuant to the European Union's Directive on Privacy and Electronic Communications, applies an opt-in approach as well. With countries around the world also adopting opt-in rather than opt-out acts, the United States seems to be one of the more spam-tolerant countries.

If international legal control of spam is possible at all, it will probably require a multilateral treaty to set uniform antispam laws worldwide. In the meantime users and ISPs must seek other means to reduce spam: denial of Internet access to known spammers, individual lawsuits, and interception and deletion of messages. Interception of messages, like detection of viruses and adware, involves an arms race, in this case between spammers on the one hand and ISPs and makers of anti-spam software on the other. But while antivirus and anti-adware software are relatively successful, antispam software is less so; a purely market-based solution may not be effective without government intervention to force spammers to internalize the costs they currently impose on others. One mechanism that has been proposed to achieve this is email postage—charging a slight fee for each message sent. While this makes sense from an economic perspective, collecting the fee and enforcing violations would be a problem—spammers who use stolen credit card numbers to open email accounts could use those numbers to pay the fee, and spam sent from zombie computers would be billed to that computer's Internet access account holder, not the spammer. Like the identification and opt-out provisions, email postage would affect spammers who comply with the law but do nothing to restrain outlaw spammers (see Hansell 2006).

Statutes
United States
- Controlling the Assault of Non-solicited Pornography and Marketing (CAN-SPAM) Act of 2003, 15 U.S.C. §§ 7701–7713

European Union
- Directive 2002/58/EC of the European Parliament and of the Council of 12 July 2002 on Privacy and Electronic Communications, 2002 O.J. (L 201) 37

England and United Kingdom
- Data Protection Act, 1998, c. 29, §§ 7–12 (Eng.)
- The Privacy and Electronic Communications Regulations, 2011, EC Directive No. 1208, §§ 19–22 (U.K.), available at http://www.legislation.gov.uk/uksi/2011/1208/contents/made

Cases
- *Mainstream Marketing Services, Inc. v. Federal Trade Commission*, 358 F.3d 1228 (10th Cir. 2004)
- *Cyber Promotions, Inc. v. America Online, Inc.*, 948 F. Supp. 436 (E.D. Pa. 1996)

See also: Advertising; Adware and Spyware; Censorship; Denial-of-Service Attack; First Amendment; Hacking; Malware; Privacy; Trademark; Trojan; Worm; Zombie

Sources and Further Reading
Elizabeth A. Alongi, "Has the U.S. Canned Spam?" 46 *Arizona Law Review* 263 (2004)

SharaelFeist, "Newsmaker: The Father of Modern Spam Speaks," CNET News (March 26, 2002), available at http://news.cnet.com/2008–1082–868483.html (visited February 18, 2013)

Credence E. Fogo, "The Postman Always Rings 4,000 Times: New Approaches to Curb Spam," 18 *John Marshall Journal of Computer & Information Law* 915 (2000)

"Getting the Message, at Last," *Economist* (December 13, 2007), available at http://www.economist.com/node/10286400 (visited February 18, 2013)

Robyn Greenspan, "The Deadly Duo: Spam and Viruses, May 2004," Internetnews.com (June 7, 2004), available at http://www.Internetnews.com/stats/article.php/3364421 (visited February 18, 2013)

Saul Hansell, "Postage Is Due for Companies Sending E-Mail," *N.Y. Times* (February 5, 2006), available at http://www.nytimes.com/2006/02/05/technology/05AOL.html?pagewanted=all&_r=0 (visited February 18, 2013)

Arik Hesseldahl, "Ten O'Clock Tech: D-Day in the Spam War," Forbes.com (February 27, 2004), available at http://www.forbes.com/2004/02/27/cx_ah_0227tentech.html (visited February 18, 2013)

M.P., To the Editor of *The Times*, June 1, 1864, reproduced at *Computer History: Telegraph "spam,"* available at http://www.computerhistory.org/revolution/the-web/20/392/2172 (visited February 18, 2013)

Ariella Mutchler, "CAN-SPAM versus the European Union E-Privacy Directive: Does Either Provide a Solution to the Problem of Spam?" 43 *Suffolk University Law Review* 957 (2010)

Vagelis Papakonstantinou & Paul de Hert, "The Amended EU Law on ePrivacy and Electronic Communications after Its 2011 Implementation; New Rules on Data Protection, Spam, Data Breaches and Protection of Intellectual Property Rights," 29 *John Marshall Journal of Computer & Information Law* 29 (2011)

"Read This and Win Million$!!!," *The Economist*, January 26, 2013, at 60

"Register of Known Spam Operations (ROKSO)," The Spamhaus Project, available at http://www.spamhaus.org/rokso/ (visited January 15, 2013)

Paul Roberts, "'Buffalo Spammer' Convicted: Howard Carmack Was Convicted on Charges of ID Theft and Falsifying Business Records," *Computer World* (April 1, 2004), available at http://www.computerworld.com/softwaretopics/software/groupware/story/0,10801,91823,00.html (visited February 18, 2013)

Jon Swartz, *"Spammers Convicted: First Felony Case,"* USAToday.com (November 3, 2004, 5:20 PM), available at http://www.usatoday.com/tech/news/2004–11–03-spam_x.htm (visited February 18, 2013)

Mike Wendland, "Spam King Lives Large Off Others' E-Mail Troubles: West Bloomfield Computer Empire Helped by Foreign Internet Servers," *Detroit Free Press*, November 22, 2002

Robert H. Zakon, "Hobbes' Internet Timeline v10.2," available at http://www.zakon.org/robert/Internet/timeline/ (visited February 7, 2013)

❖ SPYWARE ❖

See Adware and Spyware

❖ STEGANOGRAPHY ❖

The term "steganography" comes from *Steganographia*, a 1499 book by Johannes Trithemius. It refers to the process by which a message can be concealed within and later extracted from another message. The steganographic message may also be, but is not necessarily, encrypted. The fundamental difference between steganography and encryption is in the level of secrecy. In an encrypted message the content of the message is secret, but the existence of the message is not. In a steganographic message the very existence of the message is not readily apparent.

In the predigital age steganographic messages could be recorded with a variety of devices, including invisible ink, photographs compressed and used as the dot over the lowercase letter "i" in plaintext or encrypted messages, tattoos on the scalp over which hair was allowed to grow back, and writing on the back of postage stamps and the inside of envelopes, among others. Digital data files, however, present a greatly expanded scope for steganography, so much so that the word "steganography" itself, which would probably have been unknown to almost every English speaker 25 years ago, has come back into use.

At the very simplest level, steganographic content might be included in a text file by typing a plaintext message in the same color as a document's background. This is the electronic equivalent of invisible ink; it offers no significant degree of security, but can be used for such things as concealing the answers to trivia quiz questions until after the reader has had a chance to guess the answer. But digital steganography offers greater possibilities: data, in plaintext or encrypted, can be inserted into redundant or nonessential portions of files.

Any type of file can contain steganographic content; content may even be hidden in obscure areas, such as disk free space or print buffers. But data files, particularly text, image, sound, and motion picture files, are especially suited to containing steganographic content, for two reasons. First, text, image, sound, and motion picture files are well suited to serve as vehicles for steganographic content because they contain redundant or nonessential information that can easily be overwritten with steganographic content without either destroying the file's integrity or alerting the viewer to the presence of the hidden message; for example, data can be transmitted during silent pauses in a Skype conversation. And second, because the files themselves contain information, the visible message distracts the viewer from the possible existence of a hidden message.

Second, text, image, sound, and motion picture files are also often copyrighted, or contain copyrighted content; steganographic content can be used to detect and track unauthorized copying of the files. This technique is not new to the digital age. Printed maps, for instance, often include one or two nonexistent features, such as cul-de-sacs, that do not affect the usefulness of the map. A publisher of telephone directories might include names and telephone numbers for a few nonexistent persons. If these nonexistent cul-de-sacs or phone listings show up in another map or phone directory, the only likely reason is that the later map or directory was copied from the earlier one. Similarly, a copyrighted JPEG file, for instance, may steganographically identify the photographer who took the picture; if copies of the JPEG are emailed around the Internet, posted on Web pages, and so forth, the hidden message will identify the JPEG as a copy. Text files created with Adobe Acrobat may be digitally signed by the author; these files might be copied and used by anyone else with a copy of the same program, but the signature will remain, although it is not visible in the text of the document. A programmer who illegally copies large chunks of another's code and incorporates it into his program may fail to notice the steganographic content the first programmer has included to identify the work as her own.

A file that contains a hidden message is called a container. Typically, the container is unaffected by the inclusion of the steganographic content. In some cases, however, the steganographic content may be included in such a way as to make it impossible to remove without damaging or destroying the container. Steganography of this sort is called robust steganography. Robust steganography is useful for copyright protection because it prevents savvy users from removing the hidden copyright-protection information and sharing the "cleaned" file with others, and because it protects against inadvertent destruction of the hidden information through recompression of the file.

Because steganography can be used by criminals, terrorists, and spies, the government has an interest in steganalysis—the detection of steganographic content. And because steganography can be used to conceal malware, private individuals and companies also have an interest in steganalysis. As with encryption, there is an ongoing race between the development of increasingly sophisticated steganographic techniques and the development of steganalytic techniques to detect them. Advancements in steganalysis have decreased the usefulness of steganography alone as a copyright-protection tool; it will still identify the casual infringer, but protection from professional pirates requires more sophisticated digital rights management systems, in which steganography is only one element (see 17 U.S.C. § 1202).

See also: Copyright; Copyright Infringement; Digital Rights Management; Encryption

Sources and Further Reading

Eric Cole, *Hiding in Plain Sight: Steganography and the Art of Covert Communication* (Indianapolis: Wiley Publishing, Inc., 2003)

Neil F. Johnson et al., *Information Hiding: Steganography and Watermarking—Attacks and Countermeasures* (Boston, MA: Kluwer Academic Publishers, 2000)

Stefan Katzenbeisser & Fabien A. P. Petitcolas, eds., *Information Hiding Techniques for Steganography and Digital Watermarking* (Norwood, MA: Artech House, 2000)

Gregory Kipper, *Investigator's Guide to Steganography* (Boca Raton, FL: Auerbach Publications, 2003)

Chun-Shien Lu, *Multimedia Security: Steganography and Digital Watermarking Techniques for Protection of Intellectual Property* (Hershey, PA: Idea Group Publishing, 2004)

"Steganography: Speaking with Silence," *The Economist*, February 2, 2013, at 68

Johannes Trithemius, *Steganographia* (1499; Darmstadt, Germany: Ioannis Berneri Bibliopolae, 1621), available in Latin at http://www.esotericarchives.com/tritheim/stegano.htm (visited June 16, 2004)

Peter Wayner, *Disappearing Cryptography—Information Hiding: Steganography and Watermarking* (Burlington, MA: Morgan Kaufmann, 3d ed. 2008)

❖ STOP ONLINE PIRACY ACT ❖

The Stop Online Piracy Act (SOPA), with its companion bill the Preventing Real Online Threats to Economic Creativity and Theft of Intellectual Property Act (PIPA), was a proposed U.S. statute that would have advanced the protection of some intellectual property rights at the expense of Internet users, Internet service providers (ISPs), and possibly the stability of the Internet itself. SOPA was ultimately defeated by a broad-based protest movement. The battle over SOPA and PIPA became the defining struggle for information rights advocates in the early part of the second decade of the 21st century.

SOPA was introduced in the U.S. House of Representatives by Representative Lamar Smith (R-TX). In pursuit of its goals of combating online copyright piracy and sales of trademark-infringing, copyright-infringing, and patent-infringing goods, SOPA would have curtailed the safe harbor protections ISPs and search engines currently enjoy under 17 U.S.C. § 512, and might, according to its opponents and some neutral observers, have seriously undermined the integrity of the Domain Name System (DNS) on which the Internet depends. The U.S. government joined in expressing this latter concern, after which Representative Smith withdrew it from the bill. The UK government and the European Union expressed similar concerns.

SOPA and PIPA inspired a broad-based protest movement, discussed under the heading "Preventing Real Online Threats to Economic Creativity and Theft of Intellectual Property Act" in this encyclopedia. These protests probably exceeded the expectations of the bill's proponents, and were ultimately successful: following a day of online and real-world protests on January 18, 2012, Representative Smith announced that "the House Judiciary Committee will postpone consideration of the legislation until there is wider agreement on a solution."

Proposed Statute

- Stop Online Piracy Act. H.R. 3261, 112th Cong. (1st Sess. 2011)

See also: Activism and Advocacy Groups; Digital Millennium Copyright Act, Title II; Internet Service Providers; Preventing Real Online Threats to Economic Creativity and Theft of Intellectual Property Act

Sources and Further Reading

Bill D. Herman, *The Fight over Digital Rights: The Politics of Copyright and Technology* (Cambridge, UK: Cambridge University Press, 2013)

Larry Magid, "What Are SOPA and PIPA and Why All the Fuss?" *Forbes* (January 18, 2012), available at http://www.forbes.com/sites/larrymagid/2012/01/18/what-are-sopa-and-pipa-and-why-all-the-fuss/ (visited April 24, 2013)

Declan McCullagh, "How SOPA Would Affect You: FAQ," CNet (January 18, 2012), available at http://news.cnet.com/8301–31921_3–57329001–281/how-sopa-would-affect-you-faq/?tag=mncol;txt (visited April 24, 2013)

Jonathan Weisman, "After an Online Firestorm, Congress Shelves Antipiracy Bills," *New York Times* (January 20, 2012), available at http://www.nytimes.com/2012/01/21/technology/senate-postpones-piracy-vote.html?_r=0 (visited April 24, 2013)

Jenna Wortham, "Public Outcry over Antipiracy Bills Began as Grassroots Grumbling," *New York Times* (January 19, 2012), available at http://www.nytimes.com/2012/01/20/technology/public-outcry-over-antipiracy-bills-began-as-grass-roots-grumbling.html?pagewanted=all (visited April 24, 2013)

❖ TAXATION ❖

E-commerce, like all commerce, is potentially subject to taxation; as e-commerce grows, so too does government's interest in taxing that commerce. However, e-commerce presents complex issues of jurisdiction; more than one government may claim authority to tax a single transaction. Even a very simple transaction may present complex tax issues. Suppose, for example, that a Web user in California purchases a copy of *Night of the Lepus* on Blu-ray through an online auction site owned by a company incorporated in Delaware but located in Pennsylvania; the company listing the item for sale is located in Wyoming, but the copy of the DVD is actually located in, and shipped from, Nevada. At the seller's request, payment is made by a deposit into the seller's bank account in the Cayman Islands. In theory, all five states, plus the Cayman Islands, might claim jurisdiction to tax the sale (although in practice some of the U.S. jurisdictions would not be able to under the U.S. Supreme Court's holding in *Quill Corp. v. North Dakota*, 504 U.S. 298 (1992)). In comparison with some interbusiness transactions, this particular transaction is a fairly simple one, and catalog mail-order sales have forced the tax system to deal with similar problems for years.

The amount of tax revenue at stake is not trivial; about $161.5 billion was spent online in the United States in 2011(Otlacan 2012). When online sales take place within a single state, they are subject to sales taxes; when they take place across state lines, they are at least theoretically subject to use taxes imposed by the buyer's state. The Commerce Clause of the Constitution prevents states from passing laws that interfere with interstate commerce. The Supreme Court in *Quill Corp. v. North Dakota* interpreted this to mean that out-of-state retailers cannot charge sales taxes when they sell goods to consumers unless those retailers maintain a "substantial nexus" with the state, which usually means a physical presence in the taxing state. When the seller has a substantial nexus with the buyer's state, it becomes the seller's duty to collect and remit the use tax to the buyer's state; from the buyer's perspective, the process is identical to the collection of sales tax (*Quill,* 504 U.S. at 311). However, the Supreme Court has drawn a "sharp distinction . . . between mail-order sellers with [a physical presence in the taxing] State and those . . . who do no more than communicate with customers in the State by mail or common carrier as part of a general interstate business"; sellers in the latter category are not required to collect and remit the use tax (*Quill,* 504 U.S. at 311).

This does not mean that the state relinquishes its right to the use tax; the buyer remains obligated to calculate the use tax and pay it to the appropriate state authority (Swartz 2003, 144). As a practical matter, however, the tax is rarely paid; few buyers are aware of the obligation, and even those who are lack information on where and how to pay the tax. And the amounts involved in most transactions tend to be so small that the cost of education and enforcement would exceed the amount collected (Swartz 2003, 144), although enforcement may be worthwhile for high-value items such as automobiles, jewelry, and works of art.

The advent of e-commerce in the mid-1990s brought the problem of taxing interstate sales to the attention of state legislatures and Congress. State governments became concerned that they would lose tax revenues; e-commerce businesses were concerned that they would be unable to attract customers if they could not offer tax-free sales. In 1998 Congress, in order to simplify the situation and protect the nascent e-commerce industry, enacted the Internet Tax Freedom Act. The Act prevents taxes that discriminate against e-commerce and taxes on Internet access (Internet Tax Freedom Act § 1101). It also declares that "it is the sense of Congress that no new Federal taxes . . . should be enacted with respect to the Internet and Internet access" during the Act's moratorium period (Internet Tax Freedom Act § 1201) and that "the Internet should be free of foreign tariffs, trade barriers, and other restrictions" (Internet Tax Freedom Act § 1203 (header)). The Act does not prevent states from levying sales or use taxes, however. The Act originally granted protection for a three-year period; in 2001, it was renewed by the Internet Tax Nondiscrimination Act; in 2004, the Act was modified and extended; and in 2007 the Internet Tax Freedom Act Amendment Act extended the Act's protections until November 1, 2014.

Bricks-and-mortar retailers, threatened by untaxed Internet sales, have united with state governors in pushing for the Marketplace Fairness Act, which would in effect eliminate the tax advantage that e-commerce retailers currently enjoy; e-commerce, consumer advocates, and technology industry groups favor legislation incorporating the *Quill* standard. Bills along those lines have been introduced in Congress, without success (Marketplace Fairness Act; Main Street Fairness Act; Marketplace Equity Act).

Large online retailers have become fairly sophisticated at avoiding a legal obligation to collect use or sales taxes. As one author explains:

> To avoid being forced to collect sales taxes, some online retailers such as Amazon.com take advantage of the Quill physical presence requirement by using a tactic called "entity isolation." To use this tactic, a corporation sets up other companies to perform specific functions, such as order fulfillment or research and development on new products. Because the subsidiaries are legally distinct from the company selling the product, the seller is not deemed to have a physical presence in the state. Thus, under Quill, the seller cannot be required to collect sales tax (Gordon 2010, at 306).

For example, subsidiaries "will ship goods to a certain state, but not actually sell them there" (Letterio 2012, at 413).

State governments estimate that they lost up to $23 billion in tax revenues in 2012 because of the moratorium on taxing Internet sales (TaxCloud 2013). There have also been attempts by state governments to circumvent *Quill* through legislation at the state level or agreements with major e-commerce retailers under which the retailers collect the taxes voluntarily (see Peterson 2012). The legislative attempts, at least, may run afoul of the *Quill* standard (see *Amazon.com LLC*, 877 N.Y.S.2d 842; Letterio 2012). Taxation of Internet services has also become a contentious issue, especially with the advent of voice-over-Internet telephone call technology and streaming music and video services.

Statute

- Internet Tax Freedom Act, P.L. 105–277, Title XI, and subsequent Acts codified at 47 U.S.C. § 151

Proposed Legislation

- Indiana Senate Bill 309, S. 309, 118th Cong. (1st Sess. 2013), available at http://www.in.gov/legislative/bills/2013/PDF/IN/IN0309.1.pdf (visited February 24, 2013)
- Main Street Fairness Act, S. 1452, 112th Cong. (1st Sess. 2011); H.R. 2701, 112th Cong. (1st Sess. 2011)
- Marketplace Equity Act of 2011, H.R. 3179, 112th Cong. (1st Sess. 2011)
- Marketplace Fairness Act, S. 1832, 112th Cong. (1st Sess. 2011)

Cases

- *Quill Corp. v. North Dakota*, 504 U.S. 298 (1992)
- *Amazon.com LLC v. New York State Department of Taxation & Finance*, 877 N.Y.S.2d 842 (N.Y. Sup. Ct. 2009), affirmed as modified 913 N.Y.S.2d 129 (N.Y. App. Div. 2010)

See also: Choice of Law; E-Commerce; Jurisdiction; Recognition and Enforcement of Judgments

Sources and Further Reading
Arthur J. Cockfield, "Jurisdiction to Tax: A Law and Technology Perspective," 38 *Georgia Law Review* 85 (2003)
Michael R. Gordon, "Up the Amazon without A Paddle: Examining Sales Taxes, Entity Isolation, and the 'Affiliate Tax,'" 11 *North Carolina Journal of Law and Technology* 299 (2010)
Walter Hellerstein, "Jurisdiction to Tax Income and Consumption in the New Economy: A Theoretical and Comparative Perspective," 38 *Georgia Law Review* 1 (2003)
Anne Letterio, "A State's Way of Circumventing the Constitution: The Unconstitutional Taxation of Out-of-State Corporations That Do Instate Business over the Internet," 22 *Albany Law Journal of Science and Technology* 411 (2012)
Otilia Otlacan, "comScore Reports $50 Billion in Q4 2011 U.S. Retail E-Commerce Spending, Up 14% vs. Year Ago," AdOps Online (February 14, 2012), available at http://www.adoperationsonline.com/2012/02/14/comscore-reports-50-billion-in-q4–2011-u-s-retail-e-commerce-spending-up-14-vs-year-ago/ (visited February 24, 2013)
Mark Peterson, "Indiana Bill Would Force Tax Collection on Internet Sales," WNDU.com (January 11, 2013), available at http://www.wndu.com/home/headlines/Indiana-bill-would-force-tax-collection-on-internet-sales-186549551.html#.UPQuOMVhdAg.twitter (visited February 24, 2013)
Ryan J. Swartz, "The Imposition of Sales and Use Taxes on E-Commerce: A Taxing Dilemma for States and Remote Sellers," 2 *Journal of High Technology Law* 143 (2003)
TaxCloud, "Marketplace Fairness Act Questions: How Much Is at Stake?" Marketplacefairness.org, available at http://www.marketplacefairness.org/questions-and-answers/ (visited January 15, 2013)

❖ TECHNOLOGY, EDUCATION AND COPYRIGHT HARMONIZATION ACT ❖

See Digital Millennium Copyright Act, Title IV

❖ THREE-DIMENSIONAL PRINTING ❖

Three-dimensional printing, or 3D printing, is a manufacturing technology still in its infancy, or at least in its youth. The most widely used 3D printing technology uses a "printer" to build a three-dimensional object by laying down multiple layers of a "printing" material, usually but not always some form of plastic. While the technology is still too new to have produced much response from the legal system, there are already concerns on the effects it may have in areas including patent law, trademark law, product liability, bioethics, and the regulation of dangerous technologies.

While copyright law has had decades to adapt to the Internet and the challenges it brings, mass downloading of patented devices has only recently become a perceived threat to patent-holders' rights. Similarly, the idea that it might be possible not just to buy a counterfeit Gucci handbag online but also to download and print an exact duplicate of the genuine item is fairly new. Neither of these problems has yet arisen as a serious threat to patent or trademark rights, but 3D printing technology has reached a stage at which it has become possible for those threats to arise in the next few years. Archives of 3D-printable files already exist at sites like Thingiverse.com.

Nor are inanimate objects the only things that can be printed. Researchers are exploring the printing of human and animal tissue, including human organs for transplant. Presumably the most effective use of the technology will involve copying the organs of exceptionally healthy persons; at present, the possessors of those organs have no intellectual property right in their own tissues, and would be unable to control or profit from their reproduction (see Rubens 2013). Three-dimensional printing could conceivably also be used to replicate prescription medicines or illegal drugs; the former has patent consequences, and both have public health and criminal law consequences.

The renewed debate over gun control in the United States prompted some gun-rights activists to design a printable multi-cartridge magazine, possibly for use where such magazines are prohibited. More worrisome still is the possibility of downloading and printing plastic guns, undetectable by metal detectors; such guns can be downloaded and have already been printed and fired (Morelle 2013). A U.S. statute, the Undetectable Firearms Act, currently makes such weapons illegal; however, its provisions are due to expire in December 2013 unless renewed. Nor is the act readily enforceable against those who print illegal weapons. U.S. representative Steve Israel (D-NY) has proposed legislation to extend and strengthen the Undetectable Firearms Act to address the problem of home-printable weapons (Greenberg Jan. 2013), saying "When I started talking about the issue of plastic firearms months ago, I was told the idea of a plastic gun is science-fiction. Now that this technology is proven, we need to act now to extend the ban [on] plastic firearms" (Sheynin 2013).

Statute

- Undetectable Firearms Act, codified at 18 U.S.C. § 922

See also: Patent; Trademark

Sources and Further Reading

"3D Printing: Your Flexible Friend," *The Economist*, December 15, 2012, at 79

Chris Anderson, *Makers: The New Industrial Revolution* (New York: Crown Business, 2012)

Samuel Arbesman, "To Understand 3-D Printing We Need to Remember 2-D Printing," Wired Weird Science Blogs (November 28, 2012), available at http://www.wired.com/wiredscience/2012/11/to-understand-3d-printing-we-need-to-remember-2d-printing/ (visited April 2, 2013)

Andy Greenberg, "Congressman Says He'll Propose Ban on 3D-Printable Gun Magazines," *Forbes* (January 16, 2013), available at http://www.forbes.com/sites/andygreenberg/2013/01/16/congressman-says-hell-propose-ban-on-3d-printable-gun-magazines/ (visited April 2, 2013)

Andy Greenberg, "This Is the World's First Entirely 3D-Printed Gun," *Forbes* (May 3, 2013), available at http://www.forbes.com/sites/andygreenberg/2013/05/03/this-is-the-worlds-first-entirely-3d-printed-gun-photos/ (visited May 13, 2013)

Rebecca Morelle, "Working Gun Made with 3D Printer," BBC News (May 6, 2013), available at http://www.bbc.co.uk/news/science-environment-22421185 (visited May 13, 2013)

Paul Rubens, "3D Printing: A New Dimension to Faking It," BBC Future (February 10, 2013), available at http://www.bbc.com/future/story/20130208-a-new-dimension-to-faking-it (visited April 2, 2013)

Dmitry Sheynin, "3D Printed Gun Unveiled in Fight against Gun Control," iTechPost (May 3, 2013), available at http://www.itechpost.com/articles/8697/20130503/3d-printed-gun-unveiled-photo-fight-against-control.htm (visited May 13, 2013)

❖ TRADEMARK ❖

Narrowly defined, a trademark is a mark that can be placed on goods to distinguish them from other goods. The term is often used in a broader sense, however, to refer to a wide range of distinguishing marks and indications of origin, including, in addition to trademarks, service marks, certification marks, collective marks, trade dress, and trade names. The body of law governing these marks and indications of origin is referred to as trademark law.

A trademark or other mark can be a design, motto, phrase, picture, shape, slogan, symbol, or word. It serves to identify the goods, services, or other thing to which the mark is attached, as well as to identify their source—that is, the person or entity that made or authorized them. It is used to connect goods and services to advertising promoting them, and it serves consumers by providing an indication of quality. Consumers learn to associate certain levels of quality with certain marks, and are thus spared the effort of an exhaustive exploration of the quality of each particular good or service they wish to purchase. A consumer planning on buying a camera attaches certain expectations to the trademarks Vivitar, Olympus, and Hasselblad; each creates different expectations, and the owners of these trademarks have expended considerable effort to create those expectations and to ensure that their cameras match the expectations they have created.

There are limits on what may become a trademark. Generic names cannot become trademarks; Vivitar, Olympus, and Hasselblad cannot trademark the term "camera," or even "digital camera." Descriptive terms, geographic terms, and personal names can only become trademarks if they acquire a secondary meaning—that is, if they become established among the public, or at least among the audience at whom the mark is named, as referring to the particular thing described and not to the broader class of things to which it belongs

(*Abercrombie & Fitch*, 537 F.2d at 9). Once such a term acquires such a secondary meaning, however, it may become a protected mark; the personal name "Hasselblad" would fall into this category. And terms that are suggestive, arbitrary, or fanciful are always eligible to become trademarks; the name "Olympus" is arbitrary when attached to cameras rather than to Greece's highest mountain or the abode of Greek gods, and the made-up name "Vivitar" is fanciful. However, as the court in *Abercrombie & Fitch v. Hunting World* pointed out, "the difficulties are compounded because a term that is in one category for a particular product may be in quite a different one for another": for example, the term " 'Ivory' would be generic when used to describe a product made from the tusks of elephants but arbitrary as applied to soap" (*Abercrombie & Fitch*, 537 F.2d at 9 & fn. 6). In addition, "a term may shift from one category to another in light of differences in usage through time": The court's example here was "the coined word 'Escalator', originally fanciful, or at the very least suggestive," which by 1950 had become generic (*Abercrombie & Fitch*, 537 F.2d at 9 & fn. 7). In addition, "a term may have one meaning to one group of users and a different one to others," and "the same term may be put to different uses with respect to a single product" (*Abercrombie & Fitch*, 537 F.2d at 9).

Eligible trademarks and other marks are protected by both state and federal case law and statutes. The central federal trademark statute is the Lanham Trademark Act; in addition, trademarks may be registered under state law. State registration cannot narrow the protection granted to the trademark holder by the Lanham Act, but can grant broader protection within a particular state. Unregistered trademarks may also be protected in courts under state common law, and the Lanham Act provides that actions to protect unregistered marks may be brought in federal courts (15 U.S.C. § 1125). Foreign trademarks may also be entitled to special protection under international trademark protection agreements to which the United States is a party, including the Madrid Protocol, the Paris Convention, the Trademark Registration Treaty, and TRIPS.

Trademarks can be registered with the U.S. Patent and Trademark Office. However, registration does not create the trademark; in the United States, trademark protection arises from the use of the mark rather than from its registration (*International Flavors*, 183 F.3d at 1366). Trademarks, unlike patents or copyrights, are of potentially infinite duration but must be renewed periodically; registrations issued after November 16, 1989, must be renewed every 10 years (15 U.S.C. §§ 1058–1059). A somewhat similar renewable registration system for copyrights has been proposed in the Public Domain Enhancement Act, but is unlikely to be enacted because of opposition from the content industry and possible conflicts with international obligations.

Trademarks may be subject to infringement or dilution. All trademarks can be infringed upon; infringement occurs when someone other than the owner of the mark uses the mark without authorization in a way that creates a likelihood of confusion. Only strong and famous trademarks can be diluted; dilution occurs when someone other than the owner of the mark does something that tarnishes or blurs the distinctiveness of the mark (15 U.S.C. § 1125(c)(1)). As with all intellectual property rights, it is the duty of the mark owner rather than of the government to detect, pursue, and bring actions against violators. For the most part, infringement and dilution actions involving the Internet involve no unique issues; sales of fake Rolex watches resulting from spam advertising involve essentially the same trademark issues as sales of fake Rolex watches at flea markets and on street corners, although the spam itself may result in dilution of the trademark: after receiving several hundred spam messages advertising fake Rolex watches, many users may be inclined to assume that most or all of the Rolex watches they see are fakes.

The Internet does provide some unique opportunities for trademark infringement and dilution, however. Metatags incorporating trademarks are invisible to the consumer, yet may guide search engine traffic to a particular site and thus infringe upon, dilute, or tarnish a trademark. And cybersquatting—the registration and use of trademarks owned by others as Internet domain names—posed a severe problem in the early days of the Internet. As a result, Congress enacted a statute, the Anticybersquatting Consumer Protection Act, especially to address this problem (15 U.S.C. § 1125(d)).

Statutes

- Anticybersquatting Consumer Protection Act, 15 U.S.C. § 1125(d)
- Lanham Trademark Act, 15 U.S.C. §§ 1052, 1058, 1059, 1125–1127

Cases

- *Abercrombie & Fitch Co. v. Hunting World, Inc.*, 537 F.2d 4 (2d Cir. 1976)
- *CPC International, Inc. v. Skippy Inc.*, 214 F.3d 456 (4th Cir. 2000)
- *In re International Flavors & Fragrances, Inc.*, 183 F.3d 1361 (Fed. Cir. 1999)

See also: Cybersquatting; Domain Name Registrations; Fair Use (Trademark); Intellectual Property; International Trademark Protection; Madrid Agreement and Madrid Protocol; Metatags; Paris Convention; Three-Dimensional Printing; Trademark Dilution; Trademark Infringement; Trademark Registration Treaty; TRIPS (Trademark)

Sources and Further Reading

Zohar Efroni, "A Guidebook to Cybersquatting Litigation: The Practical Approach in a Post-Barcelona.com World," *University of Illinois Journal of Law, Technology and Policy* 457 (2003)

Christopher T. Marsden, ed., *Regulating the Global Information Society* (New York: Routledge, 2000)

J. Thomas McCarthy et al., *McCarthy's Desk Encyclopedia of Intellectual Property* (Washington, D.C.: Bureau of National Affairs, 3d ed. 2004)

Arthur R. Miller & Michael H. Davis, *Intellectual Property, Patents, Trademarks, and Copyright in a Nutshell* (St. Paul, MN: West, 5th ed. 2012)

Singapore Treaty on the Law of Trademarks, March 28, 2006, S. Treaty Doc. No. 110–2

Richard Stim, *Patent, Copyright & Trademark: An Intellectual Property Desk Reference* (Berkeley, CA: Nolo Press, 12th ed. 2012)

❖ TRADEMARK DILUTION ❖

Trademark dilution is a violation of an intellectual property right in famous marks; it does not apply to marks that are not famous. Dilution is addressed by federal and state trademark law; under the Federal Trademark Dilution Act, the owner of a mark that is famous as well as distinctive may obtain "an injunction against another person who, at any time after the owner's mark has become famous, commences use of a mark or trade name in commerce that is likely to cause dilution by blurring or dilution by tarnishment of the famous mark, regardless of the presence or absence of actual or likely confusion, of competition, or of actual economic injury" (15 U.S.C. § 1125(c)(1)). In other words, the owner of a famous mark may obtain a court order requiring anyone who is diluting the mark to cease doing so.

Famous marks: Determining whether a mark is famous presents a problem, of course, and the Trademark Dilution Act provides a list of factors:

> [A] mark is famous if it is widely recognized by the general consuming public of the United States as a designation of source of the goods or services of the mark's owner. In determining whether a mark possesses the requisite degree of recognition, the court may consider all relevant factors, including the following:
>
> (i) The duration, extent, and geographic reach of advertising and publicity of the mark, whether advertised or publicized by the owner or third parties.
> (ii) The amount, volume, and geographic extent of sales of goods or services offered under the mark.
> (iii) The extent of actual recognition of the mark.
> (iv) Whether the mark was registered under the Act of March 3, 1881, or the Act of February 20, 1905, or on the principal register (15 U.S.C. § 1125(c)(1)).

These are only factors, not indispensable elements. In determining whether a mark is famous a court must consider each factor; some factors may weigh in favor of finding that a mark is famous, while others may weigh against such a finding. A mark may still be famous even if some factors seem to point the opposite way; another mark may not be famous even though some of the factors indicate that it should. Some marks (such as Apple's apple-with-a-bite-out-of-it logo) may be generally famous; others may be famous only within a specific region or industry. If, for example, a trademark is famous in California but unknown elsewhere, it would be unlikely to be diluted by activities in New Jersey; similarly a trademark for a legal research service well known to lawyers but unknown to the general public would be unlikely to be diluted by the use of a similar trademark for automobiles (*Mead Data Central*, 875 F.2d at 1031–1032).

Once a mark has been determined to be famous, the next question is whether any dilution has occurred. A trademark may be diluted in two ways: by blurring or by tarnishment.

Blurring: Dilution by blurring occurs when a mark similar to the famous mark is used on some other product, resulting in a diminution in the distinctiveness of the famous mark:

> "[D]ilution by blurring" is association arising from the similarity between a mark or trade name and a famous mark that impairs the distinctiveness of the famous mark. In determining whether a mark or trade name is likely to cause dilution by blurring, the court may consider all relevant factors, including the following:
>
> (i) The degree of similarity between the mark or trade name and the famous mark.
> (ii) The degree of inherent or acquired distinctiveness of the famous mark.
> (iii) The extent to which the owner of the famous mark is engaging in substantially exclusive use of the mark.
> (iv) The degree of recognition of the famous mark.
> (v) Whether the user of the mark or trade name intended to create an association with the famous mark.
> (vi) Any actual association between the mark or trade name and the famous mark (15 U.S.C. § 1125(c)(2)(B)).

Blurring is thus related, but not identical, to the "likelihood of confusion" requirement of trademark infringement (*Mead Data Central*, 875 F.2d at 1031). *Mead Data Central v. Toyota Motor Sales* was a suit brought by the owners of the Lexis computer-assisted legal research system against the makers of Lexus automobiles. Mead, the plaintiff and the owner of the Lexis trademark, sought to enjoin Toyota from using the name Lexus for luxury cars. The federal district court for the Southern District of New York issued the injunction, but the Second Circuit reversed, holding that Mead's Lexis mark was not diluted by Toyota's use of the name Lexus, for two reasons. First, although the Lexis mark was famous within its own niche market (attorneys and legal professionals), it was all but unknown to the general public; thus, there was no likelihood of blurring in the minds of the general public, because the general public was unaware of the Lexis mark. Second, blurring was not likely in the minds of attorneys, either, because "the recognized sophistication of attorneys" rendered it "unlikely that, even in the market where Mead principally operates, there [would] be any significant amount of blurring between the LEXIS and LEXUS marks" (*Mead Data Central*, 875 F.2d at 1031–1032).

Tarnishment: Tarnishment occurs when an unauthorized person uses a trademark in a way that casts disrepute upon a famous mark or otherwise interferes with the positive mental associations created in the minds of the public by the mark: "'[D]ilution by tarnishment' is association arising from the similarity between a mark or trade name and a famous mark that harms the reputation of the famous mark" (15 U.S.C. §1125(c)(2)(C)). For example, a poster imitating the appearance of a Coca-Cola advertisement, but substituting the words "Enjoy Cocaine" for "Enjoy Coca-Cola," tarnishes the Coca-Cola mark (*Coca-Cola*, 346 F. Supp. 1183). And a cybersquatter who registers a domain name similar to a famous mark and posts pornographic content on the site is tarnishing the mark, perhaps in the hope that the owner of the mark will pay for the domain name to avoid further tarnishment.

Exceptions: Some conduct that might otherwise constitute blurring or tarnishment is protected, and excluded from the Lanham Act's coverage:

> The following shall not be actionable as dilution by blurring or dilution by tarnishment under this subsection:
> (A) Any fair use, including a nominative or descriptive fair use, or facilitation of such fair use, of a famous mark by another person other than as a designation of source for the person's own goods or services, including use in connection with—
>> (i) advertising or promotion that permits consumers to compare goods or services; or
>> (ii) identifying and parodying, criticizing, or commenting upon the famous mark owner or the goods or services of the famous mark owner.
> (B) All forms of news reporting and news commentary.
> (C) Any noncommercial use of a mark (15 U.S.C. § 1125(c)(3)).

Fair use is protected by statute and to some extent by the First Amendment to the U.S. Constitution; the latter also protects news reporting and commentary. And as the Trademark Act applies only to uses in commerce, noncommercial uses are naturally excepted.

Cybersquatting: The Anticybersquatting Consumer Protection Act (ACPA) provides that a cybersquatter is one who, with a bad faith intent to profit,

> registers, traffics in, or uses a domain name that—
>> (I) in the case of a mark that is distinctive at the time of registration of the domain name, is identical or confusingly similar to that mark;
>> (II) in the case of a famous mark that is famous at the time of registration of the domain name, is identical or confusingly similar to or dilutive of that mark (15 U.S.C. § 1125(d)(1)(A)(ii)).

The ACPA thus gives broader protection to famous marks than to other marks. A cybersquatter can safely register domain names that might blur or tarnish—that is, dilute—marks that are merely distinctive, so long as they are not actually identical or confusingly similar to those marks. Famous marks, however, are protected against blurring and tarnishing as well. In effect, the ACPA reserves all of those

potentially blurring or tarnishing domain names for the holder of the famous mark.

Relief granted and immunity: The holder of a famous mark is entitled to injunctive relief in a dilution suit; that is, the court will make the person diluting the mark stop his or her diluting activity. Money damages may also be awarded if:

> (A) the mark or trade name that is likely to cause dilution by blurring or dilution by tarnishment was first used in commerce by the person against whom the injunction is sought after October 6, 2006; and
> (B) in a claim arising under this subsection—
>> (i) by reason of dilution by blurring, the person against whom the injunction is sought willfully intended to trade on the recognition of the famous mark; or
>> (ii) by reason of dilution by tarnishment, the person against whom the injunction is sought willfully intended to harm the reputation of the famous mark (15 U.S.C. § 1125(c)(5)).

A person who holds a valid trademark registration is immune to a suit for dilution, even if brought by another person with an equal or superior right in the same mark (15 U.S.C. § 1125(c)(6)).

Statutes

- Anticybersquatting Consumer Protection Act, 15 U.S.C. § 1125(d)
- Lanham Trademark Act, 15 U.S.C. §§ 1117–1118
- Trademark Dilution Revision Act of 2006, 15 USC § 1125(c)

Cases
Federal Appellate Courts
- *Mead Data Central, Inc. v. Toyota Motor Sales, U.S.A., Inc.*, 875 F.2d 1026 (2d Cir. 1989)
- *Starbucks Corp. v. Wolfe's Borough Coffee, Inc.*, 588 F.3d 97 (2d Cir. 2009)
- *V Secret Catalogue, Inc. v. Moseley*, 605 F.3d 382 (6th Cir. 2010)

Federal Trial Courts
- *Coca-Cola Co. v. Gemini Rising, Inc.*, 346 F. Supp. 1183 (E.D.N.Y. 1972)
- *Lucent Technologies, Inc. v. Lucentsucks.com*, 95 F. Supp. 2d 528 (E.D. Va. 2000)
- *Lucent Technologies v. Johnson*, No. CV 00–05668, 2000 WL 1604055 (C.D. Cal. 2000)
- *Mattel, Inc. v. Internet Dimensions, Inc.*, No. 99 Civ. 10066(HB), 2000 WL 973745 (S.D.N.Y. 2000)

See also: Cybersquatting; Domain Name Registration; Fair Use (Trademark); Trademark; Trademark Infringement

Sources and Further Reading
Kevin J. Greene, "Abusive Trademark Litigation and the Shrinking Doctrine of Consumer Confusion: Rethinking Trademark

Paradigms in the Context of Entertainment Media and Cyberspace," 27 *Harvard Journal of Law & Public Policy* (2004)

Martha Kelley, "Is Liability Just a Link Away? Trademark Dilution by Tarnishment under the Federal Trademark Dilution Act of 1995 and Hyperlinks on the World Wide Web," 9 *Journal of Intellectual Property Law* 361 (2002)

J. Thomas McCarthy et al., *McCarthy's Desk Encyclopedia of Intellectual Property* (Washington, D.C.: Bureau of National Affairs, 3d ed. 2004)

Arthur R. Miller & Michael H. Davis, *Intellectual Property, Patents, Trademarks, and Copyright in a Nutshell* (St. Paul, MN: West, 5th ed. 2012)

Christopher R. Perry, "Trademarks as Commodities: The 'Famous' Roadblock to Applying Trademark Dilution Law in Cyberspace," 32 *Connecticut Law Review* 1127 (2000)

"Trade Secrets Acts," Uniform Law Commission, available at http://www.uniformlaws.org/Act.aspx?title=Trade%20 Secrets%20Act (visited January 15, 2013)

❖ TRADEMARK INFRINGEMENT ❖

Trademark infringement is the unauthorized use of a mark belonging to another, or the use of a similar mark in a manner that creates a likelihood of confusion (15 U.S.C. § 1114(1)). All marks, registered or unregistered, are protected against infringement creating a likelihood of confusion. Only famous marks are protected against dilution, however. When resolving claims arising under both state and federal law, courts will generally apply a single analysis to determine whether the alleged infringement creates a likelihood of confusion (McCarthy et al. 2004, 301).

Likelihood of confusion: At the heart of most trademark infringement actions is the question of likelihood of confusion. In cases of deliberate counterfeiting of trademarked goods, the question is simple to answer; in other cases it is less so. The problem is complicated by the lack of a statutory guide or a uniform rule of case law; instead, the federal circuit courts have evolved different, but not necessarily contradictory, tests. The Second Circuit's list of factors set forth in *Polaroid v. Polarad* is typical, although neither exhaustive nor identical to the lists used by other circuits. The *Polaroid* factors are (1) the strength of the mark; (2) "the degree of similarity between the two marks"; (3) "the proximity of the products"; (4) "the likelihood that the prior owner will bridge the gap" between his or her current products and the products of the alleged infringer; (5) "actual confusion"; (6) the "defendant's good faith in adopting its own mark"; (7) "the quality of defendant's product"; and (8) "the sophistication of the buyers" (*Polaroid*, 287 F.2d at 495). The *Polaroid* court noted, however, that "even this extensive catalogue does not exhaust the possibilities" (*Polaroid*, 287 F.2d at 495). The Restatement (Third) of Unfair Competition sets forth a longer and more complex list of factors to be considered in common law trademark infringement cases. Some of these add clarifications to the *Polaroid* factors; for example, the

Restatement explains that subsidiary factors to be assessed in determining the degree of similarity between the conflicting marks include

(i) the overall impression created by the designations . . .;
(ii) the pronunciation of the designations;
(iii) the translation of any foreign words contained in the designations;
(iv) the verbal translation of any pictures, illustrations, or designs contained in the designations;
(v) the suggestions, connotations, or meanings of the designations (Restatement, § 21).

Actual confusion is not a requirement for likelihood of confusion; what the mark owner must show is that some significant amount of confusion is likely, not that anyone has actually been confused. When actual confusion can be shown, however, it tends to prove a likelihood of confusion (McCarthy et al. 2004, 303).

Metatags: Two contentious areas of online trademark infringement are metatags and domain name registrations. Metatags are text inserted into an HTML document so as to be invisible when the document is viewed as a Web page. Because metatags can be used by search engines to locate a page, Web site creators may attempt to use metatags in an attempt to increase a page's search result rank. Trademarked terms may be used as metatags, triggering infringement suits when the mark holder discovers the use. Changes in search engine technology have rendered the use of metatags less profitable, but the same reasoning that applies to misuse of trademarked terms in metatags applies to other misuses of those terms as advertising keywords (such as Google AdWords) or search engine optimization tools.

Cybersquatting: Because each URL is unique, domain names are especially vulnerable to trademark abuse. Cybersquatting—the registration and use of trademarks owned by others as Internet domain names—was once a serious problem. Cybersquatters would speculatively register large numbers of domain names, then attempt to sell those domain names. Many of the names registered were identical or confusingly similar to existing marks; the holders of these marks were the primary targets of the cybersquatters. In some cases the cybersquatter would simply wait for the mark holder to attempt to register its mark as a domain name; in others the cybersquatter would approach the mark holder and offer to sell the domain name. In especially egregious cases the cybersquatter would create a Web site containing offensive content in an attempt to pressure the mark owner into purchasing the name.

Existing trademark law was ill-equipped to deal with this new form of trademark infringement, and the federal courts began to create a new form of trademark dilution—dilution by cybersquatting (*Panavision*, 141 F.3d 1316). This was an awkward fit, however, and did little to help the owners of marks that were distinctive but not famous. In 1999, Congress addressed the problem with the passage of the Anticybersquatting

Consumer Protection Act (ACPA). The ACPA addresses both dilution of famous marks and infringement of all marks; it provides that a person who, with "a bad faith intent to profit," "registers, traffics in, or uses a domain name that" at the time of registration is (1) "identical [to] or confusingly similar to" a *distinctive* mark, or (2) "identical [to] or confusingly similar to or dilutive of" a *famous* mark, is liable in a civil action by the owner of the mark (15 U.S. § 1125(d)(1)(A)). Remedies may include damages and the transfer of the domain name to the mark owner (15 U.S. § 1125(d)(1)(C)).

Fair use: Certain uses of the trademark of another, like certain uses of copyrighted material, may be protected as fair use. The fact that a particular use of a trademark is fair use does not mean that the trademark has fallen into the public domain; it means simply that a particular use is permissible. Trademark fair use may be either classic fair use or nominative fair use. Classic fair use occurs when a trademark is also a descriptive term and is used in its descriptive sense. For most courts, this analysis is inextricably linked to the "likelihood of confusion" analysis; if there is a classic fair use, there is no likelihood of confusion. Thus, classic fair use in these courts is not truly an exception to the rule of liability for trademark infringement, but an instance of the requirements of the rule not being satisfied. Some courts, however, are willing to find fair use even if a likelihood of confusion exists (see *Cosmetically Sealed Industries*, 125 F.3d 28).

Nominative fair use is the use of a trademark to describe the thing trademarked in order to draw attention to some other product or service. The Ninth Circuit Court of Appeals has set out a three-part test for determining whether a particular use is nominative fair use:

> First, the product or service in question must be one not readily identifiable without use of the trademark; second, only so much of the mark or marks may be used as is reasonably necessary to identify the product or service; and third, the user must do nothing that would, in conjunction with the mark, suggest sponsorship or endorsement by the trademark holder (*Playboy*, 279 F.3d at 801).

Under this test, for example, an independent automotive shop that specializes in Volkswagen repairs has no easy way to identify its services other than by using the trademarked name "Volkswagen"; this is fair use, although use of the Volkswagen logo (rather than merely the name) to advertise the repair shop's services would not be, because that would be more than reasonably necessary to identify the service and might suggest sponsorship or endorsement by Volkswagen corporation.

Internet Service Providers: As with copyright infringement, Internet service providers (ISPs) may be involved in trademark infringement without their knowledge if users of the ISP transmit or post infringing material. However, while the Digital Millennium Copyright ACT (DMCA) creates

a safe harbor from copyright infringement liability, it contains no similar protection from trademark infringement liability. Nor does one of the few remaining sections of the Communications Decency Act, 47 U.S.C. § 230(c)(1), provide such protection. Section 230(c)(1) provides that "no provider or user of an interactive computer service shall be treated as the publisher or speaker of any information provided by another information content provider." However, this is apparently inapplicable to trademark infringement: "Nothing in this section shall be construed to limit or expand any law pertaining to intellectual property" (47 U.S.C. § 230(e)(2)). One court has already found that the result of § 230(e)(2) is that § 230(c)(1) conveys no immunity to ISPs from liability for copyright infringement (*Gucci*, 135 F. Supp. 2d at 413–414). The exact extent of potential ISP liability for trademark infringement remains unclear, although it is ultimately limited by the First Amendment (*Name.Space*, 202 F.3d at 585–586).

Statutes

- Anticybersquatting Consumer Protection Act, 15 U.S.C. § 1125(d)
- Communications Decency Act, 47 U.S.C. § 230
- Lanham Trademark Act, 15 U.S.C. § 1114
- Digital Millennium Copyright Act, 16 U.S.C. § 512

Cases
Federal Appellate Courts

- *Bosely Medical Institute, Inc. v. Kremer*, 403 F.3d 672 (9th Cir. 2005)
- *Cosmetically Sealed Industries, Inc. v. Chesebrough-Pond's USA Co.*, 125 F.3d 28 (2d Cir. 1997)
- *Eclipse Associates Limited. v. Data General Corp.*, 894 F.2d 1114 (9th Cir.1990)
- *Falcon Rice Mill, Inc. v. Community Rice Mill, Inc.*, 725 F.2d 336 (5th Cir. 1984)
- *Frisch's Restaurants, Inc. v. Elby's Big Boy, Inc.*, 670 F.2d 642 (6th Cir. 1982), certiorari denied 459 U.S. 916 (1982)
- *Keds Corp. v. Renee International Trading Corp.*, 888 F.2d 215 (1st Cir. 1989)
- *Kellogg Co. v. Pack'em Enterprises, Inc.*, 951 F.2d 330 (Fed. Cir. 1991)
- *Name.Space, Inc. v. Network Solutions, Inc.*, 202 F.3d 573 (2d Cir. 2000)
- *Piper Aircraft Corp. v. Wag-Aero, Inc.*, 741 F.2d 925 (7th Cir. 1984)
- *Panavision International L.P. v. Toeppen*, 141 F.3d 1316 (9th Cir. 1998)
- *Playboy Enterprises, Inc. v. Welles*, 279 F.3d 796 (9th Cir. 2002)
- *Polaroid Corp. v. Polarad Electronics Corp.*, 287 F.2d 492 (2d Cir. 1961)
- *Voice of the Arab World, Inc. v. MDTV Medical News Now, Inc.*, 645 F.3d 26 (1st Cir. 2011)

Federal Trial Courts
- *Bihari v. Gross*, 119 F. Supp. 2d 309 (S.D.N.Y. 2000)
- *Coca-Cola Co. v. Gemini Rising, Inc.*, 346 F. Supp. 1183 (E.D.N.Y. 1972)
- *Gucci America, Inc. v. Hall & Associates*, 135 F. Supp. 2d 409 (S.D.N.Y. 2001)
- *Lucent Technologies v. Johnson*, No. CV 00–05668, 2000 WL 1604055 (C.D. Cal. 2000)
- *Lucent Technologies, Inc. v. Lucentsucks.com*, 95 F. Supp. 2d 528 (E.D. Va. 2000)
- *Mattel, Inc. v. Internet Dimensions, Inc.*, No. 99 Civ. 10066(HB), 2000 WL 973745 (S.D.N.Y. 2000)
- *Microsoft Corp. v. Shah*, No. C10–0653 RSM, 2011 U.S. Dist. LEXIS 2995 (W.D. Wash. 2011)
- *Ocean Bio-Chem, Inc. v. Turner Network Television, Inc.*, 741 F. Supp. 1546 (S.D. Fla. 1990)

Restatement
- *Restatement (Third) of Unfair Competition §§ 21–23* (Washington, D.C.: American Law Institute 1995 & Supp. 2004)

See also: Cybersquatting; Digital Millennium Copyright Act, Title II; Domain Name Registration; Fair Use (Trademark); Metatags; Trademark; Trademark Dilution

Sources and Further Reading

James H. Aiken, "The Jurisdiction of Trademark and Copyright Infringement on the Internet," 48 *Mercer Law Review* 1331 (1997)

Katherine E. Gasparek, "Applying the Fair Use Defense in Traditional Trademark Infringement and Dilution Cases to Internet Meta Tagging or Linking Cases," 1 *George Mason Law Review* 787 (1999)

Bryce J. Maynard, "The Initial Interest Confusion Doctrine and Trademark Infringement on the Internet," 57 *Washington and Lee Law Review* 1303 (2000)

J. Thomas McCarthy et al., *McCarthy's Desk Encyclopedia of Intellectual Property* (Washington, D.C.: Bureau of National Affairs, 3d ed. 2004)

Gregory C. Walsh, "Internet Service Provider Liability for Contributory Trademark Infringement after Gucci," 2002 *Duke Law & Technology Review* 95 (2002)

Gayle Weiswasser, "Domain Names, the Internet, and Trademarks: Infringement in Cyberspace," 13 *Santa Clara Computer and High Technology Law Journal* 137 (1996)

❖ TRADEMARK LAW TREATY ❖

The Trademark Law Treaty (TLT), promulgated by the World Intellectual Property Organization (WIPO), seeks to harmonize the trademark registration process. The treaty was concluded in 1994 and as of October 2012 had 53 parties; the United States became a party on August 12, 2000. In order to bring its law into compliance with the TLT, the United States enacted the Trademark Law Treaty Act of 1998; the Act simplified U.S. trademark registration and renewal formalities.

The TLT makes no distinction between trademarks and service marks (TLT art. 2(2)(a)), but does not apply to "collective marks, certification marks and guarantee marks" (TLT art. 2(2)(b)). Articles 3 and 13 set forth uniform filing and renewal processes to be followed by all member states. The TLT also incorporates by reference the terms of the Paris Convention (TLT art. 15), and makes the Paris Convention's terms regarding trademarks applicable to service marks as well (TLT art. 16).

Substantively, the TLT sets a uniform trademark term of 10 years, renewable an indefinite number of times for 10-year periods (TLT art. 13(7)). Prior to the Trademark Law Treaty Act, U.S. law had required that each application for renewal be accompanied by a declaration or proof that the mark was actually being used; the TLT provides that no such proof may be required (TLT art. 13(6)), and the Trademark Law Treaty Act altered U.S. law accordingly. However, the substance of the requirement remains; trademark holders in the United States now have an obligation, independent of the renewal process, to file a declaration that the mark is being used (McCarthy et al. 2004, 614).

Treaty
- Trademark Law Treaty, October 27, 1994, S. Treaty Doc. No. 105–35 (1988) available at http://www.wipo.int/treaties/en/ip/tlt/ (visited December 20, 2012)

Statute
- Trademark Law Treaty Act of 1998, 15 U.S.C. § 1051

See also: International Trademark Protection; Trademark; WIPO

Source and Further Reading

J. Thomas McCarthy et al., *McCarthy's Desk Encyclopedia of Intellectual Property* (Washington, D.C.: Bureau of National Affairs, 3d ed. 2004)

❖ TRADEMARK REGISTRATION TREATY ❖

See Madrid Agreement and Madrid Protocol

❖ TRADE-RELATED ASPECTS OF INTELLECTUAL PROPERTY RIGHTS ❖

See TRIPS

❖ TRADE SECRET ❖

Trade secrets are a difficult category of intellectual property to protect, as by their very nature they are secret and cannot be disclosed to any registering authority. To some extent, in fact, the protection of trade secrets runs contrary to one of the policy interests underpinning patent law: patent law seeks to encourage inventors to share their inventions and discoveries with the public, in exchange for an economic benefit (the patent owner's limited-term monopoly). Trade secret law, in contrast, seeks to protect those who do not wish to share their inventions and discoveries.

Trade secrets are protected in the United States primarily by the vigilance of their owners. State and federal law offer some protection, however. The first problem faced by lawmakers in dealing with trade secrets is the problem of defining them. The federal Economic Espionage Act of 1996, 18 U.S.C. § 1831 et seq., sets two requirements: the owner of the secret must have "taken reasonable measures to keep such information secret," and the material to be protected must derive "independent economic value, actual or potential, from not being generally known to, and not being readily ascertainable through proper means by, the public" (18 U.S.C. § 1839(3)). The definition of protected subject matter in the Uniform Trade Secrets Act, adopted in various modified forms in 46 states plus the District of Columbia, Puerto Rico, and the U.S. Virgin Islands, is virtually identical: a trade secret is information that "(i) derives independent economic value, actual or potential, from not being generally known to, and not being readily ascertainable by proper means by, other persons who can obtain economic value from its disclosure or use, and (ii) is the subject of efforts that are reasonable under the circumstances to maintain its secrecy." Although the order of the two elements is reversed, the only significant difference is that the federal statute requires that the secret derive its value from not being known to the public, while the Uniform Act requires that it derive its value from not being known to others in the same field.

The federal statute protects against economic espionage by any person who knowingly commits the espionage either "intending or knowing that the offense will benefit any foreign government, foreign instrumentality, or foreign agent" (18 U.S.C. § 1831) or "with intent to convert"—take—"a trade secret, that is related to a product or service used in or intended for use in interstate or foreign commerce, to the economic benefit of anyone other than the owner thereof, and intending or knowing that the offense will, injure any owner of that trade secret" (18 U.S.C. § 1832). The Uniform Act is not concerned with distinguishing between foreign and U.S. parties; it prohibits misappropriation of trade secrets, misappropriation being defined as: "(i) acquisition of a trade secret of another by a person who knows or has reason to know that the trade secret was acquired by improper means; or (ii) disclosure or use of a trade secret of another without express or implied consent by a person who" acquired the secret, directly or indirectly, by improper means, accident, or mistake, or subject to a duty to maintain the secrecy" (Uniform Trade Secrets Act § 1(2)).

Trade secrets are inherently fragile. Other forms of intellectual property can survive infringement; the owner of a copyright, patent, or trademark can sue the infringer, bring a halt to the infringement, recover damages, and continue owning the right. Once a trade secret has been disclosed, however, it is no longer secret. The owner of the secret can recover damages from the person who disclosed it—but only from the first person to do so, or any other person who does so improperly. Once the secret has been widely disseminated, it is no longer a secret, and the original owner cannot reclaim it (*Religious Technology Center*, 908 F. Supp. 1362). In addition, trade secret law protects trade secrets only against improper means of discovery. It does not, as patent law does, protect the trade secret from independent rediscovery or reverse engineering (McCarthy et al. 2004, 620).

Statute
- Economic Espionage Act of 1996, 18 U.S.C. §§ 1831 et seq.

Uniform Act
- National Conference of Commissioners on Uniform State Laws, Uniform Trade Secrets Act, as amended 1985, available at http://www.uniformlaws.org/Act.aspx?title=Trade Secrets Act (visited January 17, 2013)

Proposed Legislation
- Protecting American Trade Secrets of 2012, S. 3389, 112th Cong. (2d Sess. 2012)
- Theft of Trade Secrets Clarification Act of 2012, S. 3642, 112th Cong. (2d Sess. 2012), amending and codified 18 U.S.C. § 1832(a)

Case
- *Religious Technology Center v. Lerma*, 908 F. Supp. 1362 (E.D. Va. 1995)

See also: Patent; TRIPS (Trade Secrets)

Sources and Further Reading
"Huawei: The Company That Spooked the World," *The Economist*, August 4, 2012, at 19

J. Thomas McCarthy et al., *McCarthy's Desk Encyclopedia of Intellectual Property* (Washington, D.C.: Bureau of National Affairs, 3d ed. 2004)

"Who's Afraid of Huawei?" *The Economist*, August 4, 2012, at 9

❖ TRIPS ❖

The Agreement on Trade-Related Aspects of Intellectual Property Rights is almost invariably known by its acronym,

TRIPS. In 1994, at the conclusion of the Uruguay Round of negotiations under the General Agreement on Tariffs and Trade (GATT) that gave rise to the World Trade Organization (WTO), TRIPS was adopted as Annex 1C to the Marrakesh Agreement Establishing the World Trade Organization. All countries that become parties to the WTO become parties to TRIPS.

TRIPS is a comprehensive intellectual property treaty: it covers the traditional areas of copyright, trademark, and patent, as well as other areas such as geographical indications, industrial designs, integrated circuit layouts, and trade secrets. Some of these rights, such as copyright, have both influenced and been influenced by changes in information technology; others, such as rights in geographical indications, have had little or no application to date in a computer and Internet law context.

Articles 3 and 4 of TRIPS require national treatment and most-favored nation treatment, respectively, with regard to all intellectual property rights covered by the agreement. "National treatment" means that states that are parties to TRIPS must accord to all other parties the same level of protection that they accord to their own nationals. "Most-favored nation treatment" is a confusing term; it may create the incorrect impression that a country is being singled out for preferential treatment. In fact, most-favored nation treatment has a different effect: all parties are required to give to each other party the same level of treatment that they give to the nation they most favor, so that in effect no country is favored over any other and all receive the same level of treatment. To avoid an undue hardship on developing countries, Part VI (Articles 65–67) of TRIPS contains transitional provisions; developing countries are permitted to make some exceptions to TRIPS standards under certain conditions and are given a longer period of time to phase in their TRIPS obligations.

Treaties

- Agreement Between the World Intellectual Property Organization and the World Trade Organization, December 22, 1995, 35 I.L.M. 754 (1996)
- Agreement on Trade-Related Aspects of Intellectual Property Rights, Marrakesh Agreement Establishing the World Trade Organization, Annex 1C, April 15, 1994, 33 I.L.M. 81 (1994)

Statute

- Copyright Act of 1976, 17 U.S.C. §§ 101–1332

See also: Copyright; International Copyright Protection; International Patent Protection; International Trademark Protection; Patent; Trademark; TRIPS (Copyright); TRIPS (Industrial Designs and Integrated Circuit Layouts); TRIPS (Patent); TRIPS (Trademark); TRIPS (Trade Secrets); WIPO

Sources and Further Reading

Carlos Correa, *Trade Related Aspects of Intellectual Property Rights* (Oxford, UK: Oxford University Press, 2007)

Susan K. Sell, *Private Power, Public Law: The Globalization of Intellectual Property Rights* (Cambridge, UK: Cambridge University Press, 2003)

Terence P. Stewart, *The GATT Uruguay Round: A Negotiating History (1986–1992): Trade-Related Aspects of Intellectual Property* (Dordrecht, The Netherlands: Kluwer Academic Publishers, 1993)

❖ TRIPS (COPYRIGHT) ❖

The substantive copyright provisions of TRIPS take as their starting point the Berne Convention. Article 9(2) provides that copyright protection under TRIPS, as under U.S. copyright law, "shall extend to expressions and not to ideas, procedures, methods of operation or mathematical concepts as such." Article 9(1) of TRIPS provides that members of the WTO "shall comply with Articles 1 through 21 of the Berne Convention (1971) and the Appendix thereto," with one exception. The exception is Article 6*bis* of the Berne Convention, which deals with moral rights: members of the WTO "shall not have rights or obligations under this Agreement in respect of the rights conferred under Article 6*bis* of that Convention or of the rights derived therefrom." Moral rights, in copyright law, include noneconomic rights such as the right not to have one's work mutilated or distorted, the right to be acknowledged as the author of the work, and the right to determine when and in what fashion the work shall be presented to the public. U.S. law, in contrast to European law, historically has not been receptive to the concept of moral rights. Under the pressure of international copyright agreements, notably the Berne Convention, the United States has begun to adopt limited moral rights protections such as the Visual Artists Rights Act (17 U.S.C. § 106A). The protection of moral rights in the United States is hindered, however, both by reluctance to acknowledge a noneconomic dimension to copyright and by the First Amendment.

TRIPS reflects the concerns of the United States to a far greater degree than does the Berne Convention, as the exception of Article 6*bis* shows. The United States did not become a party to the Berne Convention for over a century after its initial adoption; in contrast, the country played a major role in the drafting of TRIPS.

The terms of the Berne Convention that are incorporated into TRIPS by the reference in Article 9(1) include provisions defining the subject-matter to be protected, setting minimum terms of protection for various classes of materials, and defining the rights to be conferred and permissible limitations to those rights. Article 12 of TRIPS, like Article 7 of the Berne Convention, sets a minimum copyright term for most works of the lifetime of the author plus 50 years. Article 9 of TRIPS specifically gives protection to computer programs, while Article 10 deals with rental rights. The 1971 revision of the Berne Convention had previously provided that computer programs were to be protected as literary works. Article 10 of TRIPS adds detail: computer programs are to be protected as literary works whether expressed in source code or object code. Compilations of data, electronic or otherwise, are also protected if (and only if) "by reason of the selection or arrangement of their contents" they "constitute intellectual creations." This may conceivably give wider protection to data compilations than is currently afforded under U.S. copyright law. In the 1991 case of *Feist Publications v. Rural Telephone Service*, the U.S. Supreme Court rejected the idea that mere effort in compiling data—the "sweat of the brow"—entitles the compiler to copyright protection. The Court held that under the Copyright Act originality, rather than mere effort, is required. The "intellectual" element of the term "intellectual creations" does not seem to require originality, although perhaps the "creations" element does (*Rural Telephone*, 499 U.S. 340).

Copyright protection of a data compilation does not create any copyright in the data itself; if the data was originally within the public domain, it remains in the public domain even if the compilation is protected by copyright. It would thus be permissible, for example, for someone else to arrange the data in a manner sufficiently different to constitute a new "intellectual creation" (TRIPS art. 10(2)).

Authors of computer programs, sound recordings, and, in certain circumstances, of motion pictures are to be provided with the right to authorize or to prohibit the commercial rental of those works, although in the case of motion pictures (cinematographic works) member states are exempt from the obligation unless motion picture rentals have led to widespread copying that materially impairs the exclusive right of reproduction; in other words, this provision is meant to be applied only against states in which video piracy is widespread. With regard to computer programs, Article 11 provides that "this obligation does not apply to rentals where the program itself is not the essential object of the rental." In other words, a company that rents out equipment—cars, boats, aircraft, power tools—is in the business of renting equipment, not software. Even though the equipment may, and probably does, contain software, the software is not the object of the rental. TRIPS would thus not require its member states to require these equipment-rental companies to first obtain the software author's consent to the rental (TRIPS art. 11).

Article 14 deals with live performances, sound recordings, and broadcasting organizations. The performers of live audio performances "shall have the possibility" (the word "right" is not used) "of preventing the fixation" or broadcast of their performances. Producers of sound recordings (phonograms) "shall enjoy the right to authorize or prohibit the direct or indirect reproduction of their phonograms." Performers and producers are to be given the exclusive reproduction and rental rights to their recordings for a minimum term of 50 years, although Article 14(4) provides that states that had

"in force a system of equitable remuneration of right holders in respect of the rental of phonograms" are grandfathered in and do not need to alter their existing laws to conform to the Article 14 standard. Articles 14(3) and 14(5) set forth the right of broadcasting organizations to prevent unauthorized recording, reproduction, or rebroadcast of their broadcasts for a minimum term of 20 years.

It is Article 13, however, that represents the greatest departure from what has gone before and consequently has triggered the greatest controversy. Article 13 states, somewhat opaquely, "[m]embers shall confine limitations or exceptions to exclusive rights to certain special cases which do not conflict with a normal exploitation of the work and do not unreasonably prejudice the legitimate interests of the right holder." This provision was ostensibly intended to prevent nations with poor records of copyright enforcement from multiplying exceptions and limitations to the point that they effectively eviscerated those nations' copyright laws. However, it is also seen as an attack on the fair use exception. It benefits United States and other developed-country content owners at the expense of content consumers. Because the content industries of the developed countries provided input during the process of drafting TRIPS, some believe that the content industry used TRIPS as an "end run" to achieve through international law what could not be achieved through the domestic political process.

Article 13 is based on the three-step test in Article 9(2) of the Berne Convention, but goes farther and can more readily be enforced. The three steps of the Article 13 test provide that exceptions to the exclusive rights of the copyright holder may be made in:

(1) Certain special cases
(2) Which do not conflict with a normal exploitation of the work, and
(3) Do not unreasonably prejudice the legitimate interests of the right holder.

In other words, a country that is a party to TRIPS can permit unauthorized reproduction of a work only in certain special cases. The permitted reproduction must not conflict with normal exploitation of the work, and must not unreasonably prejudice the legitimate interest of the content owner. There are a number of abstractions here that beg for further definition. It is not readily apparent, for example, what cases are "special," what degree of prejudice is "unreasonable," or what interests are "legitimate." A kindergarten teacher who copies a magazine article might or might not fall within the "special cases" category; the teacher's copying would conflict with the normal exploitation of the work (if, in the alternative, the teacher would have had to purchase copies of the work) and would consequently prejudice the interests of the right holder, although it is also unclear whether the right holder's interests in this case would be legitimate and even less clear whether the prejudice would be unreasonable.

Treaties

- Agreement on Trade-Related Aspects of Intellectual Property Rights, Marrakesh Agreement Establishing the World Trade Organization, Annex 1C, April 15, 1994, 33 I.L.M. 81 (1994)
- Convention Concerning the Creation of an International Union for the Protection of Literary and Artistic Works (Berne Convention), September 9, 1886, as last revised at Paris, July 24, 1971 (amended 1979), 25 U.S.T. 1341, 828 U.N.T.S. 221
- Universal Copyright Convention, September 6, 1952, 6 U.S.T. 2731, revised at Paris July 24, 1971, 25 U.S.T. 1341
- WIPO Copyright Treaty, December 20, 1996, 36 I.L.M. 65 (1997)
- WIPO Performance and Phonograms Treaty, Dec. 20, 1996, 36 I.L.M. 76 (1997)

Statutes

- Copyright Act of 1976, 17 U.S.C. §§ 101–1332
- Visual Artists' Rights Act, 17 U.S.C. § 106A

Case

- *Feist Publications, Inc. v. Rural Telephone Service Co.,* 499 U.S. 340 (1991)

See also: Berne Convention; Copyright; Copyright Infringement; International Copyright Protection; Universal Copyright Convention; WIPO; WIPO Copyright Treaty; WIPO Performance and Phonograms Treaty

Sources and Further Reading

Carlos Correa, *Trade Related Aspects of Intellectual Property Rights* (Oxford, UK: Oxford University Press, 2007)

Paul Goldstein & Bernt Hugenholtz, *International Copyright: Principles, Law, and Practice* (Oxford, UK: Oxford University Press, 3d ed. 2012)

❖ TRIPS (INDUSTRIAL DESIGNS AND INTEGRATED CIRCUIT LAYOUTS) ❖

Industrial designs that are not eligible for patent, copyright, or trademark protection may nonetheless be protected as industrial designs; an example of such protection can be found in Title V of the Digital Millennium Copyright Act (DMCA). TRIPS provides that World Trade Organization (WTO) "members shall provide for the protection of independently created industrial designs that are new or original" (TRIPS art. 25.1). The rights thus protected shall include "the right to prevent third parties . . . from making, selling or importing articles bearing or embodying a design which is a copy, or substantially a copy, of the protected design, when such acts are undertaken for commercial purposes" for a period of at least 10 years (TRIPS art. 26).

The mask work used to create semiconductor chips is another category of intellectual property that doesn't fit neatly into conventional definitions; it is protected separately from industrial designs, but the protection granted under TRIPS is similar. Members of the WTO "agree to provide protection to the layout-designs (topographies) of integrated circuits . . . in accordance with" selected substantive provisions of the Treaty on Intellectual Property in Respect of Integrated Circuits (TRIPS art. 35). As with industrial designs, the protection lasts for a minimum of 10 years (TRIPS art. 38). During that time, the owner of the right shall have the sole authority to authorize "importing, selling, or otherwise distributing for commercial purposes a protected layout-design, an integrated circuit in which a protected layout-design is incorporated, or an article incorporating such an integrated circuit only in so far as it continues to contain an unlawfully reproduced layout-design" (TRIPS art. 36), although innocent third parties are protected from liability for use of chips incorporating infringing designs (TRIPS art. 37).

Treaties

- Agreement on Trade-Related Aspects of Intellectual Property Rights, Marrakesh Agreement Establishing the World Trade Organization, Annex 1C, April 15, 1994, 33 I.L.M. 81 (1994)
- Hague Agreement Concerning the International Deposit of Industrial Designs, November 6, 1925, 74 L.N.T.S. 343, revised at London, June 2, 1934, 205 L.N.T.S. 179, revised at The Hague, November 28, 1960; supplemented by the Additional Act of Monaco, November 18, 1961, the Complementary Act of Stockholm, July 14, 1967, and the Protocol of Geneva, April 10, 1975, 26 U.S.T. 571; and as amended, September 1979
- Locarno Agreement Establishing an International Classification for Industrial Designs, October 8, 1968, as amended September 28, 1979, 23 U.S.T. 1389
- Paris Convention for the Protection of Industrial Property, March 20, 1883, as revised at Brussels on December 14, 1900, at Washington on June 2, 1911, at The Hague on November 6, 1925, at London on June 2, 1934, at Lisbon on October 31, 1958, and at Stockholm on July 14, 1967, and as amended on September 28, 1979, 21 U.S.T. 1583, 828 U.N.T.S. 305
- Treaty on Intellectual Property in Respect of Integrated Circuits, Washington, May 26, 1989, 28 I.L.M. 1477 (1989)

Statutes

- Digital Millennium Copyright Act, Title V, 17 U.S.C. §§ 1301–1332
- Semiconductor Chip Protection Act, 17 U.S.C. §§ 901–914

See also: Digital Millennium Copyright Act, Title V; Intellectual Property; Semiconductor Manufacturing Mask Work Registrations; TRIPS

❖ TRIPS (PATENT) ❖

TRIPS provides that "patents shall be available for any inventions, whether products or processes, in all fields of technology," with certain exceptions, for at least "a period of 20 years counted from the filing date" (TRIPS arts. 27, 33). The length of the patent term in the United States, originally 17 years from the date the patent was granted, was changed to 20 years from the date of filing to conform to the TRIPS norm (35 U.S.C. § 154(a)(2)). The protection "for any inventions, whether products or processes" has been interpreted as requiring members to issue business methods patents, such as the controversial patent on one-click ordering. These patents were authorized in the United States by the decision of the Federal Circuit Court of Appeals in the 1998 case of *State Street Bank & Trust* (149 F.3d 1368).

Under TRIPS, WTO members must grant patent holders the exclusive right to prevent others from "making, using, offering for sale, selling, or importing" a patented product, or products made by a patented process (TRIPS art. 28). The patent holder's rights must be alienable—that is, the inventor must be able sell, license, or give away the patent rights (TRIPS art. 28).

Treaties

- Agreement on Trade-Related Aspects of Intellectual Property Rights, Marrakesh Agreement Establishing the World Trade Organization, Annex 1C, April 15, 1994, 33 I.L.M. 81 (1994)
- Paris Convention for the Protection of Industrial Property, March 20, 1883, as revised at Brussels on December 14, 1900, at Washington on June 2, 1911, at The Hague on November 6, 1925, at London on June 2, 1934, at Lisbon on October 31, 1958, and at Stockholm on July 14, 1967, and as amended on September 28, 1979, 21 U.S.T. 1583, 828 U.N.T.S. 305
- Patent Cooperation Treaty, Washington on June 19, 1970, as amended on September 28, 1979, and as modified on February 3, 1984, and October 3, 2001, 28 U.S.T. 7645, 9 I.L.M. 978 (1970)
- Patent Law Treaty, June 1, 2000, 39 I.L.M. 1047 (2000)

Statute

- Patent Code, 35 U.S.C. §§ 1–376

Cases

- *State Street Bank & Trust Co. v. Signature Financial Group, Inc.*, 149 F.3d 1368 (Fed. Cir. 1998); certiorari denied, 525 U.S. 1093
- *In re Bilski*, 545 F.3d 943 (Fed. Cir. 2008)

See also: America Invents Act; Business Methods Patent; International Patent Protection; Paris Convention; Patent; Patent Cooperation Treaty; TRIPS; WIPO

Sources and Further Reading

Graeme B. Dinwoodie et al., *International and Comparative Patent Law* (Newark, NJ: LexisNexis, 2002)

Nuno Pires de Carvalho, *The TRIPS Regime of Patent Rights* (The Hague: Kluwer Law International, 3d ed. 2010)

❖ TRIPS (TRADEMARK) ❖

TRIPS sets uniform standards for the subject matter eligible for trademark protection and for the conditions under which trademark registration may be granted or refused. "Any sign, or any combination of signs, capable of distinguishing . . . goods or services . . . shall be capable of constituting a trademark" (TRIPS art. 15(1)). TRIPS includes a nonexhaustive list of signs that may be eligible for trademark protection: "words including personal names, letters, numerals, figurative elements and combinations of colours as well as any combination of such signs" (TRIPS art. 15(1)). Even signs "not inherently capable of distinguishing the relevant goods or services" can be trademarks, although in that case "members may make registrability depend on distinctiveness acquired through use." In addition, "members may require, as a condition of registration, that signs be visually perceptible" (TRIPS art. 15(1)).

Use of a trademark may be made a prerequisite of trademark registration, but may not be made a prerequisite of trademark application, nor may certain types of goods or services be excluded from eligibility for trademark protection (TRIPS art. 15). Once a trademark is registered, the trademark owner shall have the right to prevent others from using the mark for similar goods and services (TRIPS art. 16), although WTO members may make an exception for fair use (TRIPS art. 17). TRIPS provides for a minimum trademark term of seven years (TRIPS art. 18); U.S. law currently provides for a term of 10 years (15 U.S.C. §§ 1058–1059). Trademark registrations may be lost through nonuse of the trademark for at least three years (TRIPS art. 19). Trademarks are alienable—they may be transferred by the owner—and are not subject to compulsory licensing (TRIPS art. 21).

Treaties

- Agreement on Trade-Related Aspects of Intellectual Property Rights, Marrakesh Agreement Establishing the World Trade Organization, Annex 1C, April 15, 1994, 33 I.L.M. 81 (1994)
- Lisbon Agreement for the Protection of Appellations of Origin and their International Registration, October 31, 1958, as revised at Stockholm on July 14, 1967, and as amended on September 28, 1979, 923 U.N.T.S. 205

- Madrid Agreement Concerning the International Registration of Marks, April 14, 1891, as revised at Brussels, December 14, 1900; at Washington, June 2, 1911; at The Hague, November 6, 1925; at London, June 2, 1934; at Nice, June 15, 1957; at Stockholm, July 14, 1967; and as amended September 28, 1979, available at http://www.wipo.int/madrid/en/legal_texts/ (PDF download) (visited December 20, 2012)
- Nice Agreement Concerning the International Classification of Goods and Services for the Purposes of the Registration of Marks, June 15, 1957, as revised at Stockholm on July 14, 1967, and at Geneva on May 13, 1977, and amended on September 28, 1979, 23 U.S.T. 1336, 550 U.N.T.S. 45
- Protocol Relating to the Madrid Agreement Concerning the International Registration of Marks, June 27, 1989, available at http://www.wipo.int/madrid/en/legal_texts/ (visited December 20, 2012)
- Trademark Law Treaty, October 27, 1994, available at http://www.wipo.int/treaties/en/ip/tlt/ (visited December 20, 2012)
- Vienna Agreement Establishing an International Classification of the Figurative Elements of Marks, June 12, 1973 as amended October 1, 1985, available at http://www.wipo.int/treaties/en/classification/vienna/trtdocs_wo031.html (visited December 20, 2012)

Statute
- Lanham Trademark Act, 15 U.S.C. §§ 1058–1059

See also: Fair Use (Trademark); International Trademark Protection; Trademark; TRIPS; WIPO

❖ TRIPS (TRADE SECRETS) ❖

Article 39 of TRIPS governs the protection of trade secrets by members of the WTO. To qualify for protection as a trade secret under TRIPS, information must meet four requirements: it must be lawfully within the control of a natural or legal person; it must be "secret in the sense that it is not, as a body or in the precise configuration and assembly of its components, generally known among or readily accessible to persons within the circles that normally deal with the kind of information in question"; it must have "commercial value because it is secret"; and it must have "been subject to reasonable steps under the circumstances, by the person lawfully in control of the information, to keep it secret" (TRIPS art. 39(2)).

A person who has a trade secret is entitled to keep the information from being "disclosed to, acquired by, or used by others . . . in a manner contrary to honest commercial practices" (TRIPS art. 39(2)). WTO members are thus obliged to enact laws preventing their nationals from stealing others'

trade secrets through "practices such as breach of contract, breach of confidence and inducement to breach" (TRIPS art. 39 n. 10).

The provisions of Article 39 are broadly similar to the provisions of U.S. trade secret law, and are subject to the same difficulty in implementation: because trade secrets are, by their very nature, unknown until after they have been disclosed, regulators do not know the exact nature of the content they are protecting. Instead, they must focus on the owner's desire to keep the content secret and the conduct by which another person thwarts that desire.

Treaty
- Agreement on Trade-Related Aspects of Intellectual Property Rights, Marrakesh Agreement Establishing the World Trade Organization, Annex 1C, April 15, 1994, 33 I.L.M. 81 (1994)

See also: Trade Secret; TRIPS

❖ TROJAN ❖

A Trojan, or Trojan Horse program, is a piece of malicious software, or malware, that disguises itself as some other program in order to trick a user into installing it. Trojans may arrive as email attachments or be downloaded from Web sites; they may even perform the function of the program they purport to be. However, they also perform other, often harmful functions. They may backdoor the computer on which they are installed, making the computer into a zombie for use in spamming or denial-of-service attacks (Symantec 2004). But as this is a function better suited to worms, which can replicate themselves, than to Trojans, the purpose of a Trojan is often more sinister. Trojans may serve to provide a remote user with complete access to the computer on which they are installed; the user may then perform mischievous pranks, destroy or alter some or all of the data on the computer, or steal data from the computer that may then be used for identity theft and other forms of fraud, or even blackmail.

The federal Computer Fraud and Abuse Act (CFAA) of 1986 prohibits the malicious use of Trojan programs (18 U.S.C. § 1030). The installation of a Trojan violates the CFAA's prohibition on knowingly or intentionally obtaining unauthorized access or exceeding authorized access to another's computer, as it is accomplished by subterfuge. The subterfuge is necessarily knowing or intentional; it cannot be accomplished by accident. The access is necessarily unauthorized or in violation of the authorization granted, as the victim believes that he or she is consenting to the installation of some other program. The 2001 USA PATRIOT Act has increased the maximum penalties available under the CFAA to imprisonment for 10 years for first offenders, and 20 years for repeat offenders (18 U.S.C. § 1030 (c)(4)).

Nonetheless, Trojans persist, largely because of the difficulty of catching and convicting the perpetrators. Users can guard themselves against Trojans with a combination of software and common sense. Antivirus and anti-spyware programs will detect many, but not all, Trojans. And even if a spyware or remote-access Trojan is installed, proper use of a firewall can render it ineffective by preventing the Trojan from communicating with the outside world.

In addition, common sense should be used when installing software. Programs contained in attachments to spam or messages from unknown persons should never be trusted. Even attachments to messages purporting to be from a friend, coworker, or acquaintance should be viewed with skepticism; the return person purportedly sending the message may not actually have done so, or may have been taken in by the Trojan. Downloads offered by Web sites should be refused unless the user has made a point of seeking out that particular download and knows what is being downloaded and what conditions are attached to it.

Statute

- Computer Fraud and Abuse Act, 18 U.S.C. § 1030

See also: Advertising; Adware and Spyware; Denial-of-Service Attack; Hacking; Malware; Privacy; Spam; Trademark; Worm; Zombie

Source and Further Reading

"Security Response Glossary," Symantec U.S., available at http://securityresponse.symantec.com/avcenter/refa.html (visited December 20, 2012)

❖ TYPOSQUATTING ❖

See Cybersquatting

❖ UNIFORM COMPUTER INFORMATION TRANSACTIONS ACT ❖

The Uniform Computer Information Transactions Act (UCITA) is a uniform act approved and proposed by the National Conference of Commissioners on Uniform State Laws. The Commissioners have approved and proposed many such acts over the years; they play an important role in ensuring a relative uniformity between the laws of the states of the United States. Of course, states may deliberately choose to adopt different laws, but the Commissioners prevent the laws of the states from drifting too far apart by accident or inadvertence rather than by design.

In contrast to many of the Commissioners' other proposed uniform laws, UCITA proved unsuccessful. It has been adopted by only two states, both over a decade ago. It was opposed from the outset by consumer advocates, including the attorneys general of several states (Letter from Attorneys General 1999). In opposing UCITA, the state attorneys general constructed this scenario:

> Jane Consumer purchases a piece of software that promises analysis and advice concerning various investment options. When she installs the software, she learns from a message displayed during the installation process that she must subscribe to a proprietary information service to use it, rather than the competing service she already uses to obtain such information. Even though other similar software packages are available which do not impose such requirements, Jane is loathe to begin the shopping process over again in order to decide which of those packages to purchase, so she accepts the new terms. Jane subscribes to the new information service, selecting a discounted 1 year agreement rather than a full price month to month agreement, and logs onto the system for the first time (Letter from Attorneys General 1999).

This, it turns out, was a bad decision on Jane's part. As soon as Jane logs on, she is "presented a screen which contains a hyperlink in the upper left hand corner labeled 'important information.' She is also presented with a flashing icon calling her attention to a hot stock tip." The stock tip distracts her, and when she returns to the logon screen the "important information" button is gone. Six months later, "a package arrives in the mail. It is an upgrade to her investment analysis software. Because she did not order the upgrade and there is nothing contained in the package advising her otherwise, she assumes it is a free bug fix upgrade." It is not, of course, although it seems more likely that the upgrade, free or otherwise, would be downloaded rather than received in the mail. Jane misguidedly installs the upgrade, and uses the upgraded software for the first time a few weeks later; this time she clicks the "important information" link and learns that "she will be billed $49.95 for the software because she failed to return it within seven days of receipt as required by the upgrade service provisions of her original contract." She was unaware of this provision, because she never clicked the original "important information" link (Letter from Attorneys General 1999).

Jane's problems continue to worsen, as the software vendor finds more ways of extracting more money from her than she ever believed she would pay; she cannot escape until her original 12-month contract has run its course. The attorneys general point out that all of the vendor's actions would be legal under UCITA; all that would protect Jane would be the vendor's own scruples and its desire to maintain a good reputation. UCITA's advocates, on the other hand, argued that there was already a tendency in case law toward enforcement of contractual provisions of which consumers may be unaware, and that UCITA would actually curb this trend (Ring 2003, 35).

Uniform Act

- Uniform Computer Information Transactions Act (2002), available at http://uniformlaws.org/Act.aspx?title=Computer%20Information%20Transactions%20Act (visited January 15, 2013)

See also: Clickwrap Agreement; Contracts; E-Commerce

Sources and Further Reading

Letter to NCCUSL from Attorneys General Opposing UCITA (July 23, 1999), available at http://www.arl.org/pp/ppcopyright/ucita/agoppltr.shtml (visited December 21, 2012)

Carlyle C. Ring, Jr., *Understanding Electronic Contracting 2003 The Impact of Regulation, New Laws & New Agreements: Overview of the Legal Landscape of E-Commerce*, Practising Law Institute Patents, Copyrights, Trademarks, and Literary Property Course Handbook Series, April 2003

❖ UNIVERSAL COPYRIGHT CONVENTION ❖

Since the late nineteenth century the primary multilateral treaty governing international copyright law has been the Berne Convention. For the first century of the Berne Convention's existence, however, U.S. copyright law diverged too greatly from the Berne Convention norm for the United States to become a party to the Convention. Instead, U.S. copyright relations were governed by various bilateral treaties, by a multilateral treaty with the countries of Latin America (the Buenos Aires Convention), and, from the 1950s through the 1980s, by the Universal Copyright Convention (U.C.C.).

The U.C.C. was developed under the auspices of the United Nations Educational, Scientific and Cultural Organization and adopted in 1952; the drafters had to balance the divergent concerns of major non-parties to the Berne Convention such as the United States, which exported copyrighted information, and the Soviet Union, which was deeply suspicious of a copyright regime that would protect primarily the interests of capitalist countries. The U.C.C. came into force for the United States in 1955 and went through a major revision in 1971 to take into account certain concerns of developing countries, many of which had not existed as independent nations in 1955. The earlier and later versions of the U.C.C. are sometimes referred to as the Geneva U.C.C. and the Paris U.C.C., respectively.

As with the Berne Convention, the core requirement of the U.C.C. is national treatment: Article II of both the Geneva U.C.C. and the Paris U.C.C. require parties to the Convention to extend to foreign copyright holders and foreign copyrighted works the same copyright protections that they extend to works of their own nationals first published in their own territory.

In contrast to the Berne Convention, which requires no formalities for copyright registration other than the name of the author (and even makes allowances for works that are published without identifying the author), Article III of both the Geneva and the Paris U.C.C. includes a minimal but nonetheless real registration requirement: the use of the symbol "©" upon the work together with the year of first publication and the name of the person claiming copyright. This is all the registration that can be required for foreign works, even if a state requires a more formal registration process for its own nationals; the possibility thus exists that a state might treat foreign copyright holders more favorably than its own nationals. Not coincidentally, this was also, more or less, the notice required under the U.S. Copyright Act of 1909 and, before its amendment by the Berne Convention Implementation Act of 1988, under the Copyright Act of 1976.

Article IV deals with the duration of the copyright term. This was, at the time of the adoption of both the Geneva and the Paris U.C.C., the central and irreconcilable point of difference between U.S. law and the Berne Convention. U.S. law provided for a 28-year copyright term, renewable once; registration was required for both the initial and the renewal term. The Berne Convention required, for most printed works, a minimum term of the lifetime of the author plus 50 years. Article IV(3) of the Geneva and Paris U.C.C. requires a minimum term of the life of the author plus 25 years, but for countries (such as the United States) that computed the copyright term from the date of initial publication, the minimum term was 25 years from the date of publication. This made it possible for the United States to become a party to the Convention without revising the copyright law then in effect, the Copyright Act of 1909.

Other protections provided by the U.C.C. are also generally less broad than those provided by the Berne Convention. It was anticipated that the Berne Convention parties would want to become parties to the U.C.C. as well, in order to gain the benefits of a multilateral copyright regime that included the United States and the other non-parties to the Berne Convention. To prevent these countries from picking and choosing those provisions of each convention that they found most congenial, Article XVII of the U.C.C. includes a Berne Safeguard Clause. This clause provides that no country that is a party to the Berne Convention may denounce that convention and choose instead to rely on the U.C.C. in copyright matters relating to other Berne Convention parties.

A hundred states are now parties to the Geneva U.C.C., the Paris U.C.C., or both. However, 98 of those states (including all of the parties to the Paris U.C.C.) are also parties to the Berne Convention, making the Paris U.C.C. a dead letter in international law, and the Geneva U.C.C. very nearly so: once the United States, for example, became a party to the Berne Convention, the Berne Safeguard Clause prevented it from relying on the less stringent requirements of the U.C.C. in its relations with the other Berne Convention parties. The U.C.C. does, however, continue to govern U.S. copyright relations with Cambodia, the sole country that is a party to the Geneva U.C.C. but not to the Berne Convention. Even with regard to U.S-Cambodia copyright relations, however, the effect of the U.C.C. is probably limited, as both countries are also members of the World Trade Organization and thus parties to its Agreement on Trade-Related Aspects of Intellectual Property (TRIPS).

Treaties

- Agreement on Trade-Related Aspects of Intellectual Property Rights, Marrakesh Agreement Establishing the World Trade Organization, Annex 1C, April 15, 1994, 33 I.L.M. 81 (1994)
- Convention Concerning the Creation of an International Union for the Protection of Literary and Artistic Works (Berne Convention), September 9, 1886, as last revised at Paris, July 24, 1971 (amended 1979), 25 U.S.T. 1341, 828 U.N.T.S. 221
- Universal Copyright Convention, September 6, 1952, 6 U.S.T. 2731, revised at Paris July 24, 1971, 25 U.S.T. 1341

Statutes

- Copyright Act of 1909, 17 U.S.C. §§ 1–216 (repealed 1976)
- Copyright Act of 1976, 17 U.S.C. §§ 101–1332

See also: Berne Convention; Copyright; International Copyright Protection

Source and Further Reading
Paul Goldstein & Bernt Hugenholtz, *International Copyright: Principles, Law, and Practice* (Oxford: Oxford University Press, 3d ed. 2012)

❖ VESSEL HULL DESIGN
PROTECTION ACT ❖

See Digital Millennium Copyright Act, Title V

❖ VINTAGE SOFTWARE ❖

See Abandonware

❖ VIRUS ❖

A computer virus is a program that replicates itself by inserting copies of itself into other programs or documents, much as a biological virus reproduces by inserting its genetic material into a host cell and causing the host cell to reproduce copies of the virus. The term "virus" is sometimes used in the media to refer to other types of malware as well, especially worms. Worms, however, replicate complete copies of themselves; they do not rely on other programs for reproduction or insert copies of themselves into other files.

The etymology of the term "virus" is more clouded than that of the term "worm." By the early 1980s, however, the term was in everyday use in its present sense. In the United States, the creation, use, or dissemination of viruses is governed by the Computer Fraud and Abuse Act (CFAA) of 1986 (18 U.S.C. § 1030). The CFAA makes it unlawful for any person to intentionally or knowingly obtain unauthorized access to a computer, exceed authorized access, or transmit "a program, information, code, or command" that causes damage to another's computer. Viruses and other malware fall within this last prohibition; they may also, by replicating themselves or enabling other malware, gain access to a computer or exceed authorized access (see *Morris*, 928 F.2d 504). Criminal penalties can include fines and increasingly heavy prison terms depending on the amount of harm caused, the culpability (mens rea) of the defendant, and whether the defendant is a repeat offender (18 U.S.C. § 1030(c)(4)). Life imprisonment is possible if the virus results in death (as it might, for instance, by sabotaging traffic signals, air traffic control software, or life-sustaining hospital equipment).

As with biological viruses, many computer viruses do little or no harm. Some can be destructive, however, corrupting or deleting files on the computers they infect, or slowing down or crashing those computers. Because worms offer advantages to malicious users who wish to gain access to other users' computers, worms are replacing viruses as the Internet's most troublesome malware; matters are confused by the media's habit of referring to worms as viruses. Like worms, viruses can best be avoided through the frequent use and updating of antivirus software, and through common sense when opening attachments or downloading programs. Most antivirus programs scan incoming email for viruses; however, even if the software detects no virus, there should never be a reason to open an attachment to a spam email, or to click on any link (including the bogus "unsubscribe" link in many spam messages). And no unfamiliar downloads, or downloads from unfamiliar Web sites, should ever be accepted.

Statute
- Computer Fraud and Abuse Act, 18 U.S.C. § 1030

Case
- *United States v. Morris*, 928 F. 2d 504 (2d Cir. 1991)

See also: Hacking; Malware; Trojan; Worm; Zombie

Source and Further Reading
Mathias Klang, "A Critical Look at the Regulation of Computer Viruses," 11 *International Journal of Law and Information Technology* 162 (2003)

❖ VOLUNTARY COLLECTIVE LICENSE ❖

A voluntary collective license is a license under which a copyright owner relinquishes the right to choose the licensee, without (necessarily) relinquishing the right to be paid, typically by licensing a reproduction rights organization (RRO). Anyone may copy and distribute a copyrighted work under a voluntary license, so long as he or she pays the fee set in the license (Ginsburg 1992, 383 n. 209). The RRO collects the fees and passes them along (minus costs) to the copyright owner. Voluntary collective licensing is widely used for most types of copyrighted content. Open-source works are generally distributed under some form of voluntary license, such as the GNU General Public License; under these licenses, no payment is required (making the involvement of an RRO unnecessary in most cases), but certain other conditions are imposed. A voluntary collective license differs from a compulsory license, which requires owners of certain types of intellectual property rights to license those rights to all who pay a fee, and under which the fee is generally set and collected by a government agency (McCarthy et al. 2004, 86–90).

Voluntary collective licensing has long been advocated by the Electronic Frontier Foundation (EFF), an activist group, as a solution to the problem of file-sharing and music piracy. Under the EFF's proposal,

> The concept is simple: the music industry forms several "collecting societies," which then offer file-sharing music fans the opportunity to "get legit" in exchange for a reasonable regular payment, say a total of $5–10 per month (after all, services like Rhapsody sell all-you-can-eat music for around $10 per month, so we know the rate should be below that). So long as they pay, the fans are free to keep doing what they are going to do anyway—share the music they love using whatever software they like on whatever computer platform they prefer—without fear of lawsuits. The money collected gets divided among rights-holders based on the popularity of their music (EFF 2008).

The EFF explains that the music industry has used collective licensing in the past to confront new technology:

> Songwriters originally viewed radio exactly the way the music industry today views KaZaA users—as pirates. After trying to sue radio out of existence, the songwriters ultimately got together to form ASCAP (and later BMI and SESAC). Radio stations interested in broadcasting music stepped up, paid a fee, and in return got to play whatever music they liked, using whatever equipment worked best. Today, the performing-rights societies ASCAP and BMI collect money and pay out millions annually to their artists. Even though these collecting societies get a fair bit of criticism, there's no question that the system that has evolved for radio is preferable to one based on trying to sue radio out of existence one broadcaster at a time (EFF 2008).

The marketplace may gradually be solving this problem, although for the most part, the content industry has shown more willingness to work with companies without a pirate past, such as Spotify.

See also: Activism and Advocacy Groups; Content Industry; Copyright; File-Sharing; International Federation of Reproduction Rights Organizations; Open Source; P2P; Piracy; Recording Industry Association of America

Sources and Further Reading

"A Better Way Forward: Voluntary Collective Licensing of Music File Sharing," Electronic Frontier Foundation (April 1, 2008), available at https://www.eff.org/wp/better-way-forward-voluntary-collective-licensing-music-file-sharing (visited February 24, 2013)

Jane C. Ginsburg, "No 'Sweat'? Copyright and Other Protection of Works of Information after *Feist v. Rural Telephone*," 92 *Columbia Law Review* 338 (1992)

J. Thomas McCarthy et al., *McCarthy's Desk Encyclopedia of Intellectual Property* (Washington, D.C.: Bureau of National Affairs, 3d ed. 2004)

❖ WAREZ ❖

"Warez" is a now-dated term in now-equally dated leet-speak for unauthorized copies of copyrighted computer software, unlawfully traded over the Internet or directly between users. The term is sometimes also used to refer to unauthorized copies of other types of copyrighted material, particularly movies. Warez trading begins with the cracking of the copy protection on the program or movie, if any, and the making of an unprotected copy. This copy may then be traded among warez groups, from which it will eventually leak into the mainstream Internet community through file-sharing services. It may also be pressed onto disks and sold as a counterfeit of the original program. There are distinctions among warezers. Those who create warez and distribute them for free tend to distinguish themselves from counterfeiters who sell pirated software for a profit, although their activities may still be illegal. These nonprofit warezers seem to be motivated primarily by an interest in demonstrating their technical prowess. An element of hostility to the copyright holders is also present, although some warezers argue that the distribution of warez actually increases demand for legitimate copies of the program.

A special subcategory of warez is abandonware—software that is no longer being sold or supported by its author, copyright owner, or licensed distributor. Abandonware traders seem to see themselves as archivists or historians rather than as pirates; many are motivated by enthusiasm for outdated software rather than by the technical rivalry that is evident in much of the rest of the warez community. They make the argument that, as the software is no longer being sold, the copyright holders are losing no sales as a result of the abandonware trading. While this may be a convincing argument from an ethical standpoint, it is less so from a legal standpoint: abandonware trading, like all warez trading, is illegal (Goldman 2004, 397).

The first warez trader to be prosecuted in the United States was David LaMacchia, a student. LaMacchia was an enthusiast, rather than a commercial warez trader, and thus could not be charged with criminal copyright infringement under the law of the time, which required that the infringement be done for financial gain. Instead, he was charged with conspiracy to commit wire fraud. The trial court dismissed the charge against him, though, because an earlier Supreme

Court decision had held that an intellectual property interest in copyright could not be taken by fraud unless Congress had specifically stated otherwise (*LaMacchia*, 871 F. Supp. at 545). The dismissal of charges against LaMacchia ultimately led to the passage of the 1997 No Electronic Theft Act (NET Act), which was specifically intended "to reverse the practical consequences of *United States v. LaMacchia*" (House Report, *3). The NET Act was aimed at warez trading, and greatly expanded the scope of actions subject to criminal copyright infringement penalties. It expanded the definition of "financial gain" to include "the receipt of other copyrighted works" (17 U.S.C. § 101); it criminalized the unauthorized reproduction of copyrighted works with a value in excess of $1000 even if the infringement was *not* for financial gain (17 U.S.C. § 506); and it increased the statute of limitations for criminal copyright infringement from three years to five years (17 U.S.C. § 507).

After an initial period of inactivity, the Justice Department began to pursue warez traders aggressively, breaking up long-established groups such as the notorious DrinkOrDie (Tresco Slashdot Interview 2002). By February 2004, at least 80 warez traders had been convicted; many, including enthusiast warez traders, were sent to prison (Goldman 2004, 427).

In addition to the NET Act, warez traders may be prosecuted under the Digital Millennium Copyright Act (DMCA), the Computer Fraud and Abuse Act (CFAA), and the Economic Espionage Act (EEA). Two provisions of the DMCA are applicable: the anticircumvention provisions codified at 17 U.S.C. § 1201 and the digital rights management provisions codified at 17 U.S.C. § 1202. The anticircumvention provisions prohibit the circumvention of "a technological measure that effectively controls access to a work" (17 U.S.C. § 1201(a)(1)(A)). Ostensibly, this provision is aimed only at access, not at copying, but with some programs and most DVDs, access is necessary for copying. Cracking, or circumventing copy protection, is an essential part of the warez process.

Copyrighted programs and other material also contain copyright management information; in the course of unauthorized copying, this information may be removed or modified. Section 1202 is titled "integrity of copyright management information." Copyright management information that might be found on computer software and is protected by section 1202 includes information identifying and about the title, author, and copyright owner; terms and conditions under which the program may be used; "identifying numbers or symbols referring to such information or links to such information"; and "such other information as the Register of Copyrights may prescribe by regulation" (17 U.S.C. § 1202(c)).

The knowing use of false copyright management information "with the intent to induce, enable, facilitate, or conceal infringement" is prohibited by § 1202(a). The intentional removal or alteration of the copyright management information is prohibited by § 1202(b)(1), while the unauthorized distribution of works from which the copyright management information has been removed or altered—a charge to which warez traders are particularly vulnerable—is prohibited by § 1202(3).

Section 1204 provides criminal penalties for violations of sections 1201 and 1202, while section 1203 provides civil remedies.

The anti-hacking Computer Fraud and Abuse Act, like the DMCA, contains provisions that may be used to prosecute warez traders. Obtaining copies of works for conversion to and distribution as warez often requires hacking, or unauthorized access to the copyright owner's computer or network. This is especially true in the case of zero-day and negative-day warez, which appear online on or before the day of their commercial release. And such unreleased works may also be trade secrets, protected by the Economic Espionage Act. The physical theft of a copy of a work from the copyright owner would, of course, be a crime under state law.

Statutes
- Computer Fraud and Abuse Act, 18 U.S.C. § 1030
- Digital Millennium Copyright Act, Title I, §§ 1201–1204
- Economic Espionage Act, 18 U.S.C. §§ 1831–1839
- No Electronic Theft Act, amending and codified at 17 U.S.C. §§ 101, 506 & 507 & 18 U.S.C. §§ 2319–2320

Legislative History
- House Report on the No Electronic Theft Act, H.R. Rep. No. 339 (1997)

Cases
Supreme Court
- *Dowling v. United States*, 473 U.S. 207 (1985)

Federal District Court
- *United States v. LaMacchia*, 871 F.Supp. 535 (D. Mass. 1994)

See also: Abandonware; Copyright; Copyright Infringement; Digital Millennium Copyright Act, Title I; Digital Rights Management; File-Sharing; Hacking; No Electronic Theft Act

Sources and Further Reading
"Former DrinkOrDie Member Chris Tresco Answers," *Slashdot* (October 4, 2002), available at http://interviews.slashdot .org/interviews/02/10/04/144217.shtml?tid=123 (visited February 9, 2013)

Eric Goldman, "A Road to No Warez: The No Electronic Theft Act and Criminal Copyright Infringement," 82 *Oregon Law Review* 369 (2003)

Eric Goldman, "Warez Trading and Criminal Copyright Infringement," 51 *Journal of the Copyright Society of the U.S.A.* 395 (2004)

"Six Formerly Associated with Fox Cable Charged with Copyright Infringement for Running Warez Site That Had Pirated Movies, Software," *Cybercrime Law Report*, May 31, 2004, at 21

❖ WEB ❖

See World Wide Web

❖ WEB BROWSER ❖

A Web browser is a computer program that allows the user to browse the World Wide Web. The first Web browser was created, along with the World Wide Web itself, by Tim Berners-Lee and Robert Cailliau at the European Organization for Nuclear Research (CERN) between 1989 and 1991. Other browsers appeared during the early 1990s, but like the early Web itself, they required either sophisticated computers or sophisticated users.

At the time other technologies for locating and exchanging information over the Internet, such as Gopher, were not only difficult to use but often incorporated proprietary technologies. Early Web browsers experimented with proprietary versions of hypertext markup language (HTML), creating situations in which Web pages created with a particular vendor's software package could only be viewed using that vendor's browser. Much the same situation exists today with media players; format incompatibility, as well as copyright issues, has slowed the growth of Internet video and audio. By the mid-1990s, however, most Web browsers had abandoned this destructive format war, and the Web developed rapidly. The actions of CERN in making the underlying Web and browser technology available to all, free of charge, were a major reason a format war was avoided.

In 1993, the National Center for Supercomputing Applications (NCSA) at the University of Illinois released the Mosaic browser, which was easy to use and could run on the personal computers of the time (CERN n.d.). In April 1994, the leader of the team that developed Mosaic, Marc Andreesen, then left the NCSA to form Mosaic Communications, which released its browser, Mosaic Netscape 0.9, in October 1994 (Metzger 2004).

From the outset, Netscape was mired in legal disputes. The University of Illinois sued to prevent the company from using the name "Mosaic," and in November 1994 the company changed its name to Netscape Communications and the name of its browser to Netscape Navigator (Netscape 1994). Netscape Navigator was an immediate success, both coinciding with and contributing to the explosive growth of the World Wide Web in the mid-1990s. In mid-1994, before Mosaic Netscape 0.9 was introduced, there were fewer than 3,000 Web servers; a year later there were more than 20,000 (Zakon 2004) and Netscape's share of the browser market was over 80 percent (Metzger 2004).

In August 1995 Microsoft released its own browser, Internet Explorer, and the browser wars began in earnest. Microsoft developed Internet Explorer from software purchased from Spyglass, Inc., which like Netscape was an offshoot of the NCSA at the University of Illinois. Internet Explorer was not initially bundled with Windows, but with Microsoft's Plus! 95 package. Plus! was an add-on package for Windows 95 that included extra utilities, of which Internet Explorer was the most important, and bells and whistles. In 1996 America Online began to bundle Internet Explorer with its software. Microsoft also used a strategy of bundling Internet Explorer with other Microsoft software installed on new computer systems; Netscape's market share steadily declined, but Microsoft's bundling strategy led the Justice Department and many state attorneys general to pursue antitrust litigation against Microsoft (Levy 1999).

The outcome of the Microsoft antitrust litigation was at best ambiguous; the outcome of the browser wars, however, was not. Netscape's decline in market share was irreversible; in 1998 Netscape programmers launched Mozilla.org, releasing Netscape's source code to the open-source community. In November 1998, America Online purchased Netscape; two years later it released Netscape 6.0, a version that disappointed many Netscape loyalists, leading them to switch to Internet Explorer (Metzger 2004). A year later, America Online converted the Netscape site to a news and entertainment portal, more or less abandoning the primary identification of the Netscape brand with the Web browser. In an apparent turnaround, America Online released new versions of the browser, Netscape 7.1 in June 2003 and Netscape 7.2 in August 2004 (Metzger 2004). At that point, however, 95 percent of Web surfers were using Internet Explorer, with many of the remaining 5 percent using Mozilla or other programs in preference to America Online's Netscape Navigator (*Firefox* 2004).

Since then, the Web browser market has diversified considerably; the increased popularity of Apple products has increased the market share of Apple's Safari browser, while the increased use of mobile devices for Web browsing has decreased Internet Explorer's market share. An open-source Mozilla browser, Firefox, now has a market share of between 20 percent and 24 percent; Google's Chrome and Microsoft's Internet Explorer each have about one-third of the market, with Safari holding between 7 percent and 8 percent and Opera holding about 2 percent. Opera demonstrates the fragmentation of the browser market: it is widely used on mobile devices, but is nearly nonexistent in the traditional PC browser market.

Case

- *United States v. Microsoft Corp.*, 980 F. Supp. 537 (D.D.C. 1997), reversed, 147 F.3d 935 (D.C. Cir. 1998)

See also: Internet; Microsoft Antitrust Litigation; World Wide Web

Sources and Further Reading

Awio Web Services LLC, "Web Browser Market Share Trends," W3 Counter, available at http://www.w3counter.com/trends (visited December 21, 2012)

Michael A. Cusumano & David B. Yoffie, *Competing on Internet Time: Lessons from Netscape and Its Battle with Microsoft* (New York: The Free Press, 1998)

"Firefox Browser Takes on Microsoft," BBC News (November 9, 2004), available at http://news.bbc.co.uk/2/hi/technology/3993959.stm (visited February 24, 2013)

Robert A. Levy, "Microsoft and the Browser Wars," 31 *Connecticut Law Review* 1321 (1999)

Holger Metzger, "Netscape History," available at http://www.holgermetzger.de/Netscape_History.html (visited January 15, 2013)

Press Release, Netscape, "Mosaic Communications Corporation Changes Name to Netscape Communications Corporation," available at http://www.holgermetzger.de/netscape/NetscapeCommunicationsNewsRelease.htm (visited December 21, 2012)

StatCounter, "Top 5 Browsers from Apr 2011 to Dec 2012," StatCounter GlobalStats, available at http://gs.statcounter.com/#browser-ww-monthly-201104–201212 (visited December 21, 2012)

❖ WIKILEAKS ❖

WikiLeaks is a nonprofit organization specializing in the dissemination of classified and secret information obtained from governments and other sources, sometimes in violation of local laws. Other such organizations exist, but WikiLeaks has attracted a great deal of media attention both for its release of highly sensitive U.S. government information and for the legal troubles of its founder, Julian Assange.

In the former category are a great many documents and files relating to the U.S. wars in Afghanistan and Iraq and over a quarter of a million U.S. diplomatic cables obtained from a U.S. soldier, Private Bradley Manning (now Chelsea Manning). Manning was arrested on multiple charges, including aiding the enemy; he pled guilty to some charges in February 2013 (Coombs 2013). In August 2013, Manning was acquitted of aiding the enemy but was convicted of numerous lesser charges, and was sentenced to 35 years in prison (Final Sentencing 2013; Sink 2013).

In the latter category, WikiLeaks founder Julian Assange, while living in the United Kingdom, was sought by the prosecutor's office in Sweden in connection with one or more rapes allegedly committed there. His battle in the courts of the United Kingdom to avoid extradition to Sweden took a somewhat startling turn when he sought, and was granted, political asylum at the Ecuadorian embassy in London.

The documents provided to WikiLeaks by Manning, and by WikiLeaks to the world, included several that ignited media storms, including the controversially edited and titled "Collateral Murder" video (showing the fatal shooting of two Reuters journalists in Iraq, possibly by U.S. forces) and U.S. diplomatic cables related to government corruption in Tunisia that are widely believed to have led to the fall of that country's government at the start of 2011's "Arab Spring" series of uprisings against undemocratic governments (see Dickinson 2011).

Cases

- *American Civil Liberties Union v. United States Department of Justice*, 681 F.3d 61 (2d Cir. 2012)
- *Assange v. Swedish Prosecution Authority*, [2012] UKSC 22, [2012] 2 A.C. 471 (appeal taken from Eng. & Wales C.A.)
- *U.S. v. Manning* (court-martial), U.S. Army, 1st Judicial Cir. 2013

See also: Activism and Advocacy Groups; Censorship; First Amendment

Sources and Further Reading

Associated Press, "Full Text: Bradley Manning's Letter To President Obama Requesting Pardon" (August 22, 2013), available at http://talkingpointsmemo.com/news/full-text-bradley-mannings-letter-obama-pardon.php (visited August 28, 2013)

David E. Coombs (Attorney for Bradley Manning), "PFC Manning's Written Statement in Support of His Guilty Plea" (March 4, 2013), available at http://www.armycourtmartialdefense.info/2013/03/pfc-mannings-written-statement-in.html (visited April 29, 2013)

Elizabeth Dickinson, "The First WikiLeaks Revolution?" *Foreign Policy* (January 13, 2011), available at http://wikileaks.foreignpolicy.com/posts/2011/01/13/wikileaks_and_the_tunisia_protests?sms_ss=twitter&at_xt= 4d2ffe4d9c2649d7,1 (visited April 24, 2013)

Final Sentencing, *U.S. v. PFC Bradley E. Manning* (court-martial), U.S. Army, 1st Judicial Cir. 2013, available at https://pressfreedomfoundation.org/sites/default/files/08-21-13-final-sentence.pdf

Ian Simpson and Medina Roshan, "U.S. Soldier Manning Gets 35 Years For Passing Documents to WikiLeaks" *Reuters* (August 21, 2013), available at http://www.reuters.com/article/2013/08/21/us-usa-wikileaks-manning-idUSBRE-97J0JI20130821 (visited August 28, 2013)

Justin Sink, "White House Would Consider Manning Pardon Request" (August 21, 2013), available at, http://thehill.com/blogs/blog-briefing-room/news/318117-white-house-would-consider-manning-pardon, (visited August 28, 2013)

Wikileaks, "What Is WikiLeaks?" available at http://wikileaks.org/About.html (visited April 24, 2013)

❖ WIPO ❖

The World Intellectual Property Organization (WIPO) is an international organization dedicated to the international protection of the rights of creators and owners of intellectual property. WIPO had its origin in the late nineteenth century, which saw the emergence of an international regime of intellectual property rights protection. Notable cornerstones of this regime were the Paris Convention on patents, trademarks, and industrial designs in 1883 and the Berne Convention on copyrights in 1886. Each of these treaties created an organization for administrative purposes; these united in 1893 to form the Bureaux Internationaux Réunis pour la Protection de la Propriété Intellectuelle (United International Bureau for the Protection of Intellectual Property, or BIRPI), which also administered two other treaties. Over time, the number of treaties administered and the size of the organization increased to its present level. BIRPI moved to Geneva (from Berne) in 1960; it became WIPO in 1967 and became a part of the United Nations in 1974. Today, WIPO employs nearly a thousand people at its headquarters in Geneva, its Coordination Office in New York, and elsewhere.

In addition to the treaties regarding the structure and functions of WIPO itself (the WIPO Convention, the Agreement between the United Nations and WIPO, and the Agreement between WIPO and the WTO), WIPO is responsible in whole or in part for the administration of 25 treaties:

- Beijing Treaty on Audiovisual Performances
- Berne Convention for the Protection of Literary and Artistic Works
- Brussels Convention Relating to the Distribution of Programme-Carrying Signals Transmitted by Satellite
- Budapest Treaty on the International Recognition of the Deposit of Microorganisms for the Purposes of Patent Procedure
- Convention for the Protection of Producers of Phonograms against Unauthorized Duplication of Their Phonograms
- Hague Agreement Concerning the International Deposit of Industrial Designs
- International Convention for the Protection of New Varieties of Plants
- Lisbon Agreement for the Protection of Appellations of Origin and Their International Registration
- Locarno Agreement Establishing an International Classification for Industrial Designs
- Madrid Agreement Concerning the International Registration of Marks
- Patent Cooperation Treaty
- Madrid Agreement for the Repression of False and Deceptive Indications of Source on Goods
- Nairobi Treaty on the Protection of the Olympic Symbol

- Nice Agreement Concerning the International Classification of Goods and Services for the Purposes of the Registration of Marks
- Paris Convention for the Protection of Industrial Property
- Patent Law Treaty
- Protocol Relating to the Madrid Agreement Concerning the International Registration of Marks
- Rome Convention for the Protection of Performers, Producers of Phonograms and Broadcasting Organizations
- Singapore Treaty on the Law of Trademarks
- Strasbourg Agreement Concerning the International Patent Classification
- Trademark Law Treaty
- Vienna Agreement Establishing an International Classification of the Figurative Elements of Marks
- Washington Treaty on Intellectual Property in Respect of Integrated Circuits
- WIPO Copyright Treaty
- WIPO Performances and Phonograms Treaty

One hundred and eighty-five states—nearly all of the world's countries—are members of WIPO. Although only states can be members, 238 international nongovernmental organizations (NGOs), 68 national NGOs, 67 intergovernmental organizations (IGOs), and Palestine have observer status (WIPO *Observers* 2012). (Taiwan is a party to some WIPO-administered treaties and participates as "Taiwan, Province of China.") These observers overwhelmingly represent producers and owners of intellectual property rights rather than consumers; a few, such as the International Law Association, may be presumed to be neutral.

That does not mean, however, that WIPO exclusively represents the interests of content producers. WIPO's voting structure allots each member one vote, regardless of population or level of production or consumption of intellectual property. While superficially this may seem equitable, it has the effect of giving the 36,000 people of Liechtenstein the same voting weight as the 1.2 billion people of India. It also gives the United States, the world's third most populous country and the largest producer and consumer of intellectual property, the same voting weight as the tiny island nation of São Tomé and Principe, with only 163,000 people and hardly any participation in the global intellectual property economy.

The breakup of the European overseas colonial empires has led to an increase in the number of developing countries. The concerns of developing countries, which have few intellectual property assets, tend to be the concerns of consumers rather than of producers. They tend to be opposed to the interests of developed country intellectual property rights holders, although not necessarily of developed country consumers. From the 1960s onward, it became apparent that an international intellectual property crisis was emerging in the area of pharmaceutical patents. Almost all pharmaceutical research and development is carried out by developed-world companies, and almost all pharmaceutical patents are held by developed-world persons. This research and development is expensive; costs are recouped during the period in which the drug is protected by patent. After the patent expires, the cost of the drug usually drops dramatically, as it can be manufactured by other companies and sold under a generic name; the cost of manufacture is usually less than the cost of research and development.

Many developing countries that lack the research and development resources necessary to create new drugs nonetheless have the resources to manufacture those drugs once developed. These countries are also often faced with desperate health problems; there is a strong temptation for these countries to ignore the drug developers' patents and simply manufacture the drug themselves, at far lower cost. People in these countries may feel that the lives and health of their compatriots outweigh the intellectual property interests of a handful of mostly European and North American corporations, and that no one should die because of inability to pay patent royalties. The pharmaceutical countries counter that in the absence of profits, there will be no incentive for further research and development; if the drug companies cannot recoup their costs, new drugs will not be created.

By the 1980s, the strong representation of developing countries in WIPO had effectively stymied the efforts of the pharmaceutical companies, who then lobbied their governments, particularly the U.S. government, to include an intellectual property treaty in the General Agreement on Tariffs and Trade (GATT) negotiations then underway. The GATT negotiations ultimately led to the creation of the World Trade Organization (WTO), one of the components of which is the Agreement on Trade-Related Aspects of Intellectual Property (TRIPS). TRIPS created a separate framework for protection of international intellectual property rights outside the context of WIPO; the WTO and WIPO formalized this regime in the 1995 Agreement between the World Intellectual Property Organization and the World Trade Organization. The pharmaceutical companies, others with similar interests, and their developed-world backers thus achieved a result that might not have been possible within the WIPO process.

The emergence of TRIPS as the new standard by which international intellectual property rights are determined and national intellectual property laws are measured does not mean that WIPO is moribund, however. As international organizations go, it enjoys exceptional financial stability; it is not dependent on the dues or largesse of its members, but has a steady source of income in fees from the Patent Cooperation Treaty. It continues to maintain valuable education and outreach services, to serve a function as a forum for policy discussions, and to provide dispute resolution services. Its most important function, however, is probably the provision of registration services for patents, trademarks, and designs. All intellectual property rights are granted by national governments and have effect only within the territory governed by the granting government. Protection in other countries requires registration in other countries; without WIPO's registration services, the informational obstacles to patent, trademark, and design registration would probably prove prohibitive.

Treaties

- Agreement between the United Nations and the World Intellectual Property Organization, December 17, 1974, 956 U.N.T.S. 729
- Agreement between the World Intellectual Property Organization and the World Trade Organization, December 22, 1995, 35 I.L.M. 754 (1996)
- Agreement on Trade-Related Aspects of Intellectual Property Rights, Marrakesh Agreement Establishing the World Trade Organization, Annex 1C, April 15, 1994, 33 I.L.M. 81 (1994)
- Beijing Treaty on Audiovisual Performances, June 24, 2012, 51 I.L.M. 1211
- Brussels Convention Relating to the Distribution of Programme-Carrying Signals Transmitted by Satellite, May 21, 1974, 13 I.L.M. 1444
- Budapest Treaty on the International Recognition of the Deposit of Microorganisms for the Purposes of Patent Procedure, April 28, 1977, as amended on September 26, 1980, 32 U.S.T. 1241, 1861 U.N.T.S. 361
- Convention Concerning the Creation of an International Union for the Protection of Literary and Artistic Works (Berne Convention), September 9, 1886, as last revised at Paris, July 24, 1971 (amended 1979), 25 U.S.T. 1341, 828 U.N.T.S. 221
- Convention Establishing the World Intellectual Property Organization, July 14, 1967, as amended on September 28, 1979 (WIPO Convention), 21 U.S.T. 1749, 828 U.N.T.S. 3
- Convention for the Protection of Producers of Phonograms Against Unauthorized Duplication of Their Phonograms, October 29, 1971, 25 U.S.T. 309
- Hague Agreement Concerning the International Deposit of Industrial Designs, November 6, 1925, 74 L.N.T.S. 343, revised at London, June 2, 1934, 205 L.N.T.S. 179, revised at The Hague, November 28, 1960; supplemented by the Additional Act of Monaco, November 18, 1961, the Complementary Act of Stockholm, July 14, 1967, and the Protocol of Geneva, April 10, 1975, 26 U.S.T. 571; and as amended, September 1979
- Lisbon Agreement for the Protection of Appellations of Origin and their International Registration, October 31, 1958, as revised at Stockholm on July 14, 1967, and as amended on September 28, 1979, 923 U.N.T.S. 205
- Locarno Agreement Establishing an International Classification for Industrial Designs, October 8, 1968, as amended on September 28, 1979, 23 U.S.T. 1389
- Madrid Agreement Concerning the International Registration of Marks, April 14, 1891, as revised at Brussels on December 14, 1900, at Washington on June 2, 1911, at The Hague on November 6, 1925, at London on June 2, 1934, at Nice on June 15, 1957, and at Stockholm on July 14, 1967, and as amended on September 28, 1979, 828 U.N.T.S. 389
- Madrid Agreement for the Repression of False or Deceptive Indications of Source on Goods, April 14, 1891, as revised at Washington on June 2, 1911, at The Hague on November 6, 1925, at London on June 2, 1934, and at Lisbon on October 31, 1958, and Additional Act, Stockholm, July 14, 1967, 828 U.N.T.S. 389
- Nairobi Treaty on the Protection of the Olympic Symbol, September 26, 1981, 1863 U.N.T.S. 367
- Nice Agreement Concerning the International Classification of Goods and Services for the Purposes of the Registration of Marks, June 15, 1957, as revised at Stockholm on July 14, 1967, and at Geneva on May 13, 1977, and amended on September 28, 1979, 23 U.S.T. 1336, 550 U.N.T.S. 45
- Paris Convention for the Protection of Industrial Property, March 20, 1883, as revised at Brussels on December 14, 1900, at Washington on June 2, 1911, at The Hague on November 6, 1925, at London on June 2, 1934, at Lisbon on October 31, 1958, and at Stockholm on July 14, 1967, and as amended on September 28, 1979, 21 U.S.T. 1583, 828 U.N.T.S. 305
- Patent Cooperation Treaty, Washington on June 19, 1970, as amended on September 28, 1979, and as modified on February 3, 1984, and October 3, 2001, 28 U.S.T. 7645, 9 I.L.M. 978
- Patent Law Treaty, June 1, 2000, 39 I.L.M. 1047 (2000)
- Protocol Relating to the Madrid Agreement Concerning the International Registration of Marks, June 27, 1989, S. Treaty Doc. No 106–41 (2000)
- Rome Convention for the Protection of Performers, Producers of Phonograms and Broadcasting Organizations, October 26, 1961, 496 U.N.T.S. 43
- Singapore Treaty on the Law of Trademarks, March 28, 2006, S. Treaty Doc. No. 110–2
- Strasbourg Agreement Concerning the International Patent Classification, March 24, 1971, as amended on September, 1979, 26 U.S.T. 1793
- Trademark Law Treaty, October 27, 1994, S. Treaty Doc. No. 105–35 (1988)
- Treaty on Intellectual Property in Respect of Integrated Circuits, Washington, May 26, 1989, 28 I.L.M. 1477 (1989)
- Universal Copyright Convention, September 6, 1952, 6 U.S.T. 2731, revised at Paris July 24, 1971, 25 U.S.T. 1341

- Vienna Agreement Establishing an International Classification of the Figurative Elements of Marks, June 12, 1973, 1863 U.N.T.S. 317, as amended October 1, 1985
- WIPO Copyright Treaty, December 20, 1996, 36 I.L.M. 65 (1997)
- WIPO Performance and Phonograms Treaty, December 20, 1996, 36 I.L.M. 76 (1997)

Statute

- Copyright Act of 1976, 17 U.S.C. §§ 101–1332

See also: Berne Convention; Copyright; Copyright Infringement; Domain Name Registration; International Copyright Protection; International Patent Protection; International Trademark Protection; Patent; Patent Cooperation Treaty; Trademark; Trademark Law Treaty; TRIPS; Universal Copyright Convention; WIPO Copyright Treaty; WIPO Performance and Phonograms Treaty

Sources and Further Reading

Pamela Samuelson, "The U.S. Digital Agenda at WIPO," 37 *Virginia Journal of International Law* 369 (1997)

World Intellectual Property Organization, "List of Observers," available at http://www.wipo.int/members/en/docs/observers.pdf (visited December 21, 2012)

World Intellectual Property Organization, "Member States," available at http://www.wipo.int/members/en/ (visited December 21, 2012)

❖ WIPO COPYRIGHT AND PERFORMANCES AND PHONOGRAMS TREATIES IMPLEMENTATION ACT ❖

See Digital Millennium Copyright Act, Title I

❖ WIPO COPYRIGHT TREATY ❖

The WIPO Copyright Treaty was adopted by the World Intellectual Property Organization (WIPO) in 1996 and entered into force, by its own terms, on March 6, 2002, three months after the deposit of the 30th instrument of ratification or accession. A total of 47 countries have now become parties to the convention, the most recent being South Korea on June 24, 2004. The treaty extends copyright protections beyond those guaranteed by the Berne Convention or TRIPS.

Articles 2, 4, and 5 provide protection for computer programs and compilations of data equivalent to those provided by the Berne Convention and TRIPS; footnotes 3 and 4 provide that the protection accorded each "is consistent with Article 2 of the Berne Convention and on a par with the relevant provisions of the TRIPS Agreement." However, the WIPO Copyright Treaty's protection of rental and distribution rights, set forth in Articles 6 through 8, may exceed those contained in the Berne Convention and TRIPS. It is Articles 11 and 12, however, that represent the greatest departure from past treaties and have had the greatest impact on the domestic law of those states that have become parties to the treaty.

Article 11 requires the parties to the treaty to "provide adequate legal protection and effective legal remedies against the circumvention of effective technological measures that are used by authors in connection with the exercise of their rights under this Treaty or the Berne Convention." In other words, parties to the treaty must enact and enforce laws against the circumvention of copy-protection measures. Article 12 carries the idea a bit further, prohibiting not only the circumvention of technological measures used to prevent actual copying, but any other circumvention of any part of a digital rights management scheme. Under Article 12, the parties must "provide adequate and effective legal remedies against any person knowingly" removing or altering "any electronic rights management information," or distributing, importing for distribution, broadcasting or communicating to the public any works from which such information has been removed, if in either case the person does not have the authority to do so and knows or has reason to know that doing so "will induce, enable, facilitate or conceal an infringement of any right covered by this Treaty or the Berne Convention."

The anticircumvention provisions in Articles 11 and 12 of the WIPO Copyright Treaty have been enacted into U.S. law in the form of the anticircumvention provisions of Title I of the Digital Millennium Copyright Act (17 U.S.C. §§ 1201–1204), and into European Union law by EU Directive 2001/29/EC.

Treaty

- WIPO Copyright Treaty, December 20, 1996, 36 I.L.M. 65 (1997)

Statute

- Digital Millennium Copyright Act, 17 U.S.C. § 1201

European Union Directive

- EU Directive 2001/29/EC on the Harmonisation of Certain Aspects of Copyright and Related Rights in the Information Society, 2001 O.J. (L 167) 10

See also: Berne Convention; Copyright Infringement; DeCSS; Digital Millennium Copyright Act, Title I; Digital Rights Management; Encryption; File-Sharing; International Copyright Protection; Steganography; TRIPS

Source and Further Reading

Mihaly Ficsor, *The Law of Copyright and the Internet: The 1996 WIPO Treaties, Their Interpretation and Implementation* (Oxford, UK: Oxford University Press, 2002)

❖ WIPO PERFORMANCE AND PHONOGRAMS TREATY ❖

The WIPO Performance and Phonograms Treaty was adopted by WIPO in 1996 and entered into force, by its own terms, on May 20, 2002, three months after the deposit of the 30th instrument of ratification or accession. A total of 43 countries have now become parties to the convention, the most recent being Jordan on May 24, 2004.

With two exceptions, the WIPO Phonograms Treaty stands alone: Article 1(3) provides that "this Treaty shall not have any connection with, nor shall it prejudice any rights and obligations under, any other treaties." The first of these exceptions is set out in Article 1(1): "Nothing in this Treaty shall derogate from existing obligations . . . under the" Rome phonograms treaty (to which the United States is not a party). The second exception is more general: Article 1(2) adds that protection of phonograms under the treaty "shall leave intact and shall in no way affect the protection of copyright in literary and artistic works."

Article 3 of the treaty requires parties to provide protection under the treaty to nationals of other parties applying the Rome Convention's criteria for eligibility. Article 4 requires national treatment; that is, each party "shall accord to nationals of other Contracting Parties . . . the treatment it accords to its own nationals[.]"

Article 5 protects the moral rights of performers in sound recordings of live aural performances "independently of a performer's economic rights, and even after the transfer of those rights." In an inversion of the relative importance that the United States has traditionally accorded moral and economic rights, the article protecting moral rights precedes the article protecting economic rights. Moral rights, in copyright law, are the right not to have one's work mutilated or distorted, the right to be acknowledged as the author of the work, and the right to determine when and in what fashion the work shall be presented to the public. These rights are called, respectively, the rights of integrity, paternity, and disclosure. U.S. copyright law has traditionally been reluctant to acknowledge moral rights.

Article 6 of the treaty deals with the economic rights of performers in unfixed performances, requiring that parties to the treaty grant performers the sole right of authorizing the broadcasting, except in the case of performances that are already broadcast performances. Article 6 also requires the parties to grant performers the sole right of communication to the public and fixation of their unfixed performances. Articles 7 and 8 deal with the more familiar (from a U.S. copyright law standpoint) rights of reproduction and distribution; again, parties are required to grant these rights exclusively to the performers. Article 9 grants a similar monopoly on rental rights, while Article 10 provides that "[p]erformers shall enjoy the exclusive right of authorizing the making available to the public of their performances fixed in phonograms, by wire or wireless means, in such a way that members of the public may access them from a place and at a time individually chosen by them." Articles 11 through 14 provide parallel rights to producers of phonograms. Article 15 provides performers and producers with a right of remuneration for the broadcasting or other communication to the public of their sound recordings. The minimum term of protection is set by Article 17 at 50 years from the end of the year in which the performance was fixed (for performers and for producers of works fixed but not published), and 50 years from the end of the year of publication (for producers of published phonograms). Article 20 provides, in conformity with Berne Convention and TRIPS norms, that no formalities may be required for copyright protection.

Article 16 provides for limitations and exceptions such as the U.S. fair use doctrine: "Contracting Parties may, in their national legislation, provide for the same kinds of limitations or exceptions with regard to the protection of performers and producers of phonograms as they provide for, in their national legislation, in connection with the protection of copyright in literary and artistic works." The treaty adopts the three-step test of Article 9(2) of the Berne Convention as expressed in Article 13 of TRIPS, confining the creation of limitations or exceptions to "certain special cases which do not conflict with a normal exploitation of the performance or phonogram and do not unreasonably prejudice the legitimate interests of the performer or of the producer of the phonogram." Article 18, like Article 11 of the WIPO Copyright Treaty, requires the parties to enact and enforce laws against the circumvention of copy-protection measures: Parties to the treaty "shall provide adequate legal protection and effective legal remedies against the circumvention of effective technological measures that are used by performers or producers of phonograms in connection with the exercise of their rights under this Treaty and that restrict acts, in respect of their performances or phonograms, which are not authorized by the performers or the producers of phonograms concerned or permitted by law." Article 19, like Article 12 of the WIPO Copyright Treaty, requires the parties to prohibit any other circumvention or spoofing of any part of an electronic rights management scheme. Under Article 19, the parties must "provide adequate and effective legal remedies against any person knowingly" removing or altering "any electronic rights management information," or distributing, importing for distribution, broadcasting or communicating to the public any works from which such information has been removed, if in either case the person does not have the authority to do so and knows or has reason to know that doing so "will induce, enable, facilitate or conceal an infringement of any right covered by this Treaty."

The anticircumvention provisions in Articles 18 and 19 of the WIPO Performance and Phonograms Treaty, like the corresponding provisions of the WIPO Copyright Treaty, have been implemented in the United States by the anticircumvention provisions of the Digital Millennium Copyright Act (17 U.S.C. §§ 1201–1204) and in the European Union by EU Directive 2001/29/EC.

Treaties
- Rome Convention for the Protection of Performers, Producers of Phonograms and Broadcasting Organizations, October 26, 1961, 496 U.N.T.S. 43
- WIPO Copyright Treaty, December 20, 1996, 36 I.L.M. 65 (1997)
- WIPO Performance and Phonograms Treaty, December 20, 1996, 36 I.L.M. 76 (1997)

Statute
- Digital Millennium Copyright Act, 17 U.S.C. § 1201

European Union Directive
- EU Directive 2001/29/EC on the Harmonisation of Certain Aspects of Copyright and Related Rights in the Information Society, 2001 O.J. (L 167) 10

See also: Berne Convention; Copyright Infringement; DeCSS; Digital Millennium Copyright Act, Title I; Digital Rights Management; International Copyright Protection; TRIPS

Source and Further Reading
Mihaly Ficsor, *The Law of Copyright and the Internet: The 1996 WIPO Treaties, Their Interpretation and Implementation* (Oxford, UK: Oxford University Press, 2002)

❖ WORLD INTELLECTUAL PROPERTY ORGANIZATION ❖

See WIPO

❖ WORLD WIDE WEB ❖

The World Wide Web, or Web, is often but inaccurately referred to as the Internet. The Internet is the combination of physical infrastructure and communications protocols that supports the Web and other information networks. The Web is a collection of information, distributed on billions of hypertext pages scattered across millions of Internet-connected computers, which can be accessed using a Web browser. Any person with a Web browser and access to the Internet can view pages on the World Wide Web, interact with those pages, and follow links from one page to another (Wagner 1999). Information shared across the Web can be used to facilitate other Internet activities, such as email, messaging, and file-sharing.

The Internet itself arose from a variety of sources, and cannot readily be traced to a single inventor or originating event. The origins of the World Wide Web are less obscure, however. The Web was created in the late 1990s by an independent contractor and a researcher at CERN, the European Organization for Nuclear Research. (CERN is the French acronym for the organization's original name, Centre Européenne pour la Recherche Nucléaire; the organization is now the Organisation Européenne pour la Recherche Nucléaire.) The two, Tim Berners-Lee and Robert Cailliau, created a hypertext system they called ENQUIRE in order to find documents more quickly on CERN's computers. Hypertext systems existing at the time required two-way links; the system developed by Berners-Lee and Cailliau used unidirectional links, meaning that anyone creating a document could link to another document without the need for any alteration in that second document. By 1991 Berners-Lee had created both the first Web page and the first Web browser; the Web spread quickly, first among physics researchers and then to the world at large. In December 1991, the United States had its first Web server, at the Stanford Linear Accelerator Center in Menlo Park, California (CERN 2008).

Two factors contributed to the early growth of the World Wide Web: the ease with which unidirectional hypertext links could be created, and the fact that CERN made the underlying technology available to all, free of charge. This made the Web far more attractive than proprietary technologies for which content developers would have to obtain a license and pay a fee. Early Web browsers, however, either required sophisticated computers or were difficult to use for the technologically unsophisticated. The explosion of the Web beyond the scientific community began with the release of easy-to-use Web browsers that could run on the home computers of the time. The first of these was the Mosaic browser, released in 1993 by the National Center for Supercomputing Applications at the University of Illinois (CERN 2008). Netscape released its browser, Netscape Navigator, in 1994. Netscape Navigator was followed by Microsoft's Internet Explorer in 1995, and the browser wars began. In October 1993, before Netscape Navigator appeared on the market, there were only 228 Web servers. Eight months later, in June 1994, there were 2,738. For a time during the mid-1990s the number of Web servers continued to grow at this astonishing rate, increasing an order of magnitude each year. In June 1995, there were 23,500 servers, and in June 1996 there were 252,000. The number of Web servers had topped a million by April 1997. By September 2012, the World Wide Web included well over 600 million sites, with tens of billions or hundreds of billions of pages (Netcraft 2012).

The World Wide Web, like the Internet, has been involved in controversy from its inception. The browser wars between Netscape and Microsoft led to federal and state government lawsuits against Microsoft. The ease with which the Web provides access to information has raised concerns about its use by criminal conspiracies and terrorist organizations. The relative anonymity of Web users has made it difficult to shield minors from indecent and pornographic content. These concerns have led to attempts to censor the Internet either by restricting content or by restricting access; these attempts have met with little success both because of the ease with which sophisticated users circumvent controls and, in countries such as the United States, because of constitutional protections of free speech and access to information.

The ease with which material can be reproduced and published on the Web has also raised intellectual property concerns; holders of intellectual property rights have been more successful than censorship advocates, both in court and in Congress, in achieving some measure of control over the Internet. Laws such as the Digital Millennium Copyright Act have greatly strengthened copyright protections, taking new technology into account. The Web has also revolutionized retailing through the advent of e-commerce, requiring changes to contract law.

Statute

- Digital Millennium Copyright Act, 17 U.S.C. §§ 512, 1201–1204

See also: Censorship; Copyright; Digital Millennium Copyright Act; E-Commerce; File-Sharing; Hacking; Internet; Internet Corporation for Assigned Names and Numbers; Microsoft Antitrust Litigation; Spam; Virus; Web Browser

Sources and Further Reading

Dave Kristula, "The History of the Internet" (August 2001), available at http://www.davesite.com/webstation/net-history .shtml (visited August 16, 2012)
"September 2012 Web Server Survey," Netcraft (September 10, 2012), available at http://news.netcraft.com/ archives/2012/09/10/september-2012-web-server-survey .html (visited February 7, 2013)
Ronald L. Wagner, *Road Runner Guide to Cyberspace* (Herndon, VA: Citapei Communications, 9th ed. 1999)
"Welcome to info.cern.ch: The Website of the World's First-Ever Web Server," CERN (2008), available at http://info.cern.ch/ (visited February 7, 2013)
Robert H. Zakon, "Hobbes' Internet Timeline v10.2," available at http://www.zakon.org/robert/Internet/timeline/ (last updated December 30, 2011)

❖ WORM ❖

A worm is a program that replicates itself until it has used up all of the available space on a computer. A worm is not a computer virus, although the two terms are often confused and worms may have the same effects as some viruses. The term "worm" was first used for such a program by the late British SF author John Brunner in his 1975 novel *Shockwave Rider.* Brunner's use of the term was adopted by researchers at Xerox PARC, who created the first computer worm in 1978 (PARC History 2003). It was not until a decade later, however, that computer worms burst into the popular consciousness, with the creation and distribution of a worm by Cornell University graduate student Robert Morris, Jr. (Lessig 1999, 194–196).

Morris created the worm to point out security flaws in the then-new Internet, particularly in the open-source email distribution program Sendmail:

> Morris identified four ways in which the worm could break into computers on the network:
>
> (1) through a "hole" or "bug" (an error) in SEND MAIL, a computer program that transfers and receives electronic mail on a computer;
> (2) through a bug in the "finger demon" program, a program that permits a person to obtain limited information about the users of another computer;
> (3) through the "trusted hosts" feature, which permits a user with certain privileges on one computer to have equivalent privileges on another computer without using a password; and
> (4) through a program of password guessing, whereby various combinations of letters are tried out in rapid sequence in the hope that one will be an authorized user's password, which is entered to permit whatever level of activity that user is authorized to perform (*Morris,* 928 F.2d at 506).

Morris, whose father was a data security expert for the National Security Agency, appeared to have no malicious intent; among old-school hackers, a prank like the one Morris planned was a proper and acceptable way to point out a security flaw in an open-source program such as Sendmail (Lessig 1999, 195, 282 n.18). Morris took steps to ensure that his worm would not do undue damage:

> Therefore, Morris designed the worm to "ask" each computer whether it already had a copy of the worm. If it responded "no," then the worm would copy onto the computer; if it responded "yes," the worm would not duplicate. However, Morris was concerned that other programmers could kill the worm by programming their own computers to falsely respond "yes" to the question. To circumvent this protection, Morris programmed the worm to duplicate itself every seventh time it received a "yes" response. As it turned out, Morris underestimated the number of times a computer would be asked the question, and his one-out-of-seven ratio resulted in far more copying than he had anticipated. The worm was also designed so that it would be killed when a computer was shut down, an event that typically occurs once every week or two. This would have prevented the worm from accumulating on one computer, had Morris correctly estimated the likely rate of reinfection (*Morris,* 982 F.2d at 506).

Morris released his worm on November 2, 1988, from a computer at the Massachusetts Institute of Technology. The worm spread much faster than Morris had anticipated; alarmed, he tried to kill it, but could not. Morris and a friend sent an anonymous mass email from a computer at Harvard, explaining how to kill the worm and prevent infection. Because the worm had grown so quickly, however, the fledgling Internet of the time was unable to cope with it, and much email—including Morris's message—was unable to get through (*Morris,* 982 F.2d at 506). Before it was brought under control, Morris's worm had infected thousands of computers, causing millions of dollars worth of damage (World Almanac 2004, 713). Morris was arrested and charged with violation of § 1030(a)(5)(A) of the Computer Fraud and Abuse Act. At the time, § 1030(a)(5)(A) imposed criminal penalties on anyone who:

> (5) intentionally accesses a Federal interest computer without authorization, and by means of one or more instances of such conduct alters, damages, or destroys information in any such Federal interest computer, or prevents authorized use of any such computer or information, and thereby
>> (A) causes loss to one or more others of a value aggregating $1,000 or more during any one year period (quoted in *Morris*, 928 F. 2d at 506).

Morris was convicted of violating § 1030(a)(5)(A) (*Morris*, 928 F.2d at 506); his conviction was affirmed on appeal. Since that time the statute has been amended many times, rendering obsolete the court's discussion of terms such as "Federal interest computer." However, the basic elements of the crime of spreading a computer worm, as set forth by the court considering Morris's appeal, remain the same: intent and unauthorized access. Morris intended to create and spread the worm, even if he did not intend the effects to be as severe as they actually were. And by causing the worm to replicate itself on computers that he was not authorized to access, he obtained unauthorized access to these computers. This second part of the holding seems a bit more of a stretch, as Morris gained no control over the infected computers; he could not even prevent the worm from replicating itself on those computers once he had started. Nonetheless, the court held that a reasonable jury could have found that Morris obtained access, for a variety of reasons: The worm's password-guessing function by itself was probably enough to support a finding of unauthorized access, as was the abuse of the "trusted hosts" function. Also, "he found holes in [Sendmail and Fingerdaemon] that permitted him a special and unauthorized access route into other computers" (*Morris*, 928 F.2d at 510).

While some worms simply replicate themselves, a virtue of worms, from a malicious user's point of view, is that they can be used as vehicles to install programs on other users' computers without the consent or knowledge of those other users. Some worms install Trojans or backdoor programs on the computers they infect. These backdoors turn the infected computers into zombies; the zombies can then be turned to a variety of malicious uses. Zombies can be used to launch distributed denial-of-service (DDoS) attacks against Web sites and servers, to mail spam, or to mail other worms and viruses. Uses of this sort, of course, fit the definition of "unauthorized access" far more easily than did Morris's relatively innocuous worm.

The easiest way for users to avoid worms is to update and run antivirus software (which also checks for and removes known worms) frequently, and to exercise common sense when downloading unknown attachments. While most antivirus programs scan incoming email for worms and viruses, there is never a good reason for anyone other than a computer security professional to click on an attachment to a spam email. And users should be cautious about downloading programs from unknown Web sites.

Statute
- Computer Fraud and Abuse Act, 18 U.S.C. § 1030

Case
- *United States v. Morris*, 928 F.2d 504 (2d Cir. 1991)

See also: Adware and Spyware; Denial-of-Service Attack; Hacking; Malware; Open Source; Spam; Trojan; Virus; Zombie

Sources and Further Reading

Nonfiction
Lawrence Lessig, *Code and Other Laws of Cyberspace* (New York: Basic Books, 1999)
Tiernan Ray, "E-Mail Viruses Blamed as Spam Rises Sharply," *Seattle Times* (February 18, 2004), available at http://seattle times.nwsource.com/html/businesstechnology/2001859752_spamdoubles18.html (visited February 24, 2013)
Bruce Sterling, *The Hacker Crackdown* (Electronic edition 1992), available at http://stuff.mit.edu/hacker/hacker.html (visited December 21, 2012)
"Xerox PARC History," PARC, available at http://www.parc.xerox.com/about/history/default.html (visited December 21, 2012)
World Almanac and Book of Facts 2004 (New York: World Almanac Books, 2004)

Fiction
John Brunner, *The Shockwave Rider* (New York: Ballantine, 1976)

❖ .XXX ❖

An ".xxx" top-level domain (TLD) had long been proposed as a solution to the problem of online pornography and its availability to minors and in more socially conservative countries. After much delay, in 2011, the Internet Corporation for Assigned Names and Numbers approved the ".xxx" sTLD, sponsored by the International Foundation for Online Responsibility (IFFOR), making the TLD a sponsored top-level domain, or sTLD. IFFOR's stated goals include the promotion of user choice, parental control, and combating online child abuse images (child pornography), as well as the protection of freedom of expression, privacy, security, and consumer rights (IFFOR 2012). The .xxx registry is administered by ICM Registry LLC, a company created for that purpose.

The .xxx TLD has had less effect than its proponents had claimed, both because the online pornography industry has a substantial investment in the sites it has already developed in other domains, and more importantly because there is neither an incentive for pornographers to relocate profitable Web sites nor any disincentive attached to keeping the content where it is now. If pornographic content is to be quarantined in its own area of the Internet, a legislative stick (penalties for pornographic content in other TLDs) and carrot (a safe harbor provision exempting sites within the .xxx sTLD from those penalties) are both needed. No serious attempts to enact such legislation are currently in progress, however; the .xxx sTLD may turn out to be a good idea that came a decade or two too late.

See also: .com; Indecency

Sources and Further Reading
Paul Barrett, "How to Find Porn on the Internet," Bloomberg Business Technology (September 27, 2012), available at http://www.businessweek.com/articles/2012–09–27/how-to-find-porn-on-the-internet (visited February 24, 2013)
Tim Elfrink, ".XXX Sites Are Live Thanks to Stuart Lawley, A South Florida Brit Who Beat the Bush Admin," *Miami New Times* (December 8, 2011), available at http://blogs.miaminewtimes.com/riptide/2011/12/xxx_sites_are_live_thanks_to_s.php (visited February 7, 2013)
International Foundation for Online Responsibility, "The Organization and Our Policy Goals," available at http://www.iffor.org/ (visited January 15, 2013)

❖ YAHOO! ❖

Yahoo! Inc. is a company offering a wide range of Internet services, including news, e-mail, Web hosting, shopping, and search. Yahoo! also has foreign-language sites aimed at markets in the United States and 65 other countries.

The history of Yahoo! is the history of the commercial Internet in microcosm. Yahoo! began as the project of two Stanford University graduate students, Jerry Yang and David Filo, in 1994. Originally, it was no more than a list of links to favorite Web sites: "Jerry's Guide to the World Wide Web." The list was divided into categories and eventually renamed Yahoo!; the etymology of the name has been variously given as an acronym for "Yet Another Hierarchical Officious Oracle," "Yet Another Hierarchically Organized Outline," and more simply as a term, originally derived from *Gulliver's Travels*, meaning a person who is uncouth and unsophisticated. This meaning is carried over into the name of Yahoo's children's site, Yahooligans.

The lists maintained by Filo and Yang began to attract first hundreds, then thousands of users; at the time, in 1994, the Internet was still used mostly by a relatively small number of technically sophisticated users; its transformation to a universal medium of communication had not yet taken place. Yahoo's popularity grew by word of mouth, and by fall of 1994, the site was attracting over a hundred thousand unique visitors a day. Filo and Yang incorporated Yahoo! and raised about two million dollars from high-tech venture capital firm Sequoia Capital. The introduction of venture capitalists marked the transformation of Yahoo! from grad student hobby to serious business; the company hired professional managers and began to prepare for an initial public offering (IPO) of stock. At the time the IPO actually took place, on April 12, 1996, Yahoo! had 49 employees; its IPO raised about $34 million (History of Yahoo! 2005).

Yahoo's successful IPO and continuing post-IPO success, along with those of similar early-1990s Internet businesses, inspired wild investor enthusiasm for Internet IPOs. This led Federal Reserve Board chairman Alan Greenspan to warn of "irrational exuberance" in the stock markets (Greenspan 1996), a warning that went largely unheeded until the dot-com meltdown nearly four years later.

Following its IPO, Yahoo! began to grow from a portal site to a comprehensive provider of Web services; it did this both by adding new features to its existing business and by acquiring other businesses. Among its significant acquisitions were the free Web hosting service GeoCitie, and the search engines Inktomi and AltaVista. In recent years, Yahoo!, as befits its role as bellwether for the information economy as a whole, has apparently been in decline; the 2012 appointment of Marissa Mayer as CEO was expected to produce dramatic changes.

Throughout its history, Yahoo! has been involved in a significant amount of litigation that has contributed to the growth of Internet law in general; of the suits in which Yahoo! has been involved, the best-known and most influential is a case in a foreign country: the suits and decisions collectively referred to as the "French Yahoo! case." The French Yahoo! case involved Yahoo's U.S. auction site; some users of the auction site offered Nazi memorabilia for sale on the site. The offering of such materials for sale is illegal in France, and the "French Yahoo! cases," discussed in detail under their own heading in this encyclopedia, raised and addressed fundamental questions regarding freedom of expression in an international medium.

Cases

- *Yahoo!, Inc. v. La Ligue Contre Le Racisme et L'Antisemitisme*, 169 F.Supp.2d 1181 (N.D. Cal. 2001), reversed by *Yahoo! Inc. v. La Ligue Contre Le Racisme Et L'Antisemitisme*, 379 F.3d 1120 (9th Cir. 2004)
- Yaman Akdeniz, *Case Analysis of League against Racism and Antisemitism (LICRA), French Union of Jewish Students, v. Yahoo! Inc. (USA), Yahoo France*, Tribunal de Grande Instance de Paris (The County Court of Paris), Interim Court Order, 20 November 2000, 1 *Electronic Business Law Reports* 110 (2001), download available at http://www.cyber-rights.org/documents (visited December 21, 2012)

See also: .com; French Yahoo! Case

Sources and Further Reading
Karen Angel, *Inside Yahoo! Reinvention and the Road Ahead* (New York: John Wiley & Sons, 2002)
"Remarks by Chairman Alan Greenspan at the Annual Dinner and Francis Boyer Lecture of the American Enterprise Institute

for Public Policy Research," Washington, D.C. (December 5, 1996), available at http://www.federalreserve.gov/boarddocs/speeches/1996/19961205.htm (visited December 21, 2012)

"The History of Yahoo!—How It All Started . . . ," available at http://docs.yahoo.com/info/misc/history.html (visited December 21, 2008)

Andreas Manolopoulos, "Raising 'Cyber-Borders': The Interaction between Law and Technology," 11 *International Journal of Law and Information Technology* 40 (2003)

Julianne Pepitone, "Marissa Mayer: Yahoos Can No Longer Work from Home," CNNMoneyTech (February 25, 2013), available at http://money.cnn.com/2013/02/25/technology/yahoo-work-from-home/index.html?hpt=hp_t1 (visited February 25, 2013)

❖ ZOMBIE ❖

A zombie computer, or zombie, is a computer that has been backdoored for use in denial-of-service attacks, spamming, or other unethical or illegal Internet activity; that is, its security has been compromised and it has become available for use by an outside person. This backdooring is usually accomplished with the use of a worm or Trojan. The person who has backdoored the zombie may seek to add it to a larger group (a zombie army or botnet) for use in denial and degradation of service attacks, spamming, and other online mischief.

In a denial-of-service attack, the zombie sits quietly until it is activated; the user will not notice any difference in performance. If the backdoor is not first detected and removed, the person who created the backdoor, or some other person who is aware of it, may activate it by a signal from outside. The zombie will then attempt to access the Web site upon which the denial-of-service attack is being launched, as will a large number of other zombie computers that have been similarly backdoored and have received the same signal. The goal of a denial-of-service attack is to overwhelm the targeted Web site, which will then be inaccessible to legitimate users wishing to access it; the effect is analogous to constantly telephoning a certain telephone number so that anyone else trying to call that number will receive a busy signal or message service. A denial-of-service attack launched in this way is called a distributed denial-of-service attack.

Pulsing zombies may also be used in denial-of-service attacks. A pulsing zombie attempts to access the target site intermittently rather than continuously. This increases the target site's traffic, making access for legitimate users slower, but not making the site unavailable; an attack of this sort is also called a degradation-of-service attack. A denial-of-service attack is instantly noticeable, but a degradation-of-service attack may go on for months without being noticed. A mild "attack" by pulsing zombies may also be used to make a Web site look more popular than it actually is; like denial-of-service and degradation-of-service attacks, fraud of this sort is detectable.

Another popular use of zombies is as spam mailers. A zombie computer may be used to send email advertising to large numbers of other computers without the user's knowledge; this will continue until the user notices and removes or disables the spamming program, or until the user's ISP notices (perhaps as a result of outside complaints) and shuts off the zombie's Internet access.

The use of zombies presents legal issues in all phases of the process: the installation and operation of the backdoor without the user's consent is illegal, and the purpose for which the zombie is used is often, although not always, illegal as well. Laws in many states criminalize various types of malicious hacking, often equating unlawful, unauthorized access to another person's computer with burglary or criminal trespass. Federal statutes such as the Computer Fraud and Abuse Act (CFAA) impose penalties for computer-specific crimes that cannot readily be defined by analogy to traditional crimes (Schemmel 927–928). Under the CFAA, the use of worms (Morris, 928 F.2d 504) and Trojans is punishable by fines and jail sentences. The CFAA also prohibits the launching of denial-of-service attacks. Of course, proceeding under these statutes against a hacker outside the United States may be difficult.

Statute
- Computer Fraud and Abuse Act, 18 U.S.C. § 1030

Case
- *United States v. Morris*, 928 F.2d 504 (2d Cir. 1991), certiorari denied 502 U.S. 817

See also: Denial-of-Service Attack; Hacking; Malware; Spam; Trojan; Virus; Worm

Sources and Further Reading

Susan W. Brenner, "Toward a Criminal Law for Cyberspace: Distributed Security," 10 *Boston University Journal of Science and Technology Law* 1 (2004)

Tammy J. Schemmel, "WWW.STOPCYBERCRIME.COM: How the USA PATRIOT Act Combats Cyber-Crime," 29 *William Mitchell Law Review* 921 (2003)

This glossary includes selected legal and computer terms that may be unfamiliar; most are also defined where they appear in the text, but do not have entries of their own (an exception is DeCSS). For definitions of other terms, see the subject entries and the Table of Abbreviations in the front matter.

Advergames, advertainment: Games and entertainment that serve as advertising, often through embedded product placement.

Backdoor: Used as a noun, a backdoor is a means of accessing a program or computer that bypasses security measures. Used as a verb, to backdoor is to install or use a backdoor.

Baud: A unit formerly used for measuring modem speeds, named after nineteenth-century French telegraph engineer Jean-Maurice-Emile Baudôt. One baud is one electronic state change per second; for digital transmissions, however, it is more accurate to use bits per second (bps) as a measure, and that is the measure now used. The terms are sometimes, but incorrectly, used interchangeably.

Black hat hacker: A person who gains unauthorized access to a computer system or network for purposes that are not innocuous; the black hat hacker may steal, destroy, or alter information, plant backdoors, or otherwise take advantage of the system's or network's vulnerability.

Captcha (completely automated public Turing test to tell computers and humans apart): A test used to prevent spamming, automated registrations of Web and email addresses, and other abuses of the Internet; it consists of a task that is theoretically possible for humans but impossible for software. For example, a captcha might present a picture of distorted text spelling out a word, and ask the person or program viewing it to type the word; or it might present several images of kittens or airplanes, and ask the viewer to type the word that best describes the subject of the images. As spammers' software grows more sophisticated, captchas have increased in complexity. They are now often impossible for actual humans to figure out, and are thus often derided as worthless.

Certiorari: A writ issued by an appellate or high court to a lower court, directing the lower court to deliver the record in a particular case to the higher court for review; the most common procedural mechanism by which cases come before the U.S. Supreme Court.

Constructive: A term used by courts and lawyers to mean that something will be treated in law as if it exists or has taken place, even if in fact it does not or has not; a person might have constructive knowledge of a fact that he or she does not, in fact, know, if a reasonable person similarly situated would have known the fact or would have been motivated to make further inquiries.

Content Scramble System (CSS): A form of encryption used to protect DVDs from unauthorized copying.

Cracker: A black hat hacker; someone who breaks into protected computers or networks. Also, a person who breaks the copy protection or security software on computer programs, often as part of a warez trading operation, or on DVDs or other protected content.

Damages: Money sought by or awarded to the plaintiff in an action at law as compensation for a loss or injury.

DeCSS: A program for decrypting CSS-encrypted DVDs.

DivX: A method of compressing and decompressing video files that allows movies to be stored in relatively small files; DivX has caused some concern in the motion picture industry because smaller files may more easily be shared over file-sharing networks.

DSL: Digital Subscriber Line; a telephone line used to provide broadband Internet access.

Enjoin: To issue an injunction prohibiting someone from doing something.

Equitable relief: Relief awarded in equity rather than at law; as a practical matter, relief other than damages granted to a party in a lawsuit. An injunction is a form of equitable relief.

Estoppel: A legal device that prevents parties from asserting, and courts from considering, certain claims, defenses, or issues.

File Transfer Protocol (FTP): A protocol used to transfer files from one computer to another.

GNU/Linux: An open-source operating system based on the Linux kernel developed by Linus Torvalds at the University of Helsinki.

Gray hat: A hacker who, having identified a security vulnerability, does not exploit the vulnerability but publicizes it, possibly enabling black hat hackers (or crackers) to take advantage of it if the owner or the vulnerable system or computer does not address the problem promptly.

HTML: Hypertext markup language; the language in which Web pages are written.

HTTP: Hypertext Transfer Protocol; a protocol that runs on top of the TCP/IP layer and enables connected computers to send and receive Web pages.

HTTPS: A secure version of HTTP, in which all communications are encrypted.

Information superhighway, information highway, infobahn: Outdated nicknames for the Internet.

Injunction: A court order requiring or prohibiting a particular act or acts.

Internet Protocol (IP) address: A numeric identifier for a computer attached to the Internet.

Linux: The kernel of Linux-based operating systems such as GNU/Linux; GNU/Linux is often, although not entirely correctly, referred to simply as "Linux." The first syllable should be pronounced "Lynn," not "line."

Password cracker: A computer program used to break into password-protected systems, networks, programs, and files.

Random access memory (RAM): A computer storage device whose contents can be accessed in any order, and which can be both written to and read from; the portion of a computer in which programs and information in use are stored while the computer is turned on.

Read only memory (ROM): A computer storage device that can only be read from, not written to, by the user. Typically used to refer to chips storing BIOS or in game cartridges; also used in the term CD-ROM to refer to programs or data stored on non-rewritable CDs.

Safe harbor: A provision in a statute or regulation that provides immunity from prosecution or liability for persons who meet certain requirements and comply with certain conditions.

Script kiddies: Technically unskilled hackers who use programs written by others in hacking and cracking.

Sub nom.: Abbreviated form of *sub nomine*, Latin for "under the name [of]." Often a case on repeal or remand is decided under a different name than it had been given by the previous court; "sub nom." in a case cite, followed by the new name, indicates the name change.

Subpoena: A court order requiring witnesses to appear or documents to be made available.

TCP/IP: Transmission Control Protocol/Internet Protocol; a two-layer system of protocols that enables inter-networked computers, such as those connected to the Internet, to communicate with each other. The lower layer, IP, routes packets of information toward their correct destination. The upper layer, TCP, divides messages into packets for transmission and reassembles the packets into their original form at the receiving end. It also ensures the reliable delivery of messages by resending lost, dropped, or corrupted packets.

Tort: A civil injury for which the victim may recover damages from the tortfeasor (the person causing the harm).

Tortious: Action that constitutes a tort is tortious.

White hat: A hacker who, having identified a security vulnerability, notifies the owner of the vulnerable system or computer and does not exploit the vulnerability.

WTO: World Trade Organization; an international organization with limited governing authority over trade and economic relations between member states, and a forum for ongoing trade negotiations.

The documents in this section are just a sample of those referred to in this encyclopedia. For information on how to locate other documents, see "How to Find the Law" in the front of this volume.

The documents reproduced here trace parts of two of Internet law's stories: classic content-based censorship and protection of intellectual property rights often intertwined with or perceived as censorship. The Communications Decency Act of 1996 and the Supreme Court's opinion in Reno v. ACLU *are part of the first story: the Declaration was written in part in response to the Act, which was then struck down by the Supreme Court in* Reno. *The Digital Millennium Copyright Act (DMCA), and* Universal City Studios v. Corley *and* MGM v. Grokster *are part of the second story: The WIPO Convention obligated the United States to adopt laws preventing the circumvention of copy-protection measures; § 1201 of the DMCA fulfilled this obligation, and an attempt by activists to have § 1201 limited or declared unconstitutional failed in* Corley. *Neither story has ended there; attempts to control offensive and harmful Internet content are likely to continue, as is the struggle to define the limits of copyright protection and fair use.*

Content-Based Censorship

Communications Decency Act of 1996

When the Internet was new, as now, one of its more disturbing aspects was the amount and nature of pornographic content transmitted over it. In July 1995, Time *magazine's controversial "Cyberporn" issue aggravated fears of Internet pornography. Congress was alarmed by the prospect of minors having unrestricted access to pornography. In 1996, Congress enacted the first of its attempts to control pornographic Internet content: the ill-fated Communications Decency Act (CDA). While a House version of the Act would have limited the prohibition on Internet transmissions to content not protected by the First Amendment, the Senate version was ultimately adopted. It seems almost to have been designed to fail Constitutional scrutiny, or to attempt to force a change in U.S. First Amendment jurisprudence. The statute appears below as originally enacted; in 2003 it was amended in an attempt to bring it into conformity with the First Amendment and the Court's decision in* Reno, *reproduced below. The CDA is discussed in several entries in this encyclopedia, especially in the entry "Communications Decency Act."*

(a) Whoever –

    (1) in interstate or foreign communications –

    ***

    (B) by means of a telecommunications device knowingly –

    (i) makes, creates, or solicits, and

    (ii) initiates the transmission of,

any comment, request, suggestion, proposal, image, or other communication which is obscene or indecent, knowing that the recipient of the communication is under 18 years of age, regardless of whether the maker of such communication placed the call or initiated the communication;

    ***

    (2) knowingly permits any telecommunications facility under his control to be used for any activity prohibited by paragraph (1) with the intent that it be used for such activity,

    shall be fined under Title 18, or imprisoned not more than two years, or both.

    ***

  (d) Whoever –

    (1) in interstate or foreign communications knowingly –

    (A) uses an interactive computer service to send to a specific person or persons under 18 years of age, or

    (B) uses any interactive computer service to display in a manner available to a person under 18 years of age,

    any comment, request, suggestion, proposal, image, or other communication that, in context, depicts or describes, in terms patently offensive as measured by contemporary community standards, sexual or excretory activities or organs, regardless of whether the user of such service placed the call or initiated the communication; or

    (2) knowingly permits any telecommunications facility under such person's control to be used for an activity prohibited by paragraph (1) with the intent that it be used for such activity,

    shall be fined under Title 18, or imprisoned not more than two years, or both.

Source: Communications Decency Act of 1996. Pub.L. 104–104, § 502(2), Title V, § 502, as originally codified at 47 U.S.C. § 223.

Reno v. American Civil Liberties Union, **1997**

No sooner was the Communications Decency Act of 1996 (CDA) enacted than it was challenged by a coalition of First Amendment advocates, including the American Civil Liberties Union (ACLU). At the trial court level, three judges, in three separate opinions, agreed that the statute was unconstitutional. A seven-justice majority of the Supreme Court agreed; two other justices agreed only in part.

The decision below (from which the footnotes and citations have been omitted) is also discussed in the entry "Communications Decency Act." It is interesting not only for its effect on the law of the Internet, but as a historical document. Many of the technical details that take up the first part of the Court's opinion, for example, would probably be dealt with far more quickly today; the Internet is more widely understood. Also interesting is the Court's acceptance of the concept of cyberspace as a place. This way of viewing information networks was essential to the Declaration of the Independence of Cyberspace, just as it was to Neuromancer and other cyberpunk classics, but is almost entirely absent today.

JUSTICE STEVENS DELIVERED THE OPINION OF THE COURT

At issue is the constitutionality of two statutory provisions enacted to protect minors from "indecent" and "patently offensive" communications on the Internet. Notwithstanding the legitimacy and importance of the congressional goal of protecting children from harmful materials, we agree with the three-judge District Court that the statute abridges "the freedom of speech" protected by the First Amendment.

I

The District Court made extensive findings of fact, most of which were based on a detailed stipulation prepared by the parties. The findings describe the character and the dimensions of the Internet, the availability of sexually explicit material in that medium, and the problems confronting age verification for recipients of Internet communications. Because those findings provide the underpinnings for the legal issues, we begin with a summary of the undisputed facts.

The Internet

The Internet is an international network of interconnected computers. It is the outgrowth of what began in 1969 as a military program called "ARPANET," which was designed to enable computers operated by the military, defense contractors, and universities conducting defense-related research to communicate with one another by redundant channels even if some portions of the network were damaged in a war. While the ARPANET no longer exists, it provided an example for the development of a number of civilian networks that, eventually linking with each other, now enable tens of millions of people to communicate with one another and to access vast amounts of information from around the world. The Internet is "a unique and wholly new medium of worldwide human communication."

The Internet has experienced "extraordinary growth." The number of "host" computers—those that store information and relay communications—increased from about 300 in 1981 to approximately 9,400,000 by the time of the trial in 1996. Roughly 60% of these hosts are located in the United States. About 40 million people used the Internet at the time of trial, a number that is expected to mushroom to 200 million by 1999.

Individuals can obtain access to the Internet from many different sources, generally hosts themselves or entities with a host affiliation. Most colleges and universities provide access for their students and faculty; many corporations provide their employees with access through an office network; many communities and local libraries provide free access; and an increasing number of storefront "computer coffee shops" provide access for a small hourly fee. Several major national "online services" such as America Online, CompuServe, the Microsoft Network, and Prodigy offer access to their own extensive proprietary networks as well as a link to the much larger resources of the Internet. These commercial online services had almost 12 million individual subscribers at the time of trial.

Anyone with access to the Internet may take advantage of a wide variety of communication and information retrieval methods. These methods are constantly evolving and difficult to categorize precisely. But, as presently constituted, those most relevant to this case are electronic mail (e-mail), automatic mailing list services ("mail exploders," sometimes referred to as "listservs"), "newsgroups," "chat rooms," and the "World Wide Web." All of these methods can be used to transmit text; most can transmit sound, pictures, and moving video images. Taken together, these tools constitute a unique medium—known to its users as "cyberspace"—located in no particular geographical location but available to anyone, anywhere in the world, with access to the Internet.

E-mail enables an individual to send an electronic message—generally akin to a note or letter—to another individual or to a group of addressees. The message is generally stored electronically, sometimes waiting for the recipient to check her "mailbox" and sometimes making its receipt known through some type of prompt. A mail exploder is a sort of e-mail group. Subscribers can send messages to a common e-mail address, which then forwards the message to the group's other subscribers. Newsgroups also serve groups of regular participants, but these postings may be read by others as well. There are thousands of such groups, each serving to foster an exchange of information or opinion on a particular topic running the gamut from, say, the music of Wagner to Balkan politics to AIDS prevention to the Chicago Bulls. About 100,000 new messages are posted every day. In most newsgroups, postings are automatically purged at regular intervals. In addition to posting a message that can be read later, two or more individuals wishing to communicate more immediately can enter a chat room to engage in real-time dialogue—in other words, by typing messages to one another that appear almost immediately on the others' computer screens. The District Court found that at any given time "tens of thousands of users are engaging in conversations on a huge range of subjects." It is "no exaggeration to conclude that the content on the Internet is as diverse as human thought."

The best known category of communication over the Internet is the World Wide Web, which allows users to search for and retrieve information stored in remote computers, as well as, in some cases, to communicate back to designated sites. In concrete terms, the Web consists of a vast number of documents stored in different computers all over the world. Some of these documents are simply files containing information. However, more elaborate documents, commonly known as Web "pages," are also prevalent. Each has its own address—"rather like a telephone number." Web pages frequently contain information and sometimes allow the viewer to communicate with the page's (or "site's") author. They generally also contain "links" to other documents created by that site's author or to other (generally) related sites. Typically, the links are either blue or underlined text—sometimes images.

Navigating the Web is relatively straightforward. A user may either type the address of a known page or enter one or more keywords into a commercial "search engine" in an effort to locate sites on a subject of interest. A particular Web page may contain the information sought by the "surfer," or, through its links, it may be an avenue to other documents located anywhere on the Internet. Users generally explore a given Web page, or move to another, by clicking a computer "mouse" on one of the page's icons or links. Access to most Web pages is freely available, but some allow access only to those who have purchased the right from a commercial provider. The Web is thus comparable, from the readers' viewpoint, to both a vast library including millions of readily available and indexed publications and a sprawling mall offering goods and services.

From the publishers' point of view, it constitutes a vast platform from which to address and hear from a worldwide audience of millions of readers, viewers, researchers, and buyers. Any person or organization with a computer connected to the Internet can "publish" information. Publishers include government agencies, educational institutions, commercial entities, advocacy groups, and individuals.
***

Sexually Explicit Material

Sexually explicit material on the Internet includes text, pictures, and chat and "extends from the modestly titillating to the hardest-core." These files are created, named, and posted in the same manner as material that is not sexually explicit, and may be accessed either deliberately or unintentionally during the course of an imprecise search. "Once a provider posts its content on the Internet, it cannot prevent that content from entering any community." Thus, for example, "when the UCR/California Museum of Photography posts to its Web site nudes by Edward Weston and Robert Mapplethorpe to announce that its new exhibit will travel to Baltimore and New York City, those images are available not only in Los Angeles, Baltimore, and New York City, but also in Cincinnati, Mobile, or Beijing—wherever Internet users live. Similarly, the safer sex instructions that Critical Path posts to its Web site, written in street language so that the teenage receiver can understand them, are available not just in Philadelphia, but also in Provo and Prague."

Some of the communications over the Internet that originate in foreign countries are also sexually explicit.

Though such material is widely available, users seldom encounter such content accidentally. "A document's title or a description of the document will usually appear before the document itself . . . and in many cases the user will receive detailed information about a site's content before he or she need take the step to access the document. Almost all sexually explicit images are preceded by warnings as to the content." For that reason, the "odds are slim" that a user would enter a sexually explicit site by accident. Unlike communications received by radio or television, "the receipt of information on the Internet requires a series of affirmative steps more deliberate and directed than merely turning a dial. A child requires some sophistication and some ability to read to retrieve material and thereby to use the Internet unattended."

Systems have been developed to help parents control the material that may be available on a home computer with Internet access. A system may either limit a computer's access to an approved list of sources that have been identified as containing no adult material, it may block designated inappropriate sites, or it may attempt to block messages containing identifiable objectionable features. "Although parental control software currently can screen for certain suggestive words or for known sexually explicit sites, it cannot now screen for sexually explicit images." Nevertheless, the evidence indicates that "a reasonably effective method by which parents can prevent their children from accessing sexually explicit and other material which parents may believe is inappropriate for their children will soon be widely available."

Age Verification

The problem of age verification differs for different uses of the Internet. The District Court categorically determined that there "is no effective way to determine the identity or the age of a user who is accessing material through e-mail, mail exploders, newsgroups or chat rooms." The Government offered no evidence that there was a reliable way to screen recipients and participants in such forums for age. Moreover, even if it were technologically feasible to block minors' access to newsgroups and chat rooms containing discussions of art, politics, or other subjects that potentially elicit "indecent" or "patently offensive" contributions, it would not be possible to block their access to that material and "still allow them access to the remaining content, even if the overwhelming majority of that content was not indecent."

Technology exists by which an operator of a Web site may condition access on the verification of requested information such as a credit card number or an adult password. Credit card verification is only feasible, however, either in connection with a commercial transaction in which the card is used, or by payment to a verification agency. Using credit card possession as a surrogate for proof of age would impose costs on noncommercial Web sites that would require many of them to shut down. For that reason, at the time of the trial, credit card verification was "effectively unavailable to a substantial number of Internet content providers." Moreover, the imposition of such a requirement "would completely bar adults who do not have a credit card and lack the resources to obtain one from accessing any blocked material."

Commercial pornographic sites that charge their users for access have assigned them passwords as a method of age verification. The record does not contain any evidence concerning the reliability of these technologies. Even if passwords are effective for commercial purveyors of indecent material, the District Court found that an adult password requirement would impose significant burdens on noncommercial sites, both because they would discourage users from accessing their sites and because the cost of creating and maintaining such screening systems would be "beyond their reach."

In sum, the District Court found: "Even if credit card verification or adult password verification were implemented, the Government presented no testimony as to how such systems could ensure that the user of the password or credit card is in fact over 18. The burdens imposed by credit card verification and adult password verification systems make them effectively unavailable to a substantial number of Internet content providers."

II

The Telecommunications Act of 1996 was an unusually important legislative enactment. As stated on the first of its 103 pages, its primary purpose was to reduce regulation and encourage "the rapid deployment of new telecommunications technologies." The major components of the statute have nothing to do with the Internet; they were designed to promote competition in the local telephone service market, the multichannel video market, and the market for over-the-air broadcasting. The Act includes seven Titles, six of which are the product of extensive committee hearings and the subject of discussion in Reports prepared by Committees of the Senate and the House of Representatives. By contrast, Title V—known as the "Communications Decency Act of 1996" (CDA)—contains provisions that were either added in executive committee after the hearings were concluded or as amendments offered during floor debate on the legislation. An amendment offered in the Senate was the source of the two statutory provisions challenged in this case. They are informally described as the "indecent transmission" provision and the "patently offensive display" provision.

The first, 47 U.S.C. § 223(a), prohibits the knowing transmission of obscene or indecent messages to any recipient under 18 years of age. It provides in pertinent part:

"(a) Whoever –
"(1) in interstate or foreign communications –
. . . . .
"(B) by means of a telecommunications device knowingly –

"(i) makes, creates, or solicits, and
"(ii) initiates the transmission of,
"any comment, request, suggestion, proposal, image, or other communication which is obscene or indecent, knowing that the recipient of the communication is under 18 years of age, regardless of whether the maker of such communication placed the call or initiated the communication;

. . . . .

"(2) knowingly permits any telecommunications facility under his control to be used for any activity prohibited by paragraph (1) with the intent that it be used for such activity,
"shall be fined under Title 18, or imprisoned not more than two years, or both."

The second provision, § 223(d), prohibits the knowing sending or displaying of patently offensive messages in a manner that is available to a person under 18 years of age. It provides:

"(d) Whoever –
"(1) in interstate or foreign communications knowingly –
"(A) uses an interactive computer service to send to a specific person or persons under 18 years of age, or
"(B) uses any interactive computer service to display in a manner available to a person under 18 years of age,
"any comment, request, suggestion, proposal, image, or other communication that, in context, depicts or describes, in terms patently offensive as measured by contemporary community standards, sexual or excretory activities or organs, regardless of whether the user of such service placed the call or initiated the communication; or
"(2) knowingly permits any telecommunications facility under such person's control to be used for an activity prohibited by paragraph (1) with the intent that it be used for such activity,
"shall be fined under Title 18, or imprisoned not more than two years, or both."

The breadth of these prohibitions is qualified by two affirmative defenses. See § 223(e)(5). One covers those who take "good faith, reasonable, effective, and appropriate actions" to restrict access by minors to the prohibited communications. § 223(e)(5)(A). The other covers those who restrict access to covered material by requiring certain designated forms of age proof, such as a verified credit card or an adult identification number or code. § 223(e)(5)(B).

III

On February 8, 1996, immediately after the President signed the statute, 20 plaintiffs filed suit against the Attorney General of the United States and the Department of Justice challenging the constitutionality of §§ 223(a)(1) and 223(d). A week later, based on his conclusion that the term "indecent" was too vague to provide the basis for a criminal prosecution, District Judge Buckwalter entered a temporary restraining order against enforcement of § 223(a)(1) (B)(ii) insofar as it applies to indecent communications. A second suit was then filed by 27 additional plaintiffs, the two cases were consolidated, and a three-judge District Court was convened pursuant to § 561 of the CDA. After an evidentiary hearing, that court entered a preliminary injunction against enforcement of both of the challenged provisions. Each of the three judges wrote a separate opinion, but their judgment was unanimous.

* * *

The judgment of the District Court enjoins the Government from enforcing the prohibitions in § 223(a)(1)(B) insofar as they relate to "indecent" communications, but expressly preserves the Government's right to investigate and prosecute the obscenity or child pornography activities prohibited therein. The injunction against enforcement of §§ 223(d)(1) and (2) is unqualified because those provisions contain no separate reference to obscenity or child pornography.

The Government appealed under the CDA's special review provisions, and we noted probable jurisdiction. In its appeal, the Government argues that the District Court erred in holding that the CDA violated both the First Amendment because it is overbroad and the Fifth Amendment because it is vague. While we discuss the vagueness of the CDA because of its relevance to the First Amendment overbreadth inquiry, we conclude that the judgment should be affirmed without reaching the Fifth Amendment issue. We begin our analysis by reviewing the principal authorities on which the Government relies. Then, after describing the overbreadth of the CDA, we consider the Government's specific contentions, including its submission that we save portions of the statute either by severance or by fashioning judicial limitations on the scope of its coverage.

IV

In arguing for reversal, the Government contends that the CDA is plainly constitutional under three of our prior decisions: (1) *Ginsberg v. New York;* (2) *FCC v. Pacifica Foundation;* and (3) *Renton v. Playtime Theatres, Inc.* A close look at these cases, however, raises— rather than relieves—doubts concerning the constitutionality of the CDA.

In *Ginsberg,* we upheld the constitutionality of a New York statute that prohibited selling to minors under 17 years of age material that was considered obscene as to them even if not obscene as to adults. We rejected the defendant's broad submission that "the scope of the constitutional freedom of expression secured to a citizen to read or see material concerned with sex cannot be made to depend on whether the citizen is an adult or a minor." In rejecting that contention, we relied not only on the State's independent interest in the well-being of its youth, but also on our consistent recognition of the principle that "the parents' claim to authority in their own household to direct the rearing of their children is basic in the structure of our society."

In four important respects, the statute upheld in *Ginsberg* was narrower than the CDA. First, we noted in *Ginsberg* that "the prohibition against sales to minors does not bar parents who so desire from purchasing the magazines for their children." Under the CDA, by contrast, neither the parents' consent—nor even their participation—in the communication would avoid the application of the statute. Second, the New York statute applied only to commercial transactions, whereas the CDA contains no such limitation. Third, the New York statute cabined its definition of material that is harmful to minors with the requirement that it be "utterly without redeeming social importance for minors." The CDA fails to provide us with any definition of the term "indecent" as used in § 223(a)(1) and, importantly, omits any requirement that the "patently offensive" material covered by § 223(d) lack serious literary, artistic, political, or scientific value. Fourth, the New York statute defined a minor as a person under the age of 17, whereas the CDA, in applying to all those under 18 years, includes an additional year of those nearest majority.

In *Pacifica,* we upheld a declaratory order of the Federal Communications Commission, holding that the broadcast of a recording of a 12-minute monologue entitled "Filthy Words" that had previously been delivered to a live audience "could have been the subject of administrative sanctions." The Commission had found that the repetitive use of certain words referring to excretory or sexual activities or organs "in an afternoon broadcast when children are in the audience was patently offensive" and concluded that the monologue was indecent "as broadcast." The respondent did not quarrel with the finding that the afternoon broadcast was patently offensive, but contended that it was not "indecent" within the meaning of the relevant statutes because it contained no prurient appeal. After rejecting respondent's statutory arguments, we confronted its two constitutional arguments: (1) that the Commission's construction of its authority to ban indecent speech was so broad that its order had to be set aside even if the broadcast at issue was unprotected; and (2) that since the recording was not obscene, the First Amendment forbade any abridgment of the right to broadcast it on the radio.

In the portion of the lead opinion not joined by Justices Powell and Blackmun, the plurality stated that the First Amendment does not prohibit all governmental regulation that depends on the content of speech. Accordingly, the availability of constitutional protection for a vulgar and offensive monologue that was not obscene depended on the context of the broadcast. Relying on the premise that "of all forms of communication" broadcasting had received the most limited First Amendment protection, the Court concluded that the ease with which children may obtain access to broadcasts, "coupled with the concerns recognized in *Ginsberg,*" justified special treatment of indecent broadcasting.

As with the New York statute at issue in *Ginsberg,* there are significant differences between the order upheld in *Pacifica* and the CDA. First, the order in *Pacifica,* issued by an agency that had been regulating radio stations for decades, targeted a specific broadcast that represented a rather dramatic departure from traditional program content in order to designate when—rather than whether—it would be permissible to air such a program in that particular medium. The CDA's broad categorical prohibitions are not limited to particular times and are not dependent on any evaluation by an agency familiar with the unique characteristics of the Internet. Second, unlike the CDA, the Commission's declaratory order was not punitive; we expressly refused to decide whether the indecent broadcast "would justify a criminal prosecution." Finally, the Commission's order applied to a medium which as a matter of history had "received the most limited First Amendment protection," in large part because warnings could not adequately protect the listener from unexpected program content. The Internet, however, has no comparable history. Moreover, the District Court found that the risk of encountering indecent material by accident is remote because a series of affirmative steps is required to access specific material.

In *Renton,* we upheld a zoning ordinance that kept adult movie theaters out of residential neighborhoods. The ordinance was aimed, not at the content of the films shown in the theaters, but rather at the "secondary effects"—such as crime and deteriorating property values—that these theaters fostered: "'It is th[e] secondary effect which these zoning ordinances attempt to avoid, not the dissemination of "offensive" speech.'" According to the Government, the CDA is constitutional because it constitutes a sort of "cyberzoning" on the Internet. But the CDA applies broadly to the entire universe of cyberspace. And the purpose of the CDA is to protect children from the primary effects of "indecent" and "patently offensive" speech, rather than any "secondary" effect of such speech. Thus, the CDA is a content-based blanket restriction on speech, and, as such, cannot be "properly analyzed as a form of time, place, and manner regulation."

***

These precedents, then, surely do not require us to uphold the CDA and are fully consistent with the application of the most stringent review of its provisions.

V

In *Southeastern Promotions, Ltd. v. Conrad* we observed that "[e]ach medium of expression . . . may present its own problems." Thus, some of our cases have recognized special justifications for regulation of the broadcast media that are not applicable to other speakers. In these cases, the Court relied on the history of extensive Government regulation of the broadcast medium; the scarcity of available frequencies at its inception; and its "invasive" nature.

Those factors are not present in cyberspace. Neither before nor after the enactment of the CDA have the vast democratic forums of the Internet been subject to the type of government supervision and regulation that has attended the broadcast industry. Moreover, the Internet is not as "invasive" as radio or television. The District Court specifically found that "[c]ommunications over the Internet do not 'invade' an individual's home or appear on one's computer screen unbidden. Users seldom encounter content 'by accident'.' It also found that "[a]lmost all sexually explicit images are preceded by warnings as to the content," and cited testimony that "'odds are slim' that a user would come across a sexually explicit sight by accident."

We distinguished *Pacifica* in *Sable* on just this basis. In *Sable,* a company engaged in the business of offering sexually oriented prerecorded telephone messages (popularly known as "dial-a-porn") challenged the constitutionality of an amendment to the Communications Act of 1934 that imposed a blanket prohibition on indecent as well as obscene interstate commercial telephone messages. We held that the statute was constitutional insofar as it applied to obscene messages but invalid as applied to indecent messages. In attempting to justify the complete ban and criminalization of indecent commercial telephone messages, the Government relied on *Pacifica,* arguing that the ban was necessary to prevent children from gaining access to such messages. We agreed that "there is a compelling interest in protecting the physical and psychological well-being of minors" which extended to shielding them from indecent messages that are not obscene by adult standards, but distinguished our "emphatically narrow holding" in *Pacifica* because it did not involve a complete ban and because it involved a different medium of communication. We explained that "the dial-it medium requires the listener to take affirmative steps to receive the communication." "Placing a telephone call," we continued, "is not the same as turning on a radio and being taken by surprise by an indecent message."

Finally, unlike the conditions that prevailed when Congress first authorized regulation of the broadcast spectrum, the Internet can hardly be considered a "scarce" expressive commodity. It provides relatively unlimited, low-cost capacity for communication of all kinds. The Government estimates that "[a]s many as 40 million people use the Internet today, and that figure is expected to grow to 200 million by 1999." This dynamic, multifaceted category of communication includes not only traditional print and news services, but also audio, video, and still images, as well as interactive, real-time dialogue. Through the use of chat rooms, any person with a phone line can become a town crier with a voice that resonates farther than it could from any soapbox. Through the use of Web pages, mail exploders, and newsgroups, the same individual can become a pamphleteer. As the District Court found, "the content on the Internet is as diverse as human thought." We agree with its conclusion that our cases provide no basis for qualifying the level of First Amendment scrutiny that should be applied to this medium.

VI

Regardless of whether the CDA is so vague that it violates the Fifth Amendment, the many ambiguities concerning the scope of its coverage render it problematic for purposes of the First Amendment. For instance, each of the two parts of the CDA uses a different linguistic form. The first uses the word "indecent," while the second speaks of material that "in context, depicts or describes, in terms patently offensive as measured by contemporary community standards, sexual or excretory activities or organs," § 223(d). Given the absence of a definition of either term, this difference in language will provoke uncertainty among speakers about how the two standards relate to each other and just what they mean. Could a speaker confidently assume that a serious discussion about birth control practices, homosexuality, the First Amendment issues raised by the Appendix to our *Pacifica* opinion, or the consequences of prison rape would not violate the CDA? This uncertainty undermines the likelihood that the CDA has been carefully tailored to the congressional goal of protecting minors from potentially harmful materials.

The vagueness of the CDA is a matter of special concern for two reasons. First, the CDA is a content-based regulation of speech. The vagueness of such a regulation raises special First Amendment concerns because of its obvious chilling effect on free speech. Second, the CDA is a criminal statute. In addition to the opprobrium and stigma of a criminal conviction, the CDA threatens violators with penalties including up to two years in prison for each act of violation. The severity of criminal sanctions may well cause speakers to remain silent rather than communicate even arguably unlawful words, ideas, and images. As a practical matter, this increased deterrent effect, coupled with the "risk of discriminatory enforcement" of vague regulations, poses greater First Amendment concerns than those implicated by the civil regulation reviewed in *Denver Area Ed. Telecommunications Consortium, Inc. v. FCC.*

The Government argues that the statute is no more vague than the obscenity standard this Court established in *Miller v. California*. But that is not so. In *Miller*, this Court reviewed a criminal conviction against a commercial vendor who mailed brochures containing pictures of sexually explicit activities to individuals who had not requested such materials. Having struggled for some time to establish a definition of obscenity, we set forth in *Miller* the test for obscenity that controls to this day:

"(a) whether the average person, applying contemporary community standards would find that the work, taken as a whole, appeals to the prurient interest; (b) whether the work depicts or describes, in a patently offensive way, sexual conduct specifically defined by the applicable state law; and (c)

whether the work, taken as a whole, lacks serious literary, artistic, political, or scientific value."

Because the CDA's "patently offensive" standard (and, we assume, *arguendo*, its synonymous "indecent" standard) is one part of the three-prong *Miller* test, the Government reasons, it cannot be unconstitutionally vague.

The Government's assertion is incorrect as a matter of fact. The second prong of the *Miller* test—the purportedly analogous standard—contains a critical requirement that is omitted from the CDA: that the proscribed material be "specifically defined by the applicable state law." This requirement reduces the vagueness inherent in the open-ended term "patently offensive" as used in the CDA. Moreover, the *Miller* definition is limited to "sexual conduct," whereas the CDA extends also to include (1) "excretory activities" as well as (2) "organs" of both a sexual and excretory nature.

The Government's reasoning is also flawed. Just because a definition including three limitations is not vague, it does not follow that one of those limitations, standing by itself, is not vague. Each of *Miller*'s additional two prongs—(1) that, taken as a whole, the material appeal to the "prurient" interest, and (2) that it "lac[k] serious literary, artistic, political, or scientific value"—critically limits the uncertain sweep of the obscenity definition. The second requirement is particularly important because, unlike the "patently offensive" and "prurient interest" criteria, it is not judged by contemporary community standards. This "societal value" requirement, absent in the CDA, allows appellate courts to impose some limitations and regularity on the definition by setting, as a matter of law, a national floor for socially redeeming value. The Government's contention that courts will be able to give such legal limitations to the CDA's standards is belied by *Miller*'s own rationale for having juries determine whether material is "patently offensive" according to community standards: that such questions are essentially ones of fact.

In contrast to *Miller* and our other previous cases, the CDA thus presents a greater threat of censoring speech that, in fact, falls outside the statute's scope. Given the vague contours of the coverage of the statute, it unquestionably silences some speakers whose messages would be entitled to constitutional protection. That danger provides further reason for insisting that the statute not be overly broad. The CDA's burden on protected speech cannot be justified if it could be avoided by a more carefully drafted statute.

VII

We are persuaded that the CDA lacks the precision that the First Amendment requires when a statute regulates the content of speech. In order to deny minors access to potentially harmful speech, the CDA effectively suppresses a large amount of speech that adults have a constitutional right to receive and to address to one another. That burden on adult speech is unacceptable if less restrictive alternatives would be at least as effective in achieving the legitimate purpose that the statute was enacted to serve.

In evaluating the free speech rights of adults, we have made it perfectly clear that "[s]exual expression which is indecent but not obscene is protected by the First Amendment." Indeed, *Pacifica* itself admonished that "the fact that society may find speech offensive is not a sufficient reason for suppressing it."

It is true that we have repeatedly recognized the governmental interest in protecting children from harmful materials. But that interest does not justify an unnecessarily broad suppression of speech addressed to adults. As we have explained, the Government may not "reduc[e] the adult population . . . to . . . only what is fit for children." "[R]egardless of the strength of the government's interest" in protecting children, "[t]he level of discourse reaching a mailbox simply cannot be limited to that which would be suitable for a sandbox."

The District Court was correct to conclude that the CDA effectively resembles the ban on "dial-a-porn" invalidated in *Sable*. In *Sable,* this Court rejected the argument that we should defer to the congressional judgment that nothing less than a total ban would be effective in preventing enterprising youngsters from gaining access to indecent communications. *Sable* thus made clear that the mere fact that a statutory regulation of speech was enacted for the important purpose of protecting children from exposure to sexually explicit material does not foreclose inquiry into its validity. As we pointed out last Term, that inquiry embodies an "overarching commitment" to make sure that Congress has designed its statute to accomplish its purpose "without imposing an unnecessarily great restriction on speech."

In arguing that the CDA does not so diminish adult communication, the Government relies on the incorrect factual premise that prohibiting a transmission whenever it is known that one of its recipients is a minor would not interfere with adult-to-adult communication. The findings of the District Court make clear that this premise is untenable. Given the size of the potential audience for most messages, in the absence of a viable age verification process, the sender must be charged with knowing that one or more minors will likely view it. Knowledge that, for instance, one or more members of a 100-person chat group will be a minor—and therefore that it would be a crime to send the group an indecent message—would surely burden communication among adults.

The District Court found that at the time of trial existing technology did not include any effective method for a sender to prevent minors from obtaining access to its communications on the Internet without also denying access to adults. The Court found no effective way to determine the age of a user who is accessing material through e-mail, mail exploders, newsgroups, or chat rooms. As a practical matter, the Court also found that it would be prohibitively expensive for noncommercial—as well as some commercial—speakers who have Web sites to verify that their users are adults. These limitations must inevitably curtail a significant amount of adult communication on the Internet. By contrast, the District Court found that "[d]espite its limitations, currently available user-based software suggests that a reasonably effective method by which parents can prevent their children from accessing sexually explicit and other material which parents may believe is inappropriate for their children will soon be widely available."

The breadth of the CDA's coverage is wholly unprecedented. Unlike the regulations upheld in *Ginsberg* and *Pacifica,* the scope of the CDA is not limited to commercial speech or commercial entities. Its open-ended prohibitions embrace all nonprofit entities and individuals posting indecent messages or displaying them on their own computers in the presence of minors. The general, undefined terms "indecent" and "patently offensive" cover large amounts of nonpornographic material with serious educational or other value. Moreover, the "community standards" criterion as applied to the Internet means that any communication available to a nationwide audience will be judged by the standards of the community most likely to be offended by the message. The regulated subject matter includes any of the seven "dirty words" used in the *Pacifica* monologue, the use of which the Government's expert acknowledged

could constitute a felony. It may also extend to discussions about prison rape or safe sexual practices, artistic images that include nude subjects, and arguably the card catalog of the Carnegie Library.

For the purposes of our decision, we need neither accept nor reject the Government's submission that the First Amendment does not forbid a blanket prohibition on all "indecent" and "patently offensive" messages communicated to a 17-year-old—no matter how much value the message may contain and regardless of parental approval. It is at least clear that the strength of the Government's interest in protecting minors is not equally strong throughout the coverage of this broad statute. Under the CDA, a parent allowing her 17-year-old to use the family computer to obtain information on the Internet that she, in her parental judgment, deems appropriate could face a lengthy prison term. Similarly, a parent who sent his 17-year-old college freshman information on birth control via e-mail could be incarcerated even though neither he, his child, nor anyone in their home community found the material "indecent" or "patently offensive," if the college town's community thought otherwise.

The breadth of this content-based restriction of speech imposes an especially heavy burden on the Government to explain why a less restrictive provision would not be as effective as the CDA. It has not done so. The arguments in this Court have referred to possible alternatives such as requiring that indecent material be "tagged" in a way that facilitates parental control of material coming into their homes, making exceptions for messages with artistic or educational value, providing some tolerance for parental choice, and regulating some portions of the Internet—such as commercial Web sites—differently from others, such as chat rooms. Particularly in the light of the absence of any detailed findings by the Congress, or even hearings addressing the special problems of the CDA, we are persuaded that the CDA is not narrowly tailored if that requirement has any meaning at all.

VIII

In an attempt to curtail the CDA's facial overbreadth, the Government advances three additional arguments for sustaining the Act's affirmative prohibitions: (1) that the CDA is constitutional because it leaves open ample "alternative channels" of communication; (2) that the plain meaning of the CDA's "knowledge" and "specific person" requirement significantly restricts its permissible applications; and (3) that the CDA's prohibitions are "almost always" limited to material lacking redeeming social value.

The Government first contends that, even though the CDA effectively censors discourse on many of the Internet's modalities—such as chat groups, newsgroups, and mail exploders—it is nonetheless constitutional because it provides a "reasonable opportunity" for speakers to engage in the restricted speech on the World Wide Web. This argument is unpersuasive because the CDA regulates speech on the basis of its content. A "time, place, and manner" analysis is therefore inapplicable. It is thus immaterial whether such speech would be feasible on the Web (which, as the Government's own expert acknowledged, would cost up to $10,000 if the speaker's interests were not accommodated by an existing Web site, not including costs for data base management and age verification). The Government's position is equivalent to arguing that a statute could ban leaflets on certain subjects as long as individuals are free to publish books. In invalidating a number of laws that banned leafletting on the streets regardless of their content, we explained that "one is not to have the exercise of his liberty of expression in appropriate places abridged on the plea that it may be exercised in some other place."

The Government also asserts that the "knowledge" requirement of both §§ 223(a) and (d), especially when coupled with the "specific child" element found in § 223(d), saves the CDA from overbreadth. Because both sections prohibit the dissemination of indecent messages only to persons known to be under 18, the Government argues, it does not require transmitters to "refrain from communicating indecent material to adults; they need only refrain from disseminating such materials to persons they know to be under 18." This argument ignores the fact that most Internet forums—including chat rooms, newsgroups, mail exploders, and the Web—are open to all comers. The Government's assertion that the knowledge requirement somehow protects the communications of adults is therefore untenable. Even the strongest reading of the "specific person" requirement of § 223(d) cannot save the statute. It would confer broad powers of censorship, in the form of a "heckler's veto," upon any opponent of indecent speech who might simply log on and inform the would-be discoursers that his 17-year-old child—a "specific person . . . under 18 years of age,"—would be present.

Finally, we find no textual support for the Government's submission that material having scientific, educational, or other redeeming social value will necessarily fall outside the CDA's "patently offensive" and "indecent" prohibitions.

IX

The Government's three remaining arguments focus on the defenses provided in § 223(e)(5). First, relying on the "good faith, reasonable, effective, and appropriate actions" provision, the Government suggests that "tagging" provides a defense that saves the constitutionality of the CDA. The suggestion assumes that transmitters may encode their indecent communications in a way that would indicate their contents, thus permitting recipients to block their reception with appropriate software. It is the requirement that the good-faith action must be "effective" that makes this defense illusory. The Government recognizes that its proposed screening software does not currently exist. Even if it did, there is no way to know whether a potential recipient will actually block the encoded material. Without the impossible knowledge that every guardian in America is screening for the "tag," the transmitter could not reasonably rely on its action to be "effective."

For its second and third arguments concerning defenses—which we can consider together—the Government relies on the latter half of § 223(e)(5), which applies when the transmitter has restricted access by requiring use of a verified credit card or adult identification. Such verification is not only technologically available but actually is used by commercial providers of sexually explicit material. These providers, therefore, would be protected by the defense. Under the findings of the District Court, however, it is not economically feasible for most noncommercial speakers to employ such verification. Accordingly, this defense would not significantly narrow the statute's burden on noncommercial speech. Even with respect to the commercial pornographers that would be protected by the defense, the Government failed to adduce any evidence that these verification techniques actually preclude minors from posing as adults. Given that the risk of criminal sanctions "hovers over each content provider, like the proverbial sword of Damocles," the District Court correctly refused to rely on unproven future technology to save the statute. The Government thus failed to prove that the proffered defense would significantly reduce the heavy burden on adult speech produced by the prohibition on offensive displays.

We agree with the District Court's conclusion that the CDA places an unacceptably heavy burden on protected speech, and that the defenses do not constitute the sort of "narrow tailoring" that will save an otherwise patently invalid unconstitutional provision. In *Sable,* we remarked that the speech restriction at issue there amounted to " 'burn[ing] the house to roast the pig.' " The CDA, casting a far darker shadow over free speech, threatens to torch a large segment of the Internet community.

X

At oral argument, the Government relied heavily on its ultimate fall-back position: If this Court should conclude that the CDA is insufficiently tailored, it urged, we should save the statute's constitutionality by honoring the severability clause, see 47 U.S.C. § 608, and construing nonseverable terms narrowly. In only one respect is this argument acceptable.

A severability clause requires textual provisions that can be severed. We will follow § 608's guidance by leaving constitutional textual elements of the statute intact in the one place where they are, in fact, severable. The "indecency" provision, 47 U.S.C. § 223(a), applies to "any comment, request, suggestion, proposal, image, or other communication which is obscene or indecent." (Emphasis added.) Appellees do not challenge the application of the statute to obscene speech, which, they acknowledge, can be banned totally because it enjoys no First Amendment protection. As set forth by the statute, the restriction of "obscene" material enjoys a textual manifestation separate from that for "indecent" material, which we have held unconstitutional. Therefore, we will sever the term "or indecent" from the statute, leaving the rest of § 223(a) standing. In no other respect, however, can § 223(a) or § 223(d) be saved by such a textual surgery.

The Government also draws on an additional, less traditional aspect of the CDA's severability clause, 47 U.S.C. § 608, which asks any reviewing court that holds the statute facially unconstitutional not to invalidate the CDA in application to "other persons or circumstances" that might be constitutionally permissible. It further invokes this Court's admonition that, absent "countervailing considerations," a statute should "be declared invalid to the extent it reaches too far, but otherwise left intact." There are two flaws in this argument.

First, the statute that grants our jurisdiction for this expedited review. . . limits that jurisdictional grant to actions challenging the CDA "on its face." Consistent with § 561, the plaintiffs who brought this suit and the three-judge panel that decided it treated it as a facial challenge. We have no authority, in this particular posture, to convert this litigation into an "as-applied" challenge. Nor, given the vast array of plaintiffs, the range of their expressive activities, and the vagueness of the statute, would it be practicable to limit our holding to a judicially defined set of specific applications.

Second, one of the "countervailing considerations" mentioned in *Brockett* is present here. In considering a facial challenge, this Court may impose a limiting construction on a statute only if it is "readily susceptible" to such a construction. The open-ended character of the CDA provides no guidance whatever for limiting its coverage.

This case is therefore unlike those in which we have construed a statute narrowly because the text or other source of congressional intent identified a clear line that this Court could draw. Rather, our decision in *United States v. National Treasury Employees Union* is applicable. In that case, we declined to "dra[w] one or more lines between categories of speech covered by an overly broad statute, when Congress has sent inconsistent signals as to where the new line or lines should be drawn" because doing so "involves a far more serious invasion of the legislative domain." This Court "will not rewrite a . . . law to conform it to constitutional requirements."

XI

In this Court, though not in the District Court, the Government asserts that—in addition to its interest in protecting children—its "[e]qually significant" interest in fostering the growth of the Internet provides an independent basis for upholding the constitutionality of the CDA. The Government apparently assumes that the unregulated availability of "indecent" and "patently offensive" material on the Internet is driving countless citizens away from the medium because of the risk of exposing themselves or their children to harmful material.

We find this argument singularly unpersuasive. The dramatic expansion of this new marketplace of ideas contradicts the factual basis of this contention. The record demonstrates that the growth of the Internet has been and continues to be phenomenal. As a matter of constitutional tradition, in the absence of evidence to the contrary, we presume that governmental regulation of the content of speech is more likely to interfere with the free exchange of ideas than to encourage it. The interest in encouraging freedom of expression in a democratic society outweighs any theoretical but unproven benefit of censorship.

For the foregoing reasons, the judgment of the District Court is affirmed.

It is so ordered.

Justice O'Connor, with whom the Chief Justice [Rehnquist] joins, concurring in the judgment in part and dissenting in part.

I write separately to explain why I view the Communications Decency Act of 1996 (CDA) as little more than an attempt by Congress to create "adult zones" on the Internet. Our precedent indicates that the creation of such zones can be constitutionally sound. Despite the soundness of its purpose, however, portions of the CDA are unconstitutional because they stray from the blueprint our prior cases have developed for constructing a "zoning law" that passes constitutional muster.

Appellees bring a facial challenge to three provisions of the CDA. The first, which the Court describes as the "indecency transmission" provision, makes it a crime to knowingly transmit an obscene or indecent message or image to a person the sender knows is under 18 years old. What the Court classifies as a single "patently offensive display provision, see ante, at 2338, is in reality two separate provisions. The first of these makes it a crime to knowingly send a patently offensive message or image to a specific person under the age of 18 ("specific person" provision). The second criminalizes the display of patently offensive messages or images "in a[ny] manner available" to minors ("display" provision). None of these provisions purports to keep indecent (or patently offensive) material away from adults, who have a First Amendment right to obtain this speech. Thus, the undeniable purpose of the CDA is to segregate indecent material on the Internet into certain areas that minors cannot access.

The creation of "adult zones" is by no means a novel concept. States have long denied minors access to certain establishments frequented by adults. States have also denied minors access to speech deemed to be "harmful to minors." The Court has previously sustained such zoning laws, but only if they respect the First Amendment rights of adults and minors. That is to say, a zoning law is valid if (i) it does not unduly restrict adult access to the material; and (ii) minors have no First Amendment right to read or view the banned material. As applied to the Internet as it exists in 1997, the "display" provision and some applications of the "indecency transmission" and "specific person" provisions fail to adhere to the first of these limiting principles by restricting adults' access to protected materials in certain circumstances. Unlike the Court, however, I would invalidate the provisions only in those circumstances.

Our cases make clear that a "zoning" law is valid only if adults are still able to obtain the regulated speech. If they cannot, the law does more than simply keep children away from speech they have no right to obtain—it interferes with the rights of adults to obtain constitutionally protected speech and effectively "reduce[s] the adult population . . . to reading only what is fit for children." The First Amendment does not tolerate such interference. If the law does not unduly restrict adults' access to constitutionally protected speech, however, it may be valid. In *Ginsberg v. New York*, for example, the Court sustained a New York law that barred store owners from selling pornographic magazines to minors in part because adults could still buy those magazines.

The Court in *Ginsberg* concluded that the New York law created a constitutionally adequate adult zone simply because, on its face, it denied access only to minors. The Court did not question—and therefore necessarily assumed—that an adult zone, once created, would succeed in preserving adults' access while denying minors' access to the regulated speech. Before today, there was no reason to question this assumption, for the Court has previously only considered laws that operated in the physical world, a world that with two characteristics that make it possible to create "adult zones": geography and identity. A minor can see an adult dance show only if he enters an establishment that provides such entertainment. And should he attempt to do so, the minor will not be able to conceal completely his identity (or, consequently, his age). Thus, the twin characteristics of geography and identity enable the establishment's proprietor to prevent children from entering the establishment, but to let adults inside.

The electronic world is fundamentally different. Because it is no more than the interconnection of electronic pathways, cyberspace allows speakers and listeners to mask their identities. Cyberspace undeniably reflects some form of geography; chat rooms and Web sites, for example, exist at fixed "locations" on the Internet. Since users can transmit and receive messages on the Internet without revealing anything about their identities or ages, however, it is not currently possible to exclude persons from accessing certain messages on the basis of their identity.

Cyberspace differs from the physical world in another basic way: Cyberspace is malleable. Thus, it is possible to construct barriers in cyberspace and use them to screen for identity, making cyberspace more like the physical world and, consequently, more amenable to zoning laws. This transformation of cyberspace is already underway. Internet speakers (users who post material on the Internet) have begun to zone cyberspace itself through the use of "gateway" technology. Such technology requires Internet users to enter information about themselves—perhaps an adult identification number or a credit card number—before they can access certain areas of cyberspace, much like a bouncer checks a person's driver's license before admitting him to a nightclub. Internet users who access information have not attempted to zone cyberspace itself, but have tried to limit their own power to access information in cyberspace, much as a parent controls what her children watch on television by installing a lock box. This user-based zoning is accomplished through the use of screening software (such as Cyber Patrol or SurfWatch) or browsers with screening capabilities, both of which search addresses and text for keywords that are associated with "adult" sites and, if the user wishes, blocks access to such sites. The Platform for Internet Content Selection project is designed to facilitate user-based zoning by encouraging Internet speakers to rate the content of their speech using codes recognized by all screening programs.

Despite this progress, the transformation of cyberspace is not complete. Although gateway technology has been available on the World Wide Web for some time now, it is not available to all Web speakers, and is just now becoming technologically feasible for chat rooms and USENET newsgroups. Gateway technology is not ubiquitous in cyberspace, and because without it "there is no means of age verification," cyberspace still remains largely unzoned—and unzoneable. User-based zoning is also in its infancy. For it to be effective, (i) an agreed-upon code (or "tag") would have to exist; (ii) screening software or browsers with screening capabilities would have to be able to recognize the "tag"; and (iii) those programs would have to be widely available—and widely used—by Internet users. At present, none of these conditions is true. Screening software "is not in wide use today" and "only a handful of browsers have screening capabilities." There is, moreover, no agreed-upon "tag" for those programs to recognize.

Although the prospects for the eventual zoning of the Internet appear promising, I agree with the Court that we must evaluate the constitutionality of the CDA as it applies to the Internet as it exists today. Given the present state of cyberspace, I agree with the Court that the "display" provision cannot pass muster. Until gateway technology is available throughout cyberspace, and it is not in 1997, a speaker cannot be reasonably assured that the speech he displays will reach only adults because it is impossible to confine speech to an "adult zone." Thus, the only way for a speaker to avoid liability under the CDA is to refrain completely from using indecent speech. But this forced silence impinges on the First Amendment right of adults to make and obtain this speech and, for all intents and purposes, "reduce[s] the adult population [on the Internet] to reading only what is fit for children." As a result, the "display" provision cannot withstand scrutiny.

The "indecency transmission" and "specific person" provisions present a closer issue, for they are not unconstitutional in all of their applications. As discussed above, the "indecency transmission" provision makes it a crime to transmit knowingly an indecent message to a person the sender knows is under 18 years of age. The "specific person" provision proscribes the same conduct, although it does not as explicitly require the sender to know that the intended recipient of his indecent message is a minor. § 223(d)(1)(A). The Government urges the Court to construe the provision to impose such a knowledge requirement, and I would do so.

So construed, both provisions are constitutional as applied to a conversation involving only an adult and one or more minors— e.g., when an adult speaker sends an e-mail knowing the addressee is a minor, or when an adult and minor converse by themselves or with other minors in a chat room. In this context, these provisions are no different from the law we sustained in *Ginsberg*. Restricting what the adult may say to the minors in no way restricts the adult's ability to communicate with other adults. He is not prevented from speaking indecently to other adults in a chat room (because there are no other adults participating in the conversation) and he remains free to send indecent e-mails to other adults. The relevant universe contains only one adult, and the adult in that universe has the power to refrain from using indecent speech and consequently to keep all such speech within the room in an "adult" zone.

The analogy to *Ginsberg* breaks down, however, when more than one adult is a party to the conversation. If a minor enters a chat room otherwise occupied by adults, the CDA effectively requires the adults in the room to stop using indecent speech. If they did not, they could be prosecuted under the "indecency transmission" and "specific person" provisions for any indecent statements they make to the group, since they would be transmitting an indecent message to specific persons, one of whom is a minor. The CDA is therefore akin to a law that makes it a crime for a bookstore owner to sell pornographic magazines to anyone once a minor enters his store. Even assuming such a law might be constitutional in the physical world as a reasonable alternative to excluding minors completely from the store, the absence of any means of excluding minors from chat rooms in cyberspace restricts the rights of adults to engage in indecent speech in those rooms. The "indecency transmission" and "specific person" provisions share this defect.

But these two provisions do not infringe on adults' speech in all situations. And as discussed below, I do not find that the provisions are overbroad in the sense that they restrict minors' access to a substantial amount of speech that minors have the right to read and view. Accordingly, the CDA can be applied constitutionally in some situations. Normally, this fact would require the Court to reject a direct facial challenge. Appellees' claim arises under the First Amendment, however, and they argue that the CDA is facially invalid because it is "substantially overbroad"—that is, it "sweeps too broadly . . . [and] penaliz[es] a substantial amount of speech that is constitutionally protected," I agree with the Court that the provisions are overbroad in that they cover any and all communications between adults and minors, regardless of how many adults might be part of the audience to the communication.

This conclusion does not end the matter, however. Where, as here, "the parties challenging the statute are those who desire to engage in protected speech that the overbroad statute purports to punish, . . . [t]he statute may forthwith be declared invalid to the extent that it reaches too far, but otherwise left intact." There is no question that Congress intended to prohibit certain communications between one adult and one or more minors. There is also no question that Congress would have enacted a narrower version of these provisions had it known a broader version would be declared unconstitutional. I would therefore sustain the "indecency transmission" and "specific person" provisions to the extent they apply to the transmission of Internet communications where the party initiating the communication knows that all of the recipients are minors.

XII

Whether the CDA substantially interferes with the First Amendment rights of minors, and thereby runs afoul of the second characteristic of valid zoning laws, presents a closer question. In *Ginsberg*, the New York law we sustained prohibited the sale to minors of magazines that were "harmful to minors." Under that law, a magazine was "harmful to minors" only if it was obscene as to minors. Noting that obscene speech is not protected by the First Amendment, and that New York was constitutionally free to adjust the definition of obscenity for minors, the Court concluded that the law did not "invad[e] the area of freedom of expression constitutionally secured to minors[.]" New York therefore did not infringe upon the First Amendment rights of minors.

The Court neither "accept[s] nor reject[s]" the argument that the CDA is facially overbroad because it substantially interferes with the First Amendment rights of minors. Ante, at 2348. I would reject it. *Ginsberg* established that minors may constitutionally be denied access to material that is obscene as to minors. As *Ginsberg* explained, material is obscene as to minors if it (i) is "patently offensive to prevailing standards in the adult community as a whole with respect to what is suitable . . . for minors"; (ii) appeals to the prurient interest of minors; and (iii) is "utterly without redeeming social importance for minors." Because the CDA denies minors the right to obtain material that is "patently offensive"—even if it has some redeeming value for minors and even if it does not appeal to their prurient interests—Congress' rejection of the *Ginsberg* "harmful to minors" standard means that the CDA could ban some speech that is "indecent" (i.e., "patently offensive") but that is not obscene as to minors.

I do not deny this possibility, but to prevail in a facial challenge, it is not enough for a plaintiff to show "some" overbreadth. Our cases require a proof of "real" and "substantial" overbreadth, and appellees have not carried their burden in this case. In my view, the universe of speech constitutionally protected as to minors but banned by the CDA—i.e., the universe of material that is "patently offensive," but which nonetheless has some redeeming value for minors or does not appeal to their prurient interest—is a very small one. Appellees cite no examples of speech falling within this universe and do not attempt to explain why that universe is substantial "in relation to the statute's plainly legitimate sweep." That the CDA might deny minors the right to obtain material that has some "value," see ante, at 2348, is largely beside the point. While discussions about prison rape or nude art, may have some redeeming educational value for adults, they do not necessarily have any such value for minors, and under *Ginsberg,* minors only have a First Amendment right to obtain patently offensive material that has "redeeming social importance for minors," (emphasis added). There is also no evidence in the record to support the contention that "many e-mail transmissions from an adult to a minor are conversations between family members," and no support for the legal proposition that such speech is absolutely immune from regulation. Accordingly, in my view, the CDA does not burden a substantial amount of minors' constitutionally protected speech.

Thus, the constitutionality of the CDA as a zoning law hinges on the extent to which it substantially interferes with the First Amendment rights of adults. Because the rights of adults are infringed only by the "display" provision and by the "indecency transmission" and "specific person" provisions as applied to communications involving more than one adult, I would invalidate the CDA only to that extent. Insofar as the "indecency transmission" and "specific person" provisions prohibit the use of indecent speech in communications between an adult and one or more minors, however, they can and should be sustained. The Court reaches a contrary conclusion, and from that holding that I respectfully dissent.

Source: *Reno v. American Civil Liberties Union*, 521 U.S. 844 (1997).

U.S. Law: Federal Statutes

Selected Provisions of the Lanham Act (U.S. Trademark Law)

Provisions of the Lanham Act, the primary U.S. federal trademark law, and the many acts amending it can be found in Title 15 of the United States Code. Section 1125 of Title 15 (section 43 of the Lanham Act) describes the fundamental transgressions of trademark rights for which a remedy is available in the federal courts. Those most applicable in an Internet context are infringement, dilution, and cybersquatting. Infringement arises when there is a likelihood of confusion (§ 1125(a)), while dilution takes place when a famous mark is blurred or tarnished and is addressed in section 1125(c). Section 1125(d) deals with the Internet-specific problem of cybersquatting.

SECTION 43 OF THE LANHAM ACT— FALSE DESIGNATIONS OF ORIGIN, FALSE DESCRIPTIONS, AND DILUTION FORBIDDEN

(a) Civil action

(1) Any person who, on or in connection with any goods or services, or any container for goods, uses in commerce any word, term, name, symbol, or device, or any combination thereof, or any false designation of origin, false or misleading description of fact, or false or misleading representation of fact, which—

(A) is likely to cause confusion, or to cause mistake, or to deceive as to the affiliation, connection, or association of such person with another person, or as to the origin, sponsorship, or approval of his or her goods, services, or commercial activities by another person, or

(B) in commercial advertising or promotion, misrepresents the nature, characteristics, qualities, or geographic origin of his or her or another persons goods, services, or commercial activities,

shall be liable in a civil action by any person who believes that he or she is or is likely to be damaged by such act.

(2) As used in this subsection, the term "any person" includes any State, instrumentality of a State or employee of a State or instrumentality of a State acting in his or her official capacity. Any State, and any such instrumentality, officer, or employee, shall be subject to the provisions of this chapter in the same manner and to the same extent as any nongovernmental entity.

(3) In a civil action for trade dress infringement under this chapter for trade dress not registered on the principal register, the person who asserts trade dress protection has the burden of proving that the matter sought to be protected is not functional.

(b) Importation

Any goods marked or labeled in contravention of the provisions of this section shall not be imported into the United States or admitted to entry at any customhouse of the United States. The owner, importer, or consignee of goods refused entry at any customhouse under this section may have any recourse by protest or appeal that is given under the customs revenue laws or may have the remedy given by this chapter in cases involving goods refused entry or seized.

(c) Dilution by blurring; dilution by tarnishment

(1) Injunctive relief

Subject to the principles of equity, the owner of a famous mark that is distinctive, inherently or through acquired distinctiveness, shall be entitled to an injunction against another person who, at any time after the owners mark has become famous, commences use of a mark or trade name in commerce that is likely to cause dilution by blurring or dilution by tarnishment of the famous mark, regardless of the presence or absence of actual or likely confusion, of competition, or of actual economic injury.

(2) Definitions

(A) For purposes of paragraph (1), a mark is famous if it is widely recognized by the general consuming public of the United States as a designation of source of the goods or services of the marks owner. In determining whether a mark possesses the requisite degree of recognition, the court may consider all relevant factors, including the following:

(i) The duration, extent, and geographic reach of advertising and publicity of the mark, whether advertised or publicized by the owner or third parties.

(ii) The amount, volume, and geographic extent of sales of goods or services offered under the mark.

(iii) The extent of actual recognition of the mark.

(iv) Whether the mark was registered under the Act of March 3, 1881, or the Act of February 20, 1905, or on the principal register.

(B) For purposes of paragraph (1), "dilution by blurring" is association arising from the similarity between a mark or trade name and a famous mark that impairs the distinctiveness of the famous mark. In determining whether a mark or trade name is likely to cause dilution by blurring, the court may consider all relevant factors, including the following:

(i) The degree of similarity between the mark or trade name and the famous mark.

(ii) The degree of inherent or acquired distinctiveness of the famous mark.

(iii) The extent to which the owner of the famous mark is engaging in substantially exclusive use of the mark.

(iv) The degree of recognition of the famous mark.

(v) Whether the user of the mark or trade name intended to create an association with the famous mark.

(vi) Any actual association between the mark or trade name and the famous mark.

(C) For purposes of paragraph (1), "dilution by tarnishment" is association arising from the similarity between a mark or trade name and a famous mark that harms the reputation of the famous mark.

(3) Exclusions

The following shall not be actionable as dilution by blurring or dilution by tarnishment under this subsection:

(A) Any fair use, including a nominative or descriptive fair use, or facilitation of such fair use, of a famous mark by another person other than as a designation of source for the persons own goods or services, including use in connection with—

(i) advertising or promotion that permits consumers to compare goods or services; or

(ii) identifying and parodying, criticizing, or commenting upon the famous mark owner or the goods or services of the famous mark owner.

(B) All forms of news reporting and news commentary.

(C) Any noncommercial use of a mark.

(4) Burden of proof

In a civil action for trade dress dilution under this chapter for trade dress not registered on the principal register, the person who asserts trade dress protection has the burden of proving that—

(A) the claimed trade dress, taken as a whole, is not functional and is famous; and

(B) if the claimed trade dress includes any mark or marks registered on the principal register, the unregistered matter, taken as a whole, is famous separate and apart from any fame of such registered marks.

(5) Additional remedies

In an action brought under this subsection, the owner of the famous mark shall be entitled to injunctive relief as set forth in section 1116 of this title. The owner of the famous mark shall also be entitled to the remedies set forth in sections 1117 (a) and 1118 of this title, subject to the discretion of the court and the principles of equity if—

(A) the mark or trade name that is likely to cause dilution by blurring or dilution by tarnishment was first used in commerce by the person against whom the injunction is sought after October 6, 2006; and

(B) in a claim arising under this subsection—

(i) by reason of dilution by blurring, the person against whom the injunction is sought willfully intended to trade on the recognition of the famous mark; or

(ii) by reason of dilution by tarnishment, the person against whom the injunction is sought willfully intended to harm the reputation of the famous mark.

(6) Ownership of valid registration a complete bar to action

The ownership by a person of a valid registration under the Act of March 3, 1881, or the Act of February 20, 1905, or on the principal register under this chapter shall be a complete bar to an action against that person, with respect to that mark, that—

(A) is brought by another person under the common law or a statute of a State; and

(B)

(i) seeks to prevent dilution by blurring or dilution by tarnishment; or

(ii) asserts any claim of actual or likely damage or harm to the distinctiveness or reputation of a mark, label, or form of advertisement.

(7) Savings clause

Nothing in this subsection shall be construed to impair, modify, or supersede the applicability of the patent laws of the United States.

(d) Cyberpiracy prevention

(1)

(A) A person shall be liable in a civil action by the owner of a mark, including a personal name which is protected as a mark under this section, if, without regard to the goods or services of the parties, that person—

(i) has a bad faith intent to profit from that mark, including a personal name which is protected as a mark under this section; and

(ii) registers, traffics in, or uses a domain name that—

(I) in the case of a mark that is distinctive at the time of registration of the domain name, is identical or confusingly similar to that mark;

(II) in the case of a famous mark that is famous at the time of registration of the domain name, is identical or confusingly similar to or dilutive of that mark; or

(III) is a trademark, word, or name protected by reason of section 706 of title 18 or section 220506 of title 36.

(B)

(i) In determining whether a person has a bad faith intent described under subparagraph (A), a court may consider factors such as, but not limited to—

(I) the trademark or other intellectual property rights of the person, if any, in the domain name;

(II) the extent to which the domain name consists of the legal name of the person or a name that is otherwise commonly used to identify that person;

(III) the persons prior use, if any, of the domain name in connection with the bona fide offering of any goods or services;

(IV) the persons bona fide noncommercial or fair use of the mark in a site accessible under the domain name;

(V) the persons intent to divert consumers from the mark owners online location to a site accessible under the domain name that could harm the goodwill represented by the mark, either for commercial gain or with the intent to tarnish or disparage the mark, by creating a likelihood of confusion as to the source, sponsorship, affiliation, or endorsement of the site;

(VI) the persons offer to transfer, sell, or otherwise assign the domain name to the mark owner or any third party for financial gain without having used, or having an intent to use, the domain name in the bona fide offering of any goods or services, or the persons prior conduct indicating a pattern of such conduct;

(VII) the persons provision of material and misleading false contact information when applying for the registration of the domain name, the persons intentional failure to maintain accurate contact information, or the persons prior conduct indicating a pattern of such conduct;

(VIII) the persons registration or acquisition of multiple domain names which the person knows are identical or confusingly similar to marks of others that are distinctive at the time of registration of such domain names, or dilutive of famous marks of others that are famous at the time of registration of such domain names, without regard to the goods or services of the parties; and

(IX) the extent to which the mark incorporated in the persons domain name registration is or is not distinctive and famous within the meaning of subsection (c).

(ii) Bad faith intent described under subparagraph (A) shall not be found in any case in which the court determines that the person believed and had reasonable grounds to believe that the use of the domain name was a fair use or otherwise lawful.

(C) In any civil action involving the registration, trafficking, or use of a domain name under this paragraph, a court may order the forfeiture or cancellation of the domain name or the transfer of the domain name to the owner of the mark.

(D) A person shall be liable for using a domain name under subparagraph (A) only if that person is the domain name registrant or that registrants authorized licensee.

(E) As used in this paragraph, the term "traffics in" refers to transactions that include, but are not limited to, sales, purchases, loans, pledges, licenses, exchanges of currency, and any other transfer for consideration or receipt in exchange for consideration.

(2)

(A) The owner of a mark may file an in rem civil action against a domain name in the judicial district in which the domain name registrar, domain name registry, or other domain name authority that registered or assigned the domain name is located if—

(i) the domain name violates any right of the owner of a mark registered in the Patent and Trademark Office, or protected under subsection (a) or (c) of this section; and

(ii) the court finds that the owner—

(I) is not able to obtain in personam jurisdiction over a person who would have been a defendant in a civil action under paragraph (1); or

(II) through due diligence was not able to find a person who would have been a defendant in a civil action under paragraph (1) by—

(aa) sending a notice of the alleged violation and intent to proceed under this paragraph to the registrant of the domain name at the postal and e-mail address provided by the registrant to the registrar; and

(bb) publishing notice of the action as the court may direct promptly after filing the action.

(B) The actions under subparagraph (A)(ii) shall constitute service of process.

(C) In an in rem action under this paragraph, a domain name shall be deemed to have its situs in the judicial district in which—

(i) the domain name registrar, registry, or other domain name authority that registered or assigned the domain name is located; or

(ii) documents sufficient to establish control and authority regarding the disposition of the registration and use of the domain name are deposited with the court.

(D)

(i) The remedies in an in rem action under this paragraph shall be limited to a court order for the forfeiture or cancellation of the domain name or the transfer of the domain name to the owner of the mark. Upon receipt of written notification of a filed, stamped copy of a complaint filed by the owner of a mark in a United States district court under this paragraph, the domain name registrar, domain name registry, or other domain name authority shall—

(I) expeditiously deposit with the court documents sufficient to establish the courts control and authority regarding the disposition of the registration and use of the domain name to the court; and

(II) not transfer, suspend, or otherwise modify the domain name during the pendency of the action, except upon order of the court.

(ii) The domain name registrar or registry or other domain name authority shall not be liable for injunctive or monetary relief under this paragraph except in the case of bad faith or reckless disregard, which includes a willful failure to comply with any such court order.

(3) The civil action established under paragraph (1) and the in rem action established under paragraph (2), and any remedy available under either such action, shall be in addition to any other civil action or remedy otherwise applicable.

(4) The in rem jurisdiction established under paragraph (2) shall be in addition to any other jurisdiction that otherwise exists, whether in rem or in personam.

Source: The Lanham (Trademark) Act. Pub.L. 79–489, 60 Stat. 427, enacted July 6, 1946, codified at 15 USC § 1125.

Selected Provisions of Title 17 of the United States Code (U.S. Copyright Law)

The Copyright Act of 1976, with all of its subsequent amendments (including the Digital Millennium Copyright Act (DMCA)) is Title 17 of the United States Code. Section 102 sets out the basic rule of copyright: what can be protected, and what cannot be protected. Section 106 sets out the benefits: what rights the copyright holder gains. Section 107 sets out the most well-known, and perhaps most litigated, limitation on the copyright holder's exclusive rights: the right of fair use. Section 109 deals with another contentious limitation, the right of first sale. Section 1201, added by the DMCA, forbids the circumvention of technological copy-protection measures.

17 USC § 102—SUBJECT MATTER OF COPYRIGHT: IN GENERAL

(a) Copyright protection subsists, in accordance with this title, in original works of authorship fixed in any tangible medium of expression, now known or later developed, from which they can be perceived, reproduced, or otherwise communicated, either directly or with the aid of a machine or device. Works of authorship include the following categories:

(1) literary works;
(2) musical works, including any accompanying words;
(3) dramatic works, including any accompanying music;
(4) pantomimes and choreographic works;
(5) pictorial, graphic, and sculptural works;
(6) motion pictures and other audiovisual works;
(7) sound recordings; and
(8) architectural works.

(b) In no case does copyright protection for an original work of authorship extend to any idea, procedure, process, system, method of operation, concept, principle, or discovery, regardless of the form in which it is described, explained, illustrated, or embodied in such work.

17 USC § 106—EXCLUSIVE RIGHTS IN COPYRIGHTED WORKS

Subject to sections 107 through 122, the owner of copyright under this title has the exclusive rights to do and to authorize any of the following:

(1) to reproduce the copyrighted work in copies or phonorecords;
(2) to prepare derivative works based upon the copyrighted work;
(3) to distribute copies or phonorecords of the copyrighted work to the public by sale or other transfer of ownership, or by rental, lease, or lending;
(4) in the case of literary, musical, dramatic, and choreographic works, pantomimes, and motion pictures and other audiovisual works, to perform the copyrighted work publicly;
(5) in the case of literary, musical, dramatic, and choreographic works, pantomimes, and pictorial, graphic, or sculptural works, including the individual images of a motion picture or other audiovisual work, to display the copyrighted work publicly; and
(6) in the case of sound recordings, to perform the copyrighted work publicly by means of a digital audio transmission.

17 USC § 107—LIMITATIONS ON EXCLUSIVE RIGHTS: FAIR USE

Notwithstanding the provisions of sections 106 and 106A, the fair use of a copyrighted work, including such use by reproduction in copies or phonorecords or by any other means specified by that section, for purposes such as criticism, comment, news reporting, teaching (including multiple copies for classroom use), scholarship, or research, is not an infringement of copyright. In determining whether the use made of a work in any particular case is a fair use the factors to be considered shall include—

(1) the purpose and character of the use, including whether such use is of a commercial nature or is for nonprofit educational purposes;
(2) the nature of the copyrighted work;
(3) the amount and substantiality of the portion used in relation to the copyrighted work as a whole; and
(4) the effect of the use upon the potential market for or value of the copyrighted work.

The fact that a work is unpublished shall not itself bar a finding of fair use if such finding is made upon consideration of all the above factors.

17 USC § 109—LIMITATIONS ON EXCLUSIVE RIGHTS: EFFECT OF TRANSFER OF PARTICULAR COPY OR PHONORECORD

(a) Notwithstanding the provisions of section 106 (3), the owner of a particular copy or phonorecord lawfully made under this title, or any person authorized by such owner, is entitled, without the authority of the copyright owner, to sell or otherwise dispose of the possession of that copy or phonorecord. Notwithstanding the preceding sentence, copies or phonorecords of works subject to restored copyright under section 104A that are manufactured before the date of restoration of copyright or, with respect to reliance parties, before publication or service of notice under section 104A (e), may be sold or otherwise disposed of without the authorization of the owner of the restored copyright for purposes of direct or indirect commercial advantage only during the 12-month period beginning on—
(1) the date of the publication in the Federal Register of the notice of intent filed with the Copyright Office under section 104A (d)(2)(A), or
(2) the date of the receipt of actual notice served under section 104A (d)(2)(B), whichever occurs first.
(b)
(1)
(A) Notwithstanding the provisions of subsection (a), unless authorized by the owners of copyright in the sound recording or the owner of copyright in a computer program (including any tape, disk, or other medium embodying such program), and in the case of a sound recording in the musical works embodied therein, neither the owner of a particular phonorecord nor any person in possession of a particular copy of a computer program (including

any tape, disk, or other medium embodying such program), may, for the purposes of direct or indirect commercial advantage, dispose of, or authorize the disposal of, the possession of that phonorecord or computer program (including any tape, disk, or other medium embodying such program) by rental, lease, or lending, or by any other act or practice in the nature of rental, lease, or lending. Nothing in the preceding sentence shall apply to the rental, lease, or lending of a phonorecord for nonprofit purposes by a nonprofit library or nonprofit educational institution. The transfer of possession of a lawfully made copy of a computer program by a nonprofit educational institution to another nonprofit educational institution or to faculty, staff, and students does not constitute rental, lease, or lending for direct or indirect commercial purposes under this subsection.

(B) This subsection does not apply to—

(i) a computer program which is embodied in a machine or product and which cannot be copied during the ordinary operation or use of the machine or product; or

(ii) a computer program embodied in or used in conjunction with a limited purpose computer that is designed for playing video games and may be designed for other purposes.

(C) Nothing in this subsection affects any provision of chapter 9 of this title.

(2)

(A) Nothing in this subsection shall apply to the lending of a computer program for nonprofit purposes by a nonprofit library, if each copy of a computer program which is lent by such library has affixed to the packaging containing the program a warning of copyright in accordance with requirements that the Register of Copyrights shall prescribe by regulation.

(B) Not later than three years after the date of the enactment of the Computer Software Rental Amendments Act of 1990, and at such times thereafter as the Register of Copyrights considers appropriate, the Register of Copyrights, after consultation with representatives of copyright owners and librarians, shall submit to the Congress a report stating whether this paragraph has achieved its intended purpose of maintaining the integrity of the copyright system while providing nonprofit libraries the capability to fulfill their function. Such report shall advise the Congress as to any information or recommendations that the Register of Copyrights considers necessary to carry out the purposes of this subsection.

(3) Nothing in this subsection shall affect any provision of the antitrust laws. For purposes of the preceding sentence, "antitrust laws" has the meaning given that term in the first section of the Clayton Act and includes section 5 of the Federal Trade Commission Act to the extent that section relates to unfair methods of competition.

(4) Any person who distributes a phonorecord or a copy of a computer program (including any tape, disk, or other medium embodying such program) in violation of paragraph (1) is an infringer of copyright under section 501 of this title and is subject to the remedies set forth in sections 502, 503, 504, and 505. Such violation shall not be a criminal offense under section 506 or cause such person to be subject to the criminal penalties set forth in section 2319 of title 18.

(c) Notwithstanding the provisions of section 106 (5), the owner of a particular copy lawfully made under this title, or any person authorized by such owner, is entitled, without the authority of the copyright owner, to display that copy publicly, either directly or by the projection of no more than one image at a time, to viewers present at the place where the copy is located.

(d) The privileges prescribed by subsections (a) and (c) do not, unless authorized by the copyright owner, extend to any person who has acquired possession of the copy or phonorecord from the copyright owner, by rental, lease, loan, or otherwise, without acquiring ownership of it.

(e) Notwithstanding the provisions of sections 106 (4) and 106 (5), in the case of an electronic audiovisual game intended for use in coin-operated equipment, the owner of a particular copy of such a game lawfully made under this title, is entitled, without the authority of the copyright owner of the game, to publicly perform or display that game in coin-operated equipment, except that this subsection shall not apply to any work of authorship embodied in the audiovisual game if the copyright owner of the electronic audiovisual game is not also the copyright owner of the work of authorship.

Source: The Copyright Act of 1976 (with added amendments). P.L. 94–553, 17 USC § 102, 106, 109.

Digital Millennium Copyright Act Anticircumvention Provisions, 1998

Few copyright statutes have aroused as much consumer and activist ire as the anticircumvention provisions of the Digital Millennium Copyright Act (DMCA). Consumers detest the provisions because they make content harder to use, harder to play back, harder to transfer from one medium or player to another—in short, they limit its value as entertainment. Activists detest the provisions for these reasons and because they seem to be a symptom of a creeping loss of control over content, letting corporations dictate what consumers may do with content they have purchased and reducing the scope of fair use. Numerous battles have been fought over the provisions, which thus far have held up to Constitutional scrutiny; the cases of Corley *and* Grokster, *below, are part of perhaps the most famous of these battles—the battles over DeCSS and file-sharing. More can be read about these issues in the entries "DeCSS," "Digital Millennium Copyright Act, Title I," "Fair Use," and "File-Sharing."*

§ 1201. CIRCUMVENTION OF COPYRIGHT PROTECTION SYSTEMS

(a) Violations regarding circumvention of technological measures

(1)

(A) No person shall circumvent a technological measure that effectively controls access to a work protected under this title. The prohibition contained in the preceding sentence shall take effect at the end of the 2-year period beginning on the date of the enactment of this chapter.

(B) The prohibition contained in subparagraph (A) shall not apply to persons who are users of a copyrighted work which is in a particular class of works, if such persons are, or are likely to be in the succeeding 3-year period, adversely affected by virtue of such prohibition in their ability to make noninfringing uses of that particular class of works under this title, as determined under subparagraph (C).

(C) During the 2-year period described in subparagraph (A), and during each succeeding 3-year period, the Librarian of Congress, upon the recommendation of the Register of Copyrights, who shall consult with the Assistant Secretary for Communications and Information of the Department of Commerce and report and comment on his or her views in making such recommendation, shall make the determination in a rulemaking proceeding for purposes of subparagraph (B) of whether persons who are users of a copyrighted work are, or are likely to be in the succeeding 3-year period, adversely affected by the prohibition under subparagraph (A) in their ability to make noninfringing uses under this title of a particular class of copyrighted works. In conducting such rulemaking, the Librarian shall examine –

(i) the availability for use of copyrighted works;

(ii) the availability for use of works for nonprofit archival, preservation, and educational purposes;

(iii) the impact that the prohibition on the circumvention of technological measures applied to copyrighted works has on criticism, comment, news reporting, teaching, scholarship, or research;

(iv) the effect of circumvention of technological measures on the market for or value of copyrighted works; and

(v) such other factors as the Librarian considers appropriate.

(D) The Librarian shall publish any class of copyrighted works for which the Librarian has determined, pursuant to the rulemaking conducted under subparagraph (C), that noninfringing uses by persons who are users of a copyrighted work are, or are likely to be, adversely affected, and the prohibition contained in subparagraph (A) shall not apply to such users with respect to such class of works for the ensuing 3-year period.

(E) Neither the exception under subparagraph (B) from the applicability of the prohibition contained in subparagraph (A), nor any determination made in a rulemaking conducted under subparagraph (C), may be used as a defense in any action to enforce any provision of this title other than this paragraph.

(2) No person shall manufacture, import, offer to the public, provide, or otherwise traffic in any technology, product, service, device, component, or part thereof, that –

(A) is primarily designed or produced for the purpose of circumventing a technological measure that effectively controls access to a work protected under this title;

(B) has only limited commercially significant purpose or use other than to circumvent a technological measure that effectively controls access to a work protected under this title; or

(C) is marketed by that person or another acting in concert with that person with that person's knowledge for use in circumventing a technological measure that effectively controls access to a work protected under this title.

(3) As used in this subsection –

(A) to "circumvent a technological measure" means to descramble a scrambled work, to decrypt an encrypted work, or otherwise to avoid, bypass, remove, deactivate, or impair a technological measure, without the authority of the copyright owner; and

(B) a technological measure "effectively controls access to a work" if the measure, in the ordinary course of its operation, requires the application of information, or a process or a treatment, with the authority of the copyright owner, to gain access to the work.

(b) Additional violations

(1) No person shall manufacture, import, offer to the public, provide, or otherwise traffic in any technology, product, service, device, component, or part thereof, that –

(A) is primarily designed or produced for the purpose of circumventing protection afforded by a technological measure that effectively protects a right of a copyright owner under this title in a work or a portion thereof;

(B) has only limited commercially significant purpose or use other than to circumvent protection afforded by a technological measure that effectively protects a right of a copyright owner under this title in a work or a portion thereof; or

(C) is marketed by that person or another acting in concert with that person with that person's knowledge for use in circumventing protection afforded by a technological measure that effectively protects a right of a copyright owner under this title in a work or a portion thereof.

(2) As used in this subsection –

(A) to "circumvent protection afforded by a technological measure" means avoiding, bypassing, removing, deactivating, or otherwise impairing a technological measure; and

(B) a technological measure "effectively protects a right of a copyright owner under this title" if the measure, in the ordinary course of its operation, prevents, restricts, or otherwise limits the exercise of a right of a copyright owner under this title.

(c) Other rights, etc., not affected

(1) Nothing in this section shall affect rights, remedies, limitations, or defenses to copyright infringement, including fair use, under this title.

(2) Nothing in this section shall enlarge or diminish vicarious or contributory liability for copyright infringement in connection with any technology, product, service, device, component, or part thereof.

(3) Nothing in this section shall require that the design of, or design and selection of parts and components for, a consumer electronics, telecommunications, or computing product provide for a response to any particular technological measure, so long as such part or component, or the product in which such part or component is integrated, does not otherwise fall within the prohibitions of subsection (a)(2) or (b)(1).

(4) Nothing in this section shall enlarge or diminish any rights of free speech or the press for activities using consumer electronics, telecommunications, or computing products.

(d) Exemption for nonprofit libraries, archives, and educational institutions

(1) A nonprofit library, archives, or educational institution which gains access to a commercially exploited copyrighted work solely in order to make a good faith determination of whether to acquire a copy of that work for the sole purpose of engaging in conduct permitted under this title shall not be in violation of subsection (a)(1)(A). A copy of a work to which access has been gained under this paragraph –

(A) may not be retained longer than necessary to make such good faith determination; and

(B) may not be used for any other purpose.

(2) The exemption made available under paragraph (1) shall only apply with respect to a work when an identical copy of that work is not reasonably available in another form.

(3) A nonprofit library, archives, or educational institution that willfully for the purpose of commercial advantage or financial gain violates paragraph (1) –

(A) shall, for the first offense, be subject to the civil remedies under section 1203; and

(B) shall, for repeated or subsequent offenses, in addition to the civil remedies under section 1203, forfeit the exemption provided under paragraph (1).

(4) This subsection may not be used as a defense to a claim under subsection (a)(2) or (b), nor may this subsection permit a nonprofit library, archives, or educational institution to manufacture, import, offer to the public, provide, or otherwise traffic in any technology, product, service, component, or part thereof, which circumvents a technological measure.

(5) In order for a library or archives to qualify for the exemption under this subsection, the collections of that library or archives shall be –

(A) open to the public; or

(B) available not only to researchers affiliated with the library or archives or with the institution of which it is a part, but also to other persons doing research in a specialized field.

(e) Law enforcement, intelligence, and other government activities.—This section does not prohibit any lawfully authorized investigative, protective, information security, or intelligence activity of an officer, agent, or employee of the United States, a State, or a political subdivision of a State, or a person acting pursuant to a contract with the United States, a State, or a political subdivision of a State. For purposes of this subsection, the term "information security" means activities carried out in order to identify and address the vulnerabilities of a government computer, computer system, or computer network.

(f) Reverse engineering

(1) Notwithstanding the provisions of subsection (a)(1)(A), a person who has lawfully obtained the right to use a copy of a computer program may circumvent a technological measure that effectively controls access to a particular portion of that program for the sole purpose of identifying and analyzing those elements of the program that are necessary to achieve interoperability of an independently created computer program with other programs, and that have not previously been readily available to the person engaging in the circumvention, to the extent any such acts of identification and analysis do not constitute infringement under this title.

(2) Notwithstanding the provisions of subsections (a)(2) and (b), a person may develop and employ technological means to circumvent a technological measure, or to circumvent protection afforded by a technological measure, in order to enable the identification and analysis under paragraph (1), or for the purpose of enabling interoperability of an independently created computer program with other programs, if such means are necessary to achieve such interoperability, to the extent that doing so does not constitute infringement under this title.

(3) The information acquired through the acts permitted under paragraph (1), and the means permitted under paragraph (2), may be made available to others if the person referred to in paragraph (1) or (2), as the case may be, provides such information or means solely for the purpose of enabling interoperability of an independently created computer program with other programs, and to the extent that doing so does not constitute infringement under this title or violate applicable law other than this section.

(4) For purposes of this subsection, the term "interoperability" means the ability of computer programs to exchange information, and of such programs mutually to use the information which has been exchanged.

(g) Encryption research. –

(1) Definitions.—For purposes of this subsection –

(A) the term "encryption research" means activities necessary to identify and analyze flaws and vulnerabilities of encryption technologies applied to copyrighted works, if these activities are conducted to advance the state of knowledge in the field of encryption technology or to assist in the development of encryption products; and

(B) the term "encryption technology" means the scrambling and descrambling of information using mathematical formulas or algorithms.

(2) Permissible acts of encryption research.—Notwithstanding the provisions of subsection (a)(1)(A), it is not a violation of that subsection for a person to circumvent a technological measure as applied to a copy, phonorecord, performance, or display of a published work in the course of an act of good faith encryption research if –

(A) the person lawfully obtained the encrypted copy, phonorecord, performance, or display of the published work;

(B) such act is necessary to conduct such encryption research;

(C) the person made a good faith effort to obtain authorization before the circumvention; and

(D) such act does not constitute infringement under this title or a violation of applicable law other than this section, including section 1030 of title 18 and those provisions of title 18 amended by the Computer Fraud and Abuse Act of 1986.

(3) Factors in determining exemption.—In determining whether a person qualifies for the exemption under paragraph (2), the factors to be considered shall include –

(A) whether the information derived from the encryption research was disseminated, and if so, whether it was disseminated in a manner reasonably calculated to advance the state of knowledge or development of encryption technology, versus whether it was disseminated in a manner that facilitates infringement under this title or a violation of applicable law other than this section, including a violation of privacy or breach of security;

(B) whether the person is engaged in a legitimate course of study, is employed, or is appropriately trained or experienced, in the field of encryption technology; and

(C) whether the person provides the copyright owner of the work to which the technological measure is applied with notice of the findings and documentation of the research, and the time when such notice is provided.

(4) Use of technological means for research activities.— Notwithstanding the provisions of subsection (a)(2), it is not a violation of that subsection for a person to –

(A) develop and employ technological means to circumvent a technological measure for the sole purpose of that person performing the acts of good faith encryption research described in paragraph (2); and

(B) provide the technological means to another person with whom he or she is working collaboratively for the purpose of conducting the acts of good faith encryption research described in paragraph (2) or for the purpose of having that other person verify his or her acts of good faith encryption research described in paragraph (2).

(5) Report to Congress [omitted]

(h) Exceptions regarding minors.—In applying subsection (a) to a component or part, the court may consider the necessity for its intended and actual incorporation in a technology, product, service, or device, which –

(1) does not itself violate the provisions of this title; and

(2) has the sole purpose to prevent the access of minors to material on the Internet.

(i) Protection of personally identifying information. –

(1) Circumvention permitted.—Notwithstanding the provisions of subsection (a)(1)(A), it is not a violation of that subsection for a person to circumvent a technological measure that effectively controls access to a work protected under this title, if –

(A) the technological measure, or the work it protects, contains the capability of collecting or disseminating personally identifying information reflecting the online activities of a natural person who seeks to gain access to the work protected;

(B) in the normal course of its operation, the technological measure, or the work it protects, collects or disseminates personally identifying information about the person who seeks to gain access to the work protected, without providing conspicuous notice of such collection or dissemination to such person, and without providing such person with the capability to prevent or restrict such collection or dissemination;

(C) the act of circumvention has the sole effect of identifying and disabling the capability described in subparagraph (A), and has no other effect on the ability of any person to gain access to any work; and

(D) the act of circumvention is carried out solely for the purpose of preventing the collection or dissemination of personally identifying information about a natural person who seeks to gain access to the work protected, and is not in violation of any other law.

(2) Inapplicability to certain technological measures.—This subsection does not apply to a technological measure, or a work it protects, that does not collect or disseminate personally identifying information and that is disclosed to a user as not having or using such capability.

(j) Security testing. –

(1) Definition.—For purposes of this subsection, the term "security testing" means accessing a computer, computer system, or computer network, solely for the purpose of good faith testing, investigating, or correcting, a security flaw or vulnerability, with the authorization of the owner or operator of such computer, computer system, or computer network.

(2) Permissible acts of security testing.—Notwithstanding the provisions of subsection (a)(1)(A), it is not a violation of that subsection for a person to engage in an act of security testing, if such act does not constitute infringement under this title or a violation of applicable law other than this section, including section 1030 of title 18 and those provisions of title 18 amended by the Computer Fraud and Abuse Act of 1986.

(3) Factors in determining exemption.—In determining whether a person qualifies for the exemption under paragraph (2), the factors to be considered shall include –

(A) whether the information derived from the security testing was used solely to promote the security of the owner or operator of such computer, computer system or computer network, or shared directly with the developer of such computer, computer system, or computer network; and

(B) whether the information derived from the security testing was used or maintained in a manner that does not facilitate infringement under this title or a violation of applicable law other than this section, including a violation of privacy or breach of security.

(4) Use of technological means for security testing.— Notwithstanding the provisions of subsection (a)(2), it is not a violation of that subsection for a person to develop, produce, distribute or employ technological means for the sole purpose of performing the acts of security testing described in subsection (2), provided such technological means does not otherwise violate section (a)(2).

(k) Certain analog devices and certain technological measures [omitted]

Source: Digital Millennium Copyright Act of 1998, Anti-Circumvention Provisions, 17 U.S.C. § 1201.

Universal City Studios, Inc. v. Corley, 2001

Not long after the passage of the Digital Millennium Copyright Act (DMCA), activists opposed it with the time-honored activist tactic of civil disobedience. In this case, the civil disobedience was electronic; it involved no lying down in front of bulldozers or protest marches, but rather sharing copies of a program called DeCSS. DeCSS was capable of breaking the copy-protection encryption used on commercial DVDs; the movie studios claimed—correctly, as it turned out—that sharing the program, or even providing links to sites from which the program could be downloaded, violated the DMCA. In the following case (from which the footnotes, many of them quite lengthy, and the citations have been omitted) the federal Second Circuit Court of Appeals rejected the arguments of hacker activist and publisher Eric Corley. Corley had claimed that the anticircumvention provisions were unconstitutional or that, even if they were constitutional, Corley's acts in posting links to DeCSS did not violate the statute.

JON O. NEWMAN, CIRCUIT JUDGE

When the Framers of the First Amendment prohibited Congress from making any law "abridging the freedom of speech," they were not thinking about computers, computer programs, or the Internet. But neither were they thinking about radio, television, or movies. Just as the inventions at the beginning and middle of the 20th century presented new First Amendment issues, so does the cyber revolution at the end of that century. This appeal raises significant First Amendment issues concerning one aspect of computer technology—encryption to protect materials in digital form from unauthorized access. The appeal challenges the constitutionality of the Digital Millennium Copyright Act ("DMCA"), 17 U.S.C. § 1201 et seq. and the validity of an injunction entered to enforce the DMCA.

Defendant-Appellant Eric C. Corley and his company, 2600 Enterprises, Inc., (collectively "Corley," "the Defendants," or "the Appellants") appeal from the amended final judgment of the United States District Court for the Southern District of New York (Lewis A. Kaplan, District Judge), entered August 23, 2000, enjoining them from various actions concerning a decryption program known as "DeCSS." The injunction primarily bars the Appellants from posting DeCSS on their web site and from knowingly linking their web site to any other web site on which DeCSS is posted. We affirm.

Introduction

Understanding the pending appeal and the issues it raises requires some familiarity with technical aspects of computers and computer software, especially software called "digital versatile disks" or "DVDs," which are optical media storage devices currently designed to contain movies. Those lacking such familiarity will be greatly aided by reading Judge Kaplan's extremely lucid opinion, *Universal City Studios, Inc. v. Reimerdes, 111 F.Supp.2d 294 (S.D.N.Y.2000)*, beginning with his helpful section "The Vocabulary of this Case."

This appeal concerns the anti-trafficking provisions of the DMCA, which Congress enacted in 1998 to strengthen copyright protection in the digital age. Fearful that the ease with which pirates could copy and distribute a copyrightable work in digital form was overwhelming the capacity of conventional copyright enforcement to find and enjoin unlawfully copied material, Congress sought to combat copyright piracy in its earlier stages, before the work was even copied. The DMCA therefore backed with legal sanctions the efforts of copyright owners to protect their works from piracy behind digital walls such as encryption codes or password protections. In so doing, Congress targeted not only those pirates who would circumvent these digital walls (the "anti-circumvention provisions," contained in 17 U.S.C. § 1201(a)(1)), but also anyone who would traffic in a technology primarily designed to circumvent a digital wall (the "anti-trafficking provisions," contained in 17 U.S.C. § 1201(a)(2), (b)(1)).

Corley publishes a print magazine and maintains an affiliated web site geared towards "hackers," a digital-era term often applied to those interested in techniques for circumventing protections of computers and computer data from unauthorized access. The so-called hacker community includes serious computer-science scholars conducting research on protection techniques, computer buffs intrigued by the challenge of trying to circumvent access-limiting devices or perhaps hoping to promote security by exposing flaws in protection techniques, mischief-makers interested in disrupting computer operations, and thieves, including copyright infringers who want to acquire copyrighted material (for personal use or resale) without paying for it.

In November 1999, Corley posted a copy of the decryption computer program "DeCSS" on his web site, http://www.2600 .com ("2600.com"). DeCSS is designed to circumvent "CSS," the encryption technology that motion picture studios place on DVDs to prevent the unauthorized viewing and copying of motion pictures. Corley also posted on his web site links to other web sites where DeCSS could be found.

Plaintiffs-Appellees are eight motion picture studios that brought an action in the Southern District of New York seeking injunctive relief against Corley under the DMCA. Following a full non-jury trial, the District Court entered a permanent injunction barring Corley from posting DeCSS on his web site or from knowingly linking via a hyperlink to any other web site containing DeCSS. The District Court rejected Corley's constitutional attacks on the statute and the injunction.

Corley renews his constitutional challenges on appeal. Specifically, he argues primarily that: (1) the DMCA oversteps limits in the Copyright Clause on the duration of copyright protection; (2) the DMCA as applied to his dissemination of DeCSS violates the First Amendment because computer code is "speech" entitled to full First Amendment protection and the DMCA fails to survive the exacting scrutiny accorded statutes that regulate "speech"; and (3) the DMCA violates the First Amendment and the Copyright Clause by unduly obstructing the "fair use" of copyrighted materials. Corley also argues that the statute is susceptible to, and should therefore be given, a narrow interpretation that avoids alleged constitutional objections.

Background

For decades, motion picture studios have made movies available for viewing at home in what is called "analog" format. Movies in this format are placed on videotapes, which can be played on a video cassette recorder ("VCR"). In the early 1990s, the studios began to consider the possibility of distributing movies in digital form as well. Movies in digital form are placed on disks, known as DVDs, which can be played on a DVD player (either a stand-alone device or a component of a computer). DVDs offer advantages over analog tapes, such as improved visual and audio quality, larger data capacity, and greater durability. However, the improved quality of a movie in a digital format brings with it the risk that a virtually perfect copy, i.e., one that will not lose perceptible quality in the copying process, can be readily made at the click of a computer control and instantly distributed to countless recipients throughout the world over the Internet. This case arises out of the movie industry's efforts to respond to this risk by invoking the anti-trafficking provisions of the DMCA.

I. CSS

The movie studios were reluctant to release movies in digital form until they were confident they had in place adequate safeguards against piracy of their copyrighted movies. The studios took several steps to minimize the piracy threat. First, they settled on the DVD as the standard digital medium for home distribution of movies. The studios then sought an encryption scheme to protect movies on DVDs. They enlisted the help of members of the consumer electronics and computer industries, who in mid-1996 developed the Content Scramble System ("CSS"). CSS is an encryption scheme that employs an algorithm configured by a set of "keys" to encrypt a DVD's contents. The algorithm is a type of mathematical formula for transforming the contents of the movie file into gibberish; the "keys" are in actuality strings of 0's and 1's that serve as values for the mathematical formula. Decryption in the case of CSS requires a set of "player keys" contained in compliant DVD players, as well as an understanding of the CSS encryption algorithm. Without the player keys and the algorithm, a DVD player cannot access the contents of a DVD. With the player keys and the algorithm, a DVD player can display the movie on a television or a computer screen, but does not give a viewer the ability to use the copy function of the computer to copy the movie or to manipulate the digital content of the DVD.

The studios developed a licensing scheme for distributing the technology to manufacturers of DVD players. Player keys and other information necessary to the CSS scheme were given to manufacturers of DVD players for an administrative fee. In exchange for the licenses, manufacturers were obliged to keep the player keys confidential. Manufacturers were also required in the licensing agreement to prevent the transmission of "CSS data" (a term undefined in the licensing agreement) from a DVD drive to any "internal recording device," including, presumably, a computer hard drive.

With encryption technology and licensing agreements in hand, the studios began releasing movies on DVDs in 1997, and DVDs quickly gained in popularity, becoming a significant source of studio revenue. In 1998, the studios secured added protection against DVD piracy when Congress passed the DMCA, which prohibits the development or use of technology designed to circumvent a technological protection measure, such as CSS. The pertinent provisions of the DMCA are examined in greater detail below.

II. DeCSS

In September 1999, Jon Johansen, a Norwegian teenager, collaborating with two unidentified individuals he met on the Internet, reverse-engineered a licensed DVD player designed to operate on the Microsoft operating system, and culled from it the player keys and other information necessary to decrypt CSS. The record suggests that Johansen was trying to develop a DVD player operable on Linux, an alternative operating system that did not support any licensed DVD players at that time. In order to accomplish this task, Johansen wrote a decryption program executable on Microsoft's operating system. That program was called, appropriately enough, "DeCSS."

If a user runs the DeCSS program (for example, by clicking on the DeCSS icon on a Microsoft operating system platform) with a DVD in the computer's disk drive, DeCSS will decrypt the DVD's CSS protection, allowing the user to copy the DVD's files and place the copy on the user's hard drive. The result is a very large computer file that can be played on a non-CSS-compliant player and copied, manipulated, and transferred just like any other computer file. DeCSS comes complete with a fairly user-friendly interface that helps the user select from among the DVD's files and assign the decrypted file a location on the user's hard drive. The quality of the resulting decrypted movie is "virtually identical" to that of the encrypted movie on the DVD. And the file produced by DeCSS, while large, can be compressed to a manageable size by a compression software called "DivX," available at no cost on the Internet. This compressed file can be copied onto a DVD, or transferred over the Internet (with some patience).

Johansen posted the executable object code, but not the source code, for DeCSS on his web site. The distinction between source code and object code is relevant to this case, so a brief explanation is warranted. A computer responds to electrical charges, the presence or absence of which is represented by strings of 1's and 0's. Strictly speaking, "object code" consists of those 1's and 0's. While some people can read and program in object code, "it would be inconvenient, inefficient and, for most people, probably impossible to do so." Computer languages have been written to facilitate program writing and reading. A program in such a computer language— BASIC, C, and Java are examples—is said to be written in "source code." Source code has the benefit of being much easier to read (by people) than object code, but as a general matter, it must be translated back to object code before it can be read by a computer. This task is usually performed by a program called a compiler. Since computer languages range in complexity, object code can be placed on one end of a spectrum, and different kinds of source code can be arrayed across the spectrum according to the ease with which they are read and understood by humans. Within months of its appearance in executable form on Johansen's web site, DeCSS was widely available on the Internet, in both object code and various forms of source code.

In November 1999, Corley wrote and placed on his web site, 2600.com, an article about the DeCSS phenomenon. His web site is an auxiliary to the print magazine, *2600: The Hacker Quarterly*, which Corley has been publishing since 1984. As the name suggests, the magazine is designed for "hackers," as is the web site. While the magazine and the web site cover some issues of general interest to computer users—such as threats to online privacy—the focus of the publications is on the vulnerability of computer security systems, and more specifically, how to exploit that vulnerability in order to circumvent the security systems. Representative articles explain how to steal an Internet domain name and how to break into the computer systems at Federal Express.

Corley's article about DeCSS detailed how CSS was cracked, and described the movie industry's efforts to shut down web sites posting DeCSS. It also explained that DeCSS could be used to copy DVDs. At the end of the article, the Defendants posted copies of the object and source code of DeCSS. In Corley's words, he added the code to the story because "in a journalistic world, . . . [y]ou have to show your evidence . . . and particularly in the magazine that I work for, people want to see specifically what it is that we are referring to," including "what evidence . . . we have" that there is in fact technology that circumvents CSS. Writing about DeCSS without including the DeCSS code would have been, to Corley, "analogous to printing a story about a picture and not printing the picture." Corley also added to the article links that he explained would take the reader to other web sites where DeCSS could be found.

2600.com was only one of hundreds of web sites that began posting DeCSS near the end of 1999. The movie industry tried to stem the tide by sending cease-and-desist letters to many of these sites. These efforts met with only partial success; a number of sites refused to remove DeCSS. In January 2000, the studios filed this lawsuit.

III. The DMCA

The DMCA was enacted in 1998 to implement the World Intellectual Property Organization Copyright Treaty ("WIPO Treaty"), which requires contracting parties to "provide adequate legal protection and effective legal remedies against the circumvention of effective technological measures that are used by authors in connection with the exercise of their rights under this Treaty or the Berne Convention and that restrict acts, in respect of their works, which are not authorized by the authors concerned or permitted by law." Even before the treaty, Congress had been devoting attention to the problems faced by copyright enforcement in the digital age. Hearings on the topic have spanned several years. This legislative effort resulted in the DMCA.

The Act contains three provisions targeted at the circumvention of technological protections. The first is subsection 1201(a)(1)(A), the anti-circumvention provision. This provision prohibits a person from "circumvent[ing] a technological measure that effectively controls access to a work protected under [Title 17, governing copyright]." The Librarian of Congress is required to promulgate regulations every three years exempting from this subsection individuals who would otherwise be "adversely affected" in "their ability to make noninfringing uses."

The second and third provisions are subsections 1201(a)(2) and 1201(b)(1), the "anti-trafficking provisions." Subsection 1201(a)(2), the provision at issue in this case, provides:

No person shall manufacture, import, offer to the public, provide, or otherwise traffic in any technology, product, service, device, component, or part thereof, that –

(A) is primarily designed or produced for the purpose of circumventing a technological measure that effectively controls access to a work protected under this title;

(B) has only limited commercially significant purpose or use other than to circumvent a technological measure that effectively controls access to a work protected under this title; or

(C) is marketed by that person or another acting in concert with that person with that person's knowledge for use in circumventing a technological measure that effectively controls access to a work protected under this title.

To "circumvent a technological measure" is defined, in pertinent part, as "to descramble a scrambled work . . . or otherwise to . . . bypass . . . a technological measure, without the authority of the copyright owner."

Subsection 1201(b)(1) is similar to subsection 1201(a)(2), except that subsection 1201(a)(2) covers those who traffic in technology that can circumvent "a technological measure that effectively controls access to a work protected under" Title 17, whereas subsection 1201(b)(1) covers those who traffic in technology that can circumvent "protection afforded by a technological measure *that effectively protects a right of a copyright owner* under" [17 U.S.C. § 1201(a)(2), (b)(1)] (emphases added). In other words, although both subsections prohibit trafficking in a circumvention technology, the focus of subsection 1201(a)(2) is circumvention of technologies designed to prevent access to a work, and the focus of subsection 1201(b)(1) is circumvention of technologies designed to permit access to a work but prevent copying of the work or some other act that infringes a copyright. Subsection 1201(a)(1) differs from both of these anti-trafficking subsections in that it targets the use of a circumvention technology, not the trafficking in such a technology.

The DMCA contains exceptions for schools and libraries that want to use circumvention technologies to determine whether to purchase a copyrighted product, 17 U.S.C. § 1201(d); individuals using circumvention technology "for the sole purpose" of trying to achieve "interoperability" of computer programs through reverse-engineering, § 1201(f); encryption research aimed at identifying flaws in encryption technology, if the research is conducted to advance the state of knowledge in the field, § 1201(g); and several other exceptions not relevant here.

The DMCA creates civil remedies, § 1203, and criminal sanctions, § 1204. It specifically authorizes a court to "grant temporary and permanent injunctions on such terms as it deems reasonable to prevent or restrain a violation." [Section 1203(b)(1)].

IV. Procedural History

Invoking subsection 1203(b)(1), the Plaintiffs sought an injunction against the Defendants, alleging that the Defendants violated the anti-trafficking provisions of the statute. On January 20, 2000, after a hearing, the District Court issued a preliminary injunction barring the Defendants from posting DeCSS.

The Defendants complied with the preliminary injunction, but continued to post links to other web sites carrying DeCSS, an action they termed "electronic civil disobedience." Under the heading "Stop the MPAA [(Motion Picture Association of America)]," Corley urged other web sites to post DeCSS lest "we . . . be forced into submission."

The Plaintiffs then sought a permanent injunction barring the Defendants from both posting DeCSS and linking to sites containing DeCSS. After a trial on the merits, the Court issued a comprehensive opinion, *Universal I*, and granted a permanent injunction, *Universal II*.

The Court explained that the Defendants' posting of DeCSS on their web site clearly falls within section 1201(a)(2)(A) of the DMCA, rejecting as spurious their claim that CSS is not a technological measure that "effectively controls access to a work" because it was so easily penetrated by Johansen, and as irrelevant their contention that DeCSS was designed to create a Linux-platform DVD player. The Court also held that the Defendants cannot avail themselves of any of the DMCA's exceptions, and that the alleged importance of DeCSS to certain fair uses of encrypted copyrighted material was immaterial to their statutory liability. The Court went on to hold that when the Defendants "proclaimed on their own site that DeCSS could be had by clicking on the hyperlinks" on their site, they were trafficking in DeCSS, and therefore liable for their linking as well as their posting.

Turning to the Defendants' numerous constitutional arguments, the Court first held that computer code like DeCSS is "speech" that is "protected" (in the sense of "covered") by the First Amendment, but that because the DMCA is targeting the "functional" aspect of that speech, it is "content neutral," and the intermediate scrutiny of *United States v. O'Brien* applies. The Court concluded that the DMCA survives this scrutiny, and also rejected prior restraint, overbreadth, and vagueness challenges.

The Court upheld the constitutionality of the DMCA's application to linking on similar grounds: linking, the Court concluded, is "speech," but the DMCA is content-neutral, targeting only the functional components of that speech. Therefore, its application to linking is also evaluated under *O'Brien*, and, thus evaluated, survives intermediate scrutiny. However, the Court concluded that a blanket proscription on linking would create a risk of chilling legitimate linking on the web. The Court therefore crafted a restrictive test for linking liability (discussed below) that it believed sufficiently mitigated that risk. The Court then found its test satisfied in this case.

Finally, the Court concluded that an injunction was highly appropriate in this case. The Court observed that DeCSS was harming the Plaintiffs, not only because they were now exposed to the possibility of piracy and therefore were obliged to develop costly new safeguards for DVDs, but also because, even if there was only indirect evidence that DeCSS availability actually facilitated DVD piracy, the threat of piracy was very real, particularly as Internet transmission speeds continue to increase. Acknowledging that DeCSS was (and still is) widely available on the Internet, the Court expressed confidence in

the likelihood . . . that this decision will serve notice on others that "the strong right arm of equity" may be brought to bear against them absent a change in their conduct and thus contribute to a climate of appropriate respect for intellectual property rights in an age in which the excitement of ready access to untold quantities of information has blurred in some minds the fact that taking what is not yours and not freely offered to you is stealing.

The Court's injunction barred the Defendants from: "posting on any Internet web site" DeCSS; "in any other way . . . offering to the public, providing, or otherwise trafficking in DeCSS"; violating the anti-trafficking provisions of the DMCA in any other manner, and finally "knowingly linking any Internet web site operated by them to any other web site containing DeCSS, or knowingly maintaining any such link, for the purpose of disseminating DeCSS."

The Appellants have appealed from the permanent injunction. The United States has intervened in support of the constitutionality of the DMCA. We have also had the benefit of a number of *amicus curiae* briefs, supporting and opposing the District Court's judgment. After oral argument, we invited the parties to submit responses to a series of specific questions, and we have received helpful responses.

Discussion

I. Narrow Construction to Avoid Constitutional Doubt

The Appellants first argue that, because their constitutional arguments are at least substantial, we should interpret the statute narrowly so as to avoid constitutional problems. They identify three different instances of alleged ambiguity in the statute that they claim provide an opportunity for such a narrow interpretation.

First, they contend that subsection 1201(c)(1), which provides that "[n]othing in this section shall affect rights, remedies, limitations or defenses to copyright infringement, including fair use, under this title," can be read to allow the circumvention of encryption technology protecting copyrighted material when the material will be put to "fair uses" exempt from copyright liability. We disagree that subsection 1201(c)(1) permits such a reading. Instead, it simply clarifies that the DMCA targets the circumvention of digital walls guarding copyrighted material (and trafficking in circumvention tools), but does not concern itself with the use of those materials after circumvention has occurred. Subsection 1201(c)(1) ensures that the DMCA is not read to prohibit the "fair use" of information just because that information was obtained in a manner made illegal by the DMCA. The Appellants' much more expansive interpretation of subsection 1201(c)(1) is not only outside the range of plausible readings of the provision, but is also clearly refuted by the statute's legislative history.

Second, the Appellants urge a narrow construction of the DMCA because of subsection 1201(c)(4), which provides that "[n]othing in this section shall enlarge or diminish any rights of free speech or the press for activities using consumer electronics, telecommunications, or computing products." This language is clearly precatory: Congress could not "diminish" constitutional rights of free speech even if it wished to, and the fact that Congress also expressed a reluctance to "enlarge" those rights cuts against the Appellants' effort to infer a narrowing construction of the Act from this provision.

Third, the Appellants argue that an individual who buys a DVD has the "authority of the copyright owner" to view the DVD, and therefore is exempted from the DMCA pursuant to subsection 1201(a)(3)(A) when the buyer circumvents an encryption technology in order to view the DVD on a competing platform (such as Linux). The basic flaw in this argument is that it misreads subsection 1201(a)(3)(A). That provision exempts from liability those who would "decrypt" an encrypted DVD with the authority of a copyright owner, not those who would "view" a DVD with the authority of a copyright owner. In any event, the Defendants offered no evidence that the Plaintiffs have either explicitly or implicitly authorized DVD buyers to circumvent encryption technology to support use on multiple platforms.

We conclude that the anti-trafficking and anti-circumvention provisions of the DMCA are not susceptible to the narrow interpretations urged by the Appellants. We therefore proceed to consider the Appellants' constitutional claims.

II. Constitutional Challenge Based on the Copyright Clause

In a footnote to their brief, the Appellants appear to contend that the DMCA, as construed by the District Court, exceeds the constitutional authority of Congress to grant authors copyrights for a "limited time," because it "empower[s] copyright owners to effectively secure perpetual protection by mixing public domain works with copyrighted materials, then locking both up with technological protection measures." This argument is elaborated in the *amici curiae* brief filed by Prof. Julie E. Cohen on behalf of herself and 45 other intellectual property law professors. For two reasons, the argument provides no basis for disturbing the judgment of the District Court.

First, we have repeatedly ruled that arguments presented to us only in a footnote are not entitled to appellate consideration. Although an amicus brief can be helpful in elaborating issues properly presented by the parties, it is normally not a method for injecting new issues into an appeal, at least in cases where the parties are competently represented by counsel. Second, to whatever extent the argument might have merit at some future time in a case with a properly developed record, the argument is entirely premature and speculative at this time on this record. There is not even a claim, much less evidence, that any Plaintiff has sought to prevent copying of public domain works, or that the injunction prevents the Defendants from copying such works. As Judge Kaplan noted, the possibility that encryption would preclude access to public domain works "does not yet appear to be a problem, although it may emerge as one in the future."

III. Constitutional Challenges Based on the First Amendment
A. Applicable Principles

Last year, in one of our Court's first forays into First Amendment law in the digital age, we took an "evolutionary" approach to the task of tailoring familiar constitutional rules to novel technological circumstances, favoring "narrow" holdings that would permit the law to mature on a "case-by-case" basis. In that spirit, we proceed, with appropriate caution, to consider the Appellants' First Amendment challenges by analyzing a series of preliminary issues the resolution of which provides a basis for adjudicating the specific objections to the DMCA and its application to DeCSS. These issues, which we consider only to the extent necessary to resolve the pending appeal, are whether computer code is speech, whether computer programs are speech, the scope of First Amendment protection for computer code, and the scope of First Amendment protection for decryption code. Based on our analysis of these issues, we then consider the Appellants' challenge to the injunction's provisions concerning posting and linking.

1. Code as Speech

Communication does not lose constitutional protection as "speech" simply because it is expressed in the language of computer code. Mathematical formulae and musical scores are written in "code," i.e., symbolic notations not comprehensible to the uninitiated, and yet both are covered by the First Amendment. If someone chose to write a novel entirely in computer object code by using strings of 1's and 0's for each letter of each word, the resulting work would be no different for constitutional purposes than if it had been written in English. The "object code" version would be incomprehensible to readers outside the programming community (and tedious to read even for most within the community), but it would be no more incomprehensible than a work written in Sanskrit for those unversed in that language. The undisputed evidence reveals that even pure object code can be, and often is, read and understood by experienced programmers. And source code (in any of its various levels of complexity) can be read by many more. Ultimately, however, the ease with which a work is comprehended is irrelevant to the constitutional inquiry. If computer code is distinguishable from conventional speech for First Amendment purposes, it is not because it is written in an obscure language.

2. Computer Programs as Speech

Of course, computer code is not likely to be the language in which a work of literature is written. Instead, it is primarily the language for programs executable by a computer. These programs are essentially instructions to a computer. In general, programs may give instructions either to perform a task or series of tasks when initiated by a single (or double) click of a mouse or, once a program is operational ("launched"), to manipulate data that the user enters into the computer. Whether computer code that gives a computer instructions is "speech" within the meaning of the First Amendment requires consideration of the scope of the Constitution's protection of speech.

The First Amendment provides that "Congress shall make no law . . . abridging the freedom of speech. . . . " "Speech" is an elusive term, and judges and scholars have debated its bounds for two centuries. Some would confine First Amendment protection to political speech. Others would extend it further to artistic expression.

Whatever might be the merits of these and other approaches, the law has not been so limited. Even dry information, devoid of advocacy, political relevance, or artistic expression, has been accorded First Amendment protection.

Thus, for example, courts have subjected to First Amendment scrutiny restrictions on the dissemination of technical scientific information, and scientific research, and attempts to regulate the publication of instructions.

Computer programs are not exempted from the category of First Amendment speech simply because their instructions require use of a computer. A recipe is no less "speech" because it calls for the use of an oven, and a musical score is no less "speech" because it specifies performance on an electric guitar. Arguably distinguishing computer programs from conventional language instructions is the fact that programs are executable on a computer. But the fact that a program has the capacity to direct the functioning of a computer does not mean that it lacks the additional capacity to convey information, and it is the conveying of information that renders instructions "speech" for purposes of the First Amendment. The information conveyed by most "instructions" is how to perform a task.

Instructions such as computer code, which are intended to be executable by a computer, will often convey information capable of comprehension and assessment by a human being. A programmer reading a program learns information about instructing a computer, and might use this information to improve personal programming skills and perhaps the craft of programming. Moreover, programmers communicating ideas to one another almost inevitably communicate in code, much as musicians use notes. Limiting First Amendment protection of programmers to descriptions of computer code (but not the code itself) would impede discourse among computer scholars, just as limiting protection for musicians to descriptions of musical scores (but not sequences of notes) would impede their exchange of ideas and expression. Instructions that communicate information comprehensible to a human qualify as speech whether the instructions are designed for execution by a computer or a human (or both).

Vartuli is not to the contrary. The defendants in *Vartuli* marketed a software program called "Recurrence," which would tell computer users when to buy or sell currency futures contracts if their computers were fed currency market rates. The Commodity Futures Trading Commission charged the defendants with violating federal law for, among other things, failing to register as commodity trading advisors for their distribution of the Recurrence software. The defendants maintained that Recurrence's cues to users to buy or sell were protected speech, and that the registration requirement as applied to Recurrence was a constitutionally suspect prior restraint. We rejected the defendants' constitutional claim, holding that Recurrence "in the form it was sold and marketed by the defendants" did not generate speech protected by the First Amendment.

Essential to our ruling in *Vartuli* was the manner in which the defendants marketed the software and intended that it be used: the defendants told users of the software to follow the software's cues "with no second-guessing," and intended that users follow Recurrence's commands "mechanically" and "without the intercession of the mind or the will of the recipient." We held that the values served by the First Amendment were not advanced by these instructions, even though the instructions were expressed in words. We acknowledged that some users would, despite the defendants' marketing, refuse to follow Recurrence's cues mechanically but instead would use the commands as a source of information and advice, and that, as to these users, Recurrence's cues might very "well have been 'speech.'" Nevertheless, we concluded that the Government could require registration for Recurrence's intended use because such use was devoid of any constitutionally protected speech.

Vartuli considered two ways in which a programmer might be said to communicate through code: to the user of the program (not necessarily protected) and to the computer (never protected). However, this does not mean that *Vartuli* denied First Amendment protection to all computer programs. Since *Vartuli* limited its constitutional scrutiny to the code "as marketed," i.e., as an automatic trading system, it did not have occasion to consider a third manner in which a programmer might communicate through code: to another programmer.

For all of these reasons, we join the other courts that have concluded that computer code, and computer programs constructed from code can merit First Amendment protection.

3. The Scope of First Amendment Protection for Computer Code

Having concluded that computer code conveying information is "speech" within the meaning of the First Amendment, we next consider, to a limited extent, the scope of the protection that code enjoys. As the District Court recognized, the scope of protection for speech generally depends on whether the restriction is imposed because of the content of the speech. Content-based restrictions are permissible only if they serve compelling state interests and do so by the least restrictive means available. A content-neutral restriction is permissible if it serves a substantial governmental interest, the interest is unrelated to the suppression of free expression, and the regulation is narrowly tailored, which "in this context requires . . . that the means chosen do not 'burden substantially more speech than is necessary to further the government's legitimate interests.' "

* * *

To determine whether regulation of computer code is content-neutral, the initial inquiry must be whether the regulated activity is "sufficiently imbued with elements of communication to fall within the scope of the First . . . Amendment." Computer code, as we have noted, often conveys information comprehensible to human beings, even as it also directs a computer to perform various functions. Once a speech component is identified, the inquiry then proceeds to whether the regulation is "justified without reference to the content of regulated speech."

The Appellants vigorously reject the idea that computer code can be regulated according to any different standard than that applicable to pure speech, i.e., speech that lacks a nonspeech component. Although recognizing that code is a series of instructions to a computer, they argue that code is no different, for First Amendment purposes, than blueprints that instruct an engineer or recipes that instruct a cook. We disagree. Unlike a blueprint or a recipe, which cannot yield any functional result without human comprehension of its content, human decision-making, and human action, computer code can instantly cause a computer to accomplish tasks and instantly render the results of those tasks available throughout the world via the Internet. The only human action required to achieve these results can be as limited and instantaneous as a single click of a mouse. These realities of what code is and what its normal functions are require a First Amendment analysis that treats code as combining nonspeech and speech elements, i.e., functional and expressive elements. ("[D]ifferences in the characteristics of new media justify differences in the First Amendment standards applied to them.")

We recognize, as did Judge Kaplan, that the functional capability of computer code cannot yield a result until a human being decides to insert the disk containing the code into a computer and causes it to perform its function (or programs a computer to cause the code to perform its function). Nevertheless, this momentary intercession of human action does not diminish the nonspeech component of code, nor render code entirely speech, like a blueprint or a recipe. Judge Kaplan, in a passage that merits extensive quotation, cogently explained why this is especially so with respect to decryption code:

[T]he focus on functionality in order to determine the level of scrutiny is not an inevitable consequence of the speech-conduct distinction. Conduct has immediate effects on the environment. Computer code, on the other hand, no matter how functional, causes a computer to perform the intended operations only if someone uses the code to do so. Hence,

one commentator, in a thoughtful article, has maintained that functionality is really "a proxy for effects or harm" and that its adoption as a determinant of the level of scrutiny slides over questions of causation that intervene between the dissemination of a computer program and any harm caused by its use.

The characterization of functionality as a proxy for the consequences of use is accurate. But the assumption that the chain of causation is too attenuated to justify the use of functionality to determine the level of scrutiny, at least in this context, is not.

Society increasingly depends upon technological means of controlling access to digital files and systems, whether they are military computers, bank records, academic records, copyrighted works or something else entirely. There are far too many who, given any opportunity, will bypass security measures, some for the sheer joy of doing it, some for innocuous reasons, and others for more malevolent purposes. Given the virtually instantaneous and worldwide dissemination widely available via the Internet, the only rational assumption is that once a computer program capable of bypassing such an access control system is disseminated, it will be used. And that is not all.

There was a time when copyright infringement could be dealt with quite adequately by focusing on the infringing act. If someone wished to make and sell high quality but unauthorized copies of a copyrighted book, for example, the infringer needed a printing press. The copyright holder, once aware of the appearance of infringing copies, usually was able to trace the copies up the chain of distribution, find and prosecute the infringer, and shut off the infringement at the source.

In principle, the digital world is very different. Once a decryption program like DeCSS is written, it quickly can be sent all over the world. Every recipient is capable not only of decrypting and perfectly copying plaintiffs' copyrighted DVDs, but also of retransmitting perfect copies of DeCSS and thus enabling every recipient to do the same. They likewise are capable of transmitting perfect copies of the decrypted DVD. The process potentially is exponential rather than linear.

. . .

These considerations drastically alter consideration of the causal link between dissemination of computer programs such as this and their illicit use. Causation in the law ultimately involves practical policy judgments. Here, dissemination itself carries very substantial risk of imminent harm because the mechanism is so unusual by which dissemination of means of circumventing access controls to copyrighted works threatens to produce virtually unstoppable infringement of copyright. In consequence, the causal link between the dissemination of circumvention computer programs and their improper use is more than sufficiently close to warrant selection of a level of constitutional scrutiny based on the programs' functionality.

The functionality of computer code properly affects the scope of its First Amendment protection.

4. The Scope of First Amendment Protection for Decryption Code

In considering the scope of First Amendment protection for a decryption program like DeCSS, we must recognize that the essential purpose of encryption code is to prevent unauthorized access.

Owners of all property rights are entitled to prohibit access to their property by unauthorized persons. Homeowners can install locks on the doors of their houses. Custodians of valuables can place them in safes. Stores can attach to products security devices that will activate alarms if the products are taken away without purchase. These and similar security devices can be circumvented. Burglars can use skeleton keys to open door locks. Thieves can obtain the combinations to safes. Product security devices can be neutralized.

Our case concerns a security device, CSS computer code, that prevents access by unauthorized persons to DVD movies. The CSS code is embedded in the DVD movie. Access to the movie cannot be obtained unless a person has a device, a licensed DVD player, equipped with computer code capable of decrypting the CSS encryption code. In its basic function, CSS is like a lock on a homeowner's door, a combination of a safe, or a security device attached to a store's products.

DeCSS is computer code that can decrypt CSS. In its basic function, it is like a skeleton key that can open a locked door, a combination that can open a safe, or a device that can neutralize the security device attached to a store's products. DeCSS enables anyone to gain access to a DVD movie without using a DVD player.

The initial use of DeCSS to gain access to a DVD movie creates no loss to movie producers because the initial user must purchase the DVD. However, once the DVD is purchased, DeCSS enables the initial user to copy the movie in digital form and transmit it instantly in virtually limitless quantity, thereby depriving the movie producer of sales. The advent of the Internet creates the potential for instantaneous worldwide distribution of the copied material.

At first glance, one might think that Congress has as much authority to regulate the distribution of computer code to decrypt DVD movies as it has to regulate distribution of skeleton keys, combinations to safes, or devices to neutralize store product security devices. However, despite the evident legitimacy of protection against unauthorized access to DVD movies, just like any other property, regulation of decryption code like DeCSS is challenged in this case because DeCSS differs from a skeleton key in one important respect: it not only is capable of performing the function of unlocking the encrypted DVD movie, it also is a form of communication, albeit written in a language not understood by the general public. As a communication, the DeCSS code has a claim to being "speech," and as "speech," it has a claim to being protected by the First Amendment. But just as the realities of what any computer code can accomplish must inform the scope of its constitutional protection, so the capacity of a decryption program like DeCSS to accomplish unauthorized—indeed, unlawful—access to materials in which the Plaintiffs have intellectual property rights must inform and limit the scope of its First Amendment protection.

With all of the foregoing considerations in mind, we next consider the Appellants' First Amendment challenge to the DMCA as applied in the specific prohibitions that have been imposed by the District Court's injunction.

B. First Amendment Challenge

The District Court's injunction applies the DMCA to the Defendants by imposing two types of prohibition, both grounded on the anti-trafficking provisions of the DMCA. The first prohibits posting DeCSS or any other technology for circumventing CSS on any Internet web site. The second prohibits knowingly linking any Internet web site to any other web site containing DeCSS. The validity of the posting and linking prohibitions must be considered separately.

1. Posting

The initial issue is whether the posting prohibition is content-neutral, since, as we have explained, this classification determines the applicable constitutional standard. The Appellants contend that the anti-trafficking provisions of the DMCA and their application by means of the posting prohibition of the injunction are content-based. They argue that the provisions "specifically target . . . scientific expression based on the particular topic addressed by that expression—namely, techniques for circumventing CSS." We disagree. The Appellants' argument fails to recognize that the target of the posting provisions of the injunction—DeCSS—has both a non-speech and a speech component, and that the DMCA, as applied to the Appellants, and the posting prohibition of the injunction target only the nonspeech component. Neither the DMCA nor the posting prohibition is concerned with whatever capacity DeCSS might have for conveying information to a human being, and that capacity, as previously explained, is what arguably creates a speech component of the decryption code. The DMCA and the posting prohibition are applied to DeCSS solely because of its capacity to instruct a computer to decrypt CSS. That functional capability is not speech within the meaning of the First Amendment. The Government seeks to "justif[y]," both the application of the DMCA and the posting prohibition to the Appellants solely on the basis of the functional capability of DeCSS to instruct a computer to decrypt CSS, i.e., "without reference to the content of the regulated speech." This type of regulation is therefore content-neutral, just as would be a restriction on trafficking in skeleton keys identified because of their capacity to unlock jail cells, even though some of the keys happened to bear a slogan or other legend that qualified as a speech component.

As a content-neutral regulation with an incidental effect on a speech component, the regulation must serve a substantial governmental interest, the interest must be unrelated to the suppression of free expression, and the incidental restriction on speech must not burden substantially more speech than is necessary to further that interest. The Government's interest in preventing unauthorized access to encrypted copyrighted material is unquestionably substantial, and the regulation of DeCSS by the posting prohibition plainly serves that interest. Moreover, that interest is unrelated to the suppression of free expression. The injunction regulates the posting of DeCSS, regardless of whether DeCSS code contains any information comprehensible by human beings that would qualify as speech. Whether the incidental regulation on speech burdens substantially more speech than is necessary to further the interest in preventing unauthorized access to copyrighted materials requires some elaboration.

Posting DeCSS on the Appellants' web site makes it instantly available at the click of a mouse to any person in the world with access to the Internet, and such person can then instantly transmit DeCSS to anyone else with Internet access. Although the prohibition on posting prevents the Appellants from conveying to others the speech component of DeCSS, the Appellants have not suggested, much less shown, any technique for barring them from making this instantaneous worldwide distribution of a decryption code that makes a lesser restriction on the code's speech component. It is true that the Government has alternative means of prohibiting unauthorized access to copyrighted materials. For example, it can create criminal and civil liability for those who gain unauthorized access, and thus it can be argued that the restriction on posting DeCSS is not absolutely necessary to preventing unauthorized access to copyrighted materials. But a content-neutral regulation need not employ the least restrictive means of accomplishing the governmental objective. It need only avoid burdening "substantially more speech than is necessary to further the government's legitimate interests." The prohibition on the Defendants' posting of DeCSS satisfies that standard.

2. Linking

In considering linking, we need to clarify the sense in which the injunction prohibits such activity. Although the injunction defines several terms, it does not define "linking." Nevertheless, it is evident from the District Court's opinion that it is concerned with "hyperlinks." A hyperlink is a cross-reference (in a distinctive font or color) appearing on one web page that, when activated by the point-and-click of a mouse, brings onto the computer screen another web page. The hyperlink can appear on a screen (window) as text, such as the Internet address ("URL") of the web page being called up or a word or phrase that identifies the web page to be called up, for example, "DeCSS web site." Or the hyperlink can appear as an image, for example, an icon depicting a person sitting at a computer watching a DVD movie and text stating "click here to access DeCSS and see DVD movies for free!" The code for the web page containing the hyperlink includes a computer instruction that associates the link with the URL of the web page to be accessed, such that clicking on the hyperlink instructs the computer to enter the URL of the desired web page and thereby access that page. With a hyperlink on a web page, the linked web site is just one click away.

In applying the DMCA to linking (via hyperlinks), Judge Kaplan recognized, as he had with DeCSS code, that a hyperlink has both a speech and a nonspeech component. It conveys information, the Internet address of the linked web page, and has the functional capacity to bring the content of the linked web page to the user's computer screen (or, as Judge Kaplan put it, to "take one almost instantaneously to the desired destination."). As he had ruled with respect to DeCSS code, he ruled that application of the DMCA to the Defendants' linking to web sites containing DeCSS is content-neutral because it is justified without regard to the speech component of the hyperlink. The linking prohibition applies whether or not the hyperlink contains any information, comprehensible to a human being, as to the Internet address of the web page being accessed. The linking prohibition is justified solely by the functional capability of the hyperlink.

Applying the *O'Brien/Ward/Turner Broadcasting* requirements for content-neutral regulation, Judge Kaplan then ruled that the DMCA, as applied to the Defendants' linking, served substantial governmental interests and was unrelated to the suppression of free expression. We agree. He then carefully considered the "closer call," as to whether a linking prohibition would satisfy the narrow tailoring requirement. In an especially carefully considered portion of his opinion, he observed that strict liability for linking to web sites containing DeCSS would risk two impairments of free expression. Web site operators would be inhibited from displaying links to various web pages for fear that a linked page might contain DeCSS, and a prohibition on linking to a web site containing DeCSS would curtail access to whatever other information was contained at the accessed site.

To avoid applying the DMCA in a manner that would "burden substantially more speech than is necessary to further the government's legitimate interests," Judge Kaplan adapted the standards of *New York Times Co. v. Sullivan* to fashion a limited prohibition against linking to web sites containing DeCSS. He required clear and convincing evidence

> that those responsible for the link (a) know at the relevant time that the offending material is on the linked-to site, (b) know that it is circumvention technology that may not lawfully be offered, and (c) create or maintain the link for the purpose of disseminating that technology.

He then found that the evidence satisfied his three-part test by his required standard of proof.

In response to our post-argument request for the parties' views on various issues, including specifically Judge Kaplan's test for a linking prohibition, the Appellants replied that his test was deficient for not requiring proof of intent to cause, or aid or abet, harm, and that the only valid test for a linking prohibition would be one that could validly apply to the publication in a print medium of an address for obtaining prohibited material. The Appellees and the Government accepted Judge Kaplan's criteria for purposes of asserting the validity of the injunction as applied to the Appellants, with the Government expressing reservations as to the standard of clear and convincing evidence.

Mindful of the cautious approach to First Amendment claims involving computer technology expressed in *Name.Space*, we see no need on this appeal to determine whether a test as rigorous as Judge Kaplan's is required to respond to First Amendment objections to the linking provision of the injunction that he issued. It suffices to reject the Appellants' contention that an intent to cause harm is required and that linking can be enjoined only under circumstances applicable to a print medium. As they have throughout their arguments, the Appellants ignore the reality of the functional capacity of decryption computer code and hyperlinks to facilitate instantaneous unauthorized access to copyrighted materials by anyone anywhere in the world. Under the circumstances amply shown by the record, the injunction's linking prohibition validly regulates the Appellants' opportunity instantly to enable anyone anywhere to gain unauthorized access to copyrighted movies on DVDs.

> At oral argument, we asked the Government whether its undoubted power to punish the distribution of obscene materials would permit an injunction prohibiting a newspaper from printing addresses of bookstore locations carrying such materials. In a properly cautious response, the Government stated that the answer would depend on the circumstances of the publication. The Appellants' supplemental papers enthusiastically embraced the arguable analogy between printing bookstore addresses and displaying on a web page links to web sites at which DeCSS may be accessed. They confidently asserted that publication of bookstore locations carrying obscene material cannot be enjoined consistent with the First Amendment, and that a prohibition against linking to web sites containing DeCSS is similarly invalid.

Like many analogies posited to illuminate legal issues, the bookstore analogy is helpful primarily in identifying characteristics that distinguish it from the context of the pending dispute. If a bookstore proprietor is knowingly selling obscene materials, the evil of distributing such materials can be prevented by injunctive relief against the unlawful distribution (and similar distribution by others can be deterred by punishment of the distributor). And if others publish the location of the bookstore, preventive relief against a distributor can be effective before any significant distribution of the prohibited materials has occurred. The digital world, however, creates a very different problem. If obscene materials are posted on one web site and other sites post hyperlinks to the first site, the materials are available for instantaneous worldwide distribution before any preventive measures can be effectively taken.

This reality obliges courts considering First Amendment claims in the context of the pending case to choose between two unattractive alternatives: either tolerate some impairment of communication in order to permit Congress to prohibit decryption that may lawfully be prevented, or tolerate some decryption in order to avoid some impairment of communication. Although the parties dispute the extent of impairment of communication if the injunction is upheld and the extent of decryption if it is vacated, and differ on the availability and effectiveness of techniques for minimizing both consequences, the fundamental choice between impairing some communication and tolerating decryption cannot be entirely avoided.

In facing this choice, we are mindful that it is not for us to resolve the issues of public policy implicated by the choice we have identified. Those issues are for Congress. Our task is to determine whether the legislative solution adopted by Congress, as applied to the Appellants by the District Court's injunction, is consistent with the limitations of the First Amendment, and we are satisfied that it is.

IV. Constitutional Challenge Based on Claimed Restriction of Fair Use

Asserting that fair use "is rooted in and required by both the Copyright Clause and the First Amendment," the Appellants contend that the DMCA, as applied by the District Court, unconstitutionally "eliminates fair use" of copyrighted materials. We reject this extravagant claim.

Preliminarily, we note that the Supreme Court has never held that fair use is constitutionally required, although some isolated statements in its opinions might arguably be enlisted for such a requirement. In *Stewart v. Abend,* cited by the Appellants, the Court merely noted that fair use "'permits courts to avoid rigid application of the copyright statute when, on occasion, it would stifle the very creativity which that law is designed to foster.'" In *Campbell v. Acuff-Rose Music, Inc.,* the Court observed, "From the infancy of copyright protection, some opportunity for fair use of copyrighted materials has been thought necessary to fulfill copyright's very purpose, '[t]o promote the Progress of Science and useful Arts. . . .'"

We need not explore the extent to which fair use might have constitutional protection, grounded on either the First Amendment or the Copyright Clause, because whatever validity a constitutional claim might have as to an application of the DMCA that impairs fair use of copyrighted materials, such matters are far beyond the scope of this lawsuit for several reasons. In the first place, the Appellants do not claim to be making fair use of any copyrighted materials, and nothing in the injunction prohibits them from making such fair use. They are barred from trafficking in a decryption code that enables unauthorized access to copyrighted materials.

Second, as the District Court properly noted, to whatever extent the anti-trafficking provisions of the DMCA might prevent others from copying portions of DVD movies in order to make fair use of them, "the evidence as to the impact of the anti-trafficking provision[s] of the DMCA on prospective fair users is scanty and fails adequately to address the issues."

Third, the Appellants have provided no support for their premise that fair use of DVD movies is constitutionally required to be made by copying the original work in its original format. Their examples of the fair uses that they believe others will be prevented from making all involve copying in a digital format those portions of a DVD movie amenable to fair use, a copying that would enable the fair user to manipulate the digitally copied portions. One example is that of a school child who wishes to copy images from a DVD movie to insert into the student's documentary film. We know of no authority for the proposition that fair use, as protected by the Copyright Act, much less the Constitution, guarantees copying by the optimum method or in the identical format of the original. Although the Appellants insisted at oral argument that they should not be relegated to a "horse and buggy" technique in making fair use of DVD movies, the DMCA does not impose even an arguable limitation on the opportunity to make a variety of traditional fair uses of DVD movies, such as commenting on their content, quoting excerpts from their screenplays, and even recording portions of the video images and sounds on film or tape by pointing a camera, a camcorder, or a microphone at a monitor as it displays the DVD movie. The fact that the resulting copy will not be as perfect or as manipulable as a digital copy obtained by having direct access to the DVD movie in its digital form, provides no basis for a claim of unconstitutional limitation of fair use. A film critic making fair use of a movie by quoting selected lines of dialogue has no constitutionally valid claim that the review (in print or on television) would be technologically superior if the reviewer had not been prevented from using a movie camera in the theater, nor has an art student a valid constitutional claim to fair use of a painting by photographing it in a museum. Fair use has never been held to be a guarantee of access to copyrighted material in order to copy it by the fair user's preferred technique or in the format of the original.

Conclusion

We have considered all the other arguments of the Appellants and conclude that they provide no basis for disturbing the District Court's judgment. Accordingly, the judgment is affirmed.

Source: *Universal City Studios, Inc. v. Corley,* 273 F.3d 429 (2nd Cir. 2001).

MGM Studios Inc. v. Grokster, Ltd., 2005

The U.S. Supreme Court's decision in Grokster *marked the end of the Wild West days of file-sharing. File-sharing networks had a few years, from Napster through Grokster, of almost-legitimacy. In the late days of the 20th century, no one was quite sure what business models would emerge from the Internet revolution; Napster founder Shawn Fanning was featured on the cover of* Time *magazine in October 2000.*

Five years later, file-sharing was on the run. It remained—and remains to this day—widespread, but its legitimacy has been destroyed; it is much harder, today, to make a sincere argument that unlimited file-sharing of copyrighted material with strangers is not theft but an act of digital civil disobedience, or something of the sort. While Grokster *might appear to be a hollow victory—Pirate Bay, for one, remains as active as ever—it has been a public relations coup for the content industry; the law is now far more clearly on the industry's side than it was before the decision.*

JUSTICE SOUTER DELIVERED THE OPINION OF THE COURT

The question is under what circumstances the distributor of a product capable of both lawful and unlawful use is liable for acts of copyright infringement by third parties using the product. We hold that one who distributes a device with the object of promoting its use to infringe copyright, as shown by clear expression or other affirmative steps taken to foster infringement, is liable for the resulting acts of infringement by third parties.

I

A

Respondents, Grokster, Ltd., and StreamCast Networks, Inc., defendants in the trial court, distribute free software products that allow computer users to share electronic files through peer-to-peer networks, so called because users' computers communicate directly with each other, not through central servers. The advantage of peer-to-peer networks over information networks of other types shows up in their substantial and growing popularity. Because they need no central computer server to mediate the exchange of information or files among users, the high-bandwidth communications capacity for a server may be dispensed with, and the need for costly server storage space is eliminated. Since copies of a file (particularly a popular one) are available on many users' computers, file requests and retrievals may be faster than on other types of networks, and since file exchanges do not travel through a server, communications can take place between any computers that remain connected to the network without risk that a glitch in the server will disable the network in its entirety. Given these benefits in security, cost, and efficiency, peer-to-peer networks are employed to store and distribute electronic files by universities, government agencies, corporations, and libraries, among others.

Other users of peer-to-peer networks include individual recipients of Grokster's and StreamCast's software, and although the networks that they enjoy through using the software can be used to share any type of digital file, they have prominently employed those networks in sharing copyrighted music and video files without authorization. A group of copyright holders (MGM for short, but including motion picture studios, recording companies, songwriters, and music publishers) sued Grokster and StreamCast for their users' copyright infringements, alleging that they knowingly and intentionally distributed their software to enable users to reproduce and distribute the copyrighted works in violation of the Copyright Act, 17 U.S.C. § 101 et seq. (2000 ed. and Supp. II). MGM sought damages and an injunction.

Discovery during the litigation revealed the way the software worked, the business aims of each defendant company, and the predilections of the users. Grokster's eponymous software employs what is known as FastTrack technology, a protocol developed by others and licensed to Grokster. StreamCast distributes a very similar product except that its software, called Morpheus, relies on what is known as Gnutella technology. A user who downloads and installs either software possesses the protocol to send requests for files directly to the computers of others using software compatible with FastTrack or Gnutella. On the FastTrack network opened by the Grokster software, the user's request goes to a computer given an indexing capacity by the software and designated a supernode, or to some other computer with comparable power and capacity to collect temporary indexes of the files available on the computers of users connected to it. The supernode (or indexing computer) searches its own index and may communicate the search request to other supernodes. If the file is found, the supernode discloses its location to the computer requesting it, and the requesting user can download the file directly from the computer located. The copied file is placed in a designated sharing folder on the requesting user's computer, where it is available for other users to download in turn, along with any other file in that folder.

In the Gnutella network made available by Morpheus, the process is mostly the same, except that in some versions of the Gnutella protocol there are no supernodes. In these versions, peer computers using the protocol communicate directly with each other. When a user enters a search request into the Morpheus software, it sends the request to computers connected with it, which in turn pass the request along to other connected peers. The search results are communicated to the requesting computer, and the user can download desired files directly from peers' computers. As this description indicates, Grokster and StreamCast use no servers to intercept the content of the search requests or to mediate the file transfers conducted by users of the software, there being no central point through which the substance of the communications passes in either direction.

Although Grokster and StreamCast do not therefore know when particular files are copied, a few searches using their software would show what is available on the networks the software reaches. MGM commissioned a statistician to conduct a systematic search, and his study showed that nearly 90% of the files available for download on the FastTrack system were copyrighted works. Grokster and StreamCast dispute this figure, raising methodological problems and arguing that free copying even of copyrighted works may be authorized by the rightholders. They also argue that potential noninfringing uses of their software are significant in kind, even if infrequent in practice. Some musical performers, for example, have gained new audiences by distributing their copyrighted works for free across peer-to-peer networks, and some distributors of unprotected content have used peer-to-peer networks to disseminate files, Shakespeare being an example. Indeed, StreamCast has given Morpheus users the opportunity to download the briefs in this very case, though their popularity has not been quantified.

As for quantification, the parties' anecdotal and statistical evidence entered thus far to show the content available on the FastTrack and Gnutella networks does not say much about which files are actually downloaded by users, and no one can say how often the software is used to obtain copies of unprotected material. But MGM's evidence gives reason to think that the vast majority of users' downloads are acts of infringement, and because well over 100 million copies of the software in question are known to have been downloaded, and billions of files are shared across the FastTrack and Gnutella networks each month, the probable scope of copyright infringement is staggering.

Grokster and StreamCast concede the infringement in most downloads, and it is uncontested that they are aware that users employ their software primarily to download copyrighted files, even if the decentralized FastTrack and Gnutella networks fail to reveal which files are being copied, and when. From time to time, moreover, the companies have learned about their users' infringement directly, as from users who have sent e-mail to each company with questions about playing copyrighted movies they had downloaded, to whom the companies have responded with guidance. And MGM notified the companies of 8 million copyrighted files that could be obtained using their software.

Grokster and StreamCast are not, however, merely passive recipients of information about infringing use. The record is replete with evidence that from the moment Grokster and StreamCast began to distribute their free software, each one clearly voiced the objective that recipients use it to download copyrighted works, and each took active steps to encourage infringement.

After the notorious file-sharing service, Napster, was sued by copyright holders for facilitation of copyright infringement, StreamCast gave away a software program of a kind known as OpenNap, designed as compatible with the Napster program and open to Napster users for downloading files from other Napster and OpenNap users' computers. Evidence indicates that "[i]t was always [StreamCast's] intent to use [its OpenNap network] to be able to capture email addresses of [its] initial target market so that [it] could promote [its] StreamCast Morpheus interface to them," [I]ndeed, the OpenNap program was engineered "to leverage Napster's 50 million user base."

StreamCast monitored both the number of users downloading its OpenNap program and the number of music files they downloaded. It also used the resulting OpenNap network to distribute copies of the Morpheus software and to encourage users to adopt it. Internal company documents indicate that StreamCast hoped to attract large numbers of former Napster users if that company was shut down by court order or otherwise, and that StreamCast planned to be the next Napster. A kit developed by StreamCast to be delivered to advertisers, for example, contained press articles about StreamCast's potential to capture former Napster users, and it introduced itself to some potential advertisers as a company "which is similar to what Napster was." It broadcast banner advertisements to users of other Napster-compatible software, urging them to adopt its OpenNap. An internal e-mail from a company executive stated: "We have put this network in place so that when Napster pulls the plug on their free service . . . or if the Court orders them shut down prior to that . . . we will be positioned to capture the flood of their 32 million users that will be actively looking for an alternative."

Thus, StreamCast developed promotional materials to market its service as the best Napster alternative. One proposed advertisement read: "Napster Inc. has announced that it will soon begin charging you a fee. That's if the courts don't order it shut down first. What will you do to get around it?" Another proposed ad touted StreamCast's software as the "#1 alternative to Napster" and asked "[w]hen the lights went off at Napster . . . where did the users go?" StreamCast even planned to flaunt the illegal uses of its software; when it launched the OpenNap network, the chief technology officer of the company averred that "[t]he goal is to get in trouble with the law and get sued. It's the best way to get in the new[s]."

The evidence that Grokster sought to capture the market of former Napster users is sparser but revealing, for Grokster launched its own OpenNap system called Swaptor and inserted digital codes into its Web site so that computer users using Web search engines to look for "Napster" or "[f]ree filesharing" would be directed to the Grokster Web site, where they could download the Grokster software. And Grokster's name is an apparent derivative of Napster.

StreamCast's executives monitored the number of songs by certain commercial artists available on their networks, and an internal communication indicates they aimed to have a larger number of copyrighted songs available on their networks than other file-sharing networks. The point, of course, would be to attract users of a mind to infringe, just as it would be with their promotional materials developed showing copyrighted songs as examples of the kinds

of files available through Morpheus. Morpheus in fact allowed users to search specifically for "Top 40" songs, which were inevitably copyrighted. Similarly, Grokster sent users a newsletter promoting its ability to provide particular, popular copyrighted materials.

In addition to this evidence of express promotion, marketing, and intent to promote further, the business models employed by Grokster and StreamCast confirm that their principal object was use of their software to download copyrighted works. Grokster and StreamCast receive no revenue from users, who obtain the software itself for nothing. Instead, both companies generate income by selling advertising space, and they stream the advertising to Grokster and Morpheus users while they are employing the programs. As the number of users of each program increases, advertising opportunities become worth more. While there is doubtless some demand for free Shakespeare, the evidence shows that substantive volume is a function of free access to copyrighted work. Users seeking Top 40 songs, for example, or the latest release by Modest Mouse, are certain to be far more numerous than those seeking a free Decameron, and Grokster and StreamCast translated that demand into dollars.

Finally, there is no evidence that either company made an effort to filter copyrighted material from users' downloads or otherwise impede the sharing of copyrighted files. Although Grokster appears to have sent e-mails warning users about infringing content when it received threatening notice from the copyright holders, it never blocked anyone from continuing to use its software to share copyrighted files. StreamCast not only rejected another company's offer of help to monitor infringement, but blocked the Internet Protocol addresses of entities it believed were trying to engage in such monitoring on its networks.

B

After discovery, the parties on each side of the case cross-moved for summary judgment. The District Court limited its consideration to the asserted liability of Grokster and StreamCast for distributing the current versions of their software, leaving aside whether either was liable "for damages arising from past versions of their software, or from other past activities." The District Court held that those who used the Grokster and Morpheus software to download copyrighted media files directly infringed MGM's copyrights, a conclusion not contested on appeal, but the court nonetheless granted summary judgment in favor of Grokster and StreamCast as to any liability arising from distribution of the then current versions of their software. Distributing that software gave rise to no liability in the court's view, because its use did not provide the distributors with actual knowledge of specific acts of infringement.

The Court of Appeals affirmed. In the court's analysis, a defendant was liable as a contributory infringer when it had knowledge of direct infringement and materially contributed to the infringement. But the court read *Sony Corp. of America v. Universal City Studios, Inc.*, 464 U.S. 417 (1984), as holding that distribution of a commercial product capable of substantial noninfringing uses could not give rise to contributory liability for infringement unless the distributor had actual knowledge of specific instances of infringement and failed to act on that knowledge. The fact that the software was capable of substantial noninfringing uses in the Ninth Circuit's view meant that Grokster and StreamCast were not liable, because they had no such actual knowledge, owing to the decentralized architecture of their software. The court also held that Grokster and StreamCast did not materially contribute to their users' infringement because it was the users themselves who searched for, retrieved, and stored the infringing files, with no involvement by the defendants beyond providing the software in the first place.

The Ninth Circuit also considered whether Grokster and Stream-Cast could be liable under a theory of vicarious infringement. The court held against liability because the defendants did not monitor or control the use of the software, had no agreed-upon right or current ability to supervise its use, and had no independent duty to police infringement. We granted certiorari.

II

A

MGM and many of the amici fault the Court of Appeals's holding for upsetting a sound balance between the respective values of supporting creative pursuits through copyright protection and promoting innovation in new communication technologies by limiting the incidence of liability for copyright infringement. The more artistic protection is favored, the more technological innovation may be discouraged; the administration of copyright law is an exercise in managing the trade-off.

The tension between the two values is the subject of this case, with its claim that digital distribution of copyrighted material threatens copyright holders as never before, because every copy is identical to the original, copying is easy, and many people (especially the young) use file-sharing software to download copyrighted works. This very breadth of the software's use may well draw the public directly into the debate over copyright policy, and the indications are that the ease of copying songs or movies using software like Grokster's and Napster's is fostering disdain for copyright protection. As the case has been presented to us, these fears are said to be offset by the different concern that imposing liability, not only on infringers but on distributors of software based on its potential for unlawful use, could limit further development of beneficial technologies.

The argument for imposing indirect liability in this case is, however, a powerful one, given the number of infringing downloads that occur every day using StreamCast's and Grokster's software. When a widely shared service or product is used to commit infringement, it may be impossible to enforce rights in the protected work effectively against all direct infringers, the only practical alternative being to go against the distributor of the copying device for secondary liability on a theory of contributory or vicarious infringement.

One infringes contributorily by intentionally inducing or encouraging direct infringement, and infringes vicariously by profiting from direct infringement while declining to exercise a right to stop or limit it. Although "[t]he Copyright Act does not expressly render anyone liable for infringement committed by another," these doctrines of secondary liability emerged from common law principles and are well established in the law.

B

Despite the currency of these principles of secondary liability, this Court has dealt with secondary copyright infringement in only one recent case, and because MGM has tailored its principal claim to our opinion there, a look at our earlier holding is in order. In *Sony Corp. v. Universal City Studios*, supra, this Court addressed a claim that secondary liability for infringement can arise from the very distribution of a commercial product. There, the product, novel at the time, was what we know today as the videocassette recorder or VCR. Copyright holders sued Sony as the manufacturer, claiming it was contributorily liable for infringement that occurred when VCR owners taped copyrighted programs because it supplied the means used to infringe, and it had constructive knowledge that infringement would occur. At the trial on the merits, the evidence showed that the principal use of the VCR was for "time-shifting," or taping a program for later viewing at a more convenient time, which the Court found to be a fair, not an infringing, use. There was no evidence that Sony had expressed an object of bringing about taping in violation of copyright or had taken active steps to increase its profits from unlawful taping. Although Sony's advertisements urged consumers to buy the VCR to "record favorite shows" or "build a library" of recorded programs, neither of these uses was necessarily infringing.

On those facts, with no evidence of stated or indicated intent to promote infringing uses, the only conceivable basis for imposing liability was on a theory of contributory infringement arising from its sale of VCRs to consumers with knowledge that some would use them to infringe. But because the VCR was "capable of commercially significant noninfringing uses," we held the manufacturer could not be faulted solely on the basis of its distribution.

This analysis reflected patent law's traditional staple article of commerce doctrine, now codified, that distribution of a component of a patented device will not violate the patent if it is suitable for use in other ways. The doctrine was devised to identify instances in which it may be presumed from distribution of an article in commerce that the distributor intended the article to be used to infringe another's patent, and so may justly be held liable for that infringement. "One who makes and sells articles which are only adapted to be used in a patented combination will be presumed to intend the natural consequences of his acts; he will be presumed to intend that they shall be used in the combination of the patent."

In sum, where an article is "good for nothing else" but infringement, there is no legitimate public interest in its unlicensed availability, and there is no injustice in presuming or imputing an intent to infringe. Conversely, the doctrine absolves the equivocal conduct of selling an item with substantial lawful as well as unlawful uses, and limits liability to instances of more acute fault than the mere understanding that some of one's products will be misused. It leaves breathing room for innovation and a vigorous commerce.

The parties and many of the amici in this case think the key to resolving it is the Sony rule and, in particular, what it means for a product to be "capable of commercially significant noninfringing uses." MGM advances the argument that granting summary judgment to Grokster and StreamCast as to their current activities gave too much weight to the value of innovative technology, and too little to the copyrights infringed by users of their software, given that 90% of works available on one of the networks was shown to be copyrighted. Assuming the remaining 10% to be its noninfringing use, MGM says this should not qualify as "substantial," and the Court should quantify Sony to the extent of holding that a product used "principally" for infringement does not qualify. As mentioned before, Grokster and StreamCast reply by citing evidence that their software can be used to reproduce public domain works, and they point to copyright holders who actually encourage copying. Even if infringement is the principal practice with their software today, they argue, the noninfringing uses are significant and will grow.

We agree with MGM that the Court of Appeals misapplied Sony, which it read as limiting secondary liability quite beyond the circumstances to which the case applied. Sony barred secondary liability based on presuming or imputing intent to cause infringement solely from the design or distribution of a product capable of substantial lawful use, which the distributor knows is in fact used for infringement. The Ninth Circuit has read Sony's limitation to mean that whenever a product is capable of substantial lawful use, the producer can never be held contributorily liable for third parties' infringing use of it; it read the rule as being this broad, even when an actual purpose to cause infringing use is shown by evidence independent of design and distribution of the product, unless the distributors had "specific knowledge of infringement at a time at which they contributed to the infringement, and failed to act upon that information." Because the Circuit found the StreamCast and Grokster software capable of substantial lawful use, it concluded on the basis of its reading of Sony that neither company could be held liable, since there was no showing that their software, being without any central server, afforded them knowledge of specific unlawful uses.

This view of Sony, however, was error, converting the case from one about liability resting on imputed intent to one about liability on any theory. Because Sony did not displace other theories of secondary liability, and because we find below that it was error to grant summary judgment to the companies on MGM's inducement claim, we do not revisit Sony further, as MGM requests, to add a more quantified description of the point of balance between protection and commerce when liability rests solely on distribution with knowledge that unlawful use will occur. It is enough to note that the Ninth Circuit's judgment rested on an erroneous understanding of Sony and to leave further consideration of the Sony rule for a day when that may be required.

C

Sony's rule limits imputing culpable intent as a matter of law from the characteristics or uses of a distributed product. But nothing in Sony requires courts to ignore evidence of intent if there is such evidence, and the case was never meant to foreclose rules of fault-based liability derived from the common law. Thus, where evidence goes beyond a product's characteristics or the knowledge that it may be put to infringing uses, and shows statements or actions directed to promoting infringement, Sony's staple-article rule will not preclude liability.

The classic case of direct evidence of unlawful purpose occurs when one induces commission of infringement by another, or "entic[es] or persuad[es] another" to infringe, as by advertising. Thus at common law a copyright or patent defendant who "not only expected but invoked [infringing use] by advertisement" was liable for infringement "on principles recognized in every part of the law."

The rule on inducement of infringement as developed in the early cases is no different today. Evidence of "active steps . . . taken to encourage direct infringement," such as advertising an infringing use or instructing how to engage in an infringing use, show an affirmative intent that the product be used to infringe, and a showing that infringement was encouraged overcomes the law's reluctance to find liability when a defendant merely sells a commercial product suitable for some lawful use.

For the same reasons that Sony took the staple-article doctrine of patent law as a model for its copyright safe-harbor rule, the inducement rule, too, is a sensible one for copyright. We adopt it here, holding that one who distributes a device with the object of promoting its use to infringe copyright, as shown by clear expression or other affirmative steps taken to foster infringement, is liable for the resulting acts of infringement by third parties. We are, of course, mindful of the need to keep from trenching on regular commerce or discouraging the development of technologies with lawful and unlawful potential. Accordingly, just as Sony did not find intentional inducement despite the knowledge of the VCR manufacturer that its device could be used to infringe, mere knowledge of infringing potential or of actual infringing uses would not be enough here to subject a distributor to liability. Nor would ordinary acts incident to product distribution, such as offering customers technical support or product updates, support liability in themselves. The inducement rule, instead, premises liability on purposeful, culpable expression and conduct, and thus does nothing to compromise legitimate commerce or discourage innovation having a lawful promise.

III

A

The only apparent question about treating MGM's evidence as sufficient to withstand summary judgment under the theory of inducement goes to the need on MGM's part to adduce evidence that StreamCast and Grokster communicated an inducing message to their software users. The classic instance of inducement is by advertisement or solicitation that broadcasts a message designed to stimulate others to commit violations. MGM claims that such a message is shown here. It is undisputed that StreamCast beamed onto the computer screens of users of Napster-compatible programs ads urging the adoption of its OpenNap program, which was designed, as its name implied, to invite the custom of patrons of Napster, then under attack in the courts for facilitating massive infringement. Those who accepted StreamCast's OpenNap program were offered software to perform the same services, which a factfinder could conclude would readily have been understood in the Napster market as the ability to download copyrighted music files. Grokster distributed an electronic newsletter containing links to articles promoting its software's ability to access popular copyrighted music. And anyone whose Napster or free file-sharing searches turned up a link to Grokster would have understood Grokster to be offering the same file-sharing ability as Napster, and to the same people who probably used Napster for infringing downloads; that would also have been the understanding of anyone offered Grokster's suggestively named Swaptor software, its version of OpenNap. And both companies communicated a clear message by responding affirmatively to requests for help in locating and playing copyrighted materials.

In StreamCast's case, of course, the evidence just described was supplemented by other unequivocal indications of unlawful purpose in the internal communications and advertising designs aimed at Napster users ("When the lights went off at Napster . . . where did the users go?"). Whether the messages were communicated is not to the point on this record. The function of the message in the theory of inducement is to prove by a defendant's own statements that his unlawful purpose disqualifies him from claiming protection (and incidentally to point to actual violators likely to be found among those who hear or read the message). Proving that a message was sent out, then, is the preeminent but not exclusive way of showing that active steps were taken with the purpose of bringing about infringing acts, and of showing that infringing acts took place by using the device distributed. Here, the summary judgment record is replete with other evidence that Grokster and StreamCast, unlike the manufacturer and distributor in Sony, acted with a purpose to cause copyright violations by use of software suitable for illegal use.

Three features of this evidence of intent are particularly notable. First, each company showed itself to be aiming to satisfy a known source of demand for copyright infringement, the market comprising former Napster users. StreamCast's internal documents made constant reference to Napster, it initially distributed its Morpheus software through an OpenNap program compatible with Napster, it advertised its OpenNap program to Napster users, and its Morpheus software functions as Napster did except that it could be used to distribute more kinds of files, including copyrighted movies and software programs. Grokster's name is apparently derived from Napster, it too initially offered an OpenNap program, its software's function is likewise comparable to Napster's, and it attempted to divert queries for Napster onto its own Web site. Grokster and StreamCast's efforts to supply services to former Napster users, deprived of a mechanism to copy and distribute what were overwhelmingly infringing files, indicate a principal, if not exclusive, intent on the part of each to bring about infringement.

Second, this evidence of unlawful objective is given added significance by MGM's showing that neither company attempted to develop filtering tools or other mechanisms to diminish the infringing activity using their software. While the Ninth Circuit treated the defendants' failure to develop such tools as irrelevant because they lacked an independent duty to monitor their users' activity, we think this evidence underscores Grokster's and StreamCast's intentional facilitation of their users' infringement.

Third, there is a further complement to the direct evidence of unlawful objective. It is useful to recall that StreamCast and Grokster make money by selling advertising space, by directing ads to the screens of computers employing their software. As the record shows, the more the software is used, the more ads are sent out and the greater the advertising revenue becomes. Since the extent of the software's use determines the gain to the distributors, the commercial sense of their enterprise turns on high-volume use, which the record shows is infringing. This evidence alone would not justify an inference of unlawful intent, but viewed in the context of the entire record its import is clear.

The unlawful objective is unmistakable.

B

In addition to intent to bring about infringement and distribution of a device suitable for infringing use, the inducement theory of course requires evidence of actual infringement by recipients of the device, the software in this case. As the account of the facts indicates, there is evidence of infringement on a gigantic scale, and there is no serious issue of the adequacy of MGM's showing on this point in order to survive the companies' summary judgment requests. Although an exact calculation of infringing use, as a basis for a claim of damages, is subject to dispute, there is no question that the summary judgment evidence is at least adequate to entitle MGM to go forward with claims for damages and equitable relief.

* * *

In sum, this case is significantly different from Sony and reliance on that case to rule in favor of StreamCast and Grokster was error. Sony dealt with a claim of liability based solely on distributing a product with alternative lawful and unlawful uses, with knowledge that some users would follow the unlawful course. The case struck a balance between the interests of protection and innovation by holding that the product's capability of substantial lawful employment should bar the imputation of fault and consequent secondary liability for the unlawful acts of others.

MGM's evidence in this case most obviously addresses a different basis of liability for distributing a product open to alternative uses. Here, evidence of the distributors' words and deeds going beyond distribution as such shows a purpose to cause and profit from third-party acts of copyright infringement. If liability for inducing infringement is ultimately found, it will not be on the basis of presuming or imputing fault, but from inferring a patently illegal objective from statements and actions showing what that objective was.

There is substantial evidence in MGM's favor on all elements of inducement, and summary judgment in favor of Grokster and StreamCast was error. On remand, reconsideration of MGM's motion for summary judgment will be in order.

The judgment of the Court of Appeals is vacated, and the case is remanded for further proceedings consistent with this opinion.

It is so ordered.

Source: *MGM Studios Inc. v. Grokster, Ltd.*, 545 U.S. 913 (2005).

Selected Provisions of Title 35 of the United States Code (U.S. Patent Law)

The U.S. Patent Act is Title 35 of the United States Code. Sections 101 through 103 set out the basic requirements of patentability. In order to be patentable, an invention must be useful (§ 101), novel (§ 102), and nonobvious (§ 103).

---

35 USC § 101—INVENTIONS PATENTABLE

Whoever invents or discovers any new and useful process, machine, manufacture, or composition of matter, or any new and useful improvement thereof, may obtain a patent therefor, subject to the conditions and requirements of this title.

---

35 USC § 102—CONDITIONS FOR PATENTABILITY; NOVELTY AND LOSS OF RIGHT TO PATENT

A person shall be entitled to a patent unless—

(a) the invention was known or used by others in this country, or patented or described in a printed publication in this or a foreign country, before the invention thereof by the applicant for patent, or

(b) the invention was patented or described in a printed publication in this or a foreign country or in public use or on sale in this country, more than one year prior to the date of the application for patent in the United States, or

(c) he has abandoned the invention, or

(d) the invention was first patented or caused to be patented, or was the subject of an inventor's certificate, by the applicant or his legal representatives or assigns in a foreign country prior to the date of the application for patent in this country on an application for patent or inventor's certificate filed more than twelve months before the filing of the application in the United States, or

(e) the invention was described in

(1) an application for patent, published under section 122 (b), by another filed in the United States before the invention by the applicant for patent or

(2) a patent granted on an application for patent by another filed in the United States before the invention by the applicant for patent, except that an international application filed under the treaty defined in section 351 (a) shall have the effects for the purposes of this subsection of an application filed in the United States only if the international application designated the United States and was published under Article 21(2) of such treaty in the English language; or

(f) he did not himself invent the subject matter sought to be patented, or

(g)

(1) during the course of an interference conducted under section 135 or section 291, another inventor involved therein establishes, to the extent permitted in section 104, that before such person's invention thereof the invention was made by such other inventor and not abandoned, suppressed, or concealed, or

(2) before such person's invention thereof, the invention was made in this country by another inventor who had not abandoned, suppressed, or concealed it. In determining priority of invention under this subsection, there shall be considered not only the respective dates of conception and reduction to practice of the invention, but also the reasonable diligence of one who was first to conceive and last to reduce to practice, from a time prior to conception by the other.

35 USC § 103—CONDITIONS FOR PATENTABILITY; NON-OBVIOUS SUBJECT MATTER

(a) A patent may not be obtained though the invention is not identically disclosed or described as set forth in section 102, if the differences between the subject matter sought to be patented and the prior art are such that the subject matter as a whole would have been obvious at the time the invention was made to a person having ordinary skill in the art to which said subject matter pertains. Patentability shall not be negatived by the manner in which the invention was made.

(b)

[biotechnological processes; omitted]

(c)

(1) Subject matter developed by another person, which qualifies as prior art only under one or more of subsections (e), (f), and (g) of section 102, shall not preclude patentability under this section where the subject matter and the claimed invention were, at the time the claimed invention was made, owned by the same person or subject to an obligation of assignment to the same person.

(2) For purposes of this subsection, subject matter developed by another person and a claimed invention shall be deemed to have been owned by the same person or subject to an obligation of assignment to the same person if—

(A) the claimed invention was made by or on behalf of parties to a joint research agreement that was in effect on or before the date the claimed invention was made;

(B) the claimed invention was made as a result of activities undertaken within the scope of the joint research agreement; and

(C) the application for patent for the claimed invention discloses or is amended to disclose the names of the parties to the joint research agreement.

(3) For purposes of paragraph (2), the term "joint research agreement" means a written contract, grant, or cooperative agreement entered into by two or more persons or entities for the performance of experimental, developmental, or research work in the field of the claimed invention.

Source: The U.S. Patent Act of 1952, *35 USC § 101, 102, and 103.*

Computer Crimes: The Computer Fraud and Abuse Act, 1986

The Computer Fraud and Abuse Act (CFAA) is the primary U.S. antihacking and antimalware statute. Like many older statutes that have been forced into service in the modern information world, it is a somewhat awkward fit for its job. The CFAA was originally enacted in 1984, when home computing was in its infancy, and was intended at the time to apply to computers used by financial institutions and the federal government. The total number of protected computers at the time was probably in the tens of thousands. However, a catchall phrase applying the act to computers "used in or affecting interstate or foreign commerce" means that the statute now applies, at least potentially, to hundreds of millions or billions of devices. It has become the main tool in federal prosecutor's kit for prosecution of unauthorized access, theft of information, and distribution of viruses and other malware.

§ 1030. FRAUD AND RELATED ACTIVITY IN CONNECTION WITH COMPUTERS

(a) Whoever—

(1) having knowingly accessed a computer without authorization or exceeding authorized access, and by means of such conduct having obtained information that has been determined by the United States Government pursuant to an Executive order or statute to require protection against unauthorized disclosure for reasons of national defense or foreign relations, or any restricted data, as defined in paragraph y.[(y)] of section 11 of the Atomic Energy Act of 1954 [*42 USCS § 2014(y)*], with reason to believe that such information so obtained could be used to the injury of the United States, or to the advantage of any foreign nation willfully communicates, delivers, transmits, or causes to be communicated, delivered, or transmitted, or attempts to communicate, deliver, transmit or cause to be communicated, delivered, or transmitted the same to any person not entitled to receive it, or willfully retains the same and fails to deliver it to the officer or employee of the United States entitled to receive it;

(2) intentionally accesses a computer without authorization or exceeds authorized access, and thereby obtains—

(A) information contained in a financial record of a financial institution, or of a card issuer as defined in section 1602(n) of title 15, or contained in a file of a consumer reporting agency on a consumer, as such terms are defined in the Fair Credit Reporting Act (*15 U.S.C. 1681* et seq.);

(B) information from any department or agency of the United States; or

(C) information from any protected computer;

(3) intentionally, without authorization to access any nonpublic computer of a department or agency of the United States, accesses such a computer of that department or agency that is exclusively for the use of the Government of the United States or, in the case of a computer not exclusively for such use, is used by or for the Government of the United States and such conduct affects that use by or for the Government of the United States;

(4) knowingly and with intent to defraud, accesses a protected computer without authorization, or exceeds authorized access, and by means of such conduct furthers the intended fraud and obtains anything of value, unless the object of the fraud and the thing obtained consists only of the use of the computer and the value of such use is not more than $ 5,000 in any 1-year period;

(5)

(A) knowingly causes the transmission of a program, information, code, or command, and as a result of such conduct, intentionally causes damage without authorization, to a protected computer;

(B) intentionally accesses a protected computer without authorization, and as a result of such conduct, recklessly causes damage; or

(C) intentionally accesses a protected computer without authorization, and as a result of such conduct, causes damage and loss.[;]

(6) knowingly and with intent to defraud traffics (as defined in section 1029 [*18 USCS § 1029*]) in any password or similar information through which a computer may be accessed without authorization, if—

(A) such trafficking affects interstate or foreign commerce; or

(B) such computer is used by or for the Government of the United States;

[or]

(7) with intent to extort from any person any money or other thing of value, transmits in interstate or foreign commerce any communication containing any—

(A) threat to cause damage to a protected computer;

(B) threat to obtain information from a protected computer without authorization or in excess of authorization or to impair the confidentiality of information obtained from a protected computer without authorization or by exceeding authorized access; or

(C) demand or request for money or other thing of value in relation to damage to a protected computer, where such damage was caused to facilitate the extortion;

shall be punished as provided in subsection (c) of this section.

(b) Whoever conspires to commit or attempts to commit an offense under subsection (a) of this section shall be punished as provided in subsection (c) of this section.

(c) The punishment for an offense under subsection (a) or (b) of this section is—

(1)

(A) a fine under this title or imprisonment for not more than ten years, or both, in the case of an offense under subsection (a)(1) of this section which does not occur after a conviction for another offense under this section, or an attempt to commit an offense punishable under this subparagraph; and

(B) a fine under this title or imprisonment for not more than twenty years, or both, in the case of an offense under subsection

(a)(1) of this section which occurs after a conviction for another offense under this section; or an attempt to commit an offense punishable under this subparagraph;

(2)

(A) except as provided in subparagraph (B), a fine under this title or imprisonment for not more than one year, or both, in the case of an offense under subsection (a)(2), (a)(3), or (a)(6) of this section which does not occur after a conviction for another offense under this section, or an attempt to commit an offense punishable under this subparagraph;

(B) a fine under this title or imprisonment for not more than 5 years, or both, in the case of an offense under subsection (a)(2), or an attempt to commit an offense punishable under this subparagraph, if—

(i) the offense was committed for purposes of commercial advantage or private financial gain;

(ii) the offense was committed in furtherance of any criminal or tortious act in violation of the Constitution or laws of the United States or of any State; or

(iii) the value of the information obtained exceeds $ 5,000; and

(C) a fine under this title or imprisonment for not more than ten years, or both, in the case of an offense under subsection (a)(2), (a)(3) or (a)(6) of this section which occurs after a conviction for another offense under this section, or an attempt to commit an offense punishable under this subparagraph;

(3)

(A) a fine under this title or imprisonment for not more than five years, or both, in the case of an offense under subsection (a)(4) or (a)(7) of this section which does not occur after a conviction for another offense under this section, or an attempt to commit an offense punishable under this subparagraph; and

(B) a fine under this title or imprisonment for not more than ten years, or both, in the case of an offense under subsection (a)(4)[,] or (a)(7) of this section which occurs after a conviction for another offense under this section, or an attempt to commit an offense punishable under this section;

(4)

(A) except as provided in subparagraphs (E) and (F), a fine under this title, imprisonment for not more than 5 years, or both, in the case of—

(i) an offense under subsection (a)(5)(B), which does not occur after a conviction for another offense under this section, if the offense caused (or, in the case of an attempted offense, would, if completed, have caused)—

(I) loss to 1 or more persons during any 1-year period (and, for purposes of an investigation, prosecution, or other proceeding brought by the United States only, loss resulting from a related course of conduct affecting 1 or more other protected computers) aggregating at least $ 5,000 in value;

(II) the modification or impairment, or potential modification or impairment, of the medical examination, diagnosis, treatment, or care of 1 or more individuals;

(III) physical injury to any person;

(IV) a threat to public health or safety;

(V) damage affecting a computer used by or for an entity of the United States Government in furtherance of the administration of justice, national defense, or national security; or

(VI) damage affecting 10 or more protected computers during any 1-year period; or

(ii) an attempt to commit an offense punishable under this subparagraph;

(B) except as provided in subparagraphs (E) and (F), a fine under this title, imprisonment for not more than 10 years, or both, in the case of—

(i) an offense under subsection (a)(5)(A), which does not occur after a conviction for another offense under this section, if the offense caused (or, in the case of an attempted offense, would, if completed, have caused) a harm provided in subclauses (I) through (VI) of subparagraph (A)(i); or

(ii) an attempt to commit an offense punishable under this subparagraph;

(C) except as provided in subparagraphs (E) and (F), a fine under this title, imprisonment for not more than 20 years, or both, in the case of—

(i) an offense or an attempt to commit an offense under subparagraphs (A) or (B) of subsection (a)(5) that occurs after a conviction for another offense under this section; or

(ii) an attempt to commit an offense punishable under this subparagraph;

(D) a fine under this title, imprisonment for not more than 10 years, or both, in the case of—

(i) an offense or an attempt to commit an offense under subsection (a)(5)(C) that occurs after a conviction for another offense under this section; or

(ii) an attempt to commit an offense punishable under this subparagraph;

(E) if the offender attempts to cause or knowingly or recklessly causes serious bodily injury from conduct in violation of subsection (a)(5)(A), a fine under this title, imprisonment for not more than 20 years, or both;

(F) if the offender attempts to cause or knowingly or recklessly causes death from conduct in violation of subsection (a)(5)(A), a fine under this title, imprisonment for any term of years or for life, or both; or

(G) a fine under this title, imprisonment for not more than 1 year, or both, for—

(i) any other offense under subsection (a)(5); or

(ii) an attempt to commit an offense punishable under this subparagraph.

(5) [Deleted]

(d)

(1) The United States Secret Service shall, in addition to any other agency having such authority, have the authority to investigate offenses under this section.

(2) The Federal Bureau of Investigation shall have primary authority to investigate offenses under subsection (a)(1) for any cases involving espionage, foreign counterintelligence, information protected against unauthorized disclosure for reasons of national defense or foreign relations, or Restricted Data (as that term is defined in section 11y of the Atomic Energy Act of 1954 (42 U.S.C. 2014(y)), except for offenses affecting the duties of the United States Secret Service pursuant to section 3056(a) of this title [18 USCS § 3056(a)].

(3) Such authority shall be exercised in accordance with an agreement which shall be entered into by the Secretary of the Treasury and the Attorney General.

(e) As used in this section—

(1) the term "computer" means an electronic, magnetic, optical, electrochemical, or other high speed data processing device performing logical, arithmetic, or storage functions, and includes any data storage facility or communications facility directly related to or operating in conjunction with such device, but such term does not include an automated typewriter or typesetter, a portable hand held calculator, or other similar device;

(2) the term "protected computer" means a computer—

(A) exclusively for the use of a financial institution or the United States Government, or, in the case of a computer not exclusively for such use, used by or for a financial institution or the United States Government and the conduct constituting the offense affects that use by or for the financial institution or the Government; or

(B) which is used in or affecting interstate or foreign commerce or communication, including a computer located outside the United States that is used in a manner that affects interstate or foreign commerce or communication of the United States;

(3) the term "State" includes the District of Columbia, the Commonwealth of Puerto Rico, and any other commonwealth, possession or territory of the United States;

(4) the term "financial institution" means—

(A) an institution, with deposits insured by the Federal Deposit Insurance Corporation;

(B) the Federal Reserve or a member of the Federal Reserve including any Federal Reserve Bank;

(C) a credit union with accounts insured by the National Credit Union Administration;

(D) a member of the Federal home loan bank system and any home loan bank;

(E) any institution of the Farm Credit System under the Farm Credit Act of 1971;

(F) a broker-dealer registered with the Securities and Exchange Commission pursuant to section 15 of the Securities Exchange Act of 1934 [15 USCS § 78o];

(G) the Securities Investor Protection Corporation;

(H) a branch or agency of a foreign bank (as such terms are defined in paragraphs (1) and (3) of section 1(b) of the International Banking Act of 1978 [12 USCS § 3101(1) and (3)]); and

(I) an organization operating under section 25 or section 25(a) of the Federal Reserve Act;

(5) the term "financial record" means information derived from any record held by a financial institution pertaining to a customer's relationship with the financial institution;

(6) the term "exceeds authorized access" means to access a computer with authorization and to use such access to obtain or alter information in the computer that the accesser is not entitled so to obtain or alter;

(7) the term "department of the United States" means the legislative or judicial branch of the Government or one of the executive department enumerated in section 101 of title 5;

(8) the term "damage" means any impairment to the integrity or availability of data, a program, a system, or information;

(9) the term "government entity" includes the Government of the United States, any State or political subdivision of the United States, any foreign country, and any state, province, municipality, or other political subdivision of a foreign country;

(10) the term "conviction" shall include a conviction under the law of any State for a crime punishable by imprisonment for more than 1 year, an element of which is unauthorized access, or exceeding authorized access, to a computer;

(11) the term "loss" means any reasonable cost to any victim, including the cost of responding to an offense, conducting a damage assessment, and restoring the data, program, system, or information to its condition prior to the offense, and any revenue lost, cost incurred, or other consequential damages incurred because of interruption of service; and

(12) the term "person" means any individual, firm, corporation, educational institution, financial institution, governmental entity, or legal or other entity.

(f) This section does not prohibit any lawfully authorized investigative, protective, or intelligence activity of a law enforcement agency of the United States, a State, or a political subdivision of a State, or of an intelligence agency of the United States.

(g) Any person who suffers damage or loss by reason of a violation of this section may maintain a civil action against the violator to obtain compensatory damages and injunctive relief or other equitable relief. A civil action for a violation of this section may be brought only if the conduct involves 1 of the factors set forth in subclauses [subclause] (I), (II), (III), (IV), or (V) of subsection (c)(4)(A)(i). Damages for a violation involving only conduct described in subsection (c)(4)(A)(i)(I) are limited to economic damages. No action may be brought under this subsection unless such action is begun within 2 years of the date of the act complained of or the date of the discovery of the damage. No action may be brought under this subsection for the negligent design or manufacture of computer hardware, computer software, or firmware.

(h) The Attorney General and the Secretary of the Treasury shall report to the Congress annually, during the first 3 years following the date of the enactment of this subsection [enacted Sept. 13, 1994], concerning investigations and prosecutions under subsection (a)(5).

(i)

(1) The court, in imposing sentence on any person convicted of a violation of this section, or convicted of conspiracy to violate this section, shall order, in addition to any other sentence imposed and irrespective of any provision of State law, that such person forfeit to the United States—

(A) such person's interest in any personal property that was used or intended to be used to commit or to facilitate the commission of such violation; and

(B) any property, real or personal, constituting or derived from, any proceeds that such person obtained, directly or indirectly, as a result of such violation.

(2) The criminal forfeiture of property under this subsection, any seizure and disposition thereof, and any judicial proceeding in relation thereto, shall be governed by the provisions of section 413 of the Comprehensive Drug Abuse Prevention and Control Act of 1970 (*21 U.S.C. 853*), except subsection (d) of that section.

(j) For purposes of subsection (i), the following shall be subject to forfeiture to the United States and no property right shall exist in them:

(1) Any personal property used or intended to be used to commit or to facilitate the commission of any violation of this section, or a conspiracy to violate this section.

(2) Any property, real or personal, which constitutes or is derived from proceeds traceable to any violation of this section, or a conspiracy to violate this section[.]

Source: The Computer Fraud and Abuse Act of 1986, 18 U.S.C. § 1030.

NOLO PRESS

- Stephen R. Elias & Richard Stim, *Patent, Copyright & Trademark: An Intellectual Property Desk Reference* (Berkeley, CA: Nolo Press, 12th ed. 2012)
- Richard Stim, *Getting Permission: How to License & Clear Copyrighted Materials Online & Off* (Berkeley, CA: Nolo Press, 4th ed. 2010)

Nolo Press is a publisher of do-it-yourself legal guides. Because Nolo's guides are written for nonlawyers, they are easy to understand. However, because they are designed to deal with immediate practical problems, they may have less theoretical depth than other works on the same subject. The two works listed here are good practical guides for anyone who operates a Web site or otherwise places content on the Web and is concerned about copyright or other intellectual property issues. *Getting Permission* focuses on the use of materials copyrighted by others, rather than on protection of one's own copyrighted Web content. The *Desk Reference* provides plain-English definitions for a wide range of intellectual property law terms.

WEST'S NUTSHELL SERIES

- Jerome A. Barron & C. Thomas Dienes, *Constitutional Law in a Nutshell* (St. Paul, MN: West, 7th ed. 2009)
- Michael H. Davis & Arthur Raphael Miller, *Intellectual Property: Patents, Trademarks, and Copyright in a Nutshell* (St. Paul, MN: West, 4th ed. 2007)
- Robert H. Klonoff, *Class Actions and Other Multi-Party Litigations in a Nutshell* (St. Paul, MN: West, 2d ed. 2004)
- Claude D. Rohwer et al., *Contracts in a Nutshell* (St. Paul, MN: West, 7th ed. 2010)
- David D. Siegel, *Conflicts in a Nutshell* (St. Paul, MN: West, 2d ed. 2005)
- Bradford Stone, *Uniform Commercial Code in a Nutshell* (St. Paul, Minnesota: West, 7th ed. 2008)

West Publishing, based in St. Paul, Minnesota, is the largest, and among the oldest, legal publishing companies in the United States. The Nutshell series includes volumes covering nearly every imaginable topic. Nutshells are small (5 inches by 7 inches, and typically no more than one inch thick) paperback volumes providing an overview of the law on a particular topic. Although practicing attorneys use them, they are designed with law students in mind. As a result, they are less opaque than works aimed specifically at attorneys or law professors, if more challenging than the Nolo Press works. The titles of the aforementioned books are more or less self-explanatory. *Constitutional Law in a Nutshell* deals with a range of constitutional law issues, of which the ones most relevant to Internet law are those arising from the First Amendment's guarantee of freedom of expression. *Intellectual Property: Patents, Trademarks, and Copyright in a Nutshell* covers the three traditional areas—copyright, patents, and trademarks. All three of these are important to the Internet, but copyright most of all. *Class Actions and Other Multi-Party Litigations in a Nutshell* is much more specialized, dealing with a particular type of lawsuit; class actions may arise in a computer and Internet context when a business violates consumer rights. *Contracts in a Nutshell* and *Uniform Commercial Code in a Nutshell* deal with business transactions of all sorts, not merely e-commerce. And *Conflicts in a Nutshell* addresses the various conflicts of law that can arise when an action takes place in or affects persons, property, or interests in more than one jurisdiction, as often happens in Internet cases. These conflicts may include problems of choice of applicable law, recognition and enforcement of judgments, and territorial jurisdiction.

LEXISNEXIS'S UNDERSTANDING SERIES

- Jeffrey Ferriell & Michael Navin, *Understanding Contracts* (New York: Matthew Bender, 2d ed. 2009)
- Marshall Leaffer, *Understanding Copyright Law* (3d ed. New York: Matthew Bender, 5th ed. 2010)
- William M. Richman & William L. Reynolds, *Understanding Conflict of Laws* (New York: Matthew Bender, 3d ed. 2002)

The *Understanding* series, from the Matthew Bender division of LexisNexis, is similar to the Nutshell series but provides somewhat more detailed source notes. The books are somewhat larger, and the footnotes provided for every point of law are a useful starting point for further research. However, while there is a Nutshell for nearly every legal topic, there are fewer volumes in the Understanding series. *Understanding Contracts* includes references to such Internet issues as electronic signatures and electronic transactions. The Internet affects and is affected by nearly every area of copyright law, making *Understanding Copyright Law* especially relevant. *Understanding Conflict of Laws* provides a thorough introduction to this often-misunderstood area of law, and includes a section on jurisdiction and the Internet.

LEGAL REFERENCE WORKS

- Bryan A. Garner, ed., *Black's Law Dictionary* (St. Paul, MN: West, 9th ed. 2009)
- J. Thomas McCarthy et al., *McCarthy's Desk Encyclopedia of Intellectual Property* (Washington, D.C.: Bureau of National Affairs, 3d ed. 2004)

Black's Law Dictionary is a standard legal reference; anyone planning to spend any amount of time reading legal materials should keep *Black's* (or a similar work) handy as an aid in cutting through what at times may seem to be an impenetrable thicket of legal terminology.

McCarthy's Desk Encyclopedia of Intellectual Property is also a reference work, albeit a more specialized one, and not as recently updated as other available sources. It covers all aspects of intellectual property, United States and international, online and off, with detailed explanations and references to statutes, cases, and other sources.

INTELLECTUAL PROPERTY AND THE INTERNET

- Lawrence Lessig, *Code and Other Laws of Cyberspace* (New York: Basic Books, 1999)
- Lawrence Lessig, *The Future of Ideas* (New York: Random House, 2001)
- Lawrence Lessig, *Free Culture: How Big Media Uses Technology and the Law to Lock Down Culture and Control Creativity* (New York: Penguin, 2004)
- Lawrence Lessig, *Remix: Making Art and Commerce Thrive in the Hybrid Economy* (New York: Penguin Press, 2008)
- Siva Vaidhyanathan, *Copyrights and Copywrongs: The Rise of Intellectual Property and How It Threatens Creativity* (New York: New York University Press, 2001)
- Siva Vaidhyanathan, *The Anarchist in the Library: How the Clash between Freedom and Control Is Hacking the Real World and Crashing the System* (New York: Basic Books, 2004)
- Siva Vaidhyanathan, *The Googlization of Everything—And Why We Should Worry* (Berkeley, CA: University of California Press, 2011)

Professors Lessig and Vaidhyanathan are commentators on law (especially copyright law) and the Internet; both achieved prominence in the relatively early days of the Internet as a mass medium of communication. In the five books listed here, they developed parallel, but not identical, arguments to the effect that the apparently ongoing increase in the scope of intellectual property protection is stifling innovation and creativity, damaging the U.S. (and world) economy and polity, and will ultimately backfire, harming even those industries it is intended to protect.

Code, Lessig's 1999 work (later revised as *Code 2.0*), was a breakthrough in at least two ways: it brought awareness of the emerging field of Internet law to the wider world beyond law schools, the intellectual property profession, and a few federal regulatory agencies. Presciently, it predicted that "we will see the Net move to an architecture of control." In *The Future of Ideas*, Lessig continued to develop this theme, warning of creativity-stifling corporate control of the Internet, and warned of the need for public awareness of, and participation in, the Internet and intellectual property governance process. *Free Culture* focused on copyright law, looking at Internet law's main battleground of the moment—file-sharing—and at Lessig's involvement in *Eldred v. Ashcroft*, an ultimately unsuccessful court battle against the Sonny Bono Copyright Term Extension Act.

Vaidhyanathan, a communications professor and former journalist, reached similar conclusions by a somewhat different path. In *Copyrights and Copywrongs*, he warned of the stifling effect that overzealous protection of copyright would have on creativity. He pointed out that the effect of overzealous copyright enforcement

was to stifle all cultural expression, but that the effect was unevenly distributed, and that minority cultures were disproportionately affected. In *The Anarchist in the Library*, he carried this idea further, looking at the ways in which the tension resulting from attempts to control Internet content and attempts to avoid that control led to extremism that carried over into the larger world, feeding into the trends toward anarchy and terrorism on the one hand and totalitarianism on the other.

THE TECHNICAL SIDE OF INTERNET SECURITY

- Bruce Schneier, *Schneier on Security* (Indianapolis: John Wiley & Sons, 2008)

An understanding of the technology and business realities of Internet security is often essential to an understanding of legal problems arising from breaches of security; unfortunately, many technical books about the Internet are written in jargon at least as impenetrable as that in many legal treatises. In *Schneier on Security*, noted security expert Bruce Schneier addresses the technical side of security problems, providing a comprehensive survey of security threats and solutions. Computer and network security are often overlooked simply because they're perceived as boring; Schneier manages to counter this problem by presenting material in an accessible manner.

FREE SPEECH

- Andrea Dworkin, *Pornography: Men Possessing Women* (New York: Perigee Books, 1981)
- Mike Godwin, *Cyber Rights: Defending Free Speech in the Digital Age* (Cambridge, MA: MIT Press, 2003)
- Saul Levmore & Martha C. Nussbaum, eds., *The Offensive Internet: Speech, Privacy & Reputation* (Cambridge, MA: Harvard University Press, 2012)
- Kevin W. Saunders, *Saving Our Children from the First Amendment* (New York: New York University Press, 2004)
- Madeleine Schachter, *Law of Internet Speech* (Durham, NC: Carolina Academic Press, 2d ed. 2002)
- Micah Sifry, *WikiLeaks and the Age of Transparency* (Berkeley, CA: Counterpoint, 2011)

While the problem of freedom of expression online has many facets, it is the problem of pornography, and of minors' access to it, that attracts the most attention. In *Cyber Rights*, Mike Godwin of the Electronic Frontier Foundation discusses attempts to censor Internet pornography, as well as censorship issues relating to copyright, defamation, encryption, and warez trading. While the book takes an anticensorship position, it presents all sides of the various questions fairly and completely.

Andrea Dworkin's classic work *Pornography* predates the Internet, but is an essential starting point for anyone wishing to understand opposition to pornography from a feminist perspective. And Kevin Saunders, in *Saving Our Children from the First Amendment*, makes the difficult case for more censorship, not only of pornography but also, and perhaps especially, of violence and racist hate speech; Saunders makes a compelling argument that exposing minors to these materials will lead to an increase in hate crimes and other acts of violence.

Madeleine Schachter's book *Law of Internet Speech* presents law and policy reasoning on a wide range of Internet free speech issues objectively and in considerable depth. In *The Offensive Internet: Speech, Privacy & Reputation*, editors and noted legal scholars Saul Levmore and Martha Nussbaum present 13 essays representing a variety of cutting-edge perspectives on the intersection of the Internet and First Amendment jurisprudence. And in *WikiLeaks and the Age of Transparency*, Micah Sifry addresses the possible effect of the unauthorized release of large amounts of classified government information on the future of free speech.

FILE-SHARING

- Stuart Biegel, *Beyond Our Control? Confronting the Limits of Our Legal System in the Age of Cyberspace* (Cambridge, MA: MIT Press, 2001)
- Quang Hieu Vu, Mihai Lupu, & Beng Chin Ooi, *Peer-to-Peer Computing: Principles and Applications* (New York: Springer, 2010)
- Joseph Menn, *All the Rave: The Rise and Fall of Shawn Fanning's Napster* (New York: Crown Business, 2003)
- Trevor Merriden, *Irresistible Forces: The Business Legacy of Napster and the Growth of the Underground Internet* (New York: John Wiley & Sons, 2002)

File-sharing is the most controversial and most heavily litigated aspect of the Internet today. A great many books have been written about it; the four listed here are only a tiny sample. *Irresistible Forces* and *All the Rave* tell the history of Napster—the subject of file-sharing's first, and defining, great battle. *Irresistible Forces*, in particular, goes on to follow the post-Napster history of P2P. Stuart Biegel's *Beyond Our Control* also focuses on P2P, but uses the story of P2P file-sharing networks as a lens through which to view the evolution of Internet law. More recently, the legitimate uses of P2P have increased interest in its technical and practical aspects;

Peer-to-Peer Computing: Principles and Applications is one of many books filling the need for technical information on the topic.

THE INTERNET AS A CULTURAL PHENOMENON

- John Brunner, *The Shockwave Rider* (New York: Ballantine, 1976)
- Thomas M. Disch, *The Dreams Our Stuff Is Made Of: How Science Fiction Conquered the World* (New York: Touchstone, 1998)
- William Gibson, *Neuromancer* (New York: Ace, 1984)
- Bruce Sterling, ed., *Mirrorshades: The Cyberpunk Anthology* (New York: Arbor House, 1986)

The Internet is not, and should not be, a primarily legal phenomenon. The Internet is constantly redefining its own place in popular culture as well as in the legal system. Technological advances and their social consequences are often anticipated in fiction, which in turn creates expectations that shape the evolution of technology: it is no accident that today's cell phones resemble the communicators of the original crew of the Starship Enterprise in a television show nearly 40 years old. Thomas M. Disch, in *The Dreams Our Stuff Is Made Of*, investigates the influence of SF on the real world, and vice versa.

SF writers anticipated and wrote about information networks for decades before they became reality, but among the most eerily predictive works is *Shockwave Rider*, by the late British author John Brunner. Writing four decades ago, Brunner anticipated aspects of the Internet ranging from worms to data havens. A decade later, William Gibson wrote the novel that was to define the Internet in the popular imagination and in academia: *Neuromancer*. *Neuromancer* and its sequels brought cyberpunk to the world's attention and made information networks romantic and interesting. A good place for an introduction to cyberpunk as a genre is *Mirrorshades*, a 1986 anthology of short stories edited by Bruce Sterling.

Treaties

- Agreement between the United Nations and the World Intellectual Property Organization, December 17, 1974, 956 U.N.T.S. 729
- Agreement between the World Intellectual Property Organization and the World Trade Organization, December 22, 1995, 35 I.L.M. 754 (1996)
- Agreement on Trade-Related Aspects of Intellectual Property Rights (TRIPS), Marrakesh Agreement Establishing the World Trade Organization, Annex 1C, April 15, 1994, 33 I.L.M. 81 (1994)
- Beijing Treaty on Audiovisual Performances, June 24, 2012, Doc. No. AVP/DC/20
- Brussels Convention Relating to the Distribution of Programme-Carrying Signals Transmitted by Satellite, May 21, 1974, 13 I.L.M. 1444
- Buenos Aires Convention, August 20, 1910, 38 Stat. 1785, 155 L.N.T.S. 179
- Budapest Treaty on the International Recognition of the Deposit of Microorganisms for the Purposes of Patent Procedure, April 28, 1977, as amended on September 26, 1980, 32 U.S.T. 1241, 1861 U.N.T.S. 361
- Convention Concerning the Creation of an International Union for the Protection of Literary and Artistic Works (Berne Convention), September 9, 1886, as last revised at Paris, July 24, 1971 (amended 1979), 25 U.S.T. 1341, 828 U.N.T.S. 221
- Convention Establishing the World Intellectual Property Organization, July 14, 1967, as amended on September 28, 1979 (WIPO Convention), 21 U.S.T. 1749, 828 U.N.T.S. 3
- Convention for the Protection of Producers of Phonograms against Unauthorized Duplication of Their Phonograms, October 29, 1971, 25 U.S.T. 309
- Convention on the Grant of European Patents, 5 October 1973, 13 I.L.M. 276, text as amended through December 10, 1998, available at http://www.epo.org/law-practice/legal-texts/html/epc/2010/e/ma1.html [European Patent Convention]
- Convention Relating to the Distribution of Programme-Carrying Signals Transmitted by Satellite, May 21, 1974, 13 I.L.M. 1444
- General Agreement on Trade in Services, Marrakesh Agreement Establishing the World Trade Organization, Annex 1B, April 15, 1994, 33 I.L.M. 1168 (1994)
- Hague Agreement Concerning the International Deposit of Industrial Designs, November 6, 1925, 74 L.N.T.S. 343, revised at London, June 2, 1934, 205 L.N.T.S. 179, revised at The Hague, November 28, 1960; supplemented by the Additional Act of Monaco, November 18, 1961, the Complementary Act of Stockholm, July 14, 1967, and the Protocol of Geneva, April 10, 1975, 26 U.S.T. 571; and as amended, September 1979
- International Convention for the Protection of Performers, Producers of Phonograms and Broadcasting Organizations, October 26, 1961, 496 U.N.T.S. 43
- Lisbon Agreement for the Protection of Appellations of Origin and their International Registration, October 31, 1958, as revised at Stockholm on July 14, 1967, and as amended on September 28, 1979, 923 U.N.T.S. 205
- Locarno Agreement Establishing an International Classification for Industrial Designs, October 8, 1968, as amended September 28, 1979, 23 U.S.T. 1389
- Madrid Agreement for the Repression of False or Deceptive Indications of Source on Goods, April 14, 1891, as revised at Washington on June 2, 1911, at The Hague on November 6, 1925, at London on June 2, 1934, and at Lisbon on October 31, 1958, and Additional Act, Stockholm, July 14, 1967, 828 U.N.T.S. 389
- Madrid Agreement Concerning the International Registration of Marks, April 14, 1891, as revised at Brussels, December 14, 1900; at Washington, June 2, 1911; at The Hague, November 6, 1925; at London, June 2, 1934; at Nice, June 15, 1957; at Stockholm, July 14, 1967; and as amended September 28, 1979, available at http://www.wipo.int/madrid/en/legal_texts/
- Nairobi Treaty on the Protection of the Olympic Symbol, September 26, 1981, 1863 U.N.T.S. 367, available at http://clea.wipo.int/PDFFILES/English/WO/WO018EN.PDF
- Nice Agreement Concerning the International Classification of Goods and Services for the Purposes of the Registration of Marks, June 15, 1957, as revised at Stockholm on July 14, 1967, and at Geneva on May 13, 1977, and amended on September 28, 1979, 23 U.S.T. 1336, 550 U.N.T.S. 45
- Paris Convention for the Protection of Industrial Property, March 20, 1883, as revised at Brussels on December 14, 1900, at Washington on June 2, 1911, at The Hague on November 6, 1925, at London on June 2, 1934, at Lisbon on October 31, 1958, and at Stockholm on July 14, 1967, and as amended on September 28, 1979, 21 U.S.T. 1583, 828 U.N.T.S. 305
- Patent Cooperation Treaty, Washington on June 19, 1970, as amended on September 28, 1979, and as modified on February 3, 1984, and October 3, 2001, 28 U.S.T. 7645, 9 I.L.M. 978
- Patent Law Treaty, June 1, 2000, 39 I.L.M. 1047 (2000)
- Rome Convention for the Protection of Performers, Producers of Phonograms and Broadcasting Organizations, October 26, 1961, 496 U.N.T.S. 43
- Protocol Relating to the Madrid Agreement Concerning the International Registration of Marks, June 27, 1989, S.

Treaty Doc. No 106–41 (2000), available at http://www.wipo.int/madrid/en/legal_texts/
- Rome Convention for the Protection of Performers, Producers of Phonograms and Broadcasting Organizations, October 26, 1961, 496 U.N.T.S. 43
- Singapore Treaty on the Law of Trademarks, March 28, 2006, S. Treaty Doc. No. 110–2
- Strasbourg Agreement Concerning the International Patent Classification, March 24, 1971, as amended September 1979, 26 U.S.T. 1793
- Trademark Law Treaty, October 27, 1994, S. Treaty Doc. No. 105–35 (1988), available at http://www.wipo.int/clea/docs/en/wo/wo027en.htm
- Treaty on Intellectual Property in Respect of Integrated Circuits, Washington, May 26, 1989, 28 I.L.M. 1477 (1989)
- Universal Copyright Convention, September 6, 1952, 6 U.S.T. 2731, revised at Paris July 24, 1971, 25 U.S.T. 1341
- Vienna Agreement Establishing an International Classification of the Figurative Elements of Marks, June 12, 1973, 1863 U.N.T.S. 317, as amended October 1, 1985, available at http://www.wipo.int/clea/docs/en/wo/wo031en.htm
- WIPO Copyright Treaty, December 20, 1996, 36 I.L.M. 65 (1997)
- WIPO Performance and Phonograms Treaty, December 20, 1996, 36 I.L.M. 76 (1997)

Statutes, Rules, and Regulations
Federal
- Anticybersquatting Consumer Protection Act, 15 U.S.C. § 1125(d)
- Arms Export Control Act, 22 U.S.C. § 2778 (2010)
- Audio Home Recording Act, Pub.L. 102–563, § 1, October 28, 1992, 106 Stat. 4237, amending 17 U.S.C. §§ 1001–1010, 801, 804, 912, and 19 U.S.C.A. § 1337
- Bank Fraud Act, 18 U.S.C. § 1344
- Child Online Protection Act, 47 U.S.C. § 231
- Child Pornography Prevention Act of 1996, 18 U.S.C. §§ 2251–2260
- Children's Internet Protection Act, 47 U.S.C. § 254(h)
- Children's Online Privacy Protection Act, 15 U.S.C. §§ 6501–6506
- Children's Online Privacy Protection Rule, 64 Fed. Reg. 59, 888 (November 3, 1999) (codified at 16 C.F.R. § 312 (2001))
- Communications Act of 1934, as amended by Telecommunications Act of 1996, 47 U.S.C. §§ 151 et seq.
- Communications Assistance for Law Enforcement Act (CALEA) of 1994, Pub. L. No. 103–414, 108 Stat. 4279, amending 47 U.S.C. §§ 1001–1010Communications Decency Act of 1996, Pub. L. No. 104–104 § 502, 1996 U.S.S.C.A.N. (110 Stat.) 56, 133 (later codified at 47 U.S.C. § 223)
- Computer Fraud and Abuse Act of 1986, 18 U.S.C. § 1030
- Computer Matching and Privacy and Protection Act, 5 U.S.C. § 552a(o)
- Controlling the Assault of Non-solicited Pornography and Marketing (CAN-SPAM) Act of 2003, 15 U.S.C. §§ 7701–7713

- Copyright Act of 1976, 17 U.S.C. §§ 101–1332
- Credit Card Fraud Act, 18 U.S.C. § 1029
- Determination of Reasonable Rates and Terms for the Digital Performance of Sound Recordings and Ephemeral Recordings, Final Rule, 67 Fed. Reg. 45,239 (July 8, 2002) (codified at 37 C.F.R. § 261)
- Digital Millennium Copyright Act, Pub. L. No. 105–304, codified at 17 U.S.C. §§ 1201–1205
- Digital Performance Right in Sound Recordings Act, codified at 17 U.S.C. §§ 106, 114–15
- Economic Espionage Act of 1996, 18 U.S.C. § 1831 et seq.
- Electronic Communications Privacy Act of 1986, Pub. L. No. 99–508, codified at 18 U.S.C. § 2703
- Electronic Signatures in Global and National Commerce Act (E-Sign), 15 U.S.C. §§ 7001 et. seq.
- Exemption to Prohibition on Circumvention of Copyright Protection Systems for Access Control Technologies, 37 C.F.R § 201.40 (2010)
- Fair and Accurate Credit Transactions Act, 117 Stat. 1952, amending and codified at 15 U.S.C. §§ 1681 et seq.
- Federal Anti-Lottery Act, 18 U.S.C. §§ 1301–1304
- Federal Trade Commission Act, 15 U.S.C. § 45
- Federal Trademark Dilution Act of 1995, 15 U.S.C. § 1125(c)
- First Inventors Defense Act, 35 U.S.C. § 273
- Full Faith and Credit Statute, 28 U.S.C. § 1738
- Identity Theft and Assumption Deterrence Act of 1998, amending and codified at 18 U.S.C. § 1028
- Identity Theft Penalty Enforcement Act of 2004, amending and codified at 18 U.S.C. § 1028
- Identity Theft and Restitution Act of 2008, amending and codified 18. U.S.C. § 3663(b)
- International Traffic in Arms Regulation (ITAR), 22 C.F.R. §§ 120–130
- Internet False Identification Prevention Act, amending and codified at 18 U.S.C. § 1028
- Internet Tax Freedom Act, P.L. 105–277, Title XI, and subsequent Acts codified at 47 U.S.C. § 151
- Lanham Trademark Act, 15 U.S.C. § 1115(b)
- Mask Work Protection, 37 C.F.R. § 211
- National Information Infrastructure Protection Act (NII) of 1996, codified at 18 U.S.C. § 1030
- Neighborhood Children's Internet Protection Act, 47 U.S.C. § 254(l)
- No Electronic Theft Act, amending and codified at 17 U.S.C. §§ 101, 506 & 507 & 18 U.S.C. §§ 2319–2320
- Online Copyright Infringement Liability Limitation Act (Digital Millennium Copyright Act, Title II), 17 U.S.C. § 512
- Patent Act, 35 U.S.C. §§ 1–376
- Patent Act, Right of Priority, 35 U.S.C. § 119
- Privacy Act of 1974, 5 U.S.C. § 552a
- Prosecuting Remedies and Tools against the Exploitation of Children Today (PROTECT) Act of 2003, 18 U.S.C. § 1466A
- Secure Authentication Feature and Enhanced Identification Defense (SAFE ID) Act, amending and codified at 18 U.S.C. § 1028
- Semiconductor Chip Protection Act, 17 U.S.C. §§ 901–914
- Sherman Antitrust Act, 15 U.S.C. § 1

- Small Webcasters Settlement Act of 2002, amending and codified at 17 U.S.C. § 114(f)
- Sonny Bono Copyright Term Extension Act, Pub. L. 105–298, 112 Stat. 2827 (1998) amending and codified at 17 U.S.C. §§ 101, 108, 110, 201, 301–304, 512
- Stored Communications Act, 18 U.S.C. §§ 2701–2712 (1986)
- Technology, Education and Copyright Harmonization Act amendments, 17 U.S.C. §§ 110(2), 112
- Telecommunications Act of 1996, 47 U.S.C. §§ 151 et seq.
- Trademark Dilution Revision Act of 2006, 15 USC § 1125
- Trademark Law Treaty Act of 1998, 15 U.S.C. § 1051
- Undertaking Spam, Spyware, and Fraud Enforcement with Enforcers beyond Borders ("SAFE WEB") Act of 2006, Pub. L. No. 109–455, codified at 15 U.S.C. §§ 41 et. seq.
- Unfair Methods of Competition, 15 U.S.C. § 45
- Uniting and Strengthening America by Providing Appropriate Tools Required to Intercept and Obstruct Terrorism Act (USA PATRIOT Act) of 2001, Pub. L. No. 107–56, 115 Stat. 272 (codified as amended in scattered sections of the U.S.C.)
- Unlawful Internet Gambling Enforcement Act of 2006, 31 U.S.C. §§ 5361–5367
- Vessel Hull Design Protection Act, codified at 17 U.S.C. §§ 1301–1332
- Visual Artists Rights Act, 17 U.S.C. § 106A
- Wire Act, 18 U.S.C. § 1084
- Wire Fraud Act, 18 U.S.C. § 1343
- World Intellectual Property Organization, Regulations under the Patent Cooperation Treaty (PCT) Rule 19.1(a)(iii), available at http://www.wipo.int/pct/en/texts/rules/r19.htm (visited August 16, 2012)

State

- 10 L.P.R.A. §§ 2181–2185
- 73 P.S. 2330.1 et seq.
- Computer Crimes Act, H.B. 2215 (Va. 2005), Va. Code § 18.2–152.4
- Consumer Protection against Computer Spyware Act, S.B. 327 (Tex. 2005), Tex. Bus. & Comm. Code §§ 324.001–102
- Consumer Protection against Computer Software Act, S.B. 1436 (Cal. 2004), Cal. Bus. & Prof. Code §§ 22947 to 22947.6
- Computer Security Act, H.B. 127 (Ga. 2005), Ga. Code §§ 16-9-152 to 157
- Computer Spyware, H.B. 2414 (Ariz. 2005), Ariz. Rev. Stat. §§ 44–7301 to 44–7304
- Deceptive or Unauthorized Computer Software, H.F. 614 (Iowa. 2005), Iowa Code §§ 715.1 to 715.8
- Delaware Gaming Competiveness Act of 2012, H.B. 333 (Del. 2012), 29 Del. Code §§ 4803, 4805, 4810–4811, 4815, 4819–4820, 4824 -4826, 4834–4836, 4 Del. Code 543
- Georgia Code Ann., § 16–9-93.1
- Illinois Amending Lottery and State Finance Act, S.B. 3497 (Ill. 2012), 20 ILCS 1605/7.12, 1605/14.4
- Illinois Spyware Prevent Initiative Act, H.B. 380 (Ill. 2005), 720 ILCS 5/17–52.5

- Improper Use of Computer Spyware, H.B. 2904 (Ark. 2004), Ark. Code §§ 4–111–101, -102, -103, -104, -105, § 19–6-301, § 19–6-804
- Indiana Code §§ 24–4.8–1 et seq., §§ 24–4.8–2 et. seq, §§ 24–4.8–3 et seq.
- Louisiana Rev. Stat. §§ 51:2006 to 51:2014
- Maine An Act To Enhance Opportunities for the Sale of Lottery Tickets, S.P. 657 (Me. 2012), 8. Me. Rev. Stat. §§ 372 & 379
- Michigan McCauley-Traxler-Law-Bowman-McNeely Lottery Act, S.B. 1003 (Mich. 2012), Mich. Code § 432.9
- Nevada Rev. Stat. § 205.4737
- Regulating the Use of Computer Spyware, H.B. 47 (N.H. 2005), N.H. Rev. Stat. §§ 359-H:1 to 359-H:6
- Rhode Island Gen. Laws §§ 11–52.2–2 to 2–7
- Spyware and Unsolicited Internet Advertising, S.B. 140 (Alaska. 2005), Alaska Stat. §§ 45.45.792, -.794, -.798; § 45.50.471(51)
- Spyware Control Act, H.B. 323 (Utah 2004), Utah Code §§ 13–40–203, 13–40–204, 13–40–301, 13–40–302, 13–40–402
- Utah Internet Gambling, H.B. 108 (Utah 2012), Utah Code §§ 76–10–1101–1102
- Washington Rev. Code §§ 19.270.101–900

Proposed Legislation (Federal)

- Anti-Counterfeiting Trade Agreement, October 1, 2011, 50 I.LM. 243 (2011)
- Child Protection Act of 2012, S. 3456, 112th Cong. (2d Sess. 2011–2012)
- Children's Online Privacy Protection Act, 15 U.S.C. §§ 6501–6506
- Combating Online Infringement and Counterfeits Act, S. 3804, 111th Cong. (2d Sess. 2010)
- Consumer Broadband and Digital Television Promotion Act, S. 2048, 107th Cong. (2d Sess. 2002), available at http://thomas.loc.gov/cgi-bin/query/z?c107:S.2048
- Cybersecurity Act of 2012, S. 2105, 112th Cong. (2d Sess. 2011–2012)
- Indiana Senate Bill 309, S. 309, 118th Cong. (1st Sess. 2013), available at http://www.in.gov/legislative/bills/2013/PDF/IN/IN0309.1.pdf
- Inducing Infringement of Copyrights Act of 2004, S. 2560, 108th Cong. (2d Sess. 2004)
- Intellectual Property Enforcement Act of 2007, S. 2317, 110th Cong. (1st Sess. 2007)
- International Cyberspace and Cybersecurity Coordination Act of 2010, S. 3193, 111th Cong. (2d Sess. 2010)
- Internet Freedom Act, H.R. 96, 112th Cong. (1st Sess. 2011)
- Internet Radio Equality Act, H.R. 2060, 110th Cong. (1st Sess. 2007)
- Internet Spyware Prevention ("I-SPY") Act of 2007, H.R.1525, 110th Cong. (1st Sess. 2007–2008)
- Main Street Fairness Act, S. 1452, 112th Cong. (1st Sess. 2011); H.R. 2701, 112th Cong. (1st Sess. 2011)
- Marketplace Equity Act of 2011, H.R. 3179, 112th Cong. (1st Sess. 2011)
- Marketplace Fairness Act, S. 1832, 112th Cong. (1st Sess. 2011)
- Preventing Real Online Threats to Economic Creativity and Theft of Intellectual Property (PROTECT IP) Act of 2011, S. 968, 112th Cong. (1st Sess. 2011)

- Protect America Act of 2007, S. 1927, 110th Cong. (1st Sess. 2007)
- Protecting American Trade Secrets of 2012, S. 3389, 112th Cong. (2d Sess. 2012)
- Protecting Children from Internet Pornographers Act of 2011, H.R. 1981, 112th Cong. (1st Sess. 2011–2012)
- Protecting Intellectual Rights against Theft and Expropriation (PIRATE) Act of 2004, S. 2237, 108th Cong. (2d Sess. 2004)
- Public Domain Enhancement Act, H.R. 2601, 108th Cong. (1st Sess. 2003), available at http://thomas.loc .gov/cgi-bin/query/z?c108:H.R.2601:
- Safeguard against Privacy Invasions Act, H.R. 2929, 108th Cong. (1st Sess. 2003), reported to and passed by House of Representatives as Securely Protect Yourself against Cyber Trespass Act ("SPY ACT")
- Security and Freedom through Encryption (SAFE) Act, H.R. 850, 106th Cong. (1st Sess. 1999)
- Software Principles Yielding Better Levels of Consumer Knowledge ("SPY BLOCK") Act, S. 2145, 108th Cong. (2d Sess. 2003)
- Stop Online Piracy Act, H.R. 3261, 112th Cong. (1st Sess. 2011)
- Theft of Trade Secrets Clarification Act of 2012, S. 3642, 112th Cong. (2d Sess. 2012), amending and codified 18 U.S.C. § 1832(a)
- Undetectable Firearms Act, codified at 18 U.S.C. § 922
- Unlawful Internet Gambling Funding Prohibition Act, H.R. 2143, 108th Cong. (1st Sess. 2003)

Proposed Legislation (State)
- California Internet Gambling Consumer Protection and Public-Private Partnership Act of 2012, S.B. 1463 (Reg Sess. 2011–12)
- Colorado Prohibition of Internet Lottery, H.B. 12–135 (Reg Sess. 2012)
- Hawaii Internet and Lottery Gaming Act, H.B. 2422 (Reg Sess. 2011–12)
- Iowa Act Authorizing Licensees Authorized to Conduct Gambling, S.S.B. 1364 (2012)
- Leahy-Smith America Invents Act, H.R. 1249, 112th Cong., sec. 3 (1st Sess. 2011)
- Mississippi Internet Gaming Act of 2012, H.B. 1373 (Reg Sess. 2012)
- New Jersey Internet Wagering at Atlantic Casinos Act (Amending and Supplementing Casino Control Act), A. 2578 (Reg Sess. 2012–2013)

Administrative and Executive Materials
- 144 Cong. Rec. H9946–01, H9952 (Sonny Bono Copyright Term Extension Act, October 7, 1998) (Statement of Representative Mary Bono)
- Copyright Arbitration Royalty Panel, Report to the Librarian of Congress (February 20, 2002), Appendix A, available at http://www.copyright.gov/carp/webcast_regs .html#panel
- Guidelines for Classroom Copying in Not-for-Profit Educational Institutions, H.R. Rep. No. 94–1476 (1976)
- H. Con. Res. 127, 112th Cong. (2011–2013)
- House Report on the No Electronic Theft Act, H.R. Rep. No. 339 (1997)

- Register of Copyrights, before the Subcommittee on Intellectual Property, Senate Judiciary Committee, 109th Congress (2005) (Statement of Marybeth Peters)
- Report of the Committee on Financial Services on the Unlawful Internet Gambling Funding Prohibition Act, H.R. Rep. No. 108–133 (2003)
- Virgina A. Seitz, *Memorandum Opinion for the Assistant Attorney General, Criminal Division: Whether Proposals by Illinois and New York to Use the Internet and Out-of-State Transaction Processors to Sell Lottery Tickets to In-State Adults Violate the Wire Act*, Opinions of the Office of Legal Counsel 35 (2011), available at http://www.justice.gov/ olc/2011/state-lotteries-opinion.pdf
- United States Copyright Office, Compendium II of Copyright Office Practices § 306.02(b) (1984)
- United States Copyright Office, DMCA Section 104 Report, A Report of the Register of Copyrights Pursuant to §104 of the Digital Millennium Copyright Act (August 2001)
- United States Copyright Office, Joint Study of Section 1201(g) of The Digital Millennium Copyright Act (May 2000)
- United States Copyright Office, Report on Copyright and Digital Distance Education (May 1999)

Model Codes and Restatements
- American Law Institute, *Restatement of the Law Second: Conflict of Laws* (Philadelphia: American Law Institute, 1971)
- American Law Institute, *Restatement (Second) of Torts* (Washington, D.C.: American Law Institute, 1984 & Supp. 2003)
- American Law Institute, *Restatement (Third) of Unfair Competition §§ 21–23* (Washington, D.C.: American Law Institute 1995 & Supp. 2004)
- National Conference of Commissioners on Uniform State Laws, Uniform Trade Secrets Act, as amended 1985
- Uniform Commercial Code (2001)
- Uniform Computer Information Transactions Act (2002)
- Uniform Electronic Transactions Act (1999)

European Union Directives
- Article 9(1) of Council Regulation (EC) No 40/94 of 20 December 1993 on the Community trade mark 1994 O.J. (L11) 1
- Article 14 of Directive 2000/31/EC of the European Parliament and of the Council of 8 June 2000 on certain legal aspects of information society services, in particular electronic commerce 2000 O.J. (L 178) 1
- Council Directive 93/98/EEC of 29 October 1993 Harmonizing the Term of Protection of Copyright and Certain Related Rights, 1993 O.J. (L 290) 9
- Directive 2002/58/EC of the European Parliament and of the Council of 12 July 2002 on Privacy and Electronic Communications, 2002 O.J. (L 201) 37
- Directive 2006/116/EC of the European Parliament and of the Council of 12 December 2006 on the Term of Protection of Copyright and Certain Related Rights, 2006 O.J. (L 372) 12–18
- Directive 2009/136/EC of the European Parliament and of the Council of 25 November 2009, 2009 O.J. (L 337) 11

- Directive on the approximation of the laws, regulations and administrative provisions of the Member States relating to the advertising and sponsorship of tobacco products, 2003 O.J. (L 152) 16
- Directive on Privacy and Electronic Communications, Council Directive 2002/58/EC, 2002 O.J. (L 201) 37
- EU Directive 2001/29/EC on the Harmonisation of Certain Aspects of Copyright and Related Rights in the Information Society, 2001 O.J. (L 167) 10
- First Council Directive 89/104/EEC of 21 December 1988 to approximate the laws of the Member States relating to trade marks 1989 O.J. (L 40) 1
- Notice 11/2007 from the European Patent Office dated 1 October 2007 concerning business methods, 2007 O.J. (EPO 592)

International Directives, Laws and Regulations
- Data Protection Act, 1998, c. 29, §§ 7–12 (Eng.)
- The Personal Information Protection an Electronic Documents Act and the Telecommunications Act, amended 2011, S.C. 2010, c. 23 (Can.), available at http://laws-lois.justice.gc.ca/eng/acts/E-1.6/index.html
- The Privacy and Electronic Communications Regulations, 2011, EC Directive No. 1208 (U.K.), available at http://www.legislation.gov.uk/uksi/2011/1208/contents/made

Cases
Supreme Court
- *Ashcroft v. American Civil Liberties Union*, 524 U.S. 656 (2004)
- *Ashcroft v. Free Speech Coalition*, 535 U.S. 234 (2002)
- *Bilski v. Kappos*, 130 S. Ct. 3218 (2010)
- *Brandenburg v. Ohio*, 395 U.S. 444 (1969)
- *Brockett v. Spokane Arcades Inc.*, 472 U.S. 491 (1985)
- *Brown v. Entertainment Merchants Association*, 131 S. Ct. 2729 (2011)
- *Campbell v. Acuff-Rose Music, Inc.*, 510 U.S. 569 (1994)
- *Dastar v. Twentieth Century Fox, Inc.*, 539 U.S. 23 (2003)
- *Diamond v. Diehr, II*, 450 U.S. 175 (1981)
- *Dowling v. United States*, 473 U.S. 207 (1985)
- *Ebay Inc. v. MercExchange, L.L.C.*, 547 U.S. 388 (2006)
- *Eldred v. Ashcroft*, 537 U.S. 186 (2003)
- *Federal Communications Commission v. Fox TV Stations, Inc.*, 132 S. Ct. 2307 (2012)
- *Federal Communications Commission v. Pacifica Foundation*, 438 U.S. 726 (1978)
- *Feist Publications, Inc. v. Rural Telephone Service Co.*, 499 U.S. 340 (1991)
- *Festo Corp. v. Shoketsu Kinzoku Kogyo Kabushiki Co., Ltd.*, 535 U.S. 722 (2002)
- *Gottschalk v. Benson*, 409 U.S. 63 (1972)
- *Hamling v. United States*, 418 U.S. 87 (1974)
- *Harper & Row Publishers Inc. v. Nation Enterprises*, 471 U.S. 539 (1985)
- *Hilton v. Guyot*, 159 U.S. 113 (1895)
- *International Shoe v. Washington*, 326 U.S. 310 (1945)
- *Jacobellis v. Ohio*, 378 U.S. 184 (1964)
- *KP Permanent Make-Up, Inc. v. Lasting Impression 1, Inc.*, 543 U.S. 111 (2004)
- *KSR International Co. v. Teleflex, Inc.*, 550 U.S. 398 (2007)
- *Metro-Goldwyn-Mayer Studios, Inc. v. Grokster, Ltd.*, 545 U.S. 913 (2005)
- *Miller v. California*, 413 U.S. 15 (1973)
- *Mishkin v. New York*, 383 U.S. 502 (1966)
- *New York v. Ferber*, 458 U.S. 747 (1982)
- *Osborne v. Ohio*, 495 U.S. 103 (1990)
- *Paris Adult Theatre v. Slaton*, 413 U.S. 49 (1973)
- *Pinkus v. United States*, 436 U.S. 293 (1978)
- *Pope v. Illinois*, 481 U.S. 497 (1987)
- *Quill Corp. v. North Dakota*, 504 U.S. 298 (1992)
- *Reno v. American Civil Liberties Union*, 521 U.S. 844 (1997)
- *Roth v. United States*, 354 U.S. 476 (1957)
- *Saxlehner v. Wagner*, 216 U.S. 375 (1910)
- *Singer Manufacturing Co. v. June Manufacturing Co.*, 163 U.S. 169 (1896)
- *Sony Corp. of America v. Universal City Studios, Inc.*, 464 U.S. 417 (1984)
- *Two Pesos, Inc. v. Taco Cabana, Inc.*, 505 U.S. 763 (1992)
- *United States v. American Library Association, Inc.*, 539 U.S. 194 (2003)
- *Whalen v. Roe*, 429 U.S. 589 (1977)
- *Wheaton v. Peters*, 33 U.S. (8 Pet.) 591 (1834)
- *White v. Dunbar*, 119 U.S. 47 (1886)

Federal Appellate Courts
- *1–800 Contacts, Inc. v. WhenU.com, Inc.*, 414 F.3d 400 (2d Cir. 2005)
- *A&M Records, Inc. v. Napster, Inc.*, 239 F.3d 1004 (9th Cir. 2001), on remand, No. 00–16401, 2001 WL 227083 (N.D. Cal. 2001), affirmed, 284 F.3d 1091 (9th Cir. 2002)
- *Abercrombie & Fitch Co. v. Hunting World, Inc.*, 537 F.2d 4 (2d Cir. 1976)
- *ALS Scan, Inc. v. RemarQ Communities, Inc.*, 239 F.3d 619 (4th Cir. 2001)
- *Amazon.com, Inc. v. Barnesandnoble.com, Inc.*, 239 F.3d 1343 (Fed. Cir. 2001)
- *American Civil Liberties Union v. Ashcroft*, 322 F.3d 240 (3d Cir. 2003)
- *American Civil Liberties Union v. Mukasey*, 534 F.3d 181 (3d Cir. 2008) certiorari denied sub nom, *Mukasey v. American Civil Liberties Union*, 555 U.S. 1137 (2009)
- *American Civil Liberties Union v. Reno*, 217 F.3d 162 (3d Cir. 2000), reversed sub nom, *Ashcroft v. American Civil Liberties Union*, 535 U.S. 564 (2002), on remand, *American Civil Liberties Union v. Ashcroft*, 322 F.3d 240 (3d Cir. 2003), certiorari granted, *Ashcroft v. American Civil Liberties Union*, 540 U.S. 944 (2003), affirmed & remanded, 542 U.S. 656 (2004)
- *American Civil Liberties Union v. United States Department of Justice*, 681 F.3d 61 (2d Cir. 2012)
- *Andrews v. TRW, Inc.*, 225 F.3d 1063 (9th Cir. 2000), reversed, 534 U.S. 19 (2001)
- *Apple Computer, Inc. v. Franklin Computer Corp.*, 714 F.2d 1240 (3d Cir. 1983), abrogated by *In re Bilski*, 545 F.3d 943 (Fed. Cir. 2008)
- *Apple Inc. v. Psystar Corp.*, 658 F.3d 1150 (9th Cir. 2011)
- *AT&T Corp. v. City of Portland*, 216 F.3d 871 (9th Cir. 2000)
- *AT&T Corp. v. Excel Communications, Inc.*, 172 F.3d 1352 (Fed. Cir. 1999)

- *Network Automation, Inc. v. Advanced Systems Concepts Inc.,* 638 F.3d 1137 (9th Cir. 2011)
- *New Kids on the Block v. News America Publishing, Inc.,* 971 F.2d 302 (9th Cir. 1992)
- *Novell, Inc. v. Microsoft Corp.,* 429 F.App'x 254 (4th Cir. 2011)
- *PACCAR Inc. v. TeleScan Technologies, L.L.C.,* 319 F.3d 243 (6th Cir. 2003)
- *Panavision International L.P. v. Toeppen,* 141 F.3d 1316 (9th Cir. 1998)
- *Pebble Beach Co., v. Tour 18 I Limited,* 155 F.3d 526 (5th Cir. 1998)
- *Perfect 10, Inc. v. Amazon.com, Inc.,* 508 F.3d 1146 (9th Cir. 2007)
- *Perfect 10, Inc. v. Google, Inc.,* 653 F.3d 976 (9th Cir. 2011)
- *Pickett v. Prince,* 207 F.3d 402 (7th Cir. 2000)
- *Piper Aircraft Corp. v. Wag-Aero, Inc.,* 741 F.2d 925 (7th Cir. 1984)
- *Pippinger v. Rubin,* 129 F.3d 519 (10th Cir. 1997)
- *Playboy Enterprises Inc. v. Netscape Communications Corp.,* 354 F.3d 1020 (9th Cir. 2004)
- *Playboy Enterprises, Inc. v. Welles,* 279 F.3d 796 (9th Cir. 2002), superseded by statute, *Levi Strauss & Co. v. Abercrombie & Fitch Trading Co.,* 633 F.3d 1158 (9th Cir. 2011)
- *Polaroid Corp. v. Polarad Electronics Corp.,* 287 F.2d 492 (2d Cir. 1961)
- *Rearden LLC v. Rearden Commerce, Inc.,* 683 F.3d 1190 (9th Cir. 2012)
- *Recording Industry Association of America v. Charter Communications, Inc.,* 393 F.3d 771 (8th Cir. 2005)
- *Recording Industry Association of America v. Diamond Multimedia Systems, Inc.,* 180 F.3d 1072 (9th Cir. 1999)
- *Red Baron-Franklin Park, Inc. v. Taito Corp.,* 883 F.2d 275 (4th Cir. 1989)
- *Rescuecom Corp. v. Google, Inc.,* 562 F.3d 123 (2d Cir. 2009)
- *Rosetta Stone Ltd. v. Google, Inc.,* 676 F.3d 144 (4th Cir. 2012)
- *Salinger v. Colting,* 607 F.3d 68 (2d Cir. 2010)
- *Scott Paper Co. v. Scott's Liquid Gold, Inc.,* 589 F.2d 1225 (3d Cir. 1978)
- *Sega Enterprises Ltd. v. Accolade, Inc.,* 977 F.2d 1510 (9th Cir. 1992)
- *Shields v. Zuccarini,* 254 F.3d 476 (3d Cir. 2001)
- *Sony BMG Music Entertainment v. Tenenbaum,* 660 F.3d 487 (1st Cir. 2011)
- *Sony Computer Entertainment, Inc. v. Connectix Corp.,* 203 F.3d 596 (9th Cir. 2000)
- *Sporty's Farm L.L.C. v. Sportsman's Market, Inc.,* 202 F.3d 489 (2d Cir. 2000)
- *Starbucks Corp. v. Wolfe's Borough Coffee, Inc.,* 588 F.3d 97 (2d Cir. 2009)
- *State Street Bank & Trust v. Signature Financial Group, Inc.,* 149 F.3d 1368 (Fed. Cir. 1999), certiorari denied, 525 U.S. 1093
- *Steve Jackson Games v. United States Secret Service,* 36 F.3d 457 (5th Cir. 1994) superseded by statute as stated *in Konop v. Hawaiian Airlines, Inc.,* 236 F.3d 1035 (9th Cir. 2001)

- *Texas Instruments Inc. v. U.S. International Trade Commission,* 988 F.2d 1165 (Fed. Cir. 1993)
- *Theofel v. Farey Jones,* 341 F.3d 978 (9th Cir. 2003); 359 F.3d 1066 (9th Cir. 2004)
- *Time Warner Telecom, Inc. v. FCC,* 507 F.3d 205 (3d Cir. 2007)
- *Toyota Motor Sales, U.S.A., Inc. v. Tabari,* 610 F.3d 1171 (9th Cir. 2010)
- *United States v. Cohen,* 260 F.3d 68 (2d Cir. 2001)
- *United States v. Hsu,* 364 F.3d 192 (4th Cir. 2004)
- *United States v. Microsoft Corp.,* 253 F.3d 34 (D.C. Cir. 2001)
- *United States v. Morris,* 928 F.2d 504 (2d Cir. 1991)
- *United States v. Whorley,* 550 F.3d 326 (4th Cir. 2008)
- *Universal City Studios, Inc. v. Corley,* 273 F.3d 429 (2d Cir. 2001)
- *Universal Communication Systems, Inc. v. Lycos, Inc.,* 478 F.3d 413 (1st Cir. 2007)
- *V Secret Catalogue, Inc. v. Moseley,* 605 F.3d 382 (6th Cir. 2010)
- *Vault Corp. v. Quaid Software Ltd.,* 847 F.2d 255 (5th Cir. 1988)
- *Vernor v. Autodesk, Inc.,* 621 F.3d 1102 (9th Cir. 2010)
- *Viacom International, Inc. v. YouTube, Inc.,* 676 F.3d 19 (2d Cir. 2012)
- *Virtual Works, Inc. v. Volkswagen of America, Inc.,* 238 F.3d 262 (4th Cir. 2001)
- *Voice of the Arab World, Inc. v. MDTV Medical News Now, Inc.,* 645 F.3d 26 (1st Cir. 2011)
- *Wang Labs, Inc. v. Toshiba Corp.,* 993 F.2d 858 (Fed. Cir. 1993)
- *Williams Electronics, Inc. v. Arctic International, Inc.,* 685 F.2d 870 (3d Cir. 1982)
- *Yahoo! Inc. v. La Ligue Contre Le Racisme et L'Antisemitisme,* 379 F.3d 1120 (9th Cir. 2004), reversed and remanded, *Yahoo! Inc. v. La Ligue Contre Le Racisme et L'Antisemitisme,* 379 F.3d 1120 (9th Cir. 2004), rehearing, 433 F.3d 1199 (9th Cir. 2006), certiorari denied, 547 U.S. 1163 (2006)
- *Zango, Inc. v. Kaspersky Lab, Inc.,* 568 F.3d 1169 (9th Cir. 2009)
- *Zeran v. America Online, Inc.,* 129 F.3d 327 (4th Cir. 1997)

Federal Trial Courts

- *1–800 Contacts v. WhenU.com, Inc.,* 309 F. Supp. 2d 467 (S.D.N.Y. 2003), reversed on other (trademark) grounds, 414 F.3d 400 (2d Cir. 2005)
- *Adobe Systems, Inc. v. Stargate Software Inc.,* 216 F. Supp. 2d 1051 (N.D. Cal. 2002)
- *Aitken v. Communs. Workers of Am.,* 496 F. Supp. 2d 653 (E.D. Va. 2007)
- *American Booksellers Foundation for Free Expression v. Coakley,* No. 10–11165-RWZ, 2010 U.S. Dist. LEXIS 114750 (D. Mass. 2010)
- *American Civil Liberties Union of Georgia v. Miller,* 977 F. Supp. 1228 (N.D. Ga. 1997)
- *American Civil Liberties Union v. Gonzales,* 478 F. Supp. 2d 775 (E.D. Pa. 2007)
- *American Civil Liberties Union v. Reno,* F. Supp. 824 (E.D. Pa. 1996), affirmed sub nom, *Reno v. American Civil Liberties Union,* 521 U.S. 844 (1997)

reversed by *Yahoo! Inc. v. La Ligue Contre Le Racisme et L'Antisemitisme*, 379 F.3d 1120 (9th Cir. 2004); reversal affirmed on rehearing by Yahoo! Inc. v. La Ligue Contre Le Racisme, 433 F.3d 1199 (9th Cir. 2006)

Administrative Agency Decision (FCC)

- *In re Inquiry Concerning High-Speed Access to the Internet over Cable and Other Facilities*, 17 F.C.C. Rcd. 4798, 2002 WL 407567 (2002)

State Courts

- *Alabama Great Southern Railroad Company v. Carroll*, 97 Ala. 126 (1892)
- *Amazon.com LLC v. New York State Department of Taxation & Finance*, 877 N.Y.S.2d 842 (N.Y. Sup. Ct. 2009), affirmed as modified 913 N.Y.S.2d 129 (N.Y. App. Div. 2010)
- *Bachchan v. India Abroad Publications*, 585 N.Y.S.2d 661 (N.Y. Sup. Ct. 1992)
- *DVD Copy Control Association, Inc. v. Bunner*, 113 Cal. Rptr. 2d 338 (2001), reversed, 4 Cal. Rptr. 3d 69 (2003)
- *Ferguson v. Friendfinders, Inc.*, 94 Cal. App. 4th 1255 (Cal. App. 1st Dist. 2002)
- *In re Appeal of Application for Search Warrant*, No. 2010–479 (Vt. December 14, 2012)
- *In re Rolando S.*, 197 Cal. App. 4th. 936 (Cal. App. 5th Dist. 2011)
- *In re Schneider's Estate*, 96 N.Y.S. 2d 652 (N.Y. Sup. Ct. 1950)
- *Intel Corp. v. Hamidi*, 30 Cal. 4th 1342 (Cal. 2003)
- *Kilberg v. Northwest Airlines, Inc.*, 172 N.E.2d 34 (N.Y. App. Ct. 1961)
- *University of Chicago v. Dater*, 270 N.W. 175 (Mich. 1936)

Australia

- *Apple Inc. v. Samsung Electronics Ltd. Co.* (No. 2) 2012 FCA 1358 (Austl.), available at http://www .judgments.fedcourt.gov.au/judgments/Judgments/ fca/single/2012/2012fca1358 (visited January 12, 2013) *Gutnick v. Dow Jones & Co.* [2002] H.C.A. 56 (Austl.), available at http://www.austlii.edu.au/ cgi-bin/sinodisp/au/cases/cth/HCA/2002/56 .html?stem=0&synonyms=0&query=dow%20jones (visited February 8, 2013)

France

- *League against Racism and Antisemitism (LICRA), French Union of Jewish Students, v. Yahoo! Inc. (USA), Yahoo France*, Tribunal de Grande Instance de Paris, Interim Court Order, 20 November 2000
- Tribunal de Grand Instance de Paris [TGI], [ordinary court of jurisdiction] Paris, March 3, 2011, Case No. 0718523043 (Fr.) (*Public Prosecutor v. Weiler*), English translation available at http://www.ejiltalk.org/ wp-content/uploads/2011/03/Public-Prosecutor-v-Weiler-judgement-March-3–2011–3.pdf (visited December 18, 2012)
- Tribunal De Grand Instance de Paris [TGI], [ordinary court of jurisdiction] Paris, Case No. 11/10464, December 8, 2011 (Fr.) (*Samsung Electronics Co. Ltd and Samsung Electronics France v. Apple France et al.*), English translation

available at http://www.eplawpatentblog.com/2011/ December/2011–12–08_Samsung_Apple_comments.pdf (visited January 12, 2013)

- Yaman Akdeniz, Case Analysis of *League against Racism and Antisemitism (LICRA), French Union of Jewish Students, v. Yahoo! Inc. (USA), Yahoo France*, Tribunal de Grande Instance de Paris, Interim Court Order, 20 November 2000, 1 Elec. Bus. L. Rep. 110 (2001), download available at http://www.cyber-rights.org/ documents (visited October 11, 2004)

Italy

- Tribunale di Milano (Milan first-instance court) (preliminary proceedings) 8 Dicembre 2011, Docket No. 11/58301 (It.) (*Samsung Electronics Italia s.p.a v. Apple Inc.*)
- Tribunale Ordinario di Milano (Ordinary Tribunal of Milan) 12 aprile 2010, Case No. 1972/2010 (It.), available at http://www.giurcost.org/casi_scelti/Google .pdf (visited January 12, 2013)
- Tribunale Ordinario di Milano (Ordinary Tribunal of Milan) 24 febbraio 2010, Sentenza n. 1972/2010 (It.)

Japan

- Tōkyō Chihō Saibansho [Tokyo District Court] August 31, 2012, Case No. 2011 (Yo) No. 22027 (Japan) (*Japan Samsung Electronics Co., Ltd v. Apple Japan, Inc.*)

Korea

- Seoul Central District Court Decision, Case No. 2011 Kahap 39552, August 24, 2012 (S. Kor.) (*Samsung Electronics Co., Ltd. v. Apple Korea Ltd.*)

The Netherlands

- *Buma & Stemra v. KaZaA*, Amsterdam Court of Appeal (2002), unofficial English translation available at www.eff .org/IP/P2P/BUMA_v_Kazaa/20020328_kazaa_appeal_ judgment.html (visited December 19, 2012)

Norway

- *Sunde (for Norway) v. Johansen*, Oslo First Instance Trial Court, January 7, 2003, No. 02–507 M/94, English translation by Professor Jon Bing available at http:// w2.eff.org/IP/Video/Johansen_DeCSS_case/20030109_ johansen_decision.html (visited July 27, 2004); on appeal, Borgarting Appellate Court, December 22, 2003, No. LB-2003–00731, English translation by Professor Jon Bing available at http://www.efn.no/DVD-dom-20031222-en .html (visited July 27, 2004)

European Union Courts

- Case C-236/08, *Google France v. Louis Vuitton*, Judgment of Court (Grand Chamber) (March23, 2010), available at http://curia.europa.eu/juris/liste .jsf?language=en&num=C-236/08 (visited February 18, 2013)
- Case C-128/11, *UsedSoft GmbH v. Oracle International Corp.*, Judgment of the Court of First Instance (Grand Chamber) (July 3, 2012), available at http://curia.europa .eu/juris/document/document.jsf?text=&docid=124564& doclang=en&mode=req (visited December 14, 2012)

- Case G 0003/08, *Patentability of Programs for Computers*, Enlarged Board of Appeal of the European Patent Office pursuant to Article 112(1)(b) EPC (November 12, 2010)
- Case T-201/04, *Microsoft Corp. v Commission of the European Communities*, Judgment of the Court of First Instance (Grand Chamber) (September 17, 2007)
- Case T 0935/97–3.5.1., *International Business Machines Corporation*, Technical Board of Appeal of the European Patent Office (February 4, 1999)

United Kingdom
- *Cheavin v. Walker*, 5 Ch. Div. 850 (1877)
- *Donaldson v. Beckett*, 2 Bro. P.C. 129, 1 Eng. Rep. 837 Burr. (4th ed.) 2408, 98 Eng. Rep. 257 (H.L. 1774)
- *Samsung Electronics Co., Ltd v. Apple Retail UK et al.* [2012] EWHC 1882 (Pat) (U.K.) available at http://www.judiciary.gov.uk/Resources/JCO/Documents/Judgments/samsung-apple.pdf (visited January 12, 2013)

World Trade Organization
- *Dispute Settlement: Dispute DS285, United States—Measures Affecting the Cross-Border Supply of Gambling and Betting Services*, World Trade Organization (December 21, 2007) available at http://www.wto.org/english/tratop_e/dispu_e/cases_e/ds285_e.htm
- Measures Affecting the Cross-Border Supply of Gambling and Better Services (*U.S. v. Antigua & Barbuda*), WT/DS285/ARB, Decision by Arbitrator (World Trade Organization. 2007), available at http://docsonline.wto.org/GEN_highLightParent.asp?qu=%28%40meta%5FSymbol+WT%FCDS285%FCARB%2A%29&doc=D%3A%2FDDFDOCUMENTS%2FT%2FWT%2FDS%2F285ARB%2EDOC%2EHTM&curdoc=3&popTitle=WT%2FDS285%2FARB
- Report of the WTO Panel, United States: Section 110(5) of the U.S. Copyright Act, WT/DS160/R, June 15, 2000

Sources and Further Readings
"2012 Legislation Regarding Internet Gambling or Lotteries," National Conference of State Legislature, available at .ncsl.org/issues-research/econ/2012-online-gambling-legislation.aspx (visited January 9, 2013)

"2d Cir. to Decide Legality of Injunction against 1–800 Contacts Inc. v. WhenU.com Inc.," *Andrews Software Law Bulletin*, April 1, 2004, at 12

"3D Printing: Your Flexible Friend," *The Economist*, December 15, 2012, at 79

Abandonware: The Official Ring, available at http://www.abandonwarering.com/ (visited May 30, 2012)

Tom Abeles, "Trademark's Unfair Nominative Fair Use Defense: Protecting E-Commentary from Censorship by Corporate Monoliths," 33 *Hastings Communications and Entertainment Law Journal* 181 (2011)

Oliver Abou, *Telechargez vos DIVX et MP3 avec KaZaA et eDonkey* (Paris: Micro Application, 2003) (in French)

"About Verisign," Verisign, available at http://www.verisigninc.com/en_US/company-information/about-verisign/index.xhtml (visited October 2, 2012)

Tsan Abrahamson, "Coping with COPPA: The Practical Aspects of Children's Privacy," *Practical Lawyer*, January 2002, at 49

"Accused Movie Pirate Sues for Defamation and Millions in Damages," TorrentFreak (July 23, 2012), available at http://torrentfreak.com/accused-movie-pirate-sues-for-defamation-120723/ (visited January 28, 2013)

Richard Adhikari, "Hacker Exploits a Loophole to Score Free App Goodies," MacNewsWorld (July 14, 2012), available at http://www.macnewsworld.com/story/75637.html (visited April 4, 2013)

Advanced Access Content System ("AACS") Adopter Agreement, available at http://www.aacsla.com/license/AACS_Adopter_Agrmt_090605.pdf (visited September 23, 2012)

"Advertising on Mobile Phones: Attack of the Covert Commercials," *The Economist*, July 7, 2012, at 60

"AdWords Trademark Policy," Google, available at http://support.google.com/adwordspolicy/bin/answer.py?hl=en&answer=6118 (visited December 20, 2012)

Affirmation of Commitments by the United States Department of Commerce and the Internet Corporation for Assigned Names and Numbers, U.S.-ICANN (September 30, 2009), available at http://www.icann.org/en/news/announcements/announcement-30sep09-en.htm (visited February 7, 2013)

James H. Aiken, "The Jurisdiction of Trademark and Copyright Infringement on the Internet," 48 *Mercer Law Review* 1331 (1997)

Jenny Aker, "C U L8ter? Using Mobile Phones as a Literacy Tool in Niger," Center for Global Development (September 13, 2010), available at http://blogs.cgdev.org/globaldevelopment/2010/09/c-u-l8ter-using-mobile-phones-as-a-literacy-tool-in-niger.php (visited January 28, 2013)

G. Peter Albert, Jr. & Rita A. Abbati, "Metatags, Keywords and Links: Recent Developments Addressing Trademark Threats in Cyberspace," 40 *San Diego Law Review* 341 (2003)

Michael Albert & Lisa Vertinsky, "From Sony to Napster—and Back? Copyright Law Implications of Decentralized File-Sharing Technology," *Boston Bar Journal*, January/February 2004, at 10

John Alderman & Evan I. Schwartz, *Sonic Boom* (Boulder, CO: Perseus, 2002)

Elizabeth A. Alongi, "Has the U.S. Canned Spam?" 46 *Arizona Law Review* 263 (2004)

Xavier Amadei, "Standards of Liability for Internet Service Providers: A Comparative Study of France and the United States with a Specific Focus on Copyright, Defamation and Illicit Content," 35 *Cornell International Law Journal* 189 (2001–2002)

Amazon Web Services, Amazon Elastic Compute Cloud (EC2) User Guide (2012)

American Law Institute, *Principles of the Law of Software Contracts* (Philadelphia, PA: American Law Institute, 2010)

"An Ad-Block Shock: France v Google," *The Economist* (January 12, 2013), available at http://www.economist.com/news/business/21569414-xavier-niel-playing-rough-internet-giant-france-v-google (visited February 18, 2013)

Joe Anastasi, *The New Forensics: Investigating Corporate Fraud and the Theft of Intellectual Property* (Hoboken, NJ: John Wiley & Sons, 2003*)*

Craig Anderson, "Betting on a Retrial, Oracle Defers Copyright Damages in Java Code Case," *Los Angeles Daily Journal*, May 17, 2012, at 4

Craig Anderson, "Java Language Can't Be Copyrighted, Judge Rules," *Los Angeles Daily Journal*, June 1, 2012, at 1

Craig Anderson, "Jury Hands Google a Sweeping Win in Java Trial," *Los Angeles Daily Journal*, May 24, 2012, at 1

Chris Anderson, *Makers: The New Industrial Revolution* (New York: Crown Business, 2012)

Erik Anderson, "Protection of Trademarks from Use in Internet Advertising Banner Triggers: Playboy v. Netscape," 40 *Jurimetrics Journal* 469 (2000)

Tanya Aplin, *Copyright Law in the Digital Society: The Challenges of Multimedia* (Oxford, UK: Hart Publishing, 2005)

"Apple v. Samsung: iPhone, uCopy, iSue," *The Economist*, September 1, 2012, at 12

Samuel Arbesman, "To Understand 3-D Printing We Need to Remember 2-D Printing," Wired Weird Science Blogs (November 28, 2012), available at http://www.wired .com/wiredscience/2012/11/to-understand-3d-printing-we-need-to-remember-2d-printing/ (visited April 2, 2013)

"Articles of Incorporation of Internet Corporation for Assigned Names and Numbers," ICANN, available at http://www .icann.org/general/articles.htm (visited February 7, 2013)

"ASCAP and the Radio Music License Committee Announce Settlement in Principle," ASCAP (December 5, 2011), available at http://www.ascap.com/press/2011/1205_ ASCAP_RMLC.aspx (visited January 28, 2013)

William M. Atkinson & Joey H. Foxhall, "Stating the Obvious Gets Easier: The Supreme Court's KSR Decision," *IPL Newsletter*, Winter 2008, at 1

Audacity, available at http://audacity.sourceforge.net (visited January 7, 2013)

"Avoid Scams: Phishing," OnGuardOnline.gov (September 2011), available at http://www.onguardonline.gov/ phishing (visited February 8, 2013)

Awio Web Services LLC, "Web Browser Market Share Trends," W3 Counter, available at http://www.w3counter.com/ trends (visited December 21, 2012)

Andre Bacard, *The Computer Privacy Handbook: A Practical Guide to E-Mail Encryption, Data Protection, and PGP Privacy Software* (Berkeley, CA: Peachpit Press, 1995)

Andrew William Bagley, "Don't Be Evil: The Fourth Amendment in the Age of Google, National Security, and Digital Papers and Effects," 21 *Albany Law Journal of Science & Technology* 153 (2011)

John J. Barcelo III & Kevin M. Clermont, *A Global Law of Jurisdiction and Judgments: Lessons from the Hague* (Dordrecht, Netherlands: Kluwer Law International, 2002)

J. Cam Barker, "Grossly Excessive Penalties in the Battle against Illegal File-Sharing: The Troubling Effects of Aggregating Minimum Statutory Damages for Copyright Infringement," 83 *Texas Law Review* 525 (2004)

John Perry Barlow, *A Declaration of the Independence of Cyberspace* (February 8, 1996), available at https:// projects.eff.org/~barlow/Declaration-Final.html (visited January 28, 2013)

Michel Barreau, *KaZaA, iMesh, eDonkey et tous les autres* (Paris: CampusPress, 2003) (in French)

Paul Barrett, "How to Find Porn on the Internet," Bloomberg Business Technology (September 27, 2012), available at http://www.businessweek.com/articles/2012–09–27/ how-to-find-porn-on-the-internet (visited February 24, 2013)

Dan Barrett, "Vermont Supreme Court Agrees with the ACLU on Electronic Search Limits," ACLU (December 14, 2012), available at http://www.aclu.org/blog/criminal-law-reform-national-security-technology-and-liberty/vermont-supreme-court-addresses (visited April 4, 2013)

Jerome A. Barron & C. Thomas Dienes, *Constitutional Law in a Nutshell* (St. Paul, Minnesota: West, 7th ed. 2009)

Lori Irish Bauman, "Personal Jurisdiction and Internet Advertising," 14 *Computer Lawyer* 1 (1997)

Jessica E. Bauml, "It's a Mad, Mad Internet: Globalization and the Challenges Presented by Internet Censorship," 63 *Federal Communications Law Journal* 697 (2011)

Caron Beesley, "Five Legal Issues to Consider when Developing and Marketing a Mobile App," Small Business Administration (March 2, 2012), available at http://www .sba.gov/community/blogs/community-blogs/business-law-advisor/five-legal-issues-consider-when-developing-and- (visited April 2, 2013)

Rosalind E. Bell, "Reconciling the Protect Act with the First Amendment," 87 *New York University Law Review* 1878 (2012)

Bruce Bethke, "Cyberpunk, Amazing Science Fiction," Volume 57, Number 4 (1983), available at http://project .cyberpunk.ru/lib/cyberpunk/ (visited April 4, 2013)

Grace J. Bergen, "Litigation as a Tool against Digital Piracy," 35 *McGeorge Law Review* 181 (2004)

"A Better Way Forward: Voluntary Collective Licensing of Music File Sharing," Electronic Frontier Foundation (April 1, 2008), available at https://www.eff.org/wp/better-way-forward-voluntary-collective-licensing-music-file-sharing (visited February 24, 2013)

Stuart Biegel, *Beyond Our Control? Confronting the Limits of Our Legal System in the Age of Cyberspace* (Cambridge, MA: MIT Press, 2001)

"Binational Working Group on Cross-Border Mass Marketing Fraud," Report on Phishing: A Report to the Minister of Public Safety and Emergency Preparedness Canada and the Attorney General of the United States (October 2006), available at http://www.justice.gov/opa/report_on_ phishing.pdf (visited February 8, 2013)

Andrew Blum, *Tubes: A Journey to the Center of the Internet* (New York: Harper Collins, 2012)

Michael Boardman, "Digital Copyright Protection and Graduated Response: A Global Perspective," 33 *Loyola of Los Angeles International & Comparative Law Review* 223 (2011)

Robert Bond, "The EU E-Privacy Directive and Consent to Cookies," 68 *Business Lawyer* 215 (2012)

Rebecca Borges, "In re The Federal Trade Commission's Proposed Revisions to the Children's Online Privacy Protection Rule, Notice of Proposed Rulemaking, 76 Fed. Reg. 59804 (September 27, 2011)," 20 *CommLaw Conspectus* 293 (2011)

John Borland, Tech, "Studio Giants Team on New DVD Locks," CNET News.com (July 14, 2004), available at http:// news.com.com/Tech,+studio+giants+team+on+new+DV D+locks/2100–1025_3–5269286.html (visited April 4, 2013)

James Boyle, ed., *Collected Papers, Duke Conference on the Public Domain* (Durham, NC: Center for the Study of the Public Domain, 2003)

James Boyle, "The Second Enclosure Movement and the Construction of the Public Domain," 66 *Law & Contemporary Problems* 33 (2003)

David P. Branfman, "What Do Copyrights, Trolls, Sex, & Lawyers Have in Common?" *North County Lawyer*, February 2012, at 19

Susan W. Brenner, "Toward a Criminal Law for Cyberspace: Distributed Security," 10 *Boston University Journal of Science and Technology Law* 1 (2004)

Tom Brewster, "Super-Charged DDoS Attacks Spike in 2012," TechWeekEurope (July 23, 2012), available at http://www.techweekeurope.co.uk/news/ddos-attacks-power2012–86926 (visited January 28, 2013)

"A Brief Overview of the Federal Trade Commission's Investigative and Law Enforcement Authority," Federal Trade Commission, available at http://www.ftc.gov/ogc/brfovrvw.shtm#N_1 (visited February 3, 2013)

John Brockman, ed., *Is the Internet Changing the Way You Think? The Net's Impact on Our Minds and Future* (New York: HarperCollins, 2011)

John Brogan, "Much Ado about Squatting: The Constitutionally Precarious Application of the Anticybersquatting Consumer Protection Act," 88 *Iowa Law Review* 163 (2002)

Dan Brown, *The Da Vinci Code* (New York: Doubleday, 2003)

Bob Brown, "Sony BMG Rootkit Scandal: 5 Years Later," *Network World* (November 1, 2010), available at http://www.networkworld.com/news/2010/110110-sonybmg-rootkit-fsecure-drm.html (visited February 8, 2013)

John Brunner, *The Shockwave Rider* (New York: Ballantine, 1976)

Tracie L. Bryant, "The America Invents Act: Slaying Trolls, Limiting Joinder," 25 *Harvard Journal of Law & Technology* 673 (2012)

Budapest Open Access Initiative (February 14, 2002), available at http://www.soros.org/openaccess/read.shtml (visited April 4, 2013)

G. M. Buechlein, "Burden and Sufficiency of Proof under First Sale Doctrine in Prosecution for Copyright Infringement," 94 *American Law Reports Federal* 101 (1989 & Supp. 2004)

John Buford, Heather Yu, & Eng Keong Lua, *P2P Networking and Applications* (Burlington, MA: Morgan Kaufmann, 2008)

Henry Bursill, *Hand Shadows to Be Thrown upon the Wall: A Series of Novel and Amusing Figures Formed by the Hand* (Yorkletts, Whitstable, Kent, UK: Pryor Publications 1993 (1860)), reviews and ordering information available from Amazon UK at available at http://www.amazon.co.uk/exec/obidos/ASIN/0946014248/qid=1097002589/ref=sr_8_xs_ap_i1_xgl/202–0143568–6564612 (visited January 13, 2012)

"Businesses and Cyber-Security: A Spook Speaks," *The Economist*, June 30, 2012, at 67

"Business Computing: The Cloud Crowd," *The Economist*, October 6, 2012, at 76

Business Wire, "Trusted Computing Group TPM Adds Security to Platforms Using Windows 8 and Windows Server 2012," SOA Software (December 6, 2012), available at http://www.sys-con.com/node/2474633 (visited April 4, 2013)

Chris Butts, "The Microsoft Case 10 Years Later: Antitrust and New Leading "New Economy" Firms," 8 *Northwestern Journal of Technology and Intellectual Property* 275 (2008)

Lisa M. Byerly, "Look and Feel Protection of Web Site User Interfaces: Copyright or Trade Dress?" 14 *Santa Clara Computer and High Technology Law Journal* 221 (1998)

Bylaws for Internet Corporation for Assigned Names and Numbers, a California Nonprofit Public-Benefit Corporation: As amended 13 October 2003, available at http://www.icann.org/general/archive-bylaws/bylaws-13oct03.htm (visited February 7, 2013)

Michael A. Caloyannides, *Computer Forensics and Privacy* (Norwood, Massachusetts: Artech House, 2001)

Robert Cannon, "The Legislative History of Senator Exon's Communications Decency Act: Regulating Barbarians on the Information Superhighway," 49 *Federal Communications Law Journal* 51 (1996)

David Carnoy, "Kindle E-book Piracy Accelerates," CNET (February 18, 2011) available at http://reviews.cnet.com/8301–18438_7–20033437–82.html (visited April 4, 2013)

Mary E. Carter, *Electronic Highway Robbery: An Artist's Guide to Copyrights in the Digital Era* (Berkeley, CA: Peachpit Press, 1996)

Nuno Pires de Carvalho, *The TRIPS Regime of Patent Rights* (The Hague: Kluwer Law International, 3d ed. 2010)

Nuno Pires de Carvalho, *The TRIPS Regime of Patent Rights* (The Hague: Kluwer Law International, 2d ed. 2005)

Timothy D. Casey, *ISP Liability Survival Guide: Strategies for Managing Copyright, Spam, Cache, and Privacy Regulations* (New York: John Wiley & Sons, 2000)

Doug Casey, "Your 'Net' Investment: Then and Now," WorldNetDaily.com (February 22, 2001), available at http://www.worldnetdaily.com/news/article.asp?ARTICLE_ID=21814 (visited February 8, 2013)

Giles Castonguay, "Court Quashes Convictions in Google Video Case," *Wall Street Journal* (December 21, 2012), available at http://online.wsj.com/article/SB10001424127887324461604578193093685872724.html (visited January 28, 2013)

Fred H. Cate, *Privacy in the Information Age* (Washington, D.C.: Brookings Institution Press, 1997)

Damien Cave & Katharine Mieszkowski, "Free Dmitry! A Russian Programmer Charged with Violating the Digital Millennium Copyright Act Languishes in Jail," Salon (August 3, 2001), available at http://www.salon.com/2001/08/03/dmitry (visited January 28, 2013)

Baila H. Celedonia & Kieran Doyle, "Century 21, The New Kid in Town: The Third Circuit Crafts a New Nominative Fair Use Test," 97 *Trademark Reporter* 989 (2007)

Center for Copyright Information, The Copyright Alert System (2013), available at http://www.copyrightinformation.org/the-copyright-alert-system/ (visited April 24, 2013)

Center for Copyright Information, Memorandum of Understanding (July 6, 2011), available at http://www.copyrightinformation.org/wp-content/uploads/2013/02/Memorandum-of-Understanding.pdf (visited April 24, 2013)

Walter T. Champion, Jr. & I. Nelson Rose, *Gaming Law in a Nutshell* (St. Paul, MN: West Publishing, 2012)

Anupam Chander & Madhavi Sunder, "Everyone's a Superhero: A Cultural Theory of 'Mary Sue' Fan Fiction as Fair Use," 95 *California Law Review* 597 (2007)

Alfred Cheng, "Does Spybot Finally Have Some Allies?: An Analysis of Current Spyware Legislation," 58 *Southern Methodist University Law Review* 1497 (2005)

Jacqui Cheng, "MPAA: Teachers Should Videotape Monitors, Not Rip DVDs," *Ars Technica* (May 7, 2009), available at http://arstechnica.com/tech-policy/2009/05/mpaa-teachers-should-video-record-tv-screens-not-rip-dvds/ (visited April 4, 2013)

"Chinese E-Commerce: Pity the Parcel People," *The Economist*, November 17, 2012, at 59

Daniel C.K. Chow, *A Primer on Foreign Investment Enterprises and Protection of Intellectual Property in China* (The Hague: Kluwer Law International, 2002)

Richard Chused, ed., *A Copyright Anthology: The Technology Frontier* (Cincinnati, OH: Anderson Publishing Co., 1998)

Scott Cleland, *Search & Destroy: Why You Can't Trust Google Inc.* (St. Louis: Telescope Books, 2011)

Kevin M. Clermont, *Civil Procedure: Territorial Jurisdiction and Venue* (New York: Foundation Press, 1999)

Arthur J. Cockfield, "Jurisdiction to Tax: A Law and Technology Perspective," 38 *Georgia Law Review* 85 (2003)

Amanda Cohen, "Surveying the Microsoft Antitrust Universe," 19 *Berkeley Technology Law Journal* 333 (2004)

Eric Cole, *Hiding in Plain Sight: Steganography and the Art of Covert Communication* (Indianapolis: Wiley Publishing, Inc., 2003)

Rodger R. Cole, "Substantial Similarity in the Ninth Circuit: A 'Virtually Identical' 'Look and Feel'?" 11 *Santa Clara Computer and High Technology Law Journal* 417 (1995)

Eoin Colfer, *Artemis Fowl* series, Beginning with Artemis Fowl (New York: Hyperion Books,2001)

"Collective Management of Digital Rights," International Federation of Reproduction Rights Organizations (October 15, 1996), available at http://www.ifrro.org/issues_list/641/ (visited February 7, 2013)

"Come Stream with Me: Is There Money in Digital Radio?" *The Economist*, June 16, 2012, at 74

Computer History Museum, Exhibits: Internet History (2006), available at http://www.computerhistory.org/internet_history/internet_history_90s.html (visited January 11, 2013)

John M. Conley, "The International Law of Business Method Patents," U.S. Patent and Trademark Office Economic Review (October 2003), available at http://www.frbatlanta.org/filelegacydocs/erq403_conley.pdf (visited February 8, 2013)

"Consumer Privacy: $450,000 Payment to States—DoubleClick Reaches Agreement with States on Visibility of Consumer Tracking Activities," *Cybercrime Law Report*, September 9, 2002, at 6

"Content Protection," Rovi Corp. (2012), available at http://www.rovicorp.com/products/distribution/content-protection.htm (visited February 8, 2013)

David E. Coombs (Attorney for Bradley Manning), PFC Manning's Written Statement in Support of his Guilty Plea (March 4, 2013), available at http://www.armycourtmartialdefense.info/2013/03/pfc-mannings-written-statement-in.html (visited April 29, 2013)

Todd Cooper, "Fake Facebook Account Prompts Defamation Lawsuit," Omaha.com (July 9, 2012, 1:00AM), available at http://www.omaha.com/article/20120709/NEWS/707099925/1707 (visited January 28, 2013)

Blake Cooper, "The U.S. Libel Law Conundrum and the Necessity of Defensive Corporate Measures in Lessening

International Internet Libel Liability," 21 *Connecticut Journal of International Law* 127 (2005)

"Copyright and the Internet: Letting the Baby Dance," *The Economist*, September 1, 2012, at 60

"Copyrights: A Radical Rethink," *The Economist*, January. 25, 2003, available at http://www.economist.com/node/1547223 (visited April 4, 2013)

Carlos Correa, *Trade Related Aspects of Intellectual Property Rights* (Oxford, UK: Oxford University Press, 2007)

Greg Costikyan, "New Front in the Copyright Wars: Out-of-Print Computer Games," *N.Y. Times* (May 18, 2000), available at http://www.nytimes.com/library/tech/00/05/circuits/articles/18aban.html (visited April 4, 2013)

Andrew Couts, *U.S. Gov't Seizes 70 More Websites for Copyright Infringement—Not the Digital Kind*, Digital Trends (July 12, 2012), available at http://www.digitaltrends.com/web/u-s-govt-seizes-70-more-websites-for-copyright-infringement-not-the-digital-kind/ (visited April 4, 2013)

Terence Craig & Mary Ludloff, *Privacy & Big Data* (Sebastopol, California: O'Riley Media, Inc., 2011)

Robert W. Crandall et al., "The Empirical Case against Asymmetric Regulation of Broadband Internet Access," 17 *Berkeley Technology Law Journal* 953 (2002)

Sara Crasson, "Are DeCSS T-Shirts Dirty Laundry? Wearable, Non-Executable Computer Code as Protected Speech," 15 *Fordham Intellectual Property, Media & Entertainment Law Journal* 169 (2004)

Susan P. Crawford, "The Biology of the Broadcast Flag," 25 *Hastings Communications and Entertainment Law Journal* 603 (2003)

Creative Commons, available at http://creativecommons.org/choose/ (visited August 3, 2012)

Kevin P. Cronin & Ronald N. Weikers, *Data Security and Privacy Law: Combating Cyberthreats* § 8:44 (St. Paul, MN: West, 2004)

Kevin P. Cronin & Ronald N. Weikers, "Electronic Security Risks and the Need for Privacy, § 1.17," in *Data Security and Privacy Law: Combating Cyberthreats* (St. Paul, MN: West, 2004)

William M. Cross, "Restoring the Public Library Ethos: Copyright, E-Licensing, and the Future of Librarianship," 104 *Law Library Journal* 195 (2012)

Barbara Crutchfield George et al., "Increasing Extraterritorial Intrusion of European Union Law into U.S. Business Mergers and Competition Practices: U.S. Multinational Businesses Underestimate the Strength of the European Commission from G.E.—Honeywell to Microsoft," 19 *Connecticut Journal of International Law* 571 (2004)

Gerard V. Curtin, Jr., "The Basics of ASICs: Protection for Semiconductor Mask Works in Japan and the United States," 15 *Boston College International and Comparative Law Review* 113 (1992)

Matt Curtin & Marcus J. Ranum, "Firewalls FAQ," faqs.org (December 01, 2000), available at http://www.faqs.org/faqs/firewalls-faq/ (visited February 3, 2013)

Michael A. Cusumano & David B. Yoffe, *Competing on Internet Time: Lessons from Netscape and Its Battle with Microsoft* (New York: Touchstone, 2000)

Andrew S. Dallmann, *Life after Bilski: Is It Time to Bet on Business Method Patents Again?* Jeffer Mangels Butler & Mitchell

Patent Lawyer Blog (September 20, 2011), available at http://patentlaw.jmbm.com/2011/09/life-after-bilski-is-it-time-t.html (visited April 4, 2013)

Anthony D'Amato & Doris Estelle Long eds., *International Intellectual Property Anthology* (Cincinnati, OH: Anderson Publishing, 1996)

Ross A. Dannenberg et al., eds., *Computer Games and Virtual Worlds: A New Frontier in Intellectual Property Law* (Chicago: American Bar Association Publishing, 2010)

"Data Privacy: Out of Shape," *The Economist, July 21, 2012, at 14*

Michael H. Davis & Arthur Raphael Miller, *Intellectual Property: Patents, Trademarks, and Copyright in a Nutshell* (St. Paul, MN: West, 4th ed. 2007)

Cherie Dawson, "Creating Borders on the Internet: Free Speech, The United States, and International Jurisdiction," 44 *Virginia Journal of International Law* 637 (2004)

Clint DeBoer, "2010: The Year AACS and HDMI Kill Off Component Video," Audioholics Online A/V Magazine, available at http://www.audioholics.com/news/industry-news/aacs-hdmi-kill-component-2010 (visited February 17, 2010)

Michelle Delio, "Traveling? Take Big Brother along," *Wired* (April 4, 2003), available at http://www.wired.com/politics/security/news/2003/04/58344 (visited January 28, 2013)

George B. Delta & Jeffrey H. Matsuura, *Law of Internet* (New York: Aspen Publishers, 2d ed. 2001)

Laura DeNardis, ed., *Opening Standards: The Global Politics of Interoperability* (Cambridge, MA: MIT Press, 2011)

Doug Denison, "Delaware to Allow Online Gambling," *USA TODAY* (June 28, 2012) available at http://usatoday30.usatoday.com/news/nation/story/2012–06–28/delaware-online-gambling/55897914/1 (visited February 3, 2013)

Christina DesMarais, "10 Terrible Tech Laws That Have You in Their Bull's-Eye," *PCWorld* (June 10, 2012), available at http://www.pcworld.com/article/257247/10_terrible_tech_laws_that_have_you_in_their_bulls_eye.html (visited April 4, 2013)

Charles Dickens, *A Christmas Carol* (London: Chapman & Hall, 1843)

Elizabeth Dickinson, "The First WikiLeaks Revolution?" Foreign Policy (January 13, 2011), available at http://wikileaks.foreignpolicy.com/posts/2011/01/13/wikileaks_and_the_tunisia_protests?sms_ss=twitter&at_xt=4d2ffe4d9c2649d7,1 (visited April 24, 2013)

Whitfield Diffie & Susan Landau, *Privacy on the Line: The Politics of Wiretapping and Encryption* (Cambridge, MA: MIT Press, updated ed. 2007)

Dinwoodie et al., *International and Comparative Patent Law* (Newark, NJ: LexisNexis, 2002)

Thomas M. Disch, *The Dreams Our Stuff Is Made Of: How Science Fiction Conquered the World* (New York: Touchstone, 1998)

"Do-It-Yourself Apps: Make Your Own Angry Birds," *The Economist,* July 21, 2012, at 55

"Dow Jones Settles Gutnick Action," *ABC News* (November 12, 2004), available at http://www.abc.net.au/news/2004–11–12/dow-jones-settles-gutnick-action/584404 (visited February 8, 2013)

John Draper, Phone Phreaking Stories (2007), available at http://www.webcrunchers.com/stories/ (visited February 8, 2013)

Jesse Drucker, "Google Shifts $10b into Bermuda Subsidiary Tax Bill," Royal Gazette Online (December 11, 2012), available at http://www.royalgazette.com/article/20121211/BUSINESS/712109923 (visited February 18, 2013)

Gregory M. Duhl, "Old Lyrics, Knock-Off Videos, and Copycat Comic Books: The Fourth Fair Use Factor in U.S. Copyright Law," 54 *Syracuse Law Review* 665 (2004)

Jeffrey P. Dunning, "Whatever Happened to New Kids on the block? The Nominative Fair Use Defense to Trademark Infringement," *Intellectual Property & Technology Law Journal* (2006)

Musetta Durkee, "The Truth Can Catch the Lie: The Flawed Understanding of Online Speech in In re Anonymous Online Speakers," 26 *Berkeley Technology Law Journal* 773 (2011)

"Dutch Court Bans Pirate Party Links to the Pirate Bay," BBC News (May 10, 2012), available at http://www.bbc.co.uk/news/technology-18016819 (visited February 8, 2013)

Andrea Dworkin, *Pornography: Men Possessing Women* (New York: Perigee Books, 1981)

Wim Van Eck, "Electromagnetic Radiation from Video Display Units: An Eavesdropping Risk?" 4 *North-Holland Computers & Security* 269 (1985), available at http://cryptome.org/emr.pdf (visited February 8, 2013)

Umberto Eco, *Foucault's Pendulum* (San Diego, CA: Harcourt Brace & Company, 1989)

Umberto Eco, *The Name of the Rose* (New York: Harcourt Brace & Company, 1983)

"The Economic Cost of Piracy," Oceans Beyond Piracy (2012), available at http://oceansbeyondpiracy.org/cost-of-piracy/economic(visited February 8, 2013)

Economics & Statistics Administration, "Exploring the Digital Nation—Computer and Internet Use at Home," U.S. Dept. of Commerce (November 8, 2011), available at http://www.esa.doc.gov/Reports/exploring-digital-nation-computer-and-internet-use-home (visited January 28, 2013)

Fritz Effenberger, *Clever tauschen mit KaZaA und Co.* (Poing: Franzis 2003)(in German)

Zohar Efroni, "A Guidebook to Cybersquatting Litigation: The Practical Approach in a Post-Barcelona.com World," 2003 *University of Illinois Journal of Law, Technology and Policy* 457 (2003)

Electronic Frontier Foundation, "About EFF, General Information about the Electronic Frontier Foundation," available at http://www.eff.org/about/ (visited June 5, 2012)

Glenn Elert, ed., *Number of Cell Phones in the US, The Physics Factbook™* (2002), available at http://hypertextbook.com/facts/2002/BogusiaGrzywac.shtml (visited January 28, 2013)

Tim Elfrink, "XXX Sites Are Live Thanks to Stuart Lawley, A South Florida Brit Who Beat the Bush Admin," *Miami New Times* (December 8, 2011), available at http://blogs.miaminewtimes.com/riptide/2011/12/xxx_sites_are_live_thanks_to_s.php (visited February 7, 2013)

Stephen R. Elias, *Patent, Copyright & Trademark: An Intellectual Property Desk Reference* (Berkeley, CA: Nolo Press, 6th ed. 2003)

Christopher Elliott, "The Navigator: The TSA's Secure Flight Initiative May Be Making Your Privacy Less Secure,"

The Washington Post (July 30, 2010), available at http://www.washingtonpost.com/wp-dyn/content/article/2010/07/30/AR2010073003907.html (visited January 28, 2013)

Christian R. Eriksen, "Cable Broadband: Did the Ninth Circuit Beat the FCC to the Punch in Last Mile Regulation?" 6 *Tulane Journal of Technology and Intellectual Property* 283 (2004)

Virginia Eubanks, *Digital Dead End: Fighting for Social Justice in the Information Age* (Cambridge, MA: MIT Press, 2011)

Jonathan I. Ezor, *Privacy and Data Protection in Business: Laws & Practices* (New Providence, NJ: LexisNexis, 2012)

"Face Value: Lawrence Lessig Wants Less Copyright Protection, Including for Disney's Famous Rodent," *The Economist*, October 12, 2002, at 67

"Face Value: The Quiet Iconoclast—With KaZaA, Niklas Zennstrom Undermined the Music Industry," *The Economist* (July 1, 2004), at 54, available at http://www.economist.com/node/2876993 (visited February 3, 2013)

"Facebook and Children: Let the Nippers Network," *The Economist*, June 9, 2012, at 18

"Facebook: Work in Progress," *The Economist*, August 4, 2012, at 60

Cyrus Farivar, "Here's What an Actual 'Six Strikes' Copyright Alert Looks Like: Ars Asks and Comcast Obliges, Giving Us Copies of Alerts 1, 2, 4, and 5," *Ars Technica* (February 27, 2013), available at http://arstechnica.com/tech-policy/2013/02/heres-what-an-actual-six-strikes-copyright-alert-looks-like/ (visited April 29, 2013)

Usama M. Fayyad et al., "From Data Mining to Knowledge Discovery: An Overview," in *Advances in Knowledge Discovery and Data Mining* 6 (Cambridge, MA: MIT Press, 1996)

Federal Trade Commission, "Combating Spyware and Malware," available at http://www.ftc.gov/opa/reporter/idtheft/spymalware.shtml (visited August 28, 2012)

Federal Trade Commission, "Federal Trade Commission: A History," available at http://www.ftc.gov/opa/history/timeline.shtm (visited February 3, 2013)

Federal Trade Commission, "How Not to Get Hooked by a Phishing Scam," FTC Consumer Alert (October 2006), available at http://www.ftc.gov/bcp/edu/pubs/consumer/alerts/alt127.shtm (visited December 17, 2012)

Federal Trade Commission, "ID Theft," available at http://www.consumer.ftc.gov/features/feature-0014-identity-theft (visited December 17, 2012)

Federal Trade Commission, "Phishing" (September 2011), available at http://www.onguardonline.gov/phishing (visited December 17, 2012)

Sharael Feist, *Newsmaker:* "The Father of Modern Spam Speaks," CNET News (March 26, 2002), available at http://news.cnet.com/2008–1082–868483.html (visited February 18, 2013)

Niels Ferguson, Bruce Schneier, & Tadayoshi Kohno, *Cryptography Engineering* (Indianapolis: John Wiley & Sons, 2010)

Gerald R. Ferrera et al., *Cyberlaw: Your Rights in Cyberspace* (Mason, OH: South-Western College Publications, 2001)

Jeffrey Ferriell & Michael Navin, *Understanding Contracts* (New York: Matthew Bender, 2d ed. 2004)

Mihaly Ficsor, *The Law of Copyright and the Internet: The 1996 WIPO Treaties, Their Interpretation and Implementation* (Oxford, UK: Oxford University Press, 2002)

"A Fine Balance: How Much Copyright Protection Does the Internet Need?" *Economist Technology Quarterly* (January 25, 2003), available at http://www.economist.com/node/1534271

"Firefox Browser Takes on Microsoft," BBC News (November 9, 2004, 11:19), available at http://news.bbc.co.uk/2/hi/technology/3993959.stm (visited February 24, 2013)

Stephen Fishman, *Copyright Your Software* (Berkeley, CA: Nolo Press, 3d ed. 2001)

Stephen Fishman, *The Public Domain: How to Find & Use Copyright-Free Writings, Music, Art & More* (Berkeley, CA: Nolo Press, 2001)

Stephen Fishman, *The Public Domain: How to Find & Use Copyright-Free Writings, Music, Art & More* (Berkeley, CA: Nolo Press, 5th ed. 2010)

Peter Fleischer, "My Italian Appeal, Peter Fleischer: Privacy . . . ?" (December 6, 2012), available at http://peterfleischer.blogspot.com/ (visited January 28, 2013)

Credence E. Fogo, "The Postman Always Rings 4,000 Times: New Approaches to Curb Spam," 18 *John Marshall Journal of Computer & Information Law* 915 (2000)

Warwick Ford & Michael S. Baum, *Secure Electronic Commerce: Building the Infrastructure for Digital Signatures and Encryption* (Upper Saddle River, NJ: Prentice Hall, 2d ed. 2001)

Chris Foresman, "DRM licensing Group Presses on with Plan to Plug Analog Hole," *Ars Technica* (June 11, 2009), available at http://arstechnica.com/gadgets/2009/06/drm-licensing-group-presses-on-with-plan-to-plug-analog-hole/ (visited April 4, 2013)

"Former DrinkOrDie Member Chris Tresco Answers," Slashdot (October 4, 2002), available at http://interviews.slashdot.org/story/02/10/04/144217/former-drinkordie-member-chris-tresco-answers (visited February 9, 2013)

"Free eBooks by Project Gutenberg," Project Gutenberg, available at http://gutenberg.nl/ (visited February 17, 2013)

Free Software Foundation, available at https://my.fsf.org/associate/support_freedom? (visited December 29, 2012)

Carl Freedman, *Critical Theory and Science Fiction* (Hanover, Germany: Wesleyan University Press, 2000)

Paul Freiberger & Michael Swaine, *Fire in the Valley* (New York: McGraw-Hill, 2d ed. 1999)

Michael Froomkin, "Internet Governance: Almost Free: An Analysis of Icann's Affirmation of Commitments," 9 *Journal on Telecommunications and High Technology Law* 187 (2011)

A. Michael Froomkin, "The Metaphor Is the Key: Cryptography, the Clipper Chip, and the Constitution," 143 *University of Pennsylvania Law Review* 709 (1995)

A. Michael Froomkin, "Wrong Turn in Cyberspace: Using ICANN to Route around the APA and the Constitution," 50 *Duke Law Journal* 17 (2000)

"FTC Charges that Security Flaws in Rock You Game Exposed 32 Million Email Addresses and Passwords," Federal Trade Commission (March 27, 2012), available at http://ftc.gov/opa/2012/03/rockyou.shtm (visited April 4, 2013)

"FTC Permanently Halts Unlawful Spyware Operations," Federal Trade Commission (November 21, 2006), available at http://www.ftc.gov/opa/2006/11/seismicodysseus.shtm (visited April 4, 2013)

"FTC Receives Largest COPPA Civil Penalties to Date in Settlements with Mrs. Fields Cookies and Hershey Foods," Federal Trade Commission (February 27, 2003), available at http://www.ftc.gov/opa/2003/02/hersheyfield.shtm (visited April 4, 2013)

"FTC Releases Consumer Fraud Survey: More than One in 10 Americans Fell Victim to Fraud," Federal Trade Commission (August 5, 2004), available at http://www.ftc.gov/opa/2004/08/fraudsurvey.shtm (visited February 7, 2013)

"FTC Releases Survey of Identity Theft in U.S.: 27.3 Million Victims in Past 5 Years, Billions in Losses for Businesses and Consumers," Federal Trade Commission (September 3, 2003), available at http://www.ftc.gov/opa/2003/09/idtheft.shtm (visited February 7, 2013)

Joseph S. Fulda, "Data Mining and Privacy," 11 *Albany Law Journal of Science and Technology* 105 (2000)

Rachel Gader-Shafran, "Confessions of a Serial Infringer: Can the Audio Home Recording Act of 1992 Protect the Consumer from Copy-Protected CDs?" *Intellectual Property Law Newsletter*, Winter 2003, at 10

Alessandra Garbagnati, "The Wrath of the Blizz King: How the Ninth Circuit's Decision in MDY Industries, Inc. v. Blizzard Entertainment May Slay the Game Genie," 34 *Hastings Communications and Entertainment Law Journal* 313 (2012)

W. David Gardner, "Unlikely Alliance Seeks .xxx Top-Level Domain," TechWeb.com (April 15, 2004), available at http://www.informationweek.com/news/18901730 (visited January 28, 2013)

Simson Garfinkel, "Welcome to Sealand. Now Bugger Off," *Wired* (July 2000), available at http://www.wired.com/wired/archive/8.07/haven.html?pg=1&topic=&topic_set=(visited April 4, 2013)

Patrick P. Garlinger, "Privacy, Free Speech, and the Patriot Act: First and Fourth Amendment Limits on National Security Letters," 84 *New York University Law Review* 1105 (2009)

Nathan W. Garnett, "Dow Jones & Co. v. Gutnick: Will Australia's Long Jurisdictional Reach Chill Internet Speech World-Wide?" 13 *Pacific Rim Law and Policy Journal* 61 (2004)

Katherine E. Gasparek, "Applying the Fair Use Defense in Traditional Trademark Infringement and Dilution Cases to Internet Meta Tagging or Linking Cases," 1 *George Mason Law Review* 787 (1999)

Daniel Geer, "CyberInsecurity: The Cost of Monopoly," Cryptome.org (September 27, 2003), available at http://cryptome.org/cyberinsecurity.htm (visited January 28, 2013)

Rachel Ann Geist, "A 'License to Read': The Effect of E-Books on Publishers, Libraries, and the First Sale Doctrine," 52 *Idea: The Intellectual Property Law Review* 63 (2012)

Julius Genachowski, "FCC Chairman, The Third Way: A Narrowly Tailored Broadband Framework," Federal Communications Commission (May 6, 2010), available at http://www.broadband.gov/the-third-way-narrowly-tailored-broadband-framework-chairman-julius-genachowski.html (visited February 3, 2013)

Steven A. Hetcher, *Norms in a Wired World* (Cambridge, UK: Cambridge University Press, 2004)

Ronald H. Gertz, "Client Memo Re: Summary of Sections 106, 112 & 114 of the Copyright Act of 1976 as Amended by the Digital Performance Right in Sound Recordings Act of 1995 and the Digital Millennium Copyright Act of 1998," in *Music on the Internet: Understanding the New Rights & Solving New Problems*, edited by Anthony V. Lupo & Mark F.Radcliffe (New York: Practising Law Institute, 2001)

Daniel Gervais, "Golan v. Holder: A Look at the Constraints Imposed by the Berne Convention," 64 *Vanderbilt Law Review* 147 (2011)

"Getting the Message, At Last," *Economist* (December 13, 2007), available at http://www.economist.com/node/10286400 (visited February 18, 2013)

William Gibson, *Burning Chrome* (New York: Arbor House, 1986)

William Gibson, *Count Zero* (New York: Arbor House, 1986)

William Gibson, *Idoru* (New York: Putnam Publishing Group, 1996)

William Gibson, *Mona Lisa Overdrive* (New York: Bantam, 1988)

William Gibson, *Neuromancer* (New York: Ace, 1984) [*Neuromancer* is actually the first book in a trilogy; the second and third volumes are *Count Zero* (New York: Arbor House, 1986) and *Mona Lisa Overdrive* (New York: Bantam, 1988)

William Gibson, *Pattern Recognition* (New York, New York: Putnam Publishing Group, 2003)

Terry Gillespie, "Virtual Violence? Pornography and Violence against Women on the Internet," in *Women, Violence and Strategies for Action*, edited by Jill Radford et al., eds. (Buckingham, UK: Open University Press 2000)

Tarleton Gillespie, *Wired Shut: Copyright and the Shape of Digital Culture* (Cambridge, MA: MIT Press, 2007)

Dara B. Gilwit, "The Latest Cybersquatting Trend: Typosquatters, Their Changing Tactics, and How to Prevent Public Deception and Trademark Infringement," 11 *Washington University Journal of Law and Policy* 267 (2003)

Jane C. Ginsburg, "Copyright in the Digital Environment: Restoring the Balance," 35 *Columbia Journal of Law & the Arts* 1 (2011)

Jane C. Ginsburg, "No 'Sweat'? Copyright and Other Protection of Works of Information after Feist v. Rural Telephone," 92 *Columbia Law Review* 338 (1992)

GNU Operating System, available at http://www.gnu.org/ (last updated December 16, 2012)

Mike Godwin, *Cyber Rights: Defending Free Speech in the Digital Age* (Cambridge, MA: MIT Press, 2003)

Eric Goldman, "A Road to No Warez: The No Electronic Theft Act and Criminal Copyright Infringement," 82 *Oregon Law Review* 369 (2003)

Eric Goldman, "Warez Trading and Criminal Copyright Infringement," 51 *Journal of the Copyright Society of the U.S.A.* 395 (2004)

Jack L. Goldsmith, "What Internet Gambling Legislation Teaches about Internet Regulation," 32 *International Lawyer* 1115 (1998)

Paul Goldstein & Bernt Hugenholtz, *International Copyright: Principles, Law, and Practice* (Oxford, UK: Oxford University Press, 3d ed. 2012)

Lee Gomes, "Hot Field of Cyberlaw Is So Much Hokum, Some Skeptics Argue," *Wall Street Journal*, July 1, 2002, at B-1

Jennifer Gong, "Defining and Addressing Virtual Property in International Treaties," 17 *Boston University Journal of Science and Technology Law* 101 (2011)

"Google and Antitrust: Transatlantic Tussles," *The Economist* (December 22, 2012), at 105, available at http://www.economist.com/news/business/21568757-investigations-google-approach-climax-america-and-europe-transatlantic-tussles (visited February 18, 2013)

"Google Brazil to Take Down Controversial Brazil Video," BBC News (September 28, 2012, 5:26), available at http://www.bbc.co.uk/news/world-latin-america-19753158 (visited February 8, 2013)

"Google's Copyright Complaints Flag Up Piracy of Microsoft," BBC News (May 25, 2012), available at http://www.bbc.co.uk/news/technology-18204411 (visited February 8, 2013)

"Google in Africa: It's a Hit," *The Economist* (May 12, 2012), at 57, available at http://www.economist.com/node/21554566 (visited February 18, 2013)

"Google Threatens French Media Ban over Proposed Law," BBC News (October 18, 2012), available at http://www.bbc.co.uk/news/technology-19996351 (visited February 18, 2013)

Wendy J. Gordon, "A Property Right in Self-Expression: Equality and Individualism in the Natural Law of Intellectual Property," 102 *Yale Law Journal* 1533 (1993)

Michael R. Gordon, "Up the Amazon without a Paddle: Examining Sales Taxes, Entity Isolation, and the 'Affiliate Tax,'" 11 *North Carolina Journal of Law and Technology* 299 (2010)

Jonathan Gottfried, "The Federal Framework for Internet Gambling," 10 *Richmond Journal of Law and Technology* 26 (2004)

"Government Surveillance: Little Peepers Everywhere," *The Economist*, July 21, 2012, at 23

Stephen Graham & Simon Marvin, *Splintering Urbanism: Networked Infrastructures, Technological Mobilities and the Urban Condition* (Basingstoke, Hampshire, UK: Brunner-Routledge, 2001)

Megan E. Gray & Will Thomas DeVries, "The Legal Fallout from Digital Rights Management Technology," *Computer & Internet Lawyer*, April 2003, at 20

Patrick Gray, "Sharman Presses for Evidence," *Wired News* (May 18, 2004), available at http://www.wired.com/news/digiwood/0,1412,63509,00.html (visited February 8, 2013)

Andy Greenberg, "Congressman Says He'll Propose Ban on 3D-Printable Gun Magazines," *Forbes* (January 16, 2013), available at http://www.forbes.com/sites/andygreenberg/2013/01/16/congressman-says-hell-propose-ban-on-3d-printable-gun-magazines/ (visited April 2, 2013)

Kevin J. Greene, "Abusive Trademark Litigation and the Shrinking Doctrine of Consumer Confusion: Rethinking Trademark Paradigms in the Context of Entertainment Media and Cyberspace," 27 *Harvard Journal of Law & Public Policy* (2004)

Robyn Greenspan, "The Deadly Duo: Spam and Viruses, May 2004," Internetnews.com (June 7, 2004), available at http://www.Internetnews.com/stats/article.php/3364421 (visited February 18, 2013)

Alan N. Greenspan, *Internet Advertising Laws and Regulations, Practising Law Institute*, 19th Annual Institute on Computer Law, February-March, 1999

Shane Greenstein & Ryan McDevitt, "Why Broadband Prices Haven't Decreased: Creating the First Broadband Consumer Price Index," Kellogg Insight (September 2010), available at http://insight.kellogg.northwestern.edu/index.php/Kellogg/article/why_broadband_prices_havent_decreased/ (visited January 28, 2013)

James Grimmelman, "Death of a Data Haven: Cypherphunks, WikiLeaks, and the World's Smallest Nation," *Ars Technica* (March 27, 2012), available at http://arstechnica.com/tech-policy/2012/03/sealand-and-havenco/ (visited January 28, 2013)

Julieta Andrea Grinffiel, "Don't Shoot the Messenger: Civil Liability for ISPs after Virginia da Cunha v. Yahoo! Argentina & Google Inc.," 17 *Law & Business Review of the Americas* 111 (2011)

Grant Gross, "Advocacy Group Takes Aim at Anti-Porn Bill," *PCWorld* (February 27, 2012), available at http://www.pcworld.com/article/250803/advocacy_group_takes_aim_at_antiporn_bill_requiring_isp_data_retention.html (visited April 4, 2013)

"Growth of the World Online Gambling Market from 2003 to 2012 (in Billion U.S. Dollars)," DowJones Statista (2012), available at http://www.statista.com/statistics/168622/market-volume-of-online-gaming-worldwide-since-2003/ (visited February 3, 2013)

"Hacker Gary McKinnon Will Not Face UK Charges," BBC News (December 14, 2012), available at http://www.bbc.co.uk/news/uk-20730627 (visited February 7, 2013)

Daniel L. Hadjinian, "Clicking Away the Competition: The Legal Ramifications of Click Fraud for Companies That Offer Pay per Click Advertising Services," 3 *Shidler Journal of Law, Commerce & Technology* 5 (2006)

John O. Haley, *Fundamentals of Transnational Litigation: The United States, Canada, Japan, and the European Union* (New Providence, NJ: LexisNexis, 2012)

Charles Hamaker, "Ebooks on Fire, Controversies Surrounding Ebooks in Libraries," *Information Today, Inc.* (December 2011) available at http://www.infotoday.com/searcher/dec11/Hamaker.shtml (visited January 28, 2013)

Noah C.N. Hampson, "The Internet is Not a Lawless Prairie: Data Protection and Privacy in Italy," 34 *Boston College International & Comparative Law Review* 477 (2011)

David Hand et al., *Principles of Data Mining* (Cambridge, MA: MIT Press, 2001)

Jennifer L. Hanley, "ISP Liability and Safe Harbor Provisions: Implications of Evolving International Law for the Approach Set Out in Viacom v. Youtube," 11 *Journal of International Business & Law* 183 (2012)

William Hannah, "Major Change, New Chapter: How Inter Partes Review and Post Grant Review Proceedings Created by the America Invents Act Will Shape Litigation Strategies," 17 *Intellectual Property Law Bulletin* 27 (2012)

Saul Hansell, "Postage Is Due for Companies Sending E-Mail," *N.Y. Times* (February 5, 2006), available at http://www.nytimes.com/2006/02/05/technology/05AOL.html?pagewanted=all&_r=0 (visited February 18, 2013)

Bruce Haring, *Beyond the Charts: MP3 and the Digital Music Revolution* (Los Angeles: JM Northern Media LLC, 2000)

Michael Hart, "Project Gutenberg Mission Statement," available at http://www.gutenberg.org/wiki/Gutenberg:Project_Gutenberg_Mission_Statement_by_Michael_Hart, Project Gutenberg (visited February 17, 2013)

Amir Hassanabadi, "Viacom v. YouTube—All Eyes Blind: The Limits of the DMCA in a Web 2.0 World," 26 *Berkeley Technology Law Journal* 405 (2011)

"HavenCo 'Data Center' Offline?" Security and the Net (November 18, 2008), available at http://securityandthe.net/2008/11/18/havenco-data-center-offline/ (visited January 28, 2013)

Ben J. Hayes & Matthew J. Conigliaro, "'The Business of Betting or Wagering': A Unifying View of Federal Gaming Law," 57 *Drake Law Review* 445 (2009)

Martin Headon, "Pet Hates: The Gaming Site Neopets Is a Welcome Relief, Says Martin Headon," *The Guardian* (October 30, 2002), available at http://www.guardian.co.uk/computergames/story/0,11500,822595,00.html (visited April 4, 2013)

Sheila M. Heidmiller, "RIAA's Latest Attack on P2P File-Sharing," *Intellectual Property Law Newsletter*, Summer 2003, at 10

Walter Hellerstein, "Jurisdiction to Tax Income and Consumption in the New Economy: A Theoretical and Comparative Perspective," 38 *Georgia Law Review* 1 (2003)

Kevin Henry, Jiayuan Sui, & Ge Zhong, "An Overview of the Advanced Access Content System (AACS)," available at http://cacr.uwaterloo.ca/techreports/2007/cacr2007–25.pdf (visited September 22, 2012)

Bill D. Herman, *The Fight over Digital Rights: The Politics of Copyright and Technology* (Cambridge, UK: Cambridge University Press, 2013)

Melanie L. Hersh, "Is COPPA a Cop-Out? The Child Online Privacy Protection Act as Proof that Parents, Not Government, Should Be Protecting Children's Interests on the Internet," 28 *Fordham Urban Law Journal* 1831 (2001)

Arik Hesseldahl, "'Brandjacking' on the Web," *Bloomberg Business Week*, May 01, 2007

Arik Hesseldahl, "Ten O'Clock Tech: D-Day In the Spam War," Forbes.com (February 27, 2004), available at http://www.forbes.com/2004/02/27/cx_ah_0227tentech.html (visited February 18, 2013)

Steven A. Hetcher, *Norms in a Wired World* (Cambridge, UK: Cambridge University Press, 2004)

Kashmir Hill, "The Downside of Being a Google Executive," *Forbes* (September 27, 2012), available at http://www.forbes.com/sites/kashmirhill/2012/09/27/the-downside-of-being-a-google-executive/ (visited January 28, 2013)

Kashmir Hill, "Will the New 'Copyright Alert System' Actually Stop People from Downloading Music and Movies Illegally?" *Forbes* (February 25, 2013), available at http://www.forbes.com/sites/kashmirhill/2013/02/25/copyright-alert-system/ (visited April 24, 2013)

Kashmir Hill, "Yes, that Legal Notice You Got from Facebook Is Real," *Forbes* (January 26, 2013), available at http://www.forbes.com/sites/kashmirhill/2013/01/26/yes-that-legal-notice-you-got-from-facebook-is-real/ (visited April 24, 2013)

P. Jay Hines, "The Year that Was: Madrid Protocol Milestones in 2003," Oblon, Spivak, McClelland, Maier & Neustadt, P.C. (July 2004), available at http://www.oblon.com/publications/year-was-madrid-protocol-milestones-2003 (visited February 8, 2013)

Peter Hirtle, "May a Library Lend E-Book Readers?" LibrayLaw Blog (June 20, 2010), available at http://blog.librarylaw.com/librarylaw/2010/06/may-a-library-lend-e-book-readers.html (visited January 29, 2013)

Becky Hogge, *Barefoot into Cyberspace: Adventures in Search of Techno-Utopia* (Saffron Walden, Essex, UK: Barefoot Publishing, 2011)

Blake Holland, "The Winding Stream: Entitlement Theories and Intellectual Property Rights in Emerging Media Technologies," 25 *Berkeley Technology Law Journal* 247 (2010)

"House of Cards: Laws Banning Gambling Show the Strength of Sovereignty," *The Economist* (November 20, 2004), at 66, available at http://www.economist.com/node/3411641 (visited February 3, 2013)

Note, "How Chevron Step One Limits Permissible Agency Interpretations: Brand X and the FCC's Broadband Reclassification," 124 *Harvard Law Review* 1016 (2011)

"Huawei: The Company That Spooked the World," *The Economist*, August 4, 2012, at 19

Eric Hughes, *A Cypherpunk's Manifesto* (March 9, 1993), available at http://www.activism.net/cypherpunk/manifesto.html (visited August 7, 2012)

Justin Hughes, "American Moral Rights and Fixing the Dastar 'Gap,'" 2007 *Utah Law Review* 659 (2007)

Reed Hundt, "The Ineluctable Modality of Broadband," 21 *Yale Journal on Regulation* 239 (2004)

"I Want My P2P: Record Labels Are Trying to Do Deals with File-Sharing Networks," *The Economist* (November 18, 2004), at 65, available at http://www.economist.com/node/3407417 (visited February 3, 2013)

"ICANN and Top Level Domains: Dot Dash," *The Economist*, June 16, 2012, at 76

"ICAAN CEO Talks about the New Affirmation of Commitments," ICANN (September 30, 2009), available at http://www.icann.org/en/news/announcements/announcement-30sep09-en.htm(visited February 7, 2013)

"ICANN's Major Agreements and Related Reports," ICANN, available at http://www.icann.org/en/about/agreements (visited January 10, 2013)

ICM Registry Inc., "Application for New sTLD RFP Application .xxx, vf (2004)," available at http://www.icann.org/tlds/stld-apps-19mar04/xxx.htm (visited January 28, 2013)

"Iconix Brand Group Settles Charges Its Apparel Web Sites Violated Children's Online Privacy Protection Act," Federal Trade Commission (October 20, 2009), available at http://www.ftc.gov/opa/2009/10/iconix.shtm (visited April 4, 2013)

"ID Theft," Federal Trade Commission, available at http://www.consumer.ftc.gov/features/feature-0014-identity-theft (visited December 17, 2012)

"Identity Theft Resources," Federal Trade Commission, available at http://www.ftc.gov/bcp/edu/microsites/idtheft2012/ (last updated October 25, 2012)

IFPI Digital Music Report 2012, available at http://www.ifpi .org/content/library/DMR2012.pdf (visited September 23, 2012)

Alfredo Ilardi & Michael Blakeney, eds., *International Encyclopaedia of Intellectual Property Treaties* (Oxford, UK: Oxford University Press, 2004)

"Imbee.com Settles FTC Charges Social Networking Site for Kids Violated the Children's Online Privacy Protection Act; Settlement Includes $130,000 Civil Penalty," Federal Trade Commission (January 30, 2008), available at http://www .ftc.gov/opa/2008/01/imbee.shtm (visited April 24, 2013)

"Imitation v. Inspiration: How Poor Countries Can Avoid the Wrongs of Intellectual-Property Rights," *The Economist* (September 14, 2002), at 13, available at http://www .economist.com/node/1325360 (visited February 7, 2013)

"Impact of Marine Polymer Tech. v. Hemecon Inc. On Post-Grant and Inter Partes Review," Patent Review Blog (March 16, 2012), available at http://patentreviewblog .wordpress.com/tag/file-wrapper-estoppel/ (visited February 17, 2013)

"Internet Domain Names: Combat," *The Economist*, June 2, 2012, at 73

"Internet Governance: System Error," *The Economist*, December 1, 2012, at 67

The Industry Handbook—The Semiconductor Industry, Investopedia.com, available at http://www.investopedia .com/features/industryhandbook/semiconductor.asp (visited December 20, 2012)

"Industry News & Articles," Trusted Computed Group, available at http://www.trustedcomputinggroup.org/media_room/ industry_news_and_articles (visited January 7, 2013)

"Information for Registrars and Registrants," ICANN, available at http://www.icann.org/en/resources/registrars(visited August 16, 2012)

"Innovation in Africa: Upwardly Mobile," *The Economist*, August 25, 2012, at 53

International Foundation for Online Responsibility, "The Organization and Our Policy Goals," available at http:// www.iffor.org/ (visited January 15, 2013)

"Internet Domain Name System Structure and Delegation (ccTLD Administration and Delegation)," ICANN (May 1999), available at http://www.icann.org/icp/icp-1.htm (visited February 7, 2013)

"Internet Domain Names: Combat," *The Economist*, June 2, 2012, at 73

"Internet Free Speech," American Civil Liberties Union, available at http://www.aclu.org/technology-and-liberty/internet-free-speech (visited December 20, 2012)

"Internet Freedom: Free to Choose," *The Economist*, October 6, 2012, at 70

"Internet Governance: System Error," *The Economist*, December 1, 2012, at 67

"Internet Users in Africa 2012-Q2," Internet World Stats, available at http://www.internetworldstats.com/stats1.htm (visited January 28, 2013)

Katherine Ivancevich, "Promatek Industries, Inc. v. Equitrac Corporation: Promoting the Metatag Fallacy," 12 *DePaul-LCA Journal of Art and Entertainment Law* 351 (2002)

"Investigations: Aviation Criticism Prompts GAO Review of TSA Data Mining Program," *Cybercrime Law Report*, September 22, 2003, at 6

"ITU Data & Statistics: Digital Access Index," International Telecommunications Union (ITU), available at http:// www.itu.int/ITU-D/ict/dai/ (visited January 19, 2012)

Joab Jackson, "Google: 129 Million Different Books Have Been Published," *PCWorld* (August 6, 2010), available at http://www.pcworld.com/article/202803/google_129_ million_different_books_have_been_published.html (visited February 3, 2013)

Fredric Jameson, *Postmodernism, or the Cultural Logic of Late Capitalism* (Durham, NC: Duke University Press, 1991)

The Jammer & Jack the Ripper, *The Official Phreaker's Manual* (February 14, 1987), available at http://www.phreak.ch/ files/phreakmanual.txt (visited February 8, 2013)

Kris Jamsa, *Cloud Computing* (Burlington, MA: Jones & Bartlett Learning, 2012)

Jeff Jarvis, *Public Parts: How Sharing in the Digital Age Improves the Way We Work and Love* (New York: Simon & Schuster, 2011)

Holman W. Jenkins, Jr., "Can Data Mining Stop the Killing?" *Wall Street Journal*, available at http://online.wsj.com/ article/SB100008723963904435709045775466716932 45302.html (visited January28, 2013)

Sara Jeruss, Robin Feldman, & Joshua Walker, "The America Invents Act 500: Effects of Patent Monetization Entities on US Litigation," 11 *Duke Law & Technology Review* 357 (2012)

Neil F. Johnson et al., *Information Hiding: Steganography and Watermarking—Attacks and Countermeasures* (Boston: Kluwer Academic Publishers, 2000)

"Joint Project Agreement between the U.S. Department of Commerce and the Internet Corporation for Assigned Names and Numbers," U.S.-ICANN, September 26, 2006, Approved Resolution 06.71, available at http://www.ntia .doc.gov/files/ntia/publications/signedmou290906.pdf (visited February 7, 2013)

Michael Jones, "Eldred v. Ashcroft: The Constitutionality of the Copyright Term Extension Act," 19 *Berkeley Technology Law Journal* 85 (2004)

Gregory R. Jones, "What's in a Name? Trademark Infringements in Cyberspace," 68 *The Alabama Lawyer* 70 (2007)

Patrik Jonsson, "Boom in Internet Gambling Ahead? US Policy Reversal Clears the Way," Christian Science Monitor (December 26, 2011), available at http://www.csmonitor .com/USA/2011/1226/Boom-in-Internet-gambling-ahead-US-policy-reversal-clears-the-way (visited February 3, 2013)

Tim Jordan, *Cyberpower: The Culture and Politics of Cyberspace and the Internet* (New York: Routledge, 1999)

William H. Jordan, "Going after Internet Hackers: Civil and Criminal Responses to Denial of Service Attacks," *Electronic Banking Law and Commerce Report*, March, 2000, at 6

Rahul Joshi, "Digital Inclusion: Thailand Opens 20,000 Free Wifi Spots in Bangkok," FutureGov Asia Pacific (January 18, 2012), available at http://www.futuregov.asia/ articles/2012/jan/18/thailand-opens-20000-free-wifi-spots-bangkok/ (visited January 28, 2013)

Ari Juels, *Tetraktys* (Newport Coast, CA: Emerald Bay Books, 2009)

Jupiter Research Corporation, *File Sharing and the DMCA* [e-book] (MarketResearch.com 2001)

David Kahn, *The Codebreakers: The Story of Secret Writing* (New York: Scribner, 1967)

Pascal Kamina, *Film Copyright in the European Union* (Cambridge, UK: Cambridge University Press, 2002)

Paul N. Katz & Robert R. Riddle, "Designing around a United States Patent," 45 *South Texas Law Review* 647 (2004)

Eddan Katz & Ramesh Subramanian, eds., *The Global Flow of Information: Legal, Social, and Cultural Perspectives* (New York and London: New York University Press, 2011)

Stefan Katzenbeisser & Fabien A.P. Petitcolas, eds., *Information Hiding Techniques for Steganography and Digital Watermarking* (Norwood, MA: Artech House, 2000)

Lauren Fisher Kellner: "Trade Dress Protection for Computer User Interface 'Look and Feel,'" 61 *University of Chicago Law Review* 1011 (1994)

Martha Kelley, "Is Liability Just a Link Away? Trademark Dilution by Tarnishment under the Federal Trademark Dilution Act of 1995 and Hyperlinks on the World Wide Web," 9 *Journal of Intellectual Property Law* 361 (2002)

Drew Kelly, "Wasting Time Is New Divide in Digital Era," *New York Times* (May 29, 2012), available at http://www.nytimes.com/2012/05/30/us/new-digital-divide-seen-in-wasting-time-online.html?_r=3&pagewanted=all& (visited January 28, 2013)

Charles J. Kenny (World Bank), *Expanding Internet Access to the Rural Poor in Africa*, International Telecommunications Union, African Internet & Telecom Summit, Banjul, The Gambia, June 5–9, 2000

"Kenya's Mobile Telephones: Vital for the Poor," *The Economist*, November 10, 2012, at 52

Orin S. Kerr, "Surveillance Law: Reshaping the Framework: A User's Guide to the Stored Communications Act, and a Legislator's Guide to Amending It", 72 *George Washington Law Review* 1208 (2004)

Shahid Khan, "'Apps.Gov': Assessing Privacy in the Cloud Computing Era," 11 *North Carolina Journal of Law & Technology*, Online Edition 259 (2010)

Dennis W. K. Khong, "Orphan Works, Abandonware and the Missing Market for Copyrighted Goods," 15 *International Journal of Law & Information Technology* 54 (2007)

Kevin Khurana, "COPPA Violations? Cop a Settlement for $3 Million," Proskauer Privacy Law Blog (May 18, 2011), available at http://privacylaw.proskauer.com/2011/05/articles/childrens-online-privacy-prote/coppa-violations-cop-a-settlement-for-3-million/ (visited April 4, 2013)

Brad King, "The Day the Napster Died," *Wired* (May 15, 2002), available at http://www.wired.com/gadgets/portablemusic/news/2002/05/52540?currentPage=all (visited April 2, 2013)

Kevin F. King, "Personal Jurisdiction, Internet Commerce, and Privacy: The Pervasive Legal Consequences of Modern Geolocation Technologies," 21 *Albany Law Journal of Science & Technology* 61 (2011)

Gregory Kipper, *Investigator's Guide to Steganography* (Boca Raton, FL: Auerbach Publications, 2003)

Chad A. Kirby, "Defining Abusive Software to Protect Computer Users from the Threat of Spyware," 10 *Computer Law Review & Technology Journal* 287 (2006)

Mathias Klang," A Critical Look at the Regulation of Computer Viruses," 11 *International Journal of Law and Information Technology* 162 (2003)

Robert H. Klonoff, *Class Actions and Other Multi-Party Litigations in a Nutshell* (St. Paul, MN: West, 2d ed. 2004)

"A Knight in Digital Armour," *The Economist Technology Quarterly*, September 1, 2012, at 23

David R. Koepsell, *The Ontology of Cyberspace: Law, Philosophy and the Future of Intellectual Property* (Chicago: Open Court, 2000)

Uta Kohl, "Defamation on the Internet—Nice Decision, Shame about the Reasoning," 52 *International & Comparative Law Quarterly* 1049 (2003)

Kathryn Kolbert & Zak Mettger, eds., *Justice Talking: Censoring the Web: Leading Advocates Debate Today's Most Controversial Issues* (New York: The New Press, 2002)

"Korea, Internet Usage, Broadband and Telecommunications Report," Internet World Stats, available at http://www.internetworldstats.com/asia/kr.htm (visited January 28, 2013)

Jeffrey D. Kramer, "Seafaring Data Havens: Google's Patented Pirate Ship," 2010 *University of Illinois Journal of Law, Technology and Policy* 359 (2010)

Ken Kraus & Dan Polatsek, "Enforcement of Foreign Media Judgments in the Aftermath of Gutnick v. Dow Jones & Co.," 21 *Communications Lawyer* 1 (2003)

Jason Krause, "The National Pulse: Google Targeted in Trademark Disputes— Rulings Should Help Define What Is Protected in Internet Advertising," *ABA Journal E-Report*, May 28, 2004

Dave Kristula, *The History of the Internet*, available at http://www.davesite.com/webstation/net-history.shtml (visited August 16, 2012)

Ronald J. Krotoszynski, *The First Amendment in Cross-Cultural Perspective: A Comparative Legal Analysis of the Freedom of Speech* (New York: NYU Press, 2009)

Katarzyna Kryczka, "Ready to Join the EU Information Society? Implementation of E-Commerce Directive 2000/31/EC in the EU Acceding Countries—the Example of Poland," 12 *International Journal of Law and Information Technology* 55 (2004)

Stephanie A. Kuhlmann, "Do Not Track Me Online: The Logistical Struggles over the Right 'To Be Let Alone' Online," 22 *DePaul Journal of Art, Technology & Intellectual Property Law* 229 (2011)

Cecil C. Kuhne III, "Forcing the Copyright Genie Back into the Bottle: Public Policy Implications of Copyright Extension Legislation," 33 *Southwestern University Law Review* 327 (2004)

Ken D. Kumayama, "A Right to Pseudonymity," 51 *Arizona Law Review* 427 (2009)

Richard G. Kunkel, "Protecting Consumers from Spyware: A Proposed Consumer Digital Trespass Act," 28 *The John Marshall Journal of Computer & Information Law* 185 (2010)

Mary LaFrance, "Graduated Response by Industry Compact: Piercing the Black Box," 30 *Cardozo Arts & Entertainment Law Journal* 165 (2012)

Susan Landau, *Surveillance or Security? The Risks Posed by New Wiretapping Technologies* (Cambridge, MA: MIT Press, 2011)

Amy L. Landers, *Understanding Patent Law* (New Providence, NJ: LexisNexis, 2d ed. 2012)

William M. Landes & Richard A. Posner, "Indefinitely Renewable Copyright," 70 *University of Chicago Law Review* 471 (2003)

Frederick Lane, *Cybertraps for the Young* (Chicago: NTI Upstream, 2011)

David Lange, "Recognizing the Public Domain," 44 *Law & Contemporary Problems* 147 (1981)

Paul Lansing & Mark D. Halter, "Internet Advertising and Right to Privacy Issues,"80 *University of Detroit Mercy Law Review* 181 (2003)

Elizabeth D. Lauzon, "Validity, Construction, and Application of Anticybersquatting Consumer Protection Act, 15 U.S.C.A. § 1125 (D), 177" *American Law Reports Federal* 1 (2002)

The Law and Practice of Digital Encryption (Amsterdam, Netherlands: Institute for Information Law, 1998)

Marshall Leaffer, "International Copyright from an American Perspective," 43 *Arkansas Law Review* 373 (1990)

Marshall Leaffer, *Understanding Copyright Law* (New Providence, NJ: LexisNexis, 5th ed. 2010)

Jessica Leber, "EmTech: French Minister Says Google Faces Critical Questions over Copyright," *MIT Technology Review* (October 25, 2012), available at http://www .technologyreview.com/view/506296/emtech-french-minister-says-google-faces-critical-questions-over-copyright/ (visited February 18, 2013)

Timothy B. Lee, How 4 Microsoft Engineers Proved that the 'darknet' Would Defeat DRM," *Ars Technica* (November 30, 2012), available at http://arstechnica.com/tech-policy/2012/11/how-four-microsoft-engineers-proved-copy-protection-would-fail/ (visited January 28, 2013)

Edward Lee, "The Public's Domain: The Evolution of Legal Restraints on the Government's Power to Control Public Access through Secrecy or Intellectual Property," 55 *Hastings Law Journal* 91 (2003)

M.K. Carol Lee & J. Julian Elliot, "Semiconductor Manufacturing," in *Bay Area Air Quality Management District Permit Handbook* § 7, Chapter 4 (2006), available at http://hank.baaqmd.gov/pmt/handbook/rev02/PH_00_05_07_04_mem_1.pdf (visited December 20, 2012)

"Legislation—Homeland Security: Senate Funding Bill Requires Review of DHS Data Mining," *Cybercrime Law Report*, August 11, 2003, at 4

Nicholas Lemann, "Letter from Washington: The Chairman: He's the Other Powell, and No One Is Sure What He's up to," *New Yorker*, October 7, 2002

Mark A. Lemley & Lawrence Lessig, "The End of End-to-End: Preserving the Architecture of the Internet in the Broadband Era," 48 *UCLA Law Review* 925 (2001)

Mark A. Lemley, "Media & Content Industry: Is the Sky Falling on the Content Industries?" 9 *Journal on Telecommunications and High Technology Law* 125 (2011)

Robert Lemos, "FBI Nabs Russian Expert at DefCon," ZDNet UK (July18, 2001), available at http://news.zdnet.co.uk/internet/security/0,39020375,2091458,00.htm (visited January 29, 2013)

Lawrence Lessig, *Code and Other Laws of Cyberspace* (New York: Basic Books, 1999)

Lawrence Lessig, *Code and Other Laws of Cyberspace, Version 2.0* (New York: Basic Books, 2006)

Lawrence Lessig, *Free Culture: How Big Media Uses Technology and the Law to Lock Down Culture and Control Creativity* (New York: Penguin, 2004)

Lawrence Lessig, *The Future of Ideas* (New York: Random House, 2001)

Lawrence Lessig, *Remix: Making Art and Commerce Thrive in the Hybrid Economy* (New York: Penguin Books, 2008)

Letter to NCCUSL from Attorneys General Opposing UCITA, July 23, 1999, available at http://www.badsoftware.com/aglet1.htm (visited July 21, 2012)

Anne Letterio, "A State's Way of Circumventing the Constitution: The Unconstitutional Taxation of Our-of-State Corporations That Do Instate Business over the Internet," 22 *Albany Law Journal Science and Technology* 411 (2012

Robert Levine, *Free Ride: How the Internet is Destroying the Culture Business and How the Culture Business Can Fight Back* (New York: Doubleday, 2011)

Meridith Levinson, "Mobile Malware: Beware Drive-By Downloads on Your Smartphone," CIO (March 22, 2012), available at http://www.cio.com/article/702655/Mobile_Malware_Beware_Drive_by_Downloads_on_Your_Smartphone (visited April 4, 2013)

Saul Levmore & Martha C. Nussbaum, eds., *The Offensive Internet: Speech, Privacy, and Reputation* (Cambridge, MA: Harvard University Press, 2012)

Michal Lev-Ram, "Zuckerberg: Kids under 13 Should Be Allowed on Facebook," CNNMoney (May 20, 2011), available at http://tech.fortune.cnn.com/2011/05/20/zuckerberg-kids-under-13-should-be-allowed-on-facebook/ (visited April 4, 2013)

Steven Levy, *Crypto: How the Code Rebels Beat the Government—Saving Privacy in the Digital Age* (New York: Penguin Putnam, 2002)

Steven Levy, *Hackers: Heroes of the Computer Revolution* (Sebastopol, CA: O'Riley Media, Inc., 2010)

Robert A. Levy, "Microsoft and the Browser Wars," 31 *Connecticut Law Review* 1321 (1999)

Matt Liebowitz, "QR Tags Can Be Rigged to Attack Smart Phones," *Scientific American* (September 13, 2011), available at http://www.scientificamerican.com/article.cfm?id=qr-tags-can-be-rigged-to (visited February 17, 2013)

"Life Imprisonment for Hackers Could Be Imminent," *2600 News* (September 25, 2001), available at http://www.2600.com/news/view/article/726 (visited February 7, 2013)

George Likourezos, "Trademark Law in the Computer Age: Applying Trademark Principles to the 'Look and Feel' of Software," 77 *Journal of the Patent and Trademark Office Society* 451 (1995)

Young Joon Lim & Sarah E. Sexton, "Internet as a Human Right: A Practical Legal Framework to Address the Unique Nature of the Medium and to Promote Development," 7 *Washington Journal of Law, Technology & Arts* 295 (2012)

Brian J. Link, "Drawing a Line in Alternate Universes: Exposing the Inadequacies of the Current Four-Factor Fair Use Test through Chanslash," 33 *Thomas Jefferson Law Review* 139 (2010)

David S. Linthicum, *Cloud Computing and SOA Convergence in Your Enterprise: A Step-by-Step Guide* (Boston: Addison-Wesley Publishing Company, 2009)

Jeremy Lipschultz, *Broadcast and Internet Indecency: Defining Free Speech* (New York: Routledge, 2007)

Jeremy Lipschultz, *Free Expression in the Age of the Internet: Social and Legal Boundaries* (Boulder, CO: Perseus Books, 1999)

Jacqueline D. Lipton, "Who Owns 'Hillary.com'? Political Speech and the First Amendment in Cyberspace," 49 *Boston College Law Review* 55 (2008)

Jessica Litman, *Digital Copyright: Protecting Intellectual Property on the Internet* (Amherst, NY: Prometheus, 2000)

Jessica Litman, "The Public Domain," 39 *Emory Law Journal* 965 (1990)

Brian Loader, *The Governance of Cyberspace: Politics, Technology and Global Restructuring* (Basingstoke, Hampshire, UK: Routledge, 1997)

Josh Lowensohn, "Apple-Samsung Trial: The End is Nigh," CNET (August 17, 2012), available at http://news.cnet .com/8301–13579_3–57495807–37/apple-samsung-trial-the-end-is-nigh/ (visited February 8, 2013)

Chun-Shien Lu, *Multimedia Security: Steganography and Digital Watermarking Techniques for Protection of Intellectual Property* (Hershey, PA: Idea Group Publishing, 2004)

Lynne B. Lubash, "How the Digital Performance Right in Sound Recordings Act of 1995 Protects Copyright Owners on the Internet," 14 *Santa Clara Computer and High Technology Law Journal* 497 (1998)

Jay Lyman, "Google Pulls P2P Links over Kazaa Copyright Claims," *TechNewsWorld* (September 2, 2003), available at http://www.technewsworld.com/story/31481.html (visited February 8, 2013)

Mark D. Lynch, "The Smart Money Is on Prosecutions: Using the Federal Interstate Wire Act to Prosecute Offshore Telephone Gambling Services," 10 *Indiana International and Comparative Law Review* 177 (1999)

Courtney G. Lytle, *Skills & Values: Intellectual Property* (New Providence, NJ: LexisNexis, 2011)

Courtney Macavinta, "DoubleClick, Abacus Merge in $1.7 Billion Deal," CNET News.com (November 24, 1999), available at http://news.com.com/2100–1023–233526 .html?legacy=cnet (visited January 28, 2013)

"Macrovision Wins Preliminary Injunction against 321 Studios in Patent and Copyright Infringement Lawsuit," Macrovision Press Release (May 20, 2004), available at http://www .realwire.com/releases/macrovision-wins-preliminary-injunction-against-321-studios-in-patent-and-copyright-infringement-law (visited August 19, 2012)

Stephen B. Maebius & Harold C. Wegner, "The Honeywell Nail in the Festo Coffin: A Narrowing Amendment Does Create a Presumption of Prosecution History Estoppel," 23 *Biotechnology Law Report* 417 (2004)

Larry Magid, "What Are SOPA and PIPA and Why All the Fuss?" (January 18, 2012), available at http://www.forbes.com/ sites/larrymagid/2012/01/18/ what-are-sopa-and-pipa-and-why-all-the-fuss/ (visited April 24, 2013)

Makeen Fouad Makeen, *Copyright in a Global Information Society: The Scope of Copyright Protection under International, US, UK, and French Law* (New York: Aspen, 2001)

Ronald Mann, "Opinion Analysis: Justices Reject Publisher's Claims in Gray-Market Copyright Case," SCOTUSblog: Supreme Court of the United States Blog (March 19, 2013), available at http://www.scotusblog .com/?p=161209 (visited April 15, 2013)

David P. Manni, "National Cable & Telecommunications Ass'n v. Brand X Internet Services: A War of Words, the Effect of Classifying Cable Modem Service as an Information Service," 13 *Villanova Sports and Entertainment Law Journal* 353 (2006)

Andreas Manolopoulos, "Raising 'Cyber-Borders': The Interaction between Law and Technology," 11 *International Journal of Law and Information Technology* 40 (2003)

Wenbo Mao, *Modern Cryptography: Theory and Practice* (Upper Saddle River, NJ: Prentice Hall, 2003)

Chris Marsden, *Internet Co-Regulation: European Law, Regulatory Governance and Legitimacy in Cyberspace* (Cambridge, MA: MIT Press, 2011)

Christopher T. Marsden, ed., *Regulating the Global Information Society* (New York: Routledge, 2000)

Lauren A. Matecki, "COPPA Is Ineffective Legislation! Next Steps for Protecting Youth Privacy Rights in the Social Networking Era," 5 *Northwestern Journal of Law and Social Policy* 369 (2010)

Ramona Mateiu, "In re Microsoft Corporation Antitrust Litigation," 17 *Berkeley Technology Law Journal* 295 (2002)

Kim Maxwell, *Residential Broadband: An Insider's Guide to the Battle for the Last Mile* (New York: John Wiley & Sons, 1998)

J. David Mayberry, "Trademark Nominative Fair Use: Toward a Uniform Standard," 102 *Trademark Reporter* 820 (2012)

Bryce J. Maynard, "The Initial Interest Confusion Doctrine and Trademark Infringement on the Internet," 57 *Washington and Lee Law Review* 1303 (2000)

Meredith McCardle, "Fandom, Fan Fiction and Fanfare: What's All the Fuss?" 9 *Boston University Journal of Science and Technology Law* 443 (2003)

J. Thomas McCarthy et al., *McCarthy's Desk Encyclopedia of Intellectual Property* (Washington, D.C.: Bureau of National Affairs, 3d ed. 2004)

Douglas G. McCray, "Oh, What a Tangled Web: The Subtle Difference between Metatag Usage as 'Fair Use' and Invisible Infringement," *Michigan Bar Journal*, August 2002, at 42

Declan McCullagh, "Bill Proposes ISPs, Wi-Fi Keep Logs for Police," CNN (February 20, 2009), available at http:// www.cnn.com/2009/TECH/02/20/internet.records. bill/ (visited April 5, 2013)

Declan McCullagh, "Google Excluding Controversial Sites," CNET News.com (October 23, 2002), available at http://news.cnet.com/2100–1023–963132.html (visited February 18, 2013)

Declan McCullagh, "Has 'Haven' for Questionable Sites Sunk?" CNET News.com (August 4, 2003), available at http:// news.com.com/2100–1028_3–5059676.html?tag=fd_ top(visited January 28, 2013)

Declan McCullagh, "How SOPA Would Affect You: FAQ," CNet (January 18, 2012), available at http://news.cnet .com/8301–31921_3–57329001–281/how-sopa-would-affect-you-faq/?tag=mncol;txt (visited April 24, 2013)

Declan McCullagh & Milana Homsi, "Leave DRM Alone: A Survey of Legislative Proposals Relating to Digital Rights Management Technology and Their Problems," 2005 *Michigan State Law Review* 317 (2005)

Declan McCullagh, "Supreme Court Deals Deathblow to Antiporn Law," CNET (January 21, 2009), available at http://news.cnet.com/8301–13578_3–10147171–38 .html (visited April 5, 2013)

Ciaran McEvoy, "Listserv Privacy Unsettled Issue," *Los Angeles Daily Journal*, May 21, 2012, at 1

David McGowan, "Between Logic and Experience: Error Costs and United States v. Microsoft Corp.," 20 *Berkeley Technology Law Journal* 1185 (2005)

Brian McHale, *Postmodernist Fiction* (London, UK: Methuen Press, 1987)

J. Andrew McKinney, Jr., "The Most Significant Practical Effects of the America Invents Act ["AIA"] for Business Owners & Transactional Attorneys," *Maryland Bar Journal*, September/October 2012, at 38

Joshua McLaurin, "Making Cyberspace Safe for Democracy: The Challenge Posed by Denial-of-Service Attacks," 30 *Yale Law & Policy Review* 211 (2011)

Kembrew McLeod, *Freedom of Expression: Resistance and Repression in the Age of Intellectual Property* (Minneapolis, MN: University of Minnesota Press, 2007)

"The Meaning of iPod," *Economist Technology Quarterly* (June 12, 2004), available at http://www.economist.com/ node/2724432 (visited April 5, 2013)

"Megaupload Case: New Zealand Court Wants FBI Evidence," BBC News (August 16, 2012), available at http://www .bbc.co.uk/news/technology-19280898 (visited February 8, 2013)

Aaron L. Melville, "The Future of the Audio Home Recording Act of 1992: Has It Survived the Millennium Bug?" 7 *Boston University Journal of Science and Technology Law* 372 (2001)

Alfred J. Menezes et al., *Handbook of Applied Cryptography* (Boca Raton, FL: CRC Press, 1997)

Joseph Menn, *All the Rave: The Rise and Fall of Shawn Fanning's Napster* (New York: Crown Business, 2003)

Memorandum of Understanding between the U.S. Department of Commerce and the Internet Corporation for Assigned Names and Numbers, November 1998, available at http:// www.icann.org/general/icann-mou-25nov98.htm (visited February 7, 2013)

Robert P. Merges & Jane C. Ginsburg, *Foundations of Intellectual Property* (New Providence, NJ: LexisNexis, 2006)

Trevor Merriden, *Irresistible Forces: The Business Legacy of Napster and the Growth of the Underground Internet* (New York: John Wiley & Sons, 2002)

Rick Merritt, "Copyright Scheme Could Fuel Transition to High-Definition Systems," *EE Times* (July 15, 2004), available at http://www.eetimes.com/showArticle .jhtml?articleID=23900919 (visited April 5, 2013)

Holger Metzger, "Netscape History," available at http://www .holgermetzger.de/Netscape_History.html (visited August 22, 2012)

Alex Michael & Ben Salter, *Marketing through Search Optimization: How to Be Found on the Web* (Burlington, MA: Butterworth-Heinemann, 2d ed. 2007)

"Jason Mick, Study: One Third of Internet is Crammed with Porn," DailyTech (June 17, 2010), available at http:// www.dailytech.com/Study+One+Third+of+Internet+is+C rammed+With+Porn/article18760.htm (visited February 17, 2013)

"Microsoft and Privacy: Change of Track," *The Economist*, June 9, 2012, at 70

Arthur R. Miller & Michael H. Davis, *Intellectual Property, Patents, Trademarks, and Copyright in a Nutshell* (St. Paul, MN: West, 5th ed. 2012)

Kevin D. Mitnick et al., *The Art of Deception: Controlling the Human Element of Security* (Indianapolis: Wiley Publishing, Inc., 2002)

"Mobile Apps Developer Settles FTC Charges It Violated Children's Privacy Rule," Federal Trade Commission (August 15, 2011), available at http://www.ftc.gov/ opa/2011/08/w3mobileapps.shtm (visited April 5, 2013)

"Mobile Cellular Subscriptions (per 100 people)," World Bank, available at http://data.worldbank.org/indicator/IT.CEL .SETS.P2 (visited November 13, 2012)

Tom Moon, "Radiohead's 'In Rainbows' Sets Its Own Terms," NPR Music (October 10, 2007), available at http://www .npr.org/templates/story/story.php?storyId=15152703 (visited February 3, 2013)

Steven J. Moore, "America Invents Act: Impact on Patent Processing and Litigation Strategies," Metropolitan Corporate Counsel (October 24, 2011), available at http://www.metrocorpcounsel.com/articles/16306/ america-invents-act-impact-patent-processing-and-litigation-strategies (visited February 17, 2013)

Evgeny Morozov, *The Net Delusion: The Dark Side of Internet Freedom* (New York: PublicAffairs, 2012)

P. Sean Morris, "Knocking on the WTO's Door: International Law and the Principle of First Sale Download in UsedSoft v. Oracle," *ASIL Insights* (January 24, 2013), available at http://www.asil.org/pdfs/insights/insight130124.pdf (visited April 15, 2013)

Jeff Moss, ed., *Stealing the Network: How to Own the Box* (Rockland, Massachusetts: Syngress, 2003)

Frank Mosuch & Susan B. Hillson, "Technical Security Measures," in *Data Security and Privacy Law: Combating Cyberthreats*, edited by Kevin P. Cronin & Ronald N. Weikers (St. Paul, MN: West, 2004)

M.P., To the Editor of *The Times*, June 1, 1864, reproduced at Computer History: Telegraph "Spam," available at http://www.computerhistory.org/revolution/the-web/20/392/2172 (visited February 18, 2013)

Milton Mueller, *Ruling the Root: Internet Governance and the Taming of Cyberspace* (Cambridge, MA: MIT Press, 2002)

Joe Mullin, "Most Apps' Privacy Policies Continue to Be Missing in Action," PaidContent (May 27, 2011), available at http://paidcontent.org/2011/05/27/419-most-apps-privacy-policies-continue-to-be-missing-in-action/ (visited April 2, 2013)

"Municipal Broadband: The Need for Speed," *The Economist*, August 11, 2012, at 26

Kevin Murphy, "Apple Finally Grabs apple.co.uk—after Just 16 Years," The A Register (July 19, 2012, 11:03), available at http://www.theregister.co.uk/2012/07/19/apple_gains_ control_of_apple_dot_co_dot_uk/ (visited April 5, 2013)

Kevin Murphy, "Facebook Cyberquatter Stitched up by Own Facebook Account," The A Register (July 18, 2012), available at http://www.theregister.co.uk/2012/07/18/facebook_cybersquatter_stitched_up_by_own_facebook_account/ (visited April 5, 2013)

Jaime E. Muscar, "A Winner Is Who? Fair Use and the Online Distribution of Manga and Video Game Fan Translations," 9 *Vanderbilt Journal of Entertainment and Technology Law* 223 (2006)

"The Music Business: Universal's Gamble," *The Economist*, July 21, 2012, at 57

"Music to Their Ears: With Compact-Disc Sales Plummetting, Record Companies Are Rethinking How to Distribute Music Online," *Economist Technology Quarterly* (September 21, 2002), available at http://www.economist.com/node/1324731 (visited January 28, 2013)

Ariella Mutchler, "CAN-SPAM versus the European Union E-Privacy Directive: Does Either Provide a Solution to the Problem of Spam?" 43 *Suffolk University Law Review* 957 (2010)

"National Differences: The World Is What You Make It—Every Country Has Its Own Internet," *The Economist Special Report: Technology and Geography*, October 27, 2012, at 20

National Research Council, *Technical, Business, and Legal Dimensions of Protecting Children from Pornography on the Internet: Proceedings of a Workshop* (Washington, D.C.: National Academies Press, 2002)

"National Security—Government Databases: Pentagon Concludes DOD Data Mining Plan Doesn't Threaten Privacy Rights," *Cybercrime Law Report* June 2, 2003, at 3

Saira Nayak, "How This Cookie Crumbled: Deciphering the Compliance Obligations around the EU's Cookie Directive," *Antitrust Source* 1 (December 2012)

Samuel P. Nelson, *Beyond the First Amendment: The Politics of Free Speech and Pluralism* (Baltimore: The Johns Hopkins University Press, 2005)

Bill Nelson et al., *Guide to Computer Forensic and Investigations* (Boston: Course Technology, 3d ed. 2009)

Jeff Nemerofsky, "The Crime of 'Interruption of Computer Services to Authorized Users': Have You Ever Heard of It?" 6 *Richmond Journal of Law & Technology* 23 (2000)

NeoSmart Technologies, "The Other Great Firewall," (August 28, 2006), available at http://neosmart.net/blog/2006/the-other-great-firewall/ (visited February 3, 2013)

Chris Nerney, "Early MP3.com Investors May Be Singing Sad Tune," Internetnews.com (July 26, 1999), available at http://www.internetnews.com/bus-news/article.php/168501 (visited February 8, 2013)

Heather Newman, "Web Sites Charge up Ford's Ire: Owners Sued over Net Names," *Detroit Free Press* (January 24, 2001), available at http://www.whoisfinder.com/news/200101/ford-sue-domain-owners.html (visited January 28, 2013)

Xuan-Thao N. Nguyen, "Should It Be a Free for All? The Challenge of Extending Trade Dress Protection to the Look and Feel of Web Sites in the Evolving Internet," 49 *American University Law Review* 1233 (2000)

Lars Nielsen, *The Little Book of Cloud Computing, 2013 Edition: Including Coverage of Big Data Tools* (Wickford, RI: New Street Communications, 2013)

"Niger, Internet Usage, Broadband and Telecommunications Report," Internet World Stats, available at http://www.internetworldstats.com/af/ne.htm (visited January 29, 2013)

David Nimmer, "Codifying Copyright Comprehensibly," 51 *UCLA Law Review* 1233 (2004)

David Nimmer, *Copyright: Sacred Text, Technology, and the DMCA* (The Hague: Kluwer Academic/Plenum Publishers, 2004)

Raymond T. Nimmer, *Licensing of Intellectual Property and Other Information Assets* (Newark, NJ: LexisNexis, 2004)

"No Lanham Act Claim Where Trademark Was Used in Metatags for Web Site Criticizing Trademark Owner," *Computer & Internet Lawyer*, December 2000, at 44

Erin F. Norris, "Why the Internet Isn't Special: Restoring Predictability to Personal Jurisdiction," 53 *Arizona Law Review* 1013 (2011)

Stephen Northcutt et al., *Inside Network Perimeter Security: The Definitive Guide to Firewalls, Virtual Private Networks (VPNs), Routers, and Intrusion Detection Systems* (Indianapolis: Sams Publishing, 2d ed. 2005)

"The Number One HTTP Server on the Internet," Apache HTTP Server Project (April 2012), available at http://httpd.apache.org/ (visited January 12, 2013)

The Open Access Project, "Promoting the Free and Unrestricted World-Wide Electronic Distribution of Peer-Reviewed Journal Literature," Public Knowledge, available at http://www.publicknowledge.org/about/what/projects/open-access.html (visited June 6, 2012)

"Open Source: Beyond Capitalism?" *The Economist* (June 10, 2004), available at http://www.economist.com/node/2747734 (visited February 8, 2013)

"Operator of Celebrity Fan Websites to Pay $1 Million to Settle FTC Charges What It Illegally Collected Children's Information without Their Parent's Consent," Federal Trade Commission (October 4, 2012), available at http://www.ftc.gov/opa/2012/10/artistarena.shtm (visited April 5, 2013)

"Operator of Social Networking Website for Kids Settle Charges Site Collected Kids' Personal Information without Parental Consent," Federal Trade Commission (November 8, 2011), available at http://www.ftc.gov/opa/2011/11/skidekids.shtm (visited April 5, 2013)

Taiwo A. Oriola, "Regulating Unsolicited Commercial Electronic Mail in the United States and the European Union: Challenges and Prospects," 7 *Tulane Journal of Technology & Intellectual Property* 113 (2005)

Otilia Otlacan, "comScore Reports $50 Billion in Q4 2011 U.S. Retail E-Commerce Spending, Up 14% vs. Year Ago," AdOps Online (February 14, 2012), available at http://www.adoperationsonline.com/2012/02/14/comscore-reports-50-billion-in-q4–2011-u-s-retail-e-commerce-spending-up-14-vs-year-ago/ (visited February 24, 2013)

Laura Hazard Owen, "Ebook Sales Way Up in 2011; Overall Trade Book Sales Roughly Flat," PaidContent: The Economics of Digital Content (July 18, 2012), available at http://paidcontent.org/2012/07/18/ebooks-are-now-the-most-popular-format-for-adult-fiction/ (visited January 29, 2013)

Jason Oxman, "The FCC and the Unregulation of the Internet," FCC/OPP Working Paper 31, July 1999

"Over-the-Top Phone Services: Joyn Them or Join Them," *The Economist*, August 11, 2012, at 60

John Paczkowski, "NovellAntitrust Suit against Microsoft Sputters to a Close," All Things (July 16, 2012), available at http://allthingsd.com/20120716/novell-antitrust-suit-against-microsoft-sputters-to-a-close/ (visited February 8, 2013)

Alan Heidi S. Padawer, "Google This: Search Engine Results Weave a Web for Trademark Infringement Actions on the Internet," 81 Washington University Law Quarterly 1099 (2003)

Patricia Paoletta & Peter McElligott, "Perspectives—U.S. and European Union Stay United in Opposition to ITU Efforts to Change Internet Governance," The European Institute, available at http://www.europeaninstitute.org/EA-December-2012/patricia-paolette-and-peter-mcelligott.html (visited January 10, 2013)

Vagelis Papakonstantinou & Paul de Hert, "The Amended EU Law on ePrivacy and Electronic Communications after Its 2011 Implementation; New Rules on Data Protection, Spam, Data Breaches and Protection of Intellectual Property Rights," 29 The John Marshall Journal of Computer & Information Law 29 (2011)

Harsh P. Parikh & Heidi McNeil Staudenmaier, "Betting on i-Gambling Could Have Big Returns," Los Angeles Daily Journal, May 11, 2012, at 8

Eli Pariser, The Filter Bubble: What the Internet is Hiding from You (New York: Penguin Press, 2011)

Andy Patrizio, "XXX Domains May Be Hard Sell", Wired News (March 6, 2001), available at http://www.wired.com/news/business/0,1367,42217,00.html (visited February 17, 2013)

William Patry, How to Fix Copyright (Oxford, UK: Oxford University Press, 2011)

Vandana Pednekar-Magal & Peter Shields, "The State and Telecom Surveillance Policy: The Clipper Chip Initiative," 8 Communication Law and Policy 429 (2003)

Alan Perkins, "The Classification of Search Engine Spam," Search Mechanics, available at http://www.ebrandmanagement.com/whitepapers/spam-classification/ (visited October 28, 2004)

Christopher R. Perry, "Trademarks as Commodities: The "Famous" Roadblock to Applying Trademark Dilution Law in Cyberspace," 32 Connecticut Law Review 1127 (2000)

"Personalising Online Prices: How Deep Are Your Pockets?" The Economist, June 30, 2012, at 69

Zorik Pesochinsky, "Almost Famous: Preventing Username-Squatting on Social Networking Websites," 28 Cardozo Arts & Entertainment Law Journal 223 (2010)

Debra D. Peterson, "The Hydra of Identity Tolerance: Patent Law Heresies Involving 35 U.S.C. § 102," 85 Journal of the Patent and Trademark Office Society 639 (2003)

Mark Peterson, "Indiana Bill Would Force Tax Collection on Internet Sales," WNDU.com (January 11, 2013), available at http://www.wndu.com/home/headlines/Indiana-bill-would-force-tax-collection-on-internet-sales-186549551.html#.UPQuOMVhdAg.twitter (visited February 24, 2013)

Adam Petravicius & Joseph T. Miotke, "Beyond the NDA: Digital Rights Management Isn't Just for Music," 16 Journal of Proprietary Rights 1 (2004)

"Philosophy of the GNU Project," GNU Operating System, available at http://www.gnu.org/philosophy/ (visited January 1, 2012)

Abigail Phillips, "The Content Industry and ISPs Announce a "Common Framework for Copyright Alerts": What Does It Mean for Users?" Electronic Frontier Foundation (July 7, 2011), available at https://www.eff.org/deeplinks/2011/07/content-industry-and-isps-announce-common (visited April 24, 2013)

Andrew M. Pickett, "Much Yahoo! about Nothing: The Ninth Circuit, Jurisprudential Schizophrenia, and the Road Not Taken in Yahoo! v. La Ligue Contre le Racisme et l'Antisemitisme," 8 Tulane Journal of Technology & Intellectual Property 231 (2006)

"Pirated Rihanna Songs Land Frenchman in Court," BBC News (September 14, 2012), available at http://www.bbc.co.uk/news/technology-19597429 (visited February 9, 2013)

"Policy Online Privacy/Data Sharing Internet Advertising Trade Group Issues Guidelines on Use of Web Bugs," Cybercrime Law Report, December 16, 2002

"Polynesians Get Free Wireless Web," BBC News (June 26, 2003), available at http://news.bbc.co.uk/1/hi/technology/3020158.stm (visited April 7, 2013)

Lucille M. Ponte, "Coming Attractions: Opportunities and Challenges in Thwarting Global Movie Piracy," 45 American Business Law Journal 331 (2008)

Lucille M. Ponte, "Getting a Bad Rap? Unconscionability in Clickwrap Dispute Resolution Clauses and a Proposal for Improving the Quality of These Online Consumer "Products"," 26 Ohio State Journal on Dispute Resolution 119 (2011)

"Porn 3x More Popular than Searches: Tracking Firm Finds that 18.8% of all U.S. Users Went to 'Adult' Sites, 5.5% Went to Search Engines," CNN Money (June 4, 2002), available at http://www.freerepublic.com/focus/f-news/1147848/posts (visited February 17, 2013)

Rebecca Porter, "Prosecutors, Plaintiffs Aim to Curb Internet Gambling," Trial, August 2004, at 14

Terry W. Posey, Jr., "Tony Soprano's Privacy Rights: Internet Cookies, Wiretapping Statutes, and Federal Computer Crimes," 29 University of Dayton Law Review 109 (2003)

Jon Postel & Joyce Reynolds, "Domain Requirements," Network Working Group Request for Comments: 920 (October 1984), available at http://www.ietf.org/rfc/rfc920.txt (visited April 7, 2013)

Joseph M. Potenza, "The America Invents Act: One Year Later," Landslide, January/February 2013, at 1

Press Release, European Parliament, Parliament Approves EU Unitary Patent Rules, (December 11, 2012), available at http://www.europarl.europa.eu/news/en/pressroom/content/20121210IPR04506/html/Parliament-approves-EU-unitary-patent-rules (visited February 7, 2013)

Press Release, Netscape, "Mosaic Communications Corporation Changes Name to Netscape Communications Corporation," available at http://www.holgermetzger.de/netscape/NetscapeCommunicationsNewsRelease.htm (visited December 21, 2012)

Press Release, Optenet, "More than One Third of Web Pages Are Pornographic" (June 16, 2010), available at http://www

.optenet.com/en-us/new.asp?id=270 (visited February 17, 2013)

Cheryl B. Preston, "CyberInfants," 39 *Pepperdine Law Review* 225 (2012)

Chris Priestman, *Web Radio: Radio Production for Internet Streaming* (Boston: Focal Press, 2001)

"Privacy Legislation: Sens. Feingold, Wyden Begin Effort to Stop 'Data Mining' by Department of Defense," *Cybercrime Law Report*, January 27, 2003, at 3

Project Gutenberg, available at http://www.gutenberg.net/ (visited January 29, 2013)

"The Project Gutenberg License, License Explained (informative)," Project Gutenberg, available at http://www.gutenberg.net/license (visited January 29, 2013)

"Project Gutenberg of Australia: A Treasure-Trove of Literature," PGA, available at http://www.gutenberg.net.au/ (visited February 17, 2013)

"Protecting Networks from DoS Attacks and Malicious Traffic," Allot Communications (November 2001), available at http://al-rabbash.com/Allot/DoS%20SP%202001–11–20%20v1a.pdf (visited January 28, 2013)

"Public Knowledge Mission Statement," available at http://www.publicknowledge.org/about/what/mission (visited June 6, 2012)

"Purchase Card Data Mining Leads to Co. Indictment," *Government Contractor*, August 25, 2004, ¶ 330

Margaret Jane Radin, "Distributed Denial of Service Attacks, Who Pays? Part I," *Cyberspace Lawyer*, December 2001, at 2

Margaret Jane Radin, "Distributed Denial of Service Attacks, Who Pays? Part II," *Cyberspace Lawyer*, January 2002, at 2

Christina Ramberg, *Internet Marketplaces: The Law of Auctions and Exchanges Online* (Oxford, UK: Oxford University Press, 2002)

Tiernan Ray, "E-Mail Viruses Blamed as Spam Rises Sharply," *Seattle Times* (February 18, 2004), available at http://seattletimes.nwsource.com/html/businesstechnology/2001859752_spamdoubles18.html (visited February 24, 2013)

George Reese, *Cloud Application Architectures: Building Applications and Infrastructure in the Cloud* (Sebastopol, CA: O'Reilly Media, 2009)

"Register of Known Spam Operations (ROKSO)," The Spamhaus Project, available at http://www.spamhaus.org/rokso/ (visited January 15, 2013)

"Regulatory Affairs—Pharmaceutical: FDA to Use Data Mining to Monitor Adverse Events," 22 *Biotechnology Law Report* 481 (2003)

Alexander Reicher, "Redefining Net Neutrality after Comcast v. FCC," 26 *Berkeley Technology Law Journal* 733 (2011)

Joel R. Reidenberg, "Current Debates in the Conflict of Laws: Choice of Law and Jurisdiction on the Internet: Technology and Internet Jurisdiction," 153 *University of Pennsylvania Law Review* 1951 (2005)

Phillip E. Reiman, "Cryptography and the First Amendment: The Right to Be Unheard," 14 *John Marshall Journal of Computer & Information Law* 325 (1996)

"RIAA v. The People: Five Years Later," Electronic Frontier Foundation (September 30, 2008), available at https://www.eff.org/wp/riaa-v-people-five-years-later (visited February 3, 2013)

Joshua Rich, "You Don't Know My Name: InRe Anonymous Online Speakers and the Right to Remain Cloaked in Cyberspace," 45 *Loyola of Los Angeles Law Review* 325 (2011)

William M. Richman & William L. Reynolds, *Understanding Conflict of Laws* (New York: Matthew Bender, 3d ed. 2002)

Sam Ricketson, *The Berne Convention for the Protection of Literary and Artistic Works: 1886–1986* (London: Centre for Commercial Law Studies, Queen Mary College, 1987)

Sam Ricketson & Jane Ginsburg, *International Copyright and Neighbouring Rights: The Berne Convention and Beyond* (Oxford, UK: Oxford University Press, 2d ed. 2006)

Carlyle C. Ring, Jr., *Understanding Electronic Contracting 2003 The Impact of Regulation, New Laws & New Agreements: Overview of the Legal Landscape of E-Commerce*, Practising Law Institute Patents, Copyrights, Trademarks, and Literary Property Course Handbook Series, April 2003

Paul Roberts, "'Buffalo Spammer' Convicted: Howard Carmack Was Convicted on Charges of ID Theft and Falsifying Business Records," *Computer World* (April 1, 2004), available at available at http://www.computerworld.com/softwaretopics/software/groupware/story/0,10801,91823,00.html (visited February 18, 2013)

Mark Robichaux, *Cable Cowboy: John Malone and the Rise of the Modern Cable Business* (New York: John Wiley & Sons, 2002)

Ryan Roemer, "Trusted Computing, Digital Rights Management, and the Fight for Copyright Control on Your Computer," 2003 *UCLA Journal of Law & Technology* 8 (2003)

Claude D. Rohwer et al., *Contracts in a Nutshell* (St. Paul, MN: West, 7th ed. 2010)

Paula Rooney, "Microsoft Shelves NGSCB Project as NX Moves to Center Stage," CRN (May 05, 2004), available at http://www.crn.com/news/security/18841713/microsoft-shelves-ngscb-project-as-nx-moves-to-center-stage.htm (visited April 7, 2013)

Mark D. Rosen, "Exporting the Constitution," 53 *Emory Law Journal* 171 (2004)

Bill Rosenblatt et al., *Digital Rights Management: Business and Technology* (New York: John Wiley & Sons, 2001)

Emily R. Roxberg, "FCC Authority Post-Comcast: Finding a Happy Medium in the Net Neutrality Debate," 37 *Journal of Corporation Law* 223 (2011)

"Royalty Settlement Signals Change for Music Industry," Innovation Asset Group (April 11, 2012), available at http://www.innovation-asset.com/intellectual-property-news/index.php/2012/04/11/190569/royalty-settlement-signals-change-for-music-industry/ (visited January 28, 2013)

"RRO Members," International Federation of Reproduction Rights Organizations, available at http://www.ifrro.org/rro (visited August 16, 2012)

Paul Rubens, "3D Printing: A New Dimension to Faking It," BBC Future (February 10, 2013), available at http://www.bbc.com/future/story/20130208-a-new-dimension-to-faking-it (visited April 2, 2013)

Ira S. Rubinstein & Michael Hintze, "*Export Controls on Encryption Software*," *in Coping with US Export Controls 2000* (New York: Practising Law Institute, Commercial Law and Practice Course Handbook Series 2000), available at http://encryption_policies.tripod.com/us/ rubinstein_1200_software.htm (visited January 7, 2013)

Julie Ruvolo, "How Much of the Internet Is Actually for Porn?" *Forbes* (September 7, 2011), available at http://www .forbes.com/sites/julieruvolo/2011/09/07/how-much- of-the-internet-is-actually-for-porn/ (visited February 17, 2013)

Dan Sabbagh, "Hollywood in Turmoil as DVD Sales Drop and Downloads Steal the Show," *The Guardian* (May 3, 2011), available at http://www.guardian.co.uk/business/2011/ may/03/film-industry-turmoil-as-dvd-sales-drop (visited April 7, 2013)

Hope Viner Samborn, "Hiding in Plain Site: The Hunt for Metatags on the Internet Is Changing the Field of Trademark Law," *ABA Journal* September 2000, at 80

Edward Samuels, "The Public Domain Revisited," 36 *Loyola (Los Angeles) Law Review* 389 (2002)

Pamela Samuelson et al., "A Manifesto Concerning the Legal Protection of Computer Programs," 94 *Columbia Law Review* 2308 (1994)

Pamela Samuelson, "Benson Revisited: The Case against Patent Protection for Algorithms and Other Computer-Related Inventions," 39 *Emory Law Journal* 1025 (1990)

Pamela Samuelson, "Intellectual Property and the Digital Economy: Why the Anti-Circumvention Regulations Need to Be Revised," 14 *Berkeley Technology Law Journal* 519 (1999)

Pamela Samuelson & Suzanne Scotchmer, "The Law and Economics of Reverse Engineering," 111 *Yale Law Journal* 1575 (2002)

Pamela Samuelson, "Mapping the Digital Public Domain: Threats and Opportunities," 66 *Law and Contemporary Problems* 147 (2003)

Pamela Samuelson, "Three Reactions to MGM v. Grokster," 13 *Michigan Telecommunications and Technology Law Review* 177 (2006)

Pamela Samuelson, "Towards More Sensible Anti-Circumvention Regulations," *Cyberspace Lawyer*, July/August 2000, at 2

Pamela Samuelson, "The U.S. Digital Agenda at WIPO," 37 *Virginia Journal of International Law* 369 (1997)

Pamela Samuelson, "Will the Copyright Office Be Obsolete in the Twenty-First Century?" 13 *Cardozo Arts & Entertainment Law Journal* 55 (1994)

Kurt M. Saunders, *Practical Internet Law for Business* (Norwood, MA: Artech House, 2001)

Kevin W. Saunders, *Saving Our Children from the First Amendment* (New York: New York University Press, 2006)

Madeleine Schachter, *Law of Internet Speech* (Durham, NC: Carolina Academic Press, 3d ed. 2008)

Tammy J. Schemmel, "WWW.STOPCYBERCRIME.COM: How the USA PATRIOT Act Combats Cyber-Crime," 29 *William Mitchell Law Review* 921 (2003)

Seth Schoen, "Trusted Computing: Promise and Risk," Electronic Frontier Foundation (October 2, 2003), available at http://seclists.org/politech/2003/Oct/7 (visited April 7, 2013)

Steven Schortgen, "'Dressing' up Software Interface Protection: The Application of Two Pesos to 'Look and Feel,'" 80 *Cornell Law Review* 158 (1994)

Christopher J. Schulte, "Abracadabra International Ltd. v. Abracadabra Creations Inc.—Internet Advertising Just

Federalized the Nation's Service Mark Law," 22 *Hamline Law Review* 563 (1999)

Aaron Schwabach, *Fan Fiction and Copyright: Outsider Works and Intellectual Property Protection* (Farnham, Surrey, UK: Ashgate Publishing, 2011)

Aaron Schwabach," The Harry Potter Lexicon and the World of Fandom: Fan Fiction, Outsider Works, and Copyright," 73 *University of Pittsburgh Law Review* 387 (2009)

Aaron Schwabach, *Intellectual Property: A Reference Handbook* (Santa Barbara, CA: ABC-CLIO, 2007)

Aaron Schwabach, "Intellectual Property Piracy: Perception and Reality in China, the United States, and Elsewhere," 2 *Journal of International Media and Entertainment Law* 65 (2007)

Aaron Schwabach, "Reclaiming Copyright from the Outside in: What the Downfall Hitler Meme Means for Transformative Works, Fair Use, and Parody," 8 *Buffalo Intellectual Property Journal* 1 (2013)

Paul M. Schwartz, "Privacy Inalienability and the Regulation of Spyware," 20 *Berkeley Technology Law Journal* 1269 (2005)

Paul M. Schwartz, "Property, Privacy, and Personal Data," 117 *Harvard Law Review* 2055 (2004)

"Search Tools Listing: Open Source Search Engines," Search Tools, available at http://www.searchtools.com/tools/ tools-opensource.html (visited February 18, 2013)

"Secure DVD Content in Today's Digital Home," Rovi Corp. (2005), available at http://www.rovicorp.com/ webdocuments/PDF/acpdvd_brochure.pdf?link_ id=productsRecursos (visited September 23, 2012)

"Secure Flight Re-Engineering Welcomed but Watchlist Problems Remain Unaddressed," American Civil Liberties Union (October 22, 2008), available at http://www.aclu.org/ technology-and-liberty/secure-flight-re-engineering- welcomed-watchlist-problems-remain-unaddressed (visited January 28, 2013)

"Security Response Glossary," Symantec U.S., available at http:// securityresponse.symantec.com/avcenter/refa.html (visited August 20, 2012)

Kerry Segrave, *Piracy in the Motion Picture Industry* (Jefferson, NC: McFarland & Company, 2003)

Susan K. Sell, *Private Power, Public Law: The Globalization of Intellectual Property Rights* (Cambridge, UK: Cambridge University Press, 2003)

Wendy Seltzer, "The Imperfect Is the Enemy of the Good: Anticircumvention versus Open User·Innovation," 25 *Berkeley Technology Law Journal* 909 (2010)

Steven Semeraro, "The Antitrust-Telecom Connection," 40 *San Diego Law Review* 555 (2003)

Martin Senftleben, *Copyright, Limitations and the Three-Step Test: An Analysis of the Three-Step Test in International and EC Copyright Law* (New York: Aspen, 2004)

"September 2012 Web Server Survey," Netcraft (September 10, 2012), available at http://news.netcraft.com/ archives/2012/09/10/september-2012-web-server-survey .html (visited February 7, 2013)

Kristina M. Sesek, "Twitter or Tweeter: Who Should Be Liable for a Right of Publicity Violation under the CDA?" 15 *Marquette Intellectual Property Law Review* 237 (2011)

Scott J. Shackelford, "From Nuclear War to Net War: Analogizing Cyber Attacks in International Law," 27 *Berkeley Journal of International Law* 192 (2009)

Assif Shameen, "Korea's Broadband Revolution: What Korea Is Doing Will Have Global Impact," *Chief Executive Magazine* (April 1, 2004), available at http://chiefexecutive.net/koreas-broadband-revolution (visited January 28, 2013)

Mary Beth Sheridan, "Interviews of Muslims to Broaden: FBI Hopes to Avert a Terrorist Attack," *Washington Post*, July 17, 2004, at A01

David D. Siegel, *Conflicts in a Nutshell* (St. Paul, MN: West, 2d ed. 2005)

Micah Sifry, *WikiLeaks and the Age of Transparency* (Berkley, CA: Counterpoint, 2011)

Karen E. Simon, Comment, "The Patent Reform Act's First-to-File Standard: Needed Reform or Constitutional Blunder?" 6 *John Marshall Review of Intellectual Property Law* 129 (2006)

Simon Singh, *The Code Book: The Evolution of Secrecy from Mary, Queen of Scots to Quantum Cryptography* (New York: Doubleday, 1999)

Peter Singleton, "Personal Jurisdiction in the Ninth Circuit," 59 *Hastings Law Journal* 911 (2008)

Ben Sisario, "New Service Offers Music in Quantity, Not by Song," *New York Times* (July 13, 2011), available at http://www.nytimes.com/2011/07/14/technology/spotify-music-streaming-service-comes-to-us.html/?_r=3&adxnnl=1&pagewanted=all&adxnnlx=1355905217-fNOqqDdkR4Q47IJIOS790w& (visited January 28, 2013)

Ben Sisario, "Pandora and Spotify Rake in the Money and then Send It Off in Royalites," *New York Times, Media Decoder* (August 24, 2012), available at http://mediadecoder.blogs.nytimes.com/2012/08/24/pandora-and-spotify-rake-in-the-money-and-then-send-it-off-in-royalties/ (visited January 28, 2013)

Shira Siskind, "Crossing the Fair Use Line: The Demise and Revival of the Harry Potter Lexicon and Its Implications for the Fair Use Doctrine in the Real World and on the Internet," 27 *Cardozo Arts & Entertainment Law Journal* 291 (2009)

Leslie David Simon et al., *Democracy and the Internet: Allies or Adversaries?* (Washington, D.C.: Woodrow Wilson Center Press, 2002)

"Six Formerly Associated with Fox Cable Charged with Copyright Infringement for Running Warez Site That Had Pirated Movies, Software", *Cybercrime Law* Report, May 31, 2004, at 21

Small Business Computing Staff, "Inside Spyware," Small Business Computing.com (July 15, 2005), available at http://smallbusinesscomputing.com/webmaster/article.php/3520466/Inside-Spyware.htm (visited April 4, 2013)

Small Business Computing Staff, "Inside Spyware: Part Two—Identifying Spyware: Malicious, Annoying or Misunderstood?" Small Business Computing.com (July 18, 2005), available at http://www.smallbusinesscomputing.com/webmaster/article.php/3520791/Inside-Spyware-Part-Two.htm (visited April 4, 2013)

Roderick W. Smith, *Broadband Internet Connections: A User's Guide to DSL and Cable* (Boston: Addison-Wesley Publishing Company, 2002)

Eric Smith, "The DAT Tax," available at http://www.brouhaha.com/~eric/bad_laws/dat_tax.html (visited January 28, 2013)

Seagrumn Smith, "From Napster to KaZaA: The Battle over Peer-to-Peer Filesharing Goes International," 2003 *Duke Law & Technology Review* 8 (2003)

Tyson Smith, "Googling a Trademark: A Comparative Look at Keyword Use in Internet Advertising," 46 *Texas International Law Journal* 231 (2010)

Software Archive, Internet Archive, available at http://web.archive.org/web/20110501034314/http://www.archive.org/details/software (visited May 30, 2012)

Barbara A. "Solomon, Domain Name Disputes: New Developments and Open Issues," 91 *The Trademark Reporter* 833 (2001)

Daniel Solove, *Nothing to Hide: The False Tradeoff between Privacy and Security* (New Haven, Connecticut: Yale University Press, 2011)

Daniel Solove & Paul M. Schwartz, *Privacy Law Fundamentals* (Portsmouth, NH: IAPP Publication, 2011)

Lawrence B. Solum & Minn Chung, "The Layers Principle: Internet Architecture and the Law," 79 *Notre Dame Law Review* 815 (2004)

"Some of John Wayne Gacy's Artwork Displayed in West Palm Beach," Associated Press (June 5, 2004), available at http://www.fadp.org/news/MGBIUQQU3VD.html (visited February 8, 2013)

Joseph H. Sommer, "Against Cyberlaw," 15 *Berkeley Technology Law Journal* 1145 (2000)

"Sony BMG Music Settles Charges Its Music Fan Websites Violated the Children's Online Privacy Protection Act," Federal Trade Commission (December 11, 2008), available at http://www.ftc.gov/opa/2008/12/sonymusic.shtm (visited April 7, 2013)

Rebecca S. Sorgen, "Trademark Confronts Free Speech on the Information Superhighway: 'Cybergripers' Face a Constitutional Collision," 22 *Loyola of Los Angeles Entertainment Law Review* 115 (2001)

Barrie Sosinsky, *Cloud Computing Bible* (Indianapolis: Wiley Publishing, 2009)

James B. Speta, "Handicapping the Race for the Last Mile? A Critique of Open Access Rules for Broadband Platforms," 17 *Yale Journal on Regulation* 39 (2000)

Lawrance Kimmel Spiller, "Credit Card Companies Crave More Money and Accumulate More through Illegal Gambling on the Internet *In re Mastercard International, Inc. Internet Gambling Litigation*, 132 F. Supp. 2d 468 (E.D. La. 2002)," 22 *Temple Environmental Law and Technology Journal* 99 (2003)

Richard Spinello, *Cyberethics: Morality and Law in Cyberspace* (Burlington, MA: Jones & Barlett Learning, 4th ed. 2011)

Robert Sprague & Corey Ciocchetti, "Preserving Identities: Protecting Personal identifying Information through Enhanced Privacy Policies and Laws," 19 *Albany Law Journal of Science & Technology* 91 (2009)

Candice J. Spurlin and Patrick M. Garry, "Does Filtering Stop the Flow of Valuable Information?: A Case Study of the Children's Internet Protection Act (CIPA) in South Dakota," 54 *South Dakota Law Review* 89 (2009)

"Square Deal: After Many False Starts, QR Codes Are Finally Taking Off," *The Economist*, June 16, 2012, at 76

Lauren A. Stagnone, "Copyright Law – Computer Program Menu Command Hierarchy: An Uncopyrightable Method of Operation? *Lotus Development Corporation v. Borland*

International, Inc., 49 F.3rd 807 (1995), aff'd, 116 S. Ct. 804 (1996)," 30 *Suffolk University Law Review* 939 (1997)

William Stallings, *Cryptography and Network Security: Principles and Practice* (Upper Saddle River, NJ: Prentice Hall, 5th ed. 2010)

StatCounter, "Top 5 Browsers from Apr 2011 to Dec 2012," StatCounter GlobalStats, available at http://gs.statcounter.com/#browser-ww-monthly-201104–201212 (visited December 21, 2012)

"State of the States: The AGA Survey of Casino Entertainment 2 (2012)," available at http://www.americangaming.org/files/aga/uploads/docs/sos/aga_sos_2012_web.pdf (visited February 3, 2013)

Elizabeth H. Steele, "Examining the FCC's Indecency Regulations in Light of Today's Technology," 63 *Federal Communications Law Journal* 289 (2010)

Neal Stephenson, *Cryptonomicon* (New York: HarperCollins, 1999)

Neal Stephenson, *Snow Crash* (New York: Bantam, 1992)

Neal Stephenson, *The System of the World* (New York: HarperCollins, 2004)

Neal Stephenson, *Quicksilver: Volume One of the Baroque Cycle* (New York: HarperCollins, 2003)

Bruce Sterling, *Ascendancies: The Best of Bruce Sterling* (Burton, MI: Subterranean Press, 2007)

Bruce Sterling, *A Good Old-Fashioned Future* (New York: Bantam, 1992)

Bruce Sterling, *The Hacker Crackdown* (Electronic edition 1992), available at available at http://stuff.mit.edu/hacker/hacker.html (visited August 14, 2012)

Bruce Sterling, *Islands in the Net* (New York: Arbor House, 1988)

Bruce Sterling, ed., *Mirrorshades: The Cyberpunk Anthology* (New York: Arbor House, 1986)

- Terence P. Stewart, *The GATT Uruguay Round: A Negotiating History (1986–1992): Trade-Related Aspects of Intellectual Property* (Dordrecht, Netherlands: Kluwer Academic Publishers, 1993)

Richard Stim, *Getting Permission: How to License & Clear Copyrighted Materials Online & Off* (Berkeley, CA: Nolo Press, 4th ed. 2010)

Richard Stim, *Patent, Copyright & Trademark: An Intellectual Property Desk Reference* (Berkeley, CA: Nolo Press, 12th ed. 2012)

Bradford Stone, *Uniform Commercial Code in a Nutshell* (St. Paul, MN: West, 7th ed. 2008)

Stop Badware, available at http://www.stopbadware.org (visited September 23, 2012)

"Struggling Smart-Phone Makers: Biting Back at Apple," *The Economist*, September 1, 2012, at 62

Bob Sullivan, "Do-Not-Spam List Won't Work, FTC says," MSNBC (June 15, 2004), available at http://www.msnbc.msn.com/id/5216554/ns/technology_and_science-security/t/do-not-spam-list-wont-work-ftc-says/#.UAecOpF2r08 (visited April 7, 2013)

Liying Sun, "Who Can Fix the Spyware Problem?" 22 *Berkeley Technology Law Journal* 555 (2007)

Cass R. Sunstein, *Republic.com 2.0* (Princeton, NJ: Princeton University Press, 2009)

Edwin Suominen, "Re-Discovering Article 1, Section 8—The Formula for First-to-Invent," 83 *Journal of the Patent Office Society* 641 (2001)

Leonard R. Sussman, "The Internet in Flux," in Freedom House, "How Free?: The Web & The Press," *The Annual Survey of Press Freedom* 4 (2001), available at http://epic.org/free_speech/pfs2001.pdf (visited February 3, 2013)

John D. Sutter, "Why Internet Connections Are Fastest in South Korea," CNN Tech (March 31, 2010), available at http://articles.cnn.com/2010–03–31/tech/broadband.south.korea_1_broadband-plan-south-korea-broadband-internet?_s=PM:TECH (visited January 28, 2013)

Ryan J. Swartz, "The Imposition of Sales and Use Taxes on E-Commerce: A Taxing Dilemma for States and Remote Sellers," 2 *Journal of High Technology Law* 143 (2003)

Jon Swartz, "Spammers Convicted: First Felony Case," USAToday.com (November 3, 2004), available at http://www.usatoday.com/tech/news/2004–11–03-spam_x.htm (visited February 18, 2013)

Symposium, "Panel II: Mickey Mice? Potential Ramifications of Eldred v. Ashcroft," 13 *Fordham Intellectual Property, Media and Entertainment Law Journal* 771 (2003)

Symposium, "The Public Domain," 66 *Law & Contemporary Problems* (2003)

Berin Szoka & Adam Marcus, eds., *The Next Digital Decade: Essays on the Future of the Internet* (Washington, D.C.: TechFreedom, 2010)

Toshiko Takenaka, "The Best Patent Practice or Mere Compromise? A Review of the Current Draft of the Substantive Patent Law Treaty and a Proposal for a First-to-Invent Exception for Domestic Applicants," 11 *Texas Intellectual Property Law Journal* 259 (2003)

Mark Tamminga, "The Sweeping Ambitions of Digital Rights Management: A Potential Hammerlock on Digital Content Has Plenty of Folks Scared," *Law Practice Management*, October 2003, at 24

TaxCloud, "Marketplace Fairness Act Questions: How Much Is at Stake?" Marketplacefairness.org, available at http://www.marketplacefairness.org/questions-and-answers/ (visited January 25, 2013)

Nicolas P. Terry, "GUI Wars: The Windows Litigation and the Continuing Decline of 'Look and Feel,'" 47 *Arkansas Law Review* 93 (1994)

Adam D. Thierer & Wayne Crews, *Copy Fights: The Future of Intellectual Property in the Information Age* (Washington, D.C.: Cato Institute, 2002)

Adam Thierer, *Important Cyberlaw & Info-Tech Policy Books* (2011 Editions), The Technology Liberation Front (December 9, 2011), available at http://techliberation.com/2011/12/09/important-cyberlaw-info-tech-policy-books-2011-edition/ (visited April 7, 2013)

- Adam Thierer et al., eds., *Who Rules the Net? Internet Governance and Jurisdiction* (Washington, D.C.: Cato Institute, 2003)

- Douglas Thomas & Brian D. Loader, eds., *Cybercrime: Law Enforcement, Security and Surveillance in the Information Age* (London: Routledge, 2000)

Amy Thomas, "UN Telecom Treaty Approved amid U.S. Web-Censorship Concerns," Bloomberg (December 14, 2012), available at http://www.bloomberg.com/news/2012–12–13/u-s-and-u-k-refuse-to-sign-un-agreement-on-telecommunications.html (visited February 7, 2013)

Dick Thornburgh & Herbert S. Lin, *Youth, Pornography and the Internet* (Washington, D.C.: National Academies Press, 2002)

Shari Thurow, *Search Engine Visibility* (Berkeley, CA: New Riders Press 2d ed. 2007)

Time to Revisit Blu-Ray? AACS, Pacific Disc (2010), available at http://www.pacificdisc.com/Article19.html (visited April 7, 2013)

Holly K. Towle, "Identity Theft: Myths, Methods and New Law," 30 *Rutgers Computer and Technology Law Journal* 237 (2004)

"Trade Secrets Acts," Uniform Law Commission, available at http://www.uniformlaws.org/Act.aspx?title=Trade%20Secrets%20Act (visited January 15, 2013)

Johannes Trithemius, *Steganographia* (1499; Darmstadt, Germany: Ioannis Berneri Bibliopolae, 1621), available in Latin at http://www.esotericarchives.com/tritheim/stegano.htm (visited June 16, 2004)

Hayley Tsukayama, "Google: 'Government Surveillance is on the Rise,'" *Washington Post* (November 13, 2012), available at http://articles.washingtonpost.com/2012–11–13/business/35506267_1_dorothy-chou-google-senior-policy-analyst-requests (visited February 17, 2013)

Alexander G. Tuneski, Hey, "That's My Name! Trademark Usage on the Internet," 31 *Franchise Law Journal* 203 (2012)

Sherry Turkle, *Alone Together: Why We Expect More from Technology and Less from Each Other* (New York: Basic Books, 2012)

Barry Turner, ed., *The Statesman's Yearbook: The Politics, Cultures and Economies of the World* (Houndmills, Basingstoke, UK: Palgrave, 139th ed. 2001)

Rebecca Tushnet, "Scary Monsters: Hybrids, Mashups, and Other Illegitimate Children," 86 *Notre Dame Law Review* 2133 (2011)

Rebecca Tushnet, "User-Generated Discontent: Transformation in Practice," 31 *Columbia Journal of Law & the Arts* 497 (2008)

Stuart Turton, "Dubai's Dubious Internet 'Censorship,'" PC Pro (September 6, 2010), available at http://www.pcpro.co.uk/blogs/2010/09/06/dubais-dubious-internet-censorship/ (visited February 3, 2013)

"Uncrackable Beams of Light: Quantum Cryptography—Hailed by Theoreticians as the Ultimate of Uncrackable Codes—Is Finally Going Commercial," *Economist Technology Quarterly* (September 6, 2003), available at http://www.economist.com/node/2020013 (visited February 2, 2013)

"Unexpected Harmony: The Music and Computer Industries Make Peace, but Differences Remain," *The Economist* (January 23, 2003), available at http://www.economist.com/node/1549398 (visited April 7, 2013)

United States Patent and Trademark Office, "Patents Examination" (March 14, 2013), available at http://www.uspto.gov/aia_implementation/patents.jsp#heading-10 (visited April 7, 2013)

Ronald R. Urbach & Gary A. Kibel, "Adware/Spyware: An Update Regarding Pending Litigation and Legislation," *Journal of Proprietary Rights*, July 2004, at 12

U.S. Census Bureau, *Statistical Abstract of the United States: 2003* (Washington, D.C.: Government Printing Office, 123d ed. 2003)

U.S. Department of Education, *National Center for Education Statistics Teachers' Use of Educational Technology in U.S. Public Schools: 2009* (May 5, 2010), available at http://nces.ed.gov/pubsearch/pubsinfo.asp?pubid=2010040 (visited January 28, 2013)

U.S. Department of Justice, *Six Formerly Associated with Fox Cable Charged with Copyright Infringement for Running Warez Site that had Pirated Movies, Software* (May 14, 2004), available at http://www.justice.gov/criminal/cybercrime/press-releases/2004/sarnaCharge.htm (visited April 7, 2013)

US v. ElcomSoft Sklyarov, Electronic Frontier Foundation, available at https://www.eff.org/cases/us-v-elcomsoft-sklyarov (visited December 4, 2012)

"US and UK Refuse to Sign UN's Communications Treaty," BBC News (December 14, 2012, 7:50), available at http://www.bbc.co.uk/news/technology-20717774 (visited February 7, 2013)

Patrick Van Eecke, *Cloud Computing Legal Issues*, DLA Piper Brussels, available at http://www.isaca.org/Groups/Professional-English/cloud-computing/GroupDocuments/DLA_Cloud%20computing%20legal%20issues.pdf (visited March 29, 2013)

Siva Vaidhyanathan, *The Anarchist in the Library: How the Clash between Freedom and Control Is Hacking the Real World and Crashing the System* (New York: Basic Books, 2004)

Siva Vaidhyanathan, *Copyrights and Copywrongs: The Rise of Intellectual Property and How It Threatens Creativity* (New York: New York University Press, 2001)

Siva Vaidhyanathan, *The Googlization of Everything: (And Why We Should Worry)* (Berkeley, CA: University of California Press, 2011)

Anthony E. Varona, "Toward a Broadband Public Interest Standard," 25 *Administrative Law Review* 1 (2009)

"Video Games: Japan Fights Back," *The Economist*, November 17, 2012, at 61

Vernor Vinge, *True Names and the Opening of the Cyberspace Frontier* (New York: Tor, 2001)

"Verisign's Sale of Authentication Services Business to Symantec Closes," Verisign (August 9, 2010), available at https://investor.verisign.com/releasedetail.cfm?releaseid=497643 (visited April 7, 2013)

Heidi Wachs, "Permissive Pornography: The Selective Censorship of the Internet under CIPA," 11 *Cardozo Women's Law Journal* 441 (2005)

R. Polk Wagner, "Information Wants to Be Free: Intellectual Property and the Mythologies of Control," 103 *Columbia Law Review* 995 (2003)

Ronald L. Wagner, *Road Runner Guide to Cyberspace* (Herndon, VA: Citapei Communications, 9th ed. 1999)

Craig W. Walker, "Application of the DMCA Safe Harbor Provisions to Search Engines," 9 *Virginia Journal of Law & Technology* 1 (2004)

Gregory C. Walsh, "Internet Service Provider Liability for Contributory Trademark Infringement after Gucci," 2002 *Duke Law & Technology Review* 95 (2002)

Lawrence G. Walters & Kevin W. Wimberly, "Legal Issues Surrounding Mobile Apps: Why Apps Are Different than Websites," *Walters Law Group* (September 28, 2010), available at http://lawrencewalters.com/articles/Mobile_App_Article-Final.pdf (visited April 2, 2013)

Tracie E. Wandell, "Geolocation and Jurisdiction: From Purposeful Availment to Avoidance and Targeting on the Internet," 16 *Journal of Technology Law & Policy* 275 (2011)

Jessica Wang, "A Brave New Step: Why the Music Industry Should Follow the Hulu Model," 41 *Idea: The Intellectual Property Law Review* 511 (2011)

R. "Ray" Wang, "UsedSoft vs Oracle Ruling Opens Up Monopolistic Practices: Used Software Pioneers Gain a Small Victory in a Shrinking On-Premises Software World," *Forbes* (July 4, 2012), available at http://www.forbes.com/sites/raywang/2012/07/04/news-analysis-usedsoft-vs-oracle-ruling-opens-up-monopolistic-practices-by-software-vendors/ (visited April 15, 2013)

Jennifer Waters, "Your Right to Resell Your Own Stuff Is in Peril," *Wall Street Journal Market Watch* (October 12, 2012), available at http://www.marketwatch.com/story/your-right-to-resell-your-own-stuff-is-in-peril-2012–10–04?pagenumber=1 (visited February 3, 2013)

Wave Systems Corp., "Wave Signs Global Distribution Agreement with Lenovo," Market Wire (July 23, 2012), available at http://www.marketwire.com/press-release/wave-signs-global-distribution-agreement-with-lenovo-nasdaq-wavx-1682555.htm (visited April 7, 2013)

Peter Wayner, *Disappearing Cryptography – Information Hiding: Steganography and Watermarking* (Burlington, MA: Morgan Kaufmann, 3d ed. 2010)

"Webmaster Tools: Metatags," Google, available at http://support.google.com/webmasters/bin/answer.py?hl=en&answer=79812 (visited February 8, 2013)

Jonathan Weinberg, "Governments, Privatization, and 'Privatization': ICANN and the GAC," 18 *Michigan Telecommunications & Technology Law Review* 189 (2011)

Amy S. Weinberg, "These Cookies Won't Crumble—Yet: The Corporate Monitoring of Consumer Internet Activity, *In re DoubleClick Inc. Privacy Litigation*, 154 F.Supp.2d 497 (S.D.N.Y. 2001)," 21 *Temple Environmental Law and Technology Journal* 33 (2002)

Marc Weingarten, "Phone Phreaks," The Feature (February 25, 2002) available at http://www.thefeaturearchives.com/topic/Archive/Phone_Phreaks.html (visited April 7, 2013)

Russell J. Weintraub, *Commentary on the Conflict of Laws* (New York: Foundation Press, 6th ed. 2010)

Gayle Weiswasser, "Domain Names, the Internet, and Trademarks: Infringement in Cyberspace," 13 *Santa Clara Computer and High Technology Law Journal* 137 (1996)

Phil Weiser, "Paradigm Changes in Telecommunications Regulation," 71 *University of Colorado Law Review* 819 (2000)

Jonathan Weisman, "After an Online Firestorm, Congress Shelves Antipiracy Bills," *New York Times* (January 20, 2012), available at http://www.nytimes.com/2012/01/21/technology/senate-postpones-piracy-vote.html?_r=0 (visited April 24, 2013)

"Welcome to ICANN," ICANN, available at http://www.icann.org/en/about/welcome (visited December 17, 2012)

"Welcome to info.cern.ch: The Website of the World's First-Ever Web Server," CERN (2008), available at http://info.cern.ch/ (visited February 7, 2013)

"Welcome to the Office of International Affairs," Federal Trade Commission, available at http://www.ftc.gov/oia/index.shtml (visited February 3, 2013)

Matthew G. "Wells, Internet Business Method Patent Policy," 87 *Virginia Law Review* 729 (2001)

Mike Wendland, "Spam King Lives Large Off Others' E-mail Troubles: West Bloomfield Computer Empire Helped by Foreign Internet Servers," *Detroit Free Press*, November 22, 2002

Bettina Wendlandt, *Cybersquatting, Metatags und Spam* (München: Beck Juristischer Verlag, 2002) (in German)

Bryan P. Werley, "Aussie Rules: Universal Jurisdiction over Internet Defamation," 18 *Temple International and Comparative Law Journal* 199 (2004)

Robert Westervelt, "Microsoft Revokes Additional Digital Certificates due to Encryption Weakness," Search Security (July 11, 2012), available at http://searchsecurity.techtarget.com/news/2240159440/Microsoft-revokes-additional-digital-certificates-due-to-encryption-weakness (visited April 7, 2013)

"We've Won, for Now," www.stoppoliceware.org (visited October 22, 2004)

"What is IFRRO?" International Federation of Reproduction Rights Organizations, available at http://www.ifrro.org/content/what-ifrro (visited August 16, 2012)

"What is Online Piracy?" RIAA, available at http://riaa.com/physicalpiracy.php?content_selector=What-is-Online-Piracy (visited December 20, 2012)

"What is Macrovision?" DVD Buying Guide (2010), available at http://www.dvdbuyingguide.com/codefreedvd/tip6.html (visited February 8, 2013)

"What is a QR Code?" Denso ADC, available at http://www.denso-adc.com/learning-center/what-are-qr-codes (visited December 20, 2012)

"Who are we," Association Littéraire et Artistique Internationale, available at http://alaiorg.vincelette.net/index.php?option=com_content&task=view&id=76&Itemid=60 (visited September 24, 2012)

"Who's Afraid of Huawei?" *The Economist*, August 4, 2012, at 9

"Why Broadband Prices Haven't Decreased," Kellogg Insight (September 2010), available at http://insight.kellogg.northwestern.edu/index.php/Kellogg/article/why_broadband_prices_havent_decreased/(visited January 28, 2013)

"Why We Do What We Do," RIAA, available at http://riaa.com/physicalpiracy.php?content_selector=piracy-online-why-we-do-what-we-do (visited December 20, 2012)

Norbert Wiener, *Cybernetics: Or the Control and Communication in the Animal and the Machine* (Cambridge, MA: MIT Press, 2d ed. 1965)

Wikileaks, "What Is WikiLeaks?" available at http://wikileaks.org/About.html (visited April 24, 2013)

Marcia Wilbur, *DMCA: The Digital Millennium Copyright Act* (San Jose, CA: Writers Club Press, 2001)

Richard Wilbur, "Museum Piece," in *New and Collected Poems* 292 (Fort Washington, PA: Harvest Books, 1987)

Jo-Na Williams, "The New Symbol of "Hope" for Fair Use: Shepard Fairey v. The Associated Press," *Landslide*, September/October 2009, at 55

Peter Wilner, "The Madrid Protocol: A Voluntary Model for the Internationalization of Trademark Law," 13 *DePaul*

University Journal of Art and Entertainment Law 17 (2003)

Tim Wilson, "Find Sensitive Data in Cloud before Criminals Do," InformationWeek (July 26, 2012), available at http://www.informationweek.com/security/management/find-sensitive-data-in-cloud-before-crim/240004393 (visited January 28, 2013)

Vic (J.R.) Winkler, "Cloud Computing: Legal and Regulatory Issues," *TechNet Magazine* (May 2012), available at http://technet.microsoft.com/en-us/magazine/hh994647.aspx

Katelynn Winkler, "Functionality Failure: How Rosetta Stone v. Google Misapplies the Trademark Functionality Doctrine to AdWords," 44 *Arizona State Law Journal* 995 (2012)

WIPO, "About the Patent Cooperation Treaty," PCT, International Patent System (2012), available at http://www.wipo.int/pct/en/treaty/about.html (visited February 8, 2013)

WIPO, *Basic Facts about the Patent Cooperation Treaty* (April 2002), available at http://www.islandpatent.com/learn/BasicFactsPCT_wipo.pdf (visited February 7, 2013)

WIPO, "Direct Filing of PCT Applications with the International Bureau as PCT Receiving Office," PCT, International Patent System, available at http://www.wipo.int/pct/en/filing/filing.htm#P20_2204 (visited August 16, 2012)

WIPO, "PCT Contracting States for which a Regional Patent Can Be Obtained via the PCT," PCT, International Patent System (May 1, 2012), available at http://www.wipo.int/pct/en/texts/reg_des.html (visited February 8, 2013)

Elaine Woo, " 'Prince' Roy Bates Dies at 91; Adventuring Monarch of Sealand," *LA Times* (October 14, 2012), available at http://articles.latimes.com/2012/oct/14/local/la-me-roy-bates-20121014 (visited January 28, 2013)

Chad Woodford, "Trusted Computing or Big Brother? Putting the Rights Back in Digital Rights Management," 75 *University of Colorado Law Review* 253 (2004)

Christopher Wolf, *Digital Millennium Copyright Act: Text, History, and Caselaw* (Silver Spring, MD: Pike & Fischer, 2003)

World Almanac and Book of Facts 2004 (New York: World Almanac Books, 2004)

World Intellectual Property Organization, "List of Observers," available at http://www.wipo.int/members/en/docs/observers.pdf (visited December 21, 2012)

World Intellectual Property Organization, "Member States," available at http://www.wipo.int/members/en/ (visited December 21, 2012)

"The World Is What You Make It: Every Country Has Its Own Internet," *The Economist*, Special Report: Technology and Geography, October 27, 2012, at 20

World Telecommunications/ICT Development Report 2010 (2010), International Telecommunications Union (ITU), available at http://www.itu.int/ITU-D/ict/publications/wtdr_10/material/WTDR2010_e_v1.pdf (visited January 28, 2013)

"World v Web: America Does Not Want the United Nations to Run the Internet", *The Economist*, November 20, 2004, at 65

Jenna Wortham, "Public Outcry over Antipiracy Bills Began as Grassroots Grumbling," *New York Times* (January 19, 2012), available at http://www.nytimes.com/2012/01/20/technology/public-outcry-over-antipiracy-bills-began-as-grass-roots-grumbling.html?pagewanted=all (visited April 24, 2013)

Tim Worstall, "The Declining Economics of the Pornography Industry," *Forbes* (June 8, 2012), available at http://www.forbes.com/sites/timworstall/2012/06/08/the-declining-economics-of-the-pornography-industry/ (visited February 17, 2013)

Timothy Wu, "Cyberspace Sovereignty? The Internet and the International System," 10 *Harvard Journal of Law & Technology* 647 (1997)

Tim Wu, "Network Neutrality, Broadband Discrimination," 2 *Journal on Telecommunications & High Technology Law* 141 (2003)

Timothy Wu, "When Law & the Internet First Met," 3 *Green Bag* 2d 171 (2000)

"Xanga.com to Pay $1 Million for Violating Children's Online Privacy Protection Rule," Federal Trade Commission (September 7, 2006), available at http://www.ftc.gov/opa/2006/09/xanga.shtm (visited April 7, 2013)

"Xerox PARC History," PARC, available at http://www.parc.xerox.com/about/history/default.html (visited December 21, 2012)

Deli Yang, *Intellectual Property and Doing Business in China* (Amsterdam, Netherlands: Pergamon, 2003)

Alfred C. Yen, "Internet Service Provider Liability for Subscriber Copyright Infringement, Enterprise Liability, and the First Amendment," 88 *Georgetown Law Journal* 1833 (2000)

Gary Chan Kok Yew, "Internet Defamation and Choice of Law in Dow Jones & Company Inc. v. Gutnick," 2003 *Singapore Journal of Legal Studies* 483 (2003)

"You Shut Down Millsberry and Ruined my Life, and Many More!!!," Pissed Consumer (May 14, 2011), available at http://general-mills.pissedconsumer.com/you-shut-down-millsberry-and-ruined-my-life-and-many-more-20110514237626.html (27 pages, 265 comments) (visited April 7, 2013)

Julie Cromer Young, "From the Mouths of Babes: Protecting Child Authors from Themselves," 112 *West Virginia Law Review* 431 (2010)

Gary Younge, "US Music Industry Sues 261 for Online Song Copying," *The Guardian* (September 10, 2003), available at http://www.richardhartley.com/2003/09/us-music-industry-sues-261-for-online-song-copying/ (visited February 3, 2013)

Youth International Party Line (aka *TAP Magazine*) archive, available at http://flag.blackened.net/daver/misc/yipl/ (visited December 19, 2012)

Peter K. Yu, "Introduction to Symposium on Bridging the Digital Divide: Equality in the Information Age," 20 *Cardozo Arts and Entertainment Law* 1 (2002)

Robert H. Zakon, "Hobbes' Internet Timeline v10.2," available at http://www.zakon.org/robert/Internet/timeline/ (visited February 7, 2013)

Vittorio Zambardino, "Il Garante Privacy sulla sentenza di Milano: 'E' sbagliata, ma ora bisogna fare regole non *censorie*," La Repubblica (April 16, 2010), available at http://www.itespresso.it/il-garante-privacy-difende-in-parte-google-dalla-sentenza-di-milano-44937.html (visited August 28, 2013)

Tal Zarsky, "Cookie Viewers and the Undermining of Data Mining: A Critical Review of the Double Click Settlement," 2001 *Stanford Technology Law Review* 1 (2002)

Tal Z. Zarsky, "Desperately Seeking Solutions: Using Implementation-Based Solutions for the Troubles of Information Privacy in the Age of Data Mining and the Internet Society," 56 *Maine Law Review* 13 (2004)

Tal Z. Zarsky, "'Mine Your Own Business!' Making the Case for the Implications of the Data Mining of Personal Information in the Forum of Public Opinion," 5 *Yale Journal of Law & Technology* 4 (2002–2003)

Tal Z. Zarsky, "Thinking outside the Box: Considering Transparency, Anonymity, and Pseudonymity as Overall Solutions to the Problems of Information Privacy in the Internet Society," 58 *University of Miami Law Review* 991 (2004)

David Zax, "The 'Six Strikes' Copyright Alert System Is Toothless," *MIT Technology Review* (February 26, 2013), available at http://www.technologyreview.com/view/511841/the-six-strikes-copyright-alert-system-is-toothless/ (visited April 24, 2013)

Tom Zeller, "Jr., F.T.C. Files First Lawsuit against Spyware Concerns," *N.Y. Times* (October 13, 2004), available at http://www.nytimes.com/2004/10/13/technology/13spy.html?_r=0 (visited April 7, 2013)

Mitchell Zimmerman, *Audio Home Recording Act Does Not Protect Device Distributor against Copyright Claims Arising from Broadcaster Role*, Fenwick & West LLP (2007), available at http://www.fenwick.com/FenwickDocuments/No_AHRA_Immunity.pdf (visited April 7, 2013)

Mitchell Zimmerman, "DMCA Safe Harbors De-Coded: 17 U.S.C. Section 512 Re-Organized in More Logical Order," Fenwick & West LLP (May 7, 2012), available at http://www.fenwick.com/Publications/Pages/DMCA-Safe-Harbors-De-Coded.aspx (visited January 28, 2013)

Jonathan L. Zittrain, *Jurisdiction* (New York: Foundation Press, 2005)

Jonathan L. Zittrain, *Technological Complements to Copyright* (New York: Foundation Press, 2005)

Note: Page numbers in **boldface** reflect main entries in the book.

About the Author

Aaron Schwabach is a professor of law at Thomas Jefferson School of Law in San Diego, California. His published works include three previous books for ABC-CLIO (*Intellectual Property: A Reference Handbook*; *Internet and the Law: Technology, Society, and Compromises*; and *International Environmental Disputes: A Reference Handbook*), as well as *Fan Fiction and Copyright: Outsider Works and Intellectual Property Protection* for Ashgate Publishing (UK), and numerous scholarly articles, book chapters, and other works covering a range of subjects from international watercourse law to intellectual property, with occasional detours into such subjects as the life of Thomas Jefferson and the law of Harry Potter's world. Professor Schwabach is a graduate of the Boalt Hall School of Law at the University of California at Berkeley.